CUBA IN TRANSITION

Volume 10

Papers and Proceedings of the

**Tenth Annual Meeting
of the
Association for the Study of the Cuban Economy (ASCE)**

Miami, Florida
August 3–5, 2000

(ISBN 0-9649082-9-8)

Cuba in Transition volumes may be ordered from:

Association for the Study of the Cuban Economy
P.O. Box 7372
Silver Spring, MD 20907-7372
Tel.   301/587-1664
Fax   301/587-1664
E-mail: jalonso@erols.com

Information on availability of volumes and book order forms are available at www.ascecuba.org.

PREFACE

This volume of Cuba in Transition brings together most of the papers and selected commentaries presented at the Tenth Annual Meeting of the Association for the Study of the Cuban Economy, which was held in Coral Gables, Florida, August 3-5, 2000. As in previous volumes, the papers and commentaries included here cover a wide range of topics related to Cuba's economy and society: the current economic and political situation; macroeconomics; monetary and fiscal policy; economic reforms; foreign investment; role of small and medium size enterprises; external sector; agriculture; sugar; environment; tourism; social issues; legal issues; and sectoral economic developments.

ASCE gratefully acknowledges the support of its sponsoring members and particularly the contributions to the Tenth Annual Meeting by the Institute for Cuban and Cuban American Studies of the University of Miami.

Jorge F. Pérez-López
José F. Alonso
Editors

TABLE OF CONTENTS

Conference Program ix

Saludo a la Décima Reunión de ASCE 1
Marta Beatriz Roque

Cuba Dual: Crisis Económica, Crisis del Régimen 2
Antonio Elorza

Cuba y su Economía de Resistencia 11
Manuel David Orrio

El Estado Real de la Economía Cubana 15
Oscar Espinosa Chepe

La Economía Cubana Durante el Período Especial 19
Antonio Gayoso

The Fall and Recovery of the Cuban Economy in the 1990s: Mirage or Reality 24
Ernesto Hernández-Catá

Has Cuba Definitely Found the Path to Economic Growth? 39
Roberto Orro

The Mirage of Floating Exchange Rates 48
Carmen M. Reinhart

Evolución y Perspectiva de la Pequeña Empresa No Estatal en Cuba 54
Evaldo A. Cabarrouy

La Descentralización de las Granjas Estatales en Cuba: ¿Gérmen para una Reforma Empresarial Pendiente? 64
Hans-Jürgen Burchardt

Transition in Central and Eastern Europe: Lessons for Development of SMEs in Cuba 72
Antonio Gayoso

Intellectual Property Rights and International Trade in Cuban Products 77
Joseph M. Perry, Louis A. Woods, and Stephen L. Shapiro

The "Understanding" Between the European Union and the United States Over Investments in Cuba 88
Joaquín Roy

Differences in Agricultural Productivity in Cuba's State and Nonstate Sectors: Further Evidence 98
José Alvarez

Market Potential for U.S. Livestock Genetics in a Free Market Cuban Economy 108
James E. Ross

Comments by William E. Kost 118

Recent Changes in Management Structure and Strategies of the Cuban Fishing Industry 121
Chuck Adams

Balance of Payments: Concepts and Measurements 128
Armando S. Linde

Cuba's Balance of Payments Statistics 136
    Jorge F. Pérez-López

Interpreting Cuba's External Accounts 145
    Emily Morris

Cuba's Balance of Payments Gap, the Remittances Scam, Drug Trafficking and Money Laundering 149
    Ernesto F. Betancourt

Land Use in Cuba Before and After the Revolution: Economic and Environmental Implications 162
    Sergio Díaz-Briquets

Comments by José Alvarez 171

La Situación Ambiental de Cuba al Finalizar el Siglo XX 173
    Eudel Eduardo Cepero

Preliminary Environmental Action Plan for a Post Castro Cuba 190
    Alberto Vega and Federico Poey

Cuba: Fin de Fiesta—Castro da por Terminado el Período Especial y Retoma el Socialismo Puro y Duro 207
    Carlos Alberto Montaner

Fiscal Reforms in Transition Economies: Implications for Cuba 212
    Lorenzo L. Pérez

**Cuba y América Latina: Consideraciones Sobre el Nivel y la Evolución del Índice de Desarrollo Humano
y del Gasto Social en la Década de los Noventa** 234
    Rolando H. Castañeda

The Internationalization of Collective Behavior: Lessons From Elian 254
    Benigno E. Aguirre

The Last Wave: Cuba's Contemporary Exodus — Political or Economic Immigrants? 265
    Silvia Pedraza

Models of Development and Globalization In Cuba 277
    Nelson Amaro

Winners and Losers in Restoring Old Havana 289
    Joseph L. Scarpaci, Jr.

Toward Best Business Practices for Foreign Investors in Cuba 301
    Ambassador Anthony C.E. Quainton

Economic Reforms and Social Contradictions in Cuba 305
    Charles Trumbull

Last Resort or Bridge to the Future? Tourism and Workers in Cuba's Second Economy 321
    Ted Henken

Cuba's Trade Policy After Castro 337
    Sidney Weintraub

Education's Contribution to Economic Growth in Cuba 342
    Manuel E. Madrid-Aris

A Comparison of Cuba's Tourism Industy with the Dominican Republic and Cancún, 1988-1999 352
    Nicolas Crespo and Charles Suddaby

Cuban Tourism During the Special Period 360
    María Dolores Espino

Telecommunications and Power Sector Reforms in Latin America: Lessons Learned 374
Juan A. B. Belt

A Discussion on Institutional Research for a Transitional Cuba 382
Jorge Luis Romeu

**Cuban Flora, Endophytic and Other, as a Potential Source of Bioactive Compounds:
Two Technical Approaches to Bioactive Compound Discovery** 391
Larry S. Daley

A Constitutional Framework for a Free Cuba 399
Alfred G. Cuzán

Microeconomic Intermediation and Sectoral Integration in a Market Transition 417
Mario A. Rivera

Soldiers and Businessmen: The FAR During the Special Period 428
Armando F. Mastrapa III

FAR: Mastering Reforms 433
Domingo Amuchastegui

Comments by José A. Font 442

A Survey of Significant Legal Changes During Cuba's Special Period: Setting Parameters for Change 445
Stephen J. Kimmerling

The Contribution of BITs to Cuba's Foreign Investment Program 456
Jorge F. Pérez-López and Matías F. Travieso-Díaz

Cuban Labor Law: Issues and Challenges 481
Aldo M. Leiva

**Corrigendum: Comments on "Actuarial Model of the Impact of Linking Economic Variables
to a Life Survival Function" by Donate-Armada** 492
Diego R. Roqué

Appendix A: Authors and Discussants 497

Appendix B: Acknowledgements 503

ASSOCIATION FOR THE STUDY
OF THE CUBAN ECONOMY (ASCE)

Tenth Annual Meeting
Biltmore Hotel, Coral Gables, Florida
August 3-5, 2000

Conference Program

The Cuban Economy During the Special Period

Antonio Elorza, Universidad Complutense de Madrid

Antonio Gayoso, Consultant

Manuel David Orrio, Independent Economist, La Habana

Macroeconomics

The Fall and Recovery of the Cuban Economy in the 1990s: Myth or Reality?
    Ernesto Hernández-Catá, International Monetary Fund

Discussant: Luis R. Luis, International Research and Strategy Associates

¿Ha recorrido Cuba su propia "V"?
    Roberto Orro, Universidad de Guanajuato

Discussant: Ricardo Martínez, Inter-American Development Bank (retired)

Fear of Floating
    Carmen Reinhart, University of Maryland, and Guillermo Calvo, University of Maryland

Discussant: Ernesto Hernández-Catá, International Monetary Fund

Small and Medium Enterprises

Small and Medium Enterprises: European Experience and Relevance for Cuba
    Antonio Gayoso, Consultant

Evolución y perspectivas de la pequeña empresa no estatal en Cuba
    Evaldo Cabarrouy, University of Puerto Rico

Discussant: Guillermo Cueto, U.S.-Cuba Business Council

La descentralización del sector estatal en la agricultura: ¿Gérmen para una reforma empresarial pendiente?
    Hans-Jürgen Burchardt, University of Hannover, Germany

Discussant: William Messina, University of Florida

External Sector

Intellectual Property Rights and International Trade in Cuban Products
    Joseph M. Perry, University of North Florida

Discussant: Matías Travieso-Díaz, Shaw Pittman

An Evaluation of the U.S. Embargo on Cuba

Carlos Seiglie, Rutgers University and Universite Pierre Mendes France-Grenoble II

Discussant: Manuel Lasaga, StratInfo

The 'Understanding' Between the European Union and the U.S. Over Investment in Cuba: *Chapuza, Pasteleo,*
Creative Arrangement, or More of the Same?

Joaquín Roy, University of Miami

Discussant: Virgilio Blanco, Middlesex County College

Agriculture and Fisheries

Differences in Agricultural Productivity Between the State and Nonstate Sectors: Further Evidence
José Alvarez, University of Florida

Cuba's Livestock Sector and the Potential Market for U.S. Livestock Genetics
James E. Ross, University of Florida

Discussant: William Kost, U.S. Department of Agriculture

The Cuban Fishing Industry and Recent Changes in Fisheries Management
Charles M. Adams, University of Florida

Discussant: Doug Gregory, University of Florida

Balance of Payments

The Balance of Payments: Concepts and Measurement
Armando Linde, International Monetary Fund

Cuba's Balance of Payments Statistics
Jorge Pérez-López, U.S. Department of Labor

Interpreting Cuba's External Accounts
Emily Morris, The Economist Intelligence Unit

Remittances and the Cuban Balance of Payments
Ernesto Betancourt, Retired public sector reform consultant

Discussant: Joaquín Pujol, IMF Advisor for Central Banks of the Caribbean

Environmental Issues

Land Use in Cuba Before and After the Revolution: Economic and Environmental Implications
Sergio Díaz-Briquets, Casals & Associates

Discussant: José Alvarez, University of Florida

La situación ambiental de Cuba al finalizar el siglo XX
Eudel Eduardo Cepero, Agencia Ambiental Entorno Cubano

Preliminary Environmental Action Plan for a Post-Castro Cuba
Alberto Vega and Federico Poey, USCBC Cuba Transition Project

Discussant: María Dolores Espino, St. Thomas University

Fiscal and Monetary Issues

Fiscal Reforms in Transition Economies: Implications for Cuba
Lorenzo Pérez, International Monetary Fund

Poverty, the Budget, and Transition
Mark Gallagher, DevTech Systems

Análisis del Nivel y la Evolución del Gasto Social en Cuba y en América Latina en la Década de los Noventa
Rolando Castañeda, Inter-American Development Bank

Discussant: Rafael Romeu, University of Maryland

Globalización vs. Aislamiento en el Contexto Cubano: Patologías, Efectos Sociales y Migratorios y Políticos

The Internationalization of Collective Behavior: Lessons from Elián
Benigno Aguirre, Texas A & M University

Globalización como Modelo de Desarrollo: Afinidades y Rechazos del Modelo Cubano
Nelson Amaro, Universidad del Valle de Guatemala

Cuba's Latest Wave: Political Refugees or Economic Immigrants?
Silvia Pedraza, University of Michigan

Discussant: Gerardo Martínez-Solana, Instituto Jacques Maritain

Cuba: La enajenación del trabajo y otras patologías sociales en el año 2000
Maida Donate Armada, Cuban American National Council

Discussant: Juan Carlos Espinosa, St. Thomas University

Roundtable: Sugar Industry and Markets

José F. Alonso, Montgomery County Public Schools

Pablo A. Carreño, Chemical Engineer

Carlos Padial, Chemical Engineer

Oscar Espinosa Chepe, Independent Economist, La Habana

Diosmel Rodríguez, U.S. Support Group for Independent Cooperatives

Foreign Invesment

Best Business Practices for Foreign Investors in Cuba
Ambassador Anthony C.E. Quainton, National Planning Association

Discussant: Ambassador Otto Reich, U.S.-Cuba Business Council

Telecommunication Investments in Cuba
Enrique López, A.K.L. Group, Inc.

Discussant: John Kavulich, U.S.-Cuba Trade and Economic Council

Habaguanex: Winners and Losers in Restoring Havana's Centro Histórico
Joseph L. Scarpaci, Virginia Tech

Discussant: Ana Julia Jatar, Inter-American Dialogue.

Student Papers

Social Contradictions in Cuba
Charles Trumbull, Dartmouth College

Discusant: Sergio Díaz-Briquets, Casals & Associates

Cuba's 'Baseball Politics': Our Shared National Pastime as a Cultural Means Toward Political Ends
Christopher Perry, College of the Holy Cross

Discussant: Jeff Carrera, Catholic University of America

Last Resort or Bridge to the Future: Tourism and Workers in Cuba's Second Economy
Ted Henken, Tulane University

Discussant: Mario Rivera, University of New Mexico

Sources of Economic Growth

The Decline in Cuba's Total Factor Productivity
Luis Locay, University of Miami

Discussant: Moshe Syrquin, University of Miami

Education's Contribution to Economic Growth in Cuba
Manuel Madrid-Aris, Florida International University

Discussant: Nicolás Sánchez, College of the Holy Cross

Tourism

Tourism in Cuba: An Update of Economic Aspects
María Dolores Espino, St. Thomas University

A Comparison of Cuba's Tourism Industry with the Dominican Republic and Cancún for the Period 1989-99

Nicolás Crespo, Cuban Society of Tourism Professionals, and Charles Suddaby, Charles Suddaby & Associates, Limited

Sol-Meliá Hotels' Role in Cuba's Tourism Industry

Félix B. Godínez, Case Western Reserve University School of Law

Discussant: Artimus Keiffer, Franklin College

Panel Discussion: ASCE at Ten—Institutional Growth and Challenges

Panelists: Roger Betancourt, University of Maryland, ASCE President 1990-92

Jorge Pérez-López, U.S. Department of Labor, ASCE President 1992-94

Antonio Gayoso, Consultant, ASCE President 1996-98

Sergio Diaz-Briquets, Casals & Associates, ASCE President, 1999-2000

Carlos Quijano, World Bank (retired), ASCE President, 2000-02

Special Topics

Best Practices in Latin America Regarding the Regulatory Framework for Power and Telecommunications: Implications for Cuba
Juan A.B. Belt, Inter-American Development Bank

Discussant: Luis Locay, University of Miami

Cuban Endophytic Flora as a Potential Source of Bioactive Materials
Larry Daley, Oregon State University

Discussant: James Ross, University of Florida

Some Ideas on University Research in Post Transitional Cuba
Jorge L. Romeu, ITT Research Institute

Discussant: Benigno Aguirre, Texas A&M University.

Politics

A Constitutional Framework for a Free Cuba
Alfred G. Cuzán, The University of West Florida

Microeconomic and Micropolitical Processes in Cuba's Market Transition
Mario A. Rivera, The University of New Mexico

Discussant: Ambassador Mauricio Solaún, University of Illinois

Civil Society in Cuba at the Turn of the Millennium: Achievements and Shortcomings
Juan J. López, University of Illinois at Chicago

Discussant: Andy Gómez, University of Miami

The Military in the Economy

Soldiers and Businessmen: The FAR During the Special Period
Armando F. Mastrapa, Cuba Armed Forces Review

FAR: Mastering Reforms
Domingo Amuchastegui, Independent Researcher

Discussants: José Antonio Font, Font International; Ernesto Betancourt, Retired public sector reform consultant

Legal Issues

Cuba's Most Significant Legal Developments During the Special Period: Prospects for Change in a Comparative
   Context
   Stephen Kimmerling
Discussant: Steven Escobar, U.S. Department of Commerce
The Contribution of BITS to Cuba's Foreign Investment Program
   Jorge Pérez-López, U.S. Department of Labor, and Matías Travieso-Díaz, Shaw Pittman
Discussant: Juan Carlos Bermúdez, Bermúdez & Tomé
Labor Law Issues and Challenges
   Aldo Leiva
Discussant: Gerard Morales, Snell & Wilmer

SALUDO A LA DÉCIMA REUNIÓN DE ASCE

Marta Beatriz Roque

Primero que todo quiero saludar a los miembros de ASCE y decirles que para mí es un placer poder estar aunque sea a través del hilo telefónico y a través de esta grabación con ustedes, ya que durante muchos años en estas reuniones estuvo presente el Instituto Cubano de Economistas Independientes y nosotros también, a través de la vía telefónica y de muchos amigos que nos ayudaron, pudimos hacerles llegar nuestro reconocimiento y nuestra felicitación por el trabajo que ustedes realizan.

Desgraciadamente dos personas allegadas al Instituto Cubano de Economistas Independientes no se encuentran con nosotros. Me refiero a nuestro hermano Manuel Sánchez Guerrero, que falleció el año pasado, y también a Vladimiro Roca, que está aún en prisión; pero aunque no estén presentes con nosotros siempre los tendremos en nuestro recuerdo.

Quisiera también decirles que durante todos estos años en que hemos trabajado juntos en distintos proyectos y en distintos intercambios de informaciones, para nosotros ha sido un placer contar con la ayuda

de personas tan destacadas dentro de los economistas en los Estados Unidos, como el Dr. Armando Lago, Juan Carlos Espinosa, Jorge Sanguinetty, Plinio Montalván, Rodolfo Carrandi, la Sra. María Werlau y Beatriz Tarajano, que tanto nos ayudan.

Quisiera también recordarles que durante mucho tiempo nuestro Instituto ha estado preparándose para poder en un futuro tener soluciones a la situación nueva que va a tener nuestro país cuando llegue la transición a la democracia y que durante todo este tiempo hemos estado recopilando datos, informaciones, haciendo proyectos, estudios que ponemos a la disposición de ASCE para poder ayudar también en las buenas intenciones que ustedes tienen a resolver los problemas del futuro.

Para todos un fuerte abrazo, un fuerte cariño y el reconocimiento de todos los economistas independientes al trabajo de ustedes, en particular en mi persona.

Los estimo siempre. Gracias.

CUBA DUAL: CRISIS ECONÓMICA, CRISIS DEL RÉGIMEN

Antonio Elorza

Uno de los dichos más repetidos en La Habana hace referencia a dos de las características más salientes del régimen de Fidel Castro: "Esto no hay quien lo tumbe, pero tampoco hay quien lo arregle." Efectivamente, en contra de las previsiones apresuradas de los sovietólogos, el castrismo resistió al efecto dominó que dio en tierra con la URSS y con las llamadas democracias populares del Este europeo. Como Fidel proclamara con orgullo en la conmemoración del 26 de julio hace un año: "Lo hemos logrado." Pero tampoco ha aprovechado el régimen esa resistencia victoriosa para introducir cambios que en otros países del mundo comunista, como China o Vietnam, permiten augurar hoy en ellos una supervivencia duradera del partido comunista en el poder, en situación de monopolio, mientras tiene lugar una eficaz restauración de relaciones económicas de signo capitalista. Por un momento, después de las reformas de supervivencia, puestas en marcha entre 1993 y 1995, pudo parecer que se abría esa perspectiva. Fue un simple espejismo y la famosa Ley 88 del pasado año demuestra que cualquier cambio en la Isla acaba siempre, como el vuelo del bumerán, con un regreso al punto de partida.

Para entender lo ocurrido, amen de recordar lo que siempre significa el factor insularidad, conviene tener en cuenta que el régimen instalado en Cuba desde los años 60 no es un sistema comunista asimilable al de la URSS o a las democracias populares. Puede ser útil plantear la comparación con el franquismo de España, que ciertamente no fue un Estado totalitario, pero tampoco el régimen autoritario de que hablara Juan Linz. El franquismo, igual que el castrismo por otras vías, puede ser calificado por un cesarismo, la

dictadura ejercida con por un jefe militar cuya legitimidad procede de haber protagonizado la victoria en una contienda civil. Y a la personalización del régimen corresponde una lógica tendencia a convertir en vitalicia esa magistratura excepcional, ya que el vencedor asume una dimensión soteriológica, como salvador que pretende haber redimido para siempre a la nación de sus males históricos, fundando además un nuevo orden con vocación de eternidad. Es cierto que por su condición humana el dictador no puede aspirar por si mismo a esa eternidad, pero por lo menos, de forma natural y espontánea, intentará por todos los medios que la duración de su poder y la de su propia vida coincidan. No existe a este respecto diferencia alguna entre Franco y Castro.

Sí la hay en cuanto al contenido de ese cesarismo. En el caso de Franco, la línea de poder fue estrictamente militar. El Ejército era "la columna vertebral del régimen," no sólo en un sentido defensivo, como instrumento de represión dispuesto a aplastar cualquier disidencia, sino tamién acompañando al poder del dictador con su penetración en los altos niveles de la administración del Estado y de la justicia. El de Castro no es un cesarismo de base militar, aun cuando esta vertiente nunca pueda ser olvidada, sino un cesarismo de base comunista, en la medida que después de muchos vaivenes fue el PC el que asumió la tarea de asumir la gestión administrativa en régimen de monopolio, así como el encuadramiento y control de la población. Así que ni el franquismo fue un pretorianismo, como pudo ser el régimen argentino hasta la derrota de las Malvinas, ni el castrismo una dictadura del proletariado en cualquiera de sus formas, ya que en ambos casos el dictador es el centro último de decisiones y tanto el Ejército con Franco como el PC con Castro desempeñan un papel instrumental, estrictamente sometidos a la voluntad del líder máximo.

No nos detendremos en la diferencia radical entre el sentido arcaizante del franquismo, heredero en tantas cosas de la mentalidad de aquellos capitanes generales que gobernaban Cuba como plaza sitiada, y el populismo igualitario que cargado de buenas intenciones y resultados pésimos define al castrismo desde la toma del poder. Importa en cambio tomar en consideración que tras los escarceos de principios de los 40, una vez disipado el humo de las victorias del Tercer Reich, el franquismo asume sin reservas el legado fascista, pero sectorialmente, en las políticas de comunicación y de represión. Con la ayuda de la Iglesia, intentará sin éxito imponer la mentalidad reaccionaria del nacional-catolicismo y al constatar el fracaso se limitará a exigir el mantenimiento del orden. Para Franco, el país era un cuartel; reinando la disciplina, la intendencia podía administrarse de una u otra manera. Así, a partir de fines de los años 50 la sociedad civil va recuperando su autonomía, en el marco de un fuerte crecimiento económico, de modo que el sistema de valores que intentaba asentar el régimen está muerto cuando desaparece el dictador. En la transición democrática española, los partidos políticos se limitaron a ser los vehículos de un cambio ya realizado en los planos económico y cultural.

En cambio, el sello progresista en el discurso y en los fines no impide que el proyecto de Fidel deba ser considerado como totalitario. Un totalitarismo permanentemente enmascarado por la demagogia, pero que responde a los elementos de la definición que nos proporciona el politólogo Emilio Gentile: una forma nueva de dominación política, puesta en práctica por un movimiento revolucionario que postula una concepción global de la política, conquista el monopolio del poder, y una vez logrado éste construye un Estado nuevo, asentado sobre un partido único y sobre un sistema policial y terrorista que le permite eliminar a los enemigos interiores. La transformación buscada de la sociedad, conseguida mediante la coerción y la actuación intensiva de los aparatos ideológicos de Estado, encuentra el respaldo de una religión política cuya meta consiste en la creación de un hombre nuevo consagrado al cumplimiento de los fines del movimiento totalitario.

No resulta dudoso adscribir todos y cada uno de los rasgos de esta definición al castrismo, que merecería incluso la calificación de "totalismo," por cuanto tiene la pretensión de ejercer un control omnicomprensivo de la vida cotidiana de los cubanos, en la formación ideológica de la infancia, en el adoctrinamiento permanente por los medios de comunicación y en la actuación de las organizaciones de masas, con el resultado de un permanente lavado de cerebro, y, para cerrar el círculo, el establecimiento de un entramado general de vigilancia a través de los Comités de Defensa de la Revolución. La vida de un cubano, según el diseño oficial, debe consistir en un continuo esfuerzo para responder al prototipo de hombre (o mujer) revolucionario, lo que de paso implica la intervención permanente del Estado para perseguir y sancionar los comportamientos anómicos con el concurso de la población militante. En suma, todo cubano es el portador viviente de los valores de la Revolución, el sujeto que como pueblo protagoniza la vida del país, y por eso mismo ha de estar en todo momento sometido a vigilancia y eventual persecución desde el poder.

No resulta posible pronóstico alguno sobre la economía cubana sin tener en cuenta el peso de este sistema totalitario, por resquebrajado que esté en estos últimos tiempos. Y tampoco cabe olvidar la peculiar ideología del personaje que ocupa su centro y asume las grandes decisiones. Por muchas invocaciones que haga al comunismo o a Martí, Fidel no es ni marxista ni martiano. Se ha dicho muchas veces que gobernaba Cuba como si fuera su finca particular y no cabe excluir que la experiencia vivida en su infancia, con su padre, un gallego violento y posesivo, señor absoluto de su hacienda en Birán, constituya el único modo de explicar el peculiar modo de gestión de la isla que ya descubriera René Dumont en 1960. El ensueño igualitario bajo su poder omnímodo, el desprecio del bienestar y la oposición a todo tipo de iniciativa individual, incluso la mitificación de la figura del médico, sólo son explicables partiendo del peculiar sistema de valores del indiano gallego. Sus efectos son conocidos y pueden experimentarse con toda dureza en la Cuba de hoy: no hay posibilidad de *remake* cubana del modelo chino bajo Fidel, porque nunca estará dispuesto a admitir ese componente básico del desarrollo capitalista que es la puesta en acción del individualismo económico. Aberraciones como las doce sillas en los paladares, entre tantas otras, como lo fuera en los años 80 la supresión del mercado libre campesino, responden a esa condición de amo de personas y bienes que en el espacio de toda la isla asume el dictador. Por eso no cabe excluir que habiendo conseguido sobrevivir a la crisis del período especial Castro pìense de nuevo en relanzar la construcción de *su* socialismo.

En especial por lo que concierne a la personalidad del Comandante, esos rasgos del sistema tienen una inmediata repercusión sobre la situación económica y sus perspectivas. La principal, propia de los cesarismos, es conocida de todos: nada fundamental cambiará en tanto que no se produzca la muerte o la incapacidad de Fidel. Las expectativas alentadas en los comienzos de la década se han desvanecido. Por ahora, en cambio, ejerce más peso esa peculiar oposición de Castro a las formas individuales de capitalismo. Bloquea la posibilidad de un desarrollo cubano según el patrón chino y en ese sentido incide poderosamente sobre las formas de vida y de pensamiento de muchísimos cubanos. Adelantaremos que, a nuestro juicio, siendo ese anticapitalismo primario un factor de estrangulamiento a corto plazo de la economía cubano, puede a medio plazo ser un aliciente para la transición política. Luego intentaremos explicarlo.

Los elementos represivos del sistema tampoco pueden ser olvidados. Los rasgos específicos del castrismo en este campo constituyen una acumulación de obstáculos contra un cambio político de signo democrático, tanto por la concentración de fuerzas policiaco-militares como por ese factor de control totalitario capilar que gravita casa a casa sobre la vida de los cubanos. No será un mecanismo que se ponga automáticamente en marcha a la muerte de Fidel pero, con todas sus quiebras, especialmente en el nivel de los comités de defensa, puede ser todavía utilizable. A diferencia del caso español, las precondiciones para el tránsito no están dadas. Con una excepción en que

los dos procesos coinciden: el enorme efecto simbólico que tendrá la muerte del dictador, con la consiguiente apertura de conflictos en el vértice del régimen y la posibilidad de que entren en juego las movilizaciones derivadas de una historia, la de estos diez últimos años, cargada de frustraciones para amplias capas de la población cubana.

* * *

¿Por qué la variante castrista del comunismo no siguió la suerte de las democracias populares y de la URSS? Carmelo Mesa-Lago encontró como factores explicativos las diferencias existentes entre Cuba y sus socios protectores, encontrándose ante todo la economía cubana menos relacionada con las economías de mercado que las euroorientales. "A mediados de los 80 Cuba era el país del campo soviético más independiente políticamente de la URSS (con excepción de Rumanía), pero el más dependiente de la URSS y el COMECON. Además Cuba era uno de los países menos desarrollados e industrializados de este grupo de naciones y figuraba entre los que contaban con menos vínculos económicos con el mercado capitalista mundial." El mantenimiento de los subsidios soviéticos hasta el final de la década hizo que en Cuba, a pesar del clima de recesión económica, no se sintieran directamente los efectos de la crisis de obsolescencia que las economías del Este experimentan en ese período. La suspensión del pago de la deuda exterior en 1986 fue signo de crisis, como la propia consigna de "rectificación," pero hasta 1990-91 la población cubana no sintió el golpe de la crisis que venía de Europa. Se mantenía la imagen de que cualesquiera que fuesen las dificultades, éstas eran menores que las sufridas por las capas populares en otros países de América Latina. Sólo cuando desaparece traumáticamente la condición subsidiada de su economía, adquieren los cubanos conciencia de la realidad.

La insularidad y la capacidad represiva del castrismo hicieron lo demás. La satisfacción antes reseñada no iba muy lejos, según había probado en tiempos de bonanza el éxodo de los "marielitos," y ahorá probarán los "balseros," reaccionando casi de inmediato al empeoramiento de la situación económica. La diferencia es que por el hecho insular esa trágica huída no tenía la calidad de detonador de tensiones dentro del país de salida que tuvo el éxodo de alemanes de la RDA hacia Occidente. No había retroacción, sino vacío. El papel de imán desempeñado por los símbolos de la sociedad de consumo de tipo occidental era comparable en uno y otro caso, pero entre comunismo y capitalismo no mediaba en este caso un muro, sino el estrecho de Florida.

Y estaba, en fin, la capacidad de control y de respuesta represiva a cargo del régimen totalitario antes descrito. Control primero, tanto por la intensidad de la presencia policial como por esa inquisición capilar que son los CDRs. La disidencia individual de cara a la huída podía ocultarse, pero cualquier embrión de sociabilidad, por no hablar de organización, alternativa al régimen debe ser inmediatamente detectada y sancionada. Es el "totalismo" a que antes hacíamos referencia, un pulpo, una *piovra* por aludir a otro fenómeno de atenazamiento general de una sociedad, el de la Mafia siciliana, que ha servido hasta ahora, y lo hizo eficazmente en el tiempo de crisis de los primeros 90, para evitar en la Isla la formación de corrientes opositoras y, llegado el caso, para golpear parapolicialmente a la disidencia mediante los llamados *actos de repudio*. Una de las tareas destructivas más eficazmente realizadas por el régimen de Castro consistió en el aplastamiento de toda posibilidad de sociedad civil, y ésta fue la protagonista de las movilizaciones que en la Europa del Este dieron en tierra con las dictaduras comunistas. En Cuba, ha sido factible huir, pero no movilizarse.

Y en la pirámide represiva, el vértice cesarista también cuenta. Cualquiera que fuese el orden de los factores que incidieron sobre la decisión de Fidel de eliminarle, lo sucedido con el general Ochoa tuvo por efecto un fortalecimiento de los mecanismos de represión en manos de Raúl Castro a través del MINFAR y una aplicación del consejo de que "la letra con sangre entra" de cara a cualquier sueño de acción opositora desde el Ejército. De paso Fidel confirmó con la sentencia de muerte un mensaje que los cubanos, como los españoles de la era de Franco, tienen bien aprendido: el pulso no le tiembla para matar si está en juego la supervivencia de su poder. El lenguaje agresivo del período 1990-92, diseñando una estrategia de eliminación, incluso de aquellos que fueran

tibios en la adhesión al régimen, al grito de "Cuba será un eterno Baraguá," fue entendido por la población, aún sorprendida por un malestar económico que pudo parecer pasajero. La conciencia de rebeldía hoy visible se encontraba todavía en gérmen.

* * *

El origen de la crisis económica de los años 90 es de sobra conocido. A pesar de la ineficiencia de la economía cubana y del embargo norteamericano, la utopía socialista dirigida por Fidel Castro garantizaba un abastecimiento precario, pero regular, al conjunto de la población cubana, gracias a la importante ayuda de los países del campo socialista, y de la URSS en primer término. Era, pues, una utopía subsidiada, que sostenía ventajosamente la comparación con otras sociedades de la América Latina marcadas por fuertes desigualdades. Como es sabido, todo se vino abajo con el desplome del bloque socialista. Dispuesto a mantener a toda costa su régimen, Castro tomó las medidas necesarias para que la población soportara las restricciones derivadas de un 40 por 100 de descenso en el PIB. Obviamente, el nivel de miseria alcanzado obligaba, esta vez sí, a una rectificación. Las reformas puestas en vigor a partir de la legalización del uso del dólar en 1993-94, con la apertura a los capitales extranjeros y una incipiente autorización de las 134 actividades económicas individuales, así como la transformación de las granjas del Estado en cooperativas de producción, permitieron evitar la continuidad de la caída y lograr una cierta recuperación que se mantiene hasta hoy. La caída en picado de los indicadores económicos en 1993 y el "maleconazo" del año siguiente hicieron indispensable ese nuevo curso. Hasta aquí todo es conocido y se ha contado mil veces sin sensibles variantes. Mayor espacio para la polémica abre la caracterización de las relaciones económicas surgidas de la reforma, primero, y más tarde de las restricciones impuestas a la misma.

De entrada, se abría una brecha tan necesaria como difícil de explicar en el sistema económico del socialismo cubano. La primera vocación de éste había sido la lucha contra la dominación imperialista encarnada por el capital norteamericano. Las nacionalizaciones de las empresas y de las propiedades de este orígen fueron descritas como la principal conquista del pue-

5

blo cubano, y más tarde como la condición para emprender el camino que finalmente llevaría al comunismo. Socialismo y orgullo nacional se encontraban unidos, aun cuando, como también sabemos, patria a su vez se identificaba con los sectores populares, excluyendo a una burguesía que resultó expropiada y se vio lanzada al destierro.

El nuevo curso económico rompió esa homogeneidad propia del proyecto socialista, ya que si bien se autoriza la presencia en la Isla del capitalismo internacional, muchas veces en condiciones de privilegio si supera las trabas burocráticas, sigue manteniéndose la barrera que impide la constitución por vías regulares incluso de una pequeña burguesía nacional. Se trata de un movimiento en tijera, que garantiza la restauración del capitalismo en favor de los empresarios extranjeros, capitalistas al margen de toda condena, por cuanto colaboran con el régimen, mientras la gran mayoría de los cubanos se ven condenados, aunque en la forma favorecidos, por permanecer en un marco de relaciones económicas de tipo socialista.

Conviene recordar que esas reformas de 1993-95 debieron ser un trágala que el dictador tuvo forzosamente que asumir por una mera razón de supervivencia. La primera respuesta dada por Fidel a la crisis puso por delante los factores políticos: un numantinismo basado en la exaltación del espíritu revolucionario, la reforma constitucional para so capa de cambio reforzar aún más sus poderes discrecionales de gobernador de plaza sitiada, la represión de los disidentes, el rejuvenecimiento de los cuadros del partido a modo de relevo en la guardia. En 1992, con ocasión del IV Congreso del PCC todavía Castro condenó sin reservas todo cuanto pudiese sonar a modelo chino o economía de mercado. Sin embargo, unos meses más tarde se resignó a suscribir las reformas que hasta hoy definen el marco en que se mueve, o se debate, la economía cubana.

En principio, el diseño de organización económica que sobre el papel hubiera debido salir de las reformas implicaba una inversión en sentido favorable de la tendencia depresiva de la economía, logrando un crecimiento cuyos efectos beneficiosos habían de compensar el golpe inferido al sagrado principio de igualdad. En la cima, el Estado dejaría de ser el gestor indiscutido de toda la economía cubana, atendiendo en primer plano a los objetivos sociales y políticos, para abrir paso a un capitalismo de Estado, según el cual: (a) las decisiones debían estar guiadas por criterios de eficiencia económica, (b) hacia el interior era preciso admitir una cierta des-estatización del mundo campesino autorizando la formación de cooperativas y el regreso de los mercados libres — eso sí, férreamente controlados desde arriba — y, en fin, (c) resultaría factible constituir sociedades mixtas en que el Estado encontrase la financiación de capital exterior a cambio del reconocimiento de un status de empresario, en cuanto a la gestión, la repatriación de beneficios, etc.

Este capitalismo de Estado, con el apoyo de cierta racionalización en el terreno fiscal, debía servir para relanzar la economía, tratando por todos los medios de captar las divisas que llegaban con las inversiones exteriores, y también por la inyección en el sistema monetario cubano de las decisivas remesas de dólares procedentes de la población cubana del exilio. La transformación de las "diplotiendas" en "TRDs," tiendas de recuperación de — antes que de venta en — divisas (dólares), fue destinada a cumplir ese papel, al mismo tiempo que hacía posible a una minoría cada vez más numerosa de cubanos privilegiados satisfacer algunas de sus apetencias de consumo.

Fue preciso también atender a los puntos negros más espectaculares de la estatalización. El regreso del mercado libre campesino permitió incentivar la producción y cubrir, aunque costosamente, las demandas primarias de la población. Y por fin fue autorizado también el trabajo por cuenta propia para más de cien actividades cuidadosamente definidas y con la cláusula de reserva de que el "cuentapropista" no pudiera degenerar en explotador del trabajo ajeno. Era una invitación a poner en juego las menguadas posibilidades que cada uno tuviera, por su vivienda bien situada, el viejo carro utilizable como taxi, la capacidad culinaria, las pequeñas remesas del familiar de Miami. En definitiva, pudo pensarse en un desarrollo de tipo chino, con el Estado en posición de vigilante y de perceptor de impuestos, del que surgiera una acumulación primitiva, gérmen de una normalización económica futura, y también un entramado de relaciones económicas en la base social que hiciese posible superar la penuria generalizada que afectaba a la mayoría de la población.

"Llegó el Comandante y mandó parar," "y se acabó la diversión," cantaba Pablo Milanés con palabras aplicables al tema que nos ocupa. De acuerdo con sus principios, Fidel Castro no podía tolerar que lo que él había destruido, las figuras de su odiado comerciante al por menor, del pequeño empresario, del individuo que busca su propio bienestar, regresasen por la puerta trasera al calor de una reforma de circunstancias. Así que muy pronto el Gobierno implantó todo tipo de frenos y controles a tales actividades. El caso de los paladares, con su máximo de doce sillas, la prohibición de vender carne de res, pescado o marisco, la obligación de surtirse en tiendas en dólares, sirve de símbolo visible de una situación general plagada de obstáculos que explica las fuertes oscilaciones en el número de cuentapropistas. Como además la tasa de impuestos por profesiones es muy alta y fija, no teniendo en cuenta la cifra de ventas y sí aplicando sanciones inmediatas por cualquier infracción, de no contar con influencias oficiales, puede explicarse la situación del sector encargado de repetir el milagro chino en la Isla: salvo excepciones, el cuentapropista vive asfixiado, con el agua al cuello de las infracciones que se ve obligado a cometer para sobrevivir, y por ello unas veces abandona y otras, las más, opta por insertarse en el circuito de relaciones económicas ilegales. Con lo cual no se genera una dinámica de tipo chino, en la cual el sujeto individual, casi siempre envuelto en su familia, innova, crea, gana, e incita al gobierno y a las autoridades a ampliar la tolerancia respecto del cambio o a legislar para evitar ese tránsito hacia esa ilegalidad que en cambio se constituye con frecuencia en Cuba en la única salida posible.

En resumen, las reformas hicieron posible la supervivencia del régimen, pero no la formación de un circuito de relaciones económicas gracias al cual el capitalismo de Estado fuese el motor de un crecimiento, sustentado desde la base social por una dinámica ascendente, de formación de pequeños capitales y de mejora en el nivel de vida, favorecida esa dinámica por la cuantiosa inyección de recursos en forma de divisas que aportan las remesas procedentes del exterior.

El resultado ha sido una Cuba dual, donde la divisoria entre dos conjuntos sociales cada vez más separados viene dada por el acceso al dólar. Sin hablar de los miembros de la clase dirigente que puedan tener alegal o ilegalmente ingresos en dólares por su vinculación con las inversiones extranjeras, como indica un publicista oficial, "cerca del 20 por 100 de los asalariados, ubicados en áreas privilegiadas por la nueva dinámica económica (turismo, tecnologías de punta, industrias exportadoras) recibe ingresos monetarios o en especie adicionales al salario oficial, lo que estaría generando una virtual remodelación de la clase obrera y asalariados en general por el capital internacional." Sin duda el porcentaje es menor, y habría de tenerse en cuenta la sangría que supone el hecho de que los empleados cubanos de empresas extranjeras cobren un puñado de pesos por un trabajo que es pagado al Estado en dólares, pero la descripción resulta aceptable por cuanto define la aparición de una aristocracia de asalariados provistos de dólares a quienes se suman aquellos que reciben remesas de parientes de los Estados Unidos, de España y de otros países de la diáspora cubana, y quienes ejercen actividades ilegales pero remuneradoras, como han sido durante años las *jineteras*, cuya presencia masiva en calles y hoteles ridiculizó hasta hace poco la imagen tópica de que Fidel había acabado con el burdel que era La Habana antes de la Revolución.

En la vertiente no bañada por el sol, aquellos que carecen de dólares se sitúan en una supervivencia de mínimos, sometidos a un racionamiento cuyas entregas de artículos de primera necesidad sufren retrasos que acaban siendo muchas veces cancelaciones. La dramática situación y los siniestros contenidos del abastecimiento popular han sido recientemente evocados en el libro sobre las mujeres cubanas en la crisis de la antropóloga Isabel Holgado, cuyos datos utilizamos a continuación. Destaca la calidad vomitiva de algunos de los productos entregados: "También la composición del picadillo comienza a mostrar una tendencia positiva," proclamaba satisfecho *Granma*, el 4 de marzo de 1999, refiriéndose al "picadillo texturizado" compuesto de un 80 por 100 de soja y un

20 por 100 de residuos cárnicos. Entre otros productos dignos de ser aplicados a la alimentación del ganado, pero que Fidel hace consumir a su "pueblo revolucionario" están también el chorimorci, un extraño chorizo hecho con soja y desperdicios, la "extensión cárnica" con soja y embutidos inclasificables, que según un testimonio "sabe a rayos y se pone duro al freirlo," el perro de pollo con pellejo de pollo y otras cosas, etcétera. Son elementos que informan acerca de un nivel de vida bien alejado de la propaganda oficial, como lo es el ir transportados en "camellos" con una mezcla de hacinamiento, lentitud y, a pesar de todo, largas esperas. Hay claramente en el régimen otras prioridades, militares y represivas, tal y como muestra la paga de los nuevos policías especiales, 800 pesos, doble de la de un médico o de un profesor de Universidad, y el equipamiento moderno de que están dotados. Igual que en cualquier régimen reaccionario tradicional, y en contra del discurso del gobierno, la seguridad del poder es prioritaria respecto del bienestar de la población.

El resultado es una sociedad sometida a tensiones crecientes, que solamente la expectativa generalizada de represión puede sofocar. Y que en todos los niveles funciona a costa de niveles muy altos de corrupción. "Aquí todo el mundo roba, y gracias a eso todo el mundo vive." Este aforismo popular refleja adecuadamente una regla maestra del funcionamiento del sistema económico, y explica una de las motivaciones de la famosa "Ley 88 de protección de la independencia nacional y de la economía de Cuba" en 1999. Es la receta habitual de Fidel, consecuente leninista en este plano: si el conflicto amenaza con llegar a ser incontrolable, represión a ultranza. La reciente caza de miles de *jineteras* y proxenetas, una vez que jugaron su papel de cebo para turistas rijosos, es una muestra de esa lógica pendular, donde a la extensión sigue siempre una violenta contracción.

No existe el circuito de dinamización de la economía que buscaron las reformas de 1993-95, pero sí una superposición de niveles enlazados entre sí por relaciones informales, cuando no por la corrupción. El superior es el correspondiente al área mencionada de capitalismo de Estado, que en tiempos recientes ha recibido un creciente apoyo, con el objeto de poner a su frente una nueva clase de "empresarios socialistas," una especie de centauros que compartirían el conocimiento de las reglas de una economía capitalista avanzada y la lealtad sin fisuras al régimen de la revolución. Es la oferta que presenta ante los eventuales inversores extranjeros un alto dirigente en la XII Feria Internacional de La Habana, con palabras que recuerdan antes la tradición de la dependencia tercermundista que la revolucionaria: "Les ofrecemos un país ordenado. Una política de apertura a la inversión coherente e irreversible. Un pueblo trabajador y abnegado con un alto nivel educacional y técnico. Les ofrecemos una nación soberana y un gobierno honrado e incorruptible." Lo que ocurre es que tantas maravillas son difíciles de creer, y tampoco el propio Fidel debe creerlas él mismo, pues de otro modo no hubiera puesto a jefes militares al frente de sectores claves, como el azúcar y distintas empresas industriales y turísticas. En cualquier caso, el Estado dista de ser "honrado e incorruptible," pues por las fisuras de su engranaje económico se filtran a la sociedad todo tipo de mercancías, desde la gasolina a los materiales de construcción, que mueven la economía del sector privado alegal.

En el fondo de la sociedad, hoy más que nunca, se encuentran aquellos que tienen que sobrevivir con los salarios de hambre reglamentados. Pero la supervivencia de la sociedad cubana no podría entenderse sin el "trapicheo" permanente a que se entregan los habitantes de la Isla, al margen de y por encima de su puesto de trabajo estatal, con la pura y simple intención de sobrevivir. Surge así un subsistema económico, una especie de capa freática que subyace al mundo oficial de los dólares y al mundo oficial de los pesos, alimentada por las precipitaciones que representan las remesas del exterior y las sustracciones a los recursos del Estado que la corrupción de sus agentes hace posible. Esta economía sumergida del socialismo cubano es la que hace posible que las tensiones de la vida cotidiana de los pobladores de la isla resulte mínimamente soportable. Representa siempre una jornada de trabajo suplementaria, donde la mujer desempeña un papel primordial, pero también cualquier miembro de la unidad familiar en condiciones de desplazarse para adquirir la pieza de recambio, la botella de aceite, los alimentos que luego podrán ser vendidos con ventaja a los vecinos o a los compañeros de trabajo. En el límite, la vivienda doméstica se convierte en granja, tal y como recordaba la canción humorística del grupo "Punto y Coma," dedicada a "la puerca Caridad" (que acaba con la detención de los propietarios y de la propia cerda criada con todo cuidado en el hogar). Es un entramado de alcance general en que las relaciones de trueque, los intercambios, las adquisiciones en dólares, tienen lugar siempre al margen de la legalidad. Dentro de las reglas fijadas por el Estado, la vida se hace imposible; resulta en consecuencia imprescindible sumirse en la ilegalidad y en la corrupción para atender las necesidades mínimas, con un doble riesgo. De un lado, la supervivencia debida a las remesas del exterior o a tratos ilegales generaliza la propensión a la delincuencia y al parasitismo; de otro, el "cuentapropista" no registrado, por honrado que sea su trabajo, tiene siempre sobre sí la espada de Damocles de la represión estatal, muchas veces arbitraria (un confidente puede manejar sin problemas su taxi ilegal) y modulada en un tira y afloja de acuerdo con las estimaciones del gobierno acerca de la coyuntura social y política.

Son tensiones que la omnipresencia policial trata de hacer invisibles. Como el médico de familia, en La Habana o en Santiago hay un policía, casi siempre oriental, en cada esquina de cuadra, y casi siempre están ocupados revisando una documentación o informando por teléfono móvil a la central. Pero el incremento en la densidad de *segurosos* no basta para dibujar la imagen de renovación que el régimen aspira a presentar al exterior. La Revolución con mayúscula no ha desaparecido del imaginario, pero casi siempre se reduce a la exhibición del cromo polivalente del "Che," ese otro Cristo del siglo XX que con su sacrificio intentó redimir a la humanidad, y en primer término a América Latina. Para uso de *marketing*, las restantes figuras de la revolución pasan al desván de los trastos viejos y son sustituidas por Compay Segundo, la salsa y el bolero. En un vuelo de Cubana Madrid-La Habana, la pantalla sólo presenta hoteles de lujo, playas y cantantes con ritmo. De acuerdo con la lógica de esta Cuba dual, abierta al capitalismo exterior y que reserva para sus ciudadanos un modo de producción casi esclavista, conviene separar los espacios en la medida de lo posible. Los visitantes deben entrar lo menos posible en contacto con la población, vieja norma ahora repuesta en nombre de la seguridad, y por ello enviados cuando se puede a guettos de lujo, como los cayos. Si el guetto no existe, se le fabrica. Es lo que realiza con notable eficiencia el llamado "historiador de la Ciudad," Eusebio Leal, con su sociedad anónima Habaguanex, en una labor de reconstrucción que no sólo tiene una finalidad de embellecimiento, ya que ante todo permite mostrar al turista en los palacios y en las calles remozadas de La Habana Vieja, una ciudad ideal sembrada de tiendas de lujo y lugares de diversión; una imagen de la capital liberada de todas las miserias expuestas hasta hace poco a su vista con la acumulación de viviendas cochambrosas y casas en ruina. Es la vieja técnica de Potemkin para satisfacer a Catalina II, sólo que ahora aplicada a poner una máscara sobre el fracaso social de la revolución.

En suma, el posible crecimiento de los últimos años ha podido favorecer a la capa de los "empresarios socialistas," a los militares convertidos en gestores y al conglomerado de gentes del dólar, pero en modo alguno ha resuelto los problemas que la penuria del "período especial" había creado a la mayoría de la población, y el precio pagado por todo ello han sido una corrupción y una represión rampantes. Esta última es susceptible de evitar el estallido, pero en la misma medida se verá incrementada la frustración de tantos cubanos que del malestar económico han pasado en esta década a la puesta en cuestión del sistema político.

* * *

"¡No es fácil!" es la expresión mil veces repetida, con la que los cubanos designan las dificultades con que tropiezan en su vida cotidiana para resolver las menores cosas. Lo dicen con tristeza, a veces con un punto de angustia, reflejando una actitud de falta de esperanza, todo lo contrario de lo que proclama la retórica del régimen. En una palabra, son conscientes de que en Cuba se vive peor de lo que se podría vivir, y además sometidos a una presión insoportable del poder político.

Tal vez éste sea el efecto más importante a medio plazo de la crisis de los 90. Hasta el fin de los subsidios, las dificultades se veían compensadas por un sentimiento de seguridad, machacado una y otra vez sobre las conciencias por la propaganda oficial. Ahora ésta no surte efecto, aunque la trabajadora cubana no encuentre medio de evitar su penosa actuación como figurante en las manifestaciones por el regreso de Elián. Los corresponsales de prensa en La Habana, por puro deber de profesionalidad, debieran haber informado sobre cómo se organizaban tales movilizaciones de masas, las coacciones indirectas en el reclutamiento, la falta de asistencia a participantes enrolados de cinco de la mañana a tres de la tarde, en lugar de transmitir sin más que era poco menos que el pueblo en armas por la repatriación. Esto no quiere decir que la base social de apoyo al castrismo haya desaparecido, siendo sin duda aún fuerte entre la población negra y en Oriente, por citar sólo dos muestras visibles. Sin embargo, las capas sociales que han experimentado de un modo u otro la frustración de las reformas no son ya susceptibles de experimentar reacción alguna ante lo que les cuenta el régimen. Saben que éste es mendaz, ineficaz, represivo a veces hasta niveles ridículos, enemigo jurado del bienestar individual, corrupto, y *last but not least*, que en contra de sus sagrados principios favorece una desigualdad intolerable en favor de los nuevos privilegiados del dólar. En La Habana, la tradicional y juiciosa reserva de los ciudadanos ante el tema político ha dejado paso a unos deseos muy extendidos de expresar crudamente la propia insatisfacción. De cara a una transición política tras la muerte de Castro, esta población irreversiblemente desengañada difícilmente tolerará sin rebeldía cualquier intento continuista.

Frente a ellos, la continuidad con reformas económicas, básicamente el modelo chino, será sin duda ensayado con una u otra variante por los sectores que se benefician del capitalismo de Estado, teniendo quizás ya configuradas sus esferas de corrupción, sin olvidar a los gestores militares que Fidel ha asociado a la dirección de la economía, ni al aparato comunista. Las bazas defensivas a su disposición no son despreciables, por sus contactos con un capital internacional que puede preferir los buenos negocios con el "orden" poscomunista, y sobre todo por la importancia del aparato represivo todavía en pie, desde los servicios de inteligencia de las FAR a los CDRs, pasando por los decenas de miles de policías que pueden temer la revancha popular. La pelota de la decisión se encuentra en este campo, pues también es posible que los tecnócratas que han ascendido en el régimen apuesten por evitar el riesgo de un estallido y prefieran ensayar una apertura política controlada, algo que una administración norteamericana como la actual apoyaría sin reservas. En fin, también cuenta el tiempo, y en sentido desfavorable, dada la acumulación de frustraciones, degradación moral y corrupción que la crisis del período especial y su legado hoy vigente, la dualidad reseñada, han traído a la sociedad cubana.

CUBA Y SU ECONOMÍA DE RESISTENCIA

Manuel David Orrio

Quiero iniciar estas palabras a la Décima Reunión Anual de la Asociación para el Estudio de la Economía Cubana, con mi más cálido saludo a los participantes. Desde La Habana, me acompañan Oscar Espinosa Chepe y una persona para quien reservo mi admiración. Puede decirse que el encuentro de este día toma ribete de fiestas porque el mismo se desenvuelve teniendo entre nosotros a la economista independiente, Marta Beatriz Roque Cabello, apenas libre de una prisión que nunca mereció. Para ella, para su sacrificio, para la misión que Dios le encomendó y supo cumplir, al igual que Rene Gómez Manzano y Félix Antonio Bonne Carcassés, y tanto como aún la cumple el economista Vladimiro Roca Antúnez, vayan los mejores pensamientos de esta reunión.

Iniciar este ejercicio con una mención a los cuatro de "La Patria es de Todos," no es gratuito. Podrá discreparse del contenido de "La Patria es de Todos," pero es verdad como templo, que en el mismo aparece de manera implícita una de las palabras que a juicio de este ponente, permite comprender. Ese vocablo no es otro que el de resistencia porque el mismo nos cuenta de una política económica incapaz de conducir a Cuba por las alamedas del desarrollo sostenible, así como del proceso de emergencia de una economía y una sociedad paralela, definibles a través de concepto que propongo.

Si cuatro intelectuales cubanos fueron a las cárceles por expresar ideas no del gusto del poder y si se acepta que las cabezas pensantes están unidas al cuerpo del pueblo por hilos invisibles, al decir de un filósofo, obvio es que ellos no sólo protagonizaron un hecho resistente, sino que además, revelaron el desarrollo de una cultura de resistencia sustentada sobre una economía de igual género, que afectaría el más ortodoxo discurso marxista. Desde luego, otra conceptualización de esa resistencia pudiera ser la de informalidad, algo que entre sociólogos y economistas se define como hacer lo lícito por lo ilícito.

Un anécdota de la República Cubana de 1940 muestra cómo los avatares informales ya estaban presentes en aquella Cuba y cómo ellos creaban ciertos convenios entre las autoridades judiciales. Podría ocurrir por aquellos días que un hombre sin empleo y con hambre se presentase en aquellos restaurantes baratos, regenteados por inmigrantes chinos y, tras solicitar el menú, ordenase algún tipo de comida. La escena posterior era la misma, tras comer sin pagar el hombre abandonaba el restaurante con los pies en polvorosa, seguido del dueño y la correspondiente multitud, al viento el cubano grito ¡ataja! Si le capturaban y le llevaban a juicio, el magistrado de turno preguntaba por el menú consumido. Si se trataba de arroz y potaje de frijoles, el acusado era absuelto; si no, 30 días de cárcel.

Los jueces de aquel entonces interpretaban que no era delito aliviar el hambre, pero sí era hacerlo con un menú mejor. De este modo, lo lícito de comer por medios ilícitos, comer informal diríase, contaba con una suerte de espacio de derecho.

Vale la anécdota para comprender por qué en la Cuba del llamado período especial ha crecido tanto la informalidad económica en ribetes tanto humorísticos como dramáticos, al punto que se ha llegado a decir que ello es el motor de los pocos cambios habidos en el último decenio, en dirección de hacer de la población el verdadero sujeto de la economía. Y aunque tales aseveraciones encierran cierto reduccionismo es un hecho que esa informalidad ha jugado y está jugando un rol de presión hacia el poder, insuficientemente estudiado dentro de los procesos económicos isleños a juzgar por la secuencia de los acontecimientos, y su reflejo legislativo, así como por las resistencias gubernamentales al despliegue de una economía más cercana al mercado.

De acuerdo con datos del Instituto Nacional de Investigaciones Económicas a la altura de 1995 la economía informal abarcaba al 50% de la circulación en mercancías, algo ilustrativo de la extensión y profundidad alcanzada por el proceso. Sin embargo, en las condiciones cubanas el concepto de informalidad aparece como insuficientemente descriptivo. Una cosas es que en una economía de mercado, de menor o mayor desarrollo, un sector de la producción produzca y comercie de ese modo y algo muy distinto es que en estados como Cuba, donde las imposiciones restrictivas van contra la naturaleza humana, todo un pueblo se ve involucrado en transacciones informales. Por ello, formula hipótesis de que no se está ante una economía informal, sino ante una de resistencia, signada por una tradición ascentral de lucha contra los monopolios.

Si en el siglo XVIII existió estanco del tabaco y rebelión de los vegueros, hoy el gobierno de Fidel Castro monopoliza esa industria, pero en las calles de La Habana una rebelión de los vegueros produce y merca. ¿Cómo llamarla? Informalidad o resistencia.

Un poco de memoria histórica aceptará la existencia de esos procesos a lo largo de los primeros 30 años de gobierno de Fidel Castro, aun cuando las subvenciones soviéticas dieran a los mismos un carácter marginal, no comparable con lo ocurrido a partir de 1990, en que acontecimientos como el IV Congreso del Partido Comunista de Cuba evidenció una voluntad popular a favor de reformas promotoras del mercado.

No ocurrió casualmente que al convocarse a la discusión abierta del llamamiento a ese Congreso más de un millón de personas propusieran la reapertura de los mercados libres campesinos, hoy mercados agropecuarios, cerrados a tenor del llamado proceso de

rectificación de errores y tendencias negativas, cuyo resultado visible en las estadísticas oficiales de los ochenta, fue dar el tiro de gracia a un modelo económico estadista, ya agotado por lo menos desde cinco años atrás.

Más de una vez me he preguntado si los analistas de la situación cubana hemos sabido valorar la significación de aquel Congreso como punto de inflexión en la percepción y actitud del cubano de a pie, hacia los sucesos económicos. En tanto que oportunidad perdida para sortear o palear la crisis sin precedente que lo sucedió debido a una actitud y inmovilista gubernamental, virtualmente respondida por el pueblo de cuatro maneras: la oposición, la balsa, la inercia y una economía de resistencia que reivindicó el derecho de comer, así de simple, pero que a la vez, fue germen de lo que hoy podría llamarse el empresario informal cubano.

A través de un mirador como periodista independiente, he criticado una suerte de línea editorial de los medios de prensa al exterior de Cuba, según la cual, parece como si el gobierno de Fidel Castro hubiera adoptado algunas decisiones tímidamente aperturistas, implementadas en el último quinquenio como resultado de una voluntad política o de coyunturas económicas externas. Nada más falso. La secuencia de los acontecimientos y el movimiento legislativo demuestran que, salvo el caso de la inversión extranjera, una resistencia popular al monopolio del Estado ha sido la fuerza motriz de esos cambios, por mínimos que sean. Si ese poder guerrillero y desordenado se canalizó por vías informales, a falta de caminos institucionales, se sabe por qué, o no ha rendido suficientes y mejores frutos por falta de dinero a la mano, ambos son motivos para que los estudiosos nos preguntemos el por qué, con la actitud desprejuiciada y distintiva de los estudios.

LOS HECHOS A LA VISTA

El IV Congreso afectó a la inversión extranjera como voluntad política y no despenalizó al dólar, lógico corolario, y el pueblo traficó en esa moneda hasta imponer su legalidad. Guardó silencio acerca del restablecimiento de los mercados libres campesinos y el vulgo contrabandeó viandas hasta llegar a una frase célebre: o saco a los tanques o saco al mercado.

Se limitó aquel IV Congreso a declaraciones generales sobre el autoempleo y media nación se dedicó a los pequeños negocios clandestinos hasta que el decreto sobre el particular puso más o menos orden a regañadientes. Semejante batallas se libraron gracias al apoyo externo de las remesas familiares, hoy principal fuente de ingresos netos a la economía cubana, calculada del modo más conservador en unos 900 millones de dólares, a la altura del año pasado.

Pero no puede olvidarse que la Comisión Económica para América Latina estimó que antes de la despenalización del dólar la población cubana ya atesoraba la bicoca de 200 millones de dólares, todo un acto de la verdad profunda y testimonio paradojal de la condición también resistente de los envíos de divisas, razón por la cual vale apuntar que parece que las economías de resistencia al estilo cubano, son más globalizadas de lo que se imagina. Nunca, a mi entender, han estado más alejados los gobiernos cubano y norteamericano de los sentires profundos del pueblo cubano, uno por prohibir un despliegue económico, otro por restringir los recursos que permiten a las fuerzas económicas al interior de Cuba el forzar, desde abajo y desde adentro, ese despliegue económico.

Si se trata de ser franco, la familia cubana ha demostrado ser mejor economista que todos nosotros juntos. Primero, al salvar su lado isleño; segundo, al dotarle de al menos el sueño para mejor emplear sus calificaciones técnicas y profesionales por vía de una posible capitalización de las remesas que de hecho se está produciendo, y se ha producido.

Una investigación de 1995 realizada por el entonces periodista independiente, José Manuel Canfiano, arrojó que en La Habana Vieja existían 116 restaurantes de los llamados *paladares*, muchos de ellos ilegales pero más de las dos terceras partes creados con recursos provenientes del exterior, según confesaron sus dueños. Un decenio de manifestación de esa economía resistente invita a reflexionar. Si en un primer quinquenio obligó al gobierno de Fidel Castro a mal aceptar las realidades del mercado y dio a todo un pueblo la posibilidad de reconocerse a sí mismo como botado de una iniciativa empresarial casi genética, un segundo quinquenio evidenció que pese a los intentos gubernamentales de yugular la economía de

resistencia del pueblo de Cuba se hizo irreversible aun cuando sufra las heridas de una disminución en el número de autoempleados bajo registro, para citar un ejemplo, quienes más bien parecen haberse incorporado a los autoempleados ilegales que a la condición de trabajadores estatales o paraestatales.

De acuerdo con cifras oficiales, los ocupados en la economía disminuyeron entre 1995 y 1998 en unos 370.400 y ese número podría haberse incrementado a la fecha, habida cuenta de las tendencias demográficas. Al mismo tiempo, una sospechosa relación se observa entre el incremento de las remesas y la caída del número de ocupados al tiempo que la negativa gubernamental a otorgar más permisos de autoempleo es respondida con un número creciente de personas que se desempeñan en oficios diversos, pese a serle denegada la licencia. El caso de los taxistas clandestinos es paradigmático, pero no único, y de todo ello, sólo estamos viendo la cima del *iceberg*. Evado intencionalmente el tema de corrupción, ubicada en una invisible frontera entre lo formal y lo informal o resistente. Pero el dato del creciente abordamiento de este fenómeno por parte de la prensa oficiosa isleña, dice por sí mismo que ni el propio gobierno cubano está en capacidad de responder hasta dónde se trata de corrupción al estilo tradicional latinoamericano, o si no se sabe que hacer ante las manifestaciones de esa economía de resistencia.

Guste a quien guste, pese a quien pese, una emergente sociedad civil actúa e interactúa en las difíciles condiciones cubanas. Los proclamados resultados económicos gubernamentales, como se sabe, se basan sobre estadísticas lo suficientemente contradictorias como para dudar de ellos.

Algunos de mis artículos recientes prueban que con sólo ordenar las cifras, la interrogante de credibilidad surge cuando esos datos se comparan, además, con la observación a lo largo y ancho de las calles. La pregunta inevitable es ¿de qué vive la gente? Aún no sabemos si con embargo se mueven, pero es indudable que con embargo están viviendo, al punto de para algunos ser admisible la hipótesis de que las estadísticas gubernamentales están perdiendo la oportunidad de sumar los resultados de la economía de resistencia: ubicua, guerrillera y fantasmal.

Desde luego, es un proceso de ganadores y perdedores, donde ya se observan matices del capitalismo salvaje, como son la existencia de miles de trabajadores sin seguro social o carentes de oportunidades de asociación libre y justa.

Creo, llegado el momento, de prestar la mayor atención a esos procesos y de buscar fórmulas para prestar apoyo a los mismos, antes de que por una u otra razón deriven hacia manifestaciones de lo peor económico. De una economía informal o resistente, pueden surgir más temprano que tarde, desde un próspero sistema de pequeñas y medianas empresas hasta una corporación del crimen organizado. La economía de resistencia cubana es un vehículo de transición. Pero, ¿hacia cuál transición?

Dejo para otra ocasión discutir si las sanciones económicas unilaterales de Estados Unidos a Cuba, apoyan o no a esa economía emergente del pueblo cubano. Mas quiero invitar a pensar si ellas contribuyen a dotar a esa economía de los instrumentos para continuar llevando adelante, en las nuevas condiciones, la labor de presión objetiva que sí pudo realizar durante el primer quinquenio de la era del picadillo de soya en la Cuba de Fidel Castro.

Una pregunta pudiera bastar para comenzar a hallar muchas respuestas. ¿Es contra Fidel Castro, o es por el pueblo cubano? Desde La Habana, muchas gracias.

EL ESTADO REAL DE LA ECONOMÍA CUBANA

Oscar Espinosa Chepe

En primer término, quiero expresarles mi agradecimiento por propiciar dirigirme a ustedes, enviarles mis más calurosos saludos y desearles muchos éxitos en la celebración del décimo encuentro de esta prestigiosa asociación.

Para los profesionales que en la isla junto a miles de hermanos luchamos en muy difíciles condiciones por la democratización de la sociedad y que se haga realidad el principio martiano de una Cuba con todo y para el bien de todos, la existencia de la asociación y su actividad constituyen un gran aliento y confirma que no estamos solos y aunque todavía nos aguardan duras batallas, la hora de la libertad y la reconciliación llegará. Cuba se encuentra sumida en la crisis más terrible de su historia, la cual ha impactado en todos los aspectos de la sociedad con efectos desastrosos sobre los valores espirituales de la ciudadanía.

Para dar una idea del estado real de la economía puede señalarse que, aún basándonos en las controvertidas estadísticas oficiales, al cierre de 1999, después de diez años de período especial, el producto interno bruto cubano a precios constantes, sólo representaba el 80% del alcanzado en 1989. Calculándose con la mejor voluntad que el modesto nivel de ese año únicamente será logrado a fines de la primer década del siglo 21, si no existen cambios radicales en el modelo imperante.

La crisis realmente se agudizó a partir de la pérdida de las enormes subvenciones provenientes del bloque soviético, pero estaba latente mucho antes, manifestándose en los años ochenta con la imposibilidad del país de hacerle frente a su deuda externa, la presencia y crecimiento continuado de un gigantesco déficit comercial, el aumento constante del saldo negativo del presupuesto estatal y el estancamiento del producto interno bruto, entre otros hechos, que enuncian la falta de veracidad de los argumentos oficiales acerca de que el estado actual de la economía responde a factores externos y no como efectivamente resulta, a la obstinada aplicación de un sistema estatista extremadamente centralizado que ha llevado la nación a la ruina.

El régimen para ganar tiempo y mantenerse en el poder, a mediados de los años noventa optó por efectuar algunos cambios, dando por consecuencia un modelo económico dual, con una controlada apertura hacia el exterior y un virtual bloqueo al poder creador de los cubanos. Política acrecentada recientemente con el paulatino cierre de los pequeños espacios abiertos a la actividad individual en los años 1993 y 1994.

La inversión extranjera realizada en puntos estratégicos de la economía como el turismo, la producción niquelífera, la prospección y explotación petrolera, la telefonía, la generación eléctrica, la comercialización del tabaco, entre otros, según datos oficiales alcanza ya 4.300 millones de dólares. Estas junto a las remesas estimadas de un rango de 800 a 1000 millones de dólares de ingreso al año y el turismo internacional prácticamente inexistente antes de 1989, y con un ingreso bruto aproximado de 2.000 millones en 1999, han sido los factores fundamentales que evitaron la continuación de la caída del producto interno bruto y propiciaron desde 1995 la modesta y endeble recuperación presente hasta hoy.

Esta dicotomía ha creado una segmentación no sólo en la esfera económica, sino también en la sociedad cubana con su máxima expresión en la dolarización al dividir a las personas entre quienes tienen acceso a la divisa norteamericana y las que no pueden obtenerla. Ello está desligado, en lo esencial, de la capacidad de aporte del ciudadano a la sociedad, pues depende de la suerte de poseer una familia o amigos generosos en el exterior o buenos vínculos con el poder que faciliten la inserción en una plaza del llamado sector emergente.

En la Cuba actual, no sorprende encontrar a muchos profesionales y reconocidos expertos trabajando en hoteles como sirvientes o en otras actividades primarias, nada relacionadas con sus conocimientos, en busca del billete verde para poder adquirir artículos y servicios básicos sólo ofertados en esa moneda.

Esta situación, a la vez que provoca junto a otros factores una creciente descapitalización humana, incide desfavorablemente en los sectores donde sólo se pagan los salarios en la depreciada moneda nacional, produciéndose una fuga indetenible de los trabajadores hacia otros lugares y, el peor de los casos, los que permanecen en sus puestos de trabajo quedan imbuidosdel más completo desinterés por lo que realizan.

Este proceso que ha dañado considerablemente el papel del salario y de la moneda nacional, también representa obstáculo para la medición económica en un país que además de no poseer una contabilidad confiable, carece de una tasa de cambio para operaciones comerciales entre el peso y el dólar, con credibilidad.

Así, se generan dificultades en la jerarquización de la rama y sectores, y como reconoció meses atrás el Secretario Ejecutivo del Consejo de Ministro, Sr. Carlos Lage, a veces actividades muy priorizadas e importantes no tienen la garantía de recursos que tienen otras actividades menos priorizadas.

En este contexto, decisivas esferas de la producción y los servicios no vinculadas en lo esencial con las operaciones en dólares están en desventaja y en una coyuntura muy complicada, como es el caso del transporte público y de mercancía, la industria azucarera, la educación, la salud pública y la mayoría de las ramas agropecuarias.

La producción azucarera cubana, antaño un punto de referencia internacional por su tecnología y eficiencia, yace hoy en una crisis que parece no tener solución, tanto en la industria como en la agricultura cañera. En la pasada zafra, la última del siglo, a pesar de contar con unas excelentes condiciones meteorológicas, la producción sólo alcanzó cuatro millones de toneladas, un monto que Cuba elaboraba en 1919 cuando tenía dos millones ochocientos mil habitantes y condiciones técnicas muy inferiores a las actuales.

En adición únicamente molieron 110 ingenios de los 156 existentes al servicio de la estrategia de mantener en funcionamiento los más eficientes, teniendo en consideración la poca disponibilidad de caña para moler. No obstante, esta política de concentración productiva no dio resultado. La utilización de las capacidades fue inferior al 71%, incluso por debajo de la zafra 1998-99, mientras el rendimiento industrial no rebasó el 11,22%.

Como punto de referencia debe señalarse que desde 1935 hasta 1958 nunca una zafra tuvo un rendimiento inferior al 12% y se efectuaron en ese período, cuatro con índices superiores al 13%. En la agricultura cañera las condiciones productivas aún son más calamitosas. La producción por hectárea es inferior a las 34 toneladas, con zonas donde el rendimiento ni siquiera sobrepasa las 26 toneladas. La organización para alimentación y agricultura FAO de las Naciones Unidas en sus estadísticas indica que internacionalmente los rendimientos promedios actualmente sobrepasan las sesenta toneladas por hectárea.

La producción azucarera cubana ha mostrado una tendencia inequívoca a la ineficiencia desde los tiempos de la plenitud de recursos provenientes del bloque soviético. Investigaciones realizadas por nosotros arrojan que en el período 1962-1993 el rendimiento de caña por hectárea obtenido por el sector no estatal fue como promedio de 3,9 toneladas superior al del sector estatal, a pesar de la carencia de recursos del primero y de la abundancia de estos en el segundo. Hay que agregar que en todos esos años los campesinos carecieron de garantías para permanecer en sus tierras, estando presente siempre el temor, bien fundando por cierto, a perderla. Circunstancia que influyó junto a otros factores en la desestimulación para desarrollar un cultivo permanente que requiere importantes inversiones iniciales y un período relativamente más largo de recuperación que otras producciones agrícolas.

A pesar de lo anterior, si en la etapa 1962-1993 de la cual se tienen estadísticas más o menos confiables, toda el área cosechada hubiera obtenido el rendimiento agrícola alcanzado por el sector no estatal y a este supuesto se le añadiera que la caña fuera procesada con un rendimiento industrial base de 96 grados del 12,74%, igual al promedio de los siete años anteriores a 1959, la producción de azúcar habría sido superior en casi 52 millones de toneladas a la realmente elaborada en esos 32 años. O sea, diez zafras adicionales de más de 5 millones de toneladas cada una.

Por otra parte este estado de cosas ha incidido muy negativamente sobre el nivel de vida de la población, deteriorado en muchos aspectos, desde la falta de vivienda y transporte hasta la carencia de una adecuada alimentación. El consumo promedio diario de energéticos y proteínas en 1999, según datos oficiales, fue de 2.369 calorías y 59,4 gramos de proteína. En relación con los niveles de 1988, esto representa un consumo inferior de 19,7% y 24% respectivamente.

No obstante, a este descenso del consumo energético proteico se une el hecho de que para amplios sectores poblacionales carentes de divisas y consecuentemente en una situación mucho más desfavorable que antes del período especial, la ingestión de nutrientes podría ser bastante inferior a las cifras globales enunciadas oficialmente, incluso por debajo de los requerimientos mínimos diarios per cápita establecidos por la FAO y la Organización Mundial de la Salud (OMS) de 2.310 calorías y 35,5 gramos de proteína. También debe tenerse en consideración que en 1999 arribaron a Cuba más de un 1.600 mil visitantes extranjeros, quienes con su consumo y elementos debieron incidir notablemente en los per cápita informado por las autoridades.

Como se recordará, la cantidad de turistas que visitaron la isla antes de 1989 no era relevante. Todo esto lleva a concluir que el estado alimentario de la población es más deficiente que el sugerido por el simple examen de los datos disponibles. Este complejo escenario económico ha llevado al país a una situación financiera interna y externa muy complicada. Internamente la masa monetaria compuesta por el efectivo en circulación y el ahorro ordinario era de 9.781 millones de pesos al término de 1999. Una liquidez semejante al monto existente a fines de 1994, cuando se iniciaron las medidas de saneamiento financiero. Ello indica que éstas se han agotado con el agravante de que existe una clara tendencia al aumento del dinero en manos de la población con sus perversas consecuencias sobre los precios y la motivación laboral.

En cuanto al sector externo los problemas son más delicados. La deuda era a fines de 1998 de 11.200 millones de dólares sin considerar la contraída con el desaparecido bloque soviético, estimándose que hoy supera los 12.000 millones con una perspectiva a seguir creciendo debido al impago. Los pocos créditos obtenidos en la actualidad, casi todos a corto plazo, son otorgados con duras condiciones financieras, incluido altísimos intereses.

A su vez a causa de la escasez de excedentes exportables, el déficit comercial crece sin cesar y en 1998, por cada dólar en mercancías exportadas se importaban tres, de acuerdo con los datos disponibles. Según cifras preliminares esta relación empeoró en 1999.

En tales circunstancias la nación se ha hecho más dependiente fundamentalmente del turismo, las remesas y los ingresos por conceptos del traspaso a manos de extranjeros partes importantes del patrimonio nacional.

A pesar de las apreciables entradas brutas que genera el efecto neto en divisa del turismo, no parece muy alto a causa de provocar una gran demanda de artículos importados. Hoy la satisfacción de las necesidades de la industria turística suministradas con suministros nacionales se calcula sólo en algo más del 50%.

Frutas tropicales como el mango, hortalizas, flores y variados artículos que pueden producirse en el país son importados para hacer frente al consumo de los visitantes, lo cual reduce considerablemente su incidencia beneficiosa sobre la economía, sin olvidar también la repatriación de los dividendos obtenidos por los inversionistas extranjeros.

La tirante situación financiera externa tiende a complicarse. En primer lugar a consecuencia del incremento del precio de los combustibles y de la inestabilidad de la cotización del azúcar, a esto se añade que la proyección para el presente año de un aumento de la llegada de los turistas en un 20% en relación con 1999, difícilmente se cumplirá. Durante los primeros cuatro meses del 2000 — la etapa alta del turismo en Cuba — el crecimiento fue del 6%, a lo que se une que las utilidades fueron inferiores a las logradas en igual etapa de 1999.

Ante estos problemas el gobierno ha decidido reducir el ya menguado abastecimiento de combustible, así como aplicar medidas de ahorro con el cierre total o parcial de centros de trabajo, incremento de la tracción animal y la disminución del suministro de insumo para la agricultura, entre otras.

Esta coyuntura habrá que seguirla de cerca, pues podría promover una regresión en la modesta recuperación económica evidenciada desde 1995 con graves consecuencias para el ya menguado nivel de vida de la población y el estado social y político del país.

Estimados compatriotas y colegas, hemos querido emplear esta oportunidad para brindarles un cuadro de la economía cubana descrito, por supuesto, muy sucintamente debido a las condiciones impuestas por la distancia y sin más pretensiones que coadyuvar en alguna medida a los debates que seguramente están teniendo lugar en este encuentro. Pensamos que resulta indispensable buscar fórmulas para fortalecer la cooperación entre ustedes y nosotros los especialistas que estamos en la isla muy carentes de información y recursos.

Estimo que nuestro apoyo mutuo no debe reducirse a la importante tarea de estudiar las cuestiones económicas políticas y sociales del momento, sino también procurar hallar soluciones y proyectos que sirvan de guía a nuestro pueblo para salir de la crisis y construir una sociedad democrática sustentada en la libertad, la justicia y la solidaridad.

Por último, recabamos de ustedes los documentos que seguramente resultarán de este Décimo Encuentro así como toda la información que sea posible hacernos llegar, todo lo cual posee un valor inestimable para nosotros.

Les reitero mi agradecimiento por esta ocasión de dirigirme a ustedes, mi deseo más ferviente de que tengan muchos éxitos en sus deliberaciones y que en el futuro nuestra población se fortalezca. Muchas gracias.

LA ECONOMÍA CUBANA DURANTE EL PERÍODO ESPECIAL

Antonio Gayoso

Me siento muy honrado de participar en ésta, la décima conferencia de la Asociación para el Estudio de la Economía Cubana. Casi que pudiéramos contrastar el éxito y los logros de nuestra Asociación con el descalabro económico que observamos en Cuba durante la misma década. Me toca reseñar y, poner en contexto, en forma apretada, las peripecias de política económica que el régimen castrista ha seguido durante éste período.

Quizás sería útil, para este proposito, sentar la premisa de que Cuba, y su gobierno, nunca han sido tan autónomos del resto del mundo como en los últimos 10 años. Con la desaparición de la Unión Soviética, Cuba dejó de ser dependiente de los cuantiosos subsidios recibidos de esa antigua potencia y de las condiciones impuestas para recibirlos. Por otro lado, el diferendo con Estados Unidos ha mantenido a Cuba, desde un punto de vista estrictamente político, como autora y dueña de sus propias decisiones y acciones. En otras palabras, el gobierno cubano no puede acusar a potencias foráneas de exitosamente dictarle que tiene que hacer, como y cuando.

Por supuesto, las acciones del gobierno cubano están influenciadas por las posiciones políticas y de naturaleza económica asumidas por los países con quienes Cuba comercia o pudiera comerciar. Sin embargo, el rumbo principal de la política económica, o por asi decirlo, su rumbo ideológico no está dictado desde afuera. Es ciertamente un producto interno, el resultado de cálculos políticos que obedecen al objetivo principal del régimen cubano. Este és, en mi opinión, el mantenimiento del poder.

El hecho de que Cuba interprete la crisis económica que padece como un problema coyuntural y por lo tanto dependiente de variables externas, y no como una situación directamente enlazada con los graves problemas estructurales del sistema, no es un sino un indicio de una óptica que culpa al exterior por los problemas y que no asume responsabilidad por ellos y por su solución.

No voy a hacer sino mención rápida del deterioro masivo del transporte. Aún en el caso de las celebradas bicicletas, que vinieran a paliar la falta de transporte urbano, el número de éstas parace haber declinado de más o menos un millón, hace tres años, a menos de la mitad de esa cifra hoy en día. ¿Por qué? Por que no hay repuestos para su mantenimiento. Tampoco voy a ahondar sobre la negligencia, casi criminal conrespecto al parque de viviendas. En la ciudad de la Habana, el propio gobierno admite que más de la tercera parte de las viviendas no podrían ser reparadas, aún si hubiera voluntad oficial o recursos para hacerlo. Otros discutirán el desastroso declive de la salud pública, o la falta creciente de materiales escolares básicos, otrora dos de los llamados logros de la revolución.

Por último, no pretendo inundarlos con una lluvia de datos que documentara, a ciencia cierta, algunas de las afirmaciones que haré. En reuniones pasadas de la Asociación, se han presentado un número de excelentes estudios en que todos podemos encontrar gran detalle. Mi propósito es el de enfocar sobre las decisiones de política económica que se han tomado, recalcar sobre las que nunca se discutieron, mucho menos decidido, y usar datos selectos sólo para subrayar el entorno.

Se puede hablar de tres sub-periodos cuando se observan los acontecimientos del Período Especial: los años pre-medidas, de 1989 a 1994; post-medidas, 1995-1998; y período de regresión, desde 1998 hasta hoy en día.

ENTORNO MACROECONÓMICO

Cuba aún no ha podido rebasar el enorme impacto económico ocasionado por la desaparición de la Unión Soviética y del Bloque Socialista.

De 1989 hasta 1994, hubo enormes cambios desfavorables en todos los índices macroeconómicos. A manera de ejemplos, las importaciones de bienes y servicios, como porcentaje del Producto Interno Bruto (PIB), descendieron del 41.4 por ciento en 1989 a 11.7 por ciento en 1994. Las exportaciones descendieron del 29 por ciento del PIB en 1989 al 11 por ciento en 1994. En términos absolutos, el déficit en la balanza de comercio creció de US$150 millones en 1992 a US$615 millones en 1994. Para el año 1997, ya había llegado a US$1,700 millones. El déficit fiscal subió del 6.7 por ciento del PIB en 1989 al 30.4 en 1994. La liquidez monetaria aumentó del 20 por ciento del PIB en 1994 al 66.5 en 1993 y bajó al 48.4 por ciento en 1994. La inversión bruta declinó del 24 por ciento del PIB en 1989 al 5 por ciento en 1994, y aún no se ha recuperado. La tasa de desempleo implicita subió del 7.9 por ciento en 1989 al 33.5 en 1994. La producción de azúcar bajó de 7.6 millones de toneladas en 1989 a 4 millones en 1994.

Durante el mismo periodo, el PIB se contrajo agudamente. La tasa de crecimiento del PIB se ha estimado en -2.9 por ciento en 1990, -10.7 en 1991, -11.9 en 1992 y -14.9 en 1993. In 1994 el PIB creció 0.7 por ciento, una vez que las primeras medidas económicas se comenzaron a implementar. Para un pais tán pobre, una tasa de crecimiento tán baja és incapaz de mejorar nada.

Pero, basta de números por el momento. El punto principal és que hubo una contracción muy fuerte y, por más de cuatro años, el gobierno revolucionario no tomó ninguna medida para amortiguar la caída ó para efectuar reformas en la estructura del sistema económico que permitieran una mejor adecuación al nuevo entorno internacional.

Las balbucientes reformas comenzaron en el verano de 1993. El gobierno comenzó al fin la implementación de una serie de medidas que, aunque parciales, parecieron indicar una voluntad de cambio en la ideología económica del gobierno. La nueva ley fiscal se aprobó en 1994, dirigida a reiniciar un sistema de impuesto sobre los ingreso y que contenía medidas para reducir el deficit fiscal y la excesiva liquidez monetaria; se legalizó el trabajo por cuenta propia, aunque con restricciones severas; se reabrieron los mercados agropecuarios libres, aunque bajo un alto grado de control; se legalizó la tenencia de dólares por la población; se comenzó a alentar al turismo extranjero.

También en 1993, se crearon, basadas en las antiguas granjas estatales, las Unidades Básicas de Producción Cooperativa (UBPCs), que serían auto-gobernadas por sus miembros. En septiembre de 1995, se aprobó la ley permitiendo y regulando la inversión extranjera. En 1997, se reorganizó el sistema bancario nacional, creando un banco central separado del Banco Nacional de Cuba, ahora operando como un banco comercial del estado. Esta reforma creó 10 instituciones financieras no-bancarias nuevas, incluyendo cajas de ahorro. Finalmente, ese mismo año se autorizó el alquiler, por particulares, de cuartos a los turitas.

Estas medidas tuvieron efectos rápidos. Más de docientas mil personas obtuvieron permisos para ser cuenta propistas, y los miembros de las UBPCs comenzaron sus tareas con agobio, pero con una cierta esperanza de autonomía. Los precios de los alimentos bajaron en los mercados agrícolas. Ya en 1996, se reportó un crecimiento del PIB en el órden del 7 por ciento, gran parte del cuál fué resultado de una mejor zafra azucarera ese año.

Las medidas, sin embargo, no cambiaron el corazón de la política económica. Fueron sólo paliativos a la crisis del momento. Se rechazó la propuesta interna de autorizar la creación de empresas privadas medianas y pequeñas por los nacionales del pais. Este rechazo se fortaleció con la creación de tiendas dolarizadas para estimular el consumo de las remesas familiares en dólares, en vez de alentar su inversión por los recipientes.

El propio éxito alcanzado inicialmente amedrentó al gobierno, quien comenzó un proceso, que aún continúa, para reprimir a los grupos a quienes las medidas habían dado un espacio económico más amplio. Se ha desalentado a los cuenta propistas con altos impuestos sobre la renta, que sólo ellos como grupo pagan, multas, contínuas inspecciones y cancelación de licencias. Asimismo, los miembros de las UBPCs reconocieron que la autonomía prometida era una ilusión pues siguen sometidos en todo a las decisiones del Acopio, el monopsonio estatal de la producción agrícola.

Se hizo claro que la participación en los mercados agropecuarios y la obtención de insumos, conllevaba la necesidad de cumplir con los contratos de venta al Acopio, mencionados antes. Se hizo evidente el mecanismo confiscatorio con que el gobierno se apodera del 95 por ciento del sueldo en dólares que los inversionistas extranjeros pagan por los obreros del sector. En fin, de hecho, se restauró el sistema de control sobre el productor que se pensó había sido suavizado por las medidas tomadas.

Por último, la legalización del dólar norteamericano ha resultado en una fisura profunda entre los niveles de vida de aquellos que tienen acceso a ésta moneda y aquellos que no, por no mencionar la fractura del mercado interno ocasionada por ésto. El efecto principal ha sido de desalentar el trabajo de aquellos que sólo pueden ganar en moneda local, y que, en su gran mayoría han visto su nivel de vida declinar ó en el mejor de los casos mantenerlo a muy bajo nivel. Todas estas acciones y factores han resultado en tasas de crecimiento anuales más bajas, entre el 1.2 y el 4 por ciento desde 1997. La producción de azúcar ha subrayado esta languidez. Zafras de 3.3 y 4 millones de toneladas son hoy la regla y no la excepción. Sus variaciones han sido el efecto principal de cambios en el PIB.

ENTORNO TURÍSTICO

Un elemento positivo, que brilla por ser la excepción, ha sido el sector turístico. Basicamente una exportación de servicios, Cuba ha atraído suficiente inver-

sión extranjera para que el turismo sea, salvo por la recepción de remesas, el sector más importante y dinámico de la economía cubana. El cambio en la postura anti-turismo que el régimen mantuvo comenzó con el advenimiento del Periodo Especial. El número de visitantes ha crecido de alrededor de 400 mil en 1991 a cerca de 1.6 millones en 1999. En 1998, se estima que esto representó un ingreso bruto de alrededor de 1,800 millones de dólares

A pesar de estas cifras alagüeñas, el turismo no ha contribuido tanto como parece. El gobierno ha admitido que el ingreso neto del sector no sobrepasa el 30 por ciento del ingreso bruto. En comparación, la mayoria de los países en el Caribe reportan un ingreso neto en exceso del 50 por ciento. Este bajo índice de aprovechamiento es el resultado de la incapacidad del sistema productivo cubano de servir las necesidades del turismo. Por ejemplo, Cuba necesita importar frutas tropicales de otros países en el Caribe, frutas que siempre fueron abundantes en la isla.

ENTORNO AGRÍCOLA

Quizás uno de los mejores ejemplos de los problemas estructurales que padece la economía cubana está en el sector agrícola. Desde temprano en el proceso revolucionario, el gobierno ha mantenido al sector agrícola bajo un régimen de control tán centralizado que es difícil de concebir. La expropiación de una gran parte de la propiedad rural concentró la tierra en manos del gobierno. Lejos de repartir esta tierra a los productores y obreros agrícolas, el gobierno creó enormes granjas estatales, gigantescos latifundios.

Un porcentaje pequeño de los productores rurales, aquellos con menos de 13.2 hectareas de tierra pudo mantenerse como propietarios privados. Hoy suman solamente 150 mil. El resto de la población rural pasó a ser empleados y obreros del estado. Muchos de los campesinos privados fueron presionados para que se integraran a las llamadas Cooperativas de Producción Agropecuaria (CPAs) adonde sus labores quedaron también bajo un régimen iguálmente centralizado.

Las cifras indican que la mayoria de éstas cooperativas estatales, y las granjas del estado han operado, con un alto nivel de ineficiencia y que han dependido de inyecciones presupuestarias continuas para sobrevivir financieramente. En el año 1993, estos subsidios llegaron a más de tres mil millones de pesos. Fué en este contexto que la creación de las UBPC fué anunciada como un esfuerzo para resolver esas ineficiencias y pérdidas contínuas.

Sin embargo, las UBPCs nacieron y siguen sometidas a iguales niveles de centralización y control. A principios de este año, el gobierno cubano sugirió que la mayoría de las UBPC cañeras operaban con cuantiosas pérdidas y que algunas podrían ser abolidas, volviendo las tierras y los productores al status de granjas del estado.

Con la excepción del pequeño propietario rural, todos los otros productores están obligados a firmar contratos con el Acopio, el monopolio/monopsonio agrícola del estado. Este determina que producto se producirá y los precios que pagará por ellos. Repito, el productor debe de entregar no menos del 80 por ciento de su producción y, sólo entonces, tendrá el derecho de acudir y vender su excedente en los mercados agropecuarios, adonde los precios reflejan la carestía relativa del producto. Al mismo tiempo, Acopio es la única fuente legal para obtener insumos, que son vendidos a precios administrados y sólo a los que han firmado contrato. El productor pequeño independiente no tiene acceso a insumos a menos que firme un contrato de entrega con el monopolio.

Hemos ya mencionado el bajo desempeño de la industria azucarera. Durante la segunda mitad del Período Especial, la producción de azúcar ha figurado entre las más bajas en la historia republicana. Las exportaciones han seguido esta tendencia decreciente. Como los precios de exportación tambien han bajado, el resultado ha sido que el valor de las exportaciones de azúcar, en 1998/99, no llegó a $550 millones de dólares, un valor que, de acuerdo a fuentes fidedignas, estuvo por debajo de los préstamos a corto plazo que Cuba recibió para financiar la zafra. Similares problemas han ocurrido con los centrales. La falta de mantenimiento y el deterioro físico de la planta ha resultado en muchos centrales no poder moler durante la zafra recientemente terminada.

ENTORNO ALIMENTARIO

Hemos ya indicado el efecto de la dualidad monetaria que existe en Cuba y los efectos que ha tenido sobre el acceso a bienes de primera necesidad de aquellos que no tienen acceso a los dólares. El problema más serio que ha surgido durante la década del Período Especial es el hambre y la malnutrición. Ya en ésta década, hubo en Cuba quasi epidemias de neuritis óptica, causada por deficiencias en el consumo de micro minerales en la dieta cubana. En el verano de 1994, la carestía de alimentos fue un factor importante en las protestas que ocurrieron en la Habana. A principios del año 2000, la FAO, la Organización de Naciones Unidas para la Alimentación y la Agricultura, reveló, usando datos oficiales, que el 19 por ciento de la población cubana no tenía acceso a los requerimientos mínimos de calorías y proteínas. La única respuesta del gobierno a este problema, que yo conozca a nivel de política, fue la decisión de otorgar pequeñas parcelas, en usufructo, a familias campesinas para producir alimentos.

EPÍLOGO

¿Que caracteriza las acciones o la falta de acción del régimen cubano durante el Período Especial? Una característica principal es la preferencia por el control total de la economía y de los ciudadanos productores.

Esta preferencia se refleja en el modelo de control de la sociedad seguido por Cuba; en la exclusividad dada a la propiedad estatal, aún si ineficiente; en la parsimonia con que el gobierno toma medidas, sólo cuando no tiene otra alternativa; en la manera en que controles y trabas fueron impuestos sobre la autonomía naciente de aquellos grupos que recibieron licencia legal para operar con cierta independencia del control estatal; en la renuencia de tomar ninguna medida que amenaze el control y la dependencia de los ciudadanos; en la política discriminatoria que permite a extranjeros crear compañías privadas mientras que las mismas actividades le son prohibidas a los ciudadanos.

El mensaje que usa el gobierno de que el Período Especial es en verdad una demostración de la resistencia de Cuba a sus enemigos, revela claramente la falta de voluntad para el cambio que existe en los líderes del régimen. Las explicaciones de los problemas siempre aducen causas externas de coyuntura. El modelo de organización social y política se sigue apoyando como el ideal para Cuba y el resto del mundo. Funcionaría mejor, dicen ellos, si el capitalismo internacional tratara a Cuba con justicia y sin ánimos de explotación y pagara precios justos por los productos de exportación. El gobierno cubano niega los problemas estructurales del sistema y rehusa, por lo tanto, desarrollar políticas y enfoques que se dirijan a resolver el meollo de esos problemas.

¿Cuales serían estas políticas que el gobierno rechaza o no discute? Harían falta, y no soy totalmente inclusivo: un agresivo programa de ajuste macroeconómico; un proceso de liberalización de los precios, incluyendo la tasa de cambio; un marco legal que proteja al ciudadano común, que establezca el derecho a la propiedad privada y la proteja, y que garantize la transparencia y la probidad de la gestión pública.

Asimismo, hace falta una estrategia económica y social de desarrollo que transforme al estado de productor único con control total de la economía en facilitador de la gestión ciudadana. Como facilitador, el estado debe desarrollar la infraestructura física y social de la nación en forma de que siente las bases para un desarrollo sustentable que asegure no hayan agudas desigualdades entre diferentes grupos de la población.

Para terminar, no sé ni que decir a las muy recientes declaraciones de Fidel Castro, reportadas en la prensa oficial, en las que dice que yá la economía está lo suficientemente fuerte para terminar el Período Especial y comenzar a reconstruir el socialismo. Dios proteja al pueblo cubano. Muchas gracias.

THE FALL AND RECOVERY OF THE CUBAN ECONOMY IN THE 1990s: MIRAGE OR REALITY

Ernesto Hernández-Catá[1]

The collapse of the Cuban economy in the early 1990s ended abruptly in 1994, gave way to a relatively strong recovery for a couple of years, and then to a period of positive, albeit modest, growth in 1997-98. At least that is the story the official numbers tell. As shown in Figure 1, real GDP contracted at an average annual rate of 10 percent from 1990 to 1993, before rising at an average of almost 4 percent a year in the period 1994-1996.[2] Real GDP growth averaged less than 2 percent in 1997-98.

Can these movements be explained? It is easy to account for the economic contraction in 1990-93 on the basis of the collapse of domestic investment resulting from the cessation of Soviet assistance to Cuba, and the disruptions caused by the sharp fall in trade with Cuba's traditional trading partners in the defunct CMEA. At first sight, however, the sudden shift to positive growth in 1994-96 is more difficult to understand in view of the rough stability in the ratio of domestic investment to GDP during that period (see Figure 1). The shift may also seem quite sudden in light of the experience of those transition economies of Eastern Europe and the former Soviet Union, and particularly of those where the implementation of structural reforms was incomplete, as has been the case in Cuba.

Against this background, this paper reviews macroeconomic developments in Cuba during the 1990s and seeks to explain the jagged pattern of growth in that period. The conventional growth accounting exercise presented below suggests that the fall and recovery of output growth in the 1990s cannot be fully attributed to the behavior of capital and labor inputs, and must be explained largely by movements in total factor productivity (TFP). The paper then examines the 1994-96 recovery on the basis of three alternative explanations: (i) that the numbers are not credible; (ii) that the 1994-96 recovery actually took place and reflected a surge in productivity resulting from the policies of macroeconomic stabilization and liberalization implemented in late 1993 and 1994; and (iii) that the recovery resulted from a favorable demand shock. The second explanation, which is consistent with both the improved performance in 1994-96 and with the fairly weak growth in 1997-98, appears to be the most convincing. The analysis also suggests that a strong and durable expansion is unlikely to be achieved in the period ahead on the basis of present policies, but that the benefits of a full liberalization of the economy are likely to be considerable.

THE END OF SOVIET ASSISTANCE AND THE 1990-93 ECONOMIC COLLAPSE

For three decades, the Cuban economy had benefited from massive economic assistance by the Soviet

---

1. The views expressed in this paper are the author's and not necessarily those of the IMF.

2. These numbers are those provided by Pérez Villanueva (1998) and the Cuban Central Bank (1999 and 2000), and differ somewhat from those published in CEPAL (2000).

Figure 1. Cuba: Real GDP and the Investment/GDP Ratio

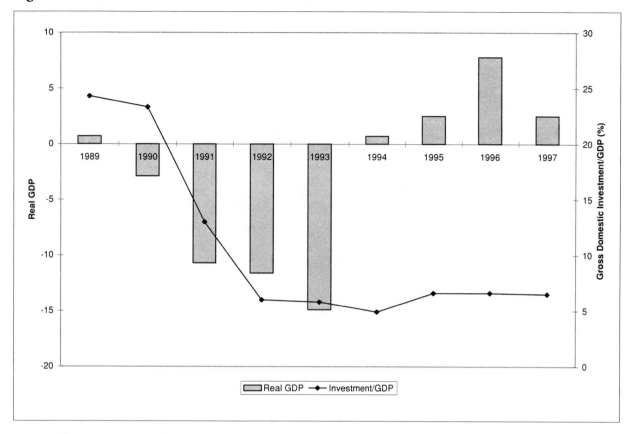

Union. The assistance mainly took the form of heavily subsidized exchanges of Cuban sugar exports for Soviet oil imports. In addition, Cuba obtained significant amounts of subsidized Soviet oil over and above its domestic consumption needs, that the Cuban government was able to sell at world market prices and use the proceeds to finance hard currency imports. These non-repayable subsidies amounted to an annual average of US$2 billion in 1986-90. In the same period, the Soviet Union extended loans to Cuba averaging US$2.3 billion a year (Pérez-López, 1998). Thus total Soviet assistance averaged US$4.3 billion in 1986-90, or 15 percent of Cuba's GDP if converted at the official rate of 1 peso per US$, and probably much more if converted at a market exchange rate.

Soviet assistance began to decline in 1989. Crumbling under the weight of budgetary problems (including the mounting external debt) and a fall in oil output, the Soviet Union under Gorbachev ended the subsidized exchange of Cuban sugar for Soviet oil and demanded payment in cash (see Alonso and Galliano, 1999). This forced Cuba to slash oil imports and buy whatever it could afford to buy in world markets, at much higher prices. What remained of Soviet assistance was slashed by the Russian Federation in 1992, and trade with the former Soviet bloc virtually disappeared.

Figure 2b illustrates the dramatic effects of these events on Cuba's flow-of-funds accounts. The ratio of foreign saving to GDP peaked at more than 14 percent in 1989, fell to 12 percent in 1990 and then plunged to 1 percent in 1994. Gross national saving also fell in relation to GDP, from 11 percent in 1990 to less than 4 percent in 1994. As a result, the ratio of gross domestic investment to GDP collapsed from just over 23 percent of GDP in 1990 to 5 percent in 1994, as the country began to consume its stock of fixed capital and to run down inventories a rapid pace.

While the domestic saving ratio fell, its composition experienced a massive change. As shown in Figure 2a,

25

Figure 2.   Cuba: Saving and Investment *(in percent of GDP)*

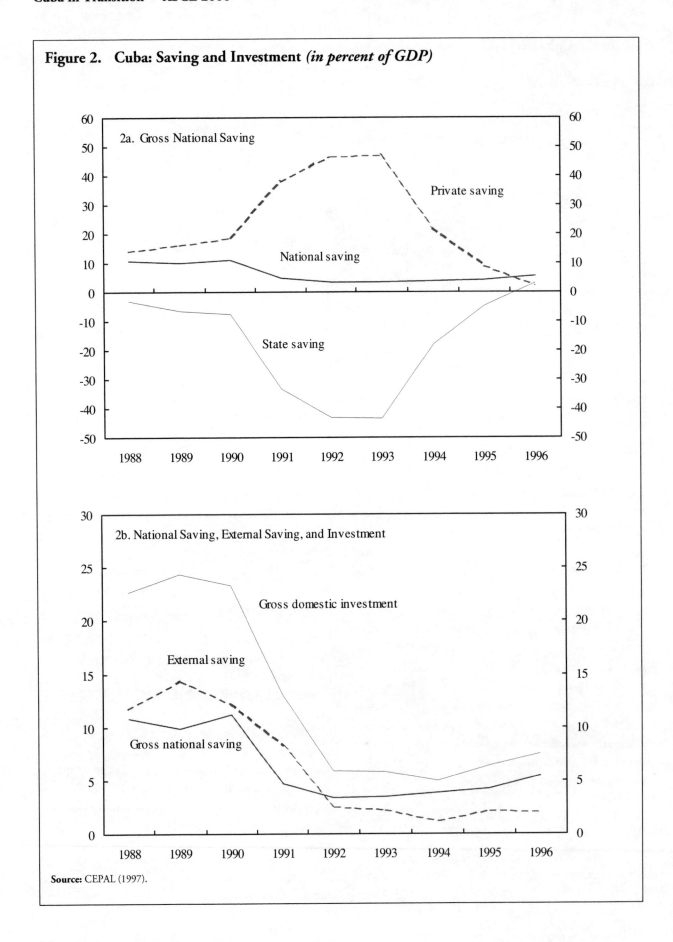

2a. Gross National Saving

Private saving

National saving

State saving

2b. National Saving, External Saving, and Investment

Gross domestic investment

External saving

Gross national saving

Source: CEPAL (1997).

Table 1. Cuba: Changes in Fiscal and Monetary Indicators During Recession and Recovery (Percentage points[a])

	1989-93	1993-96	1996-98
Revenue	**-2.8**	**-7.3**	**-1.7**
Turnover and sales tax	-4.8	-8.7	-0.4
Other	2.0	1.4	-1.3
Expenditure	**20.8**	**-35.4**	**-1.8**
Social area	6.0	-6.1	0.2
Defense & internal security	-1.8	-2.3	0.1
Subsidies	20.4	-26.5	-0.6
Investment	-2.4	-4.0	-2.2
Other	-1.4	3.7	0.4
Deficit (increase -)	-23.6	28.1	4.1
Money growth	12	-29	-0.3
Informal/free market prices	202	-230	...
GDP price deflator	14	-18	3.4

a. Fiscal variables are changes in ratios to GDP; monetary and price variables are changes in annual rates of change.

household saving surged by almost 30 percentage points from 1990 to 1993, but this was more than offset by an extraordinary increase in the use of saving by the state sector. Both changes reflected the governments' adjustment policy during this period, which can be characterized as a policy of "adjustment by brute force." With fiscal revenue falling in response to the weakening of economic activity and foreign trade, the government sought to protect social spending. More importantly from a quantitative standpoint, the government sought to keep unprofitable state enterprises afloat, thus avoiding a large contraction in state sector employment—but at the cost of a massive increase in subsidies (Tables 1 and 2). As a result, the state deficit widened from 9.4 percent of GDP in 1990 to 30.4 percent in 1993. Since financing from the Soviet Union—and the Soviet Union itself—were now things of the past, and since access to international borrowing on market terms

was limited, much of these deficits had to be financed by issuing money.[3]

With many prices still rigidly controlled well below market clearing levels, the government in effect forced the population to hold monetary balances well in excess of desired levels. This growing monetary overhang was reflected in the (involuntary) surge in household saving (see Figure 2a), and increasingly acute shortages of many goods in spite of the steep rundown in inventories. Not all prices were controlled, however. In particular black markets for agricultural products, which had existed at various levels throughout most of the communist period, were now expanding. Therefore, monetary financing of the deficit was also reflected in a rise in inflation. The rate of increase in the GDP deflator rose from 3.4 percent in 1990 to 17.4 percent in 1993 (in spite of widespread price controls), and inflation in informal and black markets surged from 2 percent in 1990 to more than 200 percent in 1993.

In the labor market, the heavy subsidization of the state sector limited the drop in state employment to 3½ percent of the labor force, which was partly offset by some employment growth in the private sector. The overall unemployment rate actually fell, as the decline in overall employment was more than offset by a 3 percent decline in the labor force that reflected a large outflow of discouraged workers (See Table 3). But the containment of unemployment came at a high price in terms of falling living standards for the population, including a severe intensification of rationing and frequent interruptions of electricity and water supply.

STABILIZATION AND RECOVERY: 1994-1996

The process of adjustment by brute force could not continue. The monetary overhang, shortages, and rationing queues were growing; inflation was threatening to get out of control; and economic activity was

---

3. The full story of how the fiscal deficit was financed is still a bit of a mystery, however. As can be seen in Table 2, seignorage accounted for much, but by no means all, of the financing in the period 1989-97. Seignorage is measured as the ratio of the change in the money supply to GDP; the money supply includes currency and peso-denominated saving deposits. There is no official explanation as to how the rest of the deficit was financed, but external borrowing, use of official reserves and state payments arrears may have been part of the story.

Table 2. Cuba: Fiscal and Monetary Indicators

Fiscal position (% of GDP)	1989	1990	1991	1992	1993	1994	1995	1996	1997	1998
Revenue	**60.1**	**58.7**	**62.4**	**56.5**	**57.3**	**62.6**	**56.6**	**50.0**	**49.5**	**48.3**
Turnover and sales taxes	24.7	24.0	22.7	24.2	19.9	16.5	13.1	11.2	10.4	10.8
Other indirect taxes	2.0	2.0	2.4	2.2	1.8	10.9	13.5	11.4	11.1	10.7
Foreign trade taxes	13.9	13.6	5.2	-1.0	0.0	0.0	0.0	0.0	0.0	0.0
Direct taxes	3.3	3.9	4.7	5.4	8.1	7.1	7.9	10.0	13.1	14.3
Other state enterprise receipts	9.1	6.7	8.1	9.7	10.4	10.9	7.6	8.3	5.9	5.6
Depreciation and asset sales	1.5	1.2	8.2	8.6	7.9	9.2	10.1	2.8	2.6	1.9
Other revenue	5.6	7.3	11.1	7.4	9.2	8.0	4.4	6.3	6.4	5.0
Expenditure	**66.9**	**68.1**	**83.8**	**86.3**	**87.7**	**69.6**	**60.0**	**52.3**	**51.3**	**50.5**
Social spending	17.5	17.9	20.9	22.6	23.5	19.3	17.6	17.4	17.6	17.6
Defense and internal security	6.1	5.5	5.0	4.5	4.3	3.2	2.6	2.0	2.6	2.1
Subsidies	16.7	18.9	26.9	34.1	37.1	20.4	12.0	10.6	9.1	10.0
Investment	14.7	13.8	20.7	14.4	12.3	13.2	7.6	8.3	7.5	6.1
Unclassified	11.9	12.0	10.3	10.7	10.5	13.9	20.3	14.2	14.3	14.6
Balance (deficit -)	**-6.8**	**-9.4**	**-21.4**	**-29.8**	**-30.4**	**-7.4**	**-3.5**	**-2.5**	**-2.0**	**-2.2**
Financing	**6.8**	**9.4**	**21.4**	**29.8**	**30.4**	**7.4**	**3.5**	**2.5**	**2.0**	**2.3**
Seignorage	1.4	3.9	9.6	10.4	17.8	-5.8	3.2	1.2	-0.4	1.1
Residual financing	5.4	5.5	11.8	19.4	12.6	13.2	0.3	1.3	2.4	1.2
Monetary and price indicators (% changes)										
Money supply (peso M2)	...	19.8	33.6	25.5	32.1	-10.1	-6.9	3.1	-1.0	2.8
Informal/free market prices	2.5	2.1	158.0	93.6	204.5	-10.1	-47.0	-25.0	...	...
GDP deflator	1.8	3.4	-7.1	3.5	17.4	23.0	12.0	-0.9	-1.0	2.5
Consumer prices	...	...	...	...	...	...	-11.5	-4.9	1.9	2.9
Exchange rate[a]	...	...	-92.9	-196.3	-95.0	-21.8	66.2	40.2	-14.6	9.1

Source: CEPAL (1997 and 2000) and Banco Central de Cuba (1999 and 2000)

Note: Data for the deficit are from Banco Central de Cuba (2000) and my differ slightly from the difference between revenue and expenditure which is based on data from CEPAL (2000).

a.   A negative sign indicates a depreciation of the peso against the U.S. dollar

Table 3. Cuba: Flows Into and Out of the Labor Force

	Thousands			Percent of Labor Force		
	1990-93	1994-96	1997-98	1990-93	1994-96	1997-98
Changes in the labor force	-131	-82	51	-2.9	-1.8	1.1
Due to changes in:						
Population of working age	471	121	-10	10.2	2.7	-0.2
Participation	-602	-203	61	-13.1	-4.5	1.3
Absorbed by changes in:						
State sector employment	-157	-569	-5	-3.4	-12.6	-0.1
Private sector employment	113	428	57	2.5	9.5	1.2
Unemployment	-87	58	0	-1.9	1.3	0.0

collapsing. Someone apparently succeeded in convincing president Castro that another method of adjustment had to be tried before the patience of the population was exhausted. While the long-term strategy of the government remained the final triumph of socialism (see Hernández-Catá, 1999), a revised economic strategy was implemented beginning in late1993 as a tactical way out of the previous, failed adjustment policy.

The new approach had two components: macroeconomic adjustment and liberalization measures.[4] In the macro-policy area, decisive measures were taken

Box 1.   Key Liberalization Measures, 1993-96

- In the **agricultural sector**, Soviet-style state farms were converted into *basic cooperative production units* (*Unidades Básicas de Producción Cooperativa*, or UBPCs) which were granted 42 percent of the country's usable land. This was followed, in October 1994 by the legalization "*farmers markets*" where farm products (with some exceptions like meat, milk and potatoes) could be sold at decontrolled prices. In 1997, an estimated 76 percent of the country's usable land was held by the non-state sector, mainly cooperatives.

- In a major policy shift, in the third quarter of 1993 the government de-criminalized both the **possession and the use of hard currency** by the population. Transfers of dollar bills from families abroad were also legalized, and travel by relatives of Cuban residents living abroad was made easier. Moreover, the government created special stores in which those able to pay in U.S. dollars could buy goods not available elsewhere. Finally, in October 1995 exchange bureaus were created and allowed to buy and sell hard currencies at close to black market rates.

- In September 1993 the government issued a decree legalizing **self-employment**. However, legalization was subject to important restrictions,[a] and was subsequently turned on and off in certain sectors, notably private restaurants. Nevertheless, it helped to create jobs and to absorb employees fired from unprofitable state enterprises, thus avoiding what could have been a massive rise in unemployment.

a.   For example, only close family members can be employed, and university graduates cannot exercise their profession as self-employed

to improve the fiscal position. Several tax measures could not arrest the decline in revenue. However state expenditure fell massively both in nominal terms and in relation to GDP. The fall affected all key sectors, including the social area. Most importantly, subsidies to enterprises, which had increased sharply during the crisis period, experienced a dramatic fall in 1994 and subsequent years. The result was an astounding drop in the fiscal deficit, from 30 percent of GDP in 1993 to 7 percent in 1994 and to 2 ½ percent in 1996. This made it possible to reduce the level of the money supply, which—together with the decontrol of prices outside the state sector—helped to reduce the monetary overhang. Monetary deflation also led to a large reduction of price levels in uncontrolled markets, and to an appreciable de-

cline of inflation as measured by the GDP deflator (see Tables 1 and 2). The level of the new consumer price index fell by 11 percent in 1995 while the GDP deflator rose by 12 percent, with the difference probably reflecting the large appreciation of the peso in that year (bottom of Table 2).

These adjustment measures had a massive impact on the flows-of-funds. As shown in Figure 2a, the huge and broadly offsetting increases in government dissaving and in forced household saving that had occurred during the crisis period were more than reversed, reflecting the fiscal adjustment and the decline in the monetary overhang. Total national saving actually rose from 1993 to 1996, particularly

---

4. The term "liberalization measures" is deliberately used instead of "structural reforms" to emphasize the tactical and potentially reversible nature of the measures.

in the latter year when transfers from abroad[5] exceeded net interest payments abroad, while foreign saving stopped falling and stabilized at around 2 percent of GDP. As a result, the contraction in the ratio of domestic investment to GDP came to an end in 1994 and the ratio rose modestly in 1995-96.

Macro-economic stabilization in the period 1994-95 was accompanied by several measures aimed at liberalizing partly certain sectors of the economy (see Box).[6] Owing largely to these measures, employment increased sharply in the private sector, almost offsetting massive layoffs in the state sector; the unemployment rate increased only by only 1.3 percent of the labor force during 1994-96, and outflows of discouraged workers from the labor force diminished considerably in comparison with 1990-93.

GROWTH ACCOUNTING

Was all this sufficient to account for the turnaround in growth? Table 4 begins to examine this question on the basis of a simple growth accounting framework. The growth of real GDP during the period 1988-98 is broken down into three components: fixed capital formation, labor force growth, and total factor productivity (TFP) growth.[7] It is clear from the table that both the fall in output in 1990-93 and its recovery beginning in 1994 reflected mostly changes in TFP. The contribution of fixed capital formation and the labor force is negligible for the period 1990-93 as a whole, although the contribution of fixed investment declines sharply within the period and becomes negative in 1992-93. In 1994-96, the net contribution of capital formation and labor force growth is negative, implying that the recovery of output during that period was more than accounted for by rapid growth in TFP.

Table 4. Cuba: Factors Accounting for Output Growth *(Percentage changes)*

	Real GDP growth	Contributions to the growth of real GDP from:		
		Capital formation	Growth of Labor force	Growth of TFP
1988	3.6	4.0	0.5	-1.0
1989	0.7	3.8	0.3	-3.4
1990	-2.9	3.1	0.1	-6.2
1991	-10.7	1.2	-0.1	-11.8
1992	-11.6	-1.2	-1.1	-9.3
1993	-14.9	-2.1	-0.4	-12.4
1994	0.7	-2.7	-1.1	4.5
1995	2.5	-2.5	0.3	4.7
1996	7.8	-1.6	-0.1	9.5
1997	2.5	-1.6	1.0	3.1
1998	1.2	-1.5	0.4	2.3
Period Averages				
1990-93	-10.0	0.3	-0.3	-9.9
1994-96	3.7	-2.3	-0.3	6.2
1997-98	1.9	-1.6	0.7	2.7

In Table 4, TFP growth is calculated residually — i.e., by subtracting the contributions of fixed capital formation and labor force growth from the rate of change in real GDP. Therefore TFP growth reflects changes in all the technological, economic and institutional factors that are not included in the measurement of capital and labor; it also reflects changes in capacity utilization, i.e., in the difference between potential and actual output. On that basis, the drop in TFP in the period 1990-93 is not surprising given the disruptions (financial, commercial and technical) associated with the end of Soviet assistance to Cuba, including the dramatic increase in the cost of imported oil. A flattening out of the *level* of TFP could have been expected in the subsequent period, given the once-and-for all nature of these shocks. But these shocks were also permanent, and therefore the huge

---

5. Transfers from abroad are calculated in part as the turnover in dollar shops minus dollar earnings accounted for by official incentive schemes (Morris, 2000). As such, these transfers are though to represent predominantly, but not exclusively, remittances from Cuban residing in the United Sates, in the form of U.S. dollar bills. Transfers may also include remittances from Cuban residents working abroad (e.g., doctors and teachers), including in African countries. Net transfers from abroad minus net interest payments abroad accounts for the difference between national and domestic saving.

6. For a fuller discussion of these liberalization measures, see Pérez-López (1995 and 1998).

7. The calculations underlying the exercise are discussed in Annex 1.

Table 5. Cuba: Selected Indicators of Economic Activity and Liberalization
(percentage changes, unless otherwise noted)

	1989	1990	1991	1992	1993	1994	1995	1996	1997	1998[a]
Economic Activity										
1. Real GDP	0.7	-2.9	-10.7	-11.6	-14.9	0.7	2.5	7.8	2.5	1.2
2. Real power consumption	4.1	-0.8	-13.1	-13.4	-7.3	6.9	2.4	7.2	7.0	1.2
3. Total factor productivity	-3.4	-6.2	-11.8	-9.3	-12.4	4.5	4.7	9.5	3.1	2.3
4. Labor productivity, industry[b]	...	-6.1	-24.0	-24.1	-9.0	21.4	14.4	14.7	5.8	8.4
5. Real GDP/total employment	...	-4.1	-15.5	-10.0	-14.6	0.0	9.0	6.8	0.3	-0.1
Indicators of liberalization										
6. Private employment	...	4.7	6.3	9.8	22.4	95.9	13.3	1.4	7.7	8.3
7. Non-state employment share[c]	5.6	5.8	6.2	6.9	8.6	19.0	22.3	22.7	24.0	26.1
8. Non-state agricultural land share	22.0	...	...	...	...	73.6	74.3	74.5	75.6	...
Indicators of distortions										
9. Price control index[d]	1.0	1.0	2.7	5.1	13.3	9.8	4.7	3.6	...	...
10. Price control index[e]	1.0	1.0	2.6	4.5	11.6	16.7	6.1	3.5	4.0	3.8
11. M2/GDP (in percent)	20.0	23.9	38.0	51.0	73.2	51.8	42.6	41.8	41.1	40.6
12. State subsidies	21.0	13.2	42.3	26.8	8.8	-44.2	-35.3	-2.2	-8.4	-4.2

Source: CEPAL (1997), Alonso and Lago (1995), Perez-Villanueva (1999), U.S. Department of Commerce, Banco Central de Cuba (1999) and author's estimates.

a. Preliminary.
b. Industrial output divided by industrial employment. Data from CEPAL (2000), exclude the sugar, fuel and electrical industries.
c. In percent of total employment.
d. Index of prices in informal markets divided by the GDP deflator (1998=100).
e. Index of U.S consumer prices converted into pesos using the unofficial exchange rate, divided by the Cuban GDP deflator (1998=100).

turnaround from negative to positive growth of TFP in 1994 is much harder to explain.

1994-96: RECOVERY INDUCED BY LIBERALIZATION OR MIRAGE?

Is such a strong and sudden increase in productivity possible? If not, it casts doubt on the credibility of the official statistics, and this likely would show up in inconsistencies in the data. If the answer is positive, there should be some explanation for the upswing in output in 1994 and the return to positive growth in 1995-96. One explanation suggested by Betancourt (1999) is that the turnaround in economic performance reflected the beneficial supply side effects of liberalization on the growth of productivity and potential output. Another, less persuasive, explanation is that the upswing in 1994 reflected a rise in capacity utilization triggered by some exogenous increase in aggregate demand.

This section examines these three possibilities in turn. It does not claim to reach strong conclusions. The publicly available base of Cuban data is limited, although for the period after 1989-98 the study of

the UN Comisión Económica para América Latina y el Caribe (CEPAL 1997, updated in 2000) provides a large number of statistical series, many of them previously unpublished. Moreover, the Central Bank of Cuba in its annual reports now provides updates for key macroeconomic time series, including on the balance of payments (but not, for example, for labor market variables). The period for which a sufficient set of key data are available is too short to allow for a thorough statistical analysis of time series. Nevertheless, the available data suggests some possible answers.

Statistical Consistency

The indicators of economic activity presented in the upper part of Table 5 point to a degree of consistency among several key variables. First, the growth of output is roughly in line with that of power consumption (lines 1 and 2.) On average, power consumption grew more rapidly—or fell less steeply—than real GDP. This pattern, which was observed in most countries of the former Soviet Union during the transition from plan to market, is often interpreted as

31

a sign that the underground economy is growing. The reason is that official statistics underestimate output in the informal and illegal sectors of the economy, while power consumption is thought to be a good proxy for total (official and underground) economic activity.[8]

Another noteworthy result in Table 5 is that total factor productivity, as derived from the growth accounting framework, is correlated with data on labor productivity growth in the industrial sector derived from official industry-by-industry data (lines 3 and 4). In particular, both productivity series show negative growth in 1990-93 and an upswing in 1994. The sharp recovery of industrial labor productivity in 1994, which reflects to a large extent labor shedding, was very broadly based across industrial sectors. The evolution of another measure of labor productivity, the ratio of real GDP to total employment, is also broadly similar to that of TFP. In sum, if there was a conspiracy to rig the numbers, someone appears to have gone to extraordinary lengths in order to establish consistency among the falsified numbers.

Liberalization as a Source of Productivity Growth?

The other variables in Table 5 illustrate the effects of labor market and price liberalization. As indicated in line 6, private employment grows throughout the period 1990-96 and surges in 1994, right after the measures liberalizing self-employment and private farming. The share of private to total employment also increases very rapidly beginning in 1994 (line 7). And the non-sate sector share of agricultural land also rises considerably from 1989 to 1994, with most of the change probably occurring in 1993-94 (line 8).

Assuming that productivity is generally higher in the private sector that in the public sector, the increase in

the private employment share should involve a rise in the average productivity of labor. In the context of the simple growth accounting framework of Table 4 (where labor is assumed to be homogenous and its productivity to be constant) this rise would show up as an increase in TFP growth. The assumption about higher productivity in the non-state sector is confirmed by Alvarez (2000) in the cases of sugar, tobacco, and a few other farm products (where the yield differential in favor of the non-state sector averages 11.4 percent in the period 1969-97). More generally, Alvarez finds that yields tend to rise as the share of the non-state sector increases, in spite of that sector's reduced access to factors of production.

Two proxies for the intensity of price controls (lines 9 and 10) show a widening gap between equilibrium prices and actual prices from 1990 to 1993, as inflation rises in black markets while price controls remain widespread, confirming anecdotal evidence of severe shortages and queues in controlled markets during that period.[9] From 1993 on, however, there is a large decline in both price controls proxies, as inflationary pressures subside and prices are liberalized in some sectors—in about one fourth to one third of the economy, judging by the private sector's 1998 shares of both employment and household purchases, but probably more given the existence of a significant underground sector.

Line 11 shows the ratio of the money supply to GDP—a proximate measure of the monetary overhang. Not surprisingly, this ratio appears to be correlated with the two indicators of price control, suggesting that the monetary overhang increased rapidly through 1993 and fell significantly thereafter, reflecting the combination of a disinflationary fiscal/monetary policy and price deregulation. It also suggests that a substantial overhang remained in 1996. Final-

---

8. Of course, other factors influence the growth differential between official GDP and power consumption, including changes in the relative price of energy, and the resulting changes in energy efficiency. These changes typically occur gradually and probably have relatively little influence on year-to-year movements in energy consumption. Energy shortages following the end of Soviet subsidies could explain why power consumption fell more rapidly than GDP in 1992-93.

9. The two indexes are (i) the ratio of the Alonso-Lago (1995) index of prices in free and black market prices to the GDP deflator (line 8); and (ii) the ratio of the U.S. consumer price index converted into pesos at the parallel market exchange rate to the Cuban GDP deflator (line 9).

Figure 3. Cuba: Total Factor Productivity and Non-State Share of Employment

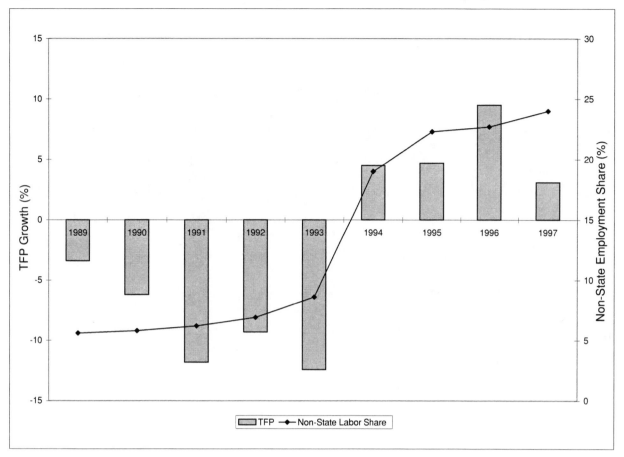

ly, line 12 shows budgetary subsidies surging in 1992-93, slowing abruptly in 1994, and then falling sharply in the next few years.

In conclusion, various indicators do suggest that the partial but significant liberalization measures introduced in 1993-94 led to an appreciable increase in the role of the private sector in goods and labor markets and in the role of prices in resource allocation. It is therefore not unreasonable to think that these measures may have contributed to a substantial increase in productivity (as illustrated in Figure 3), and therefore to an increase in output that cannot be accounted for by the growth of labor and capital inputs. What remains surprising is the magnitude of the increase, as well as the speed of the economy's response to liberalization, which, at first sight, seem quite rapid and strong in light of the experience of countries in transition. (More on that below.)

Is There a Keynesian Explanation?

It may be argued that the recovery of output in 1994-96 did not result from the favorable impact of liberalization on aggregate supply but rather from a Keynesian-type aggregate demand shock. It is clear that *capacity* output in Cuba fell in the early 1990s because of the disruptions associated with the collapse of the Soviet Union. Moreover, it is likely that the decline in *actual* output in that period was magnified by the adverse effects on aggregate *demand* of the fall household consumption and investment. Along the same lines, it could be argued that the 1994-96 recovery may have reflected, at least in part, a positive keynesian shock that boosted aggregate demand and capacity utilization, raising actual output even in the absence of an expansion in potential output. For this to be true, however, we should be able to identify a positive demand shock, i.e., a large *exogenous* increase in some component of aggregate demand occurring in 1994 or slightly earlier.

There was certainly no fiscal shock. After surging during the crisis period, the fiscal deficit contracted in relation to GDP by 23 percentage points during the recovery from 1993 to 1996 (see Table 1). Neither was there any relaxation of monetary policy—actually, money growth in the 1990s was inversely correlated with GDP growth. There was no export boom: in real terms, exports of goods and services continued to fall in 1994 and 1995, although they increased strongly in 1996. And there was certainly no sugar boom: output of sugar cane stagnated in 1994, fell in 1995 to a low of 33.6 million tons, and recovered temporarily in 1996 to 41.3 million tons—still well below the levels registered in the early 1900s. Finally, there was not much of an investment boom: real gross domestic capital formation increased from 1993 to 1996, but not by much; in the latter year it was still about one fifth of its level in 1990 (*net* investment probably fell throughout most of the 1990s).

Finally, there is no doubt that national income has been boosted in the period after the legalization on the use of foreign currency in 1993 by dollar remittances transfers from abroad—largely from Cuban relatives living in the United States—although there is uncertainty as to the precise magnitude of these remittances. (In this area, as in the area of the national accounts, CEPAL data differ from that published by Cuban official sources, notably *Banco Central de Cuba*, 1999, for reasons that remain unclear.) However, according to central bank data, these remittances have been offset in large measure by interest payments on Cuba's foreign debt. Still, the balance on net transfers and factor payments—the difference between national disposable income and GDP—appears to be an increasingly favorable element in Cuba's balance of payments, rising from zero in 1993 to the equivalent of 1 percent of GDP in 1996 and 1.5 percent in 1998.

CUBA AND THE ECONOMIES IN TRANSITION: A STATISTICAL COMPARISON

Another way to evaluate the behavior of output in Cuba during the period 1990-96 is to compare economic developments in Cuba and in the countries in transition from central planning to a market economy during that period. Figure 4 shows the behavior of output indices in Cuba and in three transition economies: Poland, Russia and Ukraine. The pattern of production in Poland is characteristic of the early and fast reformers, like the Czech Republic, Hungary and the Baltic countries: production initially falls steeply, but after a few years it flattens out and begins to increase rapidly.[10] In contrast, Ukraine represents the case of a slow reformer (like Turkmenistan and Belarus) where output initially falls less sharply than among the aggressive reformers, but then fails to recover for many years. Russia can be viewed as an "intermediate" reformer, but one with below-average performance of output, partly because of exceptionally difficult starting conditions including a particularly long period of central planning, and a large, inefficient industrial sector. It is also likely that the underground economy in Russia is underestimated in the official statistics to a greater extent than in many central and eastern European countries, including Poland.

Compared to those three countries, the evolution of real GDP in Cuba is remarkable: in the first years, i.e., through 1993, it is virtually indistinguishable from that of the slow reformer, Ukraine. Beginning in 1994, however, the Cuban output index turns up while that of Ukraine continues to decline. By 1998, Cuba's output index is still substantially below that of the rapid reformer, Poland, and well below its own level in 1989; but it is above the level of both the Ukrainian and Russian indexes.

This is a surprising pattern, but it could be rationalized along the following lines. From 1989 to 1993 both Cuba and the Ukraine made very little if any

---

10. The reasons for this pattern are associated with learning by doing by entrepreneurs, and the need to re-train the labor force (Brixiova, 1999) and to restructure the inefficient capital stock inherited from the old central panning system (Hernández-Catá, 1998).

Figure 4. Real GDP in Cuba and Selected Transition Economies

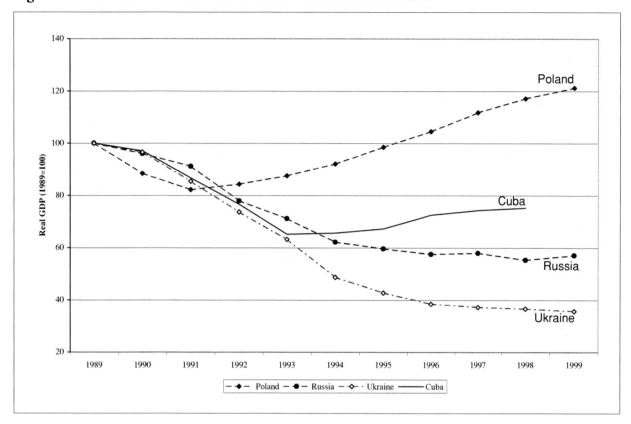

progress in reforming their economies and allowed inflation to increase to high levels (actually, to much higher levels in Ukraine than in Cuba). This similarity, coupled with the impact on both economies of the collapse of CMEA trade arrangements and the elimination of subsidies and state orders by Russia, would account for a similar evolution of economic activity in that period. Beginning in 1994, however, Cuba introduces measures to liberalize part of the economy and implements a rigorous macro-stabilization program which quickly reduces inflation to low levels. In contrast, Ukraine's liberalization program proceeds slowly, and while inflation begins to decline in 1994 it remains very high for several years. Hence the diverging evolution of the two economies after 1993. The story is plausible, but a question remains about the speed and the size of the impact of Cuba's liberalization measures on output.

A somewhat more systematic approach seeks to explain jointly Cuba's economic performance and that of the countries in transition from plan to market, in a way that allows for the impact of stabilization and liberalization. This analysis was based on a cross-section time-series regression where the rate of growth in real GDP (g) was related to the ratio of investment to GDP (I/Q); the share of the private sector in the economy (s) used as a proxy for degree of liberalization;[11] the rate of inflation (π) and the square of that rate (to capture the adverse, nonlinear effects of inflation); and a variable to capture the negative effects on growth of armed conflicts in various countries during the sample period (war). The regression was estimated for 17 countries, including Cuba, using in most cases observations for the period 1990-97. Annex 2 defines variables and provides data sources.

---

11. More general liberalization indexes, such as those developed by de Melo, Denizer and Gelb (1997) for a large number of transition countries, are not available for Cuba. The private (or non-state) share has the advantage of avoiding judgmental elements in the construction of the liberalization variables, thus avoiding possible biases.

$$g = -9.7 + 1.0 \, I/Q + 16.9 \, s - 0.36 \, \pi - 0.001 \, \pi^2 - 14.9 \, war$$
$$(4.8) \quad (1.4) \quad (6.0) \quad (3.1) \quad (2.6) \quad (5.8)$$

Adjusted $R^2 = 0.452$ Number of observations = 157

t values adjusted for heteroskedasticity are shown in parenthesis. All the coefficients have the anticipated sign and, except for the investment ratio, are significantly different from zero at the 95 percent confidence level.

The same equation was then estimated using a set of dummy variables for Cuba—one for each year from 1989 to 1997. The coefficients of these variables were negative through 1993, and positive thereafter. This indicates that Cuba's real GDP growth was higher in the first period, and lower in the second, than would have been expected on the basis of the experience of transition countries. However, the coefficients of all these dummies were insignificantly different from zero, suggesting Cuba's growth performance during the period, and particularly in 1994, was not significantly different from that of the other countries in the sample after controlling for the effects of investment, importance of the private sector, inflation, and conflicts.

TENTATIVE CONCLUSIONS

There is no definitive answer on whether the abrupt ending of the Cuban economy's post Soviet collapse and the period of subsequent growth reflected improved policies or statistical fabrication. To be sure, there are gaps in the data, and there are some puzzling differences between data released by the government and by the Economic Commission for Latin America. There are also some internal puzzles, such as the large share of the state deficits that cannot be explained by monetary financing. The Cuban government can put an end to the remaining doubts by publishing a comprehensive and up-to-date data base.

This being said, there is a degree of consistency within the available Cuban data set that argues against the possibility of a wholesale cooking of the data—a complicated enterprise in any event. Moreover, the data appears to support the hypothesis that the growth of output and productivity in 1994-96 can be explained, at least in part, by the policies of macroeconomic stabilization and structural liberalization introduced in late 1993 and 1994, following the disastrous results of the policy of "adjustment by brute force" pursued initially in reaction to the end of Soviet assistance. It seems reasonable to conclude that the 1993-94 shift in policy was instrumental in turning the economy around, even though the liberalization measures were subject to frequent flip-flops and were limited in scope and intensity, in comparison with those implemented in the successful transition countries. In this regard, it is revealing that Cuba's share of non-state employment leveled off at about one fourth in 1998, compared with 72 percent in China, 75 percent in Hungary, and 91 percent in Vietnam.

This suggests two tentative conclusions. First, the backtracking on several liberalization measures may well explain the lackluster performance of the Cuban economy in 1997-98 and suggests that, on present policies, it is unlikely that living standards can be raised appreciably. Second, the considerable, favorable effects the partial liberalization measures implemented in 1993-94 indicate that a complete reform program would have a far-reaching beneficial impact on the Cuban economy. But this would mean getting the government out of people's way and allowing the Cuban people (and not only the foreigners) to work, invest and realize profits.

REFERENCES

Alonso, José F., and Ralph J Galliano, 1999. "Russian Oil-for-Sugar Barter Deals 1989-1999," *Cuba in Transition—Volume 9.* Association for the Study of the Cuban Economy, Washington, D.C.

Alonso, José F., and Armando M. Lago, 1995. "A Frst Approximation Model of Money, Prices and Exchange Rates in Revolutionary Cuba." *Cuba in Transition—Volume 5.* Association for the

Study of the Cuban Economy, Washington, D.C.

Alvarez, José. 2000. "Differences in Agricultural Productivity in Cuba's State and Non-State Sectors: Further Evidence." *Cuba in Transition—Volume 10.* Association for the Study of the Cuban Economy, Washington, D.C.

Banco Central de Cuba, 1999 and 2000. *Informe Económico.* Ciudad de La Habana.

Betancourt, Roger, 1999. "Cuba's Economic 'Reforms': Waiting for Fidel on the Eve of the Twenty First Century." *Cuba in Transition—Volume 9.* Association for the Study of the Cuban Economy, Washington, D.C.

Brixiova, Zuzana, Wenli Li and Tarik Yousef, 1999. "Skill Acquisition and Firm Creation in Transition Economies." *IMF Working Paper* 99/130.

Comisión Económica para América Latina y el Caribe, 1997 and 2000. *La economía cubana: Reformas estructurales y desempeño en los noventa.* Fondo de Cultura Económica, Mexico.

European Bank for Reconstruction and Development, *Transition Report,* 1999.

Hernández-Catá, Ernesto, 1998. "Liberalization and the Behavior of Output During the Transition from Plan to Market." *IMF Staff Papers* (December).

Hernández-Catá, Ernesto, 1999. "Globalization, Transition, and the Outlook for the Cuban Economy." *Cuba in Transition—Volume 9.* Association for the Study of the Cuban Economy, Washington, D.C.

De Mello, Martha, Cedvet Denizer and Allan Gelb, 1996. "From Plan to Market: Patterns of Transition," *Policy Research Working Paper* No. 1564. Washington, D.C.: World Bank (January).

De Mello, Martha, Cedvet Denizer, Allan Gelb, and Stoyan Tenev, 1997. "Circumstance and Choice: The Role of Initial Conditions in Transition Economies," *Policy Research Working Paper* No. 1866. Washington, D.C.: World Bank (December).

Madrid-Aris, Manuel E., 1998. "Growth, Human Capital and Technological Change in a Centrally Planned Economy: Evidence form Cuba." Unpublished.

Morris, Emily, 2000. "Interpreting Cuba's External Accounts." *Cuba in Transition—Volume 10.* Association for the Study of the Cuban Economy, Washington, D.C.

Pérez-López, Jorge, 1995. "Coveting Beijing, but Imitating Moscow: Cuba's Economic Reforms in a Comparative Perspective." *Cuba in Transition—Volume 5.* Association for the Study of the Cuban Economy, Washington, D.C.

Pérez-López, Jorge, 1998. "The Cuban Economic Crisis of the 1990s and the External Sector." *Cuba in Transition—Volume 8.* Association for the Study of the Cuban Economy, Washington, D.C.

Pérez Villanueva, Omar Everleny, 1999. "Cuba: La Evolución Económica Reciente—Una Valoración." Unpublished, Centro de Estudios de la Economía de Cuba. La Habana.

Annex 1:
The Growth Accounting Framework

The numbers presented in Table 4 are derived from the following Cobb-Douglas production function:

$$g(Q) = \alpha\, g(K) + (1-\alpha)\, g(N) + \lambda \qquad (1)$$

where Q is real GDP, K is the capital stock, N is the labor force, and g(.) indicates the rate of growth in the relevant variable. Following Madrid (1998) the parameter α was set at 0.5. The capital stock was de- rived by accumulating gross fixed investment in con- stant prices: :

$$K(t) = I(t) + (1-\delta)\, K(t-1) \qquad (2)$$

Data for I and N are from CEPAL (2000). The de- preciation rate (δ) was assumed to be 9 percent per annum and the initial value of the real capital stock was taken form Madrid (1998).

Annex 2.
Sources of Variables Used in the Regressions

The following variables were used in the regressions discussed in the text.

g = rate of growth of real GDP, from EBRD (1999).

I /Q = ratio of gross domestic investment to GDP. For Cuba, China and Vietnam, ratio of gross fixed capital formation to GDP.

s = share of private sector in GDP. For Cuba, China, and Vietnam, non-state sector share of employment.

π = rate of consumer price inflation, annual average, from EBRD (1999). For Cuba, rate of increase in GDP deflator for goods.

War = dummy variable for years in which armed conflicts were ongoing: Armenia (1990-93), Azer- baijan (1990-94), Croatia and Macedonia (1991- 92), Georgia (1990-93), Tajikistan (1993-95).

Data for countries of the former Soviet Union, the Baltic countries and Eastern Europe are from EBRD (1999). Data for China and Vietnam are from IMF, World Economic Outlook. Data for Cuba are from CEPAL (2000) and Banco Central (2000).

HAS CUBA DEFINITELY FOUND
THE PATH TO ECONOMIC GROWTH?

Roberto Orro

One of the distinctive characteristics of the Eastern European transition process is that GDP has behaved like a "V" since the beginning of the reform process.[1] This peculiar behavior reflects the fall in production experienced during the first years of transition, followed by a recovery that seems to be permanent. Although it is impossible to talk about a real process of reforms in Cuba, the island seems to have left behind one of the worst economic crisis of its entire history. Even though production in some sectors has not yet reached the levels of the last decade, GDP has grown continuously for the last six years and there is no evidence that Cuba is on the eve of a new economic crisis.

The Cuban political system has resisted the winds of democratic change coming from Eastern Europe and elsewhere. After the end of the socialist systems in Europe and the disintegration of the Soviet Union, the perception that the end of the Cuban regime was near gained many followers. The arguments were strong: without Soviet support, Cuba's economy would become paralyzed and an economic crisis would provoke the fall of the regime. Few people predicted that Cuban socialism could confront the new challenge.

Although the break in relations between Cuba and the Soviet Union deeply affected the Cuban socialist system, the government has been able to manage the situation, maintaining the network of political control almost intact. Analyzing the factors that permitted the survival of the Cuban government is not the objective of this paper. However, it should be noted that the survival of the Cuban political-economic system required a reconfiguration of the Cuban economy, a shift to different goals and a redesigning of economic institutions. Cuba's institutions have been replaced with new ones that seek to guarantee the functioning of what we call a capitalist export monopoly. Thus, the old question "How long will the Cuban socialist regime last?" ought to be replaced by "How long will Cuba's dictatorial capitalism last?"

It is important to note that, although the political situation in Cuba is linked to the state of the economy, the two must be seen through different lenses. We believe it is incorrect to assert that a new economic crisis is a necessary condition for political change. To begin with, there are no indications that a new economic crisis is in the making. In addition, there are only two foreseeable reasons for one to occur: (1) an exogenous shock affecting exchange rates, which is presently unlikely because tourism has replaced the sugar industry as the main sector of Cuba's economy; or (2) a serious political crisis provoking a plummeting of the economy, in which case, political factors would be the cause, not the consequence, of the economic downfall.

Notwithstanding recent improvements in the reporting of statistics on the Cuban economy — due to the

---

1. See Berg, Borenstein, Sahay and Zettelmeyer, 1999.

efforts of nongovernmental institutions, Cuban economists living abroad and even economists in the island — the results presented in this paper should be taken with caution. Most of the statistics and index numbers on Cuba's economy have been developed on the basis of distorted information and using different methodologies than those common to market economies. Additionally, the lack of transparency permeating Cuban society negatively influences the results of our work.

The paper is structured as follows. In the first section we briefly review the main features of the Cuban economy during the years of close economic relations with the Soviet Union. In the second section we analyze the transformation of the Cuban economy after the disintegration of the European socialist system. The third section examines factors that could inhibit the medium and long term growth of Cuba's economy. In the final section, we present conclusions.

THE CUBAN ECONOMY BEFORE THE CRISIS OF THE 1990s

During the socialist stage, the Cuban economy had specific characteristics. In addition to elements common to any socialist economy, Cuba's economic system was characterized by a unique dependence on subsidies and other concessions from Soviet Union. Therefore, in addition to the typical distortions of socialist economies, Cuba also had those inherent to the nature of its commercial and financial relations with the former socialist community.

The topic of Soviet subsidies to Cuba has received ample attention from experts and much literature on the Cuban economy has been devoted to this issue. Quantifying the exact amount of Soviet subsidies to Cuba is an almost impossible task, because trade between Cuba and Soviet Union relied on a price system quite disconnected from the world market.[2]

This matter would be even more complicated if any attempt were made to compute the dynamic benefits to Cuba stemming from its relations with the Soviet Union. This is a very important point, because Soviet subsidies were mainly channeled through higher prices that the Soviet Union paid for Cuban sugar and the favorable conditions under which Cuba bought Soviet oil. Yet, it is often forgotten that Cuba's dependence on the Soviet Union fostered the development of an inefficient industrial sector in the island with very high oil consumption. Additionally, the advantageous trading relationship provided by the Soviet Union discouraged Cuba from developing new sources of convertible foreign exchange, consequently damaging the export sector. Moreover, a substantial share of Soviet loans was employed in monumental investment projects that, although useful in inflating national statistics, implied the use of human and material resources in projects whose contribution to welfare was insignificant.

Notwithstanding the sporadic complaints of Cuban leaders regarding the poor quality of Soviet products, without Soviet support Cuba's current political system would not have been consolidated. Trade with the Soviet Union was a necessary condition for guaranteeing minimum consumption levels to every Cuban citizen as well as to delivering education and health, which were key to preserving the political system.

Economic links with the Soviet Union conditioned the behavior of Cuba's economy on imports of Soviet oil for about 30 years.[3] Moreover, Soviet oil became one of the main Cuban export items by the end of 1980s, with exports of over three million tons in some years.[4] Such an injection of foreign exchange provided a life line to an economy that suffered a serious shortage of foreign exchange. Ironically, Cuba became an exporter of oil and an importer of sugar.

---

2. There are different estimates on the ammount of Soviet subsidies to Cuba. Alonso and Lago (1992) indicate that the figure reached 20% of Cuban GDP. According to Ritter (1990), Soviet aid represented between 26% and 37% of GDP.

3. In the official discourse of the government, Cuba was catagorized as a poor country on the basis of its lack of sources of natural energy. See *Informe Central al Primer Congreso del Partido Comunista de Cuba*, p. 52.

4. See Pérez-López (1991)

Figure 1.   Correlation between Global Social Product and Oil Consumption, 1975–1989

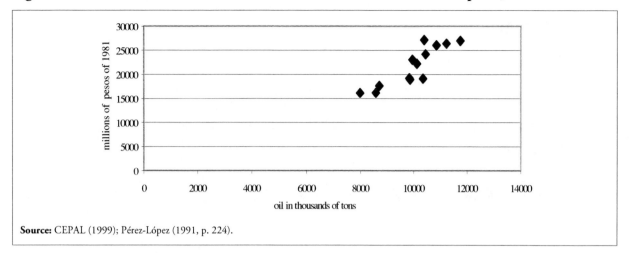

Source: CEPAL (1999); Pérez-López (1991, p. 224).

As was the case with most socialist countries, Cuban policymakers adopted as economic objective the maximization of production volumes — in physical terms as well as in value — that were determined in bureaucratic offices under premises completely divorced from the market. The Soviet oil supply was the guarantor for achieving the goals in the country's economic plans.

Trade with the Soviet Union also gave Cuba the possibility to obtain technology, intermediate inputs and replacement parts. Nonetheless, as demonstrated during the crisis of the 1990s, for 30 years investment in Cuba failed to create a national industrial plant with a low import coefficient.[5] Sugar production, which demanded considerable amounts of oil, remained the main source of foreign exchange, a fact unambiguously indicating that the monoproduction problem had not been eliminated. Because Cuba continued depending significantly on Soviet imports, an important share of economic activity consisted of distributing intermediate inputs and final goods bought from the Soviet Union.

The role of Soviet oil in the Cuban economy largely explains the decline in production at the beginning of the 1990s (Figure 1). The production-oil relation could also be used to estimate the real fall in Gross Domestic Product. In recent investigations of the evolution of output in Eastern Europe, analysts have used electric power generation as a proxy to estimate GDP. In the case of Cuba, from our point of view, oil consumption or even oil imports should be used instead as a proxy for domestic output.[6] We find three reasons to justify this: (1) the lower participation of the industrial sector in the economy in comparison with other former socialist countries; (2) the high level of oil consumption in non-industrial sectors of Cuba's economy; and (3) the existence of an informal sector whose main activity was not production, but the redistribution of imported final goods illegally taken from state enterprises.

---

5. This difficulty was openly recognized during the Third Party Congress, held in 1986. See *Informe Central al Tercer Congreso del Partido Comunista de Cuba*, p. 31.

6. According to estimates by J.M. Fernández, the generation of electric energy in Cuba en 1993 represented 72% of the level reached in 1989. Thus, if one utilizes the level of electric energy generated to estimate the real fall of production in Cuba, it is highly probable that that one would incur in an underestimation. See Werlau (1998).

Figure 2. Good Sectors Production, 1989–1998

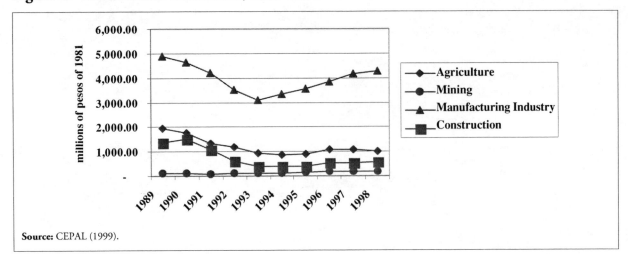

Source: CEPAL (1999).

Taking into account the high correlation between imports of Soviet oil and Gross Domestic Product, it is more plausible to assume that the real fall in output was larger than reported in CEPAL statistics.[7] Thus, while according to CEPAL and Cuban official statistics, Cuban GDP in 1993 represented 65% of the level achieved in 1989, we believe that, because oil consumption dropped by 47%, a reduction in GDP of the order of 47% makes more sense. This figure is supported by the dramatic lack of consumption goods and the monumental increases in black market prices experienced during that period.

As can be seen in Figure 2, most sectors of the economy were seriously affected by reductions in the delivery of Soviet oil. The sharp fall in economy activity was caused not only by adjustment costs in capital re-allocation. Rather, the economic contraction in 1990 is substantially the direct result of the end of Soviet oil shipments and other support to Cuba and therefore, the loss of an important source of economic resources.

THE RESTRUCTURING OF THE CUBAN ECONOMY

The recovery of Cuba's economy began in 1994. By that time, Cuban authorities were resigned to the loss of Soviet subsidies. Slowly, Cuba had been redirect-ing its economy to the West. Although facing strong financial restrictions, there was an advantage of doing business with new partners based on world market prices. This removed one of the traditional sources of distortions in the economy, as economic relations with former socialist partners were not based on market prices. The trauma provoked by the end of Soviet support was not overcome immediately, but it is evident since the middle of the decade that, as Cuba adapted itself to the new commercial relations, the crisis was progressively alleviated.

Export sectors had the most dynamic behavior and led the recovery. The case of tourism deserves special analysis. This sector, which at the end of the 1950s was one of the most important in the economy, was ignored for nearly 25 years, mainly because tourism was considered to impose large political externalities. It was not until the mid 1980s that the Cuban government decided to revive this sector as a result of its great need for convertible foreign exchange and the troublesome signals that were already coming from the Soviet Union regarding future levels of support.

One of the great advantages in the changes in Cuba's external sector is the decrease in the probability of a negative shock affecting the economy. While the dependence on sugar exports made Cuba vulnerable to

---

7. Alonso and Lago (1992) estimate that the elasticity of the consumption of petroleum with respect to GDP is 0.62. Using this estimate, the fall in GDP induced by the decline in the supply of petroleum from the USSR would be more than 47 percent.

Figure 3. Number of Tourists Visiting Cuba, 1989–1998

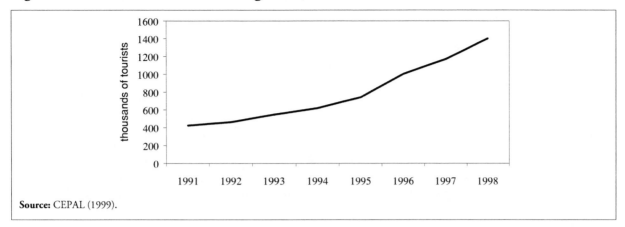

Source: CEPAL (1999).

the fluctuations in the world market price for sugar, tourism provides greater protection against external shocks. Tourism is also a superior good, which means that its demand rises as incomes rise in tourist-sending countries.

According to statistics of the World Tourism Organization, the number of tourists visiting the Caribbean has increased progressively over the last 10 years. A rise in income levels in developed countries is a guarantee of stability for countries whose economies are built on tourism. Because a shock affecting all developed countries is highly improbable, the probability of a sharp fall in the number of tourists visiting the Caribbean is extremely low. Furthermore, tourism to the Caribbean is based on natural and cultural characteristics of this region which limit competition from other geographic areas and protect these countries from dangerous disturbances. Perhaps Cuban authorities are overestimating the future possibilities for tourism on the island on the basis of the substantial growth in the 1990s (Figure 3), but no one questions that the number of tourists to Cuba will keep growing over the coming years.[8]

In recent years Cuba has succeeded in increasing other exports such as nickel, tobacco, alcoholic beverages and even some medications. It is a reality that the country has a highly qualified labor force, which positively influences economic performance. Since Cuba

has strengthened economic links to Western economies, many professionals have acquired knowledge and entrepreneurial skills which were out of reach when trade with the Soviet Union prevailed. Additionally, economic connections to Western economies provide a vehicle to obtain more advanced technologies than those coming from the Soviet Union. Cuba's portfolio of exports is, thus, far from typical third-world stock, usually comprised of primary products and poorly diversified.

The oil sector, however, is still the weakest aspect of Cuba's economy. It should be expected that the rate of oil consumption to GDP would decrease as the sectoral restructuring of the economy continues. Most of the inefficient and irrational economic activity during the Soviet period was due to the use of a stock of cars and trucks with excessive oil consumption as well as to the failed attempts to create an industrial plant like that of Eastern Europe.

Unlike most less developed countries, access to Soviet oil at below world market prices meant that Cuba was not affected by sharp rises in world market prices of oil occurring between 1973 and the beginning of the 1980s. Considering that these advantages are no longer available, a sharp rise in the price of oil could seriously affect the Cuban economy. A mitigating factor is that in the last ten years Cuba has doubled its domestic production of oil. According to Cuban

---

8. See Crespo (1999)

officials, 41% of electric power produced in 1999 was generated with domestic oil.[9]

Some sectors of the economy, such as agriculture, are still facing a critical situation. This sector began to fall into a crisis in the mid-1980s due substantially to the rectification process, designed to reduce the size of the private sector. Of course, its crisis was compounded by the end of Soviet subsidies. The creation of UBPCs — Basic Units of Cooperative Production — and the reopening of agricultural markets have not provided a definitive solution to the country's severe agricultural problem, although they have provided needed relief for the serious shortages of food. Production levels in most agricultural sectors are still significantly below both their potential and actual production levels in the 1980s. Although the Cuban people are facing a severe nutrition problem, it can be expected that agricultural production will soon recover 1989 levels. Recent experiences in China and Vietnam have proven that communist regimes can implement some reforms in agriculture without jeopardizing their monopoly over political power.

The nutrition problem has been partially attenuated by the decline in population growth.[10] This is consistent with an elemental conclusion of the Solow model, corroborated by empirical studies. Population growth rate is a variable affecting stationary levels of per capita consumption. Such a problem requires that some countries assign an important amount of resources to the poorest people, who usually exhibit the highest birth rate. With respect to Cuba, the fall in the birth rate was an endogenous change provoked by the worsening of the economic situation.[11] The latter is well suited for the new economic Cuban model, where the state is trying to get rid of traditional paternalism.

Finally, we would like to highlight the macroeconomic stability prevailing in Cuba since the middle of 1994. Cuban authorities managed to stop the devaluation of the Cuban peso and stabilize the exchange rate. Cuban dollarization, which is an unambiguous contradiction to the classical revolutionary goal of national autonomy, has played an important role in restoring macroeconomic equilibrium. It has also facilitated joint venture investments (would Sol-Meliá accept operating in Cuban pesos?) and eliminated one of the most important segments of the black market. Moreover, the government was able to bypass additional political problems, because in 1993 almost no one respected the existing penalties for holding dollars. Because the Cuban economy is extremely open, the use of dollars promotes efficiency. It could be argued that the current dual monetary system in Cuba is not optimal, but it is far better than the distorted system of the Soviet era.

PRINCIPAL OBSTACLES TO ECONOMIC GROWTH

Undoubtedly, the consolidation of economic links with the developed countries of Europe and Canada has invigorated the Cuban economy and made it more efficient. Especially important is the profound sectoral restructuring of the economy, which has permitted tourism to emerge as the most dynamic sector and driving force of the economy. We have seen that the evolution of economic indicators for the last five years provides no basis for anticipating an interruption of this secular expansion in the foreseeable future.

The behavior of Gross Domestic Product in Cuba displays the same "V" shape found in the recent economic history of Eastern Europe countries (Figure 4). This could induce people to make a false comparison between Cuba and the former socialist coun-

---

9. See the presentation of José Luis Rodríguez at the IV Extraordinary Session of the Asamblea Nacional del Poder Popular, *Granma*, 21 December 1999.

10. See CIA (1999).

11. Several factors help explain the reduction in the number of children per marriage and the decline in population growth: (1) the median level of education has increased substantially; (2) the number of marriages has probably diminished as a consequence of the housing scarcity and the additional hardships resulting from the crisis of the 1990s; (3) the legal and common practice of abortion; and (4) the high degree of incorporation of women into the labor force.

tries. In fact, the Cuban case is totally different from the process undergone by Eastern European countries. The Cuban government has failed to undertake an authentic process of reforms to eliminate the excessive power held by the Cuban state. Only a few concessions have been made to the private sector and just with the intention of bypassing a political crisis.

Figure 4. Gross Domestic Product
(Millions of Pesos of 1981)

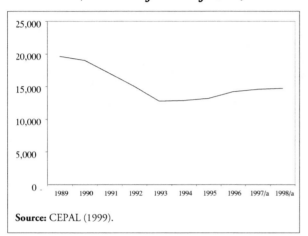

Source: CEPAL (1999).

The failure of the Cuban government to promote the private sector could affect the Cuban economy in the long and in the short run. Although the economy has grown despite the current economic model, the continuing government control over tourism and foreign trade makes it likely that the economy will suffer the problems inherent to a huge public sector. The Cuban government's commitment to retain power has led it to directly run most sectors of the economy and to impose on the private sector a heavy burden for the sole purpose of stopping its incipient development. Such an irrational policy excludes millions of people from participating fully in economic activity and obstructs the growth of the production of goods and services.

The numerous restrictions faced by professionals, peasants and workers keep the income levels of these groups depressed. This affects negatively consumption levels and domestic savings. Although the lack of financial resources has not kept the economy from growing in recent years, it is obvious that it will not

take long for these factors to become a serious obstacle to development and growth. It is improbable that remittances and incomes stemming from tourism will offset the lack of internally-generated financial resources.

The Cuban authorities have been relying heavily on direct foreign investment and joint venture projects, but this strategy also presents inconveniences and difficulties. It should be noted that the amount of foreign investment has been lower than expected. This could be explained partially by the bureaucratic barriers and obstacles faced by foreign investors and because Cuba is still classified as a high risk country for investment. The most important impediment, however, is that no country can achieve sustainable growth without relying on an efficient financial intermediation system. Data on capital inflows to developing countries show that direct foreign investment is just a portion of the resources needed by these economies: a dynamic and strong financial system is a necessary condition to giving firms and people access to private savings. Unfortunately, reforms in the Cuban banking sector undertaken in 1997 failed to bring solutions to the financial problems of small private producers, and instead was another step in strengthening the economic power of the Cuban state.

There seems to be no short run solution for the old conflict of properties seized by the Cuban government at the beginning of the Revolution. For many years, both sides have blamed each other for the persistence of this problem, but the fact remains that without a solution to this conflict, Cuba will not be able to initiate a genuine transformation. As long as the Cuban government insists on hindering the development of the private sector, there is no sense in asserting that the embargo is the source of the problems of Cuba's economy. It is worthwhile to note the dangers of a strategy that aims to compensate for the lack of financial resources by making concessions to foreign enterprises. The resources supplied by these firms have become an important factor within the Cuban economic model, but they may complicate the solution to property restitution and private property issues. The Cuban government ritually invokes the embargo to justify its position, but it is necessary to ask: Does the embargo limit the scope that can be given to the private sector? Is the embargo a reason to tax the private sector without an economic base?

CONCLUSIONS

After leaving behind one of the worst crisis in its history, the Cuban economy looks as if it were back on a growth path. The initial shock caused by the collapse of the socialist bloc has been almost overcome and a new economic model has allowed the economy to grow uninterruptedly during the last five years. As we have stressed, the successful shift in economic relations to Western economies has made it possible to obtain many of the resources needed by the government. The boom in tourism and other export sectors is the source of the recent growth. As long as these sectors continue to expand, the economy should grow.

Notwithstanding the return of economic growth, a real process of reform and liberalization aimed at establishing an economy in which the market and private sector prevail has not occurred. Although many of the distortions of the Soviet era have been removed, the monopolistic nature of the Cuban State remains. The Marxist regime has been replaced by a new state exhibiting the features of Latin American dictatorships of the nineteenth century. If the economy remains subordinated to the political interests of the Cuban government, the expectations born with the recovery will not last long. Only a real process of reform will put Cuba definitely on the path to growth.

REFERENCES

Alonso, José and Armando Lago. 1993. "A First Approximation of the Foreign Assistance Requirements of a Democratic Cuba," *Cuba in Transition—Volume 3.* Association for the Study of the Cuban Economy, Washington.

Berg, A., E. Borenstein, R. Sahay, and J. Zettelmeyer. 1999. "The Evolution of Output in Transition Economies — Explaining the Differences," IMF Working Paper No 73.

CEPAL. 1999. "Cuba: Evolución Económica durante 1998."

Crespo, N. 1998. "Back to the Future: Cuban Tourism in the Year 2007," *Cuba in Transition—Volume 8.* Association for the Study of the Cuban Economy, Washington.

CIA. 1999. *World Fact Book.* U.S. Government Printing Office, Washington.

De Melo, Martha, Cevdet Denizer, and Alan Gelb. 1996, "From Plan to Market. Patterns of Transition," Policy Research Working Paper 1564. The World Bank, April.

Hernández-Catá, Ernesto. 1997. "Liberalization and the Behavior of Output During Transition from Plan to Market," IMF Working Paper No 53.

Informe Central al Primer Congreso del Partido Comunista de Cuba. 1975. Departamento de Orientación Revolucionaria del Partido Comunista de Cuba, Ciudad de la Habana.

Informe Central al Tercer Congreso del Partido Comunista de Cuba. 1986. Editora Política, Ciudad de la Habana

Mankiw, N., D. Romer and D.N. Weil. 1992. "A contribution to the empirics of economic growth," *Quarterly Journal of Economics*, 107, pp. 407-437.

Mayoral, María Julia and Sara Más. 1999. "Crecimos y Seguiremos Avanzando Económica y Socialmente," *Granma*, 21 de Diciembre.

Pérez-López, Jorge. 1991. "Cuba's Transition to Market-Based Energy Prices," *Cuba in Transition—Volume 1.* Florida International University, Miami.

Ritter, Archibald. 1990. "The Cuban Economy in the 1990s," *Journal of Interamerican Studies and World Affairs* Vol. 32, No. 3.

Werlau, María. 1998. "Update on Foreign Investment in Cuba 1997-1998 and Focus on Energy Sector," *Cuba in Transition—Volume 8*. Association for the Study of the Cuban Economy, Washington.

THE MIRAGE OF FLOATING EXCHANGE RATES

Carmen M. Reinhart[1]

During the past few years, many countries have suffered severe currency and banking crises, producing a staggering toll on their economies, particularly in emerging market countries. In many cases, the cost of restructuring the banking sector has been in excess of twenty percent of GDP and output declines in the wake of crisis have been as large as 14 percent. An increasingly popular view blames fixed exchange rates, specifically "soft pegs," for these financial meltdowns. Not surprisingly, adherents to that view advise emerging markets to join the ranks of the United States and other industrial countries that have chosen to allow their currency to float freely.[2]

At first glance, the world—with the notable exception of Europe—does seem to be marching steadily toward floating exchange rate arrangements. According to the International Monetary Fund (IMF), ninety-seven percent of its member countries in 1970 were classified as having a pegged exchange rate; by 1980, that share had declined to thirty-nine percent and, in 1999, it was down to only eleven percent.[3] Yet, this much-used IMF classification takes at face value that countries actually do what they say they do. Even a cursory perusal of the Asian crisis countries' exchange rates prior to the 1997 crisis would suggest that their exchange rates looked very much like pegs to the U.S. dollar for extended periods of time. Only Thailand, however, was explicitly classi-

fied as a peg; the Philippines was listed as having a freely-floating exchange rate, while the others were lumped under the catch-all label of managed floating.

In this note, I summarize some of the key findings of Guillermo Calvo and Carmen Reinhart (2000), who analyze the behavior of exchange rates, foreign exchange reserves, the monetary aggregates, and interest rates across the spectrum of exchange rate arrangements to assess whether the "official labels" provide an adequate representation of actual country practice. To illustrate some of the main points, I present evidence for a few regimes that are drawn from the analysis of a much larger population of exchange rate arrangements. The data spans monthly observations for thirty-six countries during the January 1970-April 1999 period.

Some of key findings are: First, countries that say they allow their exchange rate to float mostly do not—there seems to be an epidemic case of "fear of floating." Relative to more committed floaters—such as the United States, Australia, and Japan—observed exchange rate variability is quite low. The low variability of the nominal exchange rate is not owing to the absence of real or nominal shocks in these economies—indeed, relative to the United States and Japan most of these countries are subject to larger and more frequent shocks to their terms of trade, hardly

---

1. This article is reprinted, by permission, from the May 2000 issue of the *American Economic Review*. The author thanks Guillermo Calvo and Vincent Reinhart for very useful discussions and Ioannis Tokatlidis for superb research assistance.

2. See, for example, Morris Goldstein (1999).

3. Maurice Obstfeld and Kenneth Rogoff (1995), make this point as well.

surprising, given the high primary commodity content of their exports in many cases. Second, the low relative exchange rate variability is the deliberate result of policy actions to stabilize the exchange rate. Reserve volatility (contrary to what we should expect in the context of a floating exchange rate or relative to what we observe in the more committed floaters) is very high. Third, interest rate volatility (both real and nominal) is significantly higher—and in a different league altogether—from that of the "true(r)" floaters. The high volatility in both real and nominal interest rates appears to have had two main explanations. It suggests that countries are not relying exclusively on foreign exchange market intervention to smooth fluctuations in the exchange rates—interest rate defenses are commonplace.The high variability of interest rates also suggests that there are chronic credibility problems. Lastly, since countries that are classified as having a managed float mostly resemble noncredible pegs—the so-called "demise of fixed exchange rates" is a myth. Instead, the fear of floating is pervasive, even among some of the developed countries.[4] Our finding, that most of the episodes that come under the heading of floating exchange rates look more like noncredible pegs, may help explain why earlier studies, which relied on the official classifications of regimes, failed to detect important differences in GDP growth rates and inflation, across peg and the "floating" regimes.[5]

In the next section, I present a brief review of what economic theory predicts for the behavior of exchange rates, foreign exchange reserves, the monetary aggregates, and interest rates across the spectrum of exchange rate arrangements. The following section confronts these theoretical priors with the actual data, while the concluding section discusses some of the reasons for "fear of floating."

BASIC CONCEPTS

Let, i, i^* denote the domestic and foreign nominal interest rate, respectively, while E is the nominal exchange rate. The expected devaluation rate and de-

fault risk premia are given by å and ñ, respectively, and R denotes the level of foreign exchange reserves. The variance of any variable, x, is denoted by Var (x).

Now let us first consider a floating exchange rate regime with a money supply rule, under which shocks to money demand, expectations about the exchange rate, or default risk are not accommodated. Under such circumstances, one should expect to see in the data that: $Var(E) > 0$; $Var(i) > 0$, to the extent that there are shocks to the demand for money; and $Var(R) = 0$, as there is no central bank intervention. If, as in the United States, there is no explicit targeting of monetary aggregates, the exchange rate floats, and interest rates are smoothed, then shocks to money demand are accommodated, but shocks to exchange rate expectations or the default risk premia are not. In this case, $Var(E) > 0$, $Var(i) = 0$, $Var(R) = 0$, as money supply adjusts through open market operations rather than through purchases and sales of foreign exchange reserves.

At the other extreme, if a country has a fully credible peg (which is defined to include the confidence that there would be no default), the interest rate parity condition is simply $i = i^*$. In that case, we should expect: $Var(E) = 0$; $Var(i) = Var(i^*)$ because of full credibility; and, $Var(R) > 0$, as money demand shocks are accommodated. Noncredible pegs, which include likelihood of default and are much more common, break down the one-to-one relationship between i and i^*. As before, $Var(E) = 0$ and $Var(R) > 0$, but now the interest rate parity condition is given by equation (1),

$$i = i^* + å + ñ \tag{1}$$

$$Var(i) = Var(i^*) + Var(å) + Var(ñ) + \text{covariance terms} \tag{2}$$

Hence, lack of credibility implies that $Var(i) > Var(i^*)$.

However, as noted earlier, countries frequently depart from their stated exchange rate arrangements. Pegs or quasi-pegs are not always made explicit. One increasingly common form of "peg-in-disguise" or

---

4. See Calvo and Reinhart (2000) for a fuller discussion of why there is fear of floating.

5. See Atish Ghosh, Anne-Marie Gulde, Jonathan Ostry, and Holger Wolf (1997).

"Fear of Floating I" (Table 1) is when the exchange rate is stabilized through open market operations rather than through purchases and sales of foreign exchange. Examples of this type of arrangement include Peru since August 1990 and Mexico since December 1994. Assuming imperfect credibility (since the arrangement is not made explicit), the implications are identical to that of the noncredible peg (i.e., $\text{Var}(E) = 0$, $\text{Var}(i) = \text{Var}(i^*) + \text{Var}(\mathring{a}) + \text{Var}(\tilde{n})$ + covariance terms) except $\text{Var}(R) = 0$. If, despite having an announced float, the attempt to stabilize the exchange rate is less well disguised (as is the case of South Korea in 1999 up to the present) then the predictions from theory are hardly distinguishable from a noncredible peg. This case is depicted in Table 1 under the row "Fear of Floating II."

Having reviewed the theoretical priors of what to expect from the behavior of exchange rates, international reserves and, interest rates across exchange rate regimes (which are summarized in Table 1), we proceed to confront these priors with the actual data.

Table 1. Predicted Behavior Under Alternative Exchange Rate Arrangements

Exchange rate arrangement	Var(E)	Var (i)	Var (R)
Float/ money supply rule	high	?	0
Float/ interest rate smoothing	high	low	0
Credible peg	0	Var (i^*)	?
Noncredible peg	0	high	high
Noncredible quasi-peg in disguise (Fear of Floating I)	low	high	low
Noncredible quasi-peg in less of a disguise (Fear of Floating II)	low	high	high

THE EVIDENCE

Our data are monthly for thirty six countries in Africa, Asia, Europe, and the Western Hemisphere during the January, 1970-April 1999 period. Selected examples are presented here and the full range of episodes are given in Calvo and Reinhart (2000). Countries are grouped into four types of exchange rate arrangements according to IMF classification: peg, limited flexibility, managed floating, freely-floating.

Limited flexibility has, almost exclusively, been used to classify European countries (prior to the monetary union) with exchange rate arrangements vis-a-vis one another (i.e., the Snake, the Exchange Rate Mechanism, etc.).

Despite occasional bouts of foreign exchange market intervention, sometimes even in co-ordinated fashion, the United States dollar (US $) floated about as freely against the German Deutschemark (DM) and now the euro and the Japanese Yen (¥) as any currency is allowed to float. For this reason, we compare countries that have regimes that are classified as freely-floating or managed-floating against this "G-3" benchmark. Given well-defined priors for the behavior of exchange rates, foreign exchange reserves, the monetary aggregates, and interest rates across the spectrum of exchange rate arrangements, we proceed by examining these variables one at a time. In what follows, we analyze monthly percent changes.

Table 2 presents evidence of the frequency distribution of monthly exchange rate changes (in percent). For the United States, for example, less there is about a fifty-nine percent probability that the monthly US $/DM exchange rate change falls within a relatively narrow plus/minus two-and-a-half percent band. By contrast, for Bolivia, Canada, and India (all declared floaters during that period), that probability is in the ninety-four-to-ninety-six percent range.[6] An alternative way of stating the same facts is that there is only about a five percent probability in those countries that an exchange rate change will exceed two-and-a-half percent on any given month (versus more than forty percent for the US$/DM). The absence of moderate-to-large monthly fluctuations in the exchange rate is equally absent among the so-called "managed float" episodes (Table 3). For Egypt and Bolivia, the probability of a monthly exchange rate change greater than two-and-a-half percent is nil. Even for self-proclaimed flexible-rate advocates, such as Chile and Singapore, the frequency distribution of their monthly exchange rate fluctuations relative to the U.S. dollar do not vaguely resemble that of the

---

6. These patterns are representative of a broader set of countries, see Calvo and Reinhart (2000).

Table 2. Exchange Rate Volatility in Recent or Current "Floating" Exchange Rate Regimes

Country	Period	Probability that the monthly percent change in nominal exchange rate falls within:	
		+/- 1 percent band	+/- 2.5 percent band
United States$/DM	February 1973-April 1999	26.8	58.7
Japan	February 1973-April 1999	33.8	61.2
Bolivia	September 1985-December 1997	72.8	95.9
Canada	June 1970-April 1999	68.2	93.6
India	March 1993-April 1999	82.2	93.2
Mexico	December 1994-April 1999	34.6	63.5

Table 3. Exchange Rate Volatility in Recent or Current "Managed" Exchange Rate Regimes

Country	Period	Probability that the monthly percent change in nominal exchange rate falls within:	
		+/- 1 percent band	+/- 2.5 percent band
United States$/DM	February 1973-April 1999	26.8	58.7
Japan	February 1973-April 1999	33.8	61.2
Bolivia	January 1998-April 1999	100.0	100.0
Chile	October 1982-April 1999	45.5	83.8
Egypt	February 1991-December 1998	95.7	98.9
Pakistan	January 1982-April 1999	77.8	92.8
Singapore	January 1988-April 1999	61.5	89.6

US$/DM or US$/¥, with a significantly higher proportion of observations falling within a narrow band. By this metric, post-crisis Mexico approximates a float more closely than any of the others—including Canada.

As discussed in the previous section, however, exchange rates tell only part of the story. We cannot glean from exchange rates alone what would have been the extent of exchange rate fluctuations in the absence of policy interventions—that is, we do not observe the counterfactual. To assess the extent of policy intervention to smooth out exchange rate fluctuations, we examine the behavior of foreign exchange reserves. As Table 1 highlights, the variance of reserves should be zero in a pure float. In reality, reserves may also change owing to changes in valuation. Table 4 reports excerpts from the frequency distribution of monthly reserve changes (in U.S. dollars). With the exception of the United States, most countries in Table 4 hold the lion's share of their foreign exchange reserve holdings in dollar-denominated assets, hence, valuation changes are not an issue. As Table 4 highlights, there is about a seventy-four percent probability that Japan's monthly changes in foreign exchange reserves falls in a narrow plus/minus two-and-a-half percent band. In the case of Mex-

ico, there is only a twenty-eight percent probability that changes are that small, while in the case of Bolivia that probability is even lower. Indeed for all other countries, large swings in foreign exchange reserves appear to be commonplace, consistent with a higher extent of intervention in the foreign exchange market—even relative to what is to be expected a priori from a freely floating exchange rate regime.

Policy intervention to smooth exchange rate fluctuations does not appear to be limited to transactions in foreign exchange markets. While interest rates in the United States and Japan are predominantly set with domestic policy objectives in mind, interest rate policy in most of the other countries accord a much higher weight to the stabilization of the exchange rate. It would be difficult to justify the very high relative volatility of nominal and real interest rates in these countries on the basis of changes domestic "policy fundamentals," as Table 5 makes plain. The probability that interest rate changes will be confined to a narrow plus/minus fifty-basis-point band for the United States is about eighty-two percent—even including the historically turbulent inflation stabilization period of the early 1980s. For Japan, that probability is even higher. By contrast, during Mexico's "floating exchange rate" regime, there is only a nine

Table 4. Foreign Exchange Reserve Volatility in Recent or Current "Floating" Exchange Rate Regimes

Country	Period	Probability that the monthly percent change in foreign exchange reserves falls within:	
		+/- 1 percentband	+/- 2.5 percent band
United States	February 1973-April 1999	28.6	62.2
Japan	February 1973-April 1999	44.8	74.3
Bolivia	September 1985-December 1997	8.1	19.6
Canada	June 1970-April 1999	15.9	36.6
India	March 1993-April 1999	21.6	50.0
Mexico	December 1994-April 1999	13.2	28.3

Note: Reserves are in US dollars. Since the United States holds its reserves in foreign currencies, much of the fluctuations in these simply reflect valuation changes arising from fluctuations in the dollar.

Table 5. Nominal Interest Rate Volatility in Recent or Current "Floating" Exchange Rate Regimes

Country	Period	Probability that the monthly change in nominal interest rate falls within:	
		+/- 0.25 percent (25 basis points)	+/- 0.5 percent (50 basis points)
United States	February 1973-April 1999	59.7	80.7
Japan	February 1973-April 1999	67.9	86.4
Bolivia	September 1985-December 1997	16.3	25.9
Canada	June 1970-April 1999	36.1	61.8
India	March 1993-April 1999	6.4	15.9
Mexico	December 1994-April 1999	5.7	9.4

percent probability that interest rate changes will be less-than or equal-to fifty basis points. Such stability in interest rates seems to elude most emerging markets—even those with capital controls (such as India). Indeed, major interest rate changes (by G-3 standards) appear to be the rule. While the probability that interest rates change by 500 basis points (five percent) on any given month is about zero for the United States and Japan, that probability is close to thirty percent for Mexico. A recent example of Mexico's use of high interest rates as a means to limiting exchange rate pressures (despite a slowing economy and an adverse terms-of-trade shock) comes from the aftermath of the Russian crisis in August of 1998. Nor is Mexico unique in this regard among emerging markets. Such interest volatility is not the byproduct of adhering to strict monetary targets in the face of large and frequent money demand shocks. In effect, most of these countries do not have explicit or implicit money supply rules. It is a combination of trying to stabilize the exchange rate (without giving the

explicit signal that foreign exchange market intervention yields) and lack of credibility.[7]

"FEAR OF FLOATING"

Going beyond superficial classifications and taking the wealth of evidence at hand, if results are any guide to the future, promises and statements by countries to move in the direction of a floating exchange rate may be devoid of real consequences. There appears to be a widespread "fear of floating" that is closely linked with credibility problems.

The root causes of the marked reluctance by emerging markets to float their exchange rates are multiple. When circumstances are favorable (i.e., there are capital inflows, positive terms-of-trade shocks, etc.), many emerging market countries are reluctant to allow the nominal (and real) exchange rate to appreciate. This probably stems from fears of the "Dutch disease" type problems—loss of competitiveness and serious setbacks to export diversification. When circumstances are adverse, the case against allowing

---

7. The results for real interest rates paint a similar picture; these are available from the author.

large depreciations becomes, possibly, even more compelling. The fear of a collapse in the exchange rate comes from pervasive liability dollarization, as in most emerging markets the debt of both the government and the private sector are largely denominated in hard foreign currency. For this and other reasons, devaluations in developing countries have a history of being associated with recessions, not export-led booms. Furthermore, the authorities may resist large devaluations because of their inflationary consequences and the credibility problems these may feed.

If "fear of floating" continues to be the serious policy issue it has been in the past, and if, as the stylized facts on interest rates suggest, lack of credibility remains a serious obstacle, then the only way to simultaneously avoid the "floating and credibility problems" may be full dollarization. A corner solution indeed!

REFERENCES

Calvo, Guillermo A. and Reinhart, Carmen M. "Fear of Floating." Mimeo, University of Maryland, January 2000.

Goldstein, Morris. *Safeguarding Prosperity in a Global Financial System: The Future International Financial Architecture.* Report of an Independent Task Force. Washington: Institute for International Economics for the Council on Foreign Relations, 1999.

Gosh, Atish, Gulde, Anne-Marie, Ostry, Jonathan and Wolf, Holger. "Does the Nominal Exchange Rate Regime Matter?" National Bureau of Economic Research (Cambridge MA), Working Paper No. 5874, January 1997.

Obstfeld, Maurice and Rogoff, Kenneth. "The Mirage of Fixed Exchange Rates," *Journal of Economic Perspectives*, Fall 1995, 73-96.

EVOLUCIÓN Y PERSPECTIVA DE LA
PEQUEÑA EMPRESA NO ESTATAL EN CUBA

Evaldo A. Cabarrouy

Blanco o negro, un gato sólo es bueno si sabe cómo cazar ratones

— Deng Xioaping[1]

Las medidas de política económica, instauradas por el gobierno cubano entre 1993 y 1994, redujeron el ámbito de acción y la capacidad reguladora de la planificación centralizada y dieron lugar a que surgieran actividades económicas fuera de la esfera estatal. En tales circunstancias, en la medida en que la economía se descentralizaba al permitirse diversificación de las formas de propiedad, emerge poco a poco una "segunda economía" al permitirse la formación de mercados agropecuarios, de cooperativas y pequeñas empresas individuales o familiares (trabajo por cuenta propia) y al concederse autonomía e incentivos a las asociaciones económicas con entidades extranjeras.

Sin duda, la multiplicación de actores económicos ha resultado beneficiosa para la remodelación estructural de la economía. No obstante, las reformas emprendidas alrededor de 1993, aunque en muchos aspectos exitosas, apenas han iniciado el camino de la transformación real de las estructuras productivas, las institucionales y el de la identificación de las nuevas formas de inserción productiva en la economía internacional. El país necesita saltar de un modelo de desarrollo basado en la planificación central con excesiva regulación a otro dominado por imperativos de competitividad, especialización, tecnología y flexibilidad de

adaptación al cambio en los mercados. Así lo exigen no sólo los logros de una inserción exitosa en los mercados mundiales, sino también la utilización eficiente de una fuerza de trabajo abundante en mano de obra calificada. Este trabajo, por lo tanto, pretende contribuir al debate en torno a la reorganización del sistema empresarial cubano sobre cuáles han de ser las fronteras saludables entre lo estatal y lo privado.

Los mecanismos económicos de administración y planificación centralizada presentan problemas notorios tales como: sistemas distorsionados de fijación de precios; ineficiencias al asignar recursos; inversión concentrada en la industria pesada a expensas de otros sectores; y escaso crecimiento del ingreso y del consumo por habitante, entre otros. La hipótesis que proponemos como base de este estudio postula que en Cuba un sistema industrial equilibrado estaría constituido por empresas de diferentes tipos y tamaños, y que las empresas en pequeña escala no estatales serían una buena fuente de dinamismo que ayudaría a mejorar la capacidad productiva del país dentro de un marco de progresiva equidad social.

El diseño de la política industrial cubana debe pues tomar en cuenta las diferencias funcionales entre los distintos tipos de empresas. Sin embargo, para este propósito es necesario tomar en consideración el papel que se atribuye el Estado. De manera que un aspecto importante de la viabilidad de la pequeña em-

---

1. Citado en Antonio Salinas Chávez, "Socialismo de mercado en China: 15 años de reforma económica," *Comercio Exterior* (México) 44, no. 5 (Mayo de 1994), 465.

presa no estatal en Cuba estaría vinculado al papel del Estado y su relación con la economía. El objetivo del trabajo, por lo tanto, no sólo es el de plantear que el Estado permita la concertación más amplia de estas empresas, sino también en el plano de la estrategia industrial, proponer que la pequeña empresa no estatal pueda percibir al sector gubernamental más en el papel de facilitador que de fiscalizador.

EVOLUCIÓN DE LA ACTUAL PEQUEÑA EMPRESA NO ESTATAL EN CUBA

Antes de 1959

Al igual que en otros países de la América Latina, antes de 1959 la presencia en Cuba de establecimientos de dimensión reducida en la rama de la manufactura, el comercio y los servicios era muy frecuente y generalizada. Aunque no existen datos estadísticos en torno al número y clasificación de todos estos establecimientos, en lo que respecta a las empresas industriales, los escasos datos sugieren que el tamaño de los mismos solía ser pequeño, es decir, que empleaban un número reducido de personas y representaban inversiones de capital relativamente de poca monta.

Así por ejemplo, en 1957 la Junta Nacional de Economía estimó la capitalización de la industria cubana en alrededor de $3,269 millones de pesos, con 38,384 centros de trabajo. El Cuadro 1 expresa, mejor que todo comentario, el gran número y la pequeñez de las empresas industriales no azucareras que a finales de la década de los cincuenta operaban principalmente para atender la demanda interna general. En ciertos sectores un número extraordinario de pequeñas empresas coexistía con otras de ciertos niveles de productividad más altos y en ocasiones con tecnología más avanzada y equipo mucho más moderno.[2] Debe señalarse también que en algunas de las ramas fabriles — como por ejemplo, en las industrias del calzado, vestuario y del tabaco— el segmento de las empresas que operaban en pequeña escala aportaba una fracción importante de la producción.[3] Según la Comisión Económica para América Latina y el Caribe (CEPAL), al finalizar los años cincuenta, 80 por ciento de los establecimientos de la industria no azucarera empleaban a menos de 25 personas.[4] En términos generales, puede decirse que al finalizar los años cincuenta predominaba en Cuba la producción al nivel de pequeña empresa de carácter familiar o casi artesanal.

De 1959 a 1970

En el decenio 1959-1968 se realizó en Cuba un radical proceso de transferencia de la propiedad privada de los medios de producción y parte de los inmuebles a la propiedad estatal, afectando a todos los sectores de la economía. A partir de 1959, con el triunfo de la Revolución, se inicia un proceso de colectivización de los medios de producción que transforma con rapidez las formas básicas de la organización económica del país. Como resultado de este proceso, el sistema empresarial cubano sufrió transformaciones de gran magnitud y rapidez.

Al finalizar el 1960 todo el comercio al por mayor y exterior, la banca, gran parte del transporte, la industria, la construcción y el 52 por ciento del comercio minorista, así como más de la tercera parte de la agricultura, se encontraban en manos del estado. El 48 por ciento de la actividad comercial minorista que quedaba en manos privadas estaba distribuida entre grandes y medianos comerciantes (23 por ciento) dedicados principalmente al giro de ropa, zapatos y ferretería, y el resto (25 por ciento) se encontraba en manos de pequeños comerciantes, que trabajaban directamente y con su familia, sin emplear fuerza de trabajo ajena.[5] En el sector industrial, las unidades productivas fueron organizadas, de acuerdo con la

---

2. Grupo Cubano de Investigaciones Económicas, *Un estudio sobre Cuba* (Coral Gables, FL: University of Miami Press, 1963), 1100.

3. Comisión Económica para América Latina, "La economía cubana en el período 1959-1963," en *Estudio Económico de América Latina, 1963* (Nueva York: Naciones Unidas, 1964), 272.

4. Comisión Económica para América Latina y el Caribe, *La economía cubana. Reformas estructurales y desempeño en los noventa* (México: Fondo de Cultura Económica 1997), 326.

5. Héctor Ayala Castro, "Los cambios en las relaciones de propiedad: 1961-1963," *Economía y Desarrollo* 65 (Noviembre-Diciembre 1981), 187-88.

Cuadro 1. Esquema de la economía industrial de Cuba, 1957

Grupo	Centros Trabajo	Clasificación	Capital Invertido (Valor estimado)	Estimado Obreros
I	276	Caña, azúcar y sus derivados[a]	$1,158,850,000	485,231
II	2,579	Tabaco y sus derivados[a]	55,959,400	129,141
III	666	Ganadería y sus derivados[b]	45,416,550	12,744
IV	649	Café, cacao y anexos[c]	16,290,000	7,650
V	18,086	Industrias Agrícolas[d]	60,313,000	85,005
VI	1,259	Forestal, madera, muebles, etc.	16,749,700	16,893
VII	698	Minero-metalurgia e ind. metal.[e]	524,784,300	21,972
VIII	777	Industrias marinas, pesca, etc.	7,831,500	10,866
IX	177	Combustible y anexos	130,194,000	4,345
X	316	Electricidad, gas, agua, etc.	301,521,643	8,360
XI	2,309	Transporte y comunicaciones	645,414,000	47,770
XII	599	Industria químico-farmacéutica	36,132,860	11,999
XIII	309	Construcción, materiales y anexos	17,421,000	19,343
XIV	265	Maquinaria, aparatos y anexos	5,329,000	2,179
XV	5	Materias primas varias[f]	257,600	69
XVI	2,999	Alimentos, bebidas y anexos	76,224,900	34,404
XVII	1,159	Textil, confecciones y anexos	73,270,000	23,833
XVIII	1,257	Indumentaria y tocador	8,643,800	6,970
XIX	1,252	Industrias gráficas y anexos	43,558,100	11,416
XX	122	Papel, cartón, derivados y anexos	8,883,500	2,653
XXI	1,880	Industrias cuero, pieles y anexos	18,259,500	10,019
XXII	192	Menaje, juguetería y bazar	2,260,500	1,731
XXIII	62	Apar. ortopédicos, óptica y cientif.	955,500	516
XXIV	220	Joyería, orfebrería, bisutería	3,501,500	2,063
XV	150	Alfarería, vidrio, cerámica, etc.	9,037,500	2,109
XVI	121	Industrias no especif. clasificadas	1,828,470	1,489
	38,384	Total general	$3,268,887,823	960,770

Fuente: Grupo Cubano de Investigaciones Económicas, *Un estudio sobre Cuba;* (Coral Gables, FL: University of Miami Press, 1963), 1100.

a. Incluye transformación y manufactura, no la parte agrícola.
b. Excluye valor del ganado y fincas.
c. También excluye fincas, almacenes y plantaciones de café.
d. No incluye caña, tabaco, café, ganado, sino arroz, frutos, vegetales, etc.
e. Excluye petróleo y nafta incluídos en el Grupo IX.
f. Excluye materias primas incluídas en sus propios grupos clasificados.

naturaleza de su producción, en torno a grandes "empresas consolidadas." En la segunda mitad de 1960 las empresas estatales ya representaban el 50 por ciento del valor de la producción industrial; un año más tarde esta proporción se había elevado al 75-80 por ciento de ese total. A fines de 1961, de las 38,384 empresas industriales que operaban en 1958, aproximadamente 18,500, responsables del 80 por ciento de la producción industrial, habían sido unidas en varios consolidados.[6]

En diciembre de 1962, con la promulgación de la Ley 1076, se nacionalizaron 4,600 empresas comerciales privadas grandes y medianas, y sus establecimientos, almacenes, depósitos y derechos dedicados a los giros de ropa, calzado, víveres y ferretería, las cuales fueron adjudicadas al Ministerio de Comercio Interior. La orientación que dio Comercio Interior para la aplicación de la ley definía al pequeño comercio como "aquellos en que todos los que trabajan en él son familiares o que sólo tienen un trabajador." Sin embargo, a pesar de que la ley no afectó a los pequeños propietarios, 218 establecimientos de ese tipo

6. Carmelo Mesa-Lago, *Breve historia económica de la Cuba socialista. Políticas, resultados y perspectivas* (Madrid: Alianza Editorial, S. A., 1994), 28.

fueron nacionalizados. Además, durante 1963, los comercios de pequeña propiedad seguían pasando al Estado: supuestamente sus propietarios estaban ausentes, tenían mercancías ocultas que vendían en bolsa negra, o violaron alguna disposición de la Revolución.[7]

Por otro lado, con la Reforma Agraria que se había puesto en práctica en 1959 fueron incorporadas al patrimonio estatal un 40 por ciento de la tierra en fincas. El 3 de octubre de 1963 fue dictada una nueva ley de Reforma Agraria que estableció el límite máximo de tenencia de tierra en 67 hectáreas. Las propiedades rurales con una extensión que sobrepasaba esta dimensión fueron expropiadas, eliminando con ello a los agricultores medianos. De esta manera, el 70 por ciento de las tierras y el 80 por ciento de la producción agrícola quedó bajo control estatal. A fines de 1963, sólo el 30 por ciento de las propiedades rurales y aproximadamente el 25 por ciento de la actividad comercial minorista estaban en manos privadas. El resto de la economía se encontraba en manos del Estado.[8]

En el verano de 1966 el proceso de colectivización se reanudó con nuevos bríos, concentrándose en las dos bolsas de propiedad privada remanentes: la agricultura y los servicios. En 1967 la colectivización fue reactivada en la agricultura mediante la eliminación de las pequeñas parcelas destinadas al cultivo familiar de las que disfrutaban los trabajadores de las granjas estatales, la compra de granjas privadas por el estado, la expansión del acopio, y la prohibición de ventas directas de los pequeños agricultores a los consumidores.

En marzo de 1968, con la puesta en marcha de la llamada "Ofensiva Revolucionaria," la colectivización alcanzó su punto máximo cuando se intervinieron estatalmente hasta los más pequeños negocios. El 25 por ciento del comercio minorista que aún quedaba en manos privadas además de la mayor parte del 2 a 5 por ciento de la industria y el transporte fueron co-

lectivizados de un solo golpe (véase el Cuadro 2). Entre los meses de marzo y abril de 1968 se nacionalizaron 58,012 establecimientos, "considerándose que un 10 por ciento de ellos pertenecían a propietarios capitalistas, y afectando en general a 19,450 propietarios y socios que contaban con 8,924 trabajadores. Además quedaron afectados 8,132 trabajadores por cuenta propia."[9] Los pequeños negocios nacionalizados, más de la mitad ellos establecidos después de 1961, se dedicaban principalmente al giro de comestibles y bebidas, tiendas de servicios personales, talleres de reparaciones, artesanías y vendedores ambulantes.

Cuadro 2. Cuba: Proceso de colectivización de los sectores económicos
(Por ciento de la producción)

Sectores	1961	1963	1968
Agricultura[a]	37	70	70
Industria	85	95	100
Construcción	80	98	100
Transporte	92	95	99
Comercio Minorista	52	75	100
Comercio Mayorista	100	100	100
Comercio Exterior	100	100	100
Banca	100	100	100
Educación	100	100	100

Fuente: José Acosta, "Cuba: de la neocolonia a la construcción del desarrollo del socialismo (II)," *Economía y Desarrollo* 20 (Noviembre -Diciembre 1973), 179.

a. De la superficie de la tierra

Aunque se sostuvo que estas pequeñas empresas privadas, que abarcaban casi un tercio de la distribución de bienes de consumo, estaban creciendo rápidamente y acumulando cada vez más ganancias, la verdad fue que el pequeño sector privado había estado llenando el vacío creado por el funcionamiento ineficaz de los servicios estatales. La importancia que había logrado tener el sector privado después de los primeros años de la Revolución, en la esfera del comercio y en algunos servicios y producción de artículos industriales, indicaba que la producción privada continua-

7. Ayala Castro, "Los cambios en las relaciones de propiedad: 1961-1963," 189-91.

8. Ibid., 191-95.

9. Héctor Ayala Castro, "Transformación de la propiedad en el período 1964-1980," *Economía y Desarrollo* 68 (Mayo-Junio 1982): 19.

ba desarrollándose e incluso compitiendo con éxito con el Estado debido a su mayor iniciativa y flexibilidad y que, por ello, sus productos eran preferidos incluso por el sector estatal.[10]

De hecho, la relación del sector privado con el estatal en la producción y los servicios se había desarrollado notablemente. Héctor Ayala Castro señala que se pudo comprobar que de 45,548 pequeños empresarios privados investigados, el 97 por ciento había vendido al Estado mercancías y servicios por un valor de hasta de 10,000 pesos y 3 lo habían hecho por más de medio millón de pesos en el primer semestre de 1967. Igualmente, el Estado había vendido por menos de 10,000 pesos al 91 por ciento de los privados y a uno por más de 100,000. Tanto la venta como la compra al sector privado se concentraba en unos pocos organismos estatales. En relación con los giros comerciales, los establecimientos privados predominaban sobre los estatales. En el ámbito nacional el 73.6 por ciento de las unidades eran del sector privado y el resto estatales. Si bien es cierto que esto se refiere al número de unidades y no a su volumen, ello indica que el comercio privado estaba diseminado en todo el territorio nacional en muchas pequeñas unidades.[11]

De 1970 a 1985

A partir de 1970, con la implantación del Sistema de Dirección y Planificación de la Economía (SDPE) y la incorporación de Cuba al Consejo de Ayuda Mutua Económica (CAME), se inicia una política económica distinta a la del período anterior y que prevaleció hasta 1985. En consecuencia, dentro del patrón de planificación central, se utilizaron ciertos mecanismos de mercado (incentivos materiales) y se introdujeron algunas medidas liberalizadoras en la agricultura, los servicios y la vivienda.

En la agricultura, la medida liberalizadora más significativa fue la creación de mercados libres campesinos en 1980, en los que los pequeños agricultores privados podían vender sus excedentes agrícolas (después de cumplir con el acopio del Estado y satisfacer sus propias necesidades de consumo) a precios libremente determinados por el mercado. El objetivo principal de la medida era el de alentar a los agricultores privados a aumentar la cantidad, calidad y variedad de productos agrícolas, e ir eliminando gradualmente el mercado negro y el racionamiento.[12]

En forma simultánea, se suavizaron muchas restricciones contra el autoempleo. En 1980-81 el gobierno legalizó y fomentó el empleo autónomo en servicios; por ejemplo, peluqueros, sastres, jardineros, taxistas, fotógrafos, electricistas, carpinteros y mecánicos, junto a profesionales como arquitectos, ingenieros, médicos y dentistas. Bajo un nuevo sistema de libre contratación de mano de obra, las empresas estatales podían firmas contratos con artesanos y trabajadores autónomos, proporcionándoles insumos a cambio de un 30 por ciento de sus beneficios.

Para 1980, en los principales centros urbanos, había surgido también un grupo de pequeños fabricantes que empezaron a vender sus productos en los mercados libres. Finalmente, en la primera mitad de los años ochenta el Estado relajó las anteriores restricciones sobre la construcción de viviendas privadas y esta política junto a la expansión del empleo autónomo y a un mejor acceso a los materiales de construcción generó un robusto mercado de la vivienda y un gran auge en la construcción residencial.[13]

De 1986 a 1993

En 1986, a raíz del llamado "Proceso de Rectificación de Errores y Tendencias Negativas," el gobierno cu-

---

10. Ilustra esta situación un productor de maquinaria agrícola que se estableció en 1964; éste llegó a contar con 89 trabajadores y vendió al Estado en el primer semestre de 1967 $628,000 pesos con compras por $146,347 al Estado y $300,000 a otros privados. Véase Ayala Castro, "Transformación de la propiedad en el período 1964-1980," 17-18.

11. Ibid.

12. No obstante estos objetivos y la positiva reacción de los agricultores, el gobierno les prohibió vender sus excedentes fuera de la zona donde residían y se proscribieron los intermediarios que compraban el producto para venderlo en los mercados. Véase Mesa-Lago, *Breve historia económica de la Cuba socialista*, 83-86.

13. Ibid.

bano instrumentó una serie de medidas limitando aún más las actividades privadas y el mercado mediante: la abolición de los mercados libres campesinos y la aceleración del proceso de integración de las pequeñas fincas privadas en las cooperativas bajo control estatal; la eliminación de actividades de los pequeños fabricantes privados, propietarios de camiones y vendedores ambulantes y reducción del empleo autónomo; y restricción de la construcción, las ventas y los alquileres de las viviendas privadas y de la herencia de vivienda. Se alegó que los agricultores estaban obteniendo enormes beneficios mediante la venta en dichos mercados, se resistían a la integración en las cooperativas, que muy pocos pagaban impuesto y algunos sólo entregaban al Estado 10 por ciento de sus cosechas e incluso nada.

Bajo el proceso de rectificación los pequeños fabricantes privados, transportistas y vendedores ambulantes también fueron objeto de ataque. Los pequeños empresarios vendían sus productos a un número creciente de cooperativas y empresas estatales, algunos de ellos abrían sus propias tiendas y a veces contrataban algunos trabajadores para expandir la producción y distribución. Los vendedores ambulantes que vendían cerveza y otros productos habían proliferado en las ciudades y playas. Los propietarios privados de camiones se lucraban transportando productos agrícolas de las fincas privadas, mercancías de los fabricantes y personas.[14] No obstante estas medidas antagónicas, el IV Congreso del Partido Comunista de Cuba (PCC) aprobó la reintroducción del empleo por cuenta propia en actividades privadas, pero con considerables restricciones. Por ejemplo, el empleo autónomo debía realizarse después del horario de trabajo en el sector estatal, ser complementario con la acción del Estado, estar limitado a actividades de servicios menores y estrictamente regulado para garantizar que no sea conflictivo con el socialismo. Además, los autoempleados no podían contratar fuera de la familia inmediata.[15]

Desde 1993

En 1993 el gobierno cubano introdujo reformas que modificaron profundamente el funcionamiento de la economía. Entre las medidas más importantes puestas en marcha en ese año se destacan las de diversificación de las formas de propiedad al otorgar mayor realce a las cooperativas, el trabajo por cuenta propia y las asociaciones económicas con entidades extranjeras. En este panorama, aunque el Estado continuaría interviniendo decisivamente en la economía, una de las acciones más importantes de la liberalización económica fue la desincorporación de la mayor parte de las tierras estatales mediante la creación de Unidades Básicas de Producción Cooperativa (UPBC), proceso que se inició en 1993 y concluyó en 1994. Consecuentemente con esta medida, en octubre de 1994, se formalizó la creación de los "mercados agropecuarios," donde los precios se fijan libremente en correspondencia con la oferta y demanda de los productos.[16] Los campesinos pueden participar en dichos mercados o recurrir a un representante comercial, con lo que de hecho se reconoce el papel de los intermediarios en el proceso de comercialización agrícola.

También a partir de septiembre de 1993 se comienza a aplicar una política de ampliación del ejercicio legal del trabajo por cuenta propia. En un inicio, el autoempleo estaba presente en actividades vinculadas a las necesidades familiares y personales, a la reparación de la vivienda, a la transportación y a otras, como la artesanal, por mencionar algunas. Las reglamentaciones aprobadas incrementaron el número de actividades que podían ejercerse y personas legalmente autorizadas para realizarlas. En 1993 la legislación autorizaba a ejercer el trabajo por cuenta propia, tanto a trabajadores vinculados laboralmente, así como a los jubilados, amas de casa y personas con capacidad disminuida. Aunque inicialmente se prohibió a los profesionales universitarios ejercer el empleo por cuenta propia, en 1995 se produjo una flexibilización de esta norma que les permite registrarse como traba-

---

14. Ibid., 130.

15. Ibid., 133.

16. Los únicos productos excluidos de esas transacciones son los derivados de la ganadería vacuna (carne, leche y quesos) y la papa.

jadores por cuenta propia en cualquier actividad u oficio de los que aparecen en el cuerpo legal vigente.[17]

En abril de 1996, se reconoce el cuentapropismo como una alternativa emergente de empleo. La concepción oficial del trabajo por cuenta propia define a este sector como complemento de la actividad económica estatal, como una alternativa más de empleo y una vía para incrementar los ingresos personales. Sin embargo, se prohibe la utilización del trabajo asalariado y de intermediarios para la comercialización de los productos que elaboran y los servicios que prestan los cuentapropistas. La normativa estatal también prohibe las relaciones independientes con entidades estatales, privadas o asociaciones con capital extranjero.

En tales circunstancias, reaparece poco a poco un sector no estatal de cooperativas y pequeñas empresas individuales o familiares que marca el inicio de una sociedad civil asentada en la expansión de las actividades privadas. Al mismo tiempo, estas medidas de liberalización y desregulación han facilitado operaciones comerciales que anteriormente eran consideradas ilegales, mejorando así la satisfacción de importantes necesidades básicas, sobre todo la alimentación. En términos productivos, señala la CEPAL, "la liberalización de actividades ha alentado de manera incuestionable a la producción y ha resultado socialmente benéfica por cuanto tiende a diversificar las fuentes de ingreso y a volver más tolerables los sacrificios de las crisis."[18]

Aún así, existen todavía numerosas restricciones limitativas a la expansión de las actividades del sector no estatal. Entre otras, cabría señalar las siguientes: (1) impedimento a contratar trabajadores asalariados en las actividades por cuenta propia; (2) acotamiento de los campos a elegir en el trabajo por cuenta propia; (3) limitaciones al trabajo de empleados públicos en su tiempo libre; (4) restricciones a la realización de transacciones entre el sector de empresas estatales y el sector privado emergente; (5) pago de impuestos elevados; y (6) limitaciones de acceso al crédito o a insumos estratégicos.

POSIBILIDADES ACTUALES Y PERSPECTIVAS EN CUBA

Tradicionalmente las empresas en pequeña escala han sido parte importante de la estructura industrial de muchos países y constituyen en forma invariable casi todo el universo de unidades productivas, aún en países industrializados. En años recientes y por diversas razones, las potencialidades y el desempeño de la pequeña empresa han despertado gran interés, tanto por parte de quienes manejan la política industrial como entre académicos e investigadores. Esto se debe a la importante contribución que éstas pueden hacer al desarrollo económico para mejorar la calidad de vida de la población y lograr una mejor distribución del ingreso.[19] Entre los aportes que las empresas de menor tamaño pueden realizar al desarrollo económico se destacan los siguientes: incubación de nuevos empresarios que operan en pequeña escala, incremento en el empleo, expansión de las exportaciones y estímulo al ahorro y la inversión familiar.

En Cuba se ha proclamado la necesidad de estudiar y elaborar criterios con relación al papel que puede desempeñar la pequeña y la mediana empresa, dentro del conjunto de transformaciones económicas que se vienen aplicando. Aunque aún no se han adoptado decisiones de largo alcance, se comprende la necesidad de considerar su futura presencia tomando en cuenta la función de este tipo de empresa en el desa-

---

17. No obstante, el centro de trabajo del profesional debe autorizar a éste para ejercer la actividad por cuenta propia.

18. Comisión Económica para América Latina y el Caribe, *La economía cubana*, 17-18.

19. Existe una amplia bibliografía sobre el papel que puede desempeñar la pequeña empresa no estatal en el desarrollo económico y particularmente en el sector industrial. A modo de ejemplo, véanse entre otros a Carlo Secchi, "El papel de las empresas pequeñas y medianas en el mejoramiento de la estructura productiva de los países en desarrollo," *Revista de la CEPAL* 27 (Diciembre de 1985), 139-50; Ian M. D. Little, "Small manufacturing enterprises in developing countries," *The World Bank Economic Review* 1, no. 2 (May 1987), 203-35; Mario Castillo y Claudio Cortellese, "La pequeña y mediana industria en el desarrollo de América Latina," *Revista de la CEPAL* 34 (Abril de 1988), 139-64; el trabajo clásico de Eugene Staley y Richard Morse, *Industrias pequeñas para países en desarrollo* (México: Editorial Roble, 1968) y las numerosas publicaciones de la CEPAL y del Banco Mundial.

rrollo económico contemporáneo, tanto desde el punto de vista de la flexibilidad e iniciativa que la misma pueda aportar, como por su capacidad para generar empleo con costos de inversión relativamente bajos.[20]

Igualmente, las pequeñas empresas no estatales podrían ser un factor activo en un proceso tendiente a conseguir una mayor articulación socioeconómica. Esto es así porque, a diferencia de otras empresas, la empresa de menor tamaño está más cercana a la demanda, lo que le permite responder en breve plazo a cambios en los niveles de actividad de la economía y ser funcional a la creación de un sistema industrial flexible y eficiente. Por otra parte, las relaciones entre las pequeñas empresas no estatales y las empresas del sector estatal podrían ser una de "complementariedad pasiva" por el lado de la oferta (subcontratación) y por el lado de la demanda (mercados paralelos y segmentados) y no necesariamente de dependencia o competencia. Una segunda área en la cual las empresas de menor tamaño presentan potencialidades es en el desarrollo de las capacidades empresariales. En Cuba el factor empresarial es uno de los recursos productivos más escasos. Por esta razón, la incorporación de nuevos empresarios al proceso productivo sería una de las principales funciones de la pequeña empresa no estatal. Este factor no sólo es beneficioso para una mayor eficiencia del sistema productivo, sino que también constituiría el principal semillero de nuevas iniciativas empresariales, y como tal, un importante estímulo a la oferta agregada a largo plazo.

Finalmente, entre otros aportes que las empresas de menor tamaño pueden realizar al desarrollo económico de Cuba se destacan también la expansión de las "exportaciones en frontera" que incluyen las ventas de bienes y servicios nacionales para satisfacer la creciente demanda del sector turístico y el estímulo a la producción de ámbito local a fin de potenciar el desa-

rrollo de una economía territorial en Cuba. En conclusión, el desarrollo económico es el resultado del esfuerzo organizado de toda la sociedad y no debe ser considerado tan sólo como un ejercicio de planificación desde el Estado Central. Para quienes consideramos a las empresas de menor tamaño como pieza clave en los procesos de industrialización y desarrollo coordinado, la promoción selectiva de la empresa no estatal que opera en pequeña escala puede hacer un aporte sustantivo a la transformación de las estructuras productivas en un marco de equidad social a través de su contribución a la producción, la innovación tecnológica y el desarrollo empresarial. Factor que puede ayudar a un mejor acoplamiento entre la economía emergente y la tradicional en Cuba.

CONSIDERACIONES FINALES

El desarrollo de la capacidad productiva de un sistema económico es un proceso complejo que no sólo involucra factores directamente económicos, sino que también depende de la estructura social, de los recursos existentes y de las tradiciones culturales.

En este sentido, cuando se estudia el fenómeno de la producción en pequeña escala, se quiere destacar el papel original que ésta tiene no sólo en una estructura industrial, sino también en el desarrollo económico y social de un país. En efecto, ya es tradicional reconocer el potencial de creación de empleo y de movilización de recursos que encierra el desarrollo de las empresas de menor tamaño. Asimismo, existe un creciente reconocimiento de su papel estratégico para el logro de una transformación productiva y la superación de la heterogeneidad estructural, con los siguientes efectos positivos sobre la articulación social y la evolución hacia sociedades estructuralmente más equitativas.

Las experiencias históricas de los países actualmente desarrollados sugieren que en la pequeña empresa existe considerable potencial de desarrollo de empre-

---

20. Véanse por ejemplo, Instituto de Estudios e Investigaciones del Trabajo, *Consideraciones sobre la problemática de las pequeñas y medianas empresas*, Ministerio del Trabajo y Seguridad Social, La Habana, Octubre 1995; Omar Everleny Pérez Villanueva y Viviana Togores González, "La pequeña y mediana empresa en Cuba: viabilidad o utopía," *Forum Empresarial* (San Juan PR) 2, no. 1 (Mayo de 1997), 1-17 y Gerardo Trueba, "Reflexiones sobre la reestructuración industrial en las condiciones de la actualidad cubana: las pequeñas y medianas empresas," *Economía Cubana / Boletín Informativo* 23 (Septiembre-Octubre 1995), 9-15.

sarios y de dinamismo tecnológico, así como un elemento de flexibilidad en la estructura productiva. Al mismo tiempo, en la medida en que la revolución tecnológica en curso está cambiando la noción de escala de producción, una serie de actividades abren perspectivas nuevas para la pequeña o mediana empresa moderna. Las empresas que operan en pequeña escala, lo mismo las formales y visibles que las invisibles e informales, han crecido en importancia en los países en desarrollo como fuentes de trabajo para los desempleados o subempleados y como factores que contribuirán al crecimiento económico nacional y a la igualdad económica.

En Cuba existen condiciones para que se desarrolle una mentalidad de pequeño propietario. Por una parte está la existencia histórica de una pequeña empresa, que casi desapareció abruptamente por razones políticas, y no estaba obligada a extinguirse desde el punto de vista económico. Por otra parte, ante una situación caracterizada por una restricción generalizada de recursos, el explosivo aumento de la economía informal y el desempleo, la segmentación de mercados, las rigideces de la capacidad productiva de las grandes empresas estatales y el precario liderazgo empresarial, está resurgiendo con inusitada fuerza la opción por la organización productiva no estatal a pequeña escala como un rasgo esencial de la reorganización del sistema empresarial. Sin lugar a dudas el desafío del mejoramiento de la capacidad productiva de la economía cubana es extenso y de gran envergadura. La empresa en pequeña escala no estatal podría jugar un papel relevante en una nueva estrategia de desarrollo en Cuba. La capacidad de estas empresas para cumplir con dicho papel dependerá tanto de sus características propias como de las condiciones iniciales del marco legal-normativo y del entorno financiero en el cual desarrollan sus actividades.

En su transición de una economía de planificación centralizada a otra con orientación de mercado, la República Popular de China eligió como un elemento clave en la reforma económica la política de la promoción de un sector no estatal, en lugar de recurrir a la privatización o el desmembramiento de grandes empresas estatales ineficientes. El camino escogido por China consiste en someter a todas las empresas productivas, cualesquiera que sean sus propietarios, a las fuerzas del mercado, en lugar de privatizar las fuentes de producción. De igual forma, en octubre de 1992 el XIV Congreso del Partido Comunista de China (PCCH) aprobó una resolución reafirmando una posición política de apoyo al desarrollo de la empresa privada dentro del contexto de la evolución hacia una política global orientada a la reforma con el objetivo de crear una "economía de mercado socialista." La importancia de esta resolución radica en el hecho de aceptar al mercado como un instrumento para el desarrollo económico, no como la característica definitoria de un sistema social. El carácter socialista de la economía se ha ratificado claramente y se sustenta con la preservación dominante del Estado sobre los medios de producción. La diferencia consistió en postular que la oferta y la demanda del mercado, reguladas por la influencia macroeconómica del Estado, pueden ser compatibles con el socialismo.

La propuesta de China, hasta el momento, no es que el mercado sustituya al socialismo, sino al plan, como instrumento económico.[21] Una de las metáforas favoritas del líder chino Deng Xioping, con la que pronto se identificó la filosofía de toda la reforma económica, fue la famosa frase de que "blanco o negro, un gato sólo es bueno si sabe cómo cazar ratones." En el fondo, lo verdaderamente importante es que la economía funcione bien para que genere y distribuya riqueza a todos, no tanto su "color" o apariencia sistémica. De modo que después de todo, **lo más importante no es el color del gato …**

---

21. Salinas Chávez, "Socialismo de mercado en China," 464-65.

REFERENCIAS

Ayala Castro, Héctor. "Los cambios en las relaciones de propiedad: 1961-1963." *Economía y Desarrollo* 65 (Noviembre-Diciembre 1981): 180-97.

Ayala Castro, Héctor. "Transformación de la propiedad en el período 1964-1980." *Economía y Desarrollo* 68 (Mayo-Junio 1982): 11-25.

Castillo, Mario y Claudio Cortellese. "La pequeña y mediana industria en el desarrollo de América Latina." *Revista de la CEPAL* 34 (Abril de 1988): 139-64.

Comisión Económica para América Latina. "La economía cubana en el período 1959-1963." En *Estudio Económico de América Latina, 1963*, 265-96. Nueva York: Naciones Unidas, 1964.

Comisión Económica para América Latina y el Caribe. *La economía cubana. Reformas estructurales y desempeño en los noventa*. México: Fondo de Cultura Económica, 1997.

Cuba. Instituto de Estudios e Investigaciones del Trabajo. *Consideraciones sobre la problemática de las pequeñas y medianas empresas*. Ministerio del Trabajo y Seguridad Social. La Habana, Octubre 1995.

Grupo Cubano de Investigaciones Económicas. *Un estudio sobre Cuba*. Coral Gables, FL: University of Miami Press, 1963.

Little, Ian M. D. "Small manufacturing enterprises in developing countries." *The World Bank Economic Review* 1, no. 2 (May 1987): 203-35.

Mesa-Lago, Carmelo. *Breve historia económica de la Cuba socialista. Políticas, resultados y perspectivas*. Madrid: Alianza Editorial, S. A., 1994.

Mesa-Lago, Carmelo. "La ofensiva revolucionaria." En *Cuba: Diez años después*, editado por Irving L. Horowitz, 89-114. Buenos Aires: Editorial Tiempo Contemporáneo, 1970.

Nuñez Moreno, Lilia. "Más allá del cuentapropismo en Cuba." *Temas* (La Habana), Julio-Septiembre 1997: 41-50.

Pérez Villanueva, Omar Everleny y Viviana Togores González. "La pequeña y mediana empresa en Cuba: viabilidad o utopía." *Forum Empresarial* (San Juan PR) 2, no. 1 (Mayo de 1997): 1-17.

Quintana Mendoza, Didio. "El sector informal urbano en Cuba: Algunos elementos para su caracterización." *Cuba: Investigación Económica* 3, no. 2 (Abril-Junio 1997): 101-20.

Salinas Chávez, Antonio. "Socialismo de mercado en China: 15 años de reforma económica." *Comercio Exterior* (México) 44, no. 5 (Mayo de 1994): 462-68.

Secchi, Carlo. "El papel de las empresas pequeñas y medianas en el mejoramiento de la estructura productiva de los países en desarrollo." *Revista de la CEPAL* 27 (Diciembre de 1985): 139-50.

Staley, Eugene y Richard Morse. *Industrias pequeñas para países en desarrollo*. México: Editorial Roble, 1968.

Trueba, Gerardo. "Reflexiones sobre la reestructuración industrial en las condiciones de la actualidad cubana: las pequeñas y medianas empresas." *Economía Cubana/Boletín Informativo* 23 (Septiembre-Octubre 1995): 9-15.

LA DESCENTRALIZACIÓN DE LAS GRANJAS ESTATALES EN CUBA: ¿GÉRMEN PARA UNA REFORMA EMPRESARIAL PENDIENTE?

Hans-Jürgen Burchardt[1]

Las reformas agrarias de 1959 y 1963 hechas por la Revolución cubana, de un lado llevaron al predominio estatal en la explotación de la tierra; y de otro, introdujeron patrones para la producción en gran escala. Bajo el axioma "más propiedad estatal, más socialismo," a partir de 1963 más del 70% del sector agropecuario fue estatalizado y convertidos en asalariados la gran mayoría de los trabajadores allí ocupados (Aranda 1968).

Un hecho significativo en las reformas agrarias lo constituyó la especificidad de no haber repartido tierra, sino en haber convertido en propietarios a los arrendatarios, aparceros y precaristas (Pino 1999). En otras palabras, al latifundismo colonial y "neocolonial" le siguió, casi ininterrumpidamente, un latifundismo estatal que por supuesto se distinguió de sus antecedentes por sus particularidades y, sobre todo, por su carácter social (Valdées 1997). Este se caracterizó por una racionalización fordista: "Su consecuencia inmediata fue la ampliación y reforzamiento del modelo agrícola de altos insumos en unidades productivas cada vez más gigantes para la producción en masa y bajo un fuerte régimen verticalizado de dirección" (Figueroa 1996, p. 11).

Este latifundio estatal se orientaba al uso masivo de la mecanización, introducción de la ciencia y la técnica, quimización, especialización productiva, entre los principales aspectos. Tendía además, al excesivo tamaño de las explotaciones agropecuarias (ver Cuadro 1). Los crecimientos de la producción en estas condiciones se obtenían mediante la concentración de la maquinaría y equipos y el empleo de altos insumos. Mientras las permanentes escaseces de fuerza de trabajo era suplidas con la movilización masiva de trabajadores de la ciudad.

Cuadro 1. Tamaño promedio de las empresas agropecuarias estatales, 1990

Tipo de empresa	Tamaño promedio (hectáreas)
Complejos Agro-Industriales (CAI) Azucareros	13.110
Cultivos varios	4.276
Cítricos y frutales	10.822
Arroz	32.760
Tabaco	2.778
Pecuario	24.865

Fuente: Nova 1997, p. 36

En otras palabras, la producción agrícola cubana adquirió un carácter típicamente extensivo. Entre sus deficiencias más significativas pueden señalarse que la

---

1. La base de este artículo se encuentra en el número 28 de la revista *Socialism and Democracy*, Nueva York, la cual contiene una versión en inglés que presenta un panorama más amplio de la actual política agraria en Cuba. Para un análisis más profundo y extenso sobre las reformas agrarias en Cuba consúltese mi libro, *La última reforma agraria del siglo: La agricultura cubana entre el cambio y el estancamiento*. Editorial Nueva Sociedad. Caracas, 2000.

elevación del producto agropecuario obtenido era muy inferior a los medios básicos, obras de infraestructura, ciencia y técnica empleados, al mismo tiempo que los rendimientos de los fondos y la productividad del trabajo mostraban una permanente regresión. La irrentabilidad de las empresas estatales se convirtió en un pesado fardo para el presupuesto del Estado, que subvencionaba las pérdidas, mientras en general, la agricultura no aportó los saltos productivos necesarios para alcanzar una base alimentaria que facilitara una relativa independencia en la satisfacción de los rubros principales de la alimentación de la población (Burchardt 1996).

Por otra parte, al incorporarse Cuba a la división internacional socialista del trabajo a partir de 1972, asume la especialización en la producción de azúcar y cítricos a cambio de cereales y otros bienes alimenticios. A fines de los años 80, cerca de 60% del área cultivable se destinaba a los productos exportables y algo más del 40% a la producción de alimentos. Esto arrojaba aproximadamente un 0.14 ha de superficie cultivada per cápita para la manutención. Al no lograrse los objetivos trazados en la especialización, Cuba se convirtió en dependiente de las importaciones para satisfacer las necesidades de la población. Así, en los inicios de la década de los 90, el 55% de las calorías, el 50% de las proteínas y el 90% de todas las grasas consumidas en la isla provenían del exterior (Figueras 1994). Esta dependencia, hasta hoy día, en términos generales, se mantiene.

Con el derrumbe del socialismo en Europa del Este, y con el objetivo de sustituir con producciones propias el déficit de los productos alimenticios que provenían de esa área, se instrumentó el llamado programa alimentario (1989). El objetivo central de tal política fue reducir la dependencia de las importaciones de alimentos, aumentar el nivel de autosuficiencia y garantizar a la población el suministro adecuado de calorías y proteínas. Las soluciones ensayadas, no obstante, no modificaron, en sus elementos esenciales, las bases, estructuras y condiciones de funcionamiento de la gestión y dirección de la economía agraria. La organización ramal, subordinación vertical, centralización de planes y programas, así como otras prácti-

cas, mantuvieron su vigencia, e incluso, se expandieron, abarcando el sector estatal un 83% del fondo cultivable (Figueroa 1996).

Los ambiciosos objetivos del programa alimentario no se realizaron. Las superficies previstas a poner en explotación no pudieron ser alcanzadas al reducirse drásticamente los recursos necesarios. Fuentes oficiales reconocieron que a partir de 1992 los insumos disminuyeron a una quinta parte de lo empleado antes. Al mismo tiempo, se hicieron acuciantes los déficit de fuerza de trabajo, que trataron de compensarse con movilizaciones masivas, mientras por otra parte, se manifestaron deficiencias en la distribución de los productos cosechados, llegando a reconocerse, en diferentes medios de prensa, que la red comercial recibía sólo un tercio de los productos, una tercera parte se descomponía en el campo y el otro tercio iba al mercado negro. Estos resultados convirtieron a la agricultura en el sector más subvencionado por el presupuesto estatal. "Con el Plan Alimentario fracasó el pilar básico de la estrategia económica estatal en el área de la economía interna" (Mesa-Lago 1995, p. 62).

El descalabro del programa alimentario provocó una crisis en los principales rublos de abastecimiento agropecuario, que no pudo ser totalmente amortiguada mediante las importaciones. El agudizamiento de la situación alimenticia sólo podía ser superada por medio de un cambio estructural en la agricultura. Había llegado el momento de plantearse lo que algunos especialistas han llamado una "nueva reforma agraria."

LA NUEVA POLÍTICA AGRARIA EN CUBA: AJUSTES EN LUGAR DE CAMBIOS

En septiembre de 1993 se abrió un nuevo capítulo en la historia agraria de Cuba. La propuesta del Buró Político del Comité Central del Partido Comunista de Cuba inició un proceso de reestructuración del entramado agropecuario del país. Dentro de los predios de las 735 granjas estatales cañeras y las 835 empresas agropecuarias, se crearon las Unidades Básicas de Producción Cooperativa (UBPC).[2]

Cuadro 2. Participación en el área agrícola según tipo de productor *(1995)*

Conceptos	Área/total	%	Área/agrícola	%
1) Colectivo-cooperativista	3.869,4	35	3.490,2	52
UBPC	3.143,6	29	2.844,2	42
Cañeras	1.614,3	15	1.469,6	22
No cañeras	1.529,3	14	1.374,6	20
Cooperativas de Producción Agropecuaria	725,8	7	646,0	10
2) Sector estatal	5.882,4	53	2.222,5	33
Complejo Agro-Industrial (CAI)	151,8	1	113,6	2
Empresas agropecuarias	4.469,2	41	1.579,6	23
Otras estatales	201,3	2	154,1	2
Poder Popular	788,3	7	117,1	2
Granjas militares	271,8	2	258,1	4
3) Campesinos privados	1.262,5	12	1.059,2	15
Cooperativas de Comercio y Servicio	905,4	8	739,1	11
Productores individuales	260,7	2	230,6	3
Nuevos productores	96,4	1	89,6	1
Totales	11.014,3	100	6.771,9	100

Fuente: Colectivo de Autores 1995, pp. 56-57

El Decreto Ley No. 142 dispuso la entrega de parte fundamental de las tierras estatales, en usufructo gratuito, a los colectivos obreros del sector agropecuario, así como el traspaso de los medios básicos necesarios para que asumieran sus responsabilidades productivas. Los propósitos en la creación de las UBPC estaban encaminados a lograr incrementos substanciales en las producciones agropecuarias, reducir los costos, estimular la incorporación a las labores agrícolas de nuevos productores, contribuir a la superación de la inestabilidad de la fuerza de trabajo, mejorar los niveles de vida en el agro, facilitar la solución de problemas como el de la vivienda y ampliar los servicios sociales, así como favorecer la eliminación de los subsidios a la agricultura (Díaz 1997).

Por otra parte, las UBPC han conllevado una reducción significativa del tamaño de las explotaciones agropecuarias al promediar extensiones entre las 800 y 1.000 hectáreas por unidad productiva. Esto unido a la existencia de otras formas de explotación agraria, lleva a que hoy pueda hablarse del surgimiento en la isla de una economía mixta en el sector rural (ver Cuadro 2).

Los miembros de la UBPC organizan el trabajo, deciden sobre el empleo de los medios a su disposición, disponen de áreas de autoabastecimiento y comercializan los excedentes de las producciones, una vez cumplido los contratos firmados. En tanto, sus planes productivos se fijan en convenios con las empresas estatales dentro de las cuales funcionan, compran y venden sus productos, según los precios determinados por el Estado. Hay analistas que afirman que con estas transformaciones "(...) el gigantesco sector de la granja estatal fue, en realidad, privatizado" (Deere 1994, p. 3). No obstante, el Estado se ha reservado el derecho a "(...) la disolución de cualquier Unidad Básica de Producción Cooperativa (...) por causas de interés económico o social determinado por el Gobierno" (Gaceta Oficial 1993).

Al mismo tiempo, a finales de 1994, como continuación lógica a la descentralización aplicada en el agro, se establecieron los mercados agropecuarios en todo el país (Carriazo 1994). Por esta vía las UBPC vieron ampliadas sus posibilidades de comercialización al permitírseles vender en estos establecimientos, los sobrantes y las producciones no conveniadas. En los úl-

---

2. Los siguientes comentarios reflejan algunos resultados del proyecto de investigación "La transformación de la agricultura cubana a partir de 1993," dirigido por el autor y auspiciado por la *Fundación Volkswagen*. Las instituciones que colaboraron en el proyecto fueron el *Departamento de Historia de la Universidad de Hannover*, el *Equipo de Estudios Rurales* (EER) y el *Centro de Estudios de la Economía Cubana* (CEEC) de la Universidad de La Habana.

timos tiempos, se les autorizó a acudir a esos mercados con parte importante de sus producciones fundamentales. Con ello han mejorado sus rendimientos económicos.

Por otra parte, muchos estudiosos destacan las desproporciones que se observan en el desempeño actual de la agricultura cubana. Entre ellas señalan, de una parte, el alto grado de la intervención estatal y, de otra, la autonomía reconocida a las cooperativas, lo que da por resultado la existencia de una "simbiosis" o "hibridación" en cuanto a mecanismos de gestión, asignación de recursos y criterios para medir la eficiencia de las actividades económicas. En el caso de las UBPC, se ha subrayado que constituyen, en realidad, una entidad dual a medio camino entre la empresa estatal y la verdadera cooperativa, lo que podría definirse como *dualismo estructural*. De otro lado, se encuentran a medio camino entre una empresa comercial y una simple unidad técnico-productiva, lo que podría denominarse *dualismo funcional*. En este desdoblamiento radica la complejidad actual de la cuestión agraria en Cuba y la incoherencia de las nuevas estructuras puestas en ejecución.

De acuerdo con los resultados de investigaciones de varios colectivos multidiciplinarios e investigadores individuales (EER 1996; 1998), las dificultades que presentan las transformaciones en el sector agrario son de diversa naturaleza y pueden ser desglosadas en tres dimensiones centrales: obstáculos coyunturales, socioculturales y estructurales.

Por *obstáculos coyunturales* se entienden las trabas derivadas del cambio de un modo de producción mecanizado y administrativo a otro de trabajo intensivo y autogestionado, y que, necesariamente, requiere de un proceso de consolidación y experiencia de varios años. Aquí pueden mencionarse, entre otras cosas, la falta de conocimientos empresariales, el proceso gradual de asimilación de nuevas tecnologías, el empleo de técnicas intensivas de trabajo, la institucionalización de renovados esquemas organizativos de gestión, y el perfeccionamiento y la estabilidad de las juntas directivas. No obstante, las experiencias obtenidas permiten apuntar que muchas de estas limitaciones están siendo superadas y que algunas de sus lecciones pueden ser generalizadas.

Los *problemas socioculturales*, por otra, se identifican con los patrones de comportamiento de los actores implicados en el trabajo de las UBPC. Este movimiento cooperativo surgió de una directiva gubernamental, orientada desde arriba, sin contar con un desarrollo orgánico y evolutivo desde la base. Ambos elementos se reflejan en el lento cambio de conducta de los participantes en el proceso de consolidación de las relaciones que las nuevas entidades demandan.

Este conjunto de circunstancias contribuyó a la estructuración de un extendido paternalismo, aún no totalmente erradicado, por parte de la administración estatal, al no reconocerle la autonomía indispensable a estas cooperativas. Tampoco puede desconocerse que persiste un cierto acomodamiento en las direcciones de las UBPC a aceptar el control y la injerencia de las instancias estatales. Con razón se ha destacado que "uno de los problemas más serios ha sido la imposibilidad de cambiar con rapidez la mentalidad de los agentes involucrados en el funcionamiento de las UBPC, tanto de los productores asociados en éstas, como de los funcionarios estatales relacionados. Los últimos no renuncian fácilmente a ejercer las prerrogativas y funciones que les otorgaba el esquema administrativo anterior, en tanto los primeros no se sienten dueños de lo que producen" (Carranza et al. 1995, p. 46).

El aspecto sociocultural también comprende las relaciones interempresariales. En este sentido, ante todo, vale resaltar que Cuba carecía de una gran masa de pequeños productores agrícolas; la gran mayoría de los ocupados en las labores agrarias eran asalariados con una especialización, y participación en la división del trabajo relativamente alta. Los miembros de las UBPC, en consecuencia, no disponían de una cultura autogestiónaria, ni de tiempo para desarrollar una conciencia capaz de asimilar los modos de producción e intensidad de trabajo que requiere la organización cooperativa.

Las *limitaciones estructurales* en el funcionamiento de las UBPC abarcan, ante todo, la ausencia en los niveles tanto meso como macro-económicos de cambios institucionales significativos en el papel de los órganos estatales (Rodríguez 1999). No se ha avanzado mucho en la transformación del Estado de agente productor principal y administrador central, en agente regulador de los procesos económicos; los cambios dados en el sector agrario han sido más formales que reales. Así, el Estado ha continuado ejerciendo un excesivo control, a veces directo otras indirecto, en la producción, la compra y comercialización, en la asignación de insumos, además de mantener un virtual monopolio, o cuando menos, una posición dominante en estas actividades.

Asimismo, el Estado adquiere a bajos precios los productos de las UBPC, mientras vende los suministros e insumos para la producción, así como los servicios, a precios elevados. Ya es evidente que estos mecanismos se han tornado en un freno al incremento de la productividad del trabajo (González 1998). De aquí que uno de los objetivos originales de la creación de las UBPC, incentivar el trabajo y con ello aumentar la productividad, ha sido socavado por las desproporciones de estas relaciones. De esta forma, la conexión entre productividad e ingresos no aparece debido a la monopolización estatal de precios y, sin estímulo material, no hay interés en el aumento de la producción.

Otro aspecto que incide en las trabas estructurales que afectan a las UBPC tiene que ver con la necesidad de medidas que tiendan a fortalecer la infraestructura y medios de transporte que faciliten el acceso de las cooperativas al mercado agropecuario. No obstante, la autorización para que estas unidades adquieren las producciones de productores independientes o cooperativas de consumo y servicio les abren nuevas posibilidades para incrementar sus fuentes de ingreso por la vía de la comercialización.

Otro obstáculo estructural para el funcionamiento de la UBPC tiene que ver con el sistema de asignación de los insumos. Más de un observador ha llamado la atención sobre la ausencia de mercados desregulados para los bienes intermedios industriales y medios básicos, destacando el papel que ejerce el Estado de virtual monopolio en los abastecimientos (Bu Wong 1996). Se reconoce por amplios círculos de especialistas y en eventos académicos que este proceso de asignación de recursos vigente no corresponde a la diversificación experimentada en las formas de explotación, a la multiplicación de los agentes econó-

micos y a la autonomía que, al menos, en las disposiciones oficiales se le han otorgado a las UBPC.

Por último, otra cuestión presente en las desviaciones estructurales actuantes en el trabajo de las UBPC tiene que ver con la ausencia de representación para la canalización y defensa de intereses propios. Los miembros de las cooperativas son dueños de los medios de producción (excepto la tierra) y, sin embargo, están organizados como asalariados pertenecientes al Sindicato de Trabajadores Agropecuarios y Forestales; mientras, por otra parte, están subordinados a los Ministerios de la Agricultura y del Azúcar. La condición del cooperativista-propietario-proletario y su subordinación a instancias estatales no posibilitan manifestaciones independientes de sus intereses concretos y, mucho menos, disponer de representación asociada orgánica como productores independientes (Burchardt 1999a).

EL COOPERATIVISMO CUBANO: ¿GERMEN PARA UNA REFORMA EMPRESARIAL?

Hoy por hoy, aún no puede afirmarse que las transformaciones ocurridas en el sector agropecuario y el tipo de economía mixta que parece consolidarse han dado respuesta adecuada y eficiente a los problemas históricos de la agricultura cubana: la escasez de mano de obra, el logro de una autosuficiencia alimentaria y, en consecuencia, disminución de la dependencia externa con respecto a la alimentación de la población.

Sin embargo, tomando en cuenta que el nuevo cooperativismo cubano nació en momentos de una profunda crisis económica, y que su accionar tiene que desenvolverse dentro de esa crisis, hay que reconocer que la estabilización y logros parciales de las UBPC, durante casi una década, constituyen un mérito indudable. Consolidar este éxito y convertirlo en un proceso irreversible, representa, en nuestra opinión, el principal desafío al que tiene que enfrentarse la sociedad cubana.

Un posible camino a seguir comprendería la introducción de mecanismos económicos más flexibles, referidos, ante todo, al sistema de precios y de abastecimiento técnico-material, que tendería progresivamente hacia relaciones de oferta-demanda. Junto con este paso, el área de renglones agropecuarios sujeto a distribución normada, pudieran irse reduciendo paulatinamente, al igual que los subsidios pudieran sustituirse por ayudas directas a los segmentos de menores ingresos. Así, modificar todo el entramado actual de abastecimiento técnico-material, por su adquisición en una red comercial, posibilitaría que cada UBPC establezca las combinaciones de surtido que mejor se ajusten a sus condiciones específicas. En otras palabras, sustituir las relaciones de controles administrativos por métodos económicos, parece ser el camino a transitar en el futuro próximo de las UBPC, así como lograr, en el mediano plazo, una tasa de cambio económicamente fundamentado.

Hasta el presente, un punto neurálgico en los mercados agropecuarios lo constituye la persistencia de altos precios. En el mediano plazo, la disminución de estos precios se alcanzaría — esto lo subrayan todos los especialistas — solo si se logra una ampliación de la oferta, donde las UBPC con su enorme carga de reserva productiva desempeñarían un extraordinario papel (Nova 1996). Al resolverse el problema del incremento y la eficiencia de la producción "ubepecista," se elevaría su participación en las ventas en los mercados agropecuarios y ello posibilitaría resolver sus actuales déficit financieros y de rentabilidad.

Otra cuestión sensible que han arrastrado las UBPC ha tenido que ver con la autonomía empresarial de que disponen. En este aspecto pudieran abrirse nuevas posibilidades que incluyeran, entre otras, la capacidad de decisión para establecer vínculos de cooperación con entes externos, así como facilidades para hacer inversiones a unidades que formen fondos destinados a la acumulación.

Un punto poco debatido en torno al funcionamiento de las UBPC ha sido el de su autonomía política. La autogestión de las cooperativas es condición decisiva para el éxito del modelo encarnado en las UBPC. Parece recomendable que las funciones del Estado sean menos intervencionistas, se otorguen seguridades legales más amplias y transparentes, así como se abran espacios para crear estructuras propias y más diversificadas de organización. La clave estaría aquí en el punto de equilibrio entre las aspiraciones y las potencialidades de las nuevas empresas para desarrollarse. Así,

un excesivo tutelaje castraría las bases de su consolidación y retardaría innecesariamente su protagonismo económico y social; mientras que, una excesiva autonomía, conduciría al desorden y desvirtuaría los principios del cooperativismo.

Tampoco debe olvidarse que las UBPC desarrollan sus actividades dentro de un marco local y regional. Así, una mayor racionalidad en el tamaño de las cooperativas, la diversificación de los cultivos, las posibilidades de estructurar, en el ámbito local redes de comercialización directas a la población, la autorización para la prestación de servicios, junto con la vinculación horizontal entre las cooperativas y otras empresas locales, facilitaría la integración de las UBPC en la política y las estrategias de los gobiernos municipales. Por esta vía surgirían efectos sinergéticos entre las unidades colectivas y el desarrollo local. Así, pueden crecer nuevas "local economies" que podrían ser, no sólo el fundamento de una economía sustentable y sostenible, sino también, la célula de una nueva cultura política de la sociedad cubana (Burchardt 1999b; Dilla 1996).

De lo apuntado se desprende que el proceso cooperativo engendrado por las UBPC, podría convertirse en un polo que impulse otras formas organizativas dentro de la reforma empresarial en marcha (Burchardt 2000). No resulta un secreto que el carácter que asuman los cambios en la esfera de la dirección de la economía marcarán su impronta en el entramado político y social de la isla. Dentro del marco de las transformaciones introducidas en las empresas, que aspiren a una autonomía real, a la elevación de la productividad y a un compromiso social, parece de interés promover, como una de las variantes, las cooperativas. Un efectivo modelo cooperativista contribuiría a difundir y fortalecer una distribución social más justa, así como a una democratización de la economía y de la sociedad.

Muchas son las ventajas que aportaría el desarrollo exitoso del proceso de cooperativización en el agro. En primer lugar, asegurar una base de abastecimientos de productos alimenticios, estables y a precios accesibles, a la gran mayoría de la población tendría positivos efectos psicológicos entre los consumidores. A la vez, mejores ingresos y condiciones de trabajo en la agricultura, pudieran crear las bases para absorber una masa importante de desempleados. Esto tendría una repercusión evidente e impactos directos mas dinámicos en las regiones y niveles locales. Una ampliación de las formas cooperativas, mayores descentralizaciones, así como el potenciar la creación de nuevas unidades campesinas, serían una respuesta positiva en la dirección de "recampesinar" el agro, y contribuir a detener la emigración del campo a la ciudad (Valdés 1997).

En resumen, puede adelantarse que un posible itinerario de los cambios operados en el sector agropecuario cubano, y los que son factibles de preverse para un próximo futuro reconocerían que: "... sin la reanimación de la agricultura de consumo interno y del sector agroexportador y su rentabilización, no puede hablarse de superación de la crisis económica ni de saneamiento real de las finanzas internas... Los objetivos básicos de esta reforma son la diversificación de las formas económicas de producción y de los agentes productivos, el redimensionamiento de las entidades productivas, la introducción y generalización de una agricultura de bajos insumos y alto empleo de mano de obra, la apertura del mercado y la generación de nuevos incentivos capaces de estabilizar y recapturar la fuerza de trabajo necesaria para este sector. La autonomía y la autogestión financiera y participativa son factores claves para la racionalización y la rentabilidad de la agricultura nacional. Esta es, definitivamente, la vía magistral para dar solución a los dos cuellos de botella fundamentales que aflijen al país: el

problema alimentario y la escasez de divisas" (Figueroa 1996, pp. 18-19).

Algunos estudiosos de la realidad cubana consideran, por otra parte, que las transformaciones introducidas en el funcionamiento del sector agropecuario en Cuba pueden calificarse de una "Tercera Reforma Agraria." Aún cuando la "economía mixta" que se aprecia hoy en los tipos y formas de explotación agraria en Cuba pueden dar lugar a valoraciones de este alcance, existen también cuestionamientos que no pueden pasarse por alto. Ante todo, pueden señalarse el control directo e indirecto que el Estado ejerce sobre el sector, y la ausencia de institucionalizaciones claras y precisas para validar legalmente los cambios introducidos. A estos habría que agregar la falta de promulgación de reglas transparentes para el usufructo de la tierra y la tenencia para explotaciones especializadas (tabaco, café, cacao, etc.), así como acerca de las posibilidades de hacer reversible las medidas establecidas.

Por último, alcanzar las potencialidades actuales contenidas en la política agraria de la isla plantea la necesidad de una reorientación radical. El cooperativismo cubano actualmente no es un reto de factibilidad, sino, sobre todo, una cuestión de voluntad política. Quien quiera para la Cuba del nuevo siglo una vinculación de la eficiencia económica con un sistema que priorice al hombre y su entorno social, junto a la defensa del medio ecológico, y que contenga relaciones de propiedad con una cogestión participativa, ha de promover y hacer de la llamada "Tercera Reforma Agraria" una vía irreversible.

BIBLIOGRAFÍA

Aranda, Sergio. (1968): *La revolución agraria en Cuba*. México.

Burchardt, Hans-Jürgen. (2000): Cuba: una visión desde lejos — ¿reforma económica o estancamiento?. En: *Revista de Ciencias Sociales*, No. 8, pp. 86-105.

Burchardt, Hans-Jürgen. (1999a): *Kuba: Im Herbst des Patriarchen*. Stuttgart.

Burchardt, Hans-Jürgen. (1999b): ¿Del fin del siglo a la crisis sin fin?. Cuba: El modelo híbrido en la disyuntiva entre capital social y participación o desigualdad y fracaso politico. En: *Papers*, No. 59, pp. 131-153

Burchardt, Hans-Jürgen. (1996): *Kuba: Der lange Abschied von einem Mythos*. Stuttgart.

Bu Wong, Angel. (1996): Las UBPC y su necesario perfeccionamiento. En: *Cuba: Investigación Económica*, No. 2, pp. 15-43.

Carranza Valdés, Julio; Gutiérrez Urdaneta, Luis; y Pedro Monreal González (1995): *Cuba: La restructuración de la economía - una propuesta para el debate*. La Habana.

Carriazo Moreno, George. (1994): Cambios estructurales en la agricultura cubana: La cooperativización. En: *Economía Cubana - Boletin Informativo*, No. 18, pp. 14-29.

Colectivo de Autores. (1995): *La reforma económica cubana*. La Habana.

Deere, Carmen Diana (1994): Implicaciones agrícolas del comercio cubano. En: *Economía Cubana - Boletín Informativo*, No. 18, pp. 3-14.

Díaz Vázquez, Julio. A. (1997): Cuba: Reforma económica dentro del socialismo. (Manuscrito inédito en el CIEI [Centro de Investigaciones de la Economía Internacional], La Habana).

Dilla, Haroldo. (ed.) (1996): *La participación en Cuba*. La Habana.

EER (Equipo de Estudios Rurales) (1996): *UBPC: Desarrollo rural y participación*. La Habana.

EER (Equipo de Estudios Rurales) (1998): *UBPC: Desarrollo rural y participación social*. La Habana.

Figueras, Miguel. (1994): *Aspectos estructurales de la economía cubana*. La Habana.

Figueroa, Víctor. (1996): El nuevo modelo agrario en Cuba bajo los marcos de la reforma económica. En: Equipo de Estudios Rurales (EER): *UBPC: Desarrollo rural y participación*. La Habana, pp. 1-45.

Gaceta Oficial de la República de Cuba, 21 de septiembre de 1993: Decreto-Ley 142 del Consejo de Estado. Sobre las unidades básicas de producción cooperativa.

González Gutiérrez, Alfredo. (1998): Economía y sociedad: Los retos del modelo. En: *Temas*, No. 11, pp. 4-29.

Mesa-Lago, Carmelo. (1995): Evaluación y perspectivas de la reforma económica cubana. En: Hoffmann, B. (ed.): *Cuba: Apertura y reforma económica. Perfil de un debate*. Caracas, pp. 59-89.

Nova González, Armando (1997): *Economía agropecuaria*. La Habana.

Nova González, Armando. (1996): El Mercado Agropecuario cubano: Práctica y teoría. En: *Economía y Desarrollo*, Vol. 123, No. 3-4, pp. 41-50.

Pino Santos, Oscar. (1999): La Ley de la reforma agraria de 1959 y el fin de las oligarquías en Cuba. En: *Temas*, No. 16-17, pp. 42-60.

Rodríguez Castellón, Santiago. (1999): La evolución del sector agropecuario en los noventa. En: *Balance de la economía cubana a finales de los 90's*. La Habana, pp. 61-81.

Valdés Paz, Juan. (1997): *Procesos agrarios en Cuba 1959-1995*. La Habana.

TRANSITION IN CENTRAL AND EASTERN EUROPE: LESSONS FOR DEVELOPMENT OF SMEs IN CUBA

Antonio Gayoso

The experience gained from the extraordinary process of transition, still under way in Central and Eastern Europe and in the former Soviet Union, is rich with lessons that could guide policy making and action in a Cuba of the future. This presentation attempts to distill some of these lessons and to explore those which would facilitate the growth of small and medium-size enterprises, the so-called SMEs, when transition finally unfolds in the island.

Ten years after the initiation of transition in the former command economies of Central and Eastern Europe (CEE) and the Former Soviet Union (FSU), one thing is certain: the process of transformation is far more complex and it takes far more time and resources than envisioned in 1989. The reason is that transition involves changing institutions, practices, and behaviors that have taken root in society during decades of centralized control and political repression. Another certainty is that it **is** possible to transform economic and political systems radically and end up with market economies and political democracies. Ten years after the Berlin Wall fell, most production in countries in transition originates in the private sector and is transacted under free market conditions. In addition, most of the people live under democratic rule, where the people can vote governments out of office and have done so.

OVERVIEW OF CHANGES IN CEE AND THE FSU

The decision to change came about at different times in different countries in the region. In fact, Hungary, Poland, and Yugoslavia had already started some re-

forms by the late 1980s, before the destruction of the Wall. In 1990, COMECON, the Soviet-dominated free trade area, was dissolved as members decided to start trading in hard currency and at world market prices. The disappearance of the Soviet Union, where Gorbachev had started a re-structuring program under socialism, witnessed in 1992 the start of transition in Russia and the newly independent Baltic states.

How do we define transition? In this context, transition has been the process of transforming what were non-democratic regimes, whose economic systems were centrally-controlled by the government, and where the state owned most of the means of production. The major objective of transition, at the national level, has been to develop an economic and political system that stimulates sustainable economic development and increased national wellbeing, in a context of political freedom. The move toward a private-sector based economy operating in a market context has been a key aspect of transition. Another, equally important aspect has been the move toward representative democracy.

The modus operandi of the former socialist countries in their transformation has required a number of key policy changes. To successfully divest the state of the elements used to control and to increase efficiency, most of the region's countries undertook programs of liberalization to free prices, privatization and distribution of the ownership of the means of production into private hands. In addition, the countries initiated stabilization programs that called for monetary and fiscal discipline. These stabilization programs provided the foundation for the development of financial systems that worked in market prices, and dealt with productive enterprises on the basis of their creditworthiness rather than by public subsidization. The introduction of hard budget constraints and the privatization of large firms have been, in fact, two of the most essential but also most difficult undertakings. In many of these countries this process has not been completed and has not been perfect.

A second group of changes has dealt with development of the institutional structures and processes required to support a market system and private property. Aside from developing adequate financial systems, these efforts have included the development and adoption of an appropriate legal framework and legal institutions to address, inter alia, property rights, contractual dispute adjudication, the rules for commercial transactions, and a financial regulatory framework.

Finally, and in parallel with these changes, transition has meant the development of representative, participatory democracy. This undertaking has required the development of legal rules that protect and stimulate the creation of institutions of civil society including political parties, and that prescribe periodic competitive elections.

In terms of the objectives referred to earlier, experience indicates that, generally, CEE and FSU countries have ended up into two groups.

- Most progress has been achieved in the countries of Central Europe, such as Hungary, the Czech Republic, Slovenia, Slovakia, Poland, and the Baltic countries. These are, in fact the countries that historically have had greater contact and linkages with Western Europe. This group rapidly implemented liberalization and has undertaken sustained — though sometimes controversial — stabilization programs. These, in turn, have provided the foundation for institutional change. Two powerful forces have helped. One has been the role of citizens in newly adopted representative democratic systems. The other the

tantalizing prospect of joining the European Union and NATO.

- The slow achievers, such as Belarus, Ukraine, Russia, Moldova, have been laggard in implementing liberalization programs or in mounting steady stabilization programs. In these countries, progress towards truly representative democracy has also been slow. In many, the former political elites remain powerful and unwilling to relinquish control. A great deal of rent-seeking behavior remains. As a result, markets have been less efficient, soft-budget constraints remain, and the environment for private firms has been less that ideal. Many obstacles, as well as corruption, remain and impede the growth of new private firms.

WHAT ARE THE KEY LESSONS OF THE LAST TEN YEARS?

A number of important lessons can be learned from the transition experiences of CEE and the FSU:

- The faster the liberalization and stabilization programs are put in place the easier they are to implement.

- Democratization must proceed apace in order to empower the people and weaken the former *nomenklatura* who would oppose change. To the maximum extent, the old guard must be dispossessed of power.

- Political competition is as important a factor as is market competition to assuring a sustainable transition.

- The state must assume an infinitely less controlling role than before. Yet, it must remain strong and credible to help create and support the conditions and the institutions required by a market system.

- Institutional restructuring must be implemented as rapidly as possible so that the legal, financial and regulatory frameworks are in place. Otherwise, growth of SMEs would be severely constrained.

- The transition program must have the support of the population on the whole, a fact that suggests all groups should bear equally the necessary costs of transition. Special attention must be given to programs that assure this outcome.

- The possibility of joining a successful, read rich, trading group constitutes a major incentive to undertake rapid change. Further, external alliances can encourage and facilitate change.

- There will be serious declines in output, particularly in large state-owned firms. These are also difficult to sell off before they are restructured.

- Privatization can be achieved in many ways. One is selling large state enterprises. Another is selling or transferring property of small firms to their current employees. The third way is creating the right conditions for new small and medium sized firms to appear.

WHY SMEs?

SMEs deserve the interest they have received in transition countries for three fundamental reasons: First, they are employment intensive. Second, when managed by the owner, they have proven to be efficient. And third, they are a very effective means of deepening the privatization process by making thousands of citizens private entrepreneurs with a stake in the new system. In fact, SMEs are considered to be one of the principal forces underlying transition in CEE.

SMEs play a large role in developed economies. For example, according to the United Nations Economic Commission for Europe, in 1995, 99.8 per cent of enterprises in 19 countries in Western Europe were SMEs; 92 per cent of the total number of these were firms with fewer than ten employees. In the United States, small businesses employ more than half of the labor force; in 1994, the Small Business Administration reported that of about 22 million non-primary firms in the United States, 99 per cent were small.

SMEs are attractive because of their agility in adapting to changing market and supply environments, their role in deepening managerial and entrepreneurial skills, their employment intensiveness, and their contribution to diversity and competition in the sup-

ply of products and services. Similar experiences have been observed in transition countries where agricultural lands have been transferred or sold to former rural workers.

As has been the case in the United States, many of the faster transition countries have organized institutions to stimulate growth of SMEs. The Czech Republic, Hungary, Poland, the Baltic countries, Slovenia, Slovakia, and even slower-moving Romania have all created institutions and implemented programs to assist SMEs.

PRE-TRANSITION CUBA

Cuba remains a country with an economic system closely patterned after that of the former Soviet Union, pre-Gorbachev.

- Most economic and all political decisions are made at the top.

- With few exceptions affecting a minute portion of output, all domestic prices are administered.

- In addition to the national currency, the U.S. dollar circulates legally. The official peso/U.S. dollar exchange rate has no relation to the shadow price of the national currency. A large variety of important basic needs goods can only be purchased in dollars. This dual currency system has created an acute gap between the level of living of those who have dollars and those who do not.

- The state owns the large majority of productive enterprises and most of the agricultural land. Private SMEs are prohibited and politically rejected.

- With the exception of individual work performed by a small group of licensed self-employed, the state is the only legal employer.

- Structure, level, price, and distribution patterns of output are decided administratively.

- Budget policy is directed at maintaining current institutional structure underwriting with subsidies most state enterprises, including agricultural ones.

- The tax system is rudimentary and it is used, explicitly, not to produce revenue but to control and repress those authorized to work on their own. In practice, only the self-employed pay income taxes.

- There are no standard accounting procedures nor transparency in governance.

- The political system is also closed. Political parties, other than the Communist Party, are not permitted.

- Elections which do take place are not competitive. All candidates to parliament are selected by the Party. The parliament seldom debates bills and meets only several days per year to ratify government decisions.

- There is no civil society to speak of. Dissidents and opponents are persecuted and frequently jailed.

ASSESSING FACTORS TO HELP TRANSITION

The preceding elements suggest the challenges and difficulties Cuba will face as it decides on transition. Cuba must reckon with both its assets and its liabilities.

Cuba's important assets are:

- A highly educated population, with technical skills that, though frequently not up to date, will likely allow rapid learning. Infusion of new productive technology could quickly lead to large increases in productivity and production.

- A good stock of natural resources that can be used to advantage.

- A large near-by exiled population with substantial know-how and capital, eager to assist.

- Geographical closeness to largest market on earth. In medium term, good prospect of joining the North American Free Trade Agreement (NAFTA)

Cuba's liabilities are:

- A mindset bred after 40 years of experience that leads to a high degree of avoidance of risk and individual decision making. Fear.

- No experience in participatory democracy and citizens independent action for the last two generations.

- Known but unmeasured environmental damage from past government programs and human survivalist behavior.

- Prevalence of obsolete and fuel-intensive technology.

- Outstanding claims of former property owners on a large number of confiscated properties.

- Total inadequacy of current financial system to serve the needs of citizens, entrepreneurs, and SMEs.

SEQUENCE FOR DECISIONS

The diverse experience in transition cases in Europe suggests that Cuba will have to move rapidly on a number of fronts to ensure success of transition reforms. Short-term liberalization and a massive stabilization program should be quickly put in place with help from the international financial institutions (IFIs). Their financial support will also be required to organize and implement programs to minimize welfare impact of dislocations brought about by restructuring. Acute inequalities must be avoided. This assistance from the IFIs is also needed to make available the technical expertise required to develop and support structural reform programs.

Particularly in view of the past 50 years of repressive regimes, Cuba must move decisively to restore representative democracy. The population must share responsibility and agree with the overall direction of reform.

A modern and fair tax system will be necessary so that the government can raise revenues to develop physical, financial, and human infrastructure to support the market and the private sector.

Government should move rapidly to privatize small state firms. Such a move would make economic sense and help generate popular support for reforms. There are probably few claims from former owners on these group of firms.

Special, non-subsidized, programs must be developed to stimulate investment in new SMEs. These firms would have a large short term impact on employment, output and the diversity of supply. They would provide employment for those workers let go from inefficient state-owned large firms, thus facilitating, in turn, their privatization.

It will also be of the utmost urgency to attempt and solve the issue of claims on property confiscated by the Revolution. The issue has been handled in different ways in the CEE. Some countries have effected some restitution to former owners. Others have approved compensation in diverse ways. Still a third group has not recognized any claims. The important thing in Cuba is not to let it linger without a legal, and hopefully just, decision. Undue delays will affect the political stability of a new transition regime and effectively impede the reform process and act as a drag on domestic and foreign investment.

ROLE OF THE OVERSEAS COMMUNITY

The Cuban overseas community can and, I believe, will be a major constructive factor in supporting transition in Cuba. Tens of thousands of Cubans in exile represent a reservoir of knowledge, experience, know-how and networks in a variety of fields — including a familiarity with modern technology — that could make an invaluable contribution to national recovery. In addition, there are substantial quantities of overseas Cuban capital that can fuel investment in a wide range of businesses.

Further, overseas Cubans have actively taken advantage of the opportunities to participate in the U.S. political process. This involvement and the political networks developed will be very helpful in making the case for economic assistance and eventually for Cuba's integration into the NAFTA.

The transition process needs to create a sufficient forward momentum that it may be guided but not reversed by the ups and downs of an open political system. International experience with what works is now very solid. We collectively know what needs to be done: taking advantage of participatory democracy and transparency to educate the population on the needs for transition and what will be done to minimize its costs is the responsibility of all, economists, technicians, and politicians. Without the informed support of the majority of the people, sustained transformation of Cuban society will not occur.

INTELLECTUAL PROPERTY RIGHTS
AND INTERNATIONAL TRADE IN CUBAN PRODUCTS

Joseph M. Perry, Louis A. Woods, and Stephen L. Shapiro[1]

The U. S. Department of State asserts that "the protection of intellectual property rights is an essential element of U. S. economic foreign policy. The United States government is fundamentally committed to protecting intellectual property rights on U. S. goods and services in domestic and international markets" (USDOS, 2000, June 12). The exercise of that policy has recently drawn the United States into serious confrontations with some of its major trading partners. Both Federal courts in the United States and international organizations such as the World Intellectual Property Organization (WIPO) and the World Trade Organization (WTO) have become involved. This paper investigates these recent controversies over the use of Cuban brand names and trade marks. It focuses specifically on issues regarding Cuban cigars and Cuban rum in foreign markets.

INTRODUCTION TO THE PROBLEM

When the Castro administration nationalized Cuban industry in the early 1960s, the owners of many business firms and agricultural enterprises fled the island, finding asylum in the United States and other friendly countries. They left behind the physical assets of their firms and farms. Presumably, however, they took with them the ownership of intellectual property, such as trademarks and brand names.

In time, the Castro government used the expropriated plant and equipment to produce a variety of goods and services, including cigars and rum. Many of the cigars were put on the market under brand names that were the original property of expatriate Cubans (Fruin, 1998). Havana Club rum was also marketed, although the Arechabala family originally owned that brand name. The Cuban government argued that the trademarks had also been expropriated when nationalization took place.

Expatriate Cuban businesspersons set up their own tobacco and cigar concerns in other countries, and began to use the brand names that they considered their own. In some cases, they later sold the rights to their cigar brand names to large cigar firms. These firms then produced free market cigars under the old names.

Because of the United States embargo of Cuban trade, non-Cuban cigar producers could market their wares in U. S. markets without competition from Cuba. Trademark controversies arose when Cuban and non-Cuban interests both tried to register the same brand name.

The controversies spread to rum when Bacardí purchased the rights to the Havana Club rum name from its original owners, and began to export it to the United States, where Cuba had already registered the brand name. Litigation and legislation followed.

Clearly, the existence of two sets of overlapping brand names creates problems internationally, and raises serious questions concerning the ownership of

---

1.   The authors gratefully acknowledge the comments of Matías Travieso-Díaz.

such intellectual property. The extent of the problem regarding cigars is shown in Table 1, which lists the Cuban cigar brands that were being produced in other countries in 1998. Note that 17 of those brands were also being produced in Cuba.

Table 1.   Cuban Cigar Brands Produced in Other Countries, as of 1998

Cuban Cigar Brand	U. S. Rights Owned By	Where Made
Belinda*	General Cigar	Honduras
Bolivar	General Cigar	Dominican Rep.
Cabanas*	Consolidated Cigar	United States
Cifuentes	General Cigar	Jamaica
Cohiba	General Cigar	Dominican Rep.
El Rey del Mundo	General Cigar	Honduras
Fonseca	MATASA	Dominican Rep.
Gispert	Tabacalera SA	Honduras
H. Upmann	Consolidated Cigar	Dominican Rep.
Henry Clay	Consolidated Cigar	Dominican Rep.
Hoyo de Monterrey	General Cigar	Honduras
La Gloria	El Credito	Dominican Rep.
Montecristo	Consolidated Cigar	Dominican Rep.
Partagas	General Cigar	Dominican Rep.
Por Larrañaga	Consolidated Cigar	Dominican Rep.
Punch	General Cigar	Honduras
Ramon	General Cigar	Dominican Rep.
Romeo y Julieta	Tabacalera SA	Dominican Rep.
Saint Luis Rey	Tabacalera SA	Honduras
Santa Damiana*	Consolidated Cigar	Dominican Rep.

Source: *Cigar Aficionado*, July 20, 1998.

Note: Cigar brands with an asterisk are not produced in Cuba at this time.

Fewer problems existed in other countries. The Cuban tobacco marketing organization, Habanos S. A., made an agreement with Tabacalera S. A., the Spanish tobacco firm, to distribute its cigar brands around the world. The initial years of the partnership were filled with problems and litigation, focusing on Tabacalera's purchase of some cigar brand names from large American firms. An effective working arrangement was finally reached, however. As will be noted later, Tabacalera's successor company, Altadis, ultimately bought a half interest in Habanos.

The following sections provide more detail about cigar brand name controversies and the so-called "rum wars" in the United States.

INSTITUTIONAL AND LEGAL BACKGROUND

When the United States Constitution was ratified in 1788, it gave Congress the power "to promote the Progress of Science and useful Arts, by securing for limited Times to Authors and Inventors the exclusive Right to their Respective Writings and Discoveries" (U. S. Constitution, Article II, Section 8). This provision permitted the establishment of patent and copyright laws. By extension, trade marks and service marks were later included.

A trademark is a name or a symbol that is used to distinguish one good from another. Using a popular soft drink as an example, the names, "Coca-Cola" and "Coke"; the hourglass shape of the bottle in which some Coca-Cola is sold; the special script used to write the name "Coca-Cola" on bottles; and the slogan, "Things go better with Coke," are all trademarks. They are registered with the United States Patent and Trademark Office, and are jealously guarded against use by others. Clearly, the brand name of a cigar, such as Cohiba, Punch, or Hoyo de Monterrey, is also a trade mark. Names or symbols used to identify services are called service marks (US-DOC, PTO, 1999).

Trademarks such as brand names are clearly a type of intellectual property that can have substantial commercial value. Controversies over the ownership of a brand name often involve product sales that generate large flows of revenue.

It is important to understand that intellectual property, such as a trademark, is the most legalkind of property. It was created by lawyers and the legal system, who can also change it or abolish it. Disputes regarding trademarks can be complex and lengthy. Real property, in contrast, is much easier to identify and to analyze. As a result, disputes over real property can be more quickly resolved.

Varying attitudes toward intellectual property in different countries constitute a major complicating factor. The pirating of computer software, and controversies over the ownership of Internet domain names, have given new impetus to trademark protection activities in recent years (Jussawalla, 1992).

Under U. S. common law, the sale of a product having a brand name establishes that name as a trademark. "Common law rights arise from actual use of a mark. Generally, the first to either use a mark in commerce or file an intent to use application with the Patent and Trademark Office has the ultimate right to use and registration" (USDOC, PTO, 2000).

The trademark laws of the United States are currently enforced by the U. S. Patent and Trademark Office (USPTO), which is housed in the U. S. Department of Commerce. Registration of a brand name with the USPTO gives it official government recognition, and makes it easier to defend and protect in any legal proceeding. Registration occurs only after a thorough review process, including a determination that the trademark under review does not infringe upon other trademarks already registered. In the words of the USPTO, registration gives "notice to the public of the registrant's claim of ownership of the mark, a legal presumption of ownership nationwide, and the exclusive right to use the mark on or in connection with the goods or services set forth in the registration" (USDOC, PTO, 2000).

Before 1989, a good had to be actually sold in the marketplace before its brand name could be registered as a trademark. Since that year, however, a trademark can be registered with the USPTO if the registrant has a clear intention of marketing the good. Renewal of a trademark on a good that is not on the market at that time requires the filing of a Declaration of Excusable Non-Use, explaining the reasons for no current sales.

Interestingly, the U. S. trade embargo of Cuba permits Cuban firms or the Cuban government to register trade marks and logos with the USPTO. Any citizen or organization of a foreign country may register a trademark in the United States if the trademark is already being used in interstate commerce or trade between the U. S. and other countries; if the registrant intends to place the good in interstate commerce or trade between the U. S. and foreign countries; or if the registration of the trademark is either under way or granted in a foreign country (USDOC, PTO, 2000). Cuba has exercised this right, and has

registered trademarks for a number of goods in the United States, including some cigars and rum.

The trademark situation in the United States is not unique. A foreign manufacturer who wishes to sell his or her branded good in 50 other countries must normally obtain a separate registration of the good's trademarks in all 50 countries.

Because trademark laws differ, sometimes significantly, from one country to another, questions have understandably been raised about the protection of valuable property rights. A number of international agreements now address the problem. Agreements concerning intellectual property rights were first negotiated over a century ago. The Paris Convention for the Protection of Industrial Property of 1883 and the Berne Convention for the Protection of Literary and Artistic Works of 1886 were the first such agreements, followed in 1891 by the Madrid Agreement Concerning the International Registration of Marks.

As the key international agreement relating specifically to trademarks and other marks, the Madrid Convention has been revised several times. In 1989, a Protocol Relating to the Madrid Agreement was adopted by many of the Madrid Union countries. The Madrid system of international registration is currently administered by the International Bureau of the World International Property Organization (WIPO), which was created in 1967 by the United Nations. Member countries may register their trademarks with WIPO, requesting that the mark be accorded protection in other member countries. At the present time, Cuba has 2,159 trademarks registered with WIPO (UN, WIPO, 1999).

The United States is one of the signatories to the Madrid Agreement. It is also one of the founding partners of the World Trade Organization, which now involves itself in trade disputes, including those that focus on the legitimate use of trademarks.

The World Trade Organization (WTO) was set up on January 1, 1995, as a result of the Uruguay Round of multilateral trade negotiations (1986-1994). The WTO is the successor to the General Agreement on Tariffs and Trade (GATT). One of the major functions of the WTO is to mediate and, where possible, resolve trade disputes among member countries (WTO, 1999).

In 1994, the Agreement on Trade-Related Aspects of Intellectual Property Rights (TRIPS) was concluded under the auspices of the Uruguay Round. This agreement encouraged the development of standards for the protection of intellectual property rights. It also helped to establish the means to enforce those standards, both domestically and "at the border" (USDOS, 2000). TRIPS is administered by the World Trade Organization. Developed countries were expected to implement the agreement by July 1, 1995. Developing nations were given more time.

Both WIPO and WTO facilities have been widely used by member countries to resolve intellectual property disputes. At the domestic level, trademark disputes are usually handled by a country's registering agency (such as USPTO) or by the country's courts.

THE CONTROVERSY OVER CUBAN CIGARS

While many Cuban cigar brands are produced in both Cuba and elsewhere, the brand name controversy in the United States has so far centered on only two major brands: Cohiba and Trinidad.

Culbro Corporation, which owns General Cigar Company, began to register its Cohiba cigars with the U. S. Patent and Trademark Office in 1978. It received registration in 1981, and assigned the registration to General Cigar in 1987. At that time, and for some time afterward, General Cigar produced and sold only limited quantities of Cohibas (Falk, 1998).

On January 15, 1997, the Cuban government petitioned the USPTO to cancel Culbro's Cohiba trademark. Its position was that Cuban factories had begun making Cohiba cigars in 1960, and that they were available in diplomatic stores in Havana as early as 1967. And since Cohiba is a "well-known or famous name" like Xerox, Coca-Cola or Nike, under international law it should not be appropriated by a producer in another country. At the present time, Cuba has registered the Cohiba name in at least 115 countries, other than the United States (Falk, 1998).

The facts of the matter are apparently somewhat different from the Cuban version. Cigar industry officials indicate that Cuban Cohibas did not become available on the open market until about 1981. Some Cuban advertisements refer to 1982 as the year when the island's "best kept secret" became public. Before that time, Cohibas were produced for the use of Fidel Castro and as gifts to foreign dignitaries (Tamayo, 1997).

Given the accuracy of these observations, Culbro and General Cigar had a legal right to the trademark in the United States by about the same time that Cohibas reached the commercial market in Cuba. Note that this argument is exclusive of, and in addition to, the argument that General Cigar purchased the brand name from its original, rightful owner, and that the Cuban government had expropriated the brand name.

A complicating factor is that U. S. trademark law requires actual market use of a brand name, or the submission of an affidavit justifying the absence of sales. General Cigar did not produce Cohibas in significant quantities until 1997. Early in that year, it introduced Cohibas to the national market, promoting them heavily through advertisements. The U. S. version of the Cohiba has a logo that is very similar to the Cuban Cohiba logo. It is also advertised as being made from tobacco that is grown from Cuban seed. From the point of view of Cuban producers, the effect of such similarity is to confuse consumers. Trademark registration is intended to eliminate such confusion.

Since the issue could not be resolved by the USPTO, on November 12, 1997, Cubatabaco sued General Cigar Holdings, Culbro, and their distributor for "trademark infringement, trade dress infringement, false designation of source or origin, unfair competition, misappropriation and trademark dilution" (Falk, 1998). The suit appealed to the aforementioned international treaties for relief.

With Federal legal proceedings hanging over their heads, both sides agreed to suspend litigation and to begin negotiations that might lead to a settlement. Representatives of both parties met in Mexico City to explore this possibility. A financial settlement would clearly have damaged at least the spirit of the embargo against Cuba, and would have established a precedent for negotiations about other contested brand names.

Most of the legal maneuvering by both in the controversy was eliminated or postponed by a simple piece of legislation that was sponsored by the two Senators from the State of Florida. On October 21, 1998, the Omnibus Consolidated and Emergency Supplemental Appropriations Act, 1999, was signed into law. Section 211 of that law prohibited Cuban companies or persons from registering a confiscated trademark in the United States without the permission of the original owner. U. S. courts are also prohibited from recognizing any such trademark rights unless the original owner gives his consent. The prohibition is effective even when the original owner of the trademark abandoned or relinquished it in the United States.

This law provided the basis for a clear decision in the Cohiba case. The Federal judge who heard the case found in favor of Culbro and General Cigar. As will be noted below, Section 211 also affected decisions concerning Havana Club rum.

Section 211 was phrased very broadly, although aimed primarily at Cuba. From the point of view of other foreign countries, it may also limit their ability to register or maintain trademarks in the United States.

The position of the European Union is that Section 211 violates several portions or provisions of the WTO Agreement on Trade-Related Aspects of Intellectual Property Rights (TRIPS). For example, it may treat one right-holder differently from another right-holder. And, according to TRIPS, "a trademark registration cannot be made conditional on the consent of a trademark owner who has abandoned his rights" (EU, 1999, July 9). Representatives of the United States have adamantly rejected the position of the European Union, arguing that Section 211 is in accord with TRIPS.

On July 9, 1999, the European Union asked for formal consultations with the United States under the auspices of the World Trade Organization, arguing that Section 211 is in conflict with TRIPS (EU to back Pernod, 1999). Meetings were held on September 13 and December 13, 1999, with no resolution of the dispute. Accordingly, on June 30, 2000, the European Commission formally requested that the WTO place the matter before its Dispute Settlement Body at its next meeting. And there the matter currently stands (WTO, 2000).

If the dispute settlement process follows the timelines established by the WTO, a panel report from the Dispute Settlement Body should be available for U.S. review within a year or a year and a half.

A similar controversy has arisen concerning Trinidad cigars. The Trinidad family operated one of the largest cigarette and cigar firms in Cuba, until the Castro government took it over in 1960 and formally nationalized it in 1961. The family had registered the cigar brand name, TTT Trinidad, La Habana, Cuba, with the Cuban Office of Trademarks and Patents in 1958 (Trinidad, 1999).

The Trinidad family migrated to the United States, where they set up cigarette and cigar production facilities. The brand name Trinidad y Hermano was registered for the firm's cigars.

In 1994, the Cuban government filed a petition to register the brand name, TTT Trinidad, La Habana, Cuba, with the USPTO. Permanent registration was granted to Cuba in December, 1996. At about the same time, the Trinidad family made arrangements with the Fuente organization to manufacture cigars using that brand name.

After some initial political maneuvering, the Trinidad family entered a Petition for Cancellation with the USPTO in December, 1997, asking that the Cuban registration be cancelled. The results of that petition, given Section 211, are predictably positive, although the USPTO has not yet rendered a formal decision. In the meantime, the Trinidad family is selling both Trinidad y Hermano and TTT Trinidad premium cigars in the United States.

Since 17 cigar brands are produced concomitantly in Cuba and in other countries, the resolution of these two disputes has far-ranging implications for the international cigar industry.

THE CONTROVERSY OVER CUBAN RUM

José Arechabala y Aldama migrated from Spain to Cuba in 1862, at the age of 15. In 1878, he established a small distillery in Cárdenas. The company grew over time, in spite of varying business conditions and the depredations of hurricanes. It was incorporated in 1921 as "José Arechabala, S. A." (Arechabala Industries, 1999).

Shortly before the time of the Cuban revolution, Arechabala Industries produced alcohol and fuels, refined sugar, candies, and a variety of liquors, including Havana Club rum. It also imported and distributed foreign liquors and wines.

According to Cuban government information, Arechabala Industries was in very weak financial condition at the time of the Cuban revolution. In 1955, it had permitted the Havana Club trademark to fall into the public domain in Spain and the Dominican Republic. It still maintained its trademark registration in the United States, however (Campo-Flores, 2000).

After the nationalization of Arechabala Industries in 1960, the family members migrated to the United States and to Spain. They neglected to renew the Havana Club trademark registration in the United States, although they could have done so with a Certificate of Excusable Non-Use.

Cubaexport, a Cuban state enterprise, resumed production of rum under the Havana Club name. The rum was exported primarily to Communist Bloc countries. Cubaexport registered the Havana Club brand name in Spain in 1966, and with the USPTO in 1976 (Still, October, 1999).

With the breakup of the Soviet Union and the communist bloc countries, Cuban rum lost a significant market and suffered declining revenues.

In an attempt to bring in foreign capital and to expand its marketing abilities for Havana Club rum, the Cuban government approved a new joint venture with a foreign beverage firm in 1993. The agreement formed two companies. The first was Havana Club

Holding, a holding company with equal shares of ownership going to a new Cuban company, Havana Rum & Liquor, S. A., and to the French beverage group, Pernod Ricard. The second company was Havana Club International, a distributing company which was also equally owned by Havana Rum & Liquor and Pernod Ricard.

In 1993, representatives of Pernod Ricard offered to compensate the Arechabala family, if they would give up all claims to the Havana Club name. This action by Pernod suggests that the firm may have recognized the family's right to the brand name. The family instead sold the rights to the trademark to Bacardi-Martini, in 1995, for a reported $1.25 million (Still, October, 1999).

In 1995, the U. S. Treasury Department granted a license to the Cuban government that permitted the transfer of the Havana Club trademark to Havana Club Holding. Havana Club Holding then gave Havana Club International an exclusive license to sell Havana Club Rum internationally, and to use the Havana Club trademark (Sánchez, 1998).

At this point, the Cuban government not only had tight control over the production of Havana Club Rum, but also enjoyed the use of the international distribution network provided by Pernod Ricard.

In July, 1995, Bacardi petitioned the USPTO to cancel Cuba's registration of the Havana Club trademark. At about the same time, it began to produce limited quantities of Havana Club Rum in the Bahamas, and marketed it in the United States. Production and sales continued for about a year, ending in 1996.

The arrangement was attacked by U. S. interests, but held up under initial legal review. In August, 1997, however, the Treasury Department withdrew the license it had issued to the Cuban government, placing the legality of the trademark transfer in doubt (Falk, 1998).

The New York District Court, which heard the Havana Club case, invoked Section 211 of the Omnibus Consolidated and Emergency Supplemental Appropriations Act of 1999, and ruled that the joint venture was not the owner of the trademark. Bacardi now has legal right to the brand name in the United States. Interestingly, the court's decision included no finding as to whether the Arechabala family was the rightful owner of the brand name when it was sold to Bacardi. That issue is still moot (Lopez, 1999b).

At the moment, Cuban-made Havana Club rum is being sold in 115 countries, other than the United States. The critical question of who really owns the brand name will be answered when the United States responds to the findings of the Dispute Resolution Body of the World Trade Organization in about a year. The question is the same for cigars and rum: Do the original owners of the brand names still own them?

Note that the controversy now extends only to cigars and rum. Should Cuba attempt to register other branded goods whose brand names belong to expatriates, the same question would be raised.

Although recent U. S. legislation has eased the embargo to permit the export of food and medical goods to Cuba, the major provisions of Helms-Burton and previous embargo acts still prevail. In the short run, Cuba therefore has limited options to solve the brand name problem.

Note, too, that the Clinton Administration has continued to suspend Title III of the Helms-burton Act, thus making it impossible for Cuban-Americans to sue foreign companies that traffic in properties that the Castro administration has confiscated. The latest extension of this suspension was signed by President Clinton on July 17, 2000 (Clinton suspende, 2000).

Once the transition occurs, and the island's economy is opened to U. S. trade and investment, the options open to Cuba become more numerous. At the same time, there is much uncertainty about brand name usage in international markets until some basic questions about the privatization of state-owned enterprises are resolved.

SHORT-TERM CUBAN STRATEGIES

In the short run, while the effects of Helms-Burton, Section 211, and the embargo are still being felt, the options open to the Cuban government are primarily legal.

The first such strategy is the filing of additional lawsuits, similar to the recent suits regarding Cohiba and Havana Club, in an effort to displace competing brands already in the U. S. market. Such an action would accompany the attempt by Cuba to register other cigar brand names with the USPTO, for example.

This strategy is surrounded by uncertainty, since the expatriate owners of brand names will undoubtedly also be in the courts, attempting to recover the property that was expropriated from them. Up to this point in time, U. S. courts have been largely unreceptive to claims of the Castro government. It is difficult to imagine that their position would change significantly. And the blocking action of Section 211 looms large in this scenario, although it is under attack at the WTO. Cuba has lost in the U. S. courts, and probably will continue to do so in the near future.

As an international alternative, Cuba may seek further mediation from the World Trade Organization. As noted above, the European Union has already asked the WTO to consider the dispute between Cuba and the United States, since its own interests may be affected by Section 211. This approach places the brand name dispute in the international arena, at a higher level than the domestic courts. But the United States has a record of using the WTO as it uses the United Nations and other international organizations. When the outcome of a dispute is seen to be favorable to the U. S. position, it is accepted and supported. But when the outcome goes against U. S. interests, it is very often ignored.

Fidel Castro has threatened another short-term action. If the United States persists in enforcing Section 211, he says, the Cuban government may eliminate its support of U. S. trademarks on the island. State-owned firms could produce their own versions of Coca-Cola and MacDonald's hamburgers, for example (Tamayo, 1999).

Interestingly, the WTO dispute settlement process includes the possibility of "retaliation" against the losing country in the process, if that country does not implement the terms handed down in the panel report. What form that retaliation might take in the case of the United States is uncertain.

AFTER THE TRANSITION

The short-term options open to Cuba are therefore the ones that the Castro administration is already using or is considering. As long as Helms-Burton and the embargo are in effect, wider options do not exist.

After the transition, the situation is far less predictable. The key institutional changes arethose that will take place when state-owned enterprises are privatized. What will happen to Cuban trademarks and brand names at that time? From the point of view of the Cuban expatriates who have lost their property, the ideal solution would be the return of that property to them, and the recognition that they are the rightful owners of the contested brand names. Production of Cohiba and Montecristo and H. Upmann could resume under their rightful owners, and the Cuban cigars would have free access to the U. S. market.

A possible casualty of this event would be the factories in the Dominican Republic, Honduras, and elsewhere, that now produce cigars under the old Cuban brand names. Presumably, they would phase out production of cigars such as Cohiba and Montecristo, and would shift to the production of non-competing brands. The introduction of new cigar brands would also make sense, if the market permitted. In the absence of market growth, such factories might well be shut down.

If privatization proceeds gradually, once trade with the U. S. resumes, the Cuban government may find it rational to retire some or all of the brands that are in controversy, and replace them with new brands that can be legally registered and sold in the United States.

That strategy is already being used. In recent years, Habanos has created and introduced a number of new cigar brands, probably in anticipation of a reopened U. S. market. These include Cuaba, Vegas Robaina, Trinidad, Vegueros, San Cristóbal de la Habana and La Vigía. The newest brand, San Cristóbal de la Habana, was placed on the market on November 20, 1999. None of these brands has a counterpart in the United States. But none of the older brands under controversy hasbeen retired from the market, primarily because they enjoy strong sales in other countries. It would not be rational for the Cuban government to attempt to retire and replace strongly-selling brands such as Montecristo and Cohiba.

While this new product strategy can be effective in achieving market entry, it has some disadvantages. If the Cuban government retired the Cohiba brand of cigars, and replaced it with another brand name that could be registered in the United States, it would lose all of the market advantage that accrues to a well-known, well-established cigar. Cohibas, like Montecristos, are known and prized all over the world. The new brand would be unfamiliar, untested, and, initially, perhaps unwanted by consumers. Some time would have to elapse before the new cigar could establish itself competitively. Note, too, that a stable or slowly-growing cigar market, such as exists today, presents a difficult environment for any new product. The booming cigar market of 1994-98 would have made it much easier to introduce a new cigar brand.

Gradual privatization of the Cuban manufacturing sector could also bring about the auctioning of key cigar brands to individuals in the private sector, individuals who are not necessarily the original owners of the brands. For Cohiba cigars, this policy might result in private-sector owners of the Cohiba brand name in both Cuba and the United States.

This alternative does not offer a solution, since it does not resolve the question of who legitimately owns the brand names. Litigation and petitions to international organizations could result, with a standoff that is similar to the one now in effect.

Alternatively, it has been suggested that Cuban producers might negotiate agreements with the holders of competing trademarks in the United States. Cuban producers of cigars could license the firms who hold the U. S. trademarks to sell the Cuban brands in U.S. markets.

How such agreements would work, and whether they could work at all, is uncertain. The position of General Cigar regarding its Cohiba trademark would probably be that the Cuban-made brand should be retired from the market. If both brands were to be marketed in the United States at the same time, with each identified as to country of origin, the profit levels of the producing firms could both be adversely affected. There would still be the problem of brand name confusion, especially if current cigar bands, logos, and other marks remained unchanged.

SOME CONCLUSIONS AND ADDITIONAL PROBLEMS

Given the current status of the trade embargo against Cuba and official U. S. policy as stated in the Helms-Burton Act, the Cuban government is doing all that it rationally can do to protect its expropriated cigar and rum brand names. If the WTO Dispute Resolution Body declares Section 211 to be in violation of TRIPS, then the United States must develop a policy reaction that preserves U. S. registered trademarks. That reaction is unpredictable, but may be as simple as ignoring the WTO decision, or criticizing it as being unfair.

When the transition occurs, a key consideration will be whether expatriate brand name owners can quickly and freely reclaim both their expropriated physical assets and the Cuban registration of their brand names. If this happens, economic dislocations may be minimized.

If a post-transition privatization process places brand names on the auction block, for sale to the highest bidder, the results become less predictable. If the brand names are not acquired by their original owners, then all will face a situation similar to the one that exists today, with competing claims to the brand names. The major difference will be the existence of open trade between the U. S. and Cuba.

It is clear that the resolution of these problems depends upon the answers to some very crucial legal questions. All of them bear upon the nature of intellectual property, and how it is transferred.

- Cuba expropriated the physical facilities of producers in the 1960's. Did it also legally expropriate their brand names?

- If Cuba does not own the brand names, who does?

- What is the legal standing of expropriated marks in countries other than the United States?

- How long, and under what conditions, can a person or organization assert its right to a brand name?

- Will Section 211 of the Omnibus Appropriations Act be upheld on appeal in United States courts?

- Does Section 211 conform with TRIPS? If not, how will the United States respond?

- And, importantly, how will the post-transition Cuban government handle this problem?

In sum, the resolution of the controversy will come from the legal sector, since the key questions are legal in nature.

Recent structural changes in the internationalcigar market have introduced further uncertainty. The Spanish firm, Tabacalera S. A., and the French firm, Seita, have merged to form the world's fourth-largest tobacco company, called Altadis (short for "alliance tabac distribution"). Altadis controls 25 percent of the world's cigar market. It officially came into being in December, 1999. Tabacalera owns Consolidated Cigar. Seita now owns 50 percent of the Cuban distribution agency, Habanos, S. A., through a joint venture. Altadis therefore owns or has a major interest in both of the firms that are involved in the U. S. litigation concerning the Cohiba brand name. In fact, Altadis now controls a large percentage of the cigar brands worldwide that have Cuban origins. Will Altadis attempt to find an acceptable solution to the Cohiba brand name problem, since it now has some control over both producing firms? Only time will tell.

In the meantime, the deliberations of the Dispute Settlement Body of the WTO continue. Within the next eighteen months, the United States will be pressed for a reaction to the report of that body, which will, in all probability, declare Section 211 in violation of TRIPS.

SOURCES AND WORKS CITED

Aoki, Reiko, and Thomas J. Prusa. (1993). International standards for intellectual property protection and R & D incentives. *Journal of International Economics, 35,* 251-273.

Arechabala Industries. (1999). Source material on the web site of Ernesto J. de la Fe, P. A. [Online]. http://www.delafe.com/cardenas/arechaba.htm.

Campo-Flores, Arian. (2000, January 5). Rum Warriors. Three-part article on Law NewsNetwork.com. [Online]. http://www.lawnewsnetwork.com/stories/cuba.html.

Carnevale, A. P. (1991). *America and the New Economy.* San Francisco: Jossey-Bass.

Chunko, John. (1998, July). "La Vigia" Is Born. *CNX Newswire* [Online]. http://www.cigarnexus.com/news/lavigia/ index.html.

Clinton suspende de nuevo el título III de la ley Helms-Burton. (2000, July 19). *Diario Las Américas,* 1-A.

EU to back Pernod in WTO Complaint Disputing U. S. Law. (1999, July 9). *Wall Street Journal.* A11.

European Cigar Giant Buying Half of Cuba's Habanos. (1999, December 6). *Cigar Aficionado* [Online]. What's New: Cigar News. http://www.cigaraficionado.com/Cigar/Afic... WhatsNew/Archives/19991206 .cigarnews2.wna.

European Union. Directorate-General for Trade. (1999, July 9). "Havana Club": EU to request WTO consultations on U. S. trademark law. [Online] http://europa.eu.int/comm/trade/miti/dispute/hava.htm.

Falk, Pamela S. (1998, April 5). Visions of Embargo Falling Spark U.S.-Cuba IP Battles. *National Law Journal* [Online], B07. http://www.ipcenter.com/0406ipcuba.html.

Fruin, John. (1998, June 8). Cigar Trademarks. Cigar Weekly Magazine. [Online]. http:// www.cigarweekly.com/CubaWatch/ trademarks.htm.

Gadbaw, R. Michael, and Timothy J. Richards. (1988). *Intellectual Property Rights: Global Consensus, Global Conflict?* Boulder, Colo.: Westview Press.

Gregory, Donald A., Charles W. Saber, and Jon D. Grossman. (1994). *Introduction to Intellectual Property Law.* Washington, D. C.: The Bureau of National Affairs, Inc.

Jussawalla, Meheroo. (1992). *The Economics of Intellectual Property in a World Without Frontiers: A Study of Computer Software.* New York: Greenwood Press.

Kintner, Earl W., and Jack L. Lahr. (1975). *An Intellectual Property Law Primer.* New York: Macmillan Publishing Co., Inc.

Langford, Jock. (1997). Intellectual property rights: technology transfer and resource implications. *American Journal of Agricultural Economics, 79:*5, 1576-83.

Lehman, Bruce A. (1996, Spring). Intellectual Property: America's Competitive Advantage in the 21st Century. *Columbia Journal of World Business,* 31:1, 6-16.

Lehman, Bruce A. (1998, May). *Economic Perspectives* [Online]. USIA Electronic Journals, 3:3. http://www.usia.gov/journals/ites/0598/ijee/iplehman.htm.

Lopez, Felix. (1999a, February 4). Bacardi threatened by Havana Club. *Granma International Digital Edition.* [Online]. http://www.granma.cu/ingles/febrer04/7feb 7i.html.

Lopez, Felix. (1999b, May 1). De cómo el ladrón fue declarado inocente...*Granma Internacional Digital.* [Online]. http://www.granma.cu/espanol/mayo1/17may7e.html.

Merger To Create World's Largest Cigar Company. (1999, October 4). *Cigar Aficionado* [Online].

What's New: Cigar News. http://www.cigaraficionado.com/ Cigar/Afic...WhatsNew/Archives/ 19991004 .cigarnews2.wna.

Overview of U. S. Sanctions Laws Related to Foreign Policy. (1997, September). *Economic Perspectives* [Online]. USIA Electronic Journals, 2:4. http://www.arc.org.tw/trade/ejou997/ejsanct.htm.

Samuels, Jeffrey M. (1989). *Patent Trademark and Copyright Laws.* Washington, D. C.: The Bureau of National Affairs, Inc.

Stewart, Thomas A. (1997). *Intellectual Capital: The New Wealth of Organizations.* New York: Doubleday/Currency.

Still, Torri (1999). "Red Rum" IP Journal. October Electric Version. http://www.ipmag.com/monthly/99-oct/redrum.html.

Stout, Nancy. (1997). *Habanos: The Story of the Havana Cigar.* New York: Rizzoli International Publications, Inc.

Swedes Acquiring Control of General Cigar. (2000, January 21). *Cigar Aficionado* [Online]. What's New: Cigar News column. http://www.cigaraficionado.com/Cigar/Afic ...WhatsNew/Archives/ 20000117.cigarnews 2.wna.

Tamayo, Juan O. (1997, May 15). Cuba files rum and cigar trademark challenges in U. S. *Miami Herald* [Online]. http://www.fiu.edu/~fcf/trademarkbaccub.html.

Thurow, Lester C. (1997, September-October). "Needed: A New System of Intellectual Property Rights." *Harvard Business Review,* 95-103.

Tip of the Week. (1998, July 20). *Cigar Aficionado* [Online]. What's New: Hot Tip.http://www.cigaraficionado.com/Cigar/ Afic...0.hottip.wna/1826438065286545871 955409591.

Trinidad, Diego, III. (1999). The Story of the Trinidad Family in the Cuban Tobacco Industry. Company history segment on Trinidad y Hermano website. [Online]. http://www.trinidadyhermano.com/history.htm.

Wilson, Lee. (1998). *The Trademark Guide.* New York: Allworth Press.

United Nations. World Intellectual Property Organization. (1999, April). *General information about WIPO* [Online]. http://www.wipo.org/eng/infbroch/infbro99.htm. (2000, July 6).

United States. Department of Commerce. Patent and Trademark Office. (1999, May 14). Basic Facts About Trademarks. [Online]. http://www.uspto.gov/web/offices/tac/doc/basic/.

United States. Department of Commerce. Patent and Trademark Office. (2000, February 11) Frequently Asked Questions About Trademarks. [Online]. http://www.uspto.gov/web/offices/tac/tmfaq.htm.

United States. Department of State. (2000, June 12). The Protection of Intellectual Property Rights. [Online]. http://usinfo.state.gov/topical/econ/ipr/.

United States. House of Representatives. (1998, May 22). Testimony of Ignacio Sanchez for Bacardi-Martini before the House Judiciary Subcommittee on Courts and Intellectual Property. [Online]. http://www.house.gov/judiciary/42011.htm.

United States. (1998) Omnibus Consolidated and Emergency Supplemental Appropriations Act. Public Law 105-277.

World Trade Organization. (1999, March). The World Trade Organization in Brief. [Online]. http://www.wto.org/english/thewto_e/whatis_e/inbrief_e/inbr00.htm.

World Trade Organization. (2000, July 7). United States — Section 211 Omnibus Appropriations Act of 1998. [Online]. http://www.wto.org/wto/ddf/ep/public.html.

THE "UNDERSTANDING" BETWEEN THE EUROPEAN UNION AND THE UNITED STATES OVER INVESTMENTS IN CUBA[1]

Joaquín Roy

The history of relations between revolutionary Cuba and what was called Western Europe during the Cold War provides some clues for the lack of agreement between the U.S. and European states in the 1990s over the Helms-Burton Act and investments in Cuba. During this period, most of the European countries, in response to their own political and commercial needs, maintained diplomatic and economic links with Cuba despite U.S. pressures and admonitions. Today, more than half of all joint ventures established in Cuba involve European investments.

The European perceptions and reactions to the development of the Helms-Burton bill and its approval by the U.S. Congress can be divided into two categories. First, the moves by the more influential individual countries. Second, the collective measures taken under the umbrella of the institutions of the European Union. Individually, each European state showed different approaches due to their varied degrees of commercial and political links with Cuba and their specific relations with the United States. Nonetheless, as far as attitudes are concerned, European countries showed a remarkable consensus of opposition to the Helms-Burton law. "Special relationships" (such as in the case of the UK) with the United States seemed not to be an obstacle for the creation of mechanisms of protection against the effects of the Torricelli and Helms-Burton laws.

The main European Union institutions have issued issued declarations and approved resolutions extremely critical of the policies of the United States, before and leading to the *finale* of the Helms-Burton law. Concurrently, the EU has systematically denounced violations of human rights in Cuba.[2] This two-pronged approach has been consistent over the years: opposing U.S. unilateral measures and at the same time conditioning the improvement of the treatment that Cuba has received through the EU mechanisms of humanitarian aid delivery, commercial preferences, and comprehensive cooperation agreements. In this specific terrain, Cuba has been and still is the exception in the Western Hemisphere. The political and human rights profile of the Cuban regime is the main obstacle to the implementation by the EU of a global package, which failed in March of 1996. However, the European institutions held the hope that by applying a simultaneous dual-track approach (trade and investment with Cuba, while applying pressure

1. This article expands a topic treated in my book *Cuba, the U.S. and the Helms-Burton "Doctrine": International Reactions* (Gainesville: University Press of Florida, 2000). Research was undertaken during the summer of 2000 (as a follow up of interviews carried out in the summer of 1998) in Brussels and Madrid under the partial sponsorship of a grant awarded by the North-South Center. The author would like to express his gratitude to ASCE for the kind invitation to participate in the Conference and to many members of the European Commission (most of them introduced by Angel Viñas) and the European Parliament, and the staff of the Spanish Ministry of Foreign Affairs and the Spanish Consulate in Miami. As usual, research and editorial support was provided by my Research Assistant Anna Krift.

2. See resolutions of the European Parliament for 1987, 1988, 1990, 1992, 1993 and 1996, in *Twenty Years of European-Latin American Relations* (Madrid: IRELA, 1996), pp. 769-803.

for human rights), Brussels would obtain better results than the U.S. "stick" policy.[3]

Once an initial rapprochement attempt with Cuba collapsed, a hard-line response from Brussels would come as a supplement to the EU criticism against Helms-Burton. While a planned blocking statute was a first for the EU, a critical Common Position on Cuba taken in the Fall of 1996 — the first time on a Latin American country — would also have a place in the annals of the European Union's incipient foreign policy.[4] The spirit and the letter of the Common Position have been maintained to date, with the expected protests of the Cuban government. This condition has loomed in the background of the negotiations of the failed Lomé Convention membership, with the result that the Cuban government decided to terminate the negotiations in April 2000. According to most observers (EU institutions, ACP structure, individual governments[5]), Havana's view was that the high political price to be paid (political requirements, especially in the human rights area) was not worth the economic benefits to be gained. In the words of Castro, "demasiado fastidio para tan poca plata" [too much bother for so little money].[6]

THE BLOCKING STATUTE

Under the Damocles threat of the Helms-Burton law, the European Union decided to denounce this law in the World Trade Organization (WTO). During the second half of 1996, the U.S. government made a considerable effort to convince the European Union to find an elegant face-saving solution. However, the European governments had their hands tied by a new measure adopted by the Council of Minis-

ters (also known as the Council of the European Union) in November. They could not afford to appear to be negotiating under threat. The Parliament and the Commission had already issued sufficient signs of protest.[7] By Spanish initiative, it was now the turn of the Council to counteract the consequences derived from the U.S. law.

Council Regulation (EC) No. 2271/96, the Council's Regulation containing countermeasures prohibiting the acceptance of the extraterritorial effects of the Helms-Burton law, became effective on November 22, 1996.[8] It is significant that the instrument that was chosen as a countermeasure was the highest in the ranking of EU legislation. Commission regulations are mostly administrative and technical in detail. Council Regulations, however, are concerned with important, broader, controversial matters. Regulations are binding on all member states and do not need to be translated or interpreted into national law.

Since the foundation of its predecessor, the European Community, the European Union has had as one of its objectives the contribution to "the harmonious development of world trade and to the progressive abolition of restrictions on international trade." Moreover, the EU "endeavors to achieve to the greatest extent possible the objective of free movement of capital between Member States and third countries, including the removal of any restrictions on direct investment — including investment in real estate, establishment, the provision of financial services, or the admission of securities to capital markets." In accordance with these goals, Council Regulation (EC) No.

---

3. For a review of the contrasting EU-U.S. policies towards Cuba, see my chapter included in the edited volume by Richard Haass, ed., *Transatlantic Tensions: The United States, Europe, and Problem Countries* (Washington: The Brookings Institution, 1999).

4. For a detailed review of these events, see *Cuba y la Unión Europea: Las dificultades del diálogo* (Madrid: IRELA, 1996).

5. Interviews held in Brussels and Madrid during the months of June and July of 2000.

6. Confidential conversation held with a high-level Caribbean official.

7. See especially the resolutions of the European Parliament of 1992, 1993 and 1996, and the declarations of the Council and the Presidency of the European Union of 1995. Complete texts are available in the compilation *Europa-América Latina: Veinte años de documentos (1976-1996)* (Madrid: IRELA, 1996).

8. Council Regulation (EC), No. 2271/96. *Official Journal of the European Communities* (November 29, 1997). Earlier in the process, Canadian and British press were following the preparations. As a sample, see: "Europe's Cuba law," *Maclean's*, Nov. 11, 1996, vol. 109, no. 46, p. 36; "A facade of unity: Europe's foreign policy," *The Economist*, Nov. 2, 1996, vol. 341, no. 7990, p. 49.

2271/96, the so-called "blocking statute," made the following points:

- The United States has enacted laws [the Torricelli and Helms-Burton laws[9]] that purport to regulate activities of persons under the jurisdiction of the member states of the European Union; this extra-territorial application violates international law and has adverse effects on the interests of the European Union.

  Therefore, the Regulation provides protection against the extraterritorial application of these laws and binds the persons and interests affected to inform the Commission.

- No judgment of a court outside the European Union regarding the effects of these U.S. laws will be recognized and no person shall comply with any requirement or prohibition derived from them.

- Any person affected shall be entitled to recover any damages caused by the application of these laws.

Through the Regulation, the European Union aimed to concentrate on removing the most adverse effects of Title III and Title IV of the Helms-Burton law, that is, those sections of the law perceived as having extraterritorial application.

THE FIRST "UNDERSTANDING"

Several warnings issued by the EU during the development of the Helms-Burton law demanding changes that were not heeded led Brussels and Washington to a dead-end street. After the law came into effect, the EU warned that the temporary suspension of Title III — the provision of the law that permits action against "trafficking" in expropriated properties — was not sufficient. The rest of the law was still considered a violation of the principles of commercial exchange guaranteed by the World Trade Organization (WTO). The United States countered that the Helms-Burton law was not an issue of concern to the

WTO, since the limitations imposed on trade with Cuba were a matter of national security. Ironically, this amounted to an explicit admission that the law had a *political* objective, as its most ardent advocates had made abundantly clear all along. However, this give-and-take between Europe and the United States had other additional moves. It appeared that the EU left the sensitive issue of Cuba untouched and seemed not to be concerned with the political and social evolution (or lack of it) of the Cuban regime. Brussels wanted to get the record straight.

In an effort to defuse tensions, on January 3, 1997, President Clinton suspended, for the second time, the controversial Title III of the law. The early 1997 post-electoral honeymoon between Brussels and Washington had replaced the rocky 1996 relationship. However, an important roadblock remained, as the "drop-dead date" of April 12, 1997, approached — the deadline for the European Union to formalize its first complaint about Helms-Burton in the WTO. The United States claimed exemption under national security provisions and threatened to boycott or ignore the WTO proceedings, stating that the Helms-Burton law was not fundamentally a trade issue. Europe continued the pressure. Observers pointed out that the threat to claim exemption for the United States would severely embarrass the WTO and hurt the enforcement powers of the fledgling trade organization.

On the eve of the deadline, and after fifty hours of negotiation, the United States and Europe reached an Understanding to avert the transatlantic trade dispute, or at least postpone it until the following October 15. Under the accord, the White House committed itself to work with the U.S. Congress to relax the section of the law that would penalize foreign companies for investing in Cuba (Title III) and remove the section that would deny visas to executives of corporations that have invested in expropriated property in Cuba (Title IV). In return, Europe agreed to take action to discourage investment in Cuba involving expropriated

---

9. An Annex specifically listed all US legal measures that the European Union considers unacceptable. It also included the Iran and Libya Sanctions Act of 1996. See Marc C. Hebert, "Unilateralism as Defense Mechanism: An Overview of the Iran and Libyan Sanctions Act of 1996," *Yearbook of International Law*. University of Miami Law School. Vol. 5, 1996-97, pp. 1-28.

property and to drop its WTO complaint against the United States.[10]

The unprecedented Understanding included the following major points:

- Both sides confirmed their commitment to continue their efforts to promote democracy in Cuba. On the EU side, these efforts were set out in the Common Position.

- The United States reiterated its presumption of continued suspension of Title III during the remainder of the President's term, so long as the EU and other allies continued their stepped up efforts to promote democracy in Cuba.

- The EU and the United States agreed to step up their efforts to develop agreed disciplines and principles for the strengthening of investment protection, bilaterally and in the context of the Multilateral Agreement on Investment (MAI). These disciplines should inhibit and deter the future acquisition of investments from any State which has expropriated or nationalized such investments in violation of international law.

- The United States would begin to consult with Congress with the view to obtaining an amendment providing the President with the authority to waive Title IV of the Act. In the meantime, the United States noted the President's continuing obligation to enforce Title IV.

In light of the above, the EU agreed to the suspension of the proceedings of the WTO panel. The EU reserved all rights to resume the panel procedure, or begin new proceedings, if action is taken against EU companies.[11]

Based on that agreement, both parties pledged to cooperate to bring democracy to Cuba, and claimed to have obtained mutual benefits and gains for their own respective interests. The chief EU negotiator of the Understanding, EU Commissioner Sir Leon Brittan, considered that, in exchange for withdrawing the EU claim in the WTO, the EU had obtained concessions from the United States, such as the protection of investments in other regions (such as Libya and Iran).[12] His counterpart, U.S. Under Secretary of State Stuart Eizenstat, emphasized having spared the WTO of irreparable damage by creating "a first and true opportunity for developing a multilateral discipline that will ban investment in confiscated properties."[13]

When the deal was made public, the main backers of Helms-Burton rushed to claim victory. However, while the office of Senator Helms considered the agreement positive, his co-sponsor, Representative Burton and Cuban-American Representatives Ros-Lehtinen and Díaz-Balart denounced it as a "surrender"[14] and an attempt to confuse Congress. This attitude would become the rationale for subsequent measures presented to the U.S. Congress to oppose moves to relax the U.S. embargo. Early on, European observers detected a solid front of opposition to the overtures by President Clinton.[15]

A NEW TRUCE

On May 18, 1998, at the conclusion of the EU-US Summit held in London under the chairmanship of UK Prime Minister Tony Blair (as EU president) and U.S. President Bill Clinton, the European Union and the United States announced a new agreement. Both parties declared that they had agreed to a new Understanding that in essence would freeze the application of the controversial Helms-Burton and D'Amato Acts in reference to investment

---

10. *The Washington Post*, April 12, 1997; Christopher Marquis, "Europe, U.S. Make Cuba Deal," *The Miami Herald*, April 12, 1997; Cynthia Corzo, "EU y Europa pactan sobre Ley Helms," *El Nuevo Herald*, 12 abril 1997.

11. Understanding, April 11, 1997.

12. Xavier Vidal-Folch, "La UE no ha perdido nada," *El País*, 27 abril 1997.

13. Statement released by the State Department on "Multilateral Agreement on Property Rights," transcribed under the title of "Enfoque multilateral a los derechos de propiedad," in *Diario las Américas*, 27 abril 1997.

14. Ileana Ros-Lehtinen, "La administración Clinton se rinde ante las demandas europeas," *Diario las Américas*, 20 abril 1997.

15. "Eurodiputados prevén el Congreso se niegue a suavizar Helms-Burton," EFE, 18 abril 1997.

in Cuba, Libya and Iran.[16] The agreement has to be read as a confirmation and an expansion of the spirit and the letter of the previous 1997 Understanding. Officials of the U.S. Permanent Representation to the European Union in Brussels admitted that their main task had been to convince the Europeans that the State Department and the White House were their allies and the real "enemy" was the U.S. Congress, a view confirmed by different negotiators of the EU member states and officials of the European Commission.[17]

On balance, this 1998 agreement marks a major milestone in the evolution of EU-U.S. relations. The major points of the May 1998 agreement were:

- It confirmed the 1997 promise by the EU not to pursue retaliatory measures against the United States in the WTO.

- Surprisingly, producing the protests of numerous observers and governments, the EU accepted the U.S. assessment that some of the Cuban past expropriations might have been executed in violation of international law.

- The White House, in exchange, promised to pressure the U.S. Congress to further neutralize the application of the Helms-Burton legislation.

- The United States and the European Union agreed to establish a Registry of Claims and to work jointly in the negotiation of the Multilateral Agreement of Investment (MAI), a negotiation that appeared at that time to be on track to yield a successful agreement.

- The United States agreed to respect the current status of foreign investment in Cuba and not to make pre-May 1998 expropriations the target of legal suits under Title III of the Helms-Burton law; future expropriations and subsequent investment in such properties would be mutually scrutinized.

- In a most controversial move, the EU agreed to discourage post-1998 investments in properties whose ownership was questionable by denying the customary diplomatic protection, insurance, commercial and tax incentives, and other support.

- Investment in properties illegally expropriated after May 18, 1998, would be prohibited.

In sum, the agreement confirmed the approach laid out a year earlier. EU insiders have branded this agreement as an example of "creative conflict management."[18] However, the agreement was not free of problems It was reluctantly accepted by some of the EU member states,[19] different commentators,[20] and U.S. sources.[21] Understandably, Cuba opposed the

---

16. "Understanding with Respect to Disciplines for the Strengthening of Investment Protection," *The European Union News*, May 18, 1998. For a detailed analysis of the evolution of the content and language of the agreement, see *Inside U.S. Trade* (May 1, 1998, and May 15, 1998) and *Americas Trade* (May 15, 1998).

17. Interviews held in Brussels, July 5-9, 1998.

18. Horst G. Krenzler and Gunnar Wiegand, "EU-U.S. Relations: More that Trade Disputes," *European Foreign Affairs Review*, 4: 153-180, 199.

19. AFP, "Francia y España obstacularizaron trato," *El Nuevo Herald*, 18 mayo 1998; *Inside U.S. Trade*, "Member States Poised in Fight to Accept U.S.-EU Agreement on Helms-Burton", May 22, 1998; "José Miguel Larraya, "Duro ataque de los socios del gobierno al acuerdo UE-EE.UU. sobre Cuba", *El País*, 4 junio 1998.

20. Hermenegildo Altozano, "España, la ley Helms-Burton y el Acuerdo Multilateral de Inversiones", *Expansión*, 14 mayo 1998.

21. Thomas W. Lippman, "Politicians at Odds on Sanctions as Policy," *The Washington Post*, May 19, 1998; Jonathan Miller, "How Europe forced Cuba deal," *The Miami Herald*, May 24, 1998. Studies published in U.S. legal journals have been critical and skeptical about the juridifical validity of the agreement, its effectiveness as a political tool, and its future applicability regarding property rights. For example, see Edwin D. Williamson, "U.S.-EU Understanding on Helms-Burton: A Missed Opportunity To Fix International Law on Property Rights," *Catholic University Law Review*, Vol. 48, No. 2, Winter 1999, pp. 293-322; Stefaan Smis and Kim Van der Borght, "The EU-U.S. Compromise on Helms-Burton and D'Amato Acts," *American Journal of International Law*, Vol. 93, January 1999, pp. 227-236.

arrangement.[22] Moreover, its implementation was conditioned on hard-to-get congressional cooperation.[23] The deal was linked to the overall development of policies regarding sensitive European interests in Libya and Iran.[24]

The combination of the shortness of time to develop language to be inserted into the Summit Declaration and the need for such language to please all parties generated a very confusing document. First, the EU position stressed the "political" nature of the agreement, denying legally binding status, explicitly stating that the implementation of the Understanding was void until evidence of a waiver on Title IV was in hand. Second, the EU declared that it was not obliged to follow the U.S. position on the questionable legality of the Cuban expropriations, with the clarification that investment in Cuba was still possible, and that the denying of official support was at the discretion of EU governments. Third, guidelines pointed out that any prohibition of investment in Cuba would only apply to expropriations that would take place after May 18, 1998, the date of the agreement, but not to any of the controversial expropriations that took place before. Finally, the EU Commission advised its diplomatic representations to highlight that the accord rested on the good faith of the U.S. Congress waiving Titles III and IV; only if the latter occurred would the deal be effective.[25]

The Understanding was immediately criticized by several governments. Belgium explicitly claimed that article 73C of the Maastricht Treaty prohibits limitations to capital movement and investment.[26] The French representatives insisted that the "ball is in the U.S. court," and that the EU simply has to wait for the U.S. legal modifications and waivers.[27] Legal commentators pointed out the apparent contradiction between the new political Understanding and the strict legality of the previous measures taken by the European Union, especially the Council Regulation and the Joint Action of November 1996.[28] At the political level, critical voices stressed that the new Understanding violated the spirit of the Regulation because it recognized the political aim of the Helms-Burton law in implementing restrictive economic measures with the objective of producing a change in the Cuban regime.[29] A contrast becomes evident between the explicit declarations of the European Union's Regulation (away from interference in the internal affairs of Cuba) and the explicit aim of the Helms-Burton law (conditioning the end of the embargo on the termination of the current regime). Regarding the EU constitutional field, observers questioned the competence of the sole EU negotiator, EU Commission Vice President Leon Brittan, to sign agreements that transcend the commercial boundaries of the explicitly pooled sovereignty and, in con-

22. "Castro insta a la UE a rechazar el acuerdo sobre la ley Helms-Burton," *Expansión*, 20 may 1998; AP, "Castro condemns agreement," *The Miami Herald*, May 20, 1998; AFP, "Castro califica el acuerdo entre EE.UU. y la UE de 'amenazante y no ético'," May 20, 1998; Mauricio Vicent, "Castro advierte que ningún entendimiento entre la UE y EE.UU. puede realizarse a costa de Cuba," *El País*, 25 mayo 1998.

23. "Helms Tells European Union: 'No Deal,'" Committee on Foreign Relations, May 18, 1998; "Helms Aide Tells EU to 'Drop Dead' on Request for Helms-Burton Fix," *Inside U.S. Trade*, May 29, 1998; "Congress Strongly Criticizes U.S.-EU Agreement on Helms-Burton Law," *Inside U.S. Trade*, May 22, 1998; "Ginrich critica acuerdo de Clinton con Europa," *El Nuevo Herald*, 23 mayo 1998.

24. "Senators Urge Albright Not to Grant ILSA Waivers for Libya Projects," *Inside U.S. Trade*, May 29, 1998. For a comparative review of the Helms-Burton and ILSA controversies regarding "problem" countries, see the volume edited by Haass, *Transatlantic Tensions*.

25. From European Commission sources and classified documents, June and July 1998.

26. Confidential notes of COREPER meeting, June 23, 1998.

27. Ibid.

28. See the paper by Hermenegildo Altozano, "Consideraciones sobre el entendimiento UE-EE.UU. de 18 de mayo de 1998 respecto a medidas (disciplinas) para fortalecer la protección de inversiones." Seminario sobre "Cuba: Nuevas perspectivas tras el acuerdo sobre la Ley Helms y el relajamiento del embargo," Cuba Negocios, Madrid, 3 julio 1998.

29. This view is shared by numerous sources in the Permanent Representations of the member states in Brussels. Interviews held July 5-9, 1998.

trast, pertain to the foreign policy and security sector that still is the prerogative of the member states.[30]

Spanish negotiators in Brussels admitted that the agreement was imperfect. In particular, they stressed that the new Understanding had only political value and lacked juridical force. On the one hand, they pointed out that the Helms-Burton law had acted as a deterrent to Spanish investments in Cuba. The Understanding extended the freeze of U.S. retaliation from the six-month Presidential waiver to an indefinite term. They also were pleased by the fact that no investors in "illegally" expropriated properties would be under the threat of U.S. penalties and that only official incentives would be denied. With the new deal, only certain investments would be subjected to discussion. In sum, the new pact created a climate of lessened tensions; a potential environment of permanent conflict with the United States had disappeared.

On the other hand, Spain's diplomats noted that Commissioner Brittan had acted not only in representation of the Commission but also on behalf of the European Union, in matters that exceeded strictly commercial boundaries. Second, they expressed concern about the fact that the final text apparently granted former Cuban citizens the right to have access to a future register of illegal expropriations under the setting of the MAI, a major contention point of Helms-Burton. And third, the Understanding added confusion to the concept of covered transactions.[31]

AN INTERNAL SPANISH AFFAIR

In Spain's Parliament, the Understanding became the subject of a heated and colorful confrontational debate between the Minister of Foreign Affairs and an overwhelming majority of the political opposition. The Spanish deputies were particularly irritated by the fact that the Spanish government remained si-lent on the most controversial items of the Understanding. In particular, they complained about what they considered was loss of sovereignty and the incorporation of the demands of the Helms-Burton law into the politically binding agreement.

One of the topics of the Congressional debate was the peculiar way in which Foreign Minister Matutes justified and defended the legality of the Understanding. In the course of the debate, he stated that he had a "voluminous" report (in fact, only twelve double-spaced pages) drafted (commissioned by the Ministry of Foreign Affairs) by Maximiano Bernad, a professor of International Law at the University of Zaragoza and holder of a Jean Monnet chair, endorsing the EU-U.S. deal. Although this report was not physically circulated in the hearings, it apparently was filed together with at least two other similar endorsements written by other specialists. All of this documentation has remained classified, raising more questions than answers regarding the legal status of the Understanding and the way it was negotiated by the parties, a topic which also became the target of harsh and sarcastic criticism by members of Congress and attorneys. In contrast with the expectations, the report does not add any surprising new elements to the official declarations made by the Spanish government. It simply reinforces most of the announcements made:

• The agreement does not imply unusual obligations rendered by the EU, because it does not translate into a juridical commitment. This is basically a political deal, meant to be expanded to an international agreement. The content is not strictly commercial, but it transcends the competences of the supranational "first pillar."[32] In the event that one of the parties does not fulfill the

---

30. Subsequent drafts of the "side letter" signed by Brittan show that a statement stating that the Commission was representing the European Union was finally deleted.

31. From confidential documentation dated in May of 1998 and interviews conducted in July of 1998.

32. The "First Pillar" is composed of the shared sovereignty in economic, social and cultural policies. Critics both in Spain and other EU member states have reminded that deals pertaining to foreign relations and defense belong to the "second pillar," while justice and home affairs are included in the "third pillar." Both are considered intergovernmental in nature and therefore out of bounds for the European Commission.

deal, the situation returns to step one. The EU reserves all actions.

- While it does not legally bind parties, the Understanding includes a EU declaration rejecting secondary embargoes, extraterritorial legislation, and retroactive application.

- The U.S. government promises to keep application of Title III frozen and offers to convince the U.S. Congress to do the same with Title IV.

- The potential illegality of future Cuban expropriations is a matter to be jointly decided by both parties, a mechanism that confirms the U.S. willingness to renounce unilateral declarations. Both parties agree to cooperate.[33] The absence of an additional agreement with a more convincing legal status has reduced the Understanding to a temporary — though hopefully permanent — truce between Washington and Brussels. In fact, from the U.S. point of view, the only decision that still matters is the execution of the "escape hatch" waiver provision granted to the President in the U.S. legislation for the suspension of Title III. Title IV can still be potentially activated as it is demonstrated by the frequent demands made by Senator Helms to pressure the State Department for the denial of visas to executives of "traffickers" (most noticeably, Sol Meliá of Spain).

The ambivalent atmosphere of the agreement has not been lost to Spanish critics, who disagreed with the Spanish government regarding its claim that current and future investments in Cuba were better protected than before the Understanding. During the parliamentary debate, Congressman Ignasi Guardans described the prospects of Spanish investment in Cuba as a higher risk than "opening a hotel in Rwanda."[34] Sharing the views of most of his colleagues, he protested the right that Commissioner Brittan had to enter into agreements involving issues of national sovereignty (diplomatic protection) that were not within the realm of the Commission. The fact that this parliamentarian was the spokesman for the center-right Catalan party that had insured the survival of the Spanish government with its congressional backing since the election of 1996, exemplifies the use of the Helms-Burton law in the internal politics of Spain and a confirmation that political line-up is not a guaranteed boundary when Cuba is the subject.[35]

The language in the congressional debate over the Understanding was colorful and full of expressions that normally are not in the tamed vocabulary of the Minister of Foreign Affairs. For example, he said that the displeased backers of the D'Amato law (sanctioning investment in Libya and Iran) had stated that the U.S. negotiators had caved under the pressure of the European Union, and —using an expression that today is empty of its original sexual connotation— "se han bajado los pantalones." He also added that Republican leader Gingrich expressed himself in similar terms.[36]

Confirming and expanding their different approaches and commentaries of the agreement, representatives of governments, attorneys, business representatives and academics gathered in Madrid for a symposium on the subject under the sponsorship of Cuba Negocios (a business lobby for investments in Cuba) and the Spanish government's Casa de América. Among others, the following points were made:[37]

- Representatives of the Spanish government and of the European Commission seemed on the defensive, reiterating the political nature of the agreement, its positive contribution to the pro-

---

33. "Informe sobre el Acuerdo alcanzado en Londres el 18 de mayo de 1998."

34. See complete texts of the debates: Congreso de los Diputados. *Boletín Oficial de las Cortes Generales.* 3 junio 1998. No. 107. Comisión Mixta para la UE. pp. 2211-2227. Acuerdo entre los Estados Unidos y la UE; Congreso de los Diputados. *Boletín Oficial de las Cortes Generales.* 10 junio 1998. No. 167. Pleno del Congreso. Efectos del Acuerdo entre la UE y los Estados Unidos.

35. For a panoramic review of Spain's relations with Cuba, see my book entitled *La siempre fiel* (Madrid: Universidad Complutense, 1999).

36. Congreso de los Diputados, 3 junio 1998, p. 2221.

37. *Cuba: nuevas perspectivas tras el Entendimiento sobre la Ley Helms* (Madrid: Cuba Negocios, 1999).

tection of investment, and its potential to become a legally binding measure.

- For former owners, the understanding sends the message that they have a right to be compensated by the expropriating authority (the Cuban government) and keep their rights intact regarding third parties (foreign investors); for Cuba, the agreement is considered by Cuban-American attorney Matías Travieso-Díaz as positive because it reduces confusion and confrontation over properties. However, critics (led by U.S. lawyer Robert Muse) stressed the fact that Titles I and II are still active — their purpose is to impose a certain political and social system in Cuba.

- Spanish critics protested that the agreement was negotiated in a clandestine manner. U.S. attorneys critical of the agreement raised the same protest. The commitments made surpassed the competences of the EU negotiators because they include state sovereignty.

- The distinction made between a political agreement and a juridical treaty was rejected by attorneys. Washington attorney Robert Muse offered the comparison that when "an animal walks and barks like a dog, it is because it is a dog." Spanish attorney Hermenegildo Altozano declared that the international law system does not include the figure of a "political agreement" alongside unilateral declarations, estoppel, manifest will of obligation, etc.

- The most damaging aspect of the agreement is the fact that the Helms-Burton law is still legally intact; it is only partially (Title III) suspended every six months by President Clinton; roughly, that means about two years of truce, according to Travieso-Díaz.

- The agreement legitimizes the sanctions policy of the United States, according to attorney Robert Muse. In his view, by entering into the agreement, Europe has lost negotiating leverage.

- Spanish socialists (led by Congressman Jesús Caldera) deemed the agreement as a tool for U.S. businesses to recover lost ground. After being isolated in the first part of the 1990s on its Cuba policy, the United States has made a come back. After two years of opposing the Helms-Burton law, Europeans now accept its basic terms.

- The source of the problems was a confrontation between the United and the European Union, and the agreement is only binding on the two signatories. Therefore non-EU or U.S. companies are not protected.

- The agreement reflects European cynicism by recognizing the existence of questionable investments and accepting the commitment to deny diplomatic protection and monetary incentives on future operations in targeted properties while at the same time the Spanish government has increased the number of officials visits and mission to Cuba, as an explicit endorsement of investments, as Congressman Ignasi Guardans reminded. This contradiction was dramatized by selecting a Sol Meliá hotel as the residency of Spanish premier José María Aznar while attending the Ibero-American Summit in 1999.

- In general, the business community felt that the Helms-Burton Act dissuaded investment in Cuba, meeting its main objective. In consequence, the agreement (labeled as "shameless" by Lorenzo Higuera, President of Costa Habana, a real estate joint venture) does not benefit Spanish investments in Cuba, increasing the climate of insecurity.

SOME CONCLUSIONS

The EU-U.S. Understanding has earned a place as an example of diplomatic negotiation. The agreement can be considered as a case of successful arrangement (whatever are the negative labels received from different quarters), among other reasons because it fulfilled the main objectives sought by its parties: it averted a serious confrontation. In other words, the EU has refrained from opening a process against the United States in the WTO, and the United States has maintain the partial freezing of the Helms-Burton law. Many observers agree that in effect the Understanding confirmed the death of the Helms-Burton law, although the Understanding by itself has not been the only cause for its virtual termination.

There may be some arguments in identifying the major factors behind the agreement and the subsequent neutering of the most damaging aspects of the

Helms-Burton law. For example, the Understanding was possible mainly because Cuba is not worth a commercial war between the two major world economies. The Helms-Burton law was in effect stillborn with the inclusion of the clause that allowed the President of the United States to suspend Title III, its most internationally controversial ingredient. In any event, from the point of view of the theory of negotiations, the Understanding is a model because it granted both parties a sense of success. The more times passes without conflict, the more successful the parties will feel.

As a first lesson for the future, negotiators should learn that secretive negotiations, particularly of highly politicized issues, although expeditious — apparently secrecy was crucial for the conclusion of the agreement and probably for its initial implementation — raises doubts among the public and legislators and invites confrontation. The second lesson is the legal-political frontier, where a compromise with extremely important repercussions cannot solely be based on temporary political criteria. The third lesson is that in any international controversy involving the United States and Cuba, ideological lines disappear. Cuba is a symbol (or an excuse) for standing up to the United States, especially when economic interests are at stake.

For the continued success of the agreement, some policy plan is needed on the European front. While maintaining in force all the previously approved measures, a cautious attitude (both on Cuba and U.S. policies) should continue. For example, the 1996 Council Regulation, giving legal guarantees and protection to European companies investing in Cuba while mandating the prohibition of accepting the U.S. demands, should be not only maintained but also fully implemented. The EU Common Position and Joint Action of 1996 imposed on Cuba as conditions for better economic and aid relations, should also not only remain in place, but be energetically enforced.

Coordination of policies (especially within the EU structure) should be a priority to avoid U.S. and Cu-

ban protagonists taking advantage of divisions on the European side. When possible, contradictions or violations of EU mandates should be avoided, as was the case of the STET-ITT deal, by which the Italian company compensated the U.S. communication conglomerate for the use of the previously-owned Cuban phone system. This is not an easy task. It is impaired by the fragile EU Common Foreign and Security Policy (CFSP) and the tenuous Common Position on Cuba. The latter is described by cynics as one that is neither "common" (unified and shared) nor a "position" (in means and ends).[38]

It is predicted that no major changes in the U.S. policy towards Cuba will take place before the new government is firmly in place in mid 2001. As a prelude of changes that may occur after the November 2000 U.S. presidential elections, the most reasonable expectation is a gradual and slow dismantling of the embargo, giving the impression that it is in place but in an eroded fashion. This solution is intended to award all parties a sense of accomplishment, with no clear losers or winners. It will give the U.S. hardliners and the Cuban exiles a sense of policy continuity, while affording the liberals a chance to try something else.

At the same time, the slow dismantling of the sanctions would impose on the Cuban government the pressure of the uncertainty of a transition, without the dangers of a suddenly open floodgate of political change with unforeseeable results not only in the economic sector, but also in the social minefield. This will match the wishes of U.S. security experts envisioning a scenario of a "soft landing," and an end to the Castro regime without upheavals (massive migration, partisan confrontation) that would rebound on the United States and provoke its intervention.

Both parties recognize that bringing back democracy to Cuba is a shared goal. In any event, all plans are subject to the actions of the Cuban regime. This crucial actor, however, does not seem to evolve in any encouraging direction away from maintaining its authoritarian orthodoxy.

---

38. For an updated review of EU's relations with Cuba, see IRELA's Special Report, *Revision of European Policy on Cuba? Perceptions and Interests of EU Member States.* Madrid, April 2000.

DIFFERENCES IN AGRICULTURAL PRODUCTIVITY IN CUBA'S STATE AND NONSTATE SECTORS: FURTHER EVIDENCE

José Alvarez

For more than thirty years, the Cuban state has concentrated its attention and resources on the development of the portion of the agricultural sector under its direct control, neglecting the portion outside its control, particularly private farmers and, to a lesser extent, cooperatives. Although comparative studies of agricultural productivity in the state and nonstate sectors that would show differences in the efficiency of resource allocation between them should be a priority among those devoted to research on the Cuban agricultural sector, the reality is that very few such studies have been carried out. Those by Rodríguez (1987), Forster (1989), Deere and Meurs (1992), and Deere, Meurs and Pérez (1992), were carried out with different conceptual frameworks and covered different periods of time.[1] The studies by Puerta and Alvarez (1993) and Alvarez and Puerta (1994), however, used a consistent methodology for estimating agricultural productivity in the state and nonstate sectors for the years 1970, 1975, and 1977-89, and for several crops including sugarcane, tubers and roots (potato, boniato, malanga), vegetables (tomato, onion, pepper), cereals (rice, corn), beans, and tobacco.

The changes since 1990 resulting from the Special Period in Time of Peace (September 1990) and the breakup of the state monopoly on land (1993), make it essential to update the previous research, to investigate whether the relative productivity of the state and nonstate agricultural sectors estimated for the 1980s still holds in the 1990s. The recent publication of official Cuban economic statistics for the 1990s makes it feasible to do so. Thus, the purpose of this paper is to estimate agricultural productivity for the state and nonstate sectors of the Cuban economy in the 1990s and to compare them with findings from previous periods.

THEORETICAL AND METHODOLOGICAL OVERVIEW

Let us first define the state and nonstate sectors. According to official Cuban statistical sources (*Anuario*, 1997, p. 179), the state sector is comprised of:

- state farms and enterprises (such as sugar or rice agroindustrial complexes, agricultural and livestock enterprises, forestry enterprises, etc.); and

- farms managed by the Work Youth Army (*Ejército Juvenil del Trabajo*, EJT), or by the Ministry of Interior (MININT), the local organizations of Popular Power (*Organismos Locales del Poder Popular*, OLPP), and by other state entities.

The nonstate sector includes:

- Basic Units of Cooperative Production (*Unidades Básicas de Producción Cooperativa*, UBPC);

---

1. A more recent work by Sáez (1997) relates environmental conservation and degradation to type of agricultural organization. The implications for agricultural productivity are indisputable.

- Agricultural Production Cooperatives (*Cooperativas de Producción Agropecuaria*, CPA);

- Cooperatives of Credit and Services (*Cooperativas de Crédito y Servicios*, CCS); and

- "dispersed farmers."[2]

The breakup of the state monopoly on land in 1993 changed drastically the distribution of agricultural land. At the end of 1997, the state accounted for 33.42% of total agricultural land and the nonstate sector for the remaining 66.58% (Table 1).

Our central hypothesis is that as state intervention over agricultural production units decreases, the quantity and quality of output increases despite a decreasing access to factors of production and other resources.[3] In a previous study, the analysis was based on the contribution of the nonstate sector to total production from its share of planted area, and the total production per planted area—a proxy for missing yield data in all crops except sugarcane (Alvarez and Puerta, 1994, p. 1666). Starting in 1990, official data have improved. Thus, the analysis of the performance of the nonstate sector in this study is based on its contribution to total production from its share of harvested (not planted) area, and the respective yields. No proxy for yield is used. The study period is 1990-97, except for sugarcane, for which it is 1969-97.

We conduct the analysis for more-perishable commodities (i.e., vegetables); for less-perishable commodities (i.e., tubers and roots, cereals, and beans); and for intermediate commodities such as sugarcane, which needs to be processed in the state mills, and tobacco. The specific hypotheses derive from the assumed scale of preferences of nonstate farmers: on-farm consumption → barter → black market sales. The *acopio* quota is not included at the beginning of the scale because it is not considered a "preference" but a way for farmers to gain limited

Table 1. Distribution of Cuba's Agricultural Lands, by Land Tenure and Type of Enterprise, December 31, 1997

Tenure and type of enterprise	Area 1,000 ha	Share Percentage
STATE		
Sugar Agro-Industrial Complexes	187.3	2.80
Agricultural and livestock enterprises	1382.0	20.67
Work youth army (EJT)	161.1	2.41
Ministry of the interior (MININT)	74.2	1.11
Forestry enterprises	96.7	1.45
Local organizations of popular power (OLPP)	20.7	0.31
Other	312.5	4.67
Sub-total	2234.5	33.42
NONSTATE		
Basic units of cooperative production (UBPC)	2756.0	41.22
Agricultural production cooperatives (CPA)	614.2	9.18
Cooperatives of credit and services (CCS)	779.7	11.66
Dispersed farmers	236.2	3.53
Other	66.1	0.99
Sub-total	4452.2	66.58
Total	6686.7	100.00

Source: *Anuario* (1997, p. 179).

access to inputs (Alvarez and Puerta, 1994, pp. 1666, 1674). In the current study, black market sales have been expanded to include sales in the agricultural markets established in 1994.

DIFFERENCES IN AGRICULTURAL PRODUCTIVITY
Intermediate Commodities:
Sugarcane and Tobacco

Sugarcane and tobacco share some characteristics: (a) both are important export crops; (b) they have received special attention from state managers and technicians; and (c) since they need further processing, they are not likely to be consumed in significant quantities by nonstate producers on the farm or sold

Table 2. Comparison of the Cuban Sugarcane State and Nonstate Sectors, by Area Harvested, Total Production, and Yield, 1968-69 to 1996-97

	Nonstate sector[a]		Yield (mt/ha)		Yield difference	
Season	% Area harvested (1)	% Total production (2)	Nonstate (3)	State (4)	mt/ha (5)	Percent (6)
1968-69	24.9	27.1	48.2	42.8	5.4	12.6
1969-70	21.7	23.3	59.9	54.7	5.2	9.5
1970-71[b]	20.4	21.5	44.1	41.1	3.0	7.3
1971-72	18.9	19.6	39.1	37.1	2.0	5.4
1972-73	17.5	18.5	47.1	44.4	2.7	6.1
1973-74	16.5	17.7	48.7	45.0	2.9	8.2
1974-75	16.8	18.3	48.0	43.6	4.4	10.1
1975-76	15.9	18.2	50.3	42.7	7.6	17.8
1976-77	16.8	19.9	62.8	51.1	11.7	22.9
1977-78	16.5	20.7	61.2	55.3	5.9	10.7
1978-79	15.9	17.5	64.6	57.8	6.8	11.8
1979-80	15.1	16.6	50.5	45.2	5.3	11.7
1980-81	16.3	18.2	61.3	53.8	7.5	13.9
1981-82	16.0	17.6	61.0	53.9	7.1	13.2
1982-83	19.3	21.2	63.6	56.7	6.9	12.2
1983-84	18.3	18.3	57.6	57.3	0.3	0.5
1984-85	18.2	18.4	50.7	49.8	0.9	1.8
1985-86	17.6	18.0	52.7	51.3	1.4	2.7
1986-87	17.1	17.8	54.5	51.7	2.8	5.4
1987-88	18.2	19.5	61.3	55.9	5.4	9.7
1988-89	17.2	18.0	62.8	59.4	3.4	5.7
1989-90	16.1	18.2	64.8	56.2	8.6	15.3
1990-91	16.0	18.6	63.7	53.2	10.5	19.7
1991-92	15.2	17.9	53.7	44.2	9.5	21.5
1992-93	16.4	19.0	41.4	35.0	6.4	18.3
1993-94	94.9	94.9	34.6	34.1	0.5	1.5
1994-95	NA	NA	NA	NA	NA	NA
1995-96	92.2	93.5	33.6	28.3	5.3	18.7
1996-97	91.1	93.1	31.9	24.3	7.6	31.3
Average[a]	25.6	27.1	52.5	47.2	5.1	11.4

Source: *Anuario* (1989, p. 188) until 1988-89; *Anuario* (1997, p. 183) for the remaining seasons.

a. Calculated by the author: Col. (5) = (3) - (4); col. (6) = [(5)/(4) x 100].

b. From *Anuario* (1987, p. 309).

privately in large amounts outside the official distribution channels.

Sugarcane was analyzed for the seasons 1968-69 through 1996-97, or 28 seasons (data for 1994-95 are not available), including those in the previous study because of the consistency in data reporting (Table 2). Nonstate farmers outproduced state farmers in each of the 28 seasons: while accounting for an average of 25.6% of the sugarcane area harvested, they produced an annual average of 27.1% of total sugarcane output. Yield differences ranged from 0.3 mt/ha in 1983-84 (representing a 0.5% higher average yield) to 11.7 mt/ha in 1976-77 (which translates

into a 22.9% higher average yield). The annual average yields were 52.5 mt/ha and 47.2 mt/ha for nonstate and state farms, respectively. Annual average differences were 5.1 mt/ha higher for the nonstate sector, or 11.4%. A one-way analysis of variance (ANOVA) resulted in both yields being significantly different at $P<0.05$.

Tobacco presents a similar picture. From 1990 through 1997, the nonstate sector accounted for an annual average of 81.2% of the area harvested, but was responsible for 83.1% of average annual production. Average annual yields for the nonstate sector were 0.63 mt/ha, compared with 0.58 mt/ha for the

Figure 1. Share of Harvested Area of Sugarcane and Tobacco in the Nonstate Sector, 1990–97

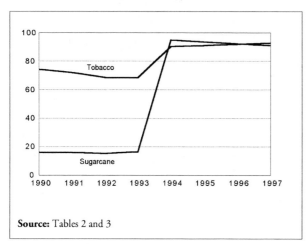

Source: Tables 2 and 3

Table 3. Comparison of the Cuban Tobacco State and Nonstate Sectors, by Area Harvested, Total Production, and Yield, 1990-97

Year	Nonstate sector		Yield	
	AH	TP	S	NS
	Percentage		mt/ha	
1990	74.2	76.2	0.64	0.72
1991	72.0	74.4	0.57	0.64
1992	68.5	75.6	0.43	0.61
1993	68.4	73.0	0.42	0.53
1994	90.3	90.0	0.49	0.47
1995	91.1	92.4	0.56	0.66
1996	92.0	92.1	0.74	0.76
1997	92.8	91.5	0.78	0.66
Average	81.2	83.1	0.58	0.63

Note: AH = area harvested; TP = total production; S = state; NS = nonstate. AH, TP, and Average were calculated by the author.

Source: *Anuario* (1996, pp. 199, 201, 202, 204, 206, 207); (1997, pp. 186, 188, 189, 191, 193, 194).

state sector (Table 3). Despite the obvious annual yield differences, the ANOVA did not return any statistical significance (P≤0.32) between the two sectors.

The data in Tables 2 and 3 reflect the breakup of the state monopoly on land in 1993 to create the UBPCs (see Figure 1). Starting with the 1993-94 season, sugarcane area harvested in the nonstate sector jumped from 16.4% to almost 95% (Table 2). In the case of tobacco, the corresponding figures are 68.4% for 1993 and 90.3% in 1994 (Table 3). Despite the disruptions resulting from that drastic change, and the lack of complete autonomy of the newly created cooperatives, agricultural productivity in the nonstate sector continues to be higher than in the state sector in these two important crops. The Special Period, and the establishment of the UBPCs, did not change the results of the previous study with respect to sugarcane and tobacco.

More-Perishable Commodities: Vegetables

The vegetables studied are tomato, onion and pepper. The period of examination is 1990-97. With regard to these commodities, nonstate farmers should perform better than state farmers because these commodities have to be moved quickly to the state's refrigeration facilities, thus avoiding large quantities devoted to on-farm consumption, bartering, and sales in the black market.

- Tomato statistics show an identical average annual share of 59% in both area harvested and share of total production for the state and nonstate sectors (Table 4), reflecting very close yields in the two sectors: 5.73 mt/ha and 5.65 mt/ha average per year, respectively. As expected, the ANOVA result indicated a lack of statistical significance (P≤0.87) between yields of the two sectors.

- For onions, while nonstate farmers were responsible on average for 56.6% of the area harvested, they contributed an annual average of 59.6% of total average production. Average annual yields in the state sector were 3.90 mt/ha, surpassed by the nonstate sector with 4.59 mt/ha per year. Despite this difference, no statistical significance (P≤0.25) was indicated in the ANOVA results.

- Pepper statistics also present a more favorable picture for nonstate than for state farmers (Table 4). Nonstate sector producers accounted for an average 72.5% of area harvested but produced an average of 79.9% of total pepper output. State farmers averaged 4.54 mt/ha per annum, while nonstate farmers averaged 6.85 mt/ha. The ANOVA results (P<0.01) confirmed the previous statement.

Table 4. **Comparison of the Cuban Vegetables State and Nonstate Sectors, by Area Harvested, Total Production and Yield, 1990-97**

	Tomato				Onion				Pepper			
	Nonstate sector		Yield		Nonstate sector		Yield		Nonstate sector		Yield	
	AH	TP	S	NS	AH	TP	S	NS	AH	TP	S	NS
Year	Percentage		mt/ha		Percentage		mt/ha		Percentage		mt/ha	
1990	50.5	52.4	5.08	5.49	31.9	36.5	3.19	3.93	73.0	85.0	4.74	9.95
1991	45.9	43.7	5.59	5.11	30.8	33.1	4.15	4.61	67.7	78.4	4.53	7.85
1992	46.2	44.0	6.55	6.00	41.4	43.5	3.46	3.77	59.4	68.0	4.88	7.09
1993	51.5	52.3	4.97	5.15	43.9	43.0	4.26	4.10	69.6	82.4	3.19	6.52
1994	69.4	63.7	5.19	4.01	66.0	66.9	3.34	3.46	76.7	82.6	2.84	4.09
1995	73.0	69.6	7.29	6.20	81.1	86.5	3.37	5.01	80.2	80.1	5.38	5.36
1996	66.8	77.7	4.22	7.34	75.9	88.2	2.61	6.22	72.6	80.2	5.10	7.82
1997	76.3	73.0	6.98	5.87	81.9	78.9	6.83	5.63	81.1	82.2	5.65	6.09
Average	59.9	59.5	5.73	5.65	56.6	59.6	3.90	4.59	72.5	79.9	4.54	6.85

Note: AH = area harvested; TP = total production; S = state; NS = nonstate. AH, TP, and Average were calculated by the author.

Source: *Anuario* (1996, pp. 199, 201, 202, 204, 206, 207); (1997, pp. 186, 188, 189, 191, 193, 194).

Figure 2. **Share of Harvested Area of Tomato, Onion and Pepper in the Nonstate Sector, 1990–97**

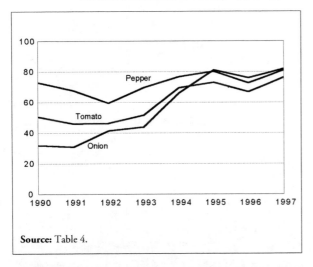

Source: Table 4.

Area harvested by the nonstate sector in the last years shows identical trends for the three vegetables (Figure 2). Although starting from different levels (31.9%, 50.5%, and 73% for onion, tomato and pepper, respectively) the upward trend associated with the establishment of the UBPCs brought the share of land under nonstate sector control to about 80% for the three crops in the last year of the period under study.

The results support strongly our hypothesis with regard to vegetables. Except for tomatoes, where yields were about equal for both sectors, it corroborates our

previous findings. The results for tomatoes may be explained by the creation of the free agricultural markets in 1994, which may force nonstate farmers to report additional quantities produced and intended for sale in these markets. This would be an important addition to the farmers' scale of preferences discussed above. The ratios of sales over production before and after the creation of the agricultural markets cannot be calculated because of lack of data.

Less-Perishable Commodities: Tubers and Roots, Cereals, and Beans

In this study, tubers and roots include potato, boniato and malanga; cereals include only rice and corn. Beans are also considered as a less-perishable commodity.

- As in the previous study, potato is the only crop in the tubers and roots category where average annual share of production (37.9%) for the nonstate sector is larger than average area harvested per year (37.3%). The difference, however, is extremely small. Average annual yield in the state sector was 17.4 mt/ha, while the nonstate sector shows a slightly higher average of 17.9 mt/ha/year (Table 5). An extremely small yield difference produced non-significant statistical results ($P \leq 0.85$) in the ANOVA.

- For boniato, the nonstate sector harvested on average 48.1% of annual area, while producing 46.4% average of total output per year. State sec-

Table 5. **Comparison of the Cuban Tubers and Roots State and Nonstate Sectors, by Area Harvested, Total Production and Yield, 1990-97**

	Potato				Boniato				Malanga			
	Nonstate sector		Yield		Nonstate sector		Yield		Nonstate sector		Yield	
	AH	TP	S	NS	AH	TP	S	NS	AH	TP	S	NS
Year	Percentage		mt/ha		Percentage		mt/ha		Percentage		mt/ha	
1990	18.3	19.2	11.89	12.64	32.7	29.1	4.04	3.41	52.9	31.0	4.80	1.92
1991	13.4	16.4	13.03	15.79	26.6	25.9	3.52	3.39	50.7	40.3	3.13	2.06
1992	14.2	13.9	18.09	17.69	26.9	26.0	3.46	3.30	55.2	42.8	3.01	1.83
1993	15.2	14.6	17.09	16.24	32.3	32.9	2.81	2.89	60.5	37.2	2.32	0.90
1994	60.7	61.2	12.80	13.05	60.9	60.3	2.73	2.65	74.4	69.8	1.53	1.22
1995	60.2	60.5	21.09	21.43	66.3	62.6	3.46	2.93	81.8	74.2	2.72	1.75
1996	59.5	59.6	26.49	26.62	68.1	65.2	3.68	3.22	86.2	80.0	3.05	1.96
1997	56.7	57.6	18.75	19.45	70.7	69.3	3.47	3.24	89.4	85.4	3.63	2.53
Average	37.3	37.9	17.4	17.9	48.1	46.4	3.4	3.1	68.9	57.6	3.0	1.8

Note: AH = area harvested; TP = total production; S = state; NS = nonstate. AH, TP, and Average were calculated by the author.

Source: *Anuario* (1996, pp. 199, 201, 202, 204, 206, 207); (1997, pp. 186, 188, 189, 191, 193, 194).

tor yields averaged 3.4 mt/ha, while the corresponding figure for the nonstate sector was 3.1 mt/ha (Table 5). The ANOVA result indicates a very low (P≤0.16) level of statistical significance.

- Malanga shows more drastic differences: 68.9% average annual area harvested by the nonstate sector contrasted with 57.6% annual average share of total production. Average annual yields of 3.0 mt/ha for the state sector contrast with a much lower 1.8 mt/ha per year for the nonstate sector (Table 5). A high level of statistical significance (P<0.01) by the ANOVA confirmed the yield differences between both sectors.

Trends in shares of area harvested for the three crops are somewhat different (Figure 3). Malanga shows the highest percentage of area harvested, followed by boniato and, finally, potato. The big jump also occurred from 1993 to 1994 as a result of the establishment of the UBPCs.

The results from the analyses of tubers and roots corroborate the results of the previous study and give credibility to the hypothesis stated for this type of less-perishable crops, namely that since these crops do not spoil soon after harvest, nonstate farmers can hide them from *Acopio* for on-farm consumption, bartering, or sales in the black market. Malanga presents the most convincing case. As stated previously

Figure 3. **Share of Harvested Area of Potato, Boniato and Malanga in the Nonstate Sector, 1990–97**

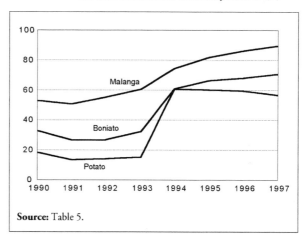

Source: Table 5.

The case of *malanga*, which reflects the poorest performance, may validate the previous explanation. The demand for this commodity is higher than for the other tubers and roots. Benjamin, Collins and Scott (1986) call *malanga* "the starchy tuber most Cubans love" while stating that "Cubans consider [*malanga*] the ideal weaning food." This commodity, however, is not legally available to the general population since it is "allocated through rationing primarily to groups with special diets—small children, the elderly, people with digestive problems, for example" (Alvarez and Puerta, 1994, pp. 1667-8).

Table 6. Comparison of the Cuban Rice, Corn, and Beans State and Nonstate Sectors, by Area Harvested, Total Production and Yield, 1990-97

	Rice				Corn				Beans			
	Nonstate sector		Yield		Nonstate sector		Yield		Nonstate sector		Yield	
	AH	TP	S	NS	AH	TP	S	NS	AH	TP	S	NS
Year	Percentage		mt/ha		Percentage		mt/ha		Percentage		mt/ha	
1990	13.2	10.8	3.14	2.50	49.3	39.0	1.05	0.69	40.0	18.5	0.36	0.12
1991	9.1	11.3	2.74	3.48	50.0	37.4	1.00	0.60	37.7	22.0	0.33	0.15
1992	15.0	10.5	2.31	1.52	50.4	39.0	1.01	0.63	33.7	19.0	0.25	0.11
1993	14.4	9.3	2.02	1.24	53.9	45.9	0.85	0.62	33.3	15.8	0.23	0.09
1994	51.0	48.9	2.43	2.23	74.4	76.1	0.89	0.97	63.9	63.7	0.20	0.19
1995	50.4	55.0	2.33	2.79	75.5	70.5	1.27	0.98	70.8	66.6	0.30	0.24
1996	50.1	50.8	2.43	2.49	74.7	72.1	1.29	1.13	72.6	72.7	0.30	0.30
1997	55.0	47.1	3.38	2.46	75.8	72.7	1.44	1.22	74.6	70.6	0.36	0.30
Average	32.3	30.5	2.60	2.34	63.0	56.6	1.10	0.85	53.3	43.6	0.29	0.19

Note: AH = area harvested; TP = total production; S = state; NS = nonstate. AH, TP, and Average were calculated by the author.

Source: *Anuario* (1996, pp. 199, 201, 202, 204, 206, 207); (1997, pp. 186, 188, 189, 191, 193, 194).

Figure 4. Share of Harvested Area of Rice, Corn and Beans in the Nonstate Sector, 1990–97

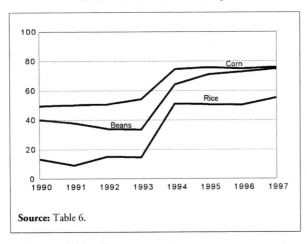

Source: Table 6.

For grains and beans, two other categories of less-perishable commodities, the current study (Table 6) corroborates previous findings:

- In the case of rice, the nonstate sector controlled 32.3% of area harvested in the nonstate sector and accounted for a yearly average of 30.5% of total production. Average annual yields in the state sector were 2.60 mt/ha, while the nonstate sector reported 2.34 mt/ha. As expected, no statistical significance (P<0.40) between yields in both sectors was found in the ANOVA.

- For corn, the nonstate sector had annual average area harvested of 63.0%, contrasting with an av-

erage share of total production of 56.6%. Average yields in the state sector were 1.10 mt/ha, while they were 0.85 mt/ha for the nonstate sector (Table 6). ANOVA results rendered a high statistical significance (P≤0.05) for yield differences between the state and nonstate sectors.

- For beans, the nonstate sector accounted for 53.3% of area harvested and obtained 43.6% of total production. Annual yields in the state sector were 0.29 mt/ha, while the figure for the nonstate sector was 0.19 mt/ha (Table 6). High statistical significance (P≤0.01) was returned by the ANOVA.

Figure 4 shows the increase in shares of area harvested by the nonstate sector since 1994. In 1990, at the beginning of the study period, the shares of agricultural land devoted to rice, corn and beans were 13.2%, 49.3% and 40.0%, respectively. By 1997, the influence of the nonstate sector in these three commodities translated into shares of area harvested of 55.0%, 75.8% and 74.6% for rice, corn and beans, respectively.

THE IMPACT OF THE SPECIAL PERIOD

As stated at the beginning of this paper, the establishment of the Special Period in September 1990 has to be considered when analyzing differences in agricultural productivity between the state and nonstate sectors. The reason is that government policy may have influenced the results because it distributed already-

Table 7. **Impact of the Special Period on the Yields of Selected Crops in the State and Nonstate Sectors, 1990 and Average 1991 through 1997**

| | Nonstate sector | | | State sector | | |
| | Yield | | | Yield | | |
Crop	1990 mt/ha	Average 1991-97 mt/ha	Impact Percentage	1990 mt/ha	Average 1991-97 mt/ha	Impact Percentage
Sugarcane	64.80	43.15	- 33.4	56.20	36.52	- 35.0
Tobacco	0.72	0.62	- 13.9	0.64	0.57	- 10.9
Tomato	5.49	5.67	3.3	5.08	5.83	14.8
Onion	3.93	4.68	19.0	3.19	4.00	25.4
Pepper	9.95	6.40	- 35.7	4.74	4.51	- 4.8
Potato	12.64	18.61	47.2	11.89	18.19	53.0
Boniato	3.41	3.09	- 9.4	4.04	3.30	- 8.3
Malanga	1.92	1.75	- 8.8	4.80	2.77	- 42.3
Rice	2.50	2.32	- 7.2	3.14	2.52	- 19.7
Corn	0.69	0.88	27.5	1.05	1.11	5.7
Bean	0.12	0.20	66.7	0.36	0.32	- 11.1

scarce resources unevenly between the state and nonstate sectors.

To elucidate this issue, the data were analyzed in a different manner. Yields for the year 1990 were considered the starting point. An average of the remaining years (1991 through 1997) was computed. This average was intended to capture the variation in yield of selected crops over several years. The negative or positive impact was calculated as the percentage change compared to the base year (1990). The results are shown in Table 7.

Starting with the intermediate commodities, it is not surprising that, given the dismal performance of the sugar industry since the beginning of the 1990s, sugarcane yields dropped by 33.4% in the nonstate sector and by 35.0% in the state sector. Tobacco yields decreased by 13.9% and by 10.9% in the nonstate and state sectors, respectively. On the surface, these data seem to contradict the relative success experienced by the tobacco industry in recent years.[4] The yield increases of the last years of the study period (from 1995 to 1997) could not compensate for the drop between 1991 and 1994 in both sectors (Table 3).

Vegetables present mixed results. There were increases in yields for tomatoes and onions but a decrease for pepper in both sectors. Tomatoes experienced an increase of 3.3% in the nonstate sector and of 14.8% in the state sector while yields for onions rose by 19.0% and 25.4% for the nonstate and state sectors, respectively. Yields of pepper, however, decreased in both the nonstate and state sectors, by 35.7% and 4.8%, respectively. The sharp decrease in pepper yield may result from an abnormally high yield in the base year (1990). In general, increases in vegetable production during the Special Period can be attributed to the extra attention given to these crops to supply the tourist sector.

Mixed results are also present in the case of tubers and roots. Potatoes show tremendous yield increases in both sectors: 47.2% in the nonstate sector and 53.0% in the state sector. The very high increase may be affected by the opposite of the phenomenon observed for pepper: an abnormally low yield for potatoes in the base year. Boniato yields declined by similar percentages in both sectors: by 9.4% in the nonstate sector and by 8.3% in the state sector. Malanga yields showed an 8.8% decrease in the nonstate sector and a much-higher 42.3% in the state sector. The yields in the starting year are also responsible for this discrepancy: the state sector started with yields more than twice those in the nonstate sector. This relates to the hypothesis and the assumed scale of preferences for farmers discussed throughout the paper.

---

4. Perry et al. (1998) contain a description and analysis of that relative success. Alvarez (1998) explains briefly the reasons why.

For cereals, while rice yields experienced a decrease of 7.2% in the nonstate sector, they dropped by 19.7% in the state sector. In addition to yield differences at the beginning of the study period, another possible explanation for the differences in behavior is the increase in yields experienced by the nonstate sector after the establishment of the UBPCs. These organizations have more governmental support than dispersed farmers. Recall that the former rice farms were part of the rice agro-industrial complexes (as UBPCs continue to be), with all the benefits derived from that association. Corn yields rose by 27.5% in the nonstate sector and by 5.7% in the state sector, probably due to the same reasons explained in the case of rice, except for the lack of agro-industrial complexes. For beans, yields in the nonstate sector were three times lower than for the state sector during the base year; this difference explains to a large extent the increase of 66.7% in yield for the nonstate sector compared to a decrease of 11.1% for the state sector.

CONCLUSIONS AND IMPLICATIONS

Several conclusions and implications can be drawn from this study:

- Results from testing the general and specific hypotheses for intermediate, more-perishable and less-perishable crops, based on the scale of preferences assumed for nonstate farmers, are positive and very convincing in every case.

- The results also corroborate those in a previous study (Alvarez and Puerta, 1994). Even in the presence of new, and potentially disruptive, events such as the breakup of the state monopoly on land, the establishment of the UBPCs, and the creation of the agricultural markets, the same results were obtained. The stability of the results in the face of new data for different time periods enhances the credibility of the theoretical and methodological framework developed to analyze differences in agricultural productivity between Cuba's state and nonstate sectors.

- The Special Period in Time of Peace, imposed in September 1990, has had different impacts on yields of the state and nonsate sectors depending on the commodity. Yields decreased in both sectors for sugarcane, tobacco, pepper, boniato, malanga, and in beans for the state sector. The remaining commodities showed from modest to significant yield increases.

- The radical transformation of the Cuban countryside after the breakup of the state monopoly on land and the establishment of the UBPCs was obvious in the change in relative shares of area harvested and total production between the state and nonstate sectors after 1993. The area harvested by the nonstate sector in the last year for which official statistics are available (1997) was as follows: 91.1% of sugarcane, 92.8% of tobacco, 76.3% of tomatoes, 81.9% of onions, 81.1% of peppers, 56.7% of potatoes, 70.7% of boniato, 89.4% of malanga, 55.0% of rice, 75.8% of corn, and 74.6% of beans.

REFERENCES

Alvarez, José. "Comments on 'The Cuban Cigar Industry as the Transition Approaches' by Joseph M. Perry, Louis A. Woods, Stephen L. Shapiro and Jeffrey W. Steagall." *Cuba in Transition— Volume 8.* Washington: Association for the Study of the Cuban Economy, 1998, pp. 426-428.

Alvarez, José and Ricardo A. Puerta. "State Intervention in Cuban Agriculture: Impact on Organization and Performance," *World Development,* 22:11 (1994), pp. 1663-1675.

Anuario Estadístico de Cuba. La Habana: Oficina Nacional de Estadísticas, various issues.

Benjamin, Medea, Joseph Collins and Michael Scott. *No Free Lunch: Food & Revolution in Cuba Today.* New York: Grove Press, 1986.

Deere, Carmen Diana and Mieke Meurs. "Markets, Markets Everywhere? Understanding the Cuban Anomaly," *World Development,* 20:6 (1992), pp. 825-839.

Deere, Carmen Diana, Mieke Meurs and Niurka Pérez. "Toward a Periodization of the Cuban Collectivization Process: Changing Incentives and Peasant Response," *Cuban Studies,* 22 (1992), pp. 115-149.

Forster, Nancy. "Cuban Agricultural Productivity," in I.L. Horowitz (Ed.) *Cuban Communism.* New Brunswick, N.J.: Transaction Publishers, 1989, pp. 235-255.

Perry, Joseph M., Louis A. Woods, Stephen L. Shapiro and Jeffrey W. Steagall. "The Cuban Cigar Industry as the Transition Approaches." *Cuba in Transition—Volume 8.* Washington: Association for the Study of the Cuban Economy, 1998, pp. 414-425.

Puerta, Ricardo A. and José Alvarez. "Organization and Performance of Cuban Agriculture at Different Levels of State Intervention," *Cuba in Transition—Volume 3.* Washington: Association for the Study of the Cuban Economy, 1993, pp. 91-122.

Rodríguez, José Luis. "Agricultural Policy and Development in Cuba," in A. Zimbalist (Ed.) *Cuba's Socialist Economy Toward the 1990s.* Boulder: Lynne Rienner Publishers, 1987, pp. 25-41.

Sáez, Héctor R. *Property Regimes, Technology, and Environmental Degradation in Cuban Agriculture,* Ph.D. Dissertation, University of Massachusetts, Amherst, May 1997.

MARKET POTENTIAL FOR U.S. LIVESTOCK GENETICS IN A FREE MARKET CUBAN ECONOMY

James E. Ross[1]

Cuba's livestock industry has undergone dramatic change from the time when Fidel Castro took control of the country's government in 1959. At the time of the revolution, cattle was the most important component of the livestock and poultry industry. Today, the cattle population in Cuba is less than at the time of the revolution. Beef and veal rank behind poultry and pork as the major source of meat in the Cuban diet. Ration stores no longer stock beef and it is illegal to serve beef at the small in-home restaurants known as *paladares*, unless the owner has paid a special tax.

What brought about this change, and what are the implications for potential U.S. exporters of livestock genetics if U.S. trade sanctions are lifted? This paper attempts to provide information bearing on this question. Livestock genetics, as used in this paper, refers to live animals for breeding purposes, semen, and embryos.

LIVESTOCK SITUATION

Cuba, with a land area approximately equal to three-fourths the size of Florida, is located in the tropics immediately south of the Tropic of Cancer. Climates in tropical countries have been considered by animal scientists as among the primary factors in the low level of returns from livestock enterprises. Other factors, such as lack of genetic improvement of breeding stock, inadequate research, and limitations of technology, have also been identified as important causes for poor performance in tropical climates.[2]

Cuban livestock production identifies with all of these factors, but Cuba also offers advantages over many other tropical and sub-tropical areas for production of livestock, especially cattle. In the eastern provinces, Cuba has a favorable climate with relatively consistent temperatures. The soil is fertile and offers prospects for improved pasture grasses. Being an island, Cuba provides opportunity for better control of animal diseases than countries bordering on other countries.

In addition to conditions affecting the tropics, Cuban livestock production during the past decade has been affected by economic problems. Since the loss of trade preferences with the Soviet Union and East European countries, an inadequate supply of animal feed has been become a major factor in limiting efficiency and yield of livestock production.

Another factor, especially in the early years following the revolution, was management. Slaughtering breeding stock to increase the supply of beef became

1. The author wishes to thank Ambassador Clarence Boonstra and Dr. Lee McDowell for reviewing the paper in draft form. Their insight into Cuba's livestock situation and tropical livestock production in general, as well as their comments on the paper, were helpful and appreciated. Responsibility for content of the paper, however, is entirely that of the author.

2. McDowell, R. E. "Problems of Cattle Production in Tropical Countries." Department of Animal Science, New York State University, Cornell University International Agricultural Development Mimeograph 17, Ithaca, New York, December 1966.

an important long-run factor hindering genetic improvement of cattle.[3] In recent years, theft and illegal slaughter of cattle have affected the cattle industry adversely.

Cattle

Spanish cattle brought to Cuba in its early history became the basis for the country's cattle population. During the administration of Cuba by the United States (1899-1902), more cattle were imported from Mexico, Venezuela, Central America, and the southern United States. The trend in importing cattle continued during the following years, mostly bulls from Latin America and the United States. Zebu cattle from India imported via U.S. southern states played a major role in improvement of the quality of Cuban cattle.[4]

In the late 1920s, imports of zebu (Brahma), Shorthorn, Jersey, Hereford, Angus, Charolais, Brown Swiss and Holstein breeds increased. In the late 1940s, the Santa Gertrudis breed was imported from Texas. At the time of the revolution, the Brahma, Brown Swiss and Santa Gertrudis were the most popular breeds.[5]

In 1962 the government began an intensive cross-breeding program. The objective was to increase production capacity through use of the Holstein breed.[6] Two of the most popular breeds developed through the cross-breeding program were given names of historical significance. The Mambi breed, a cross between the zebu and Holstein breeds, was named for the fighters against the 18 century Colonists. The Siboney breed, also a zebu-Holstein cross, was named for the inhabitants of Cuba at the time the Spanish arrived in the 15th century.[7] Artificial insemination was the basis of the cross-breeding program. Some 3,000 middle level technicians were employed in thirteen insemination centers, where semen was processed. Frozen semen in tablets, preserved in liquid nitrogen, was the technology used.[8]

In 1968 the cattle population reached 6.9 million head, but in the following years the number of cattle started to decline. By 1989, the number of cattle had fallen to 5.7 million. Currently, the number of cattle is estimated at 4.65 million, nearly a half-million less than at the time of the revolution, over two million less than 30 years ago and a million less than 10 years ago.[9]

Five provinces, generally, have been the largest cattle production areas, with more than half of the country's cattle. Camagüey, the second largest sugarcane producing province, has been the largest producer of cattle with about one-fifth of the country's total. Granma is next with 10%. Other provinces with nearly 10% each, include La Habana, Villa Clara and Pinar del Rio.[10]

Ownership of cattle is divided between the state sector and the non-state sector. The non-state sector includes the Basic Units of Cooperative Production

3. Boonstra, Clarence. Personal communique. (Boonstra was the Counselor for Economic Affairs assigned to the U.S. Embassy in Havana from 1955-57. He also was assigned to Cuba from 1942-44 by the U.S. Department of State and from 1957-60 he made frequent private visits to Cuba.)

4. Riera, Arturo J. "Cattle: The Forgotten Industry." *Cuba in Transition—Volume 4.* Washington: Association for the Study of the Cuban Economy, 1994.

5. Ibid.

6. Cuban Delegation to the X Regional F.A.O. Conference. "Agriculture and Livestock Production in Cuba." Kingston, Jamaica, 1967-68.

7. García, Anicia. Personal communique. Centro de Investigaciones de la Economía Internacional (CIEI). University of Havana, Cuba. June 2000.

8. Cuban Delegation. Op. cit.

9. FAO Website: http://apps1.fao.org/servlet/XteServlet.j. Food and Agriculture Organization, Rome, Italy, Data from 1961-1998.

10. Smith, Douglas, David Zimet, and Timothy Hewitt. *An Overview of the Cuban Livestock Sector.* International Working Paper IW95-18r, International Trade and Development Center, Food and Resource Economics Department, Institute of Food and Agricultural Sciences, University of Florida, Gainesville, Florida, October 1995.

(UBPC), the Agricultural Production Cooperatives (CPA), the Cooperatives of Credit and Services (CCS), and the small private farmers that have established "compromisos" with the Government of Cuba (GOC). Within the state sector, 97% of the cattle population is overseen by the Ministry of Agriculture. The remainder is administered by the Ministry of Sugar and provincial organizations.[11]

In 1961 the state-sector owned 24% of the country's five million head. By 1965, state ownership had increased to 57% of the nearly seven million cattle, and by 1989 the state sector managed 75% of the cattle. State farms provided most of the meat, milk and other foods for domestic consumption. Among the non-state entities, CPAs owned the largest number of cattle.

With the transformation of many of the state farms into UBPCs beginning in 1993, the majority of ownership of cattle shifted from the state sector to the non-state sector. By 1996 the importance of state farms had decreased; however, according to official data, 95% of the beef that year was produced in the public sector.[12] (Information is not available to the author to explain the high percentage; however, it could result from public ownership of the slaughtering facilities, and data could include animals produced in the non-state sector but slaughtered in state-controlled facilities.)

Official records do indicate a major shift of animal ownership from state farms to the non-state sector. In 1993, when the UBPCs were formed, 64% of the 818,600 calves born that year were in the state sector. In 1996 only 27% of the 782,000 calves born were recorded in the state sector.

In 1996 the average weight of cattle slaughtered for meat was 302 kilos (665 lbs), an increase of 56 kilos (123 lbs) from 1993 and 75 kilos (165 lbs) from

1992. This could reflect the decreased availability of foreign exchange at the end of the 1980s to import feed following loss of Soviet Bloc trade preferences, and the increased availability of inputs as a result of the improved economy beginning in the mid 1990s. It is also interesting to note that 80% of the calf mortality in 1993 was in the state sector, but only 31% in 1996.[13]

Swine

Pork, traditionally, has been a favored meat in Cuba and State planning has focused on increasing production. The number of pigs increased from 1.1 million in 1961 to 1.8 million in 1966 and then leveled off at about 1.5 million through 1981. In 1982 the number of pigs began to rise, reaching 2.8 million in 1991. Since then, the number of pigs has declined to about 2.4 million.[14]

As has been the situation with beef cattle, the average weight of hogs slaughtered increased during the last half of the past decade. In 1992 the average weight of hogs slaughtered was 50 kilos (110 lbs). It had dropped from 75 kilos (165 lbs) in 1990, a reduction of one-third. In 1993 the average weight began to increase and was 70 kilos (154 lbs) in 1996. Since then the average carcass weight has increased, but is still not at the level of the 1980s.

Consumer preference plays a role in Cuba in the weight of pigs when they are consumed. While the government effort is to increase the average weight in order to increase the meat supply, the consumer traditionally has preferred to roast pigs at a weight of under 100 pounds, preferably 60 to 70 pounds. This factor, however, probably is not reflected in the official weight data of hogs slaughtered.

Live pig births in 1996 was placed at around 2 million, with the mortality rate at 17%. This was a significant decrease in the mortality rate from 1993,

11. Nova González, Armando. "La Agricultura Cubana: Evolución y Trayectoria." Centro de Estudios de la Economía Cubana (CEEC), University of Havana, Havana, Cuba, 1998.

12. *Anuario Estadístico de Cuba* (AEC). Oficina Nacional de Estadísticas. Havana, Cuba. 1996, p. 208.

13. Centro Nacional de Control Pecuario (CENOP) in AEC, Capitulo IX, p. 208.

14. FAO Website.

when it was reported to be 29%. Mortality of swine was higher, 38%, in the state sector than the total average in 1993, but lower in 1996 at 15%. The overall decreased mortality rate indicates improved swine management, especially in the state sector. Another factor affecting the decreased mortality rate in the state sector relative to the non-state sector could be retention of the better managed operations in the state sector and the conversion of less efficient state farms to UBPCs. (Only 13 of 46 UBPCs, reportedly, showed profit in 1999.)

Swine mortality is most important from birth to weaning. Sows laying on their pigs in the early weeks after birth is an especially important factor in swine mortality. Good management, therefore, is critical. The second most important factor is hygiene, e.g. preventing diarrhea. Nutrition, genetics and, obviously, wiping out brucellosis—a serious disease that has affected swine since the pre-revolutionary days—are other important factors.[15]

Sheep

The Government of Cuba in the early years of the revolution had plans to increase sheep numbers to more than two million head in an effort to increase the meat supply and provide raw material for use in the textile industry. The number of sheep increased steadily during the 1960s, 1970s and 1980s, but began a decline in the 1990s. The number of sheep in 1961 was 220,000; in 1971 the number was 290,000; in 1981 it was 361,000; and by 1991 it was 385,000. From the peak in 1989-91, the number of sheep has declined to 310,000 and has remained at about that level.[16]

Official Cuban data showed the number of sheep in 1996 at 899,851, almost three times that of the FAO data, and the number of goats at 118, 541. Whatever the correct number might be, it is evident the plan to increase sheep numbers to two million has not materialized. Approximately one-fourth of the sheep and about 10% of the goats are held in the state sector.

Horses

Horse numbers, including donkeys and mules, are estimated to have leveled off at a little more than 600,000 (620,000 in 1999), about 200,000 more than at the time of the revolution. State farms accounted for 17% in 1996. One of the main reasons horse numbers have increased since the revolution, is that animal power has been used to a large extent to supplement, or replace, mechanical power.

In addition to horses, oxen have been used to substitute for tractors. Oxen, for example, have been used widely for working in the fields, to transport sugarcane, and for other purposes . In 1992 the Cuban government acknowledged that the country was using in excess of 100,000 oxen. Even at present, when traveling through the countryside it is apparent that oxen are used widely in the fields. Horses appear to be used mainly for transport purposes.

Live Animal Trade

In 1961 Cuba imported live animals valued at $4.9 million. The following year imports dropped to $1.5 million and remained under $1 million annually until 1990. Live animal imports that year were valued at $3.5 million. Since 1990, imports of live animals have remained insignificant. Cuba's exports of live animals, also, have remained relatively insignificant.[17]

MEAT AND MILK PRODUCTION

Prior to the loss of Soviet assistance in 1989-90, meat production—in terms of total production and on a per capita basis—was higher than during the years following the revolution. With the loss of trade preferences and the lack of foreign exchange to import feed, total meat production in recent years has fallen to less than in the 1960s. On a per capita basis, meat production has dropped dramatically.

Beef, Pork and Poultry Meat Production

Total meat production (beef, pork, poultry and other) averaged 30 metric tons per 1,000 population in the 1987-91 period. Using the same measure, pro-

---

15. McDowell. Personal electronic communication.

16. FAO Website.

17. FAO Website.

duction for the 1992-96 period averaged less than 18 tons—a reduction of more than 40%.

Table 1. Cuba: Meat Production in Metric Tons per 1,000 Capita

ITEM	1961-66 avg.	1987-91 avg.	1992-96 avg.	1997-98 avg.
Beef and Veal	20.92	12.30	6.15	6.43
Pork	4.07	8.53	5.96	6.62
Poultry Meat	3.49	8.83	5.26	5.77
Other	0.28	0.35	0.27	0.24
Total	28.76	30.01	17.64	19.06

Source: Food and Agriculture Organization Data Base.

Total meat production per person in 1987-91 was about 5% higher than the average for 1961-66, but by the 1997-98 period, production had fallen to two-thirds of the early 1960s. Production of beef and veal recorded the largest drop of the three major meats. Total beef and veal production fell from the 1961-63 average of 146,000 metric tons to 71,300 tons for the 1997-98 period, a decrease of more than half. During the last half of the 1990s, production of beef and veal per capita was slightly ahead of production in the first half of the decade. The even larger decline in production in the first half of the 1990s reflects the severity of the loss of Soviet and Eastern Bloc trade preferences.

Pork production, contrary to beef and veal production, has increased in terms of both total production and per capita production compared to the early years of the revolution. Production per person in 1997-98 was 63% higher than the average for 1961-66, but was 22% below 1987-91.

Poultry meat production increased even more than pork production in the 30 years following the revolution, however, production following the loss of trade preferences fell more than pork. Lower production of poultry meat reflected even more than pork production, the loss of foreign exchange to import feed.

Even today, many poultry production units remain idle because of the lack of feed.

Milk Production

Altitude within the tropics has a significant effect on milk production. The average milk yields and rates of growth of cattle in the lower elevations (less than 400 meters) of countries lying in the North-South 30 degree latitudes—generally considered as the area of tropical climate—are only 10-15 percent of that acceptable in the North 35-60 degree latitudes.[18]

In addition to the vagaries of the tropics, investments in livestock in Cuba in the years before the revolution were not as significant in milk production as in beef production. Although there were some entrepreneurs investing in the dairy industry in pre-revolutionary Cuba, cattle breeding generally focused on production of meat.

Following the revolution, especially the period 1962-70, the Cuban government initiated a concerted effort to increase milk production through the cross-breeding program. About 900,000 cows were inseminated annually to produce higher-yielding offspring.[19]

In 1961, Cuba's production of whole fresh milk was reported to be 350,000 metric tons. Production increased gradually reaching one million metric tons in 1979, and remained at approximately that level until 1991. During the 1990s, largely as a result of lack of animal feed, production declined to the present level of about 650,000 metric tons.[20]

Milk production per cow had increased dramatically from 1960 through 1980. The steady increase was attributed to the success of breeding programs to cross Holstein and Brown Swiss breeds with the criollo (mainly local zebu) cattle. By 1980 about 70% of the Cuban dairy herd was made up of these crosses, more than three-quarters were Holstein-criollo crosses.

---

18. McDowell. Op. cit.

19. Nova. Op. cit.

20. FAO Website.

In spite of the productivity gains in the late 1960s and 1970s, Cuba supplied only about 30% of its domestic demand for milk. Powdered milk was imported to meet the remaining demand. In years prior to the revolution, milk was supplied mainly in the form of sweetened condensed milk and evaporated milk.

Refrigeration facilities for preserving fresh milk play an important role in milk production, especially in the tropics, and undoubtedly limited refrigeration capacity has had negative impact on efforts to increase dairying in Cuba. In addition, especially in the past decade, the lack of animal feed has had a particularly negative effect on milk production. Annual production per cow in 1996 averaged 1,252 kilograms (2,754 lbs), about 600 kilos (1,348 lbs) below 1990—a decrease in yield of approximately 50%. In 1996 Florida's annual average milk production per cow was 14,588 pounds, more than five times higher than in Cuba.

The average number of cows producing milk in 1996 was 511,200, some 40,000 fewer than in 1990. Milk production in 1996 was 640,000 MT and 1,034,000 MT in 1990. Thus, while the number of dairy cows in 1996 had declined less than 10%, the total production of milk had dropped nearly 40%.

State production of milk in 1990 was 80% of the total, and in 1996 it was about 20%. As for beef cattle production, this was primarily the result of transforming state farms into UBPCs. The number of dairy cattle in the state sector in 1996 was only 16% compared to 66% in 1990.

One of the more widely publicized efforts to increase milk production in Cuba was an ambitious program supported by the United Nations World Food Program (WFP) in the province of Camagüey in 1989. Plans called for 358 new dairies and eleven new villages to encourage relocation of labor. It was referred to as the creation of the largest dairy complex in the world. In 1992 WFP introduced another project in the province of Las Tunas to benefit small farmers and cooperatives. Information is not available on the current status of these projects; however, data do not indicate any impact on increasing domestic milk production.

POTENTIAL MARKET CONSIDERATIONS

Assume that proposed legislation being considered by the U.S. Congress results in lifting the embargo on food exports, including livestock genetics, to Cuba. What are some of the major factors that will impact the market for U.S. livestock genetics?

Market Structure

Livestock products in Cuba are sold through four different markets—Ration Stores, Agricultural Markets, Dollar Stores, and the Black Market. Commodities and their availability have changed from time to time, but over the years have included beef, chicken meat, eggs, butter and canned milk. In recent years beef has not been available in the Ration Stores.

Beef, along with other kinds of meat, is sometimes available in the Dollar Stores. Reportedly, more than half of Cuba's population has access to U.S. dollars and could use those dollars to purchase beef, as well as pork, poultry and other livestock products in the Dollar Stores.

Pork and poultry meat are sold through the Agricultural Markets. Beef is not sold in these markets. Generally, beef is not offered on the menus of the *paladares*. Some *paladares*, however, do from time to time offer beef to their patrons. Reportedly, by paying a special tax, a *paladar* can provide beef on the menu. *Paladares* could purchase the beef through the Dollar Stores or in the Black Market.

Tourist and government hotels provide an additional market for livestock products. Meat and dairy products utilized in the tourist industry are largely imported.

Market Demand

Cuba's current population of more than11 million is nearly 60% greater than in 1959. The total food supply, therefore, needs to be 60% greater just to maintain the same level of per capita consumption. Production of some commodities, such as beef, is below levels prior to 1959.

Poultry meat in Cuba has surpassed both beef and pork as measured by per capita consumption. Poultry meat consumed per capita in 1998 was more than 10% greater than pork. Per capita beef consumption at 6.4 kilograms per year was about three-fourths the amount of poultry meat consumed. In the 1960s beef consumption per capita was more than six times that of poultry meat, and more than five times that of pork.

Table 2.   Cuba: Meat Supply Per Capita Per Year in Kilograms

ITEM	1961-66 avg.	1987-91 avg.	1992-96 avg.	1997-98 avg.
Beef and Veal	21.1 (65%)	13.3 (35%)	7.4 (31%)	6.4 (28%)
Pork	4.0 (12%)	8.1 (21%)	6.7 (28%)	7.3 (31%)
Poultry	3.4 (10%)	12.3 (33%)	8.3 (35%)	8.1 (35%)
Other	4.1 (13%)	4.1 (11%)	1.4 (6%)	1.2 (6%)
Total	32.6	37.8	23.8	23.2

Source: Food and Agriculture Organization Data Base.

Per capita consumption of beef has dropped steadily from the time of the revolution. The 1997-98 average consumption per capita of beef was only about 30% of the amount consumed in the 1961-66 period. Pork consumption per capita, on the other hand, increased more than 80% and poultry consumption per capita during the same time periods more than doubled.

Although at present more poultry meat is consumed than either beef or pork, consumption of poultry meat is only about two-thirds the level sustained prior to the loss of Soviet aid in 1990. Imports account for about 30% of the country's poultry meat supply, while imports have been a minor factor in the supply of other kinds of meat.

During the past decade adequate nutrition has been one of the most serious problems facing Cuba. Of particular concern has been the decline in per capita consumption of meat products. Prior to the 1990s, Cubans were consuming 20% or more of their calories in the form of animal products. During the first half of 1990s they were consuming only 15% from animal products. By the end of the 1990s, the calories derived from animal products had fallen to 12%. (Table 3)

Cuba's caloric consumption from animal origin, 12%, is slightly above the average level for developing countries—11%. In developed countries the population obtains an average of 27% of its calories from animal products.[21] Calories consumed from animal products in Cuba during 1998 (309) were less than those consumed in Costa Rica (472), Jamaica (466), Bolivia (414), or Dominican Republic (345).

Prior to the 1959 revolution, Cuba's food needs were met through domestic production and importation. For 30 years following the revolution, these endeavors were supported by favorable trade terms with the Soviet Union and Eastern Bloc countries. Soviet aid and favorable trade arrangements permitted Cuba to import production inputs needed for domestic agricultural production. Exports, primarily sugar, to the Soviet Union and Eastern Bloc countries provided foreign exchange needed to import food to fill the deficit between production and consumption.

Until the collapse of the trading relationship with the Soviet Union at the end of the 1980s, the Cuban government was able to provide adequate nutrition for its people. With the loss of Soviet aid Cuba's food situation has changed dramatically. Without the favorable trade terms, access to improved technology, and foreign exchange to import, Cuba has not been able to maintain the same level of caloric intake per capita. The country's per capita food supply, measured in terms of caloric consumption, is about three-fourths of the level held prior to the loss of Soviet assistance.

In an effort to maintain an acceptable level of nutrition, Cuba in the 1990s allocated a larger percentage of foreign exchange for food imports relative to other imports. Foreign exchange, obtained through increased family remittances, foreign investment and tourism has helped to finance the food imports.

While much of the food marketed through the tourist industry is imported, some domestic production does reach the tourist market. Reportedly, the tour-

---

21. Delgado, Christopher, et al. "Livestock to 2020: The Next Food Revolution." International Food Policy Research Institute, Washington, D.C. 2020 Brief 61, May 1999.

Table 3.   Cuba: Per Capita Caloric Consumption from Vegetable and Animal Products, Averages for the Periods Indicated

ITEM	1961-66 avg.	1987-91 avg.	1992-96 avg.	1997-98 avg.
Total Calories Per Capita Per Day	2,334	3,093	2,467	2,449
Calories from Vegetable Products	1,863 (80%)	2,436 (79%)	2,090 (85%)	2,149 (88%)
Calories from Animal Products	470 (20%)	657 (21%)	377 (15%)	301 (12%)

Source: Food and Agriculture Organization Data Base.

ism industry purchased approximately US$120 million worth of fresh produce and meat products from Ministry of Agriculture-operated companies in 1998, compared to US$75 million in 1997.

In addition to siphoning off some domestic food production for the tourist industry, lower per capita production and lack of foreign exchange to import has caused per capita supply of many food items, not only animal protein foods, to be substantially lower than before 1959. It could be argued that many of the food items currently available in smaller supplies than before the revolution are not necessary for human nutrition, but they are items that many consumers prefer.

It is obvious that there should be a pent-up demand in Cuba for livestock products, especially beef and dairy products. Increased demand would be expected to result from a larger human population, decreased imports of animal products and a smaller per capita domestic supply of meat.

Market Competition

If the market in Cuba would open for U.S. livestock genetics, it is anticipated the U.S. livestock industry would provide strong competition for suppliers from other countries. Canada has been Cuba's major source of dairy genetics. U.S. dairy and beef cattle would compete extremely well with cattle from other country sources declared foot and mouth disease free. Because of similar climatic conditions in the southern United States to that of Cuba, livestock coming from the U.S. southern states would have a strong preference to those coming from either Canada, Europe or South American livestock-producing countries, such as Argentina and Uruguay.

Countries and firms already established in the Cuban market through trade and investment could be ex-

pected to provide strong competition for U.S. exporters. Most of the international economic associations formed between Cuba and foreign entities pertaining to food and agriculture have involved financing rather than investment. Financing is used primarily to provide production inputs, such as fertilizers, chemicals, equipment, etc. It affects mainly production and processing of exportable products, e.g. citrus, sugar, tobacco and some processed foods and beverages rather than the domestic food situation, including the livestock industry.

The only major foreign investment involving livestock is a Cuban-Vietnamese joint venture in cattle and swine approved in May 1997 and inaugurated in Ninh Binh in June 1997. The Vietnamese enterprises, Phung Thuong and Don Giad, were to contribute two-thirds of the initial investment. Bacuranao, a Cuban cattle enterprise, was to contribute the remainder. The joint venture was created for production of livestock and processing of pork and beef, primarily for the tourist trade. High-quality semen was also to be produced for herd improvement. Recent reports, however, indicate the "international economic association" has not been established successfully and is in the process of dissolution.

Another international economic association in Cuba in the livestock products area is a Cuban-Spanish joint venture known as Asturia. It is an association between the Spain-based Peñasanta S.A. and Cuba's Ministry of Food Processing The joint venture will initially process and bottle powdered milk imported from Spain.

In addition to these joint ventures, the Cuban Institute of Animal Sciences is offering various opportunities for foreign institutions to collaborate on research and technical matters, e.g., on biotechnology, including protein enrichment of by-products from the sugar industry; animal physiology and nutrition, including systems to balance rations, using tropical feed; pasture improvement, including intensive management of pasture in low input systems; production systems, including calf and replacement heifer breeding systems, natural breeding in dual purpose livestock and artificial breeding with low inputs.

Once U.S. sanctions are lifted and normal commercial relations between the United States and Cuba resume, the most sought after U.S. participation in Cuba's livestock sector, according to Cuban officials, will be for collaboration on research and technology.[22]

Other Market Considerations

All sectors of Cuba's livestock industry have been impacted by the lack of animal feedstuffs, especially since 1989. Cuba has had great difficulty in substituting domestic feed production and technology for lost imports.

For the hog sector, the abrupt cessation of feed imports has been the decisive factor in the decline of swine numbers. For beef cattle, the decline in numbers began before 1989. Dairy cattle also have been affected by an inadequate feed supply. Milk production, total and on a per capita basis, in the 1990s has fallen significantly from the 1980s. Aside from internal factors, such as economic organization and management, a severe drought in the 1980s may have hit the cattle sector especially hard.

The livestock sector started the past decade from a position of heavy state involvement and, although there has been a reluctant shift toward economic decentralization, there has been little indication of any impact on overall productivity. There are indications that productivity increased in the state sector following transformation of many state farms into UBPCs; however, this could be the result of shifting less efficient units to the non-state sector.

Prospects for substantial improvement in Cuba's livestock sector are directly linked to U.S.-Cuban relations, especially the market access policies enacted by the Cuban government following normalization of commercial relations between Cuba and the United States. The vast size of the U.S. breeding stock, high level of technology in animal reproduction and physiology, advanced research on improved pasture grasses and animal feedstuffs, past experience of U.S. livestock interests in Cuba, and other factors will ultimately affect the livestock industry in Cuba.

Unique market factors will provide opportunities in Cuba for the U.S. livestock industry. Some of the factors are:

• Proximity of the U.S. livestock industry to the Cuban market. Transport of livestock genetics, especially live animals, will have a comparative advantage over other country suppliers.

• Cuba's growing tourist industry will require substantial quantities of animal protein foods. In 1998 Cuba reported 1.4 million tourists, with revenue from tourism 21% greater than the year before. Cuba's share of the Caribbean tourist trade in 1998 was 9% compared to 4% in 1989. The number of tourists has grown from 300,000 in 1989 to an estimated 1.7 million in 1999. Two million tourists are expected to visit Cuba in 2000.

• Proximity of Cuba to the tourist market in the Caribbean islands. U.S. livestock entrepreneurs who want to invest in livestock production in Cuba will have an opportunity to supply products, not only for the Cuban domestic market, but also for the export market—especially the tourist industry in nearby Caribbean countries. Utilization of free trade zones in Cuba could facilitate such investments.

Cuba offers the largest land area of any island in the Caribbean, and has favorable areas for livestock production, especially cattle in the eastern provinces. In addition, Cuba has a highly educated work force relative to many other countries. If Cuba's foreign investment climate were favorable, U.S. livestock investors could become a significant factor in livestock production in Cuba.

---

22. Private discussion with the Cuban Vice Minister of Agriculture for Research and Development. June 2000.

MARKET POTENTIAL

In the 1980s there was a growing dependency on imported feedstuffs for the livestock sector. Imports of animal and vegetable meal rose some 52% from 1980 to 1989. Certainly, the enormous drop in feed imports in the 1990s has had major impact on the numbers and productivity of the livestock sector.

While the market for U.S. swine, sheep and horse genetics will be important when U.S. economic sanctions are lifted, prospects for substantial trade and investment in the livestock sector appear to be most favorable in cattle, both beef and dairy.

Since the revolution Cuba's cattle population has decreased more than 7%, while the human population has increased nearly 60%. If Cuba were to regain the same ratio of people and cattle that existed in 1961, the cattle population would need to increase from 4.7 million to 7.5 million head. This would be a 70% increase in the number of cattle.

Following are the data used in calculating the number of cattle required to regain the number of cattle per 100 people existing in 1961:

Human population in 1961	7.1 million
Cattle population in 1961	5.0 million
Head of cattle per 100 population	70.0
Population in 1998	11.1 million
Cattle population in 1998	4.7 million
No. of cattle (at 1961 ratio)	7.8 million
No. of cattle required to restore 1961 ratio	3.1 million

While the cattle numbers stated in this paper are FAO or Cuban official data, it is estimated by Riera that the current number of cattle could be as low as two million head, or even lower.[23] But whatever the number might be, it is clear that Cuba does not have an adequate supply of beef and milk to meet the consumption demand of its people.

Building a domestic cattle industry in Cuba is going to depend to a large extent on the introduction of improved livestock genetics, but also important will be the establishment of improved pasture grasses and legumes for feed. Older literature shows phosphorus and cobalt deficiencies in Cuba, with the status of other minerals generally unknown; therefore, proper mineral nutrition will also be important.[24]

A study by the International Food Policy Research Institute (IFPRI) refers to livestock as the next food revolution in developing countries, and states there has been "a massive increase in demand for food of animal origin." The study points out that total meat production in developing countries grew at an annual rate of 5.4% between the early 1980s and mid-1990s. In most developing countries per capita production kept up with population growth.[25] In Cuba, during the same time period, total meat production declined. The rate of per capita meat consumption was negative, while the rate of population growth was positive.

Based on data and information available, it can be concluded that following resumption of normal commercial relations between Cuba and the United States:

- Cuba's population growth, urbanization and increased per capita income will generate strong demand for food products of animal origin;

- Satisfaction of that demand will depend on increased livestock production in Cuba, especially through improvement of animal genetics and nutrition, as well as the country's openness to international trade and foreign investment.

If Cuba has access to foreign exchange for importation of food, an immediate market could open for U.S. suppliers of livestock products—especially beef, dairy products, poultry meat and eggs. Refrigeration, which was not widely available in Cuba before the 1960s, could facilitate a market for these products.

The market in Cuba for U.S. suppliers of livestock genetics and livestock products will depend largely on policies established in Washington and Havana, and, if those policies are favorable, U.S. exporters and investors of livestock genetics would have an opportunity to help Cuba rebuild an industry valued in billions of dollars.

---

23. Riera. Op. cit.

24. McDowell. Personal electronic communication.

25. Delgado. Op. cit.

COMMENTS ON

"Cuba Market Potential for U.S. Livestock Genetics in a Free Market Cuban Economy" by Ross and "Differences in Agricultural Productivity in Cuba's State and Nonstate Sectors: Further Evidence" By Alvarez

William E. Kost

I have been asked to discuss two papers: Jim Ross' "Cuba Market Potential for U.S. Livestock Genetics in a Free Market Cuban Economy" and José Alvarez's "Differences in Agricultural Productivity in Cuba's State and Nonstate Sectors: Further Evidence". Both papers are quite good and raise some important issues. Given the limited time available, I'll confine my remarks to a few of the issues that came to mind as I read these papers and listened to the authors summarize them in this session.

First, Jim Ross' livestock paper. Jim provides an excellent historical perspective and summary of the current livestock situation in Cuba. He concludes that the market for livestock products in Cuba is growing and that a likely response will be an increase in Cuban livestock production. Given that both animal numbers and productivity are relatively low in Cuba, there is a need to increase the productivity through improved genetics. Were the Cuban economy opened to trade with the free market economies, particularly with a lifting of U.S. sanctions, he anticipates an increase in Cuban imports of improved breeding stock. With Cuban climatic conditions so similar to that of the U.S. southern states, much of that improved genetic stock would likely come from the United States. This would be particularly true for beef and dairy cattle.

Jim makes a good, logical argument to support these conclusions. While I think he is correct in these conclusions, I think that there are limits to the size of that market. To illustrate my point, I would like to look at the Cuban livestock and meat economy from the perspective of the constraints facing the industry. Several constraints exist.

First, demand constraints. Meat consumption is constrained by relatively low per capita income levels. Given the relatively higher prices of beef and veal, this becomes more of a constraint for beef and veal than for poultry and pork. With the limited prospects for significant income growth, meat consumption levels, particularly beef and veal, will likely remain low for the near to intermediate term.

Second, severe supply constraints that reduce the availability of meat in the marketplace. Livestock numbers are down and productivity is low. Poultry and pork production, on the other hand, have shown some production gains. Jim does a good job of discussing these supply constraints to meat and dairy production.

Third, other resource constraints that affect meat production. Land constraints preclude domestic production of the feedstuffs required to produce meat. Thus, meat production will be heavily dependent on

118

imported feeds. The foreign exchange constraint is clearly going to severely limit feed imports. Given the relatively more efficient feed conversion of poultry and pigs over cattle, it is clear why poultry and pork production have shown some gains while beef and veal production gains haven't materialized.

And fourth, another land resource constraint directly affecting cattle is the limited amount of pasture land on which to run cattle and the relatively low carrying capacity of that land. While Cuba has some lands that are uniquely suited for pasture-fed livestock, it is still limited. For much of the land suitable for livestock, cattle will have to compete with other agricultural enterprises that will likely have a comparative advantage over a livestock enterprise.

This leaves Cuba with some pent-up demand for livestock products (with a long-run potential for significant demand growth) facing low production and a constrained domestic production capacity.

The one segment of the Cuban market that has the potential to become a growing market for meat, particularly beef, veal, and dairy products, is Cuba's growing tourist industry. However, Cuban livestock and meat producers face additional constraints in this market. Demand in tourist markets will be primarily for fresh, high-quality, grain-fed beef. Serving this market will require a reasonably well developed cold-chain technology and infrastructure. Tourist hotel restaurants will want consistently high-quality food products delivered on a consistently regular basis. Cuba neither produces much of this grade quality beef nor has the market infrastructure developed to meet tourist industry needs. The tourist industry will have the foreign exchange, the fresh food storage capacity, and the links to foreign suppliers dedicated to serving a sophisticated food service industry. Therefore, Cuba's tourist industry likely will be heavily dependent on imports, including beef, veal, and dairy products. If trade restrictions are lifted, much of these tourist industry imports will likely come from U.S. food wholesalers, particularly those in Florida.

Cuba's livestock industry is also constrained by a locational disadvantage. If trade restrictions are lifted, Cuba is close to the United States: a large, efficient,

low-cost meat producer. Cuba, for the foreseeable future, will not have a comparative advantage in livestock production, particularly for high-quality grain-fed beef. Cuban meat producers will have to compete with relatively low priced imported meat and dairy products in urban domestic markets, not just the above discussed tourist industry. And once these markets are captured by imports, it will be difficult for the domestic producers to recapture them.

To the extent that a Cuban cattle industry develops, it will likely be traditional range-fed livestock focusing on meeting local domestic, not tourist and maybe not even urban, demand needs. That market is large enough and growing rapidly enough to more than absorb the domestic meat production in the near to intermediate term. That is the market segment that the southeast United States, particularly Florida, will support with exports of both genetically superior live breeding animals and genetically superior semen.

The constraints Cuban animal agriculture faces, coupled with comparative advantage market forces, will lead to Cuban animal products imports being more important than imports of genetic inputs. Given the well-developed cold-chain infrastructure in the United States for meat and dairy products, regions other than the southeast United States stand to benefit from Cuban trade. For example, meat exports and grain/oilseed feed exports will generate equally important benefits for cornbelt states.

Several things need to be in place for the United States to capture these postulated benefits. U.S. restrictions on trade with Cuba must be lifted. Cuba must continue promoting market and trade oriented policies that allow continued economic growth. Cuba needs to generate higher per capita incomes to create increased demand and more foreign exchange earnings to buy the demanded imports. Particularly for meat and dairy products, Cuba needs to improve and develop the marketing channel infrastructure required to handle perishable products.

Now, I briefly turn to José Alvarez's productivity paper. A study of Cuban agricultural productivity, particularly a comparison of state and nonstate sectors, can have a major impact on agricultural policy deci-

119

sions. Higher productivity in the nonstate sector — the sector that contains the more market-oriented enterprises — would provide a strong argument for continuing structural change in Cuban agriculture. Given the production shortages in Cuban agriculture, higher nonstate sector productivity would provide a strong impetus for continuing to reduce state intervention in agriculture.

Is there higher productivity in the nonstate sector? José's analysis showed:

- nonstate sector productivity in sugarcane and peppers was significantly higher than state sector;

- nonstate sector productivity in tobacco and onions was higher, but not significantly higher;

- nonstate sector productivity in tomatoes, potatoes, boniatos, and rice was about the same; and

- nonstate sector productivity in malanga, corn, and beans was significantly lower.

The results are clearly mixed.

José raised the issue of differences in resource allocation between the two sectors. If nonstate enterprises are allocated fewer production inputs, yields would be reduced. This would bias the productivity measures downward for nonstate produced commodities and understate any benefits to producing agricultural products in nonstate enterprises. No attempt was made to correct for this kind of bias in the analysis. I suspect the required data are not available to make that kind of adjustment. I also suspect that the results would still remain mixed — in part because of the relatively wide year-to-year variations and the short data series analyzed.

All research studies need a "more work needs to be done section." Here is my suggestion. One of the problems José faced was the short time series (1990-97, 8 observations) over which to apply the statistical tests. Creating an index of production (or productivity) would transform the data into index numbers that could be aggregated across commodities, thereby increasing the degrees of freedom for any statistical test applied. These index numbers for each commodity could aggregated simply or aggregated using quantity or value weights to capture differences in relative importance of individual commodities to the Cuban economy. This might provide a more definitive general answer to the state-nonstate productivity question (though at the expense of commodity detail).

I therefore close with a traditional "this was a good study, a good start, and more work could be done!"

RECENT CHANGES IN MANAGEMENT STRUCTURE AND STRATEGIES OF THE CUBAN FISHING INDUSTRY

Chuck Adams[1]

The commercial fishing industry of Cuba is an important source of fishery products originating from the Gulf of Mexico and Caribbean region. Cuba historically fielded a large distant-water fleet that was engaged in the harvest of many worldwide subtropical and temperate pelagic fisheries stocks. Given the evolution in the global political environment of the early 1990s, Cuba's commercial fishing industry changed dramatically. As a result, production emphasis has shifted from high volume, low-value, pelagic stocks toward high-valued, nearshore fisheries. Cuba has more recently played an increasingly important role in the world market for these high-valued finfish and shellfish seafood products harvested primarily within Cuba's nearshore waters.

As the U.S. seafood industry continues to strive to enhance its competitiveness in the global seafood market and as domestic fisheries managers attempt to be more effective in developing sustainable domestic and regional fishery management policy, a need exists to better understand the role Cuba plays in the total production of seafood products and recognize Cuba's importance in the world seafood market. And if political change in the region affords the opportunity of renewed trade between the United States and Cuba, an understanding of the resultant market impacts is crucial. In addition, given that the southeast U.S. region, Florida, in particular, and Cuba effectively share the same marine ecosystem, the sustainable utilization of the region's marine resources may be dependent on a shared understanding of appropriate management strategies. The management structure associated with Cuba's commercial and recreational fisheries has undergone significant change in the last several years. This paper will thus provide a brief history of the Cuban commercial fishing industry and discuss the recently implemented management structure.

INDUSTRY HISTORY

The commercial fishing industry of Cuba has long been an important source of fishery products from the Gulf of Mexico and Caribbean region. Prior to the Cuban Revolution, the commercial fishing industry in Cuba was characterized by a fleet composed of small boats and vessels plying the island's nearshore waters. These craft, which were typically low capacity and technically unsophisticated, primarily targeted a complement of reef fish; spiny lobster; sponge; and a few pelagic finfish species such as mackerels, tunas, and billfish. The landings were handled by small-scale processing facilities and the products were then mostly directed into the local domestic markets and the tourism industry.

1. This paper is drawn from a more comprehensive report prepared by Chuck Adams, Plácido Sánchez Vega of the Cuban Ministry of Fishing Industries and Anicia García Alvarez of the Center for the Study of the Cuban Economy at the University of Havana, which was jointly presented at the meetings of the International Institute of Fisheries Economics and Trade in Corvalis, Oregon, in July, 2000.

Following the Revolution, much attention was given to further developing the commercial fishing fleets. A viable modern fishing fleet would not only provide a badly needed source of domestic protein and export revenue, but would also enhance coastal surveillance capabilities, provide training opportunities for naval recruits, and reestablish relations with neighboring Latin American nations via bilateral fishery access agreements. However, the modernization of the Cuban commercial fishing industry would require considerable revenue, which unfortunately was in short supply as a result of production disruptions caused by, among other factors, economic sanctions imposed against Cuba by the United States.

During the early 1960s and the next two decades, a modernization program created port facilities that provided for the expansion of the Cuban fishing fleet, the seafood processing sector, and the various commercial fishing service-related industries. The Cuban fleet that emerged from this program was characterized by a level of technical sophistication and capacity unrivaled in the Caribbean and Central American region. Annual commercial fishery landings averaged about 20,000 metric tons (mt) before the Revolution (Food and Agricultural Organization of the United Nations). Following the period of commercial fishing fleet development, landings exceeded 100,000 mt by 1970 and approached 200,000 mt by 1976.

Whereas before the Revolution the Cuban commercial fishing fleet was primarily a nearshore fleet, the new Cuban fleet was comprised of four distinct components.

- The Flota Cubana de Pesca (FCP) was the distant-water fleet composed of purse seiners and midwater trawlers. This sector of the fleet represented a different form of fishing activity than that in which the Cuban fleet had traditionally engaged. The FCP developed into the largest distant-water fleet in all of Latin America and targeted low-valued species such as mackerels, herrings, and hake. These low-valued fish, harvested from southern and northwest Atlantic and Pacific regions, were destined primarily for the domestic market.

- The Flota Atunera de Cuba (FAC) was composed of tuna and swordfish longliners, which operated in the Gulf of Mexico and Mid-Atlantic regions.

- The Flota del Golfo (FG) contained bottom-longliners and other hook and line vessels that targeted bottom fish and reef fish in the Campeche Bank and in the nearshore waters.

- Finally, the Flota de Plataforma (FP) was comprised of nearshore vessels, which possessed a wide variety of gear types such as traps, hook and line, trawls, and gill nets. The FP targeted a complement of high-value, nearshore species such as shrimp, spiny lobster, sponge, reef fish, and crab.

The catch of the FCP (the fleet most supported by the preferential trading agreements with the former Soviet Union via advantageous oil prices) was primarily intended for domestic consumption, whereas the high-value catch of the FAC, FG, and FP was destined for lucrative export markets and represented an important source of new export revenue.

Although an impressive accomplishment, the development of the modern Cuban commercial fishing fleet was fraught with bad timing. This was particularly true for the FCP, FAC, and FG. Virtually all coastal nations in the Americas imposed 200-mile limits for their territorial waters in the late 1970s. With few exceptions, the exclusive rights claimed by these coastal nations excluded access by all other countries to the fisheries resources found in their territorial seas. With access denied (there were only a few exceptions throughout the region), Cuba was left with a stable of large operationally-costly vessels (FCP), which were then forced into the role of only being able to operate in the even more costly open-ocean regions. The high cost nature of the fleet, coupled with being forced to target low-valued stocks, produced an economically less efficient operation. As a result, the FCP (which targeted low-valued species) was almost totally dependent on relatively inexpensive Soviet fuel oil in order to stay operational. Such Soviet assistance did allow the FCP to continue operations for a number of years, even as the aging and costly fleet continued by necessity to target low-value species for domestic markets, rather than generating export revenue as was the case for the other fleet components.

The breakup of the Soviet Union and the tightening of U.S. embargo regulations against Cuba in the early 1990s caused the virtual shutdown of the FCP and reduced operations of the FAC and FG. Thus, during the first few years immediately following the breakup of the Soviet Union (in Cuba this is referred to as the "special period") total fleet operations were constrained. In particular, the majority of vessels comprising the FCP were standing idle in Havana harbor. The cost of operation and maintenance, coupled with the lack of fuel, was fatal to FCP fleet operations. A few former FCP trawlers are reportedly being used as transport vessels. Thus, the distant-water fleet Cuban landings of all forms of finfish and shellfish decreased dramatically, with the majority of this decrease associated with reduced operations of the FCP and declines in landings of pelagic species. The vessels, which comprised the former FP, continue to operate in the nearshore waters producing a wide variety of high-valued species, the most important of which are spiny lobster, shrimp, sponge, and reef fish. The FAC and FG also continue to operate and target pelagics such as mackerels, tunas, swordfish, reef fish, and sharks. During 1996, 12 FCP trawlers were yet targeting hake in Canadian waters. A long-standing fisheries agreement with Canada provides access by the Cuban fleet. Thus, the high-valued species harvested by the remaining fleet components, particularly the FP, represent the economic backbone of the commercial fishing industry in Cuba today.

CHANGES IN MANAGEMENT STRUCTURE AND STRATEGIES

The impact of the economic crisis of the 1990s in Cuba and the impact of the sudden lack of resources with which to maintain the existing fleets, particularly the distant-water fleet, contributed to a situation whereby the landing and processing of seafood products was significantly impaired. During the period from 1992 through 1994, the total volume of fisheries catch declined by 20%, while the volume of seafood exports declined by 8%. The sale of seafood into the domestic market also declined 8%. These

symptoms were the result, as well, of various underlying problems, including technical deficiencies in the fleets, organizational problems in the processing sector, stagnation and obsolescence in the shipbuilding sector, and insufficient integration of scientific research into the management process.

In response to this situation, a series of measures were instituted in 1995 by the Cuban government and within the fishing sector itself. The measures included organizational changes necessary for Cuba's integration into the new world economic order, as well as measures designed to improve efficiency in production, commercial activity, and financial management in order to ensure competitiveness of Cuban products in the world market.

These measures included:

- Upper level administrative changes.

- Establishment of a clear, flexible, and dynamic development strategy for fisheries management.

- Implementation of a new organizational structure.

- Provide training regarding new management techniques for directors and managerial personnel.

- Strengthen the links between the Cuban Ministry of the Fishing Industry (Ministerio de la Industria Pesquera, MIP) and the fisheries productions units.

- Imposition of regulatory guidelines to better ensure sustainable development of Cuba's fisheries.

- Decentralization of production and financial management responsibilities.

Structure

The Ministry of the Fishing Industry (MIP) is the agency in charge of directing, implementing, and governing the policy of the State and Government concerning research on and the conservation, extraction, breeding, processing, and marketing of fishing resources.

The former structure of the MIP did not correspond to the new management direction encouraged by the

Figure 1. New Organizational Structure of the Cuban Ministry of the Fishing Industry

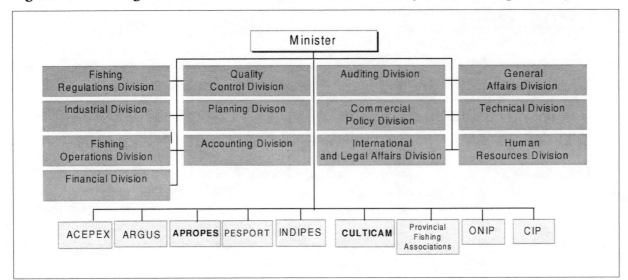

above changes, nor was it compatible with a newly instituted work method and strategy. The myriad of management entities within MIP — the enterprises engaged in fishing, processing, marketing, shipbuilding, export/import, etc. — were organized vertically with ten distinct management levels between the Minister and the actual producers. The large number of subordinate enterprises and the excessive vertical integration complicated and slowed the entire management process. The former structure made the systematic monitoring and controlling of the fishing industry virtually impossible.

With the objective of improving economic efficiency and sustainable use of fisheries resources, a change in management focus was applied. Probably the most significant change in the MIP structure was an attempt to decentralize the day-to-day operations of the harvesting sector. The MIP was left in charge of the legal and regulatory activities (i.e., administrative functions, enforcement, stock assessment, etc.), while the production enterprises were delegated to control most day-to-day productive activities and services. To facilitate the introduction of policy changes aimed at decentralization, a new overall organizational structure was instituted within the MIP. The central idea of the new MIP structure is to incorporate modern entrepreneurial and management techniques via more horizontal and flexible structures — Associations. These Associations were created for the pur-

pose of bringing decision-making and responsibility closer to the point of production, thereby increasing the efficiency of the economic activities (i.e., fleet operations) related to fisheries harvest.

The new MIP structure (Figure 1) consists of numerous Divisions, fisheries-related Associations, the National Inspection Office (ONIP) and the Fisheries Research Center (CIP). All of these units are subordinate to the Minister. The Associations consist of 15 Provincial Fishing Associations (PFAs) and six other Associations, which have specific logistical responsibilities. The latter six Associations (and their key responsibility) include:

- ACEPEX (fishery exports);

- ARGUS (shipbuilding);

- APROPES (supply distribution and fishery imports);

- PESPORT (management of the FAC, FG, and FCP fleets);

- INDIPES (seafood processing and domestic distribution); and

- CULTICAM (shrimp culture).

A Provincial Fishing Association (PFA) is located within each province, including the Isle of Youth. These PFAs are responsible for producing shellfish and finfish landings in compliance with the species-specific harvest plans. These plans are developed by the associations themselves, then consulted and approved with/by the Executive Board of the MIP. The PFAs have independent legal and jurisdictional authority, with independent control over productive resources (i.e., vessels, fuel, supplies, ice, labor, etc.). The PFAs also have control over the number of vessels, as well as ensuring the enforcement of size restrictions, gear restrictions, closed seasons, etc. The other six Associations provide the necessary resources and logistical support for the PFAs. They also assist in feasibility studies of proposed projects with the overall purpose of broadening fisheries market potential, finding new business opportunities, and further developing other activities of common interest.

Strategies

The PFAs have been given an unprecedented amount of autonomy regarding day-to-day operations of the fleet. Recent changes have interjected the notion of "profit maximizing" among vessel captains and crew. For example, each PFA has a target level of annual production for each species. With a fixed annual per-unit price per each species, the PFA (which manages a given number of vessels targeting species indigenous to the region) attempts to achieve the harvest objective at the minimum cost possible. The unit price for the target species is set with MIP staff and representatives from each PFA. In the case of the domestic market, the price is set in correspondence with operational costs, qualitative value of the product, and governmental pricing policies. In the case of foreign markets (exports), prices are determined according to costs and international market supply and demand. The Association sells the landings to the enterprises charged with fisheries product commercialization, ACEPEX and INDIPES.

Each vessel's trip expenses (i.e., ice, bait, tackle, etc.) are then covered with the revenue earned from the trip by that vessel (major repairs to the hull and deck equipment are paid for by the PFA). The Association returns the difference between total revenue and trip costs (referred to as "margin") to the individual vessels. Each vessel's captain distributes the margin for that trip to the crew via a predetermined share system. The captain uses his discretion to determine the

share each crew member receives. Thus, the crew has an incentive to minimize costs such that the net returns back to the vessel, and the crew, is maximized. The crew share is reportedly paid in dollars (20%) and pesos (80%). This process, which applies across all PFAs, is a radical departure from the previous system where the captain and crew members received a fixed annual salary along with perks determined via a complicated and generally ineffective incentive system. Because the margin is the main source of income to the crew, a strong incentive therefore exists to operate the vessels as efficiently as possible.

In addition, the price received by the vessel can be a function of quality. So, a high premium is placed on handling the catch such that quality is preserved. This new payment system for the PFAs, referred to as the "Special Working Contract," is as yet evolving and very much at the trial stage. The FP fleet, which produces the majority of high-value, exportable fin-fish and shellfish products, is the primary participant is this new program.

The structural changes instituted at the PFA level have increased the efficiency of production activity, but have created a risk situation for overexploitation of coastal fisheries resources. This results from the natural inclination to increase productivity and, thus, income, under the "Special Working Contract." The previous set of fisheries regulations, established in 1936, had become outdated with respect to the current fisheries industry. Thus, the need to develop a new regulatory framework became evident. In September 1996, the new Decreto Ley 164 ("Decree Law") went into effect. This new regulatory framework incorporates a number of new features and resolutions, including:

- Creation of a broader judicial mandate for fisheries management.

- Introduction of fisheries licensing procedures for commercial, recreational, and research purposes.

- Adoption of measures to protect threatened and endangered marine species such as sea turtles, manatees, and black coral.

- Increased monitoring and enforcement of marine resource conservation and coastal water quality measures.

- Introduction and enforcement of system of fines and penalties to ensure sustainable use of fisheries resources.

The 1996 Decree Law also provided for the establishment of the Advisory Commission on Fishing, which consults with the Minister on issues related to administration, organization, and rational use of coastal fisheries resources. Recent measures established by the Commission address creation of protected areas, species-specific closed seasons, minimum legal sizes for given species, prohibition of retention of potentially toxic species, recreational fishing quotas, gear restrictions, licensing/authorization guidelines, and sanitary/health regulations for processors. To ensure regulatory control and compliance with these measures, the MIP created the National Office for Fishing Inspection (ONIP), whose mission is to enforce the conservation and rational use of aquatic resources within Cuba's commercial zone, territorial seas, and inland waters. The ONIP utilizes 15 Provincial Offices for Fishing Inspection, with over 200 inspectors and specialists distributed on the basis of the economic importance of fishing among the provinces.

The adoption of the 1996 Decree Law, formation of the Advisory Commission on Fishing, restructuring of the MIP, creation of the Provincial Fishing Associations, and implementation of the "Special Working Contract" has reportedly resulted in a increased landings, improvement in the operational efficiency of the fleets, enhancement of the distribution of seafood products into the domestic market, and increased export revenues derived from seafood (Table 1). During the 1996-1999 period, total landings increased by 9.4%, seafood distributions to the domestic market by 5.3%, and exports by 6.9%. In addition, fuel utilized by fishing vessels per ton of catch was reduced from 0.9 tons to 0.5 tons, thus providing evidence that incentives to minimize operational costs have succeeded. The advances made since the advent of the "Special Period" demonstrate not only that the strategies adopted were effective, but that it is possible for a state enterprise to come back from the point of crisis.

Table 1. Recent Statistics on the Cuban Fishing Industry

Average Annual Growth between 1995 and 1999 (%)	
Total catch	9.4
Total catch, aquaculture (finfish)	30.0
Distribution into the domestic market	5.3
Total income	8.3
Exports	6.9
Industrial utilization levels of lobster and shrimp—65% and 84% respectively.	
The aquaculture catch reached 80,500 tons in 1999, the highest in its history.	
Fuel utilization per ton of catch was reduced to 0.467, for an average annual decrease of 15.5% between 1995-99.	

CONCLUSIONS

The Cuban fishing industry, an important source of high-valued tropical seafood for the world market, has experienced considerable change during the last decade. In an attempt to enhance the economic efficiency of the industry, the Ministry of the Fishing Industry has been substantially restructured. A key goal of this restructuring process is to decentralize the fleet management process, thereby providing incentives for vessel operations to minimize costs, enhance production, and increase revenues generated by the commercial fishing fleets. Since 1995, total fisheries catch has increased 9.4%, total income derived from fishing has increased 8.3%, and seafood exports have increased 6.9%.

REFERENCES

Adams, C.M. *An Overview of the Cuban Commercial Fishing Industry and Implications to the Florida Seafood Industry of Renewed Trade.* IW98-3. International Agricultural Trade and Development

Center, Food and Resource Economics Department. University of Florida. Gainesville, FL. 1998.

Food and Agricultural Organization of the United Nations. *Yearbook of Fishery Statistics: Landings and Catches.* Rome (various years).

Food and Agricultural Organization of the United Nations. *Yearbook of Fishery Statistics: Commodities.* Rome (various years).

García, A. Unpublished descriptive information on the Cuban fisheries industry. Centro de Investigaciones de la Economía Internacional, Universidad de la Habana. Habana, Cuba. 1996.

García, A. and P. Sánchez. "Cambios recientes en la industria pesquera cubana: Su contribución a la eficiencia." Paper presented at the seminar Role of the Agricultural Sector in Cuba's Integration into the Global Economy and Its Future Economic Structures: Implications for Florida and U.S. Agriculture, Washington, D.C., 1998.

Ministerio de la Industria Pesquera (MIP). Unpublished landings data for various years. La Habana, Cuba.

BALANCE OF PAYMENTS: CONCEPTS AND MEASUREMENTS

Armando S. Linde

I am grateful for this opportunity to participate in this panel on issues related to the measurement of Cuba's balance of payments position. My colleagues on the panel will elaborate on various problems that arise in interpreting Cuba's official balance of payments (BOP) statistics. My job today is to provide a conceptual framework for their presentations.

To begin, I will offer some thoughts on why the analysis of a country's balance of payments is important. Everyone here of course is familiar with these issues and so I can be brief. But in thinking about what we can learn from BOP data, it is always crucial to remind ourselves of the potential weaknesses of these data and the care with which policy decisions need to be taken on the basis of these data. I will next discuss the analytical presentation of balance of payments statistics; and conclude with an example of how macroeconomic imbalances can reveal themselves in a country's external accounts using Mexico's BOP data for the periods before and after the 1994/95 crisis as an example.

DEFINITION AND USES OF BALANCE OF PAYMENTS (BOP) STATISTICS

The BOP is a statistical statement designed to provide, for a specific period of time, a systematic record of a country's transactions with the rest of the world.

BOP data are most important for national and international policy formulation. External aspects— such as payments imbalances and inward and outward foreign investment—play a leading role in economic and other policy decisions in the increasingly interdependent world economy. Such data are also used for analytical studies, for example, to determine the causes of payments imbalances and the need to implement adjustment measures; relationships between merchandise trade and direct investment; aspects of international trade in services; external debt problems; income payments and growth; and effects of exchange rate changes on current and capital account flows. Similarly, BOP data constitute an indispensable link in the compilation of data for various components of the national accounts (e.g., production accounts, income accounts, capital accounts, and the related measurement of national wealth).

Careful analysis of the balance of payments is particularly important when we suspect that inappropriate economic policies—such as excessive fiscal stimulus, an imprudent monetary stance, an overvalued exchange rate, or rising labor costs unmatched by productivity gains—are leading to rising consumption and an excess of overall savings over investment in the economy. These imbalances between savings and investment can have potentially destabilizing economic and financial effects. If they are short-lived, owing perhaps to reversible policy mistakes or temporary shocks, rather than to decisions made solely on the basis of political expediency, economic entities can endure adverse policy conditions for a time by accumulating indebtedness domestically or with foreign creditors. But if inadequate policies persist and financial confidence erodes, economic growth eventually would slow, inflation and unemployment would rise, and the country's official holdings of foreign exchange could begin to decline rapidly. Early awareness of symptoms of deterioration in a country's external payments position and early diagnosis of the cause of the deterioration can make all the difference between having to deal with a full-blown currency crisis requiring economically painful correction, or weathering financial turbulence with more politically manageable policy adjustments.

BASIC BOP CONCEPTS, PROBLEMS IN DATA COMPILATION, AND CLASSIFICATIONS

Concepts and Data Problems

An *economy* is comprised of *resident* economic entities (people, corporations, governments) that trade and invest with, or transfer resources—such as grants or gifts— to *nonresident* economic entities (persons, corporations, governments, who live or operate outside the country's borders).

A basic convention of a BOP statement is the double entry accounting system in which every transaction is represented, ideally, by two entries of equal value. If, for example, an exporter receives foreign currency in payment for goods, a credit entry would be recorded in the BOP accounts for the export of goods and an offsetting debit entry would be recorded for the exporter's increase in foreign currency bank balances (or other forms of foreign currency assets).

The BOP accounting system requires that both entries for a transaction be recorded at uniform values and in the same time period. To satisfy this requirement, transactions are recorded at market value, and the time of recording is typically the point at which a change of ownership occurs. In practice, it is difficult to achieve these theoretical ideals. Different data sources are often used to measure the two entries in a transaction, and these data sources may not reflect uniform valuations and times of recording. In addition, coverage of transactions by data sources often is incomplete, a factor that results in omissions in the BOP accounts.

Income on external financial assets and liabilities is recorded on an accrued (earned) basis. This concept, which is broader than the actual payment of dividend and interest, covers dividends due for payment, interest accrued, and unremitted profits of direct investment enterprises. Again, what is theoretically desirable may not feasible in practice, and the BOP compiler may need to work with cash data for some

transactions and accrual data for others, which again will give rise to discrepancies in the BOP statement.

Another source of difficulty in compiling BOP data is the exchange rate used to convert transactions and stock positions denoted in one currency to the currency, or unit of account (usually the US dollar), in which the BOP accounts are compiled. Ideally, this conversion is made at the midpoint exchange rate applicable to the transaction and at the midpoint rate applicable on the date on which the stock position is measured, but in practice this may not always be possible.

Another difficulty is that controls also have been relied on by countries to slow inward capital movements when these are believed to have undesired effects on the conduct of monetary policy, or to stop capital flight when governments feel unable to deal with these outflows with policies that would restore macroeconomic equilibrium. With rare exceptions, these restrictions can be easily circumvented through all sorts of devices, such as under invoicing of exports, over invoicing of imports, parallel markets, and outright bribes, to name a few. Needless to say, recourse to these devices hampers the ability of data compilers to produce accurate and consistent statistics. And without good data it is difficult for policy makers to make an informed judgement on the effectiveness of a particular macroeconomic stance. At the same time, it is not too difficult to see that, with or without good data, the imposition of restrictions on trade and exchange transactions detracts from the making of sound investment decisions and drives entrepreneurial activity towards the pursuit of rent-seeking activities, with predictably negative consequences on economic efficiency and performance.

In sum, incomplete or overlapping coverage, nonuniform prices, inconsistent times of recording, inconsistent conversion practices, and trade and exchange restrictions that create incentives to conduct transactions through informal channels, all can lead to distortions and inconsistencies in BOP statistics and result in sometime large errors and omissions in the BOP statement. The foregoing suggests that BOP statistics, or statistics in general, should not be taken at face value, and that the time spent uncovering and analyzing data weaknesses is well worth the effort.

These potential data collection problems should not discourage us from looking at BOP numbers, albeit with a proper degree of caution. As we shall see below in discussing the Mexican currency crisis of 1994/95, incipient imbalances may well manifest themselves in the external accounts well before a full-blown crisis hits. This was the case with the December 1994 peso devaluation. In fact, early warnings of impending BOP pressures were also visible in the late 1990s in Argentina, Brazil, South Korea, Indonesia, Thailand and, for that matter, in the continuing external imbalances in the United States and Japan. For all of its statistical shortcomings, a BOP statement is a key macro prudential indicator: it can send an early signal that problems are brewing well before these become serious. Moreover, data deficiencies in BOP statements of individual countries tend to persist over time and tend to be of the same kind and, therefore, in analyzing BOP accounts these deficiencies would not necessarily conceal the emergence of an external imbalance.

BOP Classifications

Turning to the statistical framework of BOP statements, BOP statistics are arranged within a coherent structure to facilitate their utilization for multiple purposes, prominent among which are linkages with national accounts, debt and equity markets, and the net reserve position of the monetary authorities. These linkages are of critical importance in designing economic and financial programs, and in monitoring the implementation of these programs and, generally, the evolution of the economy. According to the IMF's *Balance of Payments Manual*,[1] the standard components of the BOP are: (a) the current account, which covers transactions in goods and services, income, and current transfers; and (b) the capital and financial accounts, which include capital transfers and other nonfinancial assets, direct investment, portfolio and other investments, and official reserve

assets and liabilities. In practice, though, to facilitate the design and monitoring of fiscal and monetary policies, and the management of the public debt and international reserves, the BOP is divided into three main components:

1. the current account;
2. the capital and financial accounts; and
3. changes in the net reserve assets of the monetary authorities (which in the Fund's BOP *Manual* are included in the financial accounts).

Each of these components are discussed briefly below.

The Current Account: The current account covers all transactions (other than those registered as financial items) that involve economic values and occur between resident and nonresident entities, or that are provided or acquired without a quid pro quo. Specifically, the major classifications are goods, services, income, and current transfers.

Goods trade involves mainly merchandise that is exported to, or imported from, nonresidents by residents and that, with a few exceptions, undergo changes in ownership. Other types of transactions classified under goods include goods crossing the frontier for processing abroad and subsequent reimport; repair activity on goods provided to or received from nonresidents on ships, aircraft, etc.; goods procured in ports by nonresident carriers, such as fuel, provisions, and supplies; and nonmonetary gold, which, when not used as a means of payment, is treated the same way as any other commodity.

Services comprise mainly transportation, travel, provision of insurance, fees and commissions for financial services, royalties and license fees, and government services such as expenditures of embassies and consulates.

Income includes compensation of employees which is paid to nonresident workers (e.g., border, seasonal, and other short-term workers), and investment in-

---

1. For full details of the standard components of a BOP statement, please consult the Fifth Edition of the IMF *Balance of Payments Manual*, Table 7.

come receipts and payments on external financial assets and liabilities. Included in the latter are receipts and payments on direct investment, portfolio and other investments, and receipts on reserve assets.

Current transfers consist of two major categories: transfers between governments or private parties in the form of grants or gifts whether in cash or in kind; and workers' remittances, which can be quite a large item in the BOP of countries with significant numbers of its citizens working abroad and considered residents there. India, China, Turkey, some of the countries of the former Soviet Union, and Mexico and Haiti in the Western Hemisphere are examples of countries benefiting from large inflows of remittances For many developing countries, particularly the poorest ones in Africa, current transfers in the form of foreign aid is one of the most significant components of their external accounts.

The Capital and Financial Accounts: The capital and financial accounts cover all transactions that involve the receipt or payment of transfers and acquisition or disposal of nonproduced, nonfinancial assets (capital account); and all transactions associated with changes of ownership in the foreign financial assets and liabilities of an economy (financial account).

In the **capital account**, a capital transfer, as distinguished from a current transfer, is one that should result in a commensurate change in the stocks of assets of one or both parties to the transaction. A current transfer, on the other hand, reduces the income and consumption possibilities of the donor and does the opposite to the recipient. Debt forgiveness is an example of a capital transfer; transactions associated with assets that may be used for production of goods and services but have not themselves been produced, such as patents, copyrights, trademarks, franchises, etc., are also considered capital account items.

The functional classification of the **financial account** comprises three main categories of investment: direct investment, portfolio investment, and other investment. Depending on the type of analysis for which BOP data are being utilized, it is sometimes helpful to make a distinction between public and private movements of capital. In those cases, the capital and financial accounts are presented on the basis of four major categories: direct investment; official capital (which would include all governmental activity with nonresidents, with placements of sovereign debt shown as the principal item); private capital, both short and medium-term; and errors and omissions.

Direct investment is used to register a transaction when an individual investor seeks a significant voice in the management of an enterprise operating outside his or her resident economy by providing a substantial amount of the equity capital of the enterprise, and/or by supplying additional capital for expansion. Over the last decade, direct investment has become a major component of the balance of payments of those countries which have undergone significant structural change. To the extent that these so-called emerging market economies have reduced their government's financing needs, updated their budget practices and tax systems, redeployed assets to the private sector, opened their economies to competition, and reformed their product and labor markets, they have benefited immensely from the advantages of the global economy, becoming recipients of large inflows of foreign direct investment.

Portfolio investment consists of cross-border investment in equity and debt securities (other than direct investment). In the current fifth edition of the IMF's *Balance of Payments Manual*, the formal distinction between long-term and short-term investment is not made for portfolio investment because it was thought that formal maturity is not likely to be a significant factor affecting the behavior of the components of the category. However, in the aftermath of the last Mexican devaluation, and more recently after the Asian Crisis and the Russian debt default, there has been a call for the IMF and the World Bank to work together to develop a set of guidelines on public debt management to assist countries in their efforts to reduce financial vulnerability. This work is now well under way. In addition, in response to large-scale changes occurring in recent decades in the size and nature of financial derivative markets, a number of modifications have been introduced in the Fund's BOP *Manual.* An important change was the recognition of interest rate swaps and forward rate agreements as financial assets and the recording of net cash settlements resulting from these contracts as financial transactions rather than investment income flows. In this connection, a new functional category, "financial derivatives," has been created for the BOP.

Other investment is a residual group which comprise many different kinds of investment, including trade credits, loans, currency and deposits.

For purposes of this paper, I will follow the presentation in the IMF's *Balance of Payments Manual*, with one exception. As noted earlier, the *Manual* classifies the net official reserves of the monetary authorities as a component of the capital and financial account. In the rest of this text and in the tables, changes in the net official reserves (assets minus liabilities) are treated as a separate line in the BOP statement. This separate line is often referred to by many in the trade as the **bottom line** of the BOP statement, because it provides one of the clearest indications, together with price data, of imbalances in the economy, and is the trigger for changes in the external value of a country's currency when the imbalances become acute.

Finally, in BOP statements, the standard practice is to show separately an item for **net errors and omissions**. Labeled by some compilers as a balancing item or statistical discrepancy, that item is intended as an offset to the overstatements or understatements of the recorded components. Some of the errors and omissions that occur in the course of compilation usually offset one another. Therefore, the size of the residual item does not necessarily provide any indication of the overall accuracy of the statement. However, large and variable residual items can be indicative, for example, of capital flight in the face of an impending devaluation, or of unrecorded outflows to bypass exchange controls. Positive net errors and omissions can be indicative of proceeds from illicit activities.

Changes in the Net Reserve Assets of the Monetary Authorities: Examining movements in the net reserve position of the monetary authorities is an essential element in the analysis of an economy's external position. Reserve assets consist of those external assets that are readily available to and controlled by

monetary authorities, usually central banks, for direct financing of payments imbalances, for directly regulating the magnitude of such imbalances through intervention in exchange markets to affect the currency exchange rate, and for creating confidence in the strength of the economy and its currency.

Typical reserve assets include monetary gold, Special Drawing Rights (SDRs), reserve positions in the IMF, foreign exchange assets (consisting of currency and deposits), and other liquid claims. It needs to be emphasized that reserve assets always refer to assets that actually exist. This is important to note because governments have been known to attempt to "dress up" the country's international reserve position, particularly at times when the currency is under pressure. For example, foreign exchange that could be obtained under swap agreements and other lines of credit, including undrawn balances with the IMF under stand-by arrangements or other IMF facilities, do not constitute existing claims. On the other hand, assets that are pledged, committed, earmarked, set aside in sinking funds, sold forward, or otherwise encumbered by the holders are nonetheless existing assets and are not precluded on those grounds alone from being included in reserve assets. However, because such arrangements may affect the availability of the assets involved, supplementary information concerning the arrangements is necessary to get a clear picture of the real strength of the reserve position. In the same vein, short-term liabilities of the central bank, including use of IMF credits, outstanding loans from correspondent banks, payments arrears, and other short-term obligations of the central bank, are netted out of its gross international reserves to arrive at the BOP "bottom line."

Timeliness in reporting reserve data is an issue that also needs to be considered. Accurate data that are reported only with several weeks' lag can be of little help in establishing or restoring financial confidence. Also, some central banks rely on the dubious practice of using short-term nondeliverable forward contracts (NDFs) with commercial banks, as opposed to buying/selling spot, to conduct foreign exchange intervention. Moreover, whereas central bank reserves are usually reported with a one- to four-week lag, NDFs often are published with as much as a four-month lag to avoid disclosing the scale and maturity profile of NDF-based operations to market participants. It is, of course, not expected that central banks disclose the extent of their involvement in the exchange market while it is in progress. However, NDFs and other similar operations and the lags in reporting them create a misleading picture of the central bank's reserve position and intervention policy. One of the principal lessons of the Asian crisis is the importance of central bank transparency, and central banks that traditionally have chosen to conduct their operations in great secrecy are slowly coming around to understanding that full integration with world financial markets demands much greater transparency than in the past.

BOP ANALYSIS: MEXICO, 1994/95

An integrated system of accounts covering national income and expenditure, as well as financial flows and associated stocks, lies at the heart of the macroeconomic appraisal and analysis of the economic performance of any economy. For each sector of the economy, the transactions between its members can be divided into two categories: transactions arising in the course of producing or acquiring goods, and financial transactions.

Imbalances in these activities are reflected in the domestic price level and in the country's external position. In open economies, excess demand pressures spill over quickly into the balance of payments. In these circumstances, a gap would emerge between national savings and investment that would need to be financed with external savings. In the BOP this "domestic resource gap" would give rise to, and be the mirror image of, a current account deficit, which in turn would need to be financed through a combinations of capital inflows—public or private—and/or a drawdown of the net international reserves of the central bank.

If external savings are not available because the country's creditworthiness has eroded, its official reserves have been depleted, or because contagion effects have denied it access to international capital markets, the adjustment to these new circumstances would occur almost instantaneously. In the external sector, trade credits and other types of financing would dry up, imports would contract, and the external current account deficit would narrow or disappear, or might even turn into a surplus, depending on the extent of the downturn in domestic activity and on any exchange rate action that might be taken to deal with the situation. On the domestic side, consumption would slow faster than capital formation, and the savings/investment gap would narrow.

Less open economies also can be engulfed very quickly in full-blown BOP crises, even if uncertainties regarding economic management, or political turmoil do not spillover immediately into the current account but instead produce capital flight. Strangely enough, when facing a run on the currency, central banks often bet the wrong way by choosing to defend the exchange rate, experiencing in the process a punishing loss of international reserves.

Although a major BOP event can unfold very rapidly, it is often years in the making. Many countries have been large net borrowers from the rest of the world for prolonged periods without adverse economic effects. Chile, for instance, had been posting current account deficits of the order of 5.5-6.0 percent of GDP for almost the entire decade of the 1990s, while GDP was growing at a rapid rate with declining inflation. The country's pursuit of sound policies, including budget surpluses, a cautious monetary stance, and trade liberalization, privatization, and other structural changes had not been lost on investors, who happily more than covered current account deficits with direct investment. In analyzing the BOP, therefore, and, in particular, the sustainability of any specific current account situation, it is important to consider the determinants of financial flows. These flows, as in the case of Chile, might be directly related to increased private capital formation in the form of direct investment, bank loans, or bonds issued in capital markets. While private financing flows tend to provide greater assurance of the sustainability of a given current account deficit than government borrowing, it is not a foregone conclusion that this is always the case. There can be circumstances in which inward movements of private capital can be quite disruptive, if they flow into the domestic banking system attracted by favorable interest rate spreads at the short-end, and if banks, when placing these loanable funds, do not appropriately weigh risk, or are poorly regulated and supervised. This was the situation in Mexico in the period leading to the late-1994 peso devaluation, and it was also at the core of the Asian economic and financial upheaval in 1997-98.

Turning to the events that led to the Mexican crisis, and how these could be discerned in the country's external accounts, the process of macroeconomic stabilization and structural transformation in Mexico that began in the wake of the 1982 debt crisis accelerated during 1988-93. The authorities' strategy was aimed at attaining external viability and laying the foundation for private sector-led growth. It was based on the following elements: the maintenance of tight financial policies; the use of the exchange rate as a nominal anchor; a comprehensive program of structural reforms; and a major restructuring of the external debt. These stabilization and reform policies produced remarkable results, and private capital inflows surged to an average of over 6 percent of GDP in 1990-93. Mexico therefore entered 1994 with a strengthened economy. But weaknesses remained—and they contained the seeds of the crisis that broke at the end of the year. In particular, the external current account deficit, running at 6.5 percent of GDP a year in 1993, was very large by most standards. It had deteriorated gradually from a position of rough balance in 1987-88; and although reflecting to some extent a rise in investment that could be expected to boost future output and net exports, the deterioration was nevertheless driven by a rapid growth in domestic consumer spending. Thus, between 1987-88 and 1993, private saving had fallen by as much as 7.5 percent of GDP. Also, associated with the widening of the current account deficit was a substantial real effective appreciation of the peso.

The sustainability of external current account deficits of this magnitude mainly to finance domestic consumption was clearly questionable, and was highly vulnerable to a sudden reversal of capital flows. Then in January 1994 there was an uprising in Chiapas; this was followed by the assassination of presidential candidate Colosio in late March; another political assassination in September; and a second Chiapas up-

rising in December. There were also significant shortcomings in Mexico's policy response. Facing significant outflows, the monetary impact of official reserve loss was sterilized, leaving interest rates virtually unchanged for most of the year; there was an attempt to maintain the peg through the issuance of short-term instruments indexed to the U.S. dollar (Tesobonos); even more damaging, political considerations led to rapid credit expansion by the government-owned development banks to the private sector; and finally, the peso was allowed to float freely in late December but only after Bank of Mexico had exhausted its international reserves.

Tables 1 and 2 show the rising trend in the current account deficit through the early 1990s, peaking at 7 percent of GDP in 1994, and the sharp drop in 1995 to close to equilibrium, in the wake of the devaluation. Most of the current account deficit in 1994 was financed with a loss of reserves and proceeds from privatization. In 1995, output contracted by more than 6 percent and inflation soared to 50 percent.

In contrast with the 1982 debt crisis, when it took several years before output recovered on a sustained basis, the economy showed much greater resilience and flexibility in both the product and labor markets, with the result that a strong supply response to the exchange rate depreciation was clearly in evidence by the last quarter of 1995. Real GDP growth averaged 6 percent a year in 1996-97. Mexico also has coped well with the contagion effect of the Asian crisis. The external current account deficit has stabilized at about 3 percent of GDP in the last four years, with foreign direct investment covering three-quarters of the deficit. Inflation is down to less than 10 percent a year, and output is expanding by some 4-5 percent in each of the last two years.

CONCLUSION

To conclude, in signaling incipient imbalances and later providing an analytical framework to aid policy makers, the BOP statement is among the most reliable statistical tools available. Because compilers depend on various sources to arrive at the BOP statement, the accuracy of the BOP account depends on the effort that is made to reduce discrepancies and inconsistencies and, in using BOP data, analysts need to be aware of its potential weaknesses.

Table 1. Mexico: Summary Balance of Payments *(In billions of U.S. dollars)*

	1990	1991	1992	1993	1994	1995	1996	1997	1998
Current account	**-7.4**	**-14.9**	**-24.8**	**-23.4**	**-29.7**	**-1.6**	**-2.3**	**-7.4**	**-16.0**
Merchandise trade balance, f.o.b.	-0.9	-7.3	-15.9	-13.5	18.5	7.1	6.5	0.6	-7.9
Exports	30.4	30.9	32.3	35.4	40.4	53.4	65.5	74.1	74.9
Of which:									
Petroleum and derivatives	10.1	8.2	8.3	7.4	7.4	8.4	11.7	11.3	7.1
Manufactures	16.9	19.8	21.5	25.2	29.9	40.4	49.8	58.5	63.5
Imports	-31.3	-38.2	-48.2	-48.9	-58.9	-46.3	-59.0	-73.5	-82.8
Factor income	-8.6	-8.6	-9.6	-10.9	-13.0	-13.3	-13.9	-12.8	-13.5
Other services and transfers	2.1	1.0	0.7	1.0	1.8	4.6	5.1	4.7	5.5
Financial account	**8.4**	**22.6**	**16.0**	**27.2**	**10.9**	**0.3**	**7.6**	**19.2**	**17.3**
Official capital	-0.2	3.0	1.5	7.5	-0.4	0.4	-3.5	-1.9	1.6
Medium- and long-term borrowing	8.4	1.2	-3.8	1.6	1.4	3.1	9.3	-3.3	1.5
Disbursements	...	...	...	...	...	...	22.7	15.1	13.2
Amortization	...	...	...	...	...	...	13.4	18.4	11.7
Other, including short-term borrowing	-8.6	2.8	5.3	5.9	-1.8	-2.8	-12.8	1.4	0.1
Private sector	8.6	19.6	14.5	26.3	12.2	-0.1	11.1	21.1	15.7
Direct investment	2.5	4.8	4.4	4.9	11.0	9.5	9.2	12.8	10.2
Portfolio investment	2.0	6.3	4.8	10.7	...	...	1.0	3.7	5.0
Other investment	4.1	8.5	5.3	10.7	1.2	-9.6	0.9	4.6	0.5
Errors and omissions	2.5	-0.1	10.7	-3.3	...	...	1.1	1.7	2.3
Net international reserves (increase -)	-3.4	-7.6	-1.9	-7.1	17.9	1.3	-6.3	-13.5	-3.7
Memorandum items:									
External current account balance (in percent of GDP)	-3.1	-5.2	-7.5	-6.4	-7.0	-0.5	-0.7	-1.9	-3.8
Real GDP (percentage change)	4.4	3.6	2.8	0.6	4.4	-6.2	5.1	6.8	4.8

Source: Bank of Mexico; and Secretariat of Finance and Public Credit.

Table 2. Mexico: Selected Economic Indicators *(In percent of GDP)*

	1990	1991	1992	1993	1994	1995	1996	1997	1998
Gross domestic investment	18.8	19.6	21.5	20.6	21.7	20.0	23.2	26.0	24.0
Gross national savings	15.7	14.4	14.0	14.2	14.7	19.5	22.5	24.2	20.2
External current account balance	-3.1	-5.2	-7.5	-6.4	-7.0	-0.5	-0.7	-1.9	-3.8
Public sector balance	-2.8	-0.6	1.6	0.7	-0.1	0.0	0.3	-1.0	-1.2
Real GDP	4.4	3.6	2.8	0.6	4.4	-6.2	5.1	6.8	4.8
CPI (end of year)	29.9	18.8	11.9	8.0	7.0	52.0	27.7	15.7	18.6
Nominal exchange rate [average depreciation (-)]	-12.5	-6.8	-2.5	-0.4	-8.2	-47.4	-14.6	-4.0	-13.3
Real effective exchange rate (CPI based) [average depreciation (-)]	2.2	10.9	7.5	7.4	-3.8	-33.2	13.0	17.9	1.9
Real effective exchange rate (CPI based) [average depreciation (-)]	...	...	...	...	-3.2	-40.8	-3.8	13.0	-0.6
Nominal interest rate, Treasury rate (period average)	26.0	16.7	15.6	15.0	14.5	48.4	31.4	19.8	24.8
Gross international reserves (months of imports)	3.9	5.6	4.8	6.2	1.3	4.5	4.0	5.9	6.0

Source: Bank of Mexico; Secretariat of Finance and Public Credit; and IMF staff projections.

135

CUBA'S BALANCE OF PAYMENTS STATISTICS

Jorge F. Pérez-López[1]

A small, island economy with a limited natural resource base, Cuba has traditionally depended on flows of goods, services and capital from abroad to increase its national wealth.[2] The high degree of openness of the Cuban economy, and hence the disproportionate importance of the external sector, can be illustrated with a few statistics.

In the 1940s and 1950s, for example, the ratio of the value of goods exports to total goods and services produced by the economy (as measured by the gross national product, GNP) averaged about 31 percent, while that of imports to GNP was nearly 26 percent, for a ratio of foreign trade turnover (the sum of exports and imports) to GNP of 57 percent.[3] Moreover, prerevolutionary Cuba had few barriers to incoming foreign investment, and foreign capital was actively sought in many sectors. Foreign capital played a key role in financing the expansion of the sugar industry and national electrical power system, the establishment of telephone service, the construction of railroads, the provision of banking and insurance services, the construction and operation of oil refineries, and the development of the commercial mining industry.

Forty years of socialism have not appreciably changed either the basic openness of the Cuban economy or its reliance on resource flows from abroad to finance development. In 1990, the last year before the serious economic crisis that has enveloped Cuba during the 1990s, merchandise exports accounted for about 28 percent of Cuban gross domestic product (GDP), while imports accounted for about 38 percent, for a ratio of trade turnover to GDP of nearly 66 percent.[4] Foreign assistance—credits, grants, nonrepayable price subsidies—from the former Soviet Union and the socialist countries of Eastern Europe was instrumental in financing economic and social development in the island throughout the 1960s, 1970s and 1980s.

In the 1990s, with the disappearance of the socialist bloc and the loss of foreign resources from these

---

1. This paper expresses only the views of the author. I am grateful to Joaquín Pujol for his detailed comments on an earlier version of the paper and for his assistance in obtaining balance of payments statistics from the International Monetary Fund.

2. The paper draws on earlier work by the author. See, e.g., Jorge F. Pérez-López, "Cuba's Foreign Economic Relationships," in *Cuba: The International Dimension*, Georges Fauriol and Eva Loser, editors, pp. 311-352 (New Brunswick: Transaction Publishers, 1990); "The Cuban Economic Crisis of the 1990s and the External Sector," *Cuba in Transition—Volume 8*, pp. 386-413 (Washington: Association for the Study of the Cuban Economy, 1998); "El sector externo de la economía," in *40 años de revolución: El legado de Castro*, Efrén Córdova, editor, pp. 91-118 (Miami: Ediciones Universal, 1999); and "The Cuban External Sector in the 1990s," in *The United States and Latin America: The New Agenda*, Victor Bulmer-Thomas and James Dunkerley, editors, pp. 267-285 (London: Institute of Latin American Studies, University of London, 1999).

3. The data, which refer to the period 1945-58, are from Carmelo Mesa-Lago, *The Economy of Socialist Cuba* (Albuquerque: University of New Mexico Press, 1981), p. 79.

4. Calculated from data at current prices from *Anuario Estadístico de Cuba 1997* (La Habana: Oficina Nacional de Estadísticas, 1999), p. 84.

countries, Cuba reversed a keystone decision made in the 1960s proscribing foreign ownership of property and began aggressively to seek capital from abroad in the form of foreign direct investment. At the same time, the Cuban government made several policy changes — among them the legalization of the holding and use of foreign currency and the creation of a network of stores where scarce goods can be purchased using foreign currency — that encourage remittances to Cuban citizens from friends and relatives residing abroad. Minister of the Economy and Planning José Luis Rodríguez and Vice President Carlos Lage have identified the lack of foreign financing as the main problem facing the Cuban economy in the second half of the 1990s.[5]

The balance of payments (BOP) is "a record of a country's money receipts from and payments to abroad, the difference between receipts and payments being the surplus or deficit."[6] BOP statistics depict the relationship between the amount of money a nation spends abroad and the income it receives from other nations in a given time period, typically one year. They consist of two accounts: (1) the current account, which tracks activity in exports and imports of goods and services, income earned from investments abroad, payments to foreign investors, and transactions for which there is no offsetting flow of goods or services (e.g., foreign aid, family remittances); and (2) the capital account, which tracks activity in capital flows, such as loans or foreign investment. BOP accounts are based on a double entry system, so that each debit is matched by a credit and therefore the balance of payments is technically always in balance. Nevertheless, the behavior of certain BOP

items or subaccounts (e.g., the goods trade subaccount, the transfers subaccount, the long-term capital subaccount) can be very informative with regard to soundness of economic policies being pursued by a nation.

Government monetary authorities such as ministries of finance or central banks generally prepare BOP statistics. In the case of Cuba, this responsibility has rested with the central bank. As will be shown in this paper, Cuba began to publish official BOP statistics in the late 1940s. Publication of official overall BOP statistics was discontinued in 1959 and did not resume until the mid-1990s.

PREREVOLUTIONARY CUBA'S BOP STATISTICS

The upheavals in international payments after World War I, followed by the outbreak of the Great Depression in the world economy, which was triggered by a financial crisis in the United States in 1929, focused international attention on the importance for countries of compiling BOP statistics as a basis for formulating economic policies.

National BOP statistics were first assembled and published by the League of Nations. With the establishment of the International Monetary Fund (IMF) in 1946, that organization took responsibility for developing a common methodology and for periodically publishing BOP statistics of member countries. The IMF published the first edition of its *Balance of Payments Manual* in 1948 and shortly after began to publish statistics in its *Balance of Payments Yearbook* and in other publications.[7] Cuba was one of the founding members of the IMF and participated actively in the Bretton Woods Conference that the created the IMF and the World Bank. Cuba joined the IMF on March 14, 1946.[8]

---

5. "Cuba necesita más divisas en 1997, advierte ministro," *El Nuevo Herald* (28 September 1996), p. 1B.

6. Poul Host-Madsen, *Balance of Payments: Its Meaning and Uses*, IMF Pamphlet Series No. 9 (Washington: International Monetary Fund, 1967), p. 1. See also Armando Linde, "The Balance of Payments: Concepts and Measurement," in this volume.

7. Poul Host-Madsen, *Macroeconomic Accounts: An Overview*, IMF Pamphlet Series No. 29 (Washington: International Monetary Fund, 1979), p. 35.

8. Joaquín P. Pujol, "Membership Requirements in the IMF: Possible Implications for Cuba," *Cuba in Transition—Volume 1* (Miami: Florida International University for the Association for the Study of the Cuban Economy, 1991), p. 96.

BOP Estimates

According to Wallich,[9] there were three attempts to construct overall BOP for Cuba before 1946, all yielding estimates of questionable quality:

- An unofficial estimate for 1937 by Moisés Porset Dumas published in 1939 in the weekly magazine *Carteles* which covered only a limited number of transactions and whose results were deemed by Pérez Cubillas and Pazos to be "purely conjectural";[10]

- An unofficial estimate by Angel Garri also published in 1939 in *Carteles* that was based on the reported operation of banks with foreign centers; Wallich deemed this exercise to be incomplete;[11] and

- Official estimates by the Cuban government issued in 1938 for bondholders and the U.S. Securities and Exchange Commission to back up the 4.5 percent bonds issued in 1937. Wallich states that the estimates include substantial double counting and deems them to be "without significance."[12]

Wallich himself estimated Cuba's BOP for the period 1919-45 by taking the Cuban bilateral payments balance with the United States — as compiled by U.S. economic statistical agencies — and expanding it into one with the world. These estimates are available in an appendix to Wallich's *Monetary Problems of an Export Economy*.[13]

Official BOP Statistics

The first comprehensive government effort to estimate the Cuban BOP — for 1946 — was conducted by the Dirección General de Estadística of the Ministry of Finance (Ministerio de Hacienda). It was published in 1947 in the form of a monograph together with an essay on the conceptual framework of BOP

Table 1. Cuba's Balance of Payments, 1946-49 *(in million pesos)*

	1946	1947	1948	1949
Current Account	142.1	117.4	85.2*	77.6*
Merchandise trade (net)	234.2	252.8	196.6	141.8
Services , income and transfers (net)	-92.1	-135.4	-112.7	-65.2
Shipping	-23.0	-33.8	-44.5	-40.8
Insurance	-2.6	-3.1	-1.8	-1.4
Commercial, financial and professional services	6.3	18.3	27.0	25.5
Foreign travel	-18.0	-31.3	-32.8	-11.6
Private remittances	-8.2	-9.3	-8.5	-6.0
Government transactions	-6.3	-2.2	-0.6	-0.5
Investment income	-40.3	-74.0	-51.5	-30.4
Capital Account (net)	-12.1	-29.6	-16.5	-8.9
Direct investments	-12.1	-29.6		
Portfolio investments	-6.5	-5.8		
Official loans	5.4	0		
Official amortization	-0.7	-12.5		
Change in Reserves	-98.9	-75.6	-61.5	-76.5
Errors and Omissions	-31.1	-12.2	-7.8	-7.5

* Individual line items to do not add up to the total because of rounding.

Note: By convention, a negative change in international reserves is a gain in such reserves.

Source: 1946-47: Dirección General de Estadística, Ministerio de Hacienda, *Balanza de Pagos Internacionales de Cuba, 1946-47* (La Habana, 1948), as reproduced in Henry C. Wallich, *Monetary Problems of an Export Economy: The Cuban Experience 1914-1947* (Cambridge: Harvard University Press, 1960), p. 338; 1948-49: Dirección General de Estadística, Ministerio de Hacienda, *Balanza de Pagos Internacionales de Cuba, 1949* (La Habana, 1950?), pp. 9-10.

statistics and detailed notes on the sources and methods used to estimate each of the components of the Cuban BOP for 1946.[14] Subsequently, BOP statistics for 1947-49 were also published by the same government agency.[15] Table 1 reproduces the overall BOP statistics for 1946-49 from this source.

In December 1948, Cuba passed legislation creating the Banco Nacional de Cuba (Cuban National Bank, BNC), the nation's first central bank. The BNC, which started operations in April 1950, took over the

---

9. Henry C. Wallich, *Monetary Problems of an Export Economy: The Cuban Experience 1914-1947* (Cambridge: Harvard University Press, 1960).

10. Wallich, *Monetary Problems of an Export Economy*, pp. 326-327.

11. Wallich, *Monetary Problems of an Export Economy*, p. 327.

12. Wallich, *Monetary Problems of an Export Economy*, pp. 327-328.

13. Wallich, *Monetary Problems of an Export Economy*, Appendix B.

14. Dirección General de Estadística, Ministerio de Hacienda, *Balanza de Pagos Internacionales de Cuba, 1946* (La Habana, 1947).

Table 2. **Cuba's Balance of Payments, 1950-58** *(in million pesos)*

	1950	1951	1952	1953	1954	1955	1956	1957	1958
Current Account	-22.6	-36.9	-130.8	27.1	-69.6	-49.5	-42.5	-71.5	-134.8
Merchandise trade (net)	94.1	91.8	-7.0	112.7	7.6	35.7	45.5	31.5	-44.3
Exports	657.0	789.6	683.0	659.4	562.5	610.8	694.5	844.7	763.2
Imports	562.9	697.8	690.0	546.7	554.9	575.1	649.0	813.2	807.5
Services trade (net)	-47.1	-57.8	-70.0	-55.0	-44.0	-44.4	-36.7	-32.4	-35.5
Exports	45.8	46.7	37.7	40.3	50.7	59.7	76.9	93.4	94.7
Imports	92.9	104.5	107.7	95.3	94.7	104.1	113.6	125.7	130.2
Income (net)	-66.1	-68.2	-52.5	-27.7	-32.2	-40.9	-50.6	-65.6	-47.9
Transfer (net)	-3.5	-2.7	-1.3	-2.9	-1.0	0.1	-0.7	-5.1	-7.1
Capital Account	68.0	77.6	45.5	-20.3	14.1	64.6	27.9	61.5	-17.6
Private capital	9.9	47.3	18.0	-25.7	9.5	57.9	35.1	49.3	23.2
Other capital	58.1	30.3	27.5	5.4	4.6	6.7	-7.2	12.2	-40.8
Change in Reserves	-76.1	-62.4	54.5	2.8	69.5	46.4	47.9	55.1	182.3
Errors and Omissions	14.5	21.7	30.8	-9.6	-14.0	-61.5	-33.3	-45.1	-29.9

Note: By convention, a negative change in international reserves is a gain in such reserves.

Source: Banco Nacional de Cuba, *Memoria 1958-59* (La Habana, 1959), pp. 183-184.

preparation of the BOP statistics from the Ministry of Finance. Overall BOP statistics, as well as statistics on selected components, were regularly published in the annual report of the BNC, *Memoria*.[16]

In 1955, the Economic Research Department of the BNC launched a monthly *Revista* intended to provide current statistical information as well as results of research studies conducted by its staff. In December 1955, the *Revista* published the first of several articles analyzing the behavior of the Cuban BOP (for 1954) and describing problems and limitations of BOP statistics.[17] BNC analysts laid blame for the time lag in compiling BOP statistics on delays in obtaining reliable foreign trade statistics — related both to merchandise and to services, such as international transportation (i.e., shipping). The BNC recognized that the BOP estimates were a work in progress, pointing to the relatively large "errors and omissions" category, which reflected transactions not properly recorded by the national statistical system. Subsequent articles in the Revista analyzed the BOP for

1955 and 1956 and discussed refinements of estimates for certain components of the BOP.[18] Table 2 presents official Cuban BOP statistics for the period 1950-58 as published by the BNC, while Table 3 presents similar statistics for the period 1946-52 compiled from publications of the International Monetary Fund.

REVOLUTIONARY CUBA'S BOP STATISTICS

Revolutionary Cuba did not publish BOP statistics for 1959 or for the 1960s, 1970s and 1980s. As is discussed below, during this period Cuba's external economic relations were segmented: the first and quantitatively most important portion with the socialist countries, transacted in "soft" or nonconvertible currencies; and the second portion with Western countries, transacted in "hard" or convertible currencies. In the 1980s, Cuba did publish some BOP statistics, but only for the hard currency portion of its external accounts. In the 1990s, with the disappearance of the socialist bloc and of Cuba's privileged

15. E.g., Dirección General de Estadística, Ministerio de Hacienda, *Balanza de Pagos Internacionales de Cuba, 1949* (La Habana, 1950?).

16. E.g., *Memoria 1950-51* (La Habana: Banco Nacional de Cuba, 1951) contained several tables of statistics on merchandise trade and a set of tables on the number of foreign tourists. The latest issue of the *Memoria* that was published appears to be for 1958.

17. "El Balance de Pagos Internacionales de Cuba," *Revista del Banco Nacional de Cuba* 1:12 (December 1955), pp. 589-600.

18. "El Balance de Pagos Internacionales de Cuba en 1955," *Revista del Banco Nacional de Cuba* 3:1 (January 1957), pp. 5-20; and "El Balance de Pagos Internacionales de Cuba en 1956," *Revista del Banco Nacional de Cuba* 3:9 (September 1957), pp. 281-298.

Table 3.   Cuba's Balance of Payments, 1946-52 *(in million pesos)*

	1946	1947	1948	1949	1950	1951	1952
Current Account Balance	142.1	117.5	93.4	83.1	61.8	61.0	-43.2
Merchandise trade balance	234.2	253.0	196.7	142.2	152.5	162.1	70.0
Exports	534.6	772.7	724.1	593.2	667.4	802.2	688.2
Imports	300.4	519.7	527.4	451.0	514.9	640.1	618.2
Services, income and transfers							
balance	-92.1	-135.5	-103.3	-59.1	-90.7	-101.1	-113.2
Travel (net)	-18.0	-31.3	-33.1	-12.0	-26.6	-24.8	-11.5
Other services (net)	-21.4	-20.3	-10.6	-11.0	-24.5	-39.7	-48.7
Investment income (net)	-40.3	-73.9	-51.5	-30.4	-36.0	-33.8	-51.5
Transfers (net)	-12.4	-10.0	-8.1	-5.7	-3.6	-2.8	-1.5
Capital Account Balance	-66.7	0.8	-38.8	1.5	18.5	56.7	28.3
Private capital (net)	-30.5	23.6	-21.1	-17.2	-9.1	19.3	17.0
Direct investment	NA	-4.6	-3.2	-1.8	4.6	26.0	13.0
Portfolio investment	NA	-8.8	-6.5	-4.8	-2.4	-2.1	1.2
Other	NA	37.0	-11.4	-10.6	-11.3	-4.6	2.8
Other capital	-36.2	-22.8	-17.7	18.7	28.4	37.4	11.3
Change in Reserves	-34.3	-80.1	29.3	-26.1	-45.5	-77.0	55.4
Official holdings of dollars	0.7	-27.1	39.3	-16.1	37.9	-10.8	15.6
Monetary gold	-35.0	-53.0	-10.0	-10.0	28.1	-40.0	96.8
Other assets of the National Bank	0.0	0.0	0.0	0.0	-111.5	-26.2	-57.0
Errors and Omissions	-41.1	-38.2	-83.9	-58.5	-34.8	-40.7	-40.5

Note: By convention, a negative change in international reserves is a gain in such reserves.

Source: International Monetary Fund, *Balance of Payments Yearbook*, Volume 1 (1946-47) and Volume 5 (1947-53).

trade and economic relations with the former socialist bloc, Cuban trade and external economic relations have been only (or at least primarily) transacted in convertible currencies. Official BOP statistics that have been published by the Cuban government for the 1990s therefore are based on transactions in hard currency and presumably reflect the universe of international transactions.

Cuba's Segmented External Accounts

In January 1959 the revolutionary government quickly began to change the nature and structure of the Cuban economy. What began as law-decrees authorizing the confiscation of property and funds controlled by the deposed dictator Batista and his collaborators turned into a much broader nationalization of private property and resulted in increased tensions with the United States over the compensation of affected U.S. citizens. In the second half of 1959 and 1960, using different pretexts, the Cuban government nationalized key industries, including those owned by foreign investors. In October 1960, Law 890 authorized the nationalization of remaining foreign investments owned by the U.S. citizens, those controlled by other foreign nationals, and key enter-

prises owned by Cuban citizens, virtually sealing the fate of private enterprise in Cuba.

As trade and investment with the United States and other traditional trading partners dried up as a result of the nationalizations, Cuba established new economic ties with the Soviet Union and the socialist bloc countries. In mid-February 1960, Cuba and the Soviet Union entered into a trade and payments agreement as well as a credit agreement. The Soviet Union committed to purchase one million tons of Cuban sugar during each of the years 1960-64, with 80 percent of the value of sugar purchases to be paid with Soviet commodities (e.g., oil) and the remaining 20 percent with convertible currencies. The credit agreement granted Cuba line of credit of $100 million for the purchase of Soviet plant and equipment.

The process of shifting trade and economic relations from the United States and the West to the Soviet Union and other socialist countries moved at a very fast pace. Prior to 1959 Cuba's economic relations with the Soviet Union and the socialist bloc countries were negligible (limited to occasional purchases by these countries of Cuban sugar at world market prices). By 1961, however, Cuba's exports to socialist bloc countries accounted for 73 percent of Cuba's total exports and imports for 70 percent of total imports.

For purposes of this paper, the significance of these changes is that through the 1960s, 1970s and 1980s, Cuba's external economic relations were segmented. Trade and economic relations with the socialist bloc countries — which accounted for about 85 percent of merchandise trade turnover in the mid-1980s[19] — were conducted through bilateral balancing agreements, tantamount to barter arrangements, in which individual transactions were made, and accounts settled, using either the currency of one of the two trading partners or "transferable rubles," an artificial currency whose sole role was to serve as the unit of account in transactions among socialist countries. Because neither the currencies of the socialist countries nor the transferable ruble could be freely exchanged into "hard currencies" (U.S. dollars, Swiss francs, Japanese yen, deutsche marks) to purchase goods and services in international markets, these countries made efforts to balance trade bilaterally each year. Socialist countries routinely financed Cuba's bilateral trade deficits by extending low-interest loans and also granted Cuba other financial assistance, including loans to finance development projects and foreign aid (grants).

Meanwhile, trade and economic relations with developed market economies and with many developing countries were conducted following common commercial practices and using hard currencies. Western governments, financial institutions, or suppliers provided Cuba with credits to finance exports, particu-

larly in the second half of the 1970s, when international lending surged in the aftermath of the 1973 oil embargo and credit was easily available as a result of the priority of financial institutions to loan "petro-dollar" balances. These interest-bearing loans had to be repaid, in hard currency, according to a predetermined schedule. Because of currency incovertibility, Cuba could not apply surpluses in trade with the socialist countries to offset deficits with developed market economies or to service debt with these nations.

Partial BOP Accounts

In August 1982, the BNC issued a report,[20] aimed at foreign audiences, in which it requested Western creditors to reschedule its hard currency debt so that Cuba could overcome a serious financial crisis caused, the BNC argued, by the drying up of short-term borrowing. According to the BNC report, as of June 30, 1982, Cuba's hard currency debt amounted to $2.9 billion, of which about $1.3 billion was owed to official lenders (i.e., foreign governments) and about $1.6 billion to private lenders.[21] (For comparison purposes, the debt to Western countries in 1959 has been estimated at $291 million.) In a nutshell, Cuba requested deferral of principal payments due in 1982-85 for a ten-year period, with a three-year grace period, and committed to continue to meet interest payments.[22] Cuba was successful in rescheduling portions of its hard currency debt in 1982-85, but a worsening of the BOP situation in 1986 led Cuba to suspend debt service payments and technically default on the hard currency foreign debt.[23]

To support the convertible debt rescheduling requests that commenced in 1982, the BNC began to publish annual reports of economic developments in

19. In 1985, 86 percent of Cuba's exports went to the Soviet Union and the six Eastern European socialist countries, and an additional 3 percent went to other socialist countries (e.g., China, Vietnam); meanwhile, 81 percent of Cuban imports that year originated from the Soviet Union and the Eastern European socialist countries and 2 percent from other socialist countries. See Jorge F. Pérez-López, "Swimming Against the Tide: Implications for Cuba of Soviet and Eastern European Reforms in Foreign Economic Relations," *Journal of Inter-American Studies and World Affairs* 33:2 (Summer 1991), p.128.

20. Banco Nacional de Cuba, *Economic Report* (La Habana, August 1982).

21. *Economic Report*, August 1982, p. 44.

22. *Economic Report*, August 1982, p. 55.

23. On Cuba's hard currency debt and its rescheduling, see Archibald R.M. Ritter, "Cuba's convertible currency debt problem," *CEPAL Review*, no. 36 (1988), pp. 117-140.

Table 4.   Cuba's Hard Currency Balance of Payments, 1980-89 *(in million pesos)*

	1980	1981	1982	1983	1984	1985	1986	1987	1988	1989
Current Account Balance	-46	51	297	263	-212	-506	-1961	-877	-900	62
Merchandise trade balance	367	285	606	441	73	67	-164	-59	65	-40
Exports	1248	1406	1356	1234	1136	1244	907	965	1113	1384
Imports	881	1121	750	793	1063	1177	1071	1024	1048	1424
Services trade balance	-414	-235	-306	-179	-294	-577	-1798	-816	-985	102
Transfers	1	1	-2	1	9	4	1	2	-	-1
Capital Account Balance	60	-52	-539	-74	106	554	1841	822	943	-76
Long-term capital	-16	-116	-136	93	138	360	799	610	311	-134
Short-term capital	76	64	-403	-167	-32	194	1042	212	632	58
Change in Reserves	-14	1	242	-189	106	-48	120	55	-43	14

Note: By convention, a negative change in international reserves is a gain in such reserves.

Source: Based on statistics of the Banco Nacional de Cuba, as compiled and adjusted by the Economic Commission for Latin America and the Caribbean. Taken from Comisión Económica para América Latina y el Caribe, *Estudio Económico de América Latina y el Caribe—Cuba, 1989*, LC/L.560/Add.20 (November 1990), p. 26.

the island, and later also quarterly reports.[24] These reports contained, for the first time since the revolutionary take-over, official statistics on the portion of the balance of payments transacted in convertible currencies, mostly transactions with Western and some developing countries. These statistics are useful since no official BOP information was available for over two decades prior to their publication, but their value is very limited since they refer probably to less than one-fifth of Cuba's overall international economic transactions during this period. Cuba's hard currency BOP statistics for the period 1980-89 are reproduced in Table 4.

BOP Statistics for the 1990s

The remarkable political and economic changes that occurred in Eastern Europe and in the former Soviet Union beginning in 1989 had a profound impact on Cuba and its economy. Within a matter of about 18 months, Cuba lost the preferential trade and economic relationship it had had for three decades with the former socialist countries. The Cuban economy experienced perhaps its deepest recession in the twentieth century, with GDP declining by more than 30 percent between 1989 and 1993.

The disappearance of the Soviet Union and of the former socialist bloc has meant that Cuba's foreign trade and economic relations since about 1990 have been conducted only hard currencies. Thus, Cuba's hard currency BOP statistics presumably refer to the universe of international transactions.

BOP statistics for the 1990s were first published by the BNC in a redesigned — and much leaner in terms of information — version of its Economic Report. The first issue of the report after a hiatus of nearly 5 years, for the year 1994, was released in August 1995.[25] The BNC, and its successor, the Cuban Central Bank (Banco Central de Cuba, BCC),[26] have published the Report for 1996-98.[27]

24. The annual reports, published in Spanish and English, were titled *Informe Económico* or *Economic Report*, and were issued generally in mid-year. The quarterly reports were titled *Informe Económico Trimestral* or *Quarterly Economic Report*.

25. Banco Nacional de Cuba, *Economic Report 1994* (August 1995).

26. In May 1997, Cuba passed legislation establishing the Cuban Central Bank as an autonomous and independent entity and assigned to it traditional central banking functions. The BNC, which had performed central and commercial banking functions since 1960 when the commercial banks were taken over the state, remained in existence, but its role was relegated to commercial banking.

27. Banco Nacional de Cuba, *Economic Report 1995* (May 1996); Banco Central de Cuba, *Informe económico 1997* (May 1998); and Banco Central de Cuba, *Informe económico 1998* (April 1999).

Box 1.   Methodological Notes on the Balance of Payments in the *Anuario estadístico de Cuba*

The Balance of Payments is presented in accordance with a framework that approximates the methodological principles set out by the International Monetary Fund, which makes it possible to make comparisons with other countries:

- Goods: Comprises goods whose property is transferred between residents and non-residents of the economy.

- Services: Includes transactions related to transportation, travel (tourism), communications, construction, finance and commerce, among others.

- Income: Includes transactions related to income, such as interest, dividends, profits, and payments, among others.

- Current transfers: Includes current transactions not included in the above-mentioned categories and that are primarily related to donations and family remittances, among others.

- Current account: The surplus or deficit reached by the national economy in its exports and imports (goods and services) as well as in its current transfers to and from the rest of the world.

- Long-term capital: Capital flows with an initial contractual date of more than 12 months or without a fixed contractual date.

- Other capital: Capital flows not classified as long-term capital.

- Change in reserves: Changes in the holdings of reserves by the authorities to finance payments imbalances.

Source: Oficina Nacional de Estadísticas, *Anuario estadístico de Cuba 1997* (La Habana, 1999), p. 114.

Moreover, Cuba's National Statistical Office (Oficina Nacional de Estadísticas, ONE), has included BOP statistics from the BNC/BCC in recent publications, making them available to a wider audience.[28] In its 1997 statistical compendium, Anuario estadístico de Cuba 1997, ONE has also provided brief methodological notes on the BOP statistics, stating that they are "presented in accordance with a framework that approximates the methodological principles set out by the International Monetary Fund, which makes it possible to make comparisons with other countries."[29] These notes are reproduced in Box 1. Cuba's official overall BOP statistics for the period 1993-98 are reported in Table 5.

CONCLUDING COMMENTS

Although the purpose of this paper has been to trace the historical development of Cuban official BOP statistics and present available data to stimulate research and analysis by specialists, some cursory comments on Cuba's BOP statistics and situation in the 1990s are in order.

First, despite the statement by Cuban statistical authorities that BOP statistics follow the methodology of the International Monetary Fund, it remains an open question whether this is in fact the case. The amount of data that the Cuban government has published is very scant, and therefore it is not possible to

---

28. E.g., Oficina Nacional de Estadísticas, *Anuario estadístico de Cuba 1997* (La Habana, 1999) and Oficina Nacional de Estadísticas, *Cuba en cifras 1998* (La Habana, 1999).

29. Oficina Nacional de Estadísticas, *Anuario estadístico de Cuba 1997* (La Habana, 1999), p. 114.

Table 5.   Cuba's Overall Balance of Payments, 1993-98 *(in million pesos)*

	1993	1994	1995	1996	1997	1998
Current Account	-371.6	-260.2	-517.7	-166.8	-436.7	-396.3
Goods and Services	-370.7	-307.6	-639.1	-417.9	-745.5	-617.1
Goods	-847.4	-971.4	-1483.3	-1790.3	-2264.5	-2785.3
Exports	1136.6	1381.4	1507.3	1866.2	1823.1	1444.4
Imports	1984.0	2352.8	2991.6	3656.5	4087.6	4229.7
Services	476.7	663.8	845.2	1372.4	1519.0	2168.2
Income	-263.8	-422.8	-524.8	-492.6	-482.9	-599.2
Current Transfers	262.9	470.2	646.2	743.7	791.7	820.0
Capital Account	356.1	262.4	596.2	174.4	457.4	413.3
Long-term Capital	118.4	817.4	24.2	307.9	786.9	632.7
Direct Investment	54.0	563.4	4.7	82.1	442.0	206.6
Other	64.4	254.0	19.5	225.8	344.9	426.1
Other Capital	237.7	-555.0	572.0	-133.5	-329.5	-219.4
Change in Reserves	15.5	-2.2	-78.5	-7.6	-20.7	-17.0

Source: By convention, a negative change in international reserves is a gain in such reserves.

Source: Sources: 1993-96—Oficina Nacional de Estadísticas, *Anuario estadístico de Cuba 1997* (La Habana, 1999), p. 117; 1997-98—Oficina Nacional de Estadísticas, *Cuba en cifras 1998* (La Habana, 1999), p. 36.

cross-check the data with other information to ascertain their reliability.

Second, the data in Tables 4 and 5 support the proposition that Cuba's external sector has shrunk significantly in the 1990s. Table 4, which refers only to the hard currency portion of the BOP — probably about 20 percent of total trade — shows goods 1989 exports and imports valued at 1384 and 1424 million pesos, respectively. By comparison, Table 5 shows that in 1993, Cuba's total goods exports and imports were only 1337 and 1984 million pesos, respectively. Thus, Cuba's overall goods trade in 1993 was roughly comparable to hard currency trade in 1989, sug-

gesting that the trade volume of the 1980s was not feasible under commercial terms.

And third, official statistics show that that revenue from services (primarily tourism and services rendered by Cuban workers laboring abroad) and remittances are the key sources of external resources for the Cuban economy. In 1998, the services account showed a surplus of 2182.6 million pesos, compared to 820 million pesos for net remittances. However, since it is estimated that tourism's net contribution to hard currency income is only about 30 percent, remittances may be the largest single contributor of external resources to the Cuban economy in the second half of the 1990s.

INTERPRETING CUBA'S EXTERNAL ACCOUNTS

Emily Morris

This paper presents data from official Cuban external accounts, from the reports of the Cuban Central Bank — Banco Nacional de Cuba (BNC) until 1996, then changed to Banco Central de Cuba (BCC) — and the UN Economic Commission for Latin America and the Caribbean (ECLAC). The BCC and ECLAC figures are broadly consistent because ECLAC uses official Cuban sources, but ECLAC has fuller back series of data and the BCC reports have the more recent data. The aim of this paper is to outline the information the official external accounts give to explain the decline and recovery of external trade and payments, and to indicate where the main gaps and uncertainties lie. These comments are as brief as possible, and are intended to serve as a basis for further discussion.

Table 1 gives an overall picture of the acute external shock, with a 73% fall in import capacity between 1989 and 1993. This decline arises from both a sharp fall in export earnings and the withdrawal of Soviet finance. Recovery of import capacity between 1993 and 1999 still leaves it at only 60% of its 1989 level. The data on the components of the current account are examined in the first section and the components of the capital account are discussed in the second section. The last section sets out brief conclusions.

THE CURRENT ACCOUNT

The collapse of sugar earnings — due to the loss of the Soviet sugar subsidy — is the main cause of the fall in merchandise export earnings (see Table 2). Total sugar export earnings have not recovered at all since 1993, and indeed reached a new low in 1999 (despite an increase in production in that year) be-

cause of unfavourable prices. Non-sugar exports have increased, but growth is concentrated among nickel, tobacco and seafood: there is little further diversification yet, as shown by the modest growth of the "other" category.

The figures for "other" exports in 1998-99 capture inaccuracies in the Economic Intelligence Unit (EIU) estimates, which probably explains the erratic behaviour in those years. Our estimates for sugar in 1999 and nickel in 1998-99 are based on information available on export volumes multiplied by the average world market prices; the actual price earned will differ from this price although the movement will be in the same direction. Our estimate for sugar in 1998 is based on press reports that may be inaccurate. "Other" exports include biotechnology goods, for which there is little information. However, indications are that earnings have been disappointing so far.

Growth of non-merchandise exports (Table 3, otherwise known as "non-factor services") has been much stronger, and the main contributor has been tourism. There is insufficient information to determine tourism's net contribution (foreign exchange earnings minus costs) to the Cuban economy. Official statements have put the net contribution at somewhere between 30% and 50% of earnings. We do not know, however, how these ratios are calculated. The EIU is seeking clarification from the ministry of tourism, but we do not yet have a clear answer.

The balance on "other" non-factor services was negative until 1996 and has started to show strong growth since 1997. Telecommunications, professional ser-

145

Table 1. Import capacity *(US$ m)*

	1989	1990	1991	1992	1993	1994	1995	1996	1997	1998	1999
Merchandise export earnings	5,400	5,415	2,980	1,779	1,157	1,331	1,492	1,866	1,819	1,540	1,466
Services export earnings	593	526	584	742	832	1,160	1,419	1,841	2,059[a]	2,738[a]	2,995[a]
Factor incomes balance	−388	−456	−334	−248	−264	−423	−525	−493	−483	−449	−569
Net current transfers	−48	−13	18	43	263	470	646	744	792	813	828
Net financing (incl. use of reserves)	3,051	2,545	1,454	420	376	−25	534	79	533	393	456
Total import capacity	8,608	8,017	4,702	2,737	2,363	2,514	3,566	4,037	4,720[a]	5,036[a]	5,136[a]
Index, 1989 = 100	100	93	55	32	27	29	41	47	55[a]	59[a]	60[a]

a. EIU estimate.

Table 2. Composition of exports *(US$ m)*

	1989	1990	1991	1992	1993	1994	1995	1996	1997	1998[a]	1999[a]
Sugar	3,942	4,333	2,282	1,236	757	759	714	976	853	601	504
Minerals (mainly nickel)	494	395	237	219	148	203	333	424	422	272	313
Tobacco	79	112	114	94	71	71	101	107	157	193	274
Seafood	126	97	125	104	68	99	121	125	127	127	128
Other	884	575	347	231	180	298	344	358	387	474	374
Total exports	5,400	5,415	2,980	1,779	1,157	1,331	1,492	1,866	1,819	1,540	1,466

a. EIU estimate.

Table 3. Non–merchandise exports *(US$ m)*

	1989	1990	1991	1992	1993	1994	1995	1996	1997	1998	1999
Gross tourism earnings	204	243	402	550	720	850	1,100	1,333	1,515	1,759	1,901
Balance other than tourism	−79	−317	−286	−230	−243	−187	−364	−48	−88	173	262
Non–factor services balance	125	−74	116	320	477	663	736	1,285	1,427	1,932	2,163

Table 4. Factor Services *(US$ m)*

	1989	1990	1991	1992	1993	1994	1995	1996	1997	1998	1999
Factor services balance	−388	−456	−333	−248	−261	−423	−525	−493	−483	−449	−569

vices, transport (air and shipping) and music will be included here. There is no information on the contribution of the different services. It is worth noting that in 1998-99 the increase in this category has almost matched the increase in tourism earnings. This could mark a "take-off" in some sectors.

The net factor services balance (Table 4) is, as would be expected, negative throughout the period. We have no published information on the composition of the flows in this category, but can observe that the degree of fluctuation is modest compared with other categories in the current account. We do not know the magnitude of factor inflows. There is a nickel factory in Canada and there have been reports of some small investments in other countries, but these flows would surely be dwarfed by interest payments and profit repatriation flowing out of the country. If the profits of Cuban state corporations registered abroad, which include some of the largest tourism corporations, were included in this category they would have a significant weight.

In the early 1990s, net factor income outflows diminished. We would expect this to happen as trade credits dried up and so interest payments on this credit also diminished. Since then, we would expect interest payments to have increased as a result of new borrowing and growing repatriated profits on foreign direct investment (FDI). However, the overall balance on factor incomes has remained relatively flat. There are several possible explanations. One is that the increase in foreign borrowing in 1994-95 was sharply curtailed from 1995, in response to the sudden growth in the burden of interest payments. In 1996 there was a large increase in "bilateral intergovernmental loans" which may have enabled the Cuban borrowers to switch from expensive private credits to

Table 5. Current transfers *(US$ m)*

	1989	1990	1991	1992	1993	1994	1995	1996	1997	1998	1999
Net current transfers	−48	−13	18	43	263	470	646	744	792	813	828
Gross tourism earnings	204	243	402	550	720	850	1,100	1,333	1,515	1,759	1,901

Table 6. Capital flows *(US$ m)*

	1989	1990	1991	1992	1993	1994	1995	1996	1997	1998	1999
Financing balance	3,051	2,545	1,454	420	376	−25	534	79	533	393	456
Net direct investment (FDI)	n/a	n/a	n/a	n/a	54	563	5	82	442	207	205
Net other long–term capital flows	n/a	n/a	n/a	n/a	64	254	20	226	345	426	413
Other capital	n/a	n/a	n/a	n/a	242a	−840[a]	588[a]	−221[a]	−234	−223	−132
Total net capital inflows	n/a	n/a	n/a	n/a	360	−22	612	87	533	409	486
Variation in reserves[b]	n/a	n/a	n/a	n/a	16	−2	−79	−8	−21	−17	−30

a. These figures are revised to make them consistent with trade figures given in the BCC's 1997 report.

b. Minus sign indicates increase in reserves.

cheaper finance. Or it could be that the growth of FDI inflows from Cuban corporations registered abroad has been sufficient to offset an increase in interest payments over the past few years. We need a more detailed breakdown here.

The final element of the current account is net transfers (Table 5). Some accounts have misleadingly suggested that net current transfers mainly represent remittances from relatives in the United States. The total also includes earnings from the informal tourist sector, which has boomed over the 1990s. If asked, Cubans offering services for tourists would of course declare that the money was remittances, because there are no laws against receiving remittances. There is a very strong correlation between the figure given for net transfers and the total for sales in the dollar shops. This is not by chance: the figures are calculated as the turnover of dollar shops minus dollar earnings accounted for by official payment of dollars (mainly through incentives schemes).

Over the past two years informal activity related to the tourist sector has faced tougher competition from the formal sector as well as a tightening of controls. This explains the falling ratio of net current transfers/gross tourism earnings, shown in Table 5. In order to find the actual level of remittances from relatives in the United States, a comprehensive survey the senders of remittances would be needed, because restrictions on transfers — and their high cost — ensure that most of the money sent does not go through formal channels. However, even if we had an accurate measure of remittances sent from the United States, that would not tell the whole story, as contact between Cubans and countries other than the United States has been greatly increased by tourism, increasing remittances flows from those countries.

THE CAPITAL ACCOUNT

The picture on the capital account is very opaque. Table 6 shows the raw figures, as far as they go. The Central Bank statisticians claim to be following the accounting rules set out by the IMF but there are major problems:

- All the figures are shown as net flows, and even those are probably incomplete.

- There is a very large "others" category. This includes net inflows of short-term capital but also includes errors and omissions.

- Official figures for changes in hard currency debt do not tie in with the capital account flows at all.

So what, if anything, can be deduced from the capital account figures?

- The "total net capital flows" is the most certain figure there is. There is a rising trend, but the flows are very lumpy. The rising trend suggests that Cuba is gradually increasing its access to the international capital market, whether FDI or loan capital, and the lumpiness is an indication of how small the level of flows is, by historical or comparative standards, meaning that an important single transaction can skew the total.

- The "net direct investment" figure does not seem to truly reflect flows of foreign direct investment. Responses from the Central bank suggest that much foreign investment in tourism is not entered here. The problem appears to be that most of the data is transmitted to the Central Bank by ministries, but since the tourism sector was reorganised into a set of relatively autonomous enterprises in the first half of the 1990s, reporting to the ministry of tourism has been disrupted. If this is the case, the FDI figure shown here is a poor indicator of the actual level of FDI. The large FDI figure in 1994 could have been mainly accounted for by a single transaction (possibly in telecommunications), with much of the finance raised having been deposited overseas, giving a large negative flow in the "other" category.

- The level of reserves is a closely guarded official secret. Annual changes only are given, since 1994. Reserves are reported to have grown since 1994, but extremely slowly. Although international reserves are likely to be low, the unhurried pace at which they are being restored suggests that they are not critically low — or that there are other, offshore, reserves.

CONCLUSIONS

In this brief overview of some very sparse data we can make some general observations about the changing structure of the external sector. The overall story described by the figures in the current account seems plausible. There are important gaps in the information, though, particularly on details of tourism earnings and expenditure and current transfers. On the capital account we can tell very little from the official data. The information provided in the Central bank reports provides in insufficient breakdown of flows and very few footnotes, so that even if we accept that there is a genuine attempt to move the accounts into line with international definitions we cannot gain much insight from the data. This is probably intentional, reflecting Cuban paranoia about economic intelligence, but contributes to the high premium paid by Cuban borrowers for foreign credits.

CUBA'S BALANCE OF PAYMENTS GAP, THE REMITTANCES SCAM, DRUG TRAFFICKING AND MONEY LAUNDERING

Ernesto F. Betancourt

Other participants of this panel will discuss Cuba's balance of payments. This paper does not address how the trade gap is met, only the remittances issue. However, you are referred to Table 5 in Jorge Pérez-López's paper.[1] Between 1993 and 1998, the cumulative trade gap reached US$10.1 billion. How can a country finance such a deficit having no foreign exchange reserves and having defaulted in its foreign debt with the Paris Club since 1986?

Sometime during the Fall of 1997, a very convenient story emerged to justify lifting the embargo while making a false accusation against the Cuban-American community. It was alleged that exiles were sending eight hundred million dollars a year to their relatives in Cuba while insisting on the preservation of the U.S. embargo. Writing in *The Washington Post*, Ambassador Ernest H. Preeg, of the Center for International and Strategic Studies, strongly criticized the Cuban-American community on the contradiction while making a subtle pitch against the embargo.[2]

Like the 20,000 murders attributed to Batista, the 20,000 prostitutes under the previous regime and the 20,000 homosexuals in the Mariel exodus, this amount of remittances became another mantra for Castro's friends. Further stories worldwide quoted the US$800 million in remittances until it became cast in concrete. By August, 2000, the figure has been raised to one billion dollars. For purposes of this discussion, we will stick to the $800 million figure. The same logic, but even with greater justification, applies to the one billion dollar level.

It is true that overseas Cubans are remitting money to their families and, in my opinion, rightly so. However, as will be shown in this paper, the US$800 million remittances estimate is mathematically impossible and politically unfeasible. This is a cynical manipulation to cover a most unpleasant truth: Castro is resorting to drug trafficking and money laundering to finance the balance of payments gap.

ECLAC IS NOT A CREDIBLE AND IMPARTIAL SOURCE

The source quoted for the US$800 million figure was an Economic Commission for Latin America and the Caribbean (ECLAC) study on the Cuban economy. Any question raised on the validity of the amount was brushed aside by referring to the supposed credibility and impartiality of the source: a United Nations agency. In the first place, ECLAC needs governmental approval to release a report. And the Cubans are very demanding before giving their approval.

Besides, for its own reasons, ECLAC has always conveyed a rosy view of the Cuban economy in its reports. These reports are based on data provided by the Cuban government. Rather than questioning the

---

1. Jorge F. Pérez-López, "Cuba's Balance of Payments Statistics," in this volume.
2. Ernest H. Preeg, "U.S. Embargo: The Illusion of Compliance," *The Washington Post*, November 2, 1997.

accuracy of the data provided by Cuban officials, ECLAC specialists have always been willing to provide the Cubans the mantle of credibility of an UN agency. As will be commented further below, the mentioned report is no exception.

In the remittances case, efforts to obtain documentation on how the US$800 million figure attributed to ECLAC was arrived at met with a wall of silence. ECLAC spokesmen in Washington and Mexico claimed the report was on hold until its official release; which, in turn, was waiting for its publication in book form by the Fondo de Cultura Económica, a left leaning publishing house in Mexico City. How, under this publication hold, the key figure on remittances was released by ECLAC to become the most important fact related to the report worldwide—to be quoted by Mr. Preeg and many others—is left to the imagination of the reader.

All we know is that the remittances estimate was legitimized by ECLAC, as a source, long before the study became public. ECLAC's spokesmen were unable or unwilling to provide any explanation. Meanwhile, Castro has been enjoying a propaganda windfall. Why are the Cubans inflating the contribution of the hated exile community to Cuba's balance of payments?

The most logical answer is that such a figure offered an excellent cover for the drug dealings and money laundering that are going on through Cuba. It is unlikely that ECLAC officials deliberately provided a story to cover for Cuban drug trafficking and money laundering. They were simply "useful idiots," to borrow Lenin's delightful label for Communist sympathizers. The source of the leak is probably some Cuban government official.

We will concentrate our efforts on the remittances and on a more realistic explanation of how the trade gap is being financed. In the first place, there is absolutely no documentation or explanation in the report of how the US$800 million figure was arrived at.

Mention of the estimate are made in passing in the text without providing any detailed basis for the calculations.[3] One would have expected from ECLAC a more thorough analysis of how the estimate was arrived at.

Particularly in view of the fact that Pedro Monreal, a Cuban government researcher, has revealed there are several studies on this matter. In an article published in *Encuentro*,[4] Monreal reports that those studies provide much lower estimates of between $300 to $400 million dollars. Regardless of that, he quotes the ECLAC report's US$800 million figure as if it were based on some serious estimate, although mentioning that his own estimate is closer to US$500 million. Unfortunately, in the rest of the article, which incorporates very interesting speculations, there is not a single table or statistical fact.

What makes ECLAC's credibility even more doubtful are the figures released by Cuba's Banco Central, which differ substantially from those given by ECLAC. In 1996, for example, the Banco Central reports Net Current Transfers amounting to US$743.7 million, while ECLAC reports US$1,112.0 million, a difference of more than US$350 million.

Having expressed our doubts about the reliability of their estimates, in this paper nevertheless we will start from what ECLAC asserts is the amount of remittances received and then try to validate its feasibility, first from the perspective of the overseas Cuban community, and second from the perspective of the impact of those transfers from abroad on Cuba's distribution of wealth and its social and political consequences. Then, some comments will be made on a possible source for the substantial financial resources entering Cuba outside conventional trading and financial exchanges: namely, drug trafficking and money laundering. Among the various sources of information for that section of the paper, the most important new one is the forthcoming *Narcotráfico y Tareas Revolucionarias*, a report by Norberto Fuentes

---

3. CEPAL, *La economía cubana: Reformas estructurales y desempeño en los noventa.* LC/MEX/R.621 (Agosto 26, 1997), pp. 89 and 107.

4. Monreal, Pedro, "Las remesas familiares en la economía cubana," *Encuentro,* Issue No. 14 (Madrid, Fall of 1999).

on the activities of the de la Guardia brothers and General Arnaldo Ochoa to be released sometime this fall by the Center for a Free Cuba.

Finally, building on ECLAC's statistical information on tourism investment, an analysis will be made of some of the issues relevant to the hypothesis raised in this paper as to the real sources of the funds for which remittances are being used as a cover. In particular, attention will be given to the massive tourist investment reported in the ECLAC report and how it may be financed through money laundering. In this respect, it is worth mentioning that in the notes presented at this panel by Emily Morris, of the Economist Intelligence Unit, she states that "the net direct investment figure does not seem to truly reflect flows of foreign direct investment. Responses from the Central Bank suggest that much tourism investment is excluded from this category, as the reporting lines from tourism corporations are atypical."[5] As our hypothesis below reveals, the sources may be atypical indeed.

CAN OVERSEAS CUBANS REMIT US$800 MILLION A YEAR?

In a very well documented demographic analysis of the Cuban expatriate community, Sergio Díaz-Briquets reaches the very reasonable conclusion that the most likely level of their remittances to Cuba in 1994, when considering not only time of arrival but also number of families and their level of income, was around US$154 million and in the most optimistic scenario between US$300 and US$400 million.[6]

The total number of immigrants has not changed significantly since 1994. The tens of thousands of raft people and the legal immigrants on visas granted under the U.S.-Cuba migration agreement—who obviously will have the highest motivation to remit to their immediate families left behind—are not enough to change the quantum of immigrants significantly. Furthermore, although in their case there is

probably a higher commitment to remit than among earlier immigrants, most of these new arrivals are at the bottom of the income scale.

In order for US$800 million to have been remitted to Cuba, about 200,000 Cuban Americans had to send US$4,000 each to their families in Cuba during that year; or, 400,000 had to send US$2,000 each; or, 800,000 had to send US$1,000 each; or some other such combination. There are no formal reports available to determine actual volume of remittances. To get an idea of which of these number is the most realistic we can draw on demographic data from a poll on Cuban public opinion, which included one category related to monthly remittances received in their homes. The poll was undertaken by the University of Florida, Gainesville, and financed by the US-AID Cuba Program. The results are given in Table 1.

Table 1. Remittances Receipts Among Recent Cuban Arrivals

Amount Received (US$/month)	Number	Percent
None	629	61.3
Less than US$90	258	25.1
US$90 to $US100	75	7.1
US$101-US$200	20	1.9
Over US$200	10	1.0
No response	37	3.6
Total	1,029	100.0

Table 1 reveals that 629 of the sample of recent Cuban arrivals, or 61.3 per cent, reported not receiving any remittances at all from abroad. The second largest group, with 258 respondents, or 25.1 per cent, reported receiving less than US$90 a month. There were 75 respondents, or 7.1 per cent, who reported receiving monthly remittances of between US$90 and US$100 and, finally, 20, or 1.9 per cent, reported receiving between US$101 and US$200. Only 10 respondents reported remittances of over US$200 per month. Since these recent arrivals were more likely to have relatives abroad and receive remittances than the rest of the population, it is reasonable to as-

---

5. Emily Morris, "Interpreting Cuba's External Accounts," in this volume. The quoted text is from an earlier version of Morris' paper.

6. Sergio Díaz-Briquets, "Emigrant Remittances in the Cuban Economy: Their Significance During and After the Castro Regime," *Cuba in Transition—Volume 4.* Washington: Association for the Study of the Cuban Economy, 1994.

sume that the level remittance receipts for the Cuban population as a whole is likely to be even lower.

Therefore, the most solid first hand information available on average remittances, based on a poll of a significant number of recent residents of Cuba, indicates that close to two-thirds receive no remittances at all and, of those receiving remittances, the overwhelming majority obtain a little over one thousand dollars a year from their relatives abroad. With such a level of remittances, it would be necessary to have almost 700,000 exiles making remittances to attain the US$ 800 million total. This is mathematically impossible, as will be demonstrated with U.S. Census data.

According to the March 1996 *Current Population Survey*, the absolute number of U.S. residents of Cuban origin 15 years of age or over, 580,000, is substantially lower than the 700,000 required to make remittances at the rate of US$1,200 a year to reach a level of US $800 million dollars (Table 2). As to the assumption that every resident would be making remittances, this is highly unrealistic. The fact is that, according to *Current Population Survey*, 412,000 out of the 580,000, or 70 per cent, earn less than US$25,000 a year, which does not leave much disposable income to remit. It is possible that household income, combining more than one income earner per family, may allow for more disposable income for remittances. However, to the extent income is pooled so that household income is higher, the absolute numbers of potential senders of remittances decrease. In view of these sobering numbers, the claim that in 1996 Cuban-Americans remitted US$800 million and in 1997 US $1,000 million to their families in Cuba, as is claimed, is just not realistic.

CAN CUBAN SOCIETY ABSORB US$800 MILLION IN REMITTANCES?

When these numbers are analyzed from the point of view of their impact within Cuban society and internal political forces, the conclusion is that these magnitudes are equally unrealistic. In any society, the distribution of income is related somehow to class

Table 2. Level of Annual Earnings of U.S. Residents of Cuban Origin

Income Category (In U.S. Dollars)	Number of Residents (thousands)
Less than $2500 to $10,000	215
$10,001 to $15,000	93
$15,001 to $25,000	104
$25,001 to $40,000	87
$40,001 to $60,000	56
Over $60,001	23
Total	580

levels. Even in supposedly socialist classless societies, where ownership of the means of production is abolished, economic rewards and privileges are distributed according to status within the *nomenklatura*. From that perspective, we can also look at the impact of the estimated remittances levels against some macro and micro magnitudes. For that, we will draw on the ECLAC report.

Present rules allow Cubans to exchange their remittances at the rate of one dollar per twenty pesos to pay taxes, make purchases or open bank accounts. In these last two cases, however, remittance recipients have the option of buying directly in dollars or opening dollar accounts. According to the ECLAC report, the Tiendas de Recuperación de Divisas (Foreign Exchange Recovery Stores, TRD) reported 627 million dollars in sales in 1996 to all groups of buyers with access to dollars. That is, in addition to those receiving remittances, this figure includes purchases by tourists, by joint ventures staff with access to dollars or credit cards, and by Cubans getting dollars through self-employment or the many special salary arrangements allowing for payments of a portion in dollars. These other TRD customers are likely to account for several hundred million dollars in purchases. Government exchange houses only reported exchanges for US$5 million and dollar bank deposits amounted to only US$2 million.[7] This accounts only for the final destination of a total of 634 million dollars. Therefore, if actual remittances amount to eight hundred million dollars, that amount exceeds the to-

---

7. CEPAL, *La economía cubana*, pp. 89-90.

tal receipts of the three destinations reported by ECLAC. In conclusion, we are left with no explanation as to the destination of whatever dollars are generated by remittances at the level reported by ECLAC. At the same time, if actual remittances were substantially lower, reconciling the level of remittances with other macroeconomic aggregates in the Cuban economy would be easier.

At the macro level, US$800 million are equivalent to 16,000 million pesos, using the exchange rate of 20 pesos to one dollar prevailing in the unofficial market. The figure of 16 billion pesos can be compared to the GDP of 25,197 million pesos and to the 18,800 million pesos of private consumption estimated in the ECLAC report for 1996 to get an idea of the concentration of buying power they represent. Granted these are value added figures. Nevertheless, this level of remittances would reflect a very high concentration of wealth in the hands of enemies of the revolution, or at least disaffected elements. Furthermore, for a small segment of the Cuban population to have such a share of total buying power within Cuban society undermines the egalitarian claims in the ECLAC report. The fact is that access to dollars has divided Cuba into two societies, creating a dual economy where economic Apartheid prevails.

The figure of 16,000 million pesos attributable to remittances represents, in turn, more than 133 percent of total government revenues of 12,124 million pesos in 1996. In other words, this group of relatives of the bitterly anti-government overseas Cubans has buying power far in excess of that of the state. Evidently, were these figures to be true, there would be a very perverse relation within Cuban society between political power and economic power. It is highly unlikely that Castro can ignore the resulting unhappiness of his followers over this situation.

A parallel situation reveals how sensitive the Castro regime is to this issue. Foreign investors are forced by law to pay salaries in dollars to Cuban government companies that provide them their workers. The government companies pay the workers on an even dollar for peso rate, that is way below the market value of twenty pesos to the dollar. At present, some midway arrangement is made to reduce the impact of such a confiscatory exchange rate practice. Castro's economic spokesmen who have come to the Cuba Project at Georgetown University, justified the policy of paying salaries in Cuban pesos at a one peso equivalent to one dollar exchange rate to the 60,000 joint venture workers on the grounds of equity to the rest of the Cuban labor force. The same logic applies, probably with more political justification, to the relatives of overseas Cubans.

To place in context the relative individual buying power of the remittances at the micro level, one must take into account that the average worker earnings in all sectors of the Cuban economy, which according to the ECLAC report, is slightly below 200 pesos per month or 2,400 pesos per year.[8] An army colonel earns around 8,400 pesos a year and a hospital director around 7,200 pesos a year. Even in the sectors where pay incentives have been introduced, the level of earnings in pesos is rather modest. The ECLAC report mentions a UBPC (Basic Unit of Cooperative Production) in which average salaries are 250 pesos a month, while highly productive workers on incentive pay can make up to 700 pesos a month.[9]

Now, how will these loyal party cadres react when they see around them the relatives of the overseas Cuban community enjoying transfers, rather than earned income, amounting to multiples of what they earn for their work? To get an idea of the magnitudes involved, to reach the US$800 million macro level, it would be necessary, for example, for 200,000 remittance receivers to get an average of 80,000 pesos per year; or, for 400,000 to receive an average of 40,000 pesos per year; or, finally, for 700,000 to receive an average of 24,000 pesos per year. The impact of such massive disparities in income between remittance receivers and party loyalists would be highly destabilizing of the internal political situation.

8. *Ibid*, p. 381

9. *Ibid*, p. 171

Castro would be forced—as he did in 1986 when he closed the Free Peasant Markets in response to complaints by party cadres—to put an end to the remittances or introduce a less disruptive exchange rate. If he did so, there would be an uproar and the willingness of people to send money would be substantially reduced. No, Cuba could not maintain internal social peace if it was really receiving such levels of remittances. The story is just not credible.

The above sections demonstrate in a better documented way than any of the estimates provided by the regime that neither can the exile community remit that much money, nor can the Castro regime tolerate the distortion in the allocation of economic rewards between its supporters and its enemies entailed by an US$800 million level of remittances. The question then is, why is the claim made? The most plausible explanation is to cover-up the income generated by drug trafficking and money laundering. This requires some background on Castro's links with drugs.

CASTRO'S LINKS WITH DRUGS

Castro's links to drugs go back to the time when he was in the Sierra Maestra. When he survived the disastrous landing of the *Granma* in 1956, the first local protector he had was Crescencio Pérez, a local peasant "capo" who controlled production and marketing of many crops, including marijuana. When some of the revolutionaries realized who their savior was and complained to Castro, he told them that for the time being they had to depend on him. Such issues would be dealt with afterwards. Later on, Crescencio became a peasant revolutionary hero.

Once in power, Castro was not, and still is not, averse to associate with drug or any illegal or unsavory activity as long as it helps him stay in power. There are four drug cases involving Cuban officials at the highest level which have resulted in U.S. grand jury indictments.

In 1982, four high ranking Cuban officials were indicted by the Guillot Lara Grand Jury for arranging a drug smuggling operation through which drugs were brought into the United States in exchange for smuggling weapons to the M-19 guerrilla movement in Colombia, which was being supported by Castro. The officers indicted included Admiral Aldo Santamaría, who was the Cuban Navy Chief and a close Castro collaborator; Fernando Ravelo, Ambassador to Colombia and later to Nicaragua; René Rodríguez Cruz, President of the Cuban People's Friendship Institute, a close Castro collaborator, since deceased; and, Gonzalo Bassols, a Cuban diplomat accredited to Colombia at the time. The most important of them in terms of relevance to the issue under discussion is Admiral Santamaría. He was a member of the Honor Tribunal condemning General Arnaldo Ochoa!

One of the central events in the Noriega indictment and trial involved Castro's mediation between Noriega and the international drug cartel over the seizure of a cocaine laboratory in Panama which Noriega had allowed to operate there in exchange for a payment of US$4 million. According to the indictment, Noriega traveled to Cuba on June 27, 1984, at Castro's request, on his way back from Paris. Castro offered his good offices to settle the disagreement between the drug cartel and General Noriega. A mediator role requires good relations with the drug lords. Good relations that extend to the present.

In 1989, Robert Vesco was indicted by the Carlos Lehder Grand Jury in Jacksonville, Florida for arranging safe passage for drug planes over Cuban air space. According to the indictment, Vesco obtained approval from Cuban authorities for this arrangement. Later on, in an interview over Radio Martí, former Cuban Air Force Deputy Chief, General Rafael del Pino, who defected in 1987, reported that all the planes flying over Cuba that veered off from the approved air corridors for commercial and private aircraft, had to be cleared with the office of Raúl Castro at MINFAR. In a program broadcast over Cuban TV on the Ochoa trial, one can see an indignant Fidel Castro calling SOBs those who pointed out Raul's involvement in drug trafficking. But his indignation does not explain away the truth: only Raúl Castro had overall command of the armed forces which allowed the smugglers to land in Cuba and provided them radar assistance and protection from U.S. Coast Guard vessels.

But the most worrisome of all the indictments for Castro was the one that ended in the conviction, on April 23, 1989, of Reinaldo Ruiz and his son Rubén. Reinaldo Ruiz was a cousin of Captain Miguel Ruiz Poo of Cuba's Ministry of the Interior. The Ruizes were allowed by Cuban authorities to land their plane at the Varadero Beach airport for refueling after dropping their drug cargoes off the Cuban coast near the Bahamas. Drug smuggling motorboats (*lancheros*), would come from Florida to pick up the cargoes. Cuban Coast Guard radar monitored U.S. Coast Guard cutters and helped the *lancheros* evade them.

These four indictments provide ample evidence, from U.S. judicial sources, that the Castro regime, at the highest level, has been involved in drug activities. It has been claimed that these activities may have been undertaken by rogue Cuban government officers on their own and without Castro's knowledge or, much less, approval. No one who has the most limited inkling of how the Cuban regime works could give credit to this explanation. True, Castro wants the world to believe there is such a possibility because he is in utmost fear of meeting the Noriega fate. As will be shown in the next section, the search for a way to deny any potential Castro involvement in drug traffic was one of the reasons for the Ochoa trial. In order to avoid falling into the trap of reductionism to a single cause, however, it is acknowledged that the need to dispose of an emerging highly popular rival also played a role. Ochoa's actions reveal the intention to challenge Castro's power monopoly in many arenas: in Cuba's relations with the Soviets, in directing military operations overseas and in managing the drug traffic.

THE OCHOA TRIAL, DRUGS AND THE CASTRO BROTHERS

The implications of the last U.S. indictment mentioned above, the Ruiz case, require some amplification because it is the central event leading to the Ochoa trial. It is precisely the use of Cuban air space and refueling facilities, as well as the provision to drug smugglers of radar support to evade the U.S. Coast Guard, that were two of the central issues raised during the trial against Ochoa. This, despite

the fact that, at no time during that period, was Ochoa in command of the forces involved in controlling Cuban air space, territorial waters or shores in the areas where these operations were taking place. However, this does not exonerate Ochoa. He just did not realize the consequences of becoming entangled with Ministry of Interior operations fully approved by Fidel Castro and directed by his brother Raúl. Once discovered, Ochoa, along with some other key operatives, were made sacrificial lambs to save Castro's good name and the reputation of the revolution.

Radio Martí was able to interview Reinaldo Ruiz in prison in the United States shortly after he was sentenced in 1989. We were informed we had to wait for the sentencing to avoid the implication that what he said was the result of some plea bargaining. In the interview with our reporter, Ruiz explained that he had been involved in a MININT people-smuggling operation through Panama and wanted to use the operation to get some of his relatives out of Cuba. It was while he was engaged in this effort that he claims he was approached by his cousin, Captain Ruiz Poo, to use his people-smuggling network for drug smuggling into the United States.

At the time, Captain Miguel Ruiz Poo was working for the Convertible Currency Department (MC) of Cuba's MININT, which was headed by Colonel Tony de la Guardia, another of the officers executed by Castro. Reinaldo Ruiz claims he agreed to the proposal after some hesitancy. His son flew as copilot of the planes landing at Varadero and he himself went into Cuba on various occasions, enjoying VIP treatment from Cuban authorities. Reinaldo Ruiz stated that, in some occasions, the Cubans even took him to Havana as a government guest. Mr. Ruiz claimed in the interview that he had no doubt that what he was doing had the approval of Castro. As an exile, he would have never taken the risk of going into Cuba had he had any doubt about who was behind those activities. A most plausible explanation.

But the Ruiz operation had been infiltrated by the U.S. Drug Enforcement Administration (DEA). The pilot of the plane was an undercover DEA agent and he recorded in videotape many of the conversations they had. The United States requested the extradition of Reinaldo Ruiz from Panama early in 1988. According to Reinaldo Ruiz, he was surprised when Panama granted the request. However, he was convinced all along that the Cubans would get him out somehow before his being convicted. According to the Norberto Fuentes report, Fidel Castro considered this setback was a consequence of Raúl's incompetence in handling the operation.

As far back as 1980, the Minister of Interior, at the time Ramiro Valdés, stopped marihuana smuggling operations ordered by Fidel when Castro refused to issue written orders to him to undertake them. In early 1983, the Minister of Interior ordered Tony de la Guardia to make a feasibility study for a drug money laundering center at Cayo Largo, south of Cuba, and de la Guardia was also asked by Fidel to establish contacts with Pablo Escobar, the Colombian drug cartel head. Castro initially delayed a proposal from the Colombian M-19 movement to engage in an exchange of weapons for coca because the proposal had been addressed directly to him by Jaime Bateman. Evidently, after Bateman's death in an airplane accident, a more discreet arrangement was made— leaving Castro out of the loop; this arrangement was brought up before the above mentioned Guillot Lara Grand Jury.

In the Fall of 1983 Fidel told Abrantes, who was really acting as Minister of Interior, and two MININT officers, José Luis Padrón and Tony de la Guardia, that he wanted to be shown the feasibility of undertaking drug operations while overcoming three obstacles: (1) the requirements established by Ramiro Valdés of written orders, (2) the clumsiness of the Chief of the Navy, Aldo Santamaría and other Raúl collaborators, already indicted in the United States; and (3) the level of formal commitment expected by the Colombian M-19. In other words, as Fidel Castro was moving towards expanding his involvement in the drug traffic, he wanted to ensure deniability for himself.

When Reinaldo Ruiz was convicted on April 23, 1989, the contents of some of the videotapes recorded by the DEA undercover agent were given ample coverage by mass media, among them one in which Reinaldo Ruiz is seen saying that the money they were paying "went straight into Castro's drawers." He also alleged that, on one occasion, while they were waiting at the Varadero Airport tarmac, Raúl Castro was at the airport and one of his bodyguards approached them requesting marijuana.

One can imagine the panic this caused among Fidel Castro and his collaborators. Neglect of the fate of a low minion in the drug operation being run by Cuban intelligence all of the sudden had entangled directly the revolutionary leadership. And in an American court of all places. Plausible denial was no longer credible.

According to one of the Cuban TV tapes of the Ochoa trial, it is precisely on April 24, 1989, the day after the conviction of the Ruizes, that Captain Miguel Ruiz Poo got a call from Major General Abelardo Colomé, a close collaborator of Raúl Castro, who is now Minister of Interior and at that time was head of MINFAR intelligence, inquiring about what was going on. In his testimony, Colonel de la Guardia stated that he tried to calm down Captain Ruiz Poo by explaining that General Colomé was inquiring about the status of collections from the operation.

It is this conversation that led to the dramatic testimony seen later on in the TV program covering the trial, showing Captain Ruiz's pathetic effort to save himself by referring to comments by other accused officers about higher ups being involved in the drug operation. After Captain Ruiz started sobbing uncontrollably on the witness stand, he is hurriedly removed from the court and the next day he is not allowed by the prosecutor to expand on his statement, while other witnesses are brought to deny that any involvement at the highest level was ever discussed and to question that anybody had grounds to even think of such a possibility. The reaction to the highly emotional revelation of a clearly terrified witness reveals that involvement by higher ups was central to the rationale for the trial.

One version of the Ochoa trial, which reached Radio Martí at the time, was that Ochoa was preparing to challenge Castro. He had some encouragement from the Soviets — Gorbachev had visited the island earlier in 1989, and was not very pleased with Castro's defiant stance towards g*lasnost* and *perestroika*. General Ochoa twice attended Soviet military schools and developed close links with Soviet generals when he commanded Cuban forces in Ethiopia and Angola. According to this version, knowing about Castro's plans to cooperate with the drug cartels in exchange for massive investments in Cuban tourism, Ochoa sent his aide Captain Martínez, also later executed by Castro, to meet Pablo Escobar in Colombia to get evidence for the challenge he was planning.

Another, much more plausible, version emerges from the Norberto Fuentes report. It reveals that Ochoa was distrusted by Raúl, who sent General Leopoldo Cintras Frías to Angola to serve as Ochoa's deputy to try to control him. In a preview of the trial that took place later on, on May 28, 1989, Raúl gave Ochoa a dressing down, while already under preliminary arrest, in the presence of Generals Ulises Rosales del Toro and Abelardo Colomé. Raúl raised with Ochoa, for the first time, the issue of sexual orgies, while adding as factors under consideration that Ochoa:

- openly disobeyed Fidel's orders in waging the last phase of the war in Angola;

- was developing too close a relationship with Soviet generals (at a time when Fidel had given orders to Minister Abrantes to start watching Soviet contacts with Cuban officials);

- had supported the attack on La Tablada garrison in Buenos Aires by Argentine guerrillas without having cleared it with his superiors; and,

- more worrisome of all, had established his own connection to Pablo Escobar to engage in drug operations.

This last issue involved a project to build a coca laboratory in Angola in association with Pablo Escobar. Ochoa had asked Tony de la Guardia to take charge of developing a marketing network in the United States and Western Europe for the output of this enterprise. Up to that time, the drug smuggling operations undertaken by Tony de la Guardia on behalf of the Ochoa/Escobar group, which had started early in 1987, had generated small amounts of money — the

rate was about US$1,200 per kg of coca — and had been aborted on several occasions due to sabotage, apparently encouraged by Castro. As a result, Ochoa was moving to set up his own smuggling operation independent of the MC Department of MININT.

From the Fuentes report, it is evident that Castro was engaged in many simultaneous drug smuggling arrangements. In the end, Fidel emerges as a distant Godfather, always in the background, having the final say in deals with Vesco, Lehder and others. Some of the deals proposed involved substantial amounts. For example, through one of Tony de la Guardia subordinates, Lt. Col. Rolando Castañeda Izquierdo, Carlos Lehder proposed a US$7 million a week arrangement for regular shipments. That would generate a flow of US$364 million a year. In another deal, Abrantes, under Fidel's orders, instructs Tony de la Guardia to find buyers in Europe for US$50 million in coca. Deals of these magnitudes could explain how Cuba finances the gap in its balance of payments.

Of all the sins of Ochoa, challenging Castro as the Cuban Godfather was his worst offense. It was not only a threat to Castro's absolute rule, it also endangered his careful efforts at covering up Cuba's involvement in drug smuggling. The Ruizes sentence precipitated events.

With his obsession to give a legal cover to the most arbitrary actions he wants to undertake, Castro decided to orchestrate a trial to eliminate the threat Ochoa presented to his leadership of the regime and, in the process, to cleanse himself from any involvement in drug traffic. To ensure their silence, he executed the four that not only knew about his entanglement with drug trafficking, but were closely involved in Ochoa's operations.

Later on, he would also get rid of the Minister of Interior, José Abrantes. Abrantes was dismissed as a result of the Ochoa trial, but not because he was involved with Ochoa. Quite the contrary. He was the executor of Castro's orders in relation to drug operations. It is quite possible that Raúl saw in the whole mess the opportunity of bringing the MININT under this control. He was able to do so by placing General Abelardo Colomé, one of his most trusted

157

officers, in charge of the MININT. After his dismissal, Abrantes was tried and sentenced to prison for omission in preventing the corrupt activities of his subordinates. While in prison in Guanajay, on January 18, 1991, he had a confrontation with General Patricio de la Guardia, Tony's twin brother and also one of the defendants at the Ochoa trial sentenced to prison. According to the Fuentes report, Abrantes told Patricio that "Fidel had authorized everything. Patricio was indignant upon the confirmation that his brother was executed for having undertaken tasks ordered by Fidel." On January 21, 1991, three days later, Abrantes died in prison. The newspaper *Granma* reported he had a heart attack. Actually, it is reported he died as a result of an overdose of a heart medication he needed, a frequent outcome in Cuba's jails.

The defendants in the Ochoa trial serving time in prison got a warning: revealing the involvement of Castro in the drug operations could be a fatal indiscretion. Meanwhile, as recent events reveal, Castro continues tolerating drug traffic through Cuba, the crime for which he executed Ochoa, free of any local competition in his role as Godfather.

For example, in January, 1996, Jorge "Gordito" Cabrera, was arrested in the Florida Keys and charged with importing 6,000 pounds of cocaine. At the time of his arrest, *El Nuevo Herald* reported he was carrying a photo of himself with Fidel Castro. Later that year, he pleaded guilty and was sentenced to 19 years in prison. To make the matter more bizarre, during the U.S. Presidential campaign finance scandal, it was revealed that three weeks before his arrest, in December 1995, Mr. Cabrera had pictures taken of him with the First Lady, Mrs. Hillary Clinton, at a White House Christmas party. Earlier he had his picture taken with Vice President Al Gore at a Miami fund raising party. It turned out Mr. Cabrera had made a US$20,000 contribution to the Democratic Presidential campaign at the urging of Mrs. Vivian Man-

nerud, a pro-Castro activist in Miami who owns a company that provides travel services to Cuba. She had approached him during a visit both had made to Havana earlier in 1995. The funds were returned, of course, but the scandal remains.[10] A more recent incident took place on December 3, 1998, in Cartagena, Colombia. That day the Colombian police seized 7 tons of cocaine bound for Cuba to be transshipped later to Europe and the United States. According to the head of the Colombian National Police, drug runners "are employing a new trend of loading cocaine into containers transported initially to Cuba for distribution in smaller shipments to the United States and other international consumer markets."[11] In this instance, the shipment was made under the disguise of raw materials for a plastic factory owned by two Spanish investors in a joint venture with a Cuban government enterprise. Later on, the Colombian police made public records of the firm revealing that there had been seven or eight earlier shipments following a similar pattern. Castro was enraged at the Colombians for making this incident public. In a speech in January 1999, he quoted drug arrests statistics to prove how hard Cuba is fighting drugs. That Cuba is fighting drug smuggling is another theme of Cuba's current propaganda. Unfortunately, there are some in the U.S. Government who believe that. They are even willing to share with Castro U.S. drug smuggling intelligence. However, others, in Colombia, claim that those Castro is arresting are from rival cartels.[12]

This idea is not as farfetched as it may appear. At the trial of the former Mexican Drug Czar General Jesús Gutiérrez Rebollo, who was arrested two weeks after being praised as an honest man by U.S. Drug Czar General Barry McCaffrey, it was revealed that General Gutiérrez Rebollo was using Mexican Army and Air Force resources to help drug capo Amado Carrillo Fuentes, the so-called Lord of the Skies, eliminate his competitors. That means that the sophisticated equipment the United States provided to the Mexi-

---

10. Don Van Natta, Jr., *The New York Times*, April 4, 1997.

11. Robert Novak, *Chicago Sun-Times*, Syndicated Column, dated February 4, 1999.

12. Marcelo Fernández-Zayas, "Cuba and Spain: Corruption, drugs and espionage," *Mundo Latino*, February 22, 1999.

Table 3. Some Relevant Indicators on Hotel Investment

	1990	1991	1992	1993	1994	1995	1996
Stock of rooms (000's)	12.9	16.6	18.7	22.1	23.3	24.2	26.9
Addition of rooms (000's)	—	3.7	2.1	3.4	1.2	0.9	2.7
Estimated investment (million US dollars)	NA	370	210	340	120	90	270
Peso equivalent of investment (million pesos at 20 pesos=US$1)	NA	7400	4200	6800	2400	1800	5400
Gross domestic investment (million pesos)	4872	2274	975	965	1036	1500	1900
Domestic savings (million pesos)	2327	820	555	577	794	985	1380
Year end market exchange rate (pesos per US$1)	7	20	45	100	60	25	19

can army to fight drug smuggling was actually used by one of the capos against his competition. Since, as is commented below, Carrillo Flores had close links with Castro, it is quite likely that the recent Castro efforts to reach an agreement to have access to U.S. intelligence and equipment were intended to replicate that experience.[13]

ARE THE DRUG CARTELS INVESTING IN CUBA IN EXCHANGE FOR CASTRO'S SUPPORT?

Cuba does not generate the savings required to finance investments. Since hotels are reported to be built with Cuban funds, one logical conclusion is that Cuba is a huge money laundering center for the cartels. After all, wasn't this Ochoa's plan? We will elaborate on this hypothesis using the figures provided in the ECLAC report.

Except the estimates for hotel investment in dollars and their conversion to Cuban pesos, all the figures in Table 3 are taken from the statistical annex of the ECLAC report. Since no table is provided in the ECLAC report for the flow of remittances, and the US$ 800 million figure is mentioned only in the text, no equivalent numbers are available to compare for the years covered in the above table. Some questions may be raised on the use of a rate of 20 pesos for US$1 for the conversion of the investments to current Cuban pesos. As can be appreciated from the last line, if anything, this rate underestimates the pesos equivalent which in 1993 reached 100 to the dollar. Therefore, it provides a conservative conversion to Cuban current pesos.

According to the tables provided in the ECLAC report, Cuba built 14,000 international-quality hotel rooms between 1990 and 1996. The ECLAC Report acknowledges that these hotels were built with Cuban financing. The benchmark figure for hotel investment in the Caribbean is between US$100,000 and US$125,000 per hotel room. Applying the lower figure to allow for lower construction labor costs in Cuba we arrive at a total investment during the period of US$1.4 billion. The amount of dollars required would be lower if Cuba could provide more inputs; however, the collapse of Cuban industry since the end of Soviet assistance does not allow for use of local components other than labor, cement and perhaps some steel bars for concrete structures. International quality hotels require equipment above Cuban production standards. According to ECLAC, even food items for tourism, such as eggs and chicken, are imported due to the poor quality of Cuban production.

The contradictions and inconsistencies these figures reveal are related to the relation between investment in hotels and total national investment and savings reported in the national accounts. As can be observed, the peso equivalent of the hotel investment for each year exceeds the figures reported by ECLAC in its report for both gross domestic investment and national savings. More so, when we consider that hotel building is not the only national investment. However, there is an unquestionable fact: hotels have been built.

As mentioned above, the information on foreign investment provided to The Economist Intelligence Unit did not include hotel investment either. The question is why do the aggregate figures from nation-

---

13. Sam Dillon and Craig Pyes, "Court files say Drug Baron used Mexican Military," *The New York Times*, May 24, 1997.

al accounts not reflect those investments? Unless there is some explanation resulting from the techniques followed for computing the national accounts, the only possible explanation is that financing for these investments has been handled outside the conventional national accounts: money laundering or drug trafficking.

WHAT IS THE EVIDENCE SUPPORTING THE MONEY LAUNDERING HYPOTHESIS?

Here is where money laundering enters as a plausible explanation for how investments in hotels are financed. First, there is the coincidence that the massive expansion of tourism hotels starts precisely the year after General Ochoa was executed. As commented above, a hypothesis is that Ochoa had uncovered this scheme and was trying to document it to justify his challenge to Castro. Second, the other, more credible, hypothesis is that Ochoa was trying to become a Castro rival as a capo in drug smuggling. Whatever the actual explanation is, when Castro discovered what Ochoa was up to, he decided to turn the tables on him and use the accusation of dealing with the drug lords to discredit Ochoa and justify his execution.

Castro's involvement with the drug lords is more than documented by the four grand jury indictments mentioned above. And this involvement did not end with the Ochoa trial. The arrest of Jorge "Gordito" Cabrera, with a photo with Castro, raises the possibility Castro was considering gaining some influence, a la Chinese, with the Clinton Administration. The cocaine shipment seized in Colombia in December 1998, after seven or eight previous ones, owned by foreign investors who were partners in a joint venture with the Cuban government could take place only with some previous clearance by Castro himself. The fact no regime official has been fired or prosecuted for acting on his own, points to Castro as the approving authority and not the doings of some rogue officer. It is evident drug smuggling has survived the

Ochoa execution, and so has money laundering, but following another track.

Over the years, Castro's practice has been to handle dollar transactions through his own substantial personal accounts overseas, the so-called "Reservas del Comandante." This was revealed by Jesús M. Fernández, who defected in May 1996 and had had access to the highest level of financial management within the regime. He reports that these private Castro accounts were used to channel Soviet financing of Cuba's military operations overseas, subversive activities and the operations of the CIMEX enterprise, later replaced by the MININT's Department of Convertible Currency. This is precisely the agency where Colonel Tony de la Guardia worked when he was involved in drug deals. According to Mr. Fernández, these private accounts are also used for those economic sectors under the direct supervision of Castro, such as pharmaceuticals and tourism, as well as Ministry of Interior overseas operations generating convertible currencies.[14]

It has been established by the DEA that the weight of the money generated by drug sales exceeds the weight of the drugs themselves. Therefore, disposing of the money involved in the United Sstates alone — with retail sales estimated at more than US$100 billion annually — is a process of industrial proportions. Trailer trucks cross the U.S.-Mexico border with full cargoes of U.S. currency. According to a 1997 report on money laundering in *The Economist*, the fee at that time for helping the cartels launder their money had increased to between 25 and 28 per cent.[15] In the argot of the money launderers, this is called "discounting," the cost of making a drug tainted dollar a tradeable dollar.

Ironically, through the prohibition of legal remittances in 1996, the U.S. Government provided an excellent cover-up for money laundering. Money started reaching Cuba through so-called "mules." That is, people who traveled to Cuba through third countries carrying tens of thousands of dollars in

---

14. DevTech Systems, "The Comandante's Reserves," *Cuba Monthly Economic Report,* Vol. 1, No. 4, August, 1997.

15. "Dirty Wars in money laundering," *The Economist,* Special Report, pp. 19-21, July 26th-August 1st, 1997.

cash. By depositing these monies in Cuban government accounts, or, more likely, in the accounts of the Comandante's reserves, the money is legitimized.

The death of the Lord of the Skies, Amado Carrillo Fuentes, has lifted the veil of another potential avenue for money laundering. According to a report published by *The Miami Herald*, Mexican authorities have obtained evidence that Carrillo Fuentes was a guest at a protocol house of the Cuban government during his frequent visits to the island. There is speculation that among the alleged activities taking Mr. Carrillo Fuentes to Cuba was money laundering.[16] Authority for assigning protocol houses is vested exclusively on Fidel Castro and his Chef de Cabinet, Dr. José Miyar Barruecos, is responsible for their administration. Finally, Cuban defectors have mentioned that, among the attractions offered to drug dealers visiting the Cayo Largo resort, a key south of the island of Cuba, is the existence of banking facilities where money laundering is performed. As was mentioned above, Tony de la Guardia was the MININT officer commissioned to undertake the feasibility study to make this key a money laundering center.

This analysis offers only an inkling of what is going on. There is no doubt that there is a huge flow of laundered money worldwide and that Cuba is one of the channels being used. It is also evident that in Cuba nothing of this sort can go on without Castro's personal approval. The hypothesis that large volumes of remittances cover the huge gap in Cuba's balance of trade stands on weak foundations. The available evidence indicates there is an impossibility of the re-

mittances option offering the main source to finance whatever is the balance of trade gap. As to other sources, there is substantial evidence to conclude that Cuba is engaged in drug smuggling and money laundering. This is a huge growing gap, as is shown in the previously mentioned Table 5 of Jorge Pérez-López's paper, which in 1998 registers a trade gap amounting to US$2,785 million. Therefore, even accepting the US$800 million estimate for remittances, there are two billion dollars more to explain.

However, there is not enough data to estimate the magnitude of the resulting financial flows. All we have is a simple rule of thumb to calculate how that gap may be met through money laundering and drug smuggling. Thus, to meet the balance of trade gap, Castro needs four dollars in money laundering transactions for each dollar in net proceeds and to smuggle a kilogram of coca for each US$1,250. Back in 1989, the U.S. Coast Guard had reports of about 300 flights per year outside of the approved air corridors over Cuba for private and commercial flights. It is such flights that make the coca drops to be picked up by the lancheros.

At some future time, reliable estimates on drug trafficking volume may be available and it may be possible to combine the data on volume with estimates of transshipment charges and money laundering fees to compute estimates of the involved financial flows. But the lack of data for quantification should not deter us from considering that drug trafficking and money laundering are the most plausible sources for financing the Cuban balance of payments gap.

---

16. Andrés Oppenheimer, "México probes drug lord's Cuban connection," *The Miami Herald*, September 9, 1997.

LAND USE IN CUBA BEFORE AND AFTER THE REVOLUTION: ECONOMIC AND ENVIRONMENTAL IMPLICATIONS

Sergio Díaz-Briquets

It is generally concluded that Cuba's poor performance in the agricultural sector since the early 1990s is the result of two primary, complementary reasons. Cuban agricultural production has faltered because of:

- a dearth of agricultural inputs since the collapse of the socialist world, and

- the adverse impact of economic policies that interfere with the sector's performance due to structural rigidities and by eliminating production incentives.

According to the first and most common line of reasoning, with the end of Soviet subsidies, Cuban agriculture has been unable to maintain 1980s production levels because the government has not been able to obtain needed imported agricultural inputs. The agricultural development model Cuba pursued since the 1960s was heavily dependent on capital and chemical inputs. These inputs were either provided by the former Soviet Union and its Eastern European allies under one subsidized scheme or another, or were purchased in international markets with the limited hard currency Cuba earned from sugar and petroleum (also provided by the Soviet Union) sales in international markets.

While most analysts embrace this reasoning, they also accept the argument that attributes the problems of Cuban agriculture to socialist economic policies. There is a wealth of documentation relating to Cuba — as well as to other countries of the former socialist community — indicating that the socialist economic

framework had disastrous production consequences, for reasons generally well understood. Aside from the systemic flaws associated with a command economy and the poor incentive framework with which it is associated, agricultural production is hampered under socialism by several dominant features of the economic system. Among the most salient are its proclivity to rely on large scale, mostly inefficient production units; undue reliance on extensive cultivation practices; excessive emphasis on mechanization; an unbounded but often unwarranted faith on technological interventions; and excessive use of agricultural inputs (for reviews see, Pryor 1992; Díaz-Briquets and Pérez-López 1998; Díaz-Briquets and Pérez-López 2000:10-13). Despite reliance on this agricultural development model, including heavy capital investments, Alvarez and Puerta (1994) have documented that productivity was considerable higher in the few small, private land holdings remaining in Cuba after 1959 than in state farms. Remarkably, this productivity advantage was achieved despite the fact that many of the agricultural inputs abundant in the state sector were not accessible to small private farmers. Furthermore, Sáenz (1994, 1995, 1997a, and 1997b) in several papers has shown that small landholders relied on agricultural practices far more favorable to environmental preservation than large-scale farms in the state sector.

While the flaws related to the characteristics of the model already represented a drag on Cuban agricultural production before the Special Period, their effects were somewhat masked by what appears to have been an ever-growing reliance on capital intensive agricultural inputs during the 1970s and 1980s. This can be seen by analyzing trends in the use of farm machinery, fertilizers, and pesticides from the 1960s to the late 1980s (see Tables 1 and 2). Between the early 1960s and 1990, for example, the stock of agricultural tractors rose by close to 300 percent. Many of the bulldozers, harvesting combines, and a substantial number of tractors, constitute heavy farm machinery, not the most appropriate for working fragile tropical soils. There were also equally impressive increases in the use of pesticides and herbicides, whether measured by physical weight or purchase value. The increase in herbicide and pesticide use, as measured in Cuban pesos, for example, rose from about 5 million in 1965 to more than 80 million in 1989, or by 1,450 percent. While extreme, this percent increase is not inconsistent with other rising trends in fertilizer and pesticide imports depicted in Table 2. To these estimates must be added agricultural inputs produced domestically, as the socialist government also made considerable investments to increase domestic production capacity, including two large nitrogen fertilizer plants built during the 1970s at Cienfuegos and Nuevitas (Díaz-Briquets and Pérez-López 2000:198).

IS THERE AN ENVIRONMENTAL CONNECTION?

While the two factors discussed above seem to be sufficient to account for the decline in Cuban agricultural production, it is surprising that hardly any attention has been directed to assess the potential effect of environmental factors in the production collapse. The work of Sáenz and others (for an overview, see Díaz-Briquets and Pérez-López 2000), as well as official Cuban sources, including those that provide agricultural statistics, suggest that an important determinant of the current situation may well be a substantial degradation of Cuba's natural resource base. The link between environmental degradation and the agricultural development policies that began to be implemented in the 1960s, leading to a radical transformation of the Cuban countryside by the late 1980s, can be readily established. To begin to appreciate the significance of the environmental underpinnings of the current agricultural situation, it is conve-

nient to review developments in land use practices before and after the revolution. Through such comparison, it is possible to reach a preliminary judgment of how changes in land use practices and environmental degradation, together with other factors, are associated with the agricultural sector's poor performance in the 1990s.

This can be done by looking at 1946 agricultural census data (with a 1945 reference date) and statistics on land use released in the last full-blown statistical compendia made public before the Special Period, the *1989 Anuario Estadístico de Cuba*. This approach has the obvious flaw of not been capable of isolating the important changes in Cuban agriculture that began after the Second World War (Grupo Cubano 1963), and that were well underway by 1959. Thus, the comparison exaggerates to a limited but indeterminate extent the effects land use changes may have had on environmental degradation and, ultimately, on agricultural production. The comparison is also contaminated by differences in definitions. The 1946 agricultural census included a large residual land use category (20.7% of the total land area) labeled "not in farms," as well as a "other uses" category (14.4% of the total land area). The 1989 data are presented inclusive of these other land use categories. While recognizing that this approach can only yield a partial and imperfect understanding of changes since the early 1960s — and some of their consequences — the comparison provides a macro glimpse of the enormous transformations experienced by the Cuban countryside under the socialist regime.

LAND USE CHANGES BETWEEN THE EARLY 1960s AND THE LATE 1980s

The data presented and discussed in this section are largely drawn from previous work by the author and Jorge Pérez-López (Díaz-Briquets and Pérez-López 2000:84-88), but enhanced by the presentation of several detailed tables that will allow the reader to analyze more closely specific trends. According to the 1946 agricultural census, farms occupied four-fifths (79.3%) of the land area (Table 3). These farms, numbering some 160,000, had an average size of 56.7 hectares. Crops accounted for 21.7% of the farm area, while 42.9% and 14%, respectively, were

Table 1.   Stock of Agricultural Tractors and Mechanized Agricultural Equipment *(units)*

	1970	1975	1980	1985	1986	1987	1988	1989
Bulldozers	—	—	—	1678	1633	1678	1720	1918
Tread tractors	3862	4151	4670	5694	6362	6752	6837	7216
Heavy wheel tractors	2760	3776	2289	2981	2713	2765	2901	3175
Light wheel tractors	37699	43118	53133	55217	59753	59969	60336	61571
Special tractors	7247	3806	8202	4693	4911	4917	4845	4821
Sugar combines	1092	1143	2776	3472	3819	3981	4014	4049
Rice harvesting combines	1153	1124	879	664	671	590	603	626
Planters				1510	1746	2031	2037	2175

Source: Comité Estatal de Estadísticas (1989, p. 214).

Table 2.   Cuban Imports of Fertilizers and Pesticides, 1970-89

		1970	1975	1980	1985	1986	1987	1988	1989
Manufactured Fertilizers	(000 pesos)	44562	88582	81449	136083	138747	130832	120191	157752
Ammonium nitrate	(000 pesos)	350	2401						
	(Tons)	6672	25868						
Urea	(000 pesos)	5316	13861	19619	37053	32772	3843	38596	53135
	(Tons)	82710	110009	151334	244354	214000	2252000	257000	351000
Simple superphosphate	(000 pesos)	2281	6418	12971	18359	21470	23191	20308	22232
	(Tons)	77429	129194	243515	255466	299000	324000	283000	311000
Triple superphosphate	(000 pesos)	3379	16150	7124	7316	7000	6899	4221	5114
	(Tons)	51185	61043	37195	40000	37000	37000	16000	26000
Ammonium sulphate	(000 pesos)	9796	24397	23128	26211	26970	17187	14042	18730
	(Tons)	301451	317723	417052	381796	393000	249000	201000	272000
Potassium chloride	(000 pesos)	4198	11695	15764	36624	34252	33404	30278	36856
	(Tons)	130321	213492	295815	390593	367000	352000	323000	394000
Potassium sulfate	(000 pesos)	1206	2578	1887	2820	2683	3584	3109	3188
	(Tons)	25859	33677	24757	24281	18000	22000	20000	20000
Mixed fertilizers	(000 pesos)	18036	11082						
	(Tons)	299598	50000						
Herbicides & pesticides	(000 pesos)	23903	52733	60476	64483	53300	76866	68768	80807
Herbicides	(000 pesos)	15324	34737	39113	35936	26285	51713	47066	55629
	(Tons)	7800	14009	15135	17500	10290	14218	12688	17151
Pesticides	(000 pesos)	5895	17996	21318	28437	26823	24846	21532	25178
	(Tons)	5914	11530	11164	14396	11952	10231	8054	9740

Source: Comité Estatal de Estadísticas (1989, pp. 282-83, 262 and earlier issues).

occupied by pastures or covered by trees. The remaining farm surface was covered by various weeds, fallow, or used by roads, buildings, etc. These same data, incorporating the land area not in farms, are presented in Table 4. In 1945, 53.8% of the country's total land surface, or 6.2 million hectares, were used for agricultural purposes. This was about 400 thousand hectares less than the country's agricultural land ceiling, as estimated through an agricultural production potential typology of Cuban soils developed during the 1980s with Soviet assistance (as described by Atienza Ambou et. al., 1992, briefly reviewed by Díaz-Briquets and Pérez-López 2000:82-83).   .

Table 3.   Land Distribution in 1945
(in hectares)

Total Land Area	Hectares	Percent
	11,452,400	100.0
In farms	(9,077,086)	(79.3)
Cultivated	1,969,728	21.7
Pasture	3,894,070	42.9
Woods	1,261,715	13.9
Marabú	272,313	3.0
Other uses	1,652,030	18.2
Fallow	27,230	0.3
Not in farms	(2,375,314)	(20.7)
Number of farms	159,958	
Average size of farms (in hectares)	56.7	

Source: World Bank (1951, Table 15, p. 87).

Table 4. Land Distribution by Type of Use, 1945 *(in thousands of hectares)*

Total	Thousands of hectares	Percent
	11,452	100.0
Agricultural	(6,614)	(53.8)
Cultivated	1,970	17.2
Not cultivated	4,194	36.6
Pastures	3,894	34.0
Fallow	300	2.6
Non-agricultural	(5,289)	(46.1)
Forests	1,262	11.0
Not in farms	2,375	20.7
Other uses	1,652	14.4

Source: World Bank (1951, Table 15, p. 87).

Land use data for 1989 are shown in Table 5. Nearly 62% of the nation's land was in agricultural and 38% in non-agricultural uses. Out of the nearly 6.8 million hectares devoted to agriculture, about 4.4 million hectares (40.1% of total land) were cultivated (including 1.082 million hectares of cultivated pastures), while 2.4 million hectares (21.4%) were natural pastures or fallow. Non-agricultural land was distributed among forests (23.7%), settlements (6.3%), not usable (5.5%), or covered by water (3%). The total amount of agricultural land in 1989 (whether cultivated or not) exceeded by nearly 200 thousand hectares the ceiling of potential agricultural soils. As can be seen in Table 6, where comparative land use data for both periods are presented, by 1989 the total amount of land being used for agriculture (61.5%) exceeded by nearly one percentage point the amount of soils considered suitable for agriculture (60.6%). More noteworthy is that the total land area cultivated had increased by nearly 23% between 1945 and 1989, whereas pastures (excluding cultivated pastures, which in 1989 accounted for 9.8 % of the total land area) had declined by half (from 34% in 1945 to 17% in 1989).

The increase in cultivated land and the decline in pastures were not as sharp when considering cultivated and natural pastures together, the total land in pasture declining by only 7% during the 1945-89 interval. Still, the amount of cultivated land (other than cultivated pastures) increased by nearly a third between 1945 and 1989. The number of hectares in fallow increased substantially, but from a much lower

Table 5. Land Distribution by Type of Use, 1989 *(in thousands of hectares)*

Total	Thousands of hectares	Percent
	11,016	100.0
Agricultural	6,772	61.5
Cultivated	4,410	40.1
Permanent	(3,620)	(32.9)
Sugar cane	1,980	18.0
Coffee	147	1.3
Cacao	10	.1
Plantain	114	1.0
Citrus	150	1.4
Fruit Trees	96	.9
Pastures	1,082	9.8
Other	41	.4
Temporary	(784)	(7.1)
Rice	206	1.9
Various	456	4.1
Tobacco	57	.5
Pastures	20	.2
Other	46	.4
Vivery	(6)	(0)
Not cultivated	2,357	21.4
Natural pastures	1,883	(17.1)
Fallow	474	(4.3)
Non-Agricultural	4,241	38.5
Forested	2,611	23.7
Not useable	606	5.5
Water	330	3.0
Settlements	694	6.3

Source: Comité Estatal de Estadísticas (1989, Tables VIII.3. VIII.4 and VIII.6, pp. 185-6).

Table 6. Comparative Land Use Pattern in 1945 and 1989 *(in percent)*

Total	1945	1989	Difference 1989/1945
	100.0	100.0	—
Agricultural Land	53.8	61.5	+7.7
Cultivated	17.2	40.0	+22.8
Pastures	34.0	17.2	-16.8
Fallow	2.6	4.3	+1.7
Forested/non-agricultural	31.7	32.2	+0.5
Settlements/other uses	14.4	6.3	-8.1

Source: Tables 4 and 5.

base. Major increases in the land area cultivated were largely achieved by bringing under the plow formerly non-agricultural land either because it was being held in reserve (e.g., by the large sugar mills), or because it was considered as agriculturally marginal. Table 7 provides more detailed information on how the expanded acreage in agricultural land was distributed. Between 1945 and 1989, the cultivated land area (the sum of land in permanent and temporary crops) increased by 1,321 hectares, or by 66.6%, from 1,982 to 3,303 thousand hectares. Of the total amount of additional land being cultivated, sugar cane accounted for 66.4%, or 877 thousand hectares. In relation to land under permanent crops, the increase attributed to sugar cane was even more pronounced, amounting to 72.8%. The increase in the amount of land dedicated to citrus plantations was minor relative to the increase in land in sugar cane plantations. Although the amount of land planted with citrus increased eight-fold between 1945 and 1989, by the latter date citrus plantations only occupied 150 thousand hectares, or 2.4% of all agricultural land, as compared to the 1,980 thousand hectares planted with sugar cane (31.5% of all agricultural land). Other notable changes were a considerable expansion in the amount of land devoted to coffee, fruit trees, and rice, and a contraction in the land area dedicated to tobacco and the residual category of "other temporary crops."

Table 7. Agricultural Land Use in 1945 and 1989

	Thousands of Hectares		Percent	
	1945	1989	1945	1989
Total Agricultural Land	5,879	6,288	100.0	100.0
Permanent Crops	1,333	2,538	22.7	40.3
Sugar Cane	1,103	1,980	18.8	31.5
Coffee	89	147	1.5	2.3
Cacao	7	10	.1	.2
Plantain	81	114	1.4	1.8
Citrus	15	150	.3	2.4
Fruit Trees	20	96	.3	1.5
Other	18	41	.3	.6
Temporary Crops	649	765	11.0	12.1
Rice	58	206	1.0	3.3
Various	330	456	5.6	7.2
Tobacco	66	57	1.1	.9
Other	195	46	3.3	.7
Pastures	3,897	2,985	66.3	47.5

Source: Ministerio de Agricultura (1951, various pages); and Comité Estatal de Estadísticas (1989, Tables VIII.3, VIII.4, and VIII.6, pp. 185-6).

A more detailed assessment of changes in land use by type of crop can be made by examining the data on Table 8. This table provides data on non-sugar land

Table 8. Non-sugar Cane Land Planted in 1945 and 1989 by Crop
(in thousands of hectares)

	1945	1989 Total	State	Non-state
TOTAL	871.0	927.9	630.8	297.1
Tubers	161.8	148.7	91.0	57.7
Potato	8.5	15.9	13.1	2.8
Boniato	53.3	53.4	35.5	17.9
Malanga	32.8	12.7	6.4	6.3
Ñame	6.7	—	—	—
Yucca	60.5	—	—	—
Vegetables	98.4	155.6	74.6	81.0
Tomatoes	72.3	42.5	17.7	24.8
Onions	.5	5.8	3.8	2.0
Peppers	1.5	5.6	1.5	4.1
Pumpkins	22.7	—	—	—
Garlic	1.4	—	—	—
Cereals	252.2	257.6	188.9	68.7
Rice	57.5	167.3	141.6	24.7
Corn	180.0	89.3	45.3	44.0
Millet	14.7	—	—	—
Leguminous	69.7	55.1	32.2	22.9
Beans	56.8	54.0	31.0	23.0
Peanuts	12.9	—	—	—
Tobacco	66.2	50.4	14.7	35.7
Henequen/Kenaf	11.2	4.6	4.6	—
Bananas	80.6	43.1	26.0	17.1
Fruit	22.6	13.1	7.4	5.7
Plantain	58.0	30.0	18.6	11.4
Citrus	14.8	5.3	4.8	.5
Orange	13.5	2.1	1.8	.3
Grapefruit	.8	2.3	2.1	.2
Lemon	.5	.7	.6	.1
Other Fruits	20.0	8.9	6.1	2.8
Mango	—	.7	.5	.2
Guava	—	.8	.6	.2
Papaya	1.1	4.8	3.1	1.7
Coconut	4.5	—	—	—
Pineapple	14.4	—	—	—
Coffee	88.9	7.5	5.5	2.0
Cacao	7.2	.6	.3	.3
Cultivated pastures	—	163.8	155.6	8.2

Source: Ministerio de Agricultura (1951, various pages); and Comité Estatal de Estadísticas (1989, Tables VIII.13, VIII.14 and VIII.15, pp. 191-3).

planted in 1946 and 1989 by type of crop (including existing and new plantings for perennial crops, and plantings for annual crops). The data suggest that the overall acreage planted in tubers declined between 1945 and 1989, even though potato plantings nearly doubled and boniato plantings remained almost unchanged. A major decline of 61% was recorded in the number of hectares planted with malanga, the data also suggesting a significant contraction in the land area planted with yuca and ñame.

Land devoted to the production of vegetables, other than tomatoes, appears to have increased considerably, with major increases in the amount of land planted with onions and peppers. A striking difference in the planting trends for rice and corn can be noted. Whereas the amount of land devoted to rice production increased three times between 1945 and 1989, the acreage devoted to corn declined by half. These divergent trends are consistent with Cuba's policy to increase domestic rice production (even before the 1959 revolution) and with the country's dependence on Soviet supplies of feed grains for livestock and poultry production. Millet, an important crop in 1945, is not even listed separately in 1989. The data suggest, finally, that the number of hectares planted with beans between 1945 and 1989 remained essentially unchanged.

In 1989, as a result of the damming of many of the country's rivers, inland water bodies accounted for 3% of the territory, while swamps did so for a further 4% to 5%. The amount of forested lands between 1945 and 1989 remained about the same, 18%, although between 1945 and 1959 it had declined to some 14%. Both estimates have little to say regarding the stock of fruit and shade trees, although it is safe to conclude that many small stands of these trees were lost during the socialist period as the capital intensive, large-scale farm model was introduced. To make up for the removal of traditional fruit tree groves, the government embarked on a program to developed fruit tree, coffee and cacao plantations, the citrus plantations being the best known. Resources were assigned to develop mango and guava tree plantations, as well as to expand coffee and cacao plantations in mountain areas, often as part of agroforestry projects.

LAND USE CHANGES BETWEEN 1959 AND 1989: SUMMARY

Despite comparability problems, several conclusions can be drawn from the data reviewed above and from other well-known information pertaining to Cuba's

agricultural economic policies during the socialist period. The first is that the total amount of agricultural land increased substantially, by as much as 8%, between 1945 and 1989, mostly by bringing marginal farm land into production. Average farm size also increased appreciably. The implementation of the socialist agricultural development model depended on the utilization of large-scale farms to facilitate mechanization of agricultural operations and intensive application of chemical inputs. These tendencies were further accentuated by:

- concentration on the production of a relatively small number of agricultural export commodities (sugar, citrus fruits);

- increasing domestic capacity to produce staple crops (rice, potatoes);

- depending on commodity imports (feed grains) to satisfy certain national needs; and,

- in some cases, neglecting the nation's capacity to produce traditional staple crops (e.g., malanga).

These decisions were reached within the framework provided by the Council for Mutual Economic Assistance (CMEA) that regulated trade relations within the socialist bloc and that assigned to Cuba a predominant role as supplier of agricultural (and mineral) commodities to the former Soviet Union and other socialist countries.

Another very important land use change was a major expansion in the amount of flooded land as hundreds of large and small reservoirs were filled behind numerous dams built during the 1970s and 1980s. Irrigation on a vast scale was an intrinsic component of the socialist approach to agricultural development. By flooding some of the most fertile soils of the country, particularly along the relatively flat western and central regions, the reservoirs removed many thousands of hectares from production.

CHANGES IN LAND USE, LAND DEGRADATION AND DECLINE IN AGRICULTURAL PRODUCTION

That the agricultural developments described above — due to land use and production practices — had adverse environmental effects is unquestionable.

Data culled by Sáez (1997) from various Cuban sources provide convincing evidence that the damage is substantial and potentially difficult and costly to reverse. According to these data, of Cuba's total agricultural land area of 6.6 million hectares, 4.2 million hectares (or 64% of the total) are eroded to one degree or another; 2.7 million hectares (or 41%) have poor drainage; soil compaction, due to excessive heavy farm machinery use, affects 1.6 million hectares (24%); 1.1 million hectares (17%) suffer from acidification; and 780 thousand hectares (12%) have been degraded by salinization.

The toll that soil degradation can take on agricultural production is well documented. I limit myself here to summarize some of its most obvious consequences. Soil erosion can have multiple consequences depending on the type of soil, but it is generally believed to have a cumulative impact. Furthermore, different soil erosion processes are usually correlated with one another. Regardless of why it occurs, the consequences of soil erosion are fairly predictable: it usually results in lower yields or in higher costs per yield when corrective measures are introduced (Pagiola 1994:22). This relationship appears to be particularly germane to Cuba's experience. The fertilizer use trend data reviewed in this paper suggests that Cuba may have been able to arrest declining yield problems during the 1980s thanks to the ever-increasing use of fertilizers and other agricultural inputs. As the availability of abundant and inexpensive imports dried out after 1989 leading to a contraction in fertilizer use, Cuban soils were no longer able to sustain their former productivity. This hypothesis merits further examination. It seems to explain the priority assigned by the Cuban agricultural authorities to the development of domestically produced organic fertilizers to substitute for the chemical fertilizers formerly acquired abroad.

The effect of poor water drainage of irrigated soils on agricultural output is well documented. Despite vast agricultural investments, Cuba's central planners gave relatively low priority to the development of a national drainage infrastructure, although the country has an abundance of flood-prone areas and the land under irrigation increased several-fold. The World Bank, in fact, has identified poor drainage as one of the most serious problems affecting countries that embraced agricultural development policies highly dependent on large-scale irrigation projects. These projects often neglect the development of a drainage infrastructure to preserve the soils. Many drainage problems are caused by the poor maintenance of canals and other irrigation facilities and more generally by inadequate attention given to the need to address drainage issues in agricultural development plans (Umali 1993:29-41). This is a fitting description of some of the issues that have affected Cuban agriculture over the last 40 years and that are likely to be having a bearing on the sector's poor performance.

In some regions of the country, salinization has become a major environmental issue. It is acknowledged to be critical in rice production areas, which were expanded by the socialist government, particularly along southwestern Cuba and in the Cauto River Basin. Important irrigation projects, involving the development of artificial water reservoirs and excessive pumping of underground water stores, together with poor drainage practices, accompanied the expansion of cultivation of rice and other crops. These tendencies are aggravated even further by the known contamination of many of Cuba's coastal aquifers, a process that appears to have been at least partly induced by perverse hydraulic development initiatives. In the southwestern section of Pinar del Río province, for example, some independent observers (Agencia Ambiental Entorno Cubano 1999) are claiming that damage is so severe that a process of desertification is underway: levels of salt concentrations are so high that few plants can survive. Even when salinization levels have not reached critical levels, it is known that "the tolerance of different plants to salinity vary greatly, but all suffer from increased salinity"(Goudie 1994:148). Thus, it seems reasonable to assert that as some of Cuban soils have become more saline, their capability to sustain former agricultural yields has been compromised. In some places the damage may be so severe so as to be virtually irreversible. Reclamation efforts (salt removal, converting more harmful salts into less harmful ones, miscellaneous control measures) in other regions may be too expensive and beyond Cuba's present day ability to pay for them (Goudie 1994:149-50).

The extent of soil compaction is also a serious concern since it can seriously damage its structure. Soil compaction, according to Goudie (1994:152-53), "tends to increase the resistance of soil to penetration by roots and emerging seedlings, and limits oxygen and carbon dioxide exchange between the root zone and the atmosphere. Moreover, it reduces the rate of water infiltration into the soil, which may change the soil moisture status and accelerate runoff and soil erosion." Goudie goes on to note that most notable effects of soil compaction can be seen on the soil's infiltration capacity, with the most damage being seen in row crops accompanied by poor rotation. Before the Special Period, these were characteristic features of Cuban socialist agriculture: the planting and harvesting of many row crops was fully mechanized and the ancient land preservation practice of crop rotation was woefully neglected. The burning of sugar cane to facilitate mechanical harvesting and frequent application of chemical fertilizers and pesticides contributed to the removal of organic matter from the soil further intensifying pressures on its fertility. The extent of the compaction damage alone suggests it must have had a noticeable impact on agricultural output.

CONCLUSION

In summary, the evidence reviewed in this paper indicates that the poor performance of the Cuban agricultural sector during the 1990s — and very likely into the future as well — responds to environmental causes, as much as it does to a shortage of imported inputs and inadequate economic policies. This conclusion is important and carries potential grave significance since soil degradation processes are expensive and difficult to reverse, and often require a long time before producing expected results. Environmental degradation, therefore, could well prove to be a major brake on Cuba's eventual economic recovery.

REFERENCES

Agencia Ambiental Entorno Cubano. "La situación ambiental de Cuba 1999." Miami, 1999.

Alvarez, José and Ricardo Puerta. "State Intervention in Cuban Agriculture: Impact on Organizatuion and Performance," *World Development* 22:1663-75, 1994.

Atienza Ambou, Aída, Anicia Gárcia Alvarez, and Oscar Echevarria Vallejo. *Repercusiones medio ambientales de las tendenciuas de desarrollo socio-económico en Cuba.* La Habana: Instituto Nacional de Investigaciones Económicas, mimeo, 1992.

Comité Estatal de Estadísticas. *Anuario Estadístico de Cuba 1989.* La Habana, 1989.

Díaz-Briquets, Sergio and Jorge Pérez-López. *Conquering Nature: The Environmental Legacy of Socialism in Cuba.* Pittsburgh: University of Pittsburgh Press, 2000.

Díaz-Briquets, Sergio and Jorge Pérez-López. "Socialism and Environmental Disruption: Implications for Cuba," in *Cuba in Transition—Volume 8*, pp. 154-172. Washington: Association for the Study of the Cuban Economy, 1998.

Goudie, Andrew. *The Human Impact on the Natural Environment.* Cambridge: The MIT Press (fourth edition), 1994.

Grupo Cubano de Investigaciones Económicas. *Un estudio sobre Cuba.* Coral Gables: University of Miami Press, 1963.

Ministerio de Agricultura. *Memoria del Censo Agrícola Nacional 1946.* La Habana, 1951.

Pagiola, Stefano. "Cost-benefit Analysis of Soil Conservation," in *Economic and Institutional Analyses of Soil Conservation Projects in Central America and the Caribbean*, edited by Ernst Lutz, Stefano Pagiola, and Carlos Reiche, pp. 21-39. World

Bank Environment Paper, No. 8. Washington: The World Bank, 1994.

Pryor, Frederick L. *The Red and the Green: The Rise and Fall of Collectivized Agriculture in Marxist Regimes.* Princeton: Princeton University Press, 1992.

Sáez, Hector R. "Agricultural Policies, Resource Degradation, and Conservation in Cuba," in *Cuban Studies* 27, pp. 40-67, 1997a.

Sáez, Hector R. "Property Rights, Technology, and Land Degradation: A Case Study of Santo Domingo, Cuba," in *Cuba in Transition—Volume 7*, pp. 472-85. Washington; Association for the Study of the Cuban Economy, 1997b.

Sáez, Hector R. "Technology, Property Rights, and Land Degradation: The Case of Santo Domingo," paper presented at the Nineteenth International Congress of the Latin American Studies Association, 1995.

Sáez, Hector R. "The Environmental Consequences of Agricultural Development in Cuba," paper presented at the Eighteenth International Congress of the Latin American Studies Association, 1994.

Umali, Dina L. *Irrigation-Induced Salinity: A Growing Problem for Development and the Environment.* World Bank Technical Paper, no. 215. Washington: The World Bank, 1993.

World Bank. *Report on Cuba.* Washington: World Bank, 1951.

COMMENTS ON

"Land Use in Cuba Before and After the Revolution: Economic and Environmental Implications" by Sergio Díaz-Briquets

José Alvarez

As it has always been the case, Sergio Díaz-Briquets has made an important contribution to the analysis of the Cuban environment. It could not have been otherwise. He and Jorge Pérez-López have been researching, and writing about, that topic for almost ten years. Such dedication culminated in the recent publication of their book *Conquering Nature: The Environmental Legacy of Socialism in Cuba* (Díaz-Briquets and Pérez-López, 2000). The present article is an expansion of the topic "Land Use Trends" discussed in chapter 4 of their book, to which they devoted less than four pages, and of other topics discussed in other sections of the book. Since the article is a solid piece of research, I have only a few minor comments which testify to the validity of its findings.

My first comment relates to the factors hampering agricultural production in socialist countries mentioned at the very beginning of the paper. Although it could be considered among what the author calls "the systemic flaws associated with a command economy," the state intervention which results in pronounced differences in agricultural productivity between the state and non-state sectors deserves being mentioned separately. In another panel of this Conference, Alvarez (2000) documents with newly released data previous results by Alvarez and Puerta (1994). Regardless of land use patterns, non-state units have been more productive than state units in Cuba.

Another factor listed is the "undue reliance on extensive cultivation." Díaz-Briquets advances solid evidence with the use of the variable planted areas. A thorough documentation for sugarcane is contained in Peña Castellanos and Alvarez (1996). The state extensive growth model, applied mainly during the 1980s, relied on extensive plantings to make up for decreases in productivity. This fact brought about the depopulation of sugarcane areas, one of the main factors responsible for the poor performance of this industry in the 1990s.

The second comment goes to the author's assertion that, by choosing 1945 and 1989 as the years for comparisons, he was unable to isolate the important changes in Cuban agriculture that began after World War II. It is obvious that the 44-year period is a big jump for this type of analysis. Díaz-Briquets' findings, however, do not change when pre-1959 data are considered. The 1946 Agricultural Census was the last one performed in pre-1959 Cuba. (The 1953 Housing, Population and Electoral Census did not include this type of information.) There are data, however, that can be used to validate the author's conclusions. In fact, Rodríguez (1963, p. 22) shows that between 1946 and 1957, area planted to sugarcane (the crop with the highest land area) increased by only 2.6%. Additional proof has been compiled by Equipo (1971, p. 70) and reproduced in Pérez Marín (1990, p. 36). When data for 1950 are compared with the 1946 Agricultural Census data, one finds that 12 out of 18 crops studied experienced negative growth, while six experienced the opposite. It is interesting to note that, in the first group, we find sugarcane, which implies that the just-mentioned growth took place after 1950. To further corroborate the author's results, all 18 crops combined experienced a decrease in area of 20%. These two sets of data contain irrefutable proof that growth was lacking between 1946 and 1959, and that the tremendous growth in planted areas occurred during the socialist revolution.

My third point is more a suggestion than a comment. The previous remarks include an implicit *ceteris paribus* assumption. We know that everything did not remain equal. An important factor to consider is population growth. It is obvious that Cuba's population did not remain unchanged from 1946 to 1989. If food imports of the type we have considered did not

increase considerably, then, in the absence of productivity gains, additional land had to be planted to feed the growing population. The author could relate a measure of land use with population. For example, a simple correlation between population and area planted could show interesting results that could further validate the author's findings.

As a final point, I would like to mention that the author states that the evidence being collected and published in recent years seem to indicate that Cuba's agricultural production decline may originate in the substantial degradation of Cuba's natural resource base. Díaz-Briquets adds that "it is surprising that hardly any attention has been directed to assess the potential effect of environmental factors in the production collapse." Those words constitute a challenge for those of us working on Cuban agricultural issues.

REFERENCES

Alvarez, José. "Differences in Agricultural Productivity Between the State and Nonstate Sectors: Further Evidence." *Cuba in Transition—Volume 10.* Washington: Association for the Study of the Cuban Economy, 2000.

Alvarez, José and Ricardo A. Puerta. "State Intervention in Cuban Agriculture: Impact on Organization and Performance." *World Development* 12:11 (1994), pp. 1663-1675.

Díaz-Briquets, Sergio and Jorge Pérez-López. *Conquering Nature: The Environmental Legacy of Socialism in Cuba.* Pittsburgh: University of Pittsburgh Press, 2000.

Equipo de Investigaciones Económicas. *El Sector Agropecuario en la Década 1959-1969: Experiencias y Perspectivas.* La Habana: Instituto de Economía, Universidad de la Habana, June 1971.

Peña Castellanos, Lázaro and José Alvarez. "The Transformation of the State Extensive Growth Model in Cuba's Sugarcane Agriculture." *Agriculture and Human Values* 13:1 (1996), pp. 59-68.

Pérez Marín, Enrique. *Agropecuaria - Desarrollo Económico.* La Habana: Editorial de Ciencias Sociales, 1990.

Rodríguez, Carlos Rafael. "Cuatro Años de Reforma Agraria." *Cuba Socialista* 21 (1963), p. 22.

LA SITUACIÓN AMBIENTAL DE CUBA AL FINALIZAR EL SIGLO XX

Eudel Eduardo Cepero

Este documento constituye un reordenamiento de las notas, artículos y comentarios escritos en los últimos cinco años del siglo pasado, unidos a los tres informes anuales de la Agencia Ambiental Entorno Cubano, 1997, 98 y 99. La estructura estará dada por capítulos dedicados a los principales elementos del entorno, a saber: suelos, vegetación, aguas, cuencas hidrográficas, zonas costeras y de playas, fauna, atmósfera, sociedad y además legislación ambiental. En ellos se exponen hechos, cifras, valoraciones y ejemplos que demuestran, lamentablemente, la critica situación ambiental del archipiélago cubano al concluir el siglo XX.

He omitido a ex profeso la introducción en aras de la síntesis pero soy conciente que la situación actual es el resultado de la concatenación de factores y accionares insostenibles practicados sobre nuestros ecosistemas, especialmente durante los últimos cuarenta años de experimentos desarrollistas caracterizados por el voluntarismo, el irraciocinio y la terquedad. Hago votos por que este manuscrito cumpla su objetivo a pesar de imperfecciones y defectos.

LOS SUELOS

En Cuba existen algo menos de 8 millones de hectáreas (ha) de tierras cultivables, de ellas más de la mitad están erosionadas. Los casos más críticos se encuentran en la provincia de Guantánamo donde 485 mil ha de las 618 mil con que cuentan, el 80%, sufren los efectos de la erosión y en la de Camagüey, donde están afectadas 1 millón de ha del área física de tierra firme, el 75% del total. Estudios publicados estiman que el 25 porciento de los suelos agrícolas está

erosionados con categoría de fuerte y muy fuerte, además se incluyen como factores degradantes de las tierras el drenaje deficiente, la salinización, la acidez, la compactación y la formación de corazas infértiles.

Todo lo anterior ha generado las siguientes consecuencias: 4.2 millones de ha degradadas por erosión artificial, un millón por salinización, 1.5 por acidez y 2.5 por compactación.

A escala nacional la correlación entre erosión de suelos y los principales cultivos es la siguiente: tabaco 97%, cítricos 91%, caña de azúcar 68%, pastos 79%, cultivos varios 86%, café y cacao 95% y forestales 90%. Como resultado el 46 porciento de los suelos está en la categoría de baja agro productividad y el 14 se considera muy baja porque en ellos no se logra el 30 porciento del potencial productivo de los cultivos, es decir que el 60 porciento de las tierras agrícolas cubanas tiene bajos rendimientos.

La salinización ha cambiado su escenario habitual en Guantánamo para manifestarse en otras zonas del país como es el caso de la región sur de La Habana y Pinar del Río donde existen afectadas por salinidad 417,916 ha cultivadas de pastos, 89,061 ha de caña de azúcar y 6,875 ha de arroz.

Otro problema es la compactación de tierras en áreas cañeras con una alta mecanización. Los camiones y remolques así como las combinadas empleadas en la cosecha pesan unas 42 toneladas (Tn) y pasan dos veces por el mismo surco durante esa labor de forma que el suelo recibe el peso de unas 84 Tn y la compactación de 60 gomas. Si se considera que un gran porciento del corte se realiza por ese método es previsible estimar la magnitud del problema.

Los terrenos ganaderos no escapan al cuadro general, constatándose una disminución en los contenidos de los principales nutrientes y un notable incremento de la acidez. Todo lo anterior ha llevado al uso oficial del término *desertificación* para definir el deterioro en que se encuentran los suelos en algunas regiones del país. La aparición de zonas desérticas en la isla es el resultado de factores políticos, económicos y sociales como la pobreza, el atraso técnico, uso inadecuado de las tierras, excesivo pastoreo, deforestación, mala gestión de las fuentes de agua y por la implementación de estrategias agrarias insostenibles con el entorno natural.

Se consideran en franco proceso hacia estadio desértico territorios en la desembocadura del río Cauto, la parte sudoccidental de Pinar del Río, norte y sur de Camagüey así como algunas zonas de Las Tunas. En Camagüey las porciones más afectadas por la desertificación se ubican en los municipios Guaimaro, Sibanicú y Najasa con tierras que apenas resisten tres o cuatro años de uso agrícola. La provincia de Pinar del Río es quizás el peor de los ejemplos pues el flagelo avanza a un ritmo de 11 kilómetros (Km) por año, afectando importantes zonas ganaderas, tabacaleras, arroceras y de cultivos varios. La salinización es patente en unas 574,000 ha, mientras la erosión se extiende por más de 279,000 ha y es en la llanura sur donde la desertificación se denota con mayor intensidad al punto de existir intrusión salina entre 15 y 20 Km tierra adentro.

Una cuestión por valorarse es la afectación económica de la degradación de tierras pues además del efecto inmediato que puede ocasionar, por ejemplo, la erosión en el campo al disminuir los rendimientos, existe otro costo fuera de este al destruir los arrastres la infraestructura agrícola y social. Por otra parte el costo ecológico de esta situación es muy alto pues los suelos constituyen en si un ecosistema y a la vez el sustento de otros que pueden ser afectados indirectamente.

Lamentablemente la degradación de los suelos cubanos alcanzó a finales del siglo XX la magnitud de catástrofe ambiental.

LA VEGETACIÓN

La actual superficie boscosa del país es un misterio dado que existen numerosas cifras al respecto.

- Un artículo aparecido en el semanario *Trabajadores* en 1997 afirma: "La superficie boscosa del país deberá llegar a un 27%. Actualmente es de un 21%." Considerando lo anterior y que la relación bosque-territorio era del 26.8% en 1993, según valores del Programa Nacional de Medioambiente (adecuación cubana de la Agenda 21), en esos tres años fue deforestado 643,347.6 ha, el 5.8% del área boscosa del país y de mantenerse ese ritmo en una década podrían desaparecer los bosques de Cuba.

- En el mismo año y medio periodístico también se publicó otro trabajo el cual refiere: "El país dispone actualmente de un 15% de área boscosa." De valorarse esta cifra entonces la relación bosque-territorio ha disminuido en un 11.8% entre 1993 y 1997 pudiendo desaparecer el área boscosa de la isla en unos cinco años.

- Sin embargo un artículo publicado en el semanario *Juventud Rebelde* en junio del 2000 indica que ha ocurrido un crecimiento espectacular del área forestal, según la fuente: "Actualmente el 23,4% de la superficie total de Cuba está cubierta por plantaciones boscosas, y en el año 1959 teníamos sólo alrededor del 18 por ciento." Si hasta el año 1998 el gobierno cubano reconocía un área forestal de 2.4 millones de hectáreas, el 21.0 porciento del archipiélago, entonces esta nueva cifra es realmente increíble pues implica un crecimiento de un 2.4 porciento en apenas dos años, mientras que entre 1959 y 1998 solo se había logrado un aumento del 3 porciento.

De cualquier forma todo hace indicar que ha ocurrido una drástica disminución del área forestal del país que puede producir un retroceso a los índices de 1959 cuando la relación bosque territorio era del 14%, según valoraciones del gobierno cubano.

La situación es grave dado que las tres cuartas partes de la explotación boscosa proviene de las forestas naturales y no de las plantaciones artificiales, las cuales son insuficientes para cubrir la demanda nacional de madera, que entre otros valores consume 1 millón de metros cúbicos de leña anualmente en la zafra azucarera. Sólo de Matanzas, se cortaron 2 millones de cujes para la producción de tabaco entre 1996 y 1997, mientras que el incremento de la producción tabacalera aumentó la tala para cujes en sitios tan sensibles como la Ciénaga de Zapata y la península de Guanahacabibes.

A lo anterior debe agregarse la mantenida explotación irracional de los bosques naturales que aún quedan en el país como lo demuestra la extracción de más de 8,000 metros cúbicos de maderas preciosas durante 1999 de las reservas arbóreas del municipio Imias, en la provincia de Guantánamo.

Los incendios forestales constituyen otro factor que influye en la deforestación de los bosques cubanos donde cada siniestro afecta como promedio 13 ha. Este tipo de flagelo tomó un dramático protagonismo durante 1998:

- Se inició la trágica secuela en el mes de abril cuando ardió la meseta de Cajálbana, en Pinar del Río, dañándose más de 500 ha de bosques naturales y plantaciones artificiales de Pino Macho, en una zona catalogada entre los mayores semilleros mundiales de esa variedad.

- Aproximadamente un mes más tarde, en la Isla de la Juventud otro siniestro de grandes proporciones destruyó el 20 porciento de la mayor reserva natural de cotorras del planeta, quedando calcinados ecosistemas de palmeras, pinares, bosques de galería y ciénagas, y junto a ellos el habitad de aves en peligro de extinción como la cotorra cubana, el tocororo, el carpintero verde, el sijú platanero y otros.

- Menos de treinta días después otro mega-incendio llevó a cenizas 2,000 ha en una importante zona de bosques naturales de la provincia de Guantánamo, destruyendo reservas con valiosas especies maderables como el guayacán, ébano negro, cuya, jatía y carbonero.

Por su parte en 1999 los incendios forestales alcanzaron record de destrucción en las exiguas y depauperadas zonas boscosas del archipiélago. De enero a mayo se produjeron 301 siniestros, 76 más que el promedio anual calculado para los últimos 15 años, en esos cinco meses fueron destruidas 16,000 ha, valor que sobrepasa espectacularmente el término medio histórico estimado para un año en 5,000 ha:

- El 8 de abril se inició un colosal incendio que destruyó 6,300 ha de plantaciones forestales con más de 30 años en un lugar conocido como Las Delicias al norte de la carretera que va a Mantua en la provincia de Pinar del Río.

- Veinticuatro días más tarde se desató otro siniestro de grandes proporciones en la misma provincia el cual dejó calcinadas 3,500 ha en una importante área protegida conocida como Cayo Ratones afectándose un listado florístico que asciende a 374 especies, 101 de ellas endémicas o únicas del lugar.

Estos dos mega-incendios forestales están catalogados entre los mayores de los últimos cuarenta años y fueron atribuidos a negligencias en la quema de un terreno así como a la caída de un rayo, respectivamente.

Según estadísticas oficiales en el país ocurre un promedio de 200 incendios forestales anuales que afectan unas 5,000 ha de bosques y se asegura que de mantenerse esa tendencia puede peligrar una extensión forestal equivalente a la existente en la Sierra del Escambray.

Un estudio validado entre 1961 y 1996 afirma que las negligencias fueron responsables del 44% de los incendios forestales, el 10 corresponde a actos intencionales y un 34 de origen desconocido pero vinculadas al hombre, mientras sólo el 12% está dado por la propia naturaleza, debido principalmente a descargas eléctricas.

Existe una extensa relación de causas y condiciones que favorecen los fuegos en los bosques, de la cual vale señalar:

- Alta incidencia de personas circulando por zonas boscosas y colindantes en busca de leña para combustible y de alimentos.

- Escasa señalización sobre el peligro de incendio.

- Insuficiente sistema de torres de observación para la detección y localización de siniestros.

- Deficiente red de comunicación radiofónica.

- Falta de mantenimientos y tratamientos silviculturales al bosque (acumulándose material combustible compuesto por maniguas, hojas, troncos, etc.).

La estrategia en la repoblación forestal del gobierno cubano se ha caracterizado por el manejo de cifras millonarias, en cuanto a posturas a plantar. Ejemplo de lo anterior es la provincia de Camagüey la cual en el pasado se propuso, y dieron por cumplidos, planes de reforestación que llegaron hasta los 100 millones de posturas en un año. A pesar de ello se mantiene como el territorio más desforestado de Cuba con una supervivencia de lo plantado que no supera el 45% en los últimos cuatro años. Esta ultima cifra es el común denominador para toda la isla.

A finales de julio de 1997 fue convocada por la Asamblea Nacional del Poder Popular una Audiencia Nacional Forestal en Pinar del Río. En la misma se discutieron los problemas de ese sector y se expuso un programa diseñando para los primeros 15 años del próximo siglo, mediante el cual se pretende la siembra de 700 mil ha de árboles con diferentes fines productivos, la mejora de 356 mil ha de bosques naturales y el incremento en 2.5 veces de la producción de madera, 78% de la cual procederá de plantaciones fomentadas con ese fin. Sin embargo, el objetivo principal de ese programa — alcanzar un 27% de área boscosa en el 2015 — implica un incremento de tan solo el 0.2% con relación al año 1993, cuando la relación bosque-territorio era del 26.8% (según datos del Programa Nacional de Medioambiente).

Un estudio nacional sobre áreas protegidas determinó la existencia de 80 zonas de significación y 287 reconocidas en todo el territorio, así como 8 reservas naturales, 22 de tipo ecológico, 11 florísticas, 14 parques naturales, 11 refugios de fauna, cuatro elementos naturales destacados y dos paisajes naturales protegidos. Vale recordar que en el país existen cuatro reservas de la biósfera proclamadas por la UNESCO: Sierra del Rosario, Península de Guanahacabibes, Baconao, y Cuchillas del Toa. No obstante el Centro Nacional de Áreas Protegidas ha insistido públicamente en la necesidad de preservar todos los espacios naturales y semi-naturales pues en muchos de ellos se llevan a cabo acciones que conspiran contra su conservación.

La publicación de *El Catalogo de Malezas de Cuba* constituye una interesante evaluación de la vegetación del archipiélago. Según el inventario existen 888 especies indeseables agrupadas en 416 géneros de 103 familias, de ese total 181 son endémicas para un 9.12 porciento.

El desarrollo por primera vez de una caña trasgénica de azúcar parece ser un hito en la "biorrevolucion verde" que promueven las autoridades cubanas en el interés de encontrar soluciones biotecnológicas que resuelvan las dificultades de la producción agrícola. La nueva gramínea posee genes resistentes a los hongos causantes de las enfermedades conocidas como roya y carbón, no necesita la aplicación de productos químicos, es auto pesticida y resistente a los herbicidas de amplio espectro. Sin embargo la utilización masiva de organismos genéticamente modificados puede generar flujos no controlados hacia otras plantas silvestres las cuales podrían transformarse en supermalezas o sea malas hierbas resistentes a herbicidas, plagas y enfermedades.

LAS AGUAS

La contaminación de ríos, arroyos, embalses, zonas costeras y bahías constituye una realidad en el entorno cubano. El río Almendares con una cuenca aproximada de 402 Kilómetros cuadrados es el ejemplo más elocuente por atravesar la ciudad de La Habana. Según estudios, a esa corriente fluvial se arrojan diariamente unos 19 315 metros cúbicos de desechos de los cuales el 80% son urbanos y el resto sólidos y desperdicios fabriles.

Otro caso es la cuenca del río San Pedro que drena más de 500 kilómetros cuadrados desde el centro hacia el sur de Camagüey, en cuyo curso superior se encuentra la ciudad del mismo nombre, escurriendo aguas contaminadas por los albañales de la capital provincial, los residuos crudos o deficientemente tratados de 17 centros industriales y de 12 instalaciones para la ceba de cerdos con más de cien cabezas. En ese cauce se puede encontrar: hidrocarburos, aguas ácidas, fibras de celulosa, cemento, esmeriles, grasas y detergentes, entre otros contaminantes.

No solo son las corrientes fluviales citadinas las contaminadas. En zonas naturales como las montañas de Pinar del Río ocho despulpadoras de café, varios asentamientos, aserríos y algunas industrias actúan como contaminantes. El asunto más critico en esta zona es el de las despulpadoras de café dado que sus aguas residuales incluyen la cáscara de grano, la cual posee un ácido muy agresivo que contamina cañadas, arroyos y ríos, constituyendo una de las causas fundamentales del deterioro ambiental en la región.

Otros ríos y arroyos son contaminados en al ámbito rural por los centrales azucareros, muchos de los cuales no tienen funcionando o no poseen sistemas para el tratamiento de residuales y vierten hidrocarburos, ácidos, grasas y cachaza licuada, situación que según los expertos esta dada en un 70% por indisciplinas tecnológicas.

Existen otras muchas fuentes contaminantes menos conocidas que los centrales azucareros, incluso pequeñas, capaces de hacer aportes considerables de sustancias agresivas como lo demuestran los siguientes datos tomados de un taller automotriz del Ministerio del Azúcar en Camagüey que procesa de 10 a 16 vehículos diarios lanzando al alcantarillado, durante un año: 2,800 litros de petróleo y 4,200 de nafta provenientes del lavado de piezas, 840 mil litros de agua emulsionada con grasa y petróleo del fregado de carros, y 56 metros cúbicos de sólidos con hidrocarburos por desecho de maquinado.

De las 2,200 principales fuentes contaminantes registradas en Cuba, 167 pertenecen al sector azucarero y precisamente los frágiles ecosistemas costeros del archipiélago son contaminados por afluentes que provienen en un 47 porciento de ingenios, destilerías y fabricas de torulas, otro 26 porciento es doméstico, un 10 de la industria alimenticia, 5 la agricultura y el resto se contabiliza en la categoría de otros.

Los Cangilones del Río Máximo

La contaminación de los "Cangilones del Río Máximo," es quizás el ejemplo más notorio en cuanto a polución de una corriente hídrica debido a que afecta

un popular elemento natural de la geografía cubana y a la demora en la solución del problema. Las reconocidas piscinas marmóreas, ubicadas en la provincia de Camagüey, permanecen cerradas al baño desde 1993 por recibir los residuales de una fábrica de alevines (juveniles de peces). Incluso las propias autoridades ambientales reconocieron el problema en el documento titulado: *Situación que Presenta el Monumento Nacional Cangilones del Río Máximo*, compilado por el Grupo de Fiscalización y Control del Ministerio de Ciencia, Tecnología y Medio Ambiente (CITMA) durante 1995, en el se expone:

> El río Máximo situado al norte de la provincia de Camagüey, al atravesar una zona de rocas calizas muy cristalizadas, cubiertas por un profundo suelo aluvial, ha cortado en la caliza subyacente un interesante cauce que por más de 350 metros constituye una piscina natural de gran belleza: Los Cangilones del Río Máximo, declarado monumento nacional.

> Sin embargo, los importantes recursos naturales que posee esta área han sido afectados en gran medida por el desarrollo económico experimentado en el territorio, las piscinas casi marmóreas han perdido su blancura y belleza y las aguas su transparencia y calidad.

Las principales afectaciones por "el desarrollo económico experimentado en el territorio," comenzaron en 1969 al terminarse la presa *Hidráulico Cubana* con capacidad para embalsar 20 millones de metros cúbicos (m3) de agua en el río Santa Cruz, afluente del Máximo, a escasos kilómetros aguas arriba de los Cangilones. Esto comenzó a limitar el escurrimiento natural por las piscinas y si bien no ocasionó gran impacto sirvió de fuente a la futura acción contaminadora del lugar. Once años más tarde es cerrado el dique de la presa *Máximo*, ubicada en el río de igual nombre también aguas arriba de los baños marmóreos, represándose 70 millones de m3 para regar las áreas citrícolas del municipio Sierra de Cubitas mediante un complejo sistema hidráulico (1,014 caballerías), lo cual implicaba pasar por las piscinas 10 m3/segundo de agua en los meses de junio, julio y agosto pero afortunadamente solo se construyeron unas 500 caballerías del regadío, hoy inactivo.

En 1982 se terminó un centro para la cria intensiva de alevines (tilapias, tencas, etc.), en la margen izquierda del río Santa Cruz, formado por 78 estanques que utilizan 10 millones de m3 de agua al año de la presa *Hidráulico Cubana*, los cuales son fertilizados en los reservorios para acelerar el crecimiento de los alevines. En este fin se utilizan anualmente 800 Tn de pienso orgánico (compuesto por maíz, soya, aceites minerales, harina de pescado y paja de arroz), o gallinaza (excretas de gallinas), y 400 Tn de urea y superfosfatos, aplicadas en dosis de 70 Kg/ha con una periodicidad de diez días. El llenado y vaciado alterno de los estanques produce vertimientos diarios de residuales al río Santa Cruz; éste los conduce por su cauce hasta mezclarlos con las aguas del Máximo el cual los hace pasar por los Cangilones. También en 1982, la Empresa de Campismo Popular inaugura la base turística *Los Cangilones*, ubicada muy próxima a las piscinas naturales pero sin incluirlas dentro de su jurisdicción a pesar de ser el principal atractivo. En la actualidad la Empresa Agropecuaria Militar es el tenente del sitio.

Diez años después, durante los estudios para el *Proyecto de Ordenación, Manejo y Desarrollo de la Cuenca del Río Máximo*, un muestreo de aguas realizado en los Cangilones indicó altas concentraciones de coliformes fecales (excretas), desatándose una aguda polémica entre especialistas y funcionarios de diferentes instituciones sobre la magnitud de la contaminación y su peligro para la salud humana, esto, además, dio vigencia a primarios llamados de alerta sobre el particular.

La disyuntiva llegó el 22 de noviembre de 1993 cuando se dieron a conocer los resultados de un estudio sobre las aguas de los Cangilones, realizado por especialistas del Centro Provincial de Higiene y Epidemiología (CPHE). El mismo dice:

> Tal como pudo comprobarse con los muestreos realizados el agua de baño de los Cangilones no reúne los requisitos establecidos para el agua de baño por la norma cubana 93-07:1986.

> Se encontró en el área de baño de los Cangilones presencia de gérmenes patógenos peligrosos para la salud.

> La calidad del agua de baño se ve afectada por el vertimiento de los residuales líquidos de la Estación de Alevinaje.

Esta investigación fue avalada por el director del CPHE en Camagüey y fundamentó el cierre de la base de campismo así como la prohibición del baño en el lugar.

Otra valoración que describe correctamente la situación prevaleciente se encuentra en el *Informe sobre la reunión celebrada el día 7 de noviembre en los Cangilones del Río Máximo, con vistas a trazar la estrategia de trabajo para la rehabilitación de esta área natural*, elaborado por el CITMA en 1995:

> Contaminación: En primer lugar por su incidencia la estación de alevinaje, que se encuentra muy cercana al área y no posee sistema de tratamiento de residuales, contamina el arroyo Santa Cruz cerca de su confluencia con el Máximo...

> Manejo: Los grandes volúmenes de agua que en ocasiones alivian los embalses "Máximo" y "Santa Cruz," situados aguas arriba del área, provocan un impacto negativo en el río, ... limitando su uso para el baño.

> La falta de una protección efectiva por parte de la unidad agropecuaria militar, ha permitido también la deforestación del entorno...

Las primeras acciones para rehabilitar los Cangilones se iniciaron dos años antes del citado informe, cuando el 14 de septiembre de 1993 especialistas de la Empresa Nacional de Proyectos Agropecuarios de Camagüey, expusieron tres ideas de solución ante un consejo de expertos formado por profesionales del Instituto de Hidroeconomía, Planificación Física y la extinta Academia de Ciencias, determinándose avalar la de los primeros. Las ultimas referencias al respecto de los Cangilones indican que finalmente las autoridades ambientales comenzaron a ejecutar la idea propuesta hace ocho años.

Las Zonas Costeras

Las zonas costeras reciben todos los residuales antes relacionados que son transportados precisamente por los ríos contaminados, siendo muy elocuente el ejemplo de la bahía de La Habana donde el contenido de oxígeno por litro es de 1.2 miligramos, los hidrocarburos flotantes de 24 Tn por día y la materia orgánica 105 Tn/día. Además se mantienen muy altos los contenidos de coliformes fecales (organismos excretados por el hombre) haciendo imposible cualquier tipo de contacto humano con las aguas.

Igual de crítico es el caso de la bahía de Nuevitas, al norte de Camagüey, cuyas aguas contienen azufre, ácido clorhídrico, plomo e hidrocarburos provenientes de cinco fuentes contaminantes, a saber: fábrica de alambres de púas y electrodos, fábrica de fertilizantes, central termoeléctrica, fábrica de cemento y terminal marítima de combustible.

La "Laguna de la Leche," reservorio natural con 27 millones de metros cúbicos de agua dulce ubicado en la costa norte de Ciego de Ávila está sufriendo serios y quizás irreversibles daños ecológicos. Los talleres ferroviarios de Morón, el combinado porcino y la industria pesquera de Turiguanó, así como los centrales azucareros "Patria" y "Enrique José Varona,"entre otros vierten sus aguas cargadas de desechos tóxicos en el otrora paradisíaco lago. Ineficientes e insostenibles obras hidrotécnicas construidas en la década de los ochenta al calor de la llamada "Voluntad Hidráulica" propiciaron la penetración del mar y con ello la salinización del mencionado acuatorio. Posteriormente a principios de los noventa un programa para la recuperación de la laguna implicó el cierre de un canal que comunicaba con la costa así como la construcción de un sistema de compuertas que nunca funcionó y si bien se disminuyó la concentración de sal en el agua también bajaron considerablemente los niveles de oxigeno en las mismas.

El derrame de unas 500 Tn de petróleo en la bahía de Matanzas, debido a la colisión de dos buques el 26 de marzo de 1998, fue el hecho más significativo relacionado con las radas. El hidrocarburo afectó entre 250 y 500 metros de costas en una zona de playas urbanas siendo necesario extraer unos 10,000 metros cúbicos de arena contaminada. Dos meses después del accidente se mantenía sumergido un volumen importante del combustible vertido y los especialistas aseguran que el proceso de recuperación será largo y lento.

Aunque en sentido general las aguas de la plataforma insular cubana no pueden considerarse contaminadas existen zonas identificadas por su afectación, con mención especial para la región de Moa y Nicaro debido a la polución por metales pesados.

En cuanto a los corales se afirma que el factor más dañino para los mismos es la sedimentación orgánica, y si bien oficialmente se asegura que sólo el tres porciento de los 3,000 km de estas formaciones alrededor del archipiélago están afectadas por ese flagelo existe una importante latencia de peligro, al estar expuestos al mal el 47 porciento de ese total debido a su cercanía a las costas y el alto grado de erosión que existe en los suelos de la isla.

Embalses e Irrigación

Por su parte los embalses no están exceptos de contaminación. Un estudio confirmó la existencia de altas concentraciones de mercurio en los sedimentos de la presa "Niña Bonita," ubicada en los límites de los municipios La Lisa y Bauta, en La Habana. La investigación detectó en los peces del lago artificial concentraciones de cadmio en el orden límite máximo admisible para el consumo humano y en el caso del mercurio por encima de lo estipulado para igual fin, señalando, entre otros, como focos contaminantes del reservorio a: Fábrica de Sueros y Hemoderivados, Instituto "Pedro Kourí" así como los repartos "Villa Pol" y "XX Aniversario."

El empleo del agua y sobretodo el precio del agua a pagar por la agricultura, la industria y otros productores es fijo: 5 pesos por cada mil metros cúbicos si el agua proviene de cuencas superficiales y solo $1.80 pesos cuando se trata de las subterráneas. Estas tarifas son bajas y no estimulan el ahorro ni representan el valor real del recurso siendo peligroso vender a tan bajo precio el agua de los mantos freáticos, estimulando el sobre consumo y por ende el agotamiento de los mismos con la ocurrencia de impredecibles costos ecológicos y económicos porque la recuperación de las cuencas subterráneas es un proceso natural demorado.

Acueductos

El despilfarro de agua se mantiene como otro de los problemas ambientales que afectan los recursos hídricos. Baste considerar que de los 30 millones m3 bombeados mensualmente hacia la capital del país 12 se pierden en derroches y salideros. Precisamente en la ciudad de La Habana existen 357 entidades consideradas como grandes consumidoras del líquido, sin embargo en el primer semestre de 1999 solo pudo medirse el gasto en 189 de ellas y en 82 la tasa supera los 4 millones 200,000 metros cúbicos. La anterior situación es similar en todo el país, incluso existe una mayor incidencia hacia el interior pues solo La Habana y Varadero posee parte de la infraestructura necesaria para medir el uso del agua.

La necesidad de mantenimientos en las obras hidráulicas, el alto costo operacional de muchos sistemas, el excesivo represamiento de las cuencas, la falta de disciplina tecnológica y de cultura ecológica hacen del actual un momento infeliz para el uso sostenible del agua en Cuba.

LAS CUENCAS HIDROGRÁFICAS

El deterioro de suelos, aguas y vegetación no son fenómenos aislados. Se manifiestan concatenados en los territorios topográficamente delimitados y drenados por ríos que son denominadas cuencas hidrográficas.

En Cuba existen 632 cuencas hidrográficas mayores de 5 kilómetros, de ellas sobresalen por su tamaño la de los ríos Cauto, Zaza y Sagua la Grande, las tres mayores en ese orden.

Los principales problemas ambientales de las cuencas son el vertimiento de residuales urbanos, industriales y agropecuarios, la deforestación, la salinización de aguas y suelos, y la erosión de tierras.

La Cuenca del Cauto

Una cuenca donde ocurren todos esos fenómenos degradantes es en la del Cauto. El mayor río del archipiélago es envenenado por 652 focos contaminantes que irradian sus cargas desde las provincias Santiago de Cuba, Holguín y Las Tunas. El índice de evaporación promedio (1,951 mm) de la cuenca es superior al de precipitación (1,190 mm) lo cual se debe en buena parte a la deforestación. Esto último aceleró la erosión de riberas en una región que tiene el 36 porciento de sus tierras consideradas como muy fuerte y fuertemente erosionadas, donde incluso es posible observar cárcavas gigantes con más de 30 metros de profundidad y espectaculares deslizamientos de tierra en las márgenes del río.

Desde la desembocadura del Cauto hacia adentro, hasta 62 Km, las aguas están salinizadas. Un ejemplo tragicómico es *Cabezada*, poblado que desde 1985 solo recibe el agua potable mediante una patana a pesar de estar ubicado en la orilla de la mayor corriente de agua dulce del país. Para colmo, en su curso final el río corre al revés pues el gasto natural debe ser de cinco metros cúbicos por segundo y dado el represamiento es de tan solo dos.

El conocimiento público de la situación ambiental en esa corriente fluvial ha causado un fuerte impacto en la opinión nacional por ser uno de los elementos naturales más conocidos del país. El estado en que se encuentra ha sido el motivo de que se le nombre popularmente como el *excusado de oriente*.

Las causas de tanta destrucción algunos las remontan a la llegada de Colón pero los testimonios de personas que aún viven en las orillas del Cauto confirman que hace 40 o 50 años la situación era bien diferente. La realidad es que desde mediados de la década del sesenta el curso inferior de la cuenca del río Cauto sirvió de polígono de pruebas a los planes para el desarrollo agrícola del país diseñados sin tener en cuenta la dimensión ambiental.

El irracional desbroce mecanizado de extensas zonas boscosas que fueron sustituidas por pastizales y cultivos de arroz así como la construcción de faraónicos sistemas de riego unido al excesivo represamiento de la cuenca por embalses como el de Cauto-El Paso, son reconocidos entre las principales causas de la actual situación. La tala incontrolada del bosque de galería ubicado en las márgenes fue otro proceso negativo acentuado en el "período especial" por la falta de combustible doméstico lo que unido al libre pastoreo de reses y el asentamiento de aparceros en esas frágiles zonas coadyuvaron a completar el desastre.

En 1996 fue creado el Consejo de la Cuenca del Río Cauto, encargado de dar respuestas integrales a los problemas que inciden en ese territorio, el cual elaboró un informe titulado *Caracterización General Ambiental de la Cuenca Hidrográfica del Río Cauto* donde, entre otros tópicos, se considera que solo para rehabilitar los suelos afectados por salinidad se necesitan $179,500 mil pesos.

Otras Cuencas

Otro ejemplo lo constituye la zona drenada por el río Zaza, considerada la segunda más extensa del país, donde coexisten 100 especies de la flora, 20 de mamíferos, 119 de aves, 19 de reptiles y 5 de anfibios, la mayoría endémicos y varios en peligro de extinción. Los diagnósticos coinciden en señalar la desforestación como el primer problema ambiental en la cuenca del Zaza, seguido por la contaminación hídrica que propician 64 fuentes, de las cuales el 80 porciento lanza sus residuales sin tratar, además del excesivo represamiento de sus aguas por tres embalses, incluido el mayor de Cuba y 41 micropresas. Además se encuentran seriamente afectadas otras seis cuencas, a saber: Toa, Guantánamo-Guaso, Hanabanilla, Almendares-Vento, y Cuyaguateje.

Otra cuenca incluida en la nefasta lista de las más afectadas es la del río Ariguanabo, en la provincia de La Habana donde drena 188 Km cuadrados de los municipios Bauta, Bejucal y Caimito. Esta cuenca también presenta una situación ambiental critica motivada por la contaminación de las aguas, la deforestación y la erosión de los suelos. Se contabilizan 42 focos contaminantes y una singular situación debido a la existencia, a lo largo del río, de un tipo de alga sembrada hace mas de 20 años la cual al crecer hasta la superficie perjudica la navegación y daña la estabilidad de las aguas.

La situación ambiental en estos territorios llevó a la creación en 1997 del Consejo Nacional de Cuencas Hidrográficas, a fin de revertir el deterioro ambiental existente y propiciar su protección y rehabilitación. La ministra de Ciencia, Tecnología y Medio Ambiente (CITMA) preside el consejo que tiene entre sus funciones proponer al gobierno la relación de aquellas cuencas que por su importancia ambiental requieren de una atención priorizada además de evaluar y aprobar los programas de manejo. Sin embargo en abril de 1999 el Consejo Nacional de Cuencas informó que se mantenía la pérdida de la capacidad productiva de los suelos como el principal problema ambiental en esos territorios, además solamente se habían solucionado el 35 porciento de las 2,153 fuentes contaminates que polucionan los principales

ríos de la nación mientras se avanza aún con menos impulso en la reforestación de las márgenes.

LAS ZONAS COSTERAS Y DE PLAYAS

El archipiélago cubano está formado por unas 4,195 islas, cayos y cayuelos que se agrupan en cuatro sub-archipiélagos a saber: Los Canarreos, De Los Colorados, Jardines de la Reina y Jardines del Rey. Este ultimo, el más extenso con unos 400 islotes, hasta finales de los ochenta poseía un paisaje casi prístino con formaciones vegetales de manglar, en sus diferentes variables florísticas, matorral y bosque siempre verde. En él se concentraban las mayores poblaciones de la fauna terrestre con unas 1,249 especies de las cuales el 20 porciento se consideran únicas de la cayería. Mención especial merece los recursos marinos: lagunas interiores y playas protegidas por extensos sistemas de dunas fósiles.

El 23 de marzo de 1987 a las tres de la tarde una brigada elite de construcción del gobierno cubano comenzó a lanzar piedras en la costa norte de Ciego de Ávila para cimentar una carretera sobre los bajos mares de La Bahía de Los Perros, el pedraplen a Cayo Coco, y con ello se dio inicio a la destrucción de los antes descritos ecosistemas. Dieciséis meses más tarde se daba por terminado el primer pedraplen del país.

Las consecuencias no se hicieron esperar en La Bahía de Los Perros, cortada en dos por un inmenso "dique-pedraplen": variaron la salinidad, densidad, temperatura y el oxígeno disuelto en el agua, desapareciendo el 83 porciento de las especies marinas comerciales lo cual eliminó prácticamente la actividad pesquera en el tradicional puerto de Punta Alegre al registrarse en 1990 uno de los más bajos niveles de captura de su historia con 854.8 toneladas. Algo similar pasó con los manglares, de las aproximadamente 10,000 hectáreas solo el 47 porciento sobrevivió mientras que el 95 porciento del mangle rojo murió, al tiempo que se reducía en más de un 60 porciento las zonas propicias para el habitat del flamenco y la corúa.

La magnitud del desastre obligó a la publicación de algunas referencias en la prensa y a la confirmación oficial por parte de la ministra de Medio Ambiente. Además se comenzó a tratar de paliar la situación poniendo alcantarillas que los peces no cruzan, así como construyendo puentes que no logran el intercambio de aguas necesario y han trastocado el sistema natural de corrientes marinas.

Lo realmente increíble es que diez años después de inaugurarse el gobierno cubano reconoció públicamente la ineficiencia económica del pedraplen a Cayo Coco. Según un articulo del periódico *Granma*, la transportación de los materiales e insumos necesarios para el desarrollo y funcionamiento turístico del cayo es sumamente costosa a través del pedraplen, lo cual encarece las obras y disminuye los beneficios de los servicios que se ofertan. Para resolver esa situación se ha generado un nuevo impacto ambiental al construirse, al nordeste del islote, un puerto con atraque de 60 metros, dársena de maniobra y dragado de acceso para recibir patanas de hasta 1,000 Tn de capacidad. La fuente asegura que la puesta en operación del fondeadero reducirá considerablemente los costos de transportación al poder traspasar la mayoría de las cargas a la vía marítima.

La construcción de un aeropuerto internacional, sin la obligada licencia ambiental, es otra antiecológica obra justificada por la necesidad de disminuir los costos de transportar vacacionistas desde la terminal aérea de Ciego de Ávila.

Con el pedraplen llegó la colonización turística a los cayos para completar la estrategia de generar divisas con rapidez y lograr el milagro de la recuperación económica a costa de ese patrimonio natural de la nación. La destrucción se lleva a cabo a pesar de que el gobierno conoce las recomendaciones hechas para manejar la cayería norte por un grupo de especialistas cubanos bajo la asesoría del consultante de la ONU James Dobbin, a saber:

- La altura de las edificaciones no sobrepasará las dos plantas;

- No se podrán realizar movimientos de tierra que modifiquen el relieve;

- No se permitirá el relleno de lagunas o la construcción sobre el manglar;

- Solo será talada la vegetación estrictamente necesaria, etc.

Una valoración ambiental de los proyectos construidos en el sub-archipiélago confirma que se obvió la opinión del señor Dobbin: desbroce indiscriminado de la vegetación, empleo excesivo de movimientos de tierra, terraceo, terraplenado y rellenos, insistencia en la destrucción de lagunas costeras y primer línea de playas, tipología urbana de las construcciones contemplado estructuras grandes y pesadas no acordes con zonas costeras, etc.

Algo inverosímil es la explotación de canteras y prestamos en los cayos Coco, Guillermo y Romano generando profundos cambios en esos bellos paisajes ahora con unas 428.4 hectáreas de huecos.

Para colmo los efectos de todas esas acciones comienzan a reflejarse precisamente en la playa. Recientes valoraciones indican que la franja de arena en el sector conocido como El Peñón, en cayo Coco, ha disminuido con relación a 1984.

La colonización turística del litoral norte parece estar completándose con la terminación de las primeras obras en 11 islotes vírgenes ubicados frente a las costas de Villa Clara. El nuevo "polo turístico" se nombra "La Rosa Blanca de los Jardines del Rey" y contempla la explotación de unas 1,200 capacidades en cuatro hoteles que deberán estar listos para el año 2002.

Al mismo tiempo se dan los primeros pasos organizativos para desarrollar un turismo de alto confort encaminado al buceo, las actividades náuticas así como las playas, sobre los paradisíacos ecosistemas del archipiélago Jardines de la Reina, impresionante y delicado entorno ubicado al sureste de Cuba formado por 66 cayos e islas donde se destacan los extensos manglares y los bosques de coral negro.

Por su parte la salinidad en las bahías de San Juan de los Remedios y Buenavista aumentó en un 6.3 y un 11.3 porciento, respectivamente, luego de terminada la construcción del pedraplen a Cayo Santamaría, en la costa norte de Cuba. Según una investigación realizada por especialistas de Estudios Marinos de la empresa GEOCUBA, entre los años 1982 y 1996, el muro del pedraplen propicia que se acumule el agua en las márgenes derecha e izquierda provocando el aumento de la salinidad en estos lugares con gradientes espaciales muy altos, lo cual incide negativamente en esos ecosistemas. La misma fuente comprobó cambios espectaculares en la velocidad de las corrientes marinas en los antes mencionados acuatorios. Antes de la construcción de la obra la velocidad media tenía valores máximos de 60 centímetros por segundo actualmente llegan a 122 centímetros por segundo.

Si bien la inauguración de obras turísticas es tema cotidiano en la prensa oficial del país por otra parte no es común encontrar referencias sobre los efectos que causan esas construcciones sobre el entorno y tampoco son conocidos los resultados de los permisos ambientales a los cuales están obligados los inversionistas.

LA FAUNA

Unas 20 especies de pájaros cubanos se consideran desaparecidas mientras otras, como el gavilán caguarero están críticamente amenazadas. La perdida de sus hábitat por la acelerada deforestación de los bosques naturales, la cacería furtiva, la colecta de ejemplares con fines comerciales y otros desmanes constituyen las causas de la actual situación. Por otra parte, el ave más grande de las Antillas, la grulla cubana, tiene fuertemente amenazado su hábitat debido a la agricultura, la ganadería y la construcción de pedraplenes que afectan a los humedales de costa.

El gobierno afirma que especialistas de la Empresa de Flora y Fauna lograron detener la disminución de las poblaciones de cotorras que se encuentran estables debido a que se desarrollan en la red nacional de áreas protegidas. Así mismo avistaron y protegieron unos cinco ejemplares de la jutiíta de la tierra, la segunda más pequeña de Cuba, especie considerada extinguida desde 1982.

Por lo menos dos nuevas especies fueron introducidas a escala comercial en las factorías acuícolas del país durante 1999.

- La lubina especie marina del sur europeo ha comenzado a cebarse en una zona de la costa norte pinareña. Según los especialistas estos alevines deben alcanzar un peso de 400 gramos al cabo de los 10 meses y poseen una carne de alta calidad. Por tal motivo esperan tener unos 100,000 ejem-

plares a principios del próximo año y lograr producciones que superen las 10,000 Tn anuales de pescado.

- El otro ejemplar en la ya larga lista de especies foráneas aclimatadas es la langosta de agua dulce, oriunda de la región tropical del nordeste de Australia, la cual ha comenzado a ser comercializada por primera vez luego de dos años de implantación y pruebas de sobre vivencia en la estación de alevinaje "Los Molinos," ubicada en la periferia de Matanzas.

Se desconocen los efectos que pueden ocasionar la introducción de estas dos nuevas especies en la isla, cuyos ecosistemas están saturados de extranjeras como la tenca, la amura y la tilapia las cuales desplazan a las criollas truchas y biajacas de sus habituales nichos naturales.

Otra especie cubana ha sido reportada internacionalmente amenazada de extinción: el majá de Santa María debido a la desaparición su hábitat, la histórica persecución por parte de los campesinos y el incremento del consumo como alimento. Los ofidios de la isla no son venenosos y están catalogados en cuatro familias, ocho géneros así como unas 20 especies.

Un caso polémico parece ser el de las tortugas marinas, las cuales según las autoridades cubanas se encuentran fuera de peligro dentro de las aguas del archipiélago con una población que excede los 10,000 ejemplares. Sin embargo, la conferencia de las partes de la Convención para el Comercio Internacional de Especies Amenazadas de la Fauna y la Flora Silvestre (CITES), el cual recoge las especies en extremo peligro de extinción, celebrada en Harare, rechazó una propuesta cubana para la explotación comercial del Carey.

LA ATMÓSFERA

La contaminación atmosférica no es problema generalizado en Cuba; existe localmente en zonas industriales como ciudad de La Habana, Moa, Nicaro o Nuevitas. También el hecho de que el crudo nacional posee un elevado contenido de azufre provoca contaminación ácida de la atmósfera en algunos lugares y otro tanto ocurre con el hollín, el polvo y las cenizas.

La contaminación atmosférica en el caso de la ciudad de Nuevitas, en la provincia de Camagüey, viene dada por una fábrica de cemento mal ubicada con respecto a la dirección de los vientos, la cual envuelve a la población en polvo de cemento y gotas de azufre en suspensión debido a desperfectos en sus electro-filtros. Algo similar ocurre en la industria cementera del Mariel, al oeste de ciudad de La Habana, cuyas emanaciones producen una nube de polvo que puede alcanzar entre 2 y 4 Km de ancho por una longitud de hasta 14 Km, afectando más del 60 porciento de los asentamientos poblacionales de ese territorio, incluida la propia fábrica, una termoeléctrica, el puerto y otras instalaciones así como la flora y fauna del lugar.

El gobierno afirma que logró sustituir en 200,000 refrigeradores domésticos y en 5,000 de tipo comercial el gas Freón 12, agotador de la capa de ozono, por un sustituto cubano que no causa ese efecto. De esa forma continúa trabajando por reducir el empleo de los refrigerantes dañinos hasta su total desaparición en el año 2000.

LA SOCIEDAD

El deterioro de la higiene ambiental no es ajeno del entorno cubano. Camagüey, una de las ciudades más limpias de la isla, posee 110 vertederos no tratados adecuadamente, los ríos y arroyos que la atraviesan están contaminados visibles y olfativamente, en no pocos lugares de sus riberas existen basureros clandestinos. Durante 1997 el tratamiento del agua para consumo tuvo altas y bajas por falta de cloro y ocurrió un déficit en la limpieza de fosas sanitarias dada la escasez de repuestos para los insuficientes carros dedicados a esa labor. Esta situación, unida a otros problemas, hace que dicha capital sea una de las más afectadas, provincialmente, por enfermedades diarreicas agudas, shigueelosis y hepatitis A.

En Villa Clara el 97% de la población está servida por el servicio de recogida de basuras, predominando el sistema de carretones tirados por caballos (66%) haciéndose solo el 13% con vehículos automotores. La disposición final se realiza en 100 lugares autorizados. De estos uno es relleno sanitario y los restantes vertederos a cielo abierto, 86 de los cuales presentan malas condiciones. Además existen 273 basureros clandestinos.

En la capital la última campaña de higienización del año 1998 preveía remover 12,000 metros cúbicos de desechos sólidos en solares, aceras y calles. Sin embargo la situación se mantenía crítica debido a las limitaciones de combustible, neumáticos, contenedores de basuras y otros que presenta el sistema de saneamiento comunal en La Habana, a lo cual debe sumarse la indisciplina estatal y social. Por ello a finales de agosto de 1999 aun se contabilizaban más de 10,000 metros cúbicos de basuras en la vía publica, mientras el principal vertedero de la urbe, que recibe diariamente más de 15,000 m3 de desperdicios, se encuentra en pésimas condiciones técnicas.

Un ejemplo es el municipio capitalino 10 de Octubre, uno de los más poblados del país. El exiguo parque de vehículos con que cuentan las autoridades sanitarias del mismo no da abasto para recopilar toda la basura del territorio ni tan solo una vez por semana. Por otra parte la arraigada indisciplina social de las propias entidades estatales y los ciudadanos mantiene volúmenes desconocidos de cajas de cigarros, latas de cervezas, nylon vacíos, botellas, periódicos y envolturas de todo tipo dispersas en los rincones de las urbes cubanas.

También en la capital los residuos de la dolarización y la falta de cestos generan molestos desperdicios que pululan en centros turísticos, playas y los más insospechados lugares. Las latas vacías de refrescos y cervezas constituyen el principal ingrediente de esta basura turística cuya abundancia motivo un artículo del semanario *Juventud Rebelde*. A lo anterior debe agregarse el uso de estuches, envoltorios, envases y presentaciones plásticas de todo tipo que se venden en las tiendas para la recaudación de divisas y terminan como basura.

Cifras de la Unión de Empresas de Recuperación de Materias Primas indican que el país genera diariamente más de 8,400 toneladas de residuos sólidos urbanos. Sin embargo no se ha logrado mejorar la efectividad de los sistemas para el tratamiento y reciclado de la basura. El caso de las latas de aluminio es bien elocuente para ilustrar el bajo nivel de recobrado, pues de unos 170 millones de unidades en circulación solo se reutiliza el 17 porciento.

También la escasez — pero en este caso de camiones limpia-fosas — creó serias dificultades con el vaciado de los depósitos para evacuar los residuales albañales en la provincia de Ciego de Ávila, donde el 40 porciento de la población utiliza esos sistemas.

Este tipo de situación, relacionado con deficiencias en la higiene ambiental, unido a la cría de cerdos en lugares inadecuados para paliar las dificultades alimentarias, incrementó en un cinco porciento la posibilidad de contraer leptospirosis; enfermedad que se transmite de los animales al hombre principalmente por la orina y es capaz de producir una muerte rápida.

La muerte de 15 personas en el poblado matancero de Manguito al ingerir alimentos contaminados con un plaguicida fue el hecho más impactante del año 1999. La venta negligente de frituras que contenían Thiodan, por parte de un trabajador por cuenta propia ocasionó el desastre donde se afectaron un total de 63 ciudadanos. Seis meses después, el 14 de agosto, otra intoxicación masiva con plaguicida fue reportada en la playa La Altura, de Bahía Honda, Pinar del Río, por suerte sin consecuencias fatales. En esta oportunidad resultaron contaminadas 54 personas, incluidos 21 niños, que habían consumido pizzas elaboradas con el mismo producto que asoló Manguito.

El Thiodan es un plaguicida de tipo organoclorado, con textura y color similares a la harina de trigo, de muy rápida reacción entre el momento de la ingestión y la aparición de los síntomas, caracterizados por náuseas, pérdida de la fuerza muscular, convulsiones y trastornos respiratorios. Escasez de alimentos, negligencia y la más absoluta falta de escrúpulos, entre otras, son las causas que conllevan a la ocurrencia de estas lamentables intoxicaciones químicas en Cuba.

Una constante mantenida en la sociedad cubana es la ausencia de una conciencia ecológica, demostrado por el mantenimiento de acciones y conductas que dañan al medio ambiente, y por tanto a las propias personas que las realizan. La educación y la divulgación ambiental sigue siendo insuficiente. Por ejemplo, durante el año 1997 fueron publicados unos cincuenta artículos relacionados con el tema en los periódicos y semanarios nacionales en los que no

existen secciones fijas para la ecología, como también ocurre en las emisoras radiales que transmiten a toda la nación. La televisión mantiene un pequeño programa semanal mientras se promueve la negativa práctica de saturar con campañas divulgativas, científicas y de todo tipo las semanas que preceden el día mundial por el medio ambiente, quedando posteriormente el tema en el olvido hasta el próximo año lo cual hace inefectivo el mensaje ecológico por carecer de continuidad y reiteración.

Durante 1998 el único periódico de circulación nacional no mencionó de forma directa la celebración del día mundial del medio ambiente en su edición del 5 de junio. La escasa referencia pública a los problemas ambientales propios está creando la intuición equivocada en muchos ciudadanos de que la degradación del entorno es una cuestión foránea y no parte de la realidad nacional, lo cual disminuye el sentido de urgencia necesario para introducir procederes y costumbres que permitan el desarrollo sostenible.

El movimiento ecologista reconocido por las autoridades mantuvo un protagonismo secundario durante el período a pesar que se existen alrededor de 30 organizaciones y asociaciones que trabajan ese campo. La única alternativa en el reducido ámbito editorial dedicado a la ecología lo constituyen la pequeña revista *Se Puede Vivir en Ecopolis* editado por el Proyecto Permacultura, Fundación Antonio Núñez Jiménez de la Naturaleza y el Hombre, así como la publicación *Agricultura Orgánica* del grupo gestor de la Asociación Cubana de Técnicos Agrícolas y Forestales, ambas controladas por la censura oficial.

Por su parte el movimiento ambientalista no reconocido mantiene una modesta participación en el debate ecologista, destacándose por sus iniciativas y actividad la organización NATURPAZ al recabar en diferentes instancias gubernamentales acciones de monitoreo, divulgación y protección ambiental.

Durante el periodo Cuba fue sede de varios eventos dedicados a la ecología. Entre otros se pueden relacionar: la Primera Convención Internacional sobre el Medio Ambiente y el Desarrollo, efectuada en La Habana; el IV Congreso de la Sociedad Cubana de la Ciencia del Suelo, sesionado en Matanzas; el V Congreso Cubano de Microbiología y Parasitología; el II Congreso Cubano de Medicina Tropical, reunido en La Habana; el Segundo Congreso Forestal de Cuba, efectuado en la capital; la Reunión Internacional sobre Océanos y Costas también en La Habana; así como otras jornadas de carácter regional y provincial.

LEGISLACIÓN AMBIENTAL

El 11 de junio de 1997 se publicó en la *Gaceta Oficial* la Ley No 81 del Medio Ambiente. Conformada por 14 títulos, 34 capítulos, 163 artículos y 3 disposiciones, la Ley No 81 viene a constituir el marco legal indispensable para la organización de las normas jurídicas que regulan el medio ambienta en Cuba.

La Ley del Medio Ambiente, además de recoger acciones ya en práctica como las evaluaciones de impacto ambiental, introduce elementos novedosos, entre éstos: la creación de un fondo nacional del medio ambiente, de un sistema nacional de información ambiental e incluso una sección para las cuencas hidrográficas y un capítulo dedicado a la educación. A pesar del avance que constituye la actual Ley No 81 se mantiene una gran dispersión de los actos normativos vigentes para regular la protección ambiental al existir alrededor de 300, entre los que se cuentran: 37 leyes, 36 decretos- leyes, 83 decretos, 95 resoluciones, 78 normas técnicas y 9 con otras denominaciones.

Por su parte, el procedimiento correctivo estas formado por un grupo de contravenciones muy benignas dictadas entre 1981 y 1992, aunque a partir de ese año aumentaron en algo el valor de las multas. Un caso ilustrativo es el articulo 34 del decreto 179 — "Protección, uso y conservación de los suelos y contravenciones" — que establece una multa de 50 pesos para quien no conserve la capa fértil del suelo, independientemente de si la afectación es en una, 2 o infinitas hectáreas. De esta forma el valor de la multa no es superior al beneficio que se puede obtener de tales acciones y por ende la sanción deja de ser eficaz.

Si bien la Ley No 81 en su tercer por cuanto señala "Es necesario consagrar, como un decreto elemental de la sociedad y los ciudadanos, el derecho a un medio ambiente sano," este particular no se encuentra recogido como tal en la Constitución del país y por ende tampoco en los articulados de la propia Ley del

Medio Ambiente. El artículo 27 de la Constitución de la República de Cuba postula: "El estado protege el medio ambiente. Así mismo: Es deber de los ciudadanos contribuir a la protección del agua, la flora, la fauna y todo el rico potencial de la naturaleza." La ausencia en la Constitución del derecho irrenunciable de toda persona a gozar de un ambiente saludable, ecológicamente equilibrado y adecuado para el desarrollo de la vida, y así mismo a la preservación del paisaje y la naturaleza, limita las acciones de amparo y tutela de las personas, individualmente consideradas, para accionar en defensa y obtener una inmediata protección contra la degradación del medio ambiente, independientemente de si el efecto es directo o indirecto por no constituir entonces una violación de los derechos fundamentales.

La Ley No 81 es un paso en el desarrollo de la legislación ambiental cubana pero aún restan importantes cambios para lograr un cuerpo legislativo armónico que partiendo de la Constitución llegue hasta las resoluciones en un entramado factible, práctico y efectivo.

El 21 de julio de 1998 la Asamblea Nacional del Poder Popular aprobó la Ley No 85, Ley Forestal, lo cual constituye otro paso en la creación de un ordenamiento jurídico que permita el desarrollo sostenible y la protección efectiva de los recursos naturales. La Ley Forestal consta de 8 capítulos y 72 artículos, e introduce, entre otras las siguientes innovaciones:

- Establece la clasificación de los bosques, la promoción e incentivación de la repoblación forestal y el uso múltiple y sostenible del patrimonio arbóreo.

- Oficializa la constitución y funcionamiento del Servicio Estatal Forestal como órgano de control encargado de exigir y velar por el cumplimiento de las regulaciones sobre el patrimonio forestal, la flora y la fauna silvestre, al cual se someten los tenentes, administradores, usuarios, etc.

- Crea el Fondo Nacional de Desarrollo Forestal para promover y financiar proyectos dedicados a conservar esos recursos,

- Dedica un capítulo al manejo forestal en el cual se introduce y regula la ordenación de los bosques y se reconocen los derechos de los habitantes de las forestas.

- Crea el Registro Forestal en el cual deberán inscribirse los centros de almacenamiento, transformación y utilización de materias primas forestales.

- Prohibe los desmontes para evitar la reducción de los bosques, salvo autorización del Consejo de Ministros.

A pesar de las severas afectaciones por erosión que padecen los suelos no se aplicó con la necesaria efectividad ni cuantía el sistema de regulaciones y multas establecido en el decreto 179, "Protección, Uso y Conservación de los Suelos y Contravenciones."

Otra carencia mantenida se encuentra en las deficiencias del sistema de normas técnicas para la protección del medio ambiente, las cuales en su mayoría no se ajustan a la actualidad, y solo se limitan a describir los métodos para indentificar sustancias contaminantes, no regulan las emisiones de las industrias al medio y se carece de los recursos materiales para poder realizar muchas de las mediciones requeridas.

A finales del 1999 se encontraban en proceso de análisis los siguientes instrumentos jurídicos:

- Decreto-Ley del sistema nacional de áreas protegidas.

- Decreto-Ley de seguridad biológica.

- Decreto-Ley de protección de la capa de ozono.

- Decreto-Ley de la bahía de La Habana.

- Decreto-Ley de costas.

Este último de gran importancia y necesidad pues incluye la definición de área no constructiva hasta 50 metros como mínimo en zonas de playas.

La mayoría de esos proyectos legislativos generalmente son debatidos en medios académicos, jurídicos y ministeriales oficiales pero no trascienden hacia los foros públicos siendo desconocidos por importantes sectores de opinión.

La publicación en la *Gaceta Oficial* de la República de Cuba los días 10 y 17 de septiembre de 1999 de la Resolución No 330-99 y el Decreto No 268, respectivamente, agregó dos nuevos instrumentos jurídicos a la legislación ambiental del país. El Reglamento de la Ley Forestal, Resolución No 330-99 del Ministerio de la Agricultura, establece una serie de disposiciones para la aplicación de la Ley Forestal de 1998 y consta de once capítulos así como de 168 artículos. Del reglamento valido es reseñar el Capitulo III, De la Clasificación y Categorización de los Bosques, dirigido a ordenar y conocer el patrimonio forestal de la nación así como la Sección Séptima, "Prohibiciones y Limitaciones de Talas," donde se relacionan 21 especies cuya corta es vedada y otras 40 con fuertes restricciones para su utilización, en ese listado se encuentran, entre otras, ébano, sabina, guayacán, roble y jiquí.

Por su parte el Decreto No 268 del Consejo de Ministros, "Contravenciones de las Regulaciones Forestales," cuyo objetivo es establecer las sanciones aplicables en materia forestal, recoge dentro de sus tres capítulos y 16 artículos multas que van desde 25 hasta 1000 pesos así como la obligación de resarcir los daños causados. Por ejemplo, el que tale u ordene talar árboles sin la autorización debida, de especies diferentes a las autorizadas, o en cantidades superiores y en lugares diferentes a los autorizados, 100 pesos por cada árbol y el decomiso de lo talado; si se trata de especies vedadas o palma real la multa será de $3000. Las autoridades facultadas para imponer las multas y demás medidas son los miembros del Servicio Estatal Forestal del Ministerio de la Agricultura. Así mismo el Cuerpo de Guarda Bosques perteneciente al Ministerio del Interior está autorizados para aplicar 7 capítulos y 11 artículos del mencionado decreto.

CONCLUSIONES

Existe una nefasta reiteración en la situación ecológica de Cuba al ser los suelos, la vegetación y las aguas los elementos del entorno con mayor degradación. Esta reincidencia ha creado un efecto acumulativo en algunas de esas variables ambientales, haciéndolas escalar en una clasificación de moderado, severo, crítico y hasta irreversible.

Ejemplo de lo anterior es la llegada a un estadío casi terminante de la variable suelos, en algunas áreas, y con ello la implantación de un nuevo paisaje en la geografía de la isla: las zonas desérticas.

Lamentablemente durante décadas el accionar proteccionista se mantuvo sin centrase en el mejoramiento y la conservación de las tierras, a pesar de ser la destrucción de ese recurso el principal problema ecológico del país. Así mismo es importante notar como se incluye una nueva dimensión dado por los impactos que la colonización turística está creando en apreciables sistemas litorales, es decir, la degradación de zonas costeras y de playas ha comenzado a ocupar

el cuarto lugar en la funesta lista de los elementos naturales más afectados.

Al finalizar el siglo XX el estado del medioambiente cubano es crítico y han comenzado a manifestarse catástrofes como la de los suelos. La situación ambiental de Cuba en el nuevo milenio estará determinada en última instancia por el accionar político-económico-social y puede ser mejor o peor pero de ocurrir lo último aumentará el saldo negativo en los principales elementos naturales del archipiélago, lo cual acercará peligrosamente la alternativa de una quiebra en la cuenta ecológica nacional.

FUENTES CONSULTADAS

Academia de Ciencias de Cuba. *Bases Ambientales para la Elaboración del Plan Estratégico para el Desarrollo Turístico de los Cayos Santa María, Guillermo, Cayo Coco y Sabinal.* 1995.

Agencia Ambiental Entorno Cubano. *La Situación Ambiental de Cuba 1997.*

Agencia Ambiental Entorno Cubano. *La Situación Ambiental de Cuba 1998.*

Agencia Ambiental Entorno Cubano. *La Situación Ambiental de Cuba 1999.*

Agricultura Orgánica. Revista del Grupo Gestor Asociación Cubana de Técnicos Agrícolas y Forestales, abril 1998.

Cubaecos. Servicio de noticias ambientales de la Agencia Ambiental Entorno Cubano. Internet. 1997, 1998, 1999, 2000.

Cuba Forestal. Revista del Ministerio de la Agricultura (MINAGRI), 1998.

Fundación Antonio Núñez Jiménez de la Naturaleza y El Hombre. Proyecto Permacultura. *Se Puede Vivir en Ecopolis.* Revista. 1998 y 1999.

Instituto de Geografía de la Academia de Ciencias de Cuba. *Atlas de Camagüey.* 1989.

Instituto de Geografía de la Academia de Ciencias de Cuba. *Atlas Nacional de Cuba.* 1970.

Instituto Nacional de Recursos Hidraúlicos. *Tecnología Apropiada.* Revista. 1997.

"Ley Forestal." *Gaceta Oficial.* 1998.

"Ley No 81 del Medio Ambiente." *Gaceta Oficial.* 1997.

Ministerio de Ciencia, Tecnología y Medio Ambiente (CITMA). *Evaluación de Impacto Ambiental en Cuba. Valoración de los Resultados Obtenidos a partir de la Implementación de la Resolución 163/95.* 1998.

Ministerio de Ciencia, Tecnología y Medio Ambiente (CITMA). *Programa Nacional de Medio Ambiente y Desarrollo.* 1995.

Ministerio de Ciencia, Tecnología y Medio Ambiente (CITMA). *Programas y resúmenes. I Convenio Internacional sobre el Medio Ambiente y el Desarrollo.* 1997.

Ministerio de Ciencia, Tecnología y Medio Ambiente (CITMA). *Resolución No 168\95 Reglamento para la realización de las Evaluaciones de Impacto Ambiental.* 1996.

Ministerio de Ciencia, Tecnología y Medio Ambiente (CITMA). *Resumen del proyecto de Ley de Costas.* 1998.

NATURPAZ. *Manifiesto del Río Almendares.* 1995.

Programas y Resúmenes. IV Congreso de la Sociedad Cubana del Suelo. Universidad de Matanzas. 1997.

Programas y Resúmenes. V Congreso Cubano de Microbiología y Parasitología. II Congreso Cubano de Medicina Tropical. Instituto Pedro Kouri. 1997.

Programas y Resúmenes. Evento Geología y Minería 98. Centro Nacional de Información Geológica, 1998.

Programas y Resúmenes. Segundo Congreso Forestal de Cuba. MINAGRI. 1998.

Programas y Resúmenes. II Congreso de Educación Ambiental 1999

Programas y Resúmenes. Convención Trópico 1999.

"Resolución No 330-99." *Gaceta Oficial.* 1999.

PRELIMINARY ENVIRONMENTAL ACTION PLAN FOR A POST CASTRO CUBA[1]

Alberto Vega and Federico Poey

This paper was prepared to identify some of the priority areas in which environmental management must be implemented to facilitate lasting and sustainable economic growth and social development in Cuba. The goal is to outline the initial effort required to support the Cuban Government to assess, structure and implement its environmental management, when a transition to democracy and market economy begins. Recognizing the close relationship between a healthy environment and a prosperous economy, this paper is an attempt to define the priority actions to recover environmental quality and to promote a wise use of natural resources. However, this paper does not pretend to be exhaustive or cover all possible aspects for the restoration of environmental quality in Cuba. That is a major undertaken that must be the result of careful and detailed planning effort by an eclectic team of experts comprising various disciplines of the natural and social sciences.

The need to anticipate the nature and extent of an environmental program for a free Cuba can not be overemphasized. As has been demonstrated by the Eastern European countries, during a transition to a market economy, there exists the danger that market, policy and institutional failures might impede the emergence or effective use of environmental control mechanisms and further allow the deterioration of environmental conditions. This could happen to Cuba. The process of economic restructuring in other former socialist states showed the limitations new governments have in terms of their abilities to finance environmental projects. Some remedies must be derived from the experience of other systems in transition in the former Soviet Union and Eastern European states.

Therefore, this paper provides a rationale and a general background on current environmental conditions in Cuba, identifies key policy flaws and points out possible environment impacts on specific areas. It also describes the nature of the program that should be implemented during the first few (3-5) years after the return to a free, Western style economic system and democratic government in Cuba. After a general background section, some of the most sensitive areas are pointed out where past and current government directed policy interventions have led to deterioration of natural resources and environmental quality, including:

- Tourism

- Surface Water Resources - Rivers and Wetlands

- Groundwater Resources

- Coastal and Marine Resources

- Mining Areas

- Sugar Production

---

1. This contribution is based on a research paper sponsored by the US-Cuba Business Council. The authors assume full and sole responsibility for its content. USCBC does not necessarily share or support the viewpoints of the authors.

- Soil Resources

- Forest Ecosystems

- Hazardous Materials

This article also anticipates future activities that may lead to further deterioration of renewable natural resources and environmental quality, for those same areas. This may be of potential importance as investment from the United States and other Western democracies takes place primarily derived from government policies and decisions. Present impacts are usually not economically impaired since they take place in resource-intensive areas of tourism development disregarding ecological safeguards. When current restrictive economic limitations are removed, the natural ecosystems will face larger risks.

On the other hand, the planning section outlines the nature of the future environmental work that is recommended in Cuba in support of the sustainable economic growth and development desired by the Cuban people and the international community at large. This planning effort includes the work needed to:

- conduct a comprehensive environmental diagnosis;

- analyze and adjust legal and institutional policy;

- provide support to improve water supply and sanitation in small to mid size towns;

- implement an action plan for coastal and marine management and conservation;

- establish a national watershed management initiative;

- facilitate efforts for the national management and conservation of biological diversity and cultural heritage;

- promote environmental improvement of living conditions in the Metropolitan Havana area;

- implement an environmental education and awareness campaign; and

- program a series of transitional planning workshops.

The estimated cost for said environmental program is approximately $236 million (M), for a five-year period. A summary of the cost per component is indicated in Table 1. Details explaining the rationale behind these figures are included in the last section of the paper.

The paper also proposes to continue working on the conceptualization and development of the overall program in two ways. The first one is a deeper analysis of said components, particularly tourism, in the north western coast of Cuba, around Varadero. The second, is a broad effort to look for consensus among the various environmental concerned groups of the Cuban and U.S. community through a series of workshops in selected U.S. cities to further expand on several of the program components.

Table 1. Estimated Cost of the Cuban Environmental Program

No.	Description	Cost $
1	Comprehensive Environmental Diagnosis	6,000,000
2	Institutional, Legal and Policy Analysis and Support	17,500,000
3	Water Supply and Sanitation. Phase I.	125,000,000
4	Coastal and Marine Management and Conservation	22,000,000
5	National Watershed Management	27,000,000
6	National Management and Conservation of Biological Diversity and Cultural Heritage	12,000,000
7	Environmental Improvement of the Metropolitan Havana Area	23,000,000
8	Environmental Education and Awareness Campaign	3,500,000
	TOTAL	236,000,000

BACKGROUND

Cuba is an archipelago, part of the West Indies in the Caribbean Antilles, composed of the island of Cuba and about 1600 smaller islands and cays, with a total population of about 12 million people. Most cays and islets are low lying and uninhabited. Cuba is the largest and western-most of the Greater Antilles and lies strategically between Florida and the Yucatan Peninsula. The island of Cuba is the 15th largest island in the world, with a total surface area of 104,945 sq km, 1250 km long and 191 km wide at its widest point. Cuba also lays claim to the 220 sq km Isla de la Juventud. Havana is less than 150 km from Florida's Key West, in the United States, and Pinar del Río Province is 210 km from Mexico's Yucatan Peninsula. Cuba's other close neighbors are Jamaica, the Bahamas and Haiti, with the latter only 77 km away across the Windward Passage.

General Environmental Conditions

Much of Cuba is made up of fertile flatlands, where cattle are grazed and sugarcane, coffee, grain, tobacco and other horticultural crops are grown. The Oriental, Central and Occidental mountain ranges cover 25% of the country, the highest point being Pico Turquino (1972 m). Cuba's longest river, the 343 km Río Cauto, is barely navigable, even for small boats. The North American and Caribbean tectonic plates[2] meet in the 7200 m deep Cayman Trench between Jamaica and Cuba, and the region is thus prone to earthquakes.

There are more than 6000 plant species in Cuba, around half of which are endemic. The well known *royal palm* (*Roystonia regia*) is represented on the country's coat of arms; there are said to be 20 million palms in Cuba. Cuba's other flora includes the rare and prehistoric *cork palm* (*Microcycas calocoma*), a throwback to the Cretaceous period; the *jagüey*, a fig tree which has aerial roots; the *palma barrigona* (big belly palm); the *ceiba*, the sacred silk-cotton tree; and the *mariposa* (butterfly jasmine), the white national flower. Much of the southern coast has mangrove swamps that support small fish and bird life while the majority of the northern coast is bordered by sandy beaches.

Cuba's most abundant land fauna is reptilian, and includes crocodiles, iguanas, lizards, salamanders, turtles and 15 species of nonpoisonous snakes. The largest land mammal is the *jutía* (*Capromys*), a tree rat which grows to about 60 cm in length. The world's smallest bird comes from Cuba: the bee hummingbird, or *zunzuncito* (*Mellisuga helenae*), is just bigger than a grasshopper and weighs only two grams. The *tocororo* (*Priotelus temnuros*) is dubbed

Cuba's national bird due to its red, white and blue plumage — the colors of the Cuban flag.

There are no great differences in seasonal temperature in Cuba, its pleasant subtropical climate being augmented by the gentle northeasterly trade winds. The wet summer season is between May and October, and the drier winter season runs from November through April. The average temperature reaches 27°C (81°F) in July and August and 22°C (72°F) in February. An average of 80% humidity exists all year round.

Effect of Recent Political Events

The most important political event in recent Cuban history was the revolution that led to Castro's military alliance with the Soviet Union and Warsaw Pact that substituted pre-1959 intense and close trade with the United States. For the first 30 years of the revolution, this geopolitical, economic and philosophical shift reduced trade with the United States that was offset by large economic subsidies from the former Soviet Union and by favorable trading relations with the members of the former Soviet Bloc (COMECON).

Between the early 1960s and the late 1980s the environmental situation worsened despite Cuba's achieving one of the lowest population growth rates in the world and reducing extreme living standard differentials in rural areas, two of the primary reasons often blamed for environmental deterioration in developing countries. The government's approach was to "conquer nature" and under its central planning approach, it did not take local circumstances into consideration. This disregard for the environmental consequences of development projects continues to this day despite official allegations to the contrary—as the country pursues an economic survival strategy based on the crash development of the tourist sector and exploitation of natural resources.

Therefore, the concept that environmental disruption was not supposed to occur under socialism since

---

2. Tectonic plates are the geologic masses of the earth that are in constant movement and that are responsible for the displacement of the earth's continents. At the meeting point one of the plates goes under the other causing a deepening of the earth's crust and releasing energy responsible for earthquakes and other telluric phenomena.

it was guided by scientific policies, and could only beget environmentally benign economic development, is not true. In reality, the socialist environmental record proved to be far different from the utopian view and it is now perceived that the environmental legacy of socialism will present serious challenges to future Cuban generations. In the next section, are a few examples of the abuses that the totalitarian regime has carried out in the country.

The collapse of communism and its favorable economic arrangements and subsidies from the COMECON countries to Cuba in 1989 led to greatly increased economic hardships and rising international debt. This economic situation translated in increasing pressure on the natural systems (indigenous resources) within the country. Table 2 compares key Cuban economic statistics before and after the end of the former Soviet Union. By 1999, the economic situation seemed to have improved somewhat although official figures are elusive. The dramatic drop off in subsidized oil imports from the Soviet Bloc has been partially offset by renewed imports of oil, mainly from Venezuela and Mexico.

Table 2. Key Economic Statistics for Cuba in 1989 and 1994

Indicator	1989	1994
GDP ($ Million)	32,700	18,600
Exports ($ Million)	5,400	1,700
Sugar Harvest (Million Tons)	8	4
Nickel Production (Thousand tons)	35	22
Foreign Tourists	340,000	600,000

Cuba's determination to permit foreign investment is limited to tourism, joint ventures and very few other associations in areas of the economy principally related to nickel, oil and telecommunications. These partnerships reflect Cuba's eagerness to join the world's economy, to acquire some of the badly needed hard currencies. However, this expansion does not reflect either the conceptual/theoretical or practical methodology used in Cuba in its totalitarian approach. New foreign investment regulations promulgated in 1995 were designed to encourage foreign entities to include joint ventures, cooperative production agreements and autonomous enterprises in partnership with the Cuban Government. European countries,

Canada, and Mexico are the main economies taking advantage of the opportunities in Cuba at this time.

With sugar production declining, the Cuban government is encouraging investment in tourism as a way to increase foreign exchange and to boost production in other sectors of the Cuban economy—mainly food and building materials. Most of the growth, however, has been in the tourism sector. This sector grew by over 14% in 1994. Growth of 8.5% in non-sugar related industrial production helped the Cuban economy grow overall by about 1% in 1994.

Nowadays, Cuban authorities are promoting a greater dialog on environmental issues. For example, a conference was held in January 2000 to investigate the use of environmental accounting to evaluate overall environmental policy and development, with participants from the Center for Environmental Policy of the University of Florida. The main areas of discussion included the most pressing environmental concerns in Cuba and included: tourism, coastal areas, wetlands and hydrological systems, forest systems, urban area environmental problems and use of sugar and mineral resources for trade initiatives. Cuban authorities have indicated that sustainability is a key factor when assessing potential impacts of proposed natural resource development projects. However, this idea remains an elusive concept. In light of fuel shortages and decreased imports consumer goods, Cubans have seen a real decline in living standards that have had a direct impact on the environment.

Policy and Institutional Framework

The approach to environmental management from the Cuban authorities departed from the idealistic concept that human development in the new society would not hurt the environment or alter renewable natural resources. From an ideological point of view, the revolution should protect the environment and all development should be sustainable. Consistent with that ideology, the socialist constitution of 1976 explicitly endorsed the protection of soils and water resources as well as the atmosphere.

Then, following the same line of thought, in 1983 the socialist Government enacted the Environmental

Protection and Rational Use of Natural Resources Act. After passing this law, there was an avalanche of mandatory regulations that had to be enforced. During this period, the schools devoted significant efforts to study ecology and natural resources management and a great number of environmentalists were formed.

However, these laws and regulations could not be efficiently implemented, since the decision making in the communist society occurs at the highest level of the government. The environmental professionals did not really have the option to assess the environmental impacts and introduce preventive measures. They were consulted on how to minimize impacts once the negative consequences were already out of control. Therefore, many of the more serious professionals made efforts to avoid participating on the evaluations councils. In that way the arrogance of the Cuban administration completely neutralized all potential benefits from the environmental framework previously discussed.

This environmental mismanagement became more critical as Cuba lost the favorable trading terms and subsidies from the Soviet Bloc countries, after the collapse of the former Soviet Union. Particularly important was the loss of the oil subsidy, which stopped after 1989.

In 1994, Cuba promulgated Law 147 granting authority to the newly created Ministry of Science, Technology and Environment to direct and control the development of policies to protect the environment and provide for the rational use of resources for the sustainable development of the country. Other ministries, including agriculture, sugar, industry, international trade, energy and mining, also have an interest in how their sphere of influence may perform against national environmental parameters. Beneath the ministries are several agencies, most importantly, the Environmental Agency, that are involved in the day to day administration of environmental concerns. Several institutes (dealing with Ecology, Geography and Oceanography), as well as academic and research institutions, are involved in environmental assessments, technologies and planning.

Although economic and environmental concerns are increasingly addressed at the higher levels of the Cuban government, it is unfortunate that decision making has usually been *ad hoc* and in the absence of strong assessment tools and policy. The initial response of the Cuban government in 1990 to fuel shortages was to try and use indigenous reserves or alternatives to fossil fuels. With the economy in tatters by 1995, Cuba's dependence on fossil fuels became apparent. If Cuba does not use imported goods and services from outside to amplify the country's environmental resource base, it will continue to fall behind and living conditions will continue to deteriorate. However, at the same time, development should be scaled to the local conditions so as not to overload the natural systems on which the country depends.

Overall, environmental decisions are still very centralized (in Havana), with only some provincial universities and research stations concerned with environmental studies outside of the capital. In spite of abundance of academically trained scientific and environmental professionals in Cuba, it is the Central Committee of the Communist Party that directs overall environmental policy. To the Party, these concerns are secondary to the economic, trade and development ones. In addition, the armed forces must approve all major plans for use of the country's natural resources including forestry, coastal areas, water and infrastructure. The result is fractured decision making with a tendency to override sound environmental policy initiatives because of perceived short-term economic imperatives.

In spite of some improvements since 1994, Cuba's environmental legislation — as it currently exists — is inappropriate to deal with many of the negative impacts from land use, large-scale development, restructuring of the infrastructure and foreign investment. The main source of new policy has been the inclusion of recommendations from international conventions such as Agenda 21.[3] International environmental standards have been adopted by Cuban institutions usually after the ratification of international law in Cuban legislation. Cuba is a signatory to all major international environmental conventions including: the Global Environment Conventions (the Stockholm Convention and the Rio Convention), the United Nations Convention on the Law of the Sea (UNCLOS III), Bonn Convention (Global Warming), Basel Convention (Control of Hazardous Substances), CITES (Convention on International Trade in Endangered Species of Wild Fauna and Flora), etc.

While many of the recommendations contained within these conventions are sound, they are very general, and must be modified for use with empirical data from the environment in which they are to be applied. The limited and somewhat vague policies and inadequate legal structure for the development of Cuba's natural resources was apparent at the January 2000 conference in Havana. Cuban environmental law should be based on the recognition that increasing population, industrialization and urbanization place growing pressures on the limited assimilative capacity of the environment, and on the finite stock of natural resources.

Cuban environmental institutions in the future should be dedicated to this task and charged with the responsibility to safeguard and improve the quality of the environment, both nationally and in a global context, and at the same time to promote economic development within the reach of the national economy. The following key endeavors should be undertaken:

1. Development of proper environmental policy and legislation for the protection and progressive improvement of the environment. In order to achieve this, policy efforts should be directed to control the main polluter — the Cuban government, which controls most of the country's resources. Changes to the current system will require greater institutional strengthening and legislation as it contains no mechanisms for conflict resolution, enforcement of non-government entities and quantitative project analysis. The Cuban Agency for the Environment will

need in the future to develop real enforcement capabilities.

2. The improvement of the environment should reflect and promote a new approach to economic growth that will take into account all components of the quality of life and not only the quantity of resources spent or even the goods produced. Therefore, economic and social development policies must be pursued in close connection with sound environmental policies, in order to ensure a balanced contribution to the improvement of human well-being.

3. The development, extraction, transportation, storage, use of energy and related waste disposal from existing and new sources as well as of other scarce resources, should take place under conditions that safeguard environmental values. When feasible, energy should be imported rather than produced locally. The Cuban economy is dependent on imports. Evaluation of Cuba's economy in 1989 showed that around 60% of its real wealth was imported as oil. In 1990, the initial response of the Cuban government to fuel shortages was to try and use indigenous reserves or alternatives to fossil fuels. This policy may not be sound as indigenous reserves are of poor quality, costly to mine and environmentally unfriendly. Most known fossil fuel reserves are on Cuba's environmentally sensitive northern continental shelf. Use of these reserves has failed to make up the shortfall.

4. The Government should actively seek to protect the environment by encouraging the promotion of non-polluting technologies, conservation of energy and other scarce resources, intensified efforts to recycle materials, and the development of substitutes for scarce or environmentally harmful substances. These technologies should be identified in the project cycle. Cuba was forced to implement recycling technologies in the 1990s as cost saving initiatives brought on by

---

3. Agenda 21 is the consolidated position of the Latin American countries to the Global Convention on the Environment of Rio de Janeiro, the Rio Convention.

lack of foreign exchange to buy replacement products. The reverse side of this is the lack of technology, equipment and fuel to undertake adequate solid waste collection, recycling and disposal. Analysis into better systems to reuse and dispose of solid wastes are required.

5. The Cuban Government should promote observance of the "Polluter-Pays Principle" to encourage environmental protection and to avoid international economic distortions, and where desirable encourage the harmonization of environmental policies. The Polluter-Pays Principle can be used as the basis of funding environmental projects.

6. Comprehensive environmental planning, including for land use, should constitute an important element of government policy. The first step in developing empirical subjectivity in Cuba's development policy is to undertake a complete analysis of the entire Cuban economy and its resource base. In 1999, a project to update the geological/land use maps of Cuba was undertaken. It lacks, however, the ecosystem classification for management. Although GIS capability does exist in Cuba, most institutions rely on outdated, Soviet-era cartography. In the future, this should be undertaken using high resolution satellite imagery digitized and classified according to ecosystem function. Institutions that may undertake in the compilations of GIS information include the Geography Institute, with input from the Institutes of Hydrogeology, Ecology and Oceanography. Classifying by ecosystem defines an ecosystem type according to its dominant sources of energy. This may be the most appropriate approach for classifying the system as a whole for sustainability because ecosystems develop their prominent characteristics as part of self organization to maximize use of all sources and storages. Sound land use policy can only follow if first class land use data are provided. Future environmental standards applicable to Cuba may follow these initiatives.

7. Systematic assessment of environmental impacts of existing and new economic activities. In order to prevent future environmental deterioration, prior assessment of the environmental consequences of significant public and private activities should be an essential element of policies applied at the national, regional and local levels. Environmental assessments should be undertaken as a comprehensive tool useful in properly scaling developments to prevailing environmental conditions. Results from these assessments will be useful for the development of policies for improving economic vitality and make better use of the environment in order to further Cuba's human and environmental prosperity.

8. Continued attention should be given to the environmental education, ratification and implementation of international conventions for the protection and conservation of the environment and to the development of new conventions.

IMPACTS ON SPECIFIC AREAS

This section is an effort to illustrate how the current mismanagement of Cuban resources and the lack of democratic institutions have impacted critical and valuable resources along the entire geography of the Cuban archipelago. Furthermore, potential areas of concern are discussed.

Tourism

Tourism is Cuba's fastest growing industry and a vital source of foreign exchange with which to buy goods and services internationally. Tourism increased dramatically in the 1990s because of new policies and because of Cuba's attractive culture and relatively intact natural systems (coral reefs, coastal and high diversity forest areas). These attributes create a positive image and attract visitors seeking a pristine environment that is not overloaded by tourism development. At the same time, tourism connected the most pristine forest and reef areas in Cuba with the world economy. In addition, diversion of resources for high intensity (luxury) tourism has led to considerable social and economic disruption.

The local resources that may be impacted by tourism include potable water supplies, waste disposal, solid waste systems, loss of wilderness areas, and excess loading on energy, food and transportation systems.

The pattern emerging in areas of high tourist use such as Varadero (Matanzas), Ciénaga de Zapata (Matanzas), Guarda la Vaca (Holguín), Viñales (Pinar del Rio), Cayo Largo (Havana) and Cayo Coco (Ciego de Avila), are similar to elsewhere in the Caribbean, i.e.:

- Environmental impacts from the operation of the resort complexes are greatest when developed in ecologically sensitive areas.

- The greater the intensity of the tourism development and foreign involvement, the greater the potential to disrupt local ecological and economic systems.

Albeit ineffectively, tourism concerns have caught the attention of the Central Committee of the Cuban Communist Party as well as of the scientific/engineering community because of its economic importance and also because of the disruption it can cause to ecological and social systems. With any development, the local environment may see declines in productivity, an increase in pollutant loads and conversion of wilderness areas. The local population has found itself excluded from traditional fishing and recreational areas.

The tourism center of Varadero, in particular, is close to offshore oil platforms and the recent downturn in tourism to this part of the country may be partially attributed to the negative impacts of oil spills on its beaches. As investment in tourism in the past decade was rarely carefully planned, negative impacts will decrease the destinations' appeal. As was anticipated in a 1995 study, tourism numbers for the most recent years have been less than anticipated.

In sensitive coastal areas, coral reefs have been negatively impacted by nutrient loading,[4] marina and infrastructure development and the decline in the population of the most desirable marine species because of demand by tourists.

In sum, a great deal of the capital from Cuba's tourism development goes into the necessary purchase of fossil fuels. Saving of fossil fuel can be made in some areas by using ecological engineering approaches to waste water disposal including recycling of wastewater through wetland systems, and solar driven limestone settling pools close to beach side hotels.

Almost no resources or attention is currently devoted to careful selection of new construction sites, the state of existing infrastructure such as local water supplies, transportation, or waste disposal capabilities. Typically development does not take in consideration the regional economy, or the potential role of the local population. In the medium and long term this lack of planning and social and environmental consideration may cause the failure of those investments and the perpetuation of poverty within the Cuban frontiers.

SURFACE WATER RESOURCES—RIVERS AND WETLANDS

Because of its geography, most river systems in Cuba are relatively short. Because of the porous nature of the karst geology[5] they are non existent in some parts of the country (i e., Pinar del Río). Rivers and streams within urban areas are reported to be almost all heavily polluted. For example, Río Almendares in Havana is heavily polluted with nutrient loads; a natural wetland recycling system is being proposed as part of a woodland restoration design for the headwaters of this river.

Because of the large quantity of wastewater in urban areas, improvements to processing may require re-engineering and the use of modern water treatment systems. A complete revision of the cities wastewater treatment systems is long overdue. Among other reasons because no immediate solution is apparent due to the critical economic situation.

Cuba's most important wetland area is the Ciénaga de Zapata in Matanzas province. Other smaller saw-

4. Nutrient loading refers to the increased levels of nutrients such as nitrogen and phosphorus coming from point and non point sources that are normally conducive to the deterioration of water quality and the quality of the aquatic ecosystems.

5. Karst geology is that dominated by dissolution of limestone.

grass dominated wetland areas are found on the south coast. Important mangrove areas are found all around the Cuban archipelago and include all four Caribbean species. In the areas of karst geology there are many lagoons and lakes. In many ways it is similar to the Florida Everglades, with similar environmental problems including the invasion of exotic species.

Changes to the hydrological cycle because of peat mining for fuel and earlier earthworks diverted water for rice and sugar production is manifest in these changes of wetland floral species. For example the expansion of *Casuarina* sp and other exotic species and the succession of saw-grass to cattail (*Thyfa* sp) due to increased nutrient loads. Examples of exotic fauna include species of deer and mongoose.

Some initiatives are being made to restore the original hydrological cycle for this important wetland area as it represents important concentrations of bio-mass for highly migratory bird species.

Another example of environmental mismanagement that severely impacted water resources is the Havana South Dike. This 70 km dike made mainly out of clay material, was built with the purpose of increasing the level of ground water recharge to improve the potential pumping from this critical water source and to reverse the saline intrusion trend affecting the aquifer. Although the measure has been partially successful, similar benefit could have been achieved at a fraction of the economic and ecological costs. Literally the dike has destroyed the ecological balance of the region including: flooding of valuable lowland areas with seawater, loss of a strip of mangrove swamps that protected the coast, increased erosion, and loss of valuable fertile soil resources, which are now carried in the form of sediment to the ocean. There they will interfere with light penetration and induce coral mortality due to reduced productivity and direct suffocation.

Elsewhere, smaller wetland areas and streams have been modified and dammed into permanent lakes. Mangrove areas in Cuba are protected although cutting continues for charcoal and in Pinar del Rio, large areas are being cleared for marina development.

The important position that wetland areas occupy in the landscape with regard to its energy signature needs to be appreciated in Cuba. This energy signature means that wetlands are concentrated areas of high production and capable of making large and free economic contribution for food production, waste assimilation, recreation, aesthetics and biodiversity.

Wetlands in Cuba provide important opportunities to increase food production and possible low cost disposal of wastewater. The use of wetlands for waste water treatment and recycle has caught the attention of Cuban environmental and tourism officials because of:

- The low cost of construction and operation.

- Low use of fossil fuels and capital expenditure.

- Flexible nature in isolated parts of the country.

Groundwater Resources

Another well documented phenomenon in the Cuban professional literature and in journalistic accounts, and validated in recent years by defectors with backgrounds in agronomy and hydrology, is the growing salinization of many of the country's major aquifers. This contamination is occurring along coastal and other areas, as well as the contamination of others. Various factors have contributed to this state of affairs, including over-pumping of underground water stores and the damming of many of the country's rivers and streams.

Beginning in the early 1960s the country saw a major expansion in the land area devoted to water stores, primarily but not exclusively, to expand the acreage under irrigation. Large-scale interference with the ecosystem has resulted in major disruptions of natural water flows, by allowing seawater to filtrate inland and preventing aquifer recharge. Large-scale irrigation projects unaccompanied by the development of an effective drainage infrastructure are also to be blamed for the salinization of many of the country's soils. Restoring the fertility of the damaged soils will take years. Wholesale discharges of contaminants by agriculture and industry and the severe and growing deterioration of the urban sanitary infrastructure have produced further damage.

Coastal and Marine Resources

Near Havana, the coastal areas have been negatively impacted by development and cutting of strand and wetland vegetation. Havana Bay is heavily polluted from direct wastewater disposal, dumping and oil pollution. Water within the Bay has a high retention time and the sediments undoubtedly contain high levels of organic and metal contaminants. Metal contamination is originated by industry (paint, chemical processing, oil spills and run-off from roads). Swimming is banned near the downtown areas of Havana and tropical fish poisoning (ciguartoxin) is commonplace. Others coastal towns, Santiago, Guantánamo and Manzanillo are reported to have similar problems to Havana harbor.

Mining Areas

The principal minerals in Cuba include nickel, copper, and iron. Mining occurs in the Eastern highlands areas of Cuba and has a negative impact on the wet dry forest areas covering serpentine and olivine igneous rocks. At present the areas are reforested after use, mainly with pine species plantings.

Alternatively, impacted areas may be reforested using ecological engineering approach, i.e. using the natural vegetation that is adapted to the high metal content of the soils. The seeds of this unique vegetation is contained within the soils and can be re-spread over mined areas if the soil is removed and stored before the mining begins.

Cuba's trade policy for nickel and other minerals needs re-evaluation. Heavy metals such as nickel have high value because of their concentration, and contribute much to the economy. Cuban policy may be better off mining this material more rationally and using it indigenously to make batteries and other products for export and domestic use rather than exporting the raw material.

Sugar Production

An evaluation of the sugar industry conducted in 1994 showed that Cuba's principal export is costly to produce (uses lots of resources like soil, water, fossil fuels, fertilizer, and human labor) and has a low value

in the world market. With sugar harvests declining in recent years, some areas have been allowed to revert to a secondary forest, for pasture, and close to urban areas for vegetable production.

Environmental impacts from sugar production include extensive loss of low land forest, which has been cleared all across the country for this purpose; high use of phosphates and other fertilizers; negative impact to water resources during sugar refining; and diversion of important and limited resources for a crop of low international market value. Cuba may be better off reducing its emphasis on sugar production for export and using the resources dedicated to this production to grow food for local consumption and export or by replanting degraded areas with forests to restore soils and the hydrological cycle.

Soil Resources

The deterioration of the country's soils responds to a variety of reasons, many of them associated with the capital intensive agricultural development approach pursued by Cuba from the early 1960s up to the late 1980s. This development strategy rested on the organization of production in vast agricultural holdings, high levels of mechanization, reliance on chemical inputs, and a major expansion in irrigation.

Compounding the detrimental impact of this development approach were the inherent flaws associated with the nature of socialist management practices generally and in agriculture in particular. In Cuba and elsewhere in the socialist world, production directives issued by central planners were often oblivious to local circumstances, while farm managers were rewarded for their compliance with those directives, rather than for decentralized initiatives more likely to result in improved production outcomes with more benign environmental impacts.

As a result, by the late 1990s, 60% of the arable lands are affected by erosion, with 25% of those in the strong severe erosion categories. Other important degradation processes include poor drainage, salinization, acidification, and compaction. The areas affected by this process are as follows:

• close to 4.2 million hectares by erosion;

- 2.5 million hectares were suffering from various degrees of soil compaction;

- salinization was a problem in 0.8 million hectares;

- acidification was a problem in 1.3 million hectares; and

- poor drainage affected 2.7 million hectares.

An extreme case is the southern plain in Pinar del Río, where land is now considered to be unproductive due to excessive use without proper soil management required for its naturally low fertility. Cattle ranges have also been severely affected with a notorious decline in soil nutrients and increasing soil acidity. Many scientists consider the deterioration of soil resources as the worst environmental problem in Cuba.

Forest Ecosystems

Because of the diverse geology of Cuba, its location and other geographical features, Cuban forests have high diversity in relation to the size of the country, particularly in the highland areas of Eastern Cuba (high endemism and biodiversity). Several nature reserves and protected areas are found here.

Some areas of upland old growth forest still have populations of the ivory-billed woodpecker — a species now extinct in the United States. Several projects proposed to produce energy from hydro-electricity in these mountainous areas were delayed in the 1990s because of economic limitations rather than environmental concerns. In Western Cuba, the secondary growth areas in the Havana province are characterized by low diversity and arrested succession due to the large distances to natural seed areas necessary for high diversity succession.

One major initiative of the government from the 1960s was the reforestation of cleared mountain areas across the country. Some areas have been planted with fast growing but relatively low value pine species such as *Pinus caribea*. Although this is preferable to leaving areas without cover, more reforestation using natural succession or enrichment with high value native species is required to increase the value of these forests from an economic and ecological perspective.

Hazardous Materials

The most important considerations in terms of the risks posed by the handling and management of hazardous materials in Cuba is associated with the construction of the Juraguá nuclear power plant (NPP) in Cienfuegos, with Russian technology and standards. The plant may be regarded as the most important endeavor of the Cuban Nuclear Program, which began in the late 1960s.

The agreement between the former Soviet Union and Cuba for construction of the Jaraguá plant occurred in 1976, and its construction began in 1983. Plans included the development of two 440-megawatt nuclear power reactors. The site is located in the Province of Cienfuegos, on the south central coast of Cuba, about 288 km south of Key West, Florida. The two reactors at Juraguá are the most advanced model (V318) of the Soviet-designed VVER-440 series of pressurized water reactors.

Concerns for the United States derive from potential malfunction of the Cuban reactors, which could lead to a radioactive fallout in the Southern United States, reaching as far west as Texas, or north as far as Washington, D.C. According to air weather patterns around Cienfuegos, it would take only 24 hours for radioactive materials to reach Southern Florida and approximately 48 hours to reach the Eastern United States. Therefore, as many as 80 million Americans could be exposed to a virtually deadly radioactive cloud. The alarm with respect to the Juraguá NPP is not only for the United States. Cuba, Caribbean and Central America countries; Colombia, Venezuela, Brazil and Mexico are also highly concerned.

Sub-standard technology and inadequate safety measures have been included in the design and the construction process of the Juraguá NPP. Among the design defects of the Soviet VVER-440 Pressurized Water Reactors is the containment dome, which was designed to withstand only 14% of the pressure required by U.S. standards. The construction process is even worse than the design. Perhaps as many as 60 percent of the soviet-made parts in the Juraguá reactors are defective, according to estimates.

Furthermore, nearly all of the reactor parts, excluding the materials for civil construction, such as concrete, were supplied by the Soviet Union under mutual economic collaboration arrangements. Breakdown of the Soviet Bloc led to the suspension of the reactors' construction in September, 1992. When construction was discontinued, critical components of the nuclear reactors, including the reactor vessel, six steam generators, five main coolant pumps, 12 isolation valves and other essential equipment were left exposed for more than six years to highly corrosive salt air and rain, thus increasing the risk of severe damage. Their quality and safety are questionable.

Other potential flaws are related to:

- the feeble emergency core cooling mechanism, which would be used to prevent a meltdown of the nuclear fuel and its vicinity;

- the emergency cooling system, which has no backup;

- the reactor protection systems and diagnosis, which are insufficient;

- the control rod insertion system; and

- the design of the electrical and emergency power supply.

The possibility of an accident occurring at Juraguá upon its operation, according to experts, is 15 percent. According to international standards the probability of an accident at nuclear facilities should be less than one percent, and therefore the Juraguá NPP should not be completed, at least not without significant safety improvements. Additional safety concerns are posed by the fact that the Cuban nuclear program lost its fundamental base after the disintegration of the former Soviet Union, and the lack of a proper nuclear safety culture in Cuba.

The geological situation at Juraguá NPP site is also a risk. U.S. federal officials believe that the reactors rest on an active earthquake fault line. A relatively small tremor could have large consequences.

Furthermore, if concluded, the Cuban NPP, will produce radioactive wastes, which will pose an additional threat to the radioactive waste management. Around 1.4 metric tons of radioactive wastes are produced by a standard nuclear fission plant in one year. Other nuclear wastes, originating from the nuclear research centers, hospitals, food irradiation plants and other Cuban nuclear facilities, represent added risk to the Cuban population and environment.

THE NATURE OF THE WORK AHEAD

The environmental effort required to promote vigorous and sustainable development in Cuba may be envisioned as a Comprehensive National Environmental Program, with at least the following components:

- conduct a comprehensive environmental diagnosis;

- analyze and adjust legal and institutional policy;

- provide support to improve water supply and sanitation in small to mid size towns;

- implement an action plan for coastal and marine management and conservation;

- establish a national watershed management initiative;

- facilitate efforts for the national management and conservation of biological diversity and cultural heritage;

- procure environmental improvement of living conditions in the Metropolitan Havana area;

- implement an environmental education awareness campaign; and

- program a series of transitional planning workshops.

A brief description of each one of these components follows, including a preliminary rationale for costing. The environmental program outlined herein represents an investment of over $236M (see Table 1 above) which will contribute to fuel the Cuban economy during the initial years of its re-insertion into the world economy. But most importantly, it will provide the bases for the establishment of an effective environmental management system in Cuba.

Comprehensive Environmental Diagnosis

Description of general environmental conditions and problems in this document is based on reference material and it serves well for illustration purpose. However, the basis for a complete environmental program in Cuba must be broadened and established on scientific evidence. In essence the diagnosis will include an environmental base line study of Cuba that could be used for several purposes in the future.

The main report from this effort will be the first state of the Comprehensive Natural Environment Program that will be prepared as a routine output of the environmental management system that must be established. The information contained in this report will provide the basis for future environmental planning and serve as a point of departure for comparison and assessment of specific intervention for economic development and growth and for improving environmental conditions and restoring the rates of renewal of natural resources.

The effort should be carried out over a three-year period and should produce intermediate reports on specific topics or regions where additional efforts are required to properly characterize the current conditions. These intermediate reports will have the form of Terms of Reference for additional work to be performed in a collaborative approach between Cuban and foreign engineers, environmental, and social scientists. The general format for these additional studies should follow the Strategic Environmental Assessment Format that has been developed by international funding organizations under the leadership of the World Bank.

Strategic environmental assessments should be implemented for the most important economic sectors as well as critical geographic regions within the country. World Bank guidelines should also be used as a point of comparison to establish the seriousness of the problem encountered and the need for remediation work.

Expected Results: The expected results from this effort should include at least the following:

- a main report following the format of a national environmental profile;

- strategic sectorial environmental assessments of the Cuban economy listed below. Emphasis in this case should be made on the establishment of existing environmental liabilities:

  – sugar cane production and industrialization;
  – coffee production and industrialization;
  – tourism;
  – mining industry ;
  – food processing and packing industry;
  – textile industry;
  – metallurgy;
  – nuclear program;
  – ports and harbors

- strategic critical regional environmental assessment of Cuba to include at least the areas mentioned below. In this case the emphasis should be placed on the identification of key obstacles for sustainable development and recommendations to overcome them effectively and efficiently:

  – Western Provinces: Pinar del Río, Havana and Matanzas;
  – Southern Coastal Areas: Isla de la Juventud and Cayo Largo, Jardines de la Reina and the Gulf of Guacanayabo;
  – Northern Coastal Areas; Archipelagos of Sabana and Camagüey; and
  – Eastern Provinces: Guantánamo, Holguín, and Santiago de Cuba.

Estimated Costs: $6M. Costs are based on an estimated effort of three years in order to complete both the environmental profile report as well as the strategic environmental assessment reports. The costs are mainly associated with personal services for both Cuban ($1.4M) and expatriate specialists ($2.5M). Additional costs include travel, lodging, meals and incidental expenses ($600K); sample collection and laboratory analysis ($1.0M) report preparation and distribution ($500K).

Institutional, Legal and Policy Analysis

The basis of future environmental law in Cuba will require the adoption of principles of strict liability for environmental damage along the lines envisaged in the UNCED Conventions of the last decade.

A legal system with appropriate reforms in the burden of proof and conflict resolution mechanisms can be summarized as 'The Polluter-Pays Principle." This principle started out as an economic incentive that has become a cornerstone of environmental law. A legal system with strict liability can be developed with the Polluter-Pays Principle so that the polluter bears the costs of pollution and control measures.

Reforms to Cuban environmental law requires that liability be placed on the polluter and to alleviate the economic burden on the state. The principle is not exclusively designed to punish polluters but to set appropriate signals in place in the economic systems so that the environmental costs are incorporated in the decision-making process so as to promote sustainable development in Cuba.

As a result of this analysis it is anticipated that an institutional strengthening and legislation support project will be designed. The purpose of this project should be to promote efficient environmental management in Cuba by strengthening the legal and institutional framework at the national, provincial and municipal levels. The main objectives of this project are anticipated to include the following:

- promote the implementation of policy and strategies through proposals for additional legislation, reforms in existing legislation, as well as supplementary rules and regulations;

- support the framing of a national environmental policy;

- lay the foundation for a national environmental system; and

- strengthen the technical and operating capacity of the executing national agency and of the agencies responsible for the environment at the national and provincial levels.

The typical activities that will be implemented under this project may include the following:

- establish demonstration programs for the prevention and control of environmental deterioration, to be applied at the level of specific provinces in the area of environmental monitoring,

sustainable development of tourism, development of institutional structures for watershed management, and control of industrial pollution;

- support the national environmental system, including technical assistance in the areas of policy, legislation, institutional strengthening, education and environmental information; and

- finance the preparation of other environmental projects.

Estimated costs: Costs for this initiative are estimated to be approximately $17.5M for a period of about 5 years. Roughly $1.5M is estimated for the design of the project and $16M for its implementation.

Water Supply and Sanitation

Since another proposed initiative focuses on the broader environmental problems around the City of Havana, other beneficiaries of this effort shall be the mid and small towns of the interior. The basic objectives of this effort shall include:

- improve living conditions in towns with 5,000 to 50,000 inhabitants by increasing water supply and sanitation services; and

- support the utilities that provide water supply and sanitation services to maintain and enhance their administrative, financial and operating mechanisms, as well as the agency responsible for sector planning, policy-setting and regulation.

Estimated Cost: The project shall include the following components, with an estimated cost of $125M.

- consultant services to prepare studies and designs for projects, update national water supply standards, conduct environmental control of projects and compile data for future program evaluations ($12M);

- supervision of construction work, program execution and contract administration to be carried out by the executing agency ($2.5M);

- multiple works, including construction or expansion of water supply, sanitary sewerage, or individual sanitation systems, including sewage and sludge treatment ($100M);

• technical support and training, institutional strengthening of the utilities providing services and of the agency responsible for sector planning, policy-setting and regulation ($10.5M).

Coastal and Marine Management and Conservation

The main objectives of this effort shall include the development of a national integrated Coastal Zone Management Program including the design and implementation of the institutional reforms necessary for successful execution of the proposed activities. Some specific objectives of this effort include:

• carry out diagnostic studies, and develop a Coastal Zone Management Plan for the Cuban coasts and develop community participation and demonstration projects in coastal zone management;

• conduct institutional strengthening activities such as the preparation of an income-generating strategy for coastal management, legal and regulatory reforms;

• establish a Geographic Information System (GIS), professional training in coastal management, public awareness and education activities, and the upgrading of environmental laboratory analysis services in support of coastal zone management; and

• design a nationwide investment program and make an assessment of its socio-economic, institutional, financial, legal and environmental feasibility, including cost recovery mechanisms for the investments.

Estimated Costs: Costs are anticipated to run in the order of $22M including: $2.2M for project design and related feasibility studies; $6.5M for technical assistance and training for project implementation; $11M for vehicles (both terrestrial and aquatic) and equipment for enforcement and control) and $2.3M for quality control and evaluation

National Watershed Management

The overall objective of this effort shall be to improve the environmental quality of the Cuban watersheds by reducing pollution and preserving its natural resources. Specific objectives may include:

• monitor and reduce industrial pollution;

• implement soil conservation practices and improve the management of toxic agricultural chemicals in priority watersheds;

• support the consolidation of conservation units;

• set up educational programs on environmental issues; and

• strengthen the environmental management capacity of state institutions.

In order to achieve these objectives, actions will be taken to:

• expand the coverage of sewage systems and treatment plants in rural and urban areas;

• control pollution in major rivers and its tributaries;

• implement a rural extension program that targets soil management, reforestation and pollution control;

• strengthen the infrastructure of selected conservation units;

• implement a pilot environmental education program for medium size cities and draw up an environmental education plan for the country; and

• provide institutional strengthening for participating agencies.

Estimated Costs: The cost for execution of this component has been estimated to run in the order of $27M during a period of 5 years. These costs include an estimated 5% for the design and preparation of several feasibility studies.

National Management and Conservation of Biological Diversity and Cultural Heritage

The objective of this effort shall be to protect the archaeological sites and ecosystem of the Cuban archipelago. The project shall consist of the following components:

- conservation and documentation of archaeological sites;

- basic protection, infrastructure and maintenance works, including construction of entrances and control structures to selected parks, rehabilitation and maintenance of parkways providing access to pre-colonial and colonial sites and observation points;

- works to minimize erosion, and rehabilitation and/or establishment of water reservoirs; and

- support actions, including strengthening of the executing agency's business and marketing management, educational training for the surrounding communities, and promotion of artisan activities.

Estimated Costs: Costs for this component are estimated to be $12M to include:

- specialized assistance in restoration and identification of causes of deterioration;

- supervision of construction and other engineering works;

- strengthening of the executing agency's management ability for the preparation of management and marketing plans;

- specialized assistance for the elaboration and publication of educational materials, teacher training, and artisan production;

- construction equipment and materials for conservation;

- computerized video technology;

- materials for drainage and water protection;

- vehicles; and

- educational equipment and materials.

Environmental Improvement of Metropolitan Havana Area

The objective of this effort is to make a sustainable improvement in the quality of life in the City of Havana Metropolitan Area. The specific objectives shall include:

- improve metropolitan management of environmental services by encouraging private sector and community involvement;

- improve the quality and coverage of environmental services, thus reducing the environmental degradation caused by improper solid and liquid waste collection and disposal;

- provide technical assistance, training, equipment and specialized tools in the areas of municipal management modernization, and environmental public services modernization;

- strengthen environmental monitoring and control capacity;

- introduce new solid waste collection systems that involve the private sector, micro-entrepreneurial and community collection systems;

- introduce systems to sort, process and dispose of solid wastes collected from throughout the metropolitan area, including the establishment of sorting and composting plants and sanitary landfills;

- develop a master plan for conveying and treating sewage, including treatment plants;

- introduce sewage collection and treatment alternatives (septic tanks) in priority areas; and

- manage green spaces to finance investments in reforestation, forest rehabilitation and management of priority green spaces, including reforestation and improving the Bosque de la Habana

Estimated Costs: Costs have been roughly estimated in $23M, to include:

- the design for the solid waste component, the sewage component and the green spaces component;

- advisory services and works supervision;

- training for solid waste collectors;

- institutional reforms for the water and sewer department;

- technical assistance in administrative and financial matters;

- programs to monitor services;

- industrial pollution studies;

- purchase of waste sorting units, solid waste collection vehicles, and equipment for treatment plants; and

- civil works to recondition and build sewage treatment plants, septic tanks and sanitary landfills.

Environmental Education and Awareness Campaign

Environmental education is not a well developed part of the current general curriculum in Cuba. Greatest improvements could be made through greater emphasis at the junior school level. Development of this curriculum may take one year and require another two years for implementation. Cuban universities already produce many teachers with a background in science and natural history, so further investment in teacher training may not be very high.

For adults, various environmental documentaries are currently produced by Cuban television or imported from overseas. However, the quality could be improved with greater funding and a dedicated environmental/natural history promotion.

Estimated Costs: Costs have been estimated in $3.5M for an initial three-year effort, after which an evaluation should be conducted and adjustments made to the overall approach as required.

Further Development of the Cuban Environmental Program

Finally it is proposed that the planning effort be started in advance to the actual changes in Cuba. The rationale behind this proposal is to assure that a Cuban environmental program will be far more developed than it is now, and to avoid problems similar to those encountered by the Eastern European countries. The proposal includes further development of the topics described in this paper including two main types of actions:

- Specific development to the pre-feasibility level of the tourism sector, particularly the beach tourism around the well known area of Varadero, in the north eastern coast of Cuba; and

- Further development of the other topics to the level of project profiles. The recommended actions include the development of position papers that can then be discussed in specialized workshops with different groups from the private sector and academic organizations related to the issues. Depending on the subject and the concerned groups attending and/or sponsoring, the workshops may be arranged and held in several cities of the United States, including Miami, Washington, and New Orleans, among others. Ideally these workshops will be carried over a one-year period. After that, a reevaluation of the program should take place according to the actual changes observed in Cuba and the likelihood of the transition to a free, democratic society.

REFERENCES

Díaz-Briquets, Sergio and Jorge Pérez-López.. 2000. *Conquering Nature: The Environmental Legacy of Cuban Socialism.* University of Pittsburgh Press. Pittsburgh.

Portela, Armando H. 1998. "El Medio Ambiente Cubano, La Fantasía y La Realidad." PROXIMO No. 6, Madrid.

US-Cuba Business Council. 2000. "Social and Environmental Impact of the Cuban Nuclear Program." US-Cuba Business Council Newsletter. Special Edition, January, 2000. Washington, D.C.

Wotzkow, Carlos. 1998. "S.O.S. For Cuba's Natural Environment." CUBA BRIEF. Center for a Free Cuba. Winter, Washington. D.C.

CUBA: FIN DE FIESTA—CASTRO DA POR TERMINADO EL *PERIODO ESPECIAL* Y RETOMA EL SOCIALISMO PURO Y DURO

Carlos Alberto Montaner

A principios de los noventa Castro tuvo miedo. Pero estaba convencido de que la vieja guardia estalinista sería capaz de desalojar del Krenlim a Gorbachov y retomar el glorioso camino del marxismo-leninismo. Esas ilusiones se desvanecieron tras el fallido golpe de agosto del 91 y el ascenso definitivo de Yeltsin al poder. Entonces la reacción del Comandante fue de pánico, pero, como suele ser propio de su carácter, huyó hacia delante. De esa época son sus discursos sobre la muerte que les esperaba a todos los dirigentes, uno a uno, en el Buró Político, en el Comité Central, en el Consejo de Estado. Padecía entonces una depresión aguda y se le habían disparado todos los sintomas de la paranoia. Estaba enfermo y había sufrido una hemiplejia que lo obligó a fuertes ejercicios de rehabilitación.

INMOVILISMO O MUERTE

¿Cómo sería el final? No sabía. Sin embargo, no estaba dispuesto a ceder un milímetro en materia ideológica y mucho menos a abrir los cauces de participación de la sociedad cubana. De ninguna manera cambiaría el perfil de su régimen. No obstante, la decisión de "resistir, resistir y resistir"—como entonces se dijo—tenía que ir acompañada con una propuesta económica creíble. Castro la hizo: la desaparecida ayuda de la URSS sería sustituida por varias medidas tomadas a regañadientes. Surgía el *periodo especial*. El "ajuste" a que sometería al país parecía dictado por el más ortodoxo asesor del *Fondo Monetario Internacional*: drástica disminución del gasto público, devaluación real de la moneda, aumento de impuestos, equi-

librio fiscal, enérgico recorte de los gastos sociales. Castro lo cumplió a rajatabla. Fue el más brutal y austero de cuantos se han ensayado en América Latina.

El costo social resultó altísimo. Los cubanos vieron disminuir su ya mermada capacidad de consumo en un cincuenta por ciento. Inmediatamente aumentaron los delitos y el comercio ilícito. La prostitución alcanzó proporciones nunca vistas. Escapar de Cuba se convirtió en la obsesión de millones de personas. Para paliar la hambruna, se permitió la reaparición de los mercados campesinos, se autorizó a los *cuentapropistas*, las granjas estatales fueron descentralizadas y se convirtieron en una suerte de semicooperativas. Asimismo, se liberalizó la tenencia de dólares con el propósito de estimular las remesas de los exiliados a sus familiares y amigos. Las Fuerzas Armadas, con el objeto de hacerlas económicamente autosuficientes, fueron reducidas sustancialmente y se trasformaron en un *holding* económico que opera hoteles, restaurantes y empresas agropecuarias.

Pero había más. El gobierno se propuso entonces impulsar las exportaciones de biotecnología. Comercializar productos con gran valor agregado sería la salida. Castro hasta llegó a anunciar la inminente aparición de una vacuna cubana contra el SIDA. Se retomaría en serio la producción azucarera y se potenciaría el turismo, una industria siempre sospechosa por los riesgos ideológicos que comporta. También habría que recurrir a varias dolorosas medidas transitorias.

Las dos más amargas eran la creación de *zonas francas* y la aceptación de *joint-ventures* con inversionistas extranjeros dispuestos a participar como socios en el capitalismo de Estado. El matiz era importante: no se abría el país a la empresa privada, sino se invitaba a ciertos empresarios sin demasiados escrúpulos para que, asociados al gobierno cubano, explotaran la excelente mano de obra disponible: dócil, educada, carente de derechos sindicales, y a la que se le arrebataba el noventa y cinco por ciento de sus salarios por medio de contratos leoninos. Esta amalgama—ajuste macroeconómico, dolarización, *joint-ventures* y vestigios de economía de mercado—tendría, repito, un nombre: *periodo especial*. Y también tendría un destino anunciado: desaparecer cuando las circunstancias lo permitieran.

RETOMAR EL SOCIALISMO

Es exactamente en ese punto en el que estamos: Castro está seguro de que ha pasado el peligro y comienza a desmantelar las medidas tomadas durante la década de los noventa. Aumenta la presión sobre los *cuentapropistas* y Carlos Lage anuncia, satisfecho, que han pasado de 180 000 a 150 000. El objetivo es que no haya ninguno. Cierran numerosos *paladares* e intentan sustituirlos por restaurantes oficiales de precios más accesibles. ¿Método para liquidar a la "competencia"? Una alta presión fiscal, multas y prohibiciones absurdas. Los paladares privados, por ejemplo, no pueden vender carne de res o mariscos. Con la misma lógica, junto a los mercados campesinos surgen instituciones públicas que venden alimentos en dólares. El gobierno se propone recuperar el monopolio total del comercio minorista, tanto en pesos—que nunca lo perdió—como en dólares. Se agrava la persecución a quienes alquilan habitaciones en sus domicilios y compiten con los hoteles. El presidente del Banco Nacional anuncia que, eventualmente, terminará la dolarización de la economía. Ya se están preparando para ello y lo ensayan en el sector turístico. Proyectan una especie de caja de conversión donde cada dólar que entre al país sea sustituido por una moneda de circulación exclusiva. Cuando tengan todos los controles en la mano bajarán artificialmente la tasa de cambio de la nueva moneda con relación al dólar. Las remesas de los exiliados podrán seguir fluyendo, mas los dólares tendrán que ser canjeados por la nueva moneda. En ese momento la tenencia de dólares volverá a ser penada por la ley.

Pero no sólo son los cubanos quienes sufren esta recaída en esa enfermedad crónica y fatal llamada "socialismo". A los inversionistas extranjeros también les ha llegado su turno. Hay el propósito de cerrar las zonas francas creadas en el país. A los pocos bufetes internacionales que operan en la Isla se les ha pedido que se vayan con sus leyes a otra parte. En el mes de mayo se anunció una paralización de las ventas en dólares de propiedades inmuebles a extranjeros y a cubanos radicados en el exterior. Ya se les notificó a los contratistas que el gobierno estudia la posibilidad de ejercer el derecho de "tanteo y retracto" previsto en los contratos. Y quienes se asoman a La Habana con el ánimo de hacer negocio lo que escuchan son propuestas de compra de suministros, o de contratos de administración—como sucede con la mayor parte de los hoteles—, pero sin compartir propiedad con el Estado cubano. El extranjero debe aportar crédito, vender y cobrarle al gobierno con mercancías o con los beneficios que produzca las empresas, pero sin establecer sociedades complejas "que menoscaben la soberanía nacional." Los hoteleros de Meliá han visto con preocupación cómo entre las directrices recientes está la obligatoriedad que tienen sus empleados de acentuar el fortalecimiento ideológico. Los incentivos importantes son los morales. Es otra vuelta guevarista a la tuerca. Ni siquiera sería extraña una renegociación de los pactos originales con la Sherritt canadiense. Castro no está nada feliz con los canadienses y muy especialmente con el Primer Ministro Jean Chrétien.

EN EL TERRENO POLÍTICO

En efecto, la recuperación del proyecto comunista también tiene una preocupante lectura política: disminuye la tolerancia con la disidencia—que siempre ha sido mínima—y se desmiente rotundamente que el régimen estudie ampliar los márgenes de participación de la sociedad cubana. Ya no hay espacio para el ambiguo lenguaje de "Robertico" Robaina. De la misma manera que se reivindica la economía planificada y la propiedad estatal como un modelo viable y moralmente superior de organización económica, se asegura que el sistema de partido único y de ideología marxista leninista es ética y políticamente superior al que exhiben las podridas naciones capitalistas, encharcadas en la politiquería pluripartidista. Por eso el gobierno mantiene en la cárcel a Vladimiro Roca o condena a varios años al médico Elías Biscet, un opositor casi ghandiano. Le da igual. No hay nada que ocultar. Castro ha comprobado que el precio que paga por la represión contra sus opositores casi nunca trasciende del plano retórico. Desde la pupila orgullosamente estalinista del régimen se trata de enemigos del pueblo. La verdadera democracia es la que se practica en Cuba, dice Castro desafiante y reiteran sus corifeos constantemente, con Ricardo Alarcón a la cabeza de ellos. "No hay alternativa al marxismo-leninismo," repiten como un *mantra* José Ramón Machado Ventura, José Ramón Balaguer y Raúl Valdés Vivó en la Escuela Superior del Partido "Ñico López." Son los encargados de velar por la ideología de la secta. Son los "ideólogos", algo que en este caso no quiere decir teóricos creativos, capaces de conceptualizar novedosamente, sino comisarios encargados de que nadie se mueva un milímetro de la línea oficial. Son sólo policías del pensamiento.

LAS RAZONES DEL CAMBIO

¿Por qué Castro ha dado este giro? En realidad nadie debe sorprenderse. Hoy se siente seguro. Desde el primer momento anunció que las "aperturas" y las "concesiones" eran sólo coyunturales. No ha engañado a nadie. Lo dijo y lo reiteró veinte veces: en el momento en que la revolución recuperara el pulso, retornaría al punto de partida. Sus tres temores principales se han desvanecido y cree que ese momento ha llegado. Primero, ya no hay temor al colapso. La economía se ha estabilizado. ¿Qué quiere eso decir? Muy sencillo: la sociedad cubana ya encajó el golpe. Se acostumbró a vivir en unos nuevos niveles de miseria, y experimenta un lento crecimiento vegetativo. Ahora el país es considerablemente más pobre de lo que era en la década de los ochenta, pero la sensación general es que "pasó lo peor". Con los ingresos de las remesas de los emigrantes, más los réditos del turismo, a lo que se suman algunas exportaciones—azúcar, níquel, tabaco—, agregados a otros ingresos *non sanctos* (lavado de dinero en la Banca oficial, doscientos millones por el uso de la Base de Lourdes que operan los soviéticos, unos cuarenta millones que ge-

nera el arrendamiento de esclavos profesionales a otros gobiernos o empresas privadas), alcanza para importar petróleo, ciertos alimentos básicos, y algunas medicinas y fertilizantes. Es decir, lo suficiente para sostener el precario nivel de la población cubana, sin tener en cuenta, por supuesto, ni la depreciación de los activos ni las inversiones que un país moderno necesita para mejorar realmente la calidad de vida de la población. Castro ya tiene lo que necesita para procurarles a los cubanos una existencia oscura y sin esperanzas: ¿para qué necesita más? El país, día a día, se irá distanciando paulatina e insensiblemente del perfil técnico y científico de las naciones más desarrolladas, pero nada de eso le quita el sueño al Comandante.

El segundo temor tenía que ver con Estados Unidos. Aunque Castro sabe que desde la muerte de John Kennedy, a partir de noviembre de 1963, no hay en Washington planes serios para derribarlo, era natural que, ante la desaparición de la protección de la UR-SS, temiera un nuevo esfuerzo en ese sentido. Pero los dos periodos de Clinton—y especialmente el segundo—lo convencieron de que el único objetivo de Estados Unidos con relación a Cuba es evitar el éxodo salvaje de la población rumbo a tierras norteamericanas. Comprobada la indiferencia de sus vecinos, incluso la fatiga de la clase dirigente de Estados Unidos tras cuatro décadas de hostilidad, y totalmente seguro de que a quien gobierne en Washington le trae sin cuidado el tipo de sistema que impera en la Isla, retomar el modelo socialista no entrañaba el menor riesgo.

El tercer obstáculo superado era la oposición interna y externa. ¿Conseguirían sus enemigos de adentro y de fuera forjar una alianza con los "blandos" o "reformistas" de su gobierno? ¿Lograría esa alianza legitimidad y ayuda exterior hasta convertirse en un peligro parecido al que liquidó el comunismo en Hungría o en Polonia? ¿Se solivantaría el ejército? Nada de eso sucedió: la oposición externa e interna se enfrascó en conflictos bizantinos ("dialogueros" frente a "intransigentes", "moderados" contra "principistas"), mientras los pocos reformistas del gobierno—casi todos temblorosamente avecindados en el mundillo académico—fueron atemorizados hasta que sus voces dejaron de oírse o hasta que se sumaron al coro habitual (Rafael Hernández, por ejemplo). Los militares, a su vez, quedaron escarmentados tras las ejecuciones y la purga de 1989. Tienen tanto miedo como el resto de la población. La prioridad de los mandos altos y medios ya no es salvar la patria de una hipotética invasión yanqui ni conquistar el Tercer Mundo para la causa sagrada del socialismo. El plan de batalla hoy consiste en buscar dólares para mejorar la calidad de la canasta familiar.

La comunidad internacional, por su parte, también aceptó el carácter inmodificable del comunismo cubano y se sentó cómodamente a esperar la muerte de Castro. Nadie—menos los cubanos, claro—parece tener prisa por ver el fin de la dictadura. Es como la lenta agonía de uno de esos enfermos terminales aquejados por una mala salud de hierro. Nada puede hacerse por salvarlos. Tampoco nada desean hacer por acelerar su muerte.

LA REVOLUCIÓN CUBANA DE AHORA EN ADELANTE

Salvados los principales escollos, Fidel Castro con gran entusiasmo, ha vuelto a lo que él supone que es la política: la agitación callejera. Para Castro, política y alboroto son sinónimos. Sufre una variante leninista y pugnaz del síndrome de Peter Pan. No ha podido superar su revoltosa adolescencia y vive convencido de que su principal enemigo es la inacción o la falta de enemigos. La atmósfera en la que mejor se siente es en el enfrentamiento. Cuando les dice a sus subalternos que deben priorizar el trabajo político por encima de cualquier otro, lo que les está comunicando es que congreguen a los cubanos para repetir consignas mitineras y para establecer algún punto de vista "revolucionario" que sustente la causa de turno. Eso hoy puede ser Elián, la oposición a la globalización, la Ley de Ajuste, el embargo. Ayer fue la deuda externa, la estructura de la ONU o las multinacionales. Mañana serán otros los pretextos. De lo que se trata es de que la población marche, aplauda y grite. Castro, siempre al frente de la muchedumbre, cree que esa es la política. Más que el Máximo Líder es el Máximo *Cheer-Leader*.

La respuesta de casi todos los cubanos ante este nuevo espasmo revolucionario es una mezcla entre la im-

potencia y la total desilusión. Marchan, aplauden y gritan porque con esos signos externos de sumisión y acatamiento se evitan daños mayores. Es la liturgia salvadora. Sin embargo, secretamente sueñan con largarse del país o con poner a salvo a sus hijos de tanto absurdo, de tanta sinrazón. Y esa reacción no es sólo propia de los opositores. Desde el primer círculo de poder hacia abajo la mayor parte de la jerarquía revolucionaria también comparte la misma sensación de frustración y desaliento. También tratan de salvar a sus hijos y familiares, colocándolos discretamente en el extranjero, bajo el previo compromiso de que se hagan invisibles.

¿Cómo lo hacen? Aprovechan sus contactos con los visitantes extranjeros y el acceso al patrimonio nacional. Uno de los más destacados jerarcas revolucionarios sacó medio millón de dólares en cuadros valiosos y le montó a su hijo un restaurant en Europa. Otros les consiguen becas universitarias fuera de Cuba o trabajos en empresas que tienen algún tipo de interés dentro de la Isla. Puro tráfico de influencias. Los muchachos suelen salir con libros valiosos en sus maletas, o con obras de arte, que luego venden en el extranjero. A veces, como tienen acceso a dólares, les "compran" ese destino a sus hijos. Por ocho o diez mil dólares logran que un italiano o un español con las conexiones adecuadas le procure al hijo o hija un puesto de trabajo o la posibilidad de realizar un misterioso "Master" en alguna universidad extranjera. En algún caso, en un claro ejemplo de corrupción, se premia al extranjero amante de la hija y futura tabla de salvación de la familia, con una asesoría pagada en dólares a cuenta del Estado cubano.

El cinismo y el doble lenguaje a veces se mantienen hasta dentro de la intimidad del hogar. Conozco el caso de un importante general—uno de los más represivos—que antes de "salvar" a su hija del paraíso que él había ayudado a construir le hizo repasar el guión como si fuera una obra de teatro: "¿Si te preguntan qué haces en el extranjero qué debes contestar?" "Que me preparo para defender la revolución, papi," contesta la muchacha. Es una buena chica. Quiere a su padre, pero odia profundamente a la revolución. "¿Y por qué no te vas tú también, papi?" "Porque yo estoy muy viejo y tengo que morirme con esta mierda. Ya es muy tarde para cambiar," le responde el general con tristeza. Los hijos de la *nomenklatura* situados en el exterior, cientos de jóvenes generalmente bien educados, atrapados entre el cariño y la lealtad a sus padres, de una parte, y el rechazo a la revolución, por otra, resuelven su dolorosa disonancia con el silencio. A su manera, son también víctimas de un sistema de terror capaz de pasar las fronteras. Son víctimas, claro, de baja intensidad.

COLOFÓN

¿En qué va a parar este triste espectáculo? Por ahora, en un creciente deterioro moral y físico de la nación cubana. El entorno material se irá degradando con cada aguacero que inunde las ciudades, con cada huracán que estremeza los campos y derribe casuchas y edificios, con el implacable desgaste del sol tropical. El país deshace, o se "desconstruye," como les gusta decir a los palabreros. En el terreno ético ocurrirá más o menos lo mismo: la mala conciencia que genera el doble lenguaje irá aumentando el malestar sicológico de la población. Unos, somatizarán esas contradicciones en forma de angustias. Otros, convertirán la huida en una dolorosa obsesión. Todos, más impotentes que resignados, esperaran impacientes la muerte del caudillo. Suponen que entonces comenzará el amanecer.

FISCAL REFORMS IN TRANSITION ECONOMIES: IMPLICATIONS FOR CUBA

Lorenzo L. Pérez[1]

This paper reviews the fiscal policy reform experience of economies in transition to a market economy, summarizes best practices, and with this background assesses the fiscal policy reforms taking place in Cuba. The paper addresses four main areas: tax policy, tax administration, budgetary and accounting practices, and public expenditure policy.

One comment is warranted at the outset. For fiscal policy reform to be effective in a country like Cuba that has a large public sector and where strong elements of a centralized planned economy still persist, significant steps have to be taken to move towards a market economy, particularly in terms of liberalizing the price system, the assignment of factors of production, the financial sector, and the external sector. These reforms do not appear to be taking place in Cuba with the speed that circumstances warrant them. Although the Cuban government does not advocate officially a transition to a full fledged market economy, this paper takes the position that a transition to a market economy would be the most efficient path to improve the welfare of the Cuban people. It is from this perspective that the ongoing fiscal reforms in Cuba are evaluated.

TAX POLICY REFORMS IN TRANSITION ECONOMIES

After the breakdown of the Soviet Union, the former republics of the Soviet Union faced the difficult task of enacting their own tax laws and establishing independent tax and customs administrations.[2] At the beginning, the new countries simply maintained the former Soviet tax system but as the transition to a market economy proceeded, the tax and customs administrations had to shift from handling the transactions of a highly controlled state sector to dealing with the more challenging compliance activities of the emerging private sector and increasingly autonomous state-owned firms. All the countries of the former Soviet Union but the three Baltic countries, have struggled to adapt their tax policy and tax administration practices in these areas and have experienced declining and inadequate revenue in varying degrees of severity.[3]

---

1. The views expressed here are those of the author and do not necessarily represent the official views of the International Monetary Fund. The author would like to thank Mr. Jorge Mattar of CEPAL (Mexico) for making available before publication the chapter on public finances of the 2000 CEPAL report on the Cuban economy written by Juan Carlos Moreno Brid; Messrs. John Norregaard and Jorge Pérez-López for providing other reference material; and Mr. Joaquín Pujol for presenting the paper on his behalf at the 10th Annual Meetings of ASCE.

2. The sections on tax policy and tax administration of the former Soviet Union countries draws on *Tax Reform in the Baltics, Russia, and Other Countries of the Former Soviet Union,* by an IMF staff team led by Liam Ebrill and Oleh Havrylyshyn, Occasional Paper 182, International Monetary Fund, Washington, D.C. 1999.

3. Ibid, p. 1.

It can be argued that socialist economies in transition to a market economy need tax reform urgently.[4] Tax reform is a necessary condition for transition because socialist tax systems are incompatible with a market oriented economy. Tax reform can help many other economic reforms which are necessary to restructure the economy, and it is also essential for macroeconomic stability in the transition process. Furthermore, the existing systems of taxation found in socialist economies are not tax systems in the usual sense and tend to be incompatible with a market-oriented economy. In socialist economies, laws of taxation were frequently subservient to laws on wages, input and output prices, and production targets among other things. Frequently, when wages and input prices were raised, tax rates were reduced to accommodate them instead of raising product or consumer prices. This practice did not leave these countries with adequate tax rates when the process of transition began. Since in socialist countries the governments had complete power to introduce taxation there was little need to educate taxpayers or to seek their acceptance. This advantage quickly becomes a disadvantage at the time of the transition because there is very little culture of tax paying.

Tax Systems of Socialist Economies

The dominant tax instruments of socialist economies, the enterprise and turnover taxes, were not suited to market economies. The tax base was defined fairly arbitrarily for enterprise taxes in socialist countries— for example, minimum levels of profits were established by the Council of Ministers in Bulgaria; indirectly, the level of profits was affected by wages, interest rates, exchange rates and pricing policies. Extreme arbitrariness also characterized the definition of allowable expenses, exemptions, and deductions which served as an open invitation to bargaining. A practice of differentiating the applica-

ble tax rates, by branches of industry and even by enterprises was widespread. Enterprise taxes were frequently waived if the enterprise could show a financial need. As the state was both the tax collector and the taxpayer, the payment of profits tax as well as other budgetary contributions of enterprises were often negotiated and determined ex post at levels consistent with the planned allocation of resources between enterprises and industries within the public sector.

Turnover taxes were not taxes in the way that they are understood in market economies. They really represented predetermined margins between the producer and consumer prices. The tax typically was expressed in three ways: (1) as the retail-wholesale price differential which varied across commodities; (2) in a specific form; or (3) as an ad valorem rate applied to some measure of turnover. As a result, the number of turnover tax rates tended to be almost as great as the number of different commodities and kept changing over time with changes in price differentials. The number of transactions to which the reduced rates of turnover tax or exemptions were applied was great too. Thus, the tax base tended to be narrow and turnover tax revenues were generally raised from a few selected commodities (for example, the alcohol tax in the Soviet Union). The efficiency impact of this tax was, not surprisingly, disastrous.[5]

As Ghandi and Mihaljek noted, the transition to a market economy, and the introduction of comprehensive price liberalization, amounted to a death blow to the system of turnover taxation. Once the producers and retailers are free to set their prices in accordance with the perceived relation between supply and demand, it is harder to set a tax equivalent to retail-wholesale price differentials, nor it is possible to defend a multi-rate and cascading-type turnover

---

4. See Ved P. Ghandi and Dubravko Mihaljek, "Scope for Reform of Socialist Tax Systems," in Vito Tanzi: *Fiscal Policies in Economies in Transition*, 1992.

5. At the same time, it should be noted that the administration of this tax was easy within the central planning system. Since the only legal form of payment between the enterprises and retailers was transfers on accounts in the state bank, and since prices were administratively fixed and the volume of their turnover closely monitored, the possibilities for tax evasion or for tax arrears were small.

tax.[6] Tax administration becomes more difficult in general.

Other important sources of revenue in socialist countries were social contributions and payroll taxes, both of which were collected from enterprises. Wage payments to workers were net of income tax and thus the burden of paying these taxes fell on the enterprises. Personal income tax applied only to incomes of performing artists, writers, sportsmen, inventors, and the smallest of retailers and service providers, who were the ones required to file tax returns. This tax was extremely progressive, if not confiscatory. The reform of personal income taxes become necessary once wage determination becomes a market determined process. The entire structure of the tax base and tax rates have to be redesigned with a view to encouraging instead of discouraging the private sector. Payroll taxes also have to be restructured to ensure that individuals make appropriate contributions to the social security system.

Taxes on foreign trade were important in socialist countries. In most cases, customs duties were not considered to be an element of tax policy. Nominal import tariffs were relatively low and the preferred protective devices were quantitative restrictions. However, most raw materials and intermediate goods were imported duty free, so the effective rates of protection varied considerably. The distortive effects of the different rates of protection need to be taken into account as economies are transformed into one where market forces play a greater role.

Tax Reform Objectives of Economies in Transition

Tax reform in economies in transition face constraints due to the revenue needs of restructuring and the limited technical capacity of tax administration.[7] In the short run, efforts need to concentrate on the rationalization of existing revenue sources (enterprise income taxes, turnover taxes, payroll taxes, and tariffs). Based on the experience of the countries of the former Soviet Union, fiscally and economically more efficient forms of taxation, such as the value-added

tax (VAT) and the comprehensive personal income tax, cannot be introduced quickly. In the economies in transition in Europe, a clear exception to this was the reform of the existing system of profit taxes on enterprises which was often among the biggest obstacles for successful reform of microeconomic decision making and had to be reformed at an early stage in the transition process.

In the short run, tax reform should aim at meeting the large revenue needs of macroeconomic stabilization and the creation of a social safety net; at restructuring the existing tax system toward a structure appropriate for the longer run; at making the existing taxes more stable and transparent; and at making the tax system supportive of other market oriented economic reforms, in ways which are incentive-enhancing and equity improving. Once a process of liberalization starts, the major revenue sources of socialist economies can be expected to come under stress. For example, as a consequence of a price reform, the government is likely to lose control over output and input pricing and the profitability of state owned enterprises will be affected. Turnover taxes are likely to decline because of a drop in aggregate demand, while payroll taxes will also drop because of loss of full employment.

As a building block for restructuring the tax system, the existing taxes need to be made more transparent and stable. A balance has to be stricken between implementing tax reform as the political opportunities appear and keeping taxes stable for the sake of investors. Domestic and foreign investors need to know what their various tax liabilities would be when they undertake specific investments. The tax liabilities need to remain stable for a foreseeable period of time as many investments have long gestation periods. The adoption of appropriate measures of taxation can also help support the implementation of price and labor reforms, and external and financial sectors liberalization.

---

6. Ghandi and Mihaljek, op.cit., page 148.

7. The discussion in the following paragraphs draws on Ghandi and Mihaljek, op.cit., pp. 155-166.

To achieve these short run objectives, tax reform should begin in transition economies through the reform of the turnover taxes because price liberalization normally has priority in the sequence of reforms. Negative turnover tax rates (used to provide price subsidies) need to be eliminated; ad valorem rates should be introduced and the number of rates reduced; selected excises need to be introduced; and work begun to introduce a VAT. One thing that need not be overlooked is to widen the tax bases which, unless is done, can limit the benefits of the rationalization of this tax.

The main reforms of enterprise taxes that should be introduced are the elimination of the practice of placing arbitrary claims on enterprise profits; and the unification and reduction of tax rates. Other technical issues would need to be addressed such as what type of enterprises will be subject to corporate income tax. For example, the enterprise income tax can be made uniform between corporations, partnerships, and proprietary firms, and the physical owners, be they shareholders, partners, or proprietors, can be taxed only on profits they take out of the enterprise in the form of dividends, profit shares, or salary. Tax systems can adapt to alternative legal forms of business which provide some more flexibility for enterprise growth.[8] Should enterprises continue to be state-owned, a charge, in addition to the legislative enterprise profits tax can be levied to reflect a minimum return on past state equity and toward interest on past loans from the governments.

In many cases, generous tax holidays for joint ventures and foreign enterprises have been given in transition economies under the mistaken impression that they will be sufficient to attract foreign investment given the presumed comparative advantage in terms of unit labor costs. Frequently, the importance of the economic fundamentals for investment were underestimated and an effort was made to substitute them with the generous tax benefits, while not taking into account the distortions introduced by these tax holi-

days. At the same time, paradoxically, frequently allowed company tax provisions (e.g. loss carry over provisions) for which a stronger case can be made were not provided for.

A transitional step toward the introduction of a personal income tax can be the introduction of a final withholding tax on wages and salaries of those workers whose incomes have come to be determined by market forces. Initially, the withholding tax could be a flat tax at a low nominal rate, collected on pay-as-you-earn basis, without too many complexities of family size, etc. Similar low-rate withholding taxes can also be introduced on other forms of incomes such as interest, pensions, and rentals, without aggregating all incomes earned by an income earner.

Although import tariffs are not the first best form of taxation, they can be used as an important source of revenue in the transition. This is particularly important because imports are likely to increase as a result of trade liberalization and trade taxes generally have much lower collection costs than other taxes that also have large revenue potential. Other aspects of trade liberalization as the elimination of quantitative restrictions would have a beneficial revenue effect. However, for import tariffs to play a useful role, highly differentiated structures of implicit import taxes need to be replaced by simpler, preferably uniform, set of ad valorem tariffs applicable to all imports. In order to avoid the potential problem of longer-term industrial inefficiency, there ought to be a phased program of tariff reductions. This should be announced at the beginning of the period of tax reform.

Finally, some forms of property taxes can be introduced, particularly at the local level. This can be introduced at the same time that privatization of land and housing is launched. An initial problem is how to determine the assessed value of the properties; if market values are not available they can be based on existing rental values properly indexed.

8. As the reader can appreciate there are complex technical issues regarding enterprise taxation that would need to be decided as a transition economy successfully turn into a market economy that are beyond the scope of this paper.

In the medium to long run, tax reform has to emphasize more the attainment of the familiar properties of a good tax system: neutrality to minimize distortions, equity to ensure fairness, and simplicity to facilitate its administration. With these objectives in mind, policy makers need to avoid provisions usually intended as short run remedies, which tend to become entrenched in the tax code once adopted. To avoid this problem, it is important at the outset to articulate the nature and characteristics of the desired long run tax system

Experience in market economies has been dominated by two common and simple themes that can be incorporated into the long run planning of economies in transition: simplification of existing income tax systems and the expansion of consumption based taxes, usually by adopting some variants of the VAT. While not abandoning the objective of equity by limiting or eliminating tax deductions that benefit mainly the rich, the reform of the income tax needs to give more weight to efficiency to have the intended effects of stimulating economic growth. At this stage, more informed decisions will have to be made regarding family allowances and indexation of rate schedules and allowances; whether the income tax will be based on individual or household income, on worldwide income or territorial income; to what extent taxation of income in kind will take place; and the extent that capital gains and interest income taxation will occur. These decisions are important in deciding the importance that the income tax will play as a revenue source. In Latin America during the 1990s there has been a decline in the reliance on the personal income tax.[9]

For the long run, the adoption of the VAT is recommended due to the well known fact that, in its ideal form, it is the least distortive broad-based consumption tax that at the same time has a built in self-enforcing mechanism. This new sales tax structure helps to break the vicious circle of the price formation mechanism and ad hoc intervention to correct microeconomic imbalances. It helps the economy move toward a fiscal system characterized with greater certainty for economic agents and more transparency for the authorities. But it is worthwhile undertaking only if relative prices are allowed to change. The adoption of the VAT does not preclude the use of excise taxes that could be used to meet social objectives.[10]

Two key issues will need to be decided: which enterprises will be subject to the VAT and to what sectors the VAT should apply. It has been recommended that the liability to VAT in transition economies should be defined for all traders through the retail stage with an exemption applied only on the basis of turnover.[11] The choice of the threshold for liability to the tax should be made with an eye to simplifying the administration of the tax. In principle, the base of the VAT should be as wide as possible, and exemptions should be avoided that would quickly generate a strong lobby for further exemptions. The limited availability of consumption goods in transition economies argues for making food subject to the tax. But to the extent that there are a lot of sales of basic foodstuffs sold directly from the farm to consumers, probably makes the taxation of these commodities unrealistic at the outset. Financial services are frequently not taxed under the VAT and it should not be recommended for transition economies at a time when they are trying to promote this key sector. For the full economic benefit of the VAT to be realized it should have other desirable features such as, for example, the exclusion of purchases of capital and intermediate goods from the tax base, a single structure with few exemptions, and a zero rating of exports.

9. P. Shome points to a number of factors behind this trend: the top personal income tax rate has fallen continuously, the personal exemption level in terms of per capita GDP has been steadily raised, and the authorities have not been successful in removing existing personal allowances, deductions and incentives that erode the tax base. See P. Shome, *Taxation in Latin America: Structural Trends and Impact of Administration*, IMF Working Paper, WP/99/19, February 1999.

10. Some key implementation issues for adopting a VAT are discussed in the tax administration section.

11. Alan A. Tait, "Introducing Value-Added Taxes," in Vito Tanzi, op.cit.

In transition economies moving to democracy and as a reaction to central government control, there was an upsurge of enthusiasm for local minority issues. The temptation arose to use the VAT as a major revenue source for subnational governments, but in a federation, the VAT is not a good state or local tax. Those countries which have tried to use the VAT at the subnational level, have had to use very complex administrative systems. The basic problem is that for VAT revenue to be apportioned within a federation, the VAT content of goods and services crossing state or provincial boundaries must be checked and settlements made. As success is achieved in putting in place a consumption tax of the form of the VAT at the national level, further steps should be taken to lower the ad valorem import tariffs and make the tariff schedule as uniform as possible to avoid resource misallocation. Any remaining nontariff barriers should be dismantled. With the adoption of a realistic exchange rate, import liberalization (to eliminate anti-export bias), and the removal of export taxes should be possible.

Reforming Tax Administration

A major role of the tax administration in socialist countries was to verify that the correct amount of revenue was transferred from one government account to another. This was a crucial role given the existence of state ownership. As an economy reforms toward a more market-oriented economy, the tax administration will have to shift resources into ensuring the compliance of an increasing number of private enterprises that will be responding to market incentives rather than to incentives created by the economic plan. This shift from simple verification of transfers to more challenging compliance activities will demand entirely new skills and abilities from tax officials and a totally different operational strategy from tax administration.[12]

The implications of state ownership permeated the basic practices and procedures of tax administration in these countries. For example, the relationship between the tax assessor and the state-owned enterprise's tax accountant was less adversarial than in market-oriented economies, primarily because the two are both employed by the state. Another feature of state ownership was that the number of taxpayers was relatively small compared with market economies. Most tax revenue is obtained from the few large state-owned enterprises or collectively owned enterprises through turnover taxes and a profits tax. Also, state-owned banks played a major role in monitoring the tax payments of these state-owned enterprises. As the private sector gained in importance in these countries, the number of tax payers increased and private banks were created that were not necessarily willing to play the same role as state-owned banks.

The reform of the tax administration has to start with changes in systems and procedures. The systems and procedures in the former Soviet Union countries were not appropriate for the administration requirements of a market economy. There existed a tradition of manual systems and outdated tax administration procedures: tax payers frequently registered at the local office where they were assigned a local number, as opposed to a national taxpayer identification number that could be used for computerized files. Tax offices in these countries provided limited assistance when there existed questions on how to fill out tax forms. The notion that tax administrators should attempt to reduce taxpayer compliance costs by providing information and assistance, simplifying procedures, or requiring only a minimum amount of information on returns was not clearly understood. Taxpayers typically required that the taxpayer physically make a trip to either a tax office or a bank, as the mail was not reliable. If the payments were made at the bank, the information was sent to tax offices that verified manually the payments.

Audit coverage was extremely broad, especially for state-owned enterprises where coverage was often 100 percent. Because the number of taxpayers was relatively small, it was possible for tax officials to visit

---

12. This section draws on Milka Casanegra de Jantscher, Carlos Silvani, and Charles L. Vehorn, "Modernizing Tax Administration," in V. Tanzi, op. cit.

almost every one of these firms on annual basis to check tax compliance. This is a practice that cannot be continued as the number of enterprises increases, particularly as many small and medium-sized firms and service-oriented activities appear, which by their very nature are harder to tax. In these circumstances, the taxpayers did not bother to keep up with changes in the legislation and negotiated with the tax officials the amount that should be paid. Frequently, the audits were conducted based on the targets in the annual plans of enterprises, in effect auditing the plan rather than the tax liability of the state enterprises. Tax penalties rarely went beyond a general interest payment to specific automatic fines for specific tax offenses that in real terms were very small. Taxpayers had very little room for appealing.

The modernization of tax administration in socialist countries requires a major reform. An important step is the elevation of the status of the tax administration to a semi-autonomous organization within the Ministry of Finance to raise the image of tax administration and be able to pay competitive salaries. The long term objective ought to be to organize tax administration on a functional basis cutting across all taxes to allow staff to gain special skills with respect to the function they perform. It facilitates the development of a system of checks and balances where one tax official does not handle all the functions of a given taxpayer.

A tax administration system based on manual processing has great difficulties in coping with the rapid expansion in the number of taxpayers and the administrative changes imposed by the new tax laws. For this reason, after designing a broad administrative framework, an electronic data processing system has to be adopted. In designing the broad administrative framework, the existing constraints and available resources should be considered. Issues such as, for example, how the taxpayers are going to be identified, will taxpayers assess their own taxes and how

will they pay them, will need to be decided. Other issues such how the tax data are going to be collected and the processing systems for the different taxes will also need to be addressed (e.g., should they be the same for all taxes?). The task of computerizing the tax administration is formidable and in a country like Cuba, it is advisable to approach the conversion to computers in stages. At the beginning what is crucial from an administration perspective is to establish a taxpayer register, taxpayer identification numbers, a master file, and to process returns and payments smoothly. The establishment of a national taxpayer identification number is the essential key to identifying all documents related to a taxpayer. This is really a prerequisite to computerization and monitoring the taxpayer population.[13]

Modern audit procedures must be adopted with specific guidelines to address different conditions, for example, auditing large enterprises versus auditing small enterprises or VAT audits versus income tax audits. Audits should not be performed until the auditors can visit taxpayers with sufficient background information. At the same time, it must be realized that tax administration cannot cope with auditing 100 percent of the taxpayers. Audit coverage may vary by class of taxpayer and type of tax, but to the extent that resources are available, the coverage should include cases related to each type of tax and each category of taxpayer. Using single-item audits relative to the number of in-depth audits will increase coverage. It is important to realize that the audit function will evolve as tax officials develop more information on taxpayer behavior and learn how to use a wide variety of audit tools. Most former Soviet Union countries have had difficulties in making progress in improving critical compliance activities—especially audit planning, and audit selection—and have not developed reporting systems to ensure that resources are allocated in the most productive manner.[14]

---

13. Several transition economies have only required individuals who carry out business activities to register. Individuals for whom wages are the only source of income have not been required to register and file tax returns.

14. Ebrill and Havrylyshyn, op.cit., p. 12.

As the tax system modernizes, more reliance will have to be put on tax payers self-assessment that would need to be complemented by a strict enforcement of penalties and a fair appeals process. A sound penalty structure should include financial and nonfinancial penalties for both civil and criminal offenses. The amount of the penalty should be automatic and sufficiently high to deter evasion. Care should be taken to ensure that penalties bear a relationship to the actual tax liability to ensure that it is within the capacity of the enterprises to pay. However, a well designed structure may fail to deter evasion unless taxpayers see that penalties are being rigorously and fairly applied. Finally, taxpayer rights must not be dismissed. The appeals process should allow the taxpayer a chance to voice his or her case before the tax administration, and, if not fully satisfied with the results, before some institution outside the tax administration.

Progress in Tax Policy and Tax Administration Reforms in the Republics of the Former Soviet Union

Ebrill and Havrylyshyn report that tax policy reforms have begun in almost all the republics of the former Soviet Union, with some countries having made considerably progress.[15] Several countries have substantially drafted their tax laws so that they are more congruent with the demands of a market economy. Most progress has been achieved in the elimination of export taxes and excess wage taxes. Mixed progress has occurred in the introduction of the appropriate VAT. Least progress has been made in the removal of inappropriate exemptions. Regarding excise taxes, specific rates have been adopted for alcohol and tobacco but least progress has been made in restricting the coverage to a few important appropriate commodities and giving a symmetric treatment to domestic production and imports. For the personal income tax, most progress has been made in adopting appropriate rate structures but least progress in effectively taxing small businesses. There has been an almost universal abolition of export taxes. These authors note that, not surprisingly, the least amount of

progress has taken place on aspects that are either technically very difficult to implement or politically sensitive, such as the introduction of new accounting systems and standards, and the elimination of exemptions. Their overall assessment of the tax policy experience is that it is clear that these countries need to continue to take important steps to address the shortcomings mentioned above to attain a comprehensive tax reform.

Progress in tax administration reform has been more slow and more uneven. The pervasiveness of non-cash transactions in the economy and the uncertain legislative framework for tax administration has made difficult progress in this area. Lack of strong political commitment to major institutional and procedural reforms and the absence of a strong management team and trained tax administrators to design and implement tax administration reforms have been major hurdles. Ebrill and Havrylysshyn conclude that with only few exceptions, progress in most aspects of organization, collection, and enforcement has been sporadic at best. They recommend that urgent actions are needed to focus arrears collection on the taxpayers with the largest arrears and with arrears that have arisen in the most recent period; establish fully functioning large taxpayer units; develop procedures to impose reasonable penalties; and establish a single, nationwide taxpayer registration system with unique taxpayer identification numbers.

The revenue performance of the former Soviet Union republics in the late 1990s, after almost a decade of adopting policies to turn their countries into market economies, including tax policy and tax administration reforms, can be summarized as follows: experience ranged from a sizable decline in the revenue-to-GDP ratios—for example, in strife torn Georgia and Tajikistan, where revenues dropped to 10-12 percent of GDP—to little if any change in places such as Ukraine and Belarus where economic and structural reforms were less advanced and revenue remained as high as 40-45 percent of GDP.[16]

---

15. Ebrill and Havrylyshyn, op.cit., Chapter III
16. See Ebrill and Havrylyshyn, op.cit.. Chapter II.

Countries like Belarus, Turkmenistan and Uzbekistan that significantly delayed reforms and retained more of the Soviet-period mechanisms of control over enterprises were generally able to maintain high levels of revenue collection. Countries that proceeded with reforms and that were not affected by civil strife, such as Kazakhstan, the Kyrgyz Republic and Russia, all experienced a clear trend reduction in their revenue ratios. In the Baltic countries, where reforms came early and advanced rapidly, there was neither a perceptible revenue decline nor indications of revenue levels that were too low for reasonable government operations.

Not surprisingly, the most noteworthy feature as regards the pattern of changes in the major revenue components is the uniform decline in enterprise profits taxation, largely independent of overall revenue developments. This has been a reflection of, among other things, a combination of falling profitability, growing difficulty in administering profit taxes in economic transition, and the removal of excess wage taxes.

These developments suggest that while avoiding economic reform might have helped maintain revenue close to levels of the Soviet period for some period of time, substantial and sustained progress in reform gave better results. This is a similar conclusion with that for growth recovery in economies in transition. Delaying reforms can minimize the output decline of transition, but the best result comes form strong reforms that lead to early recovery and sustained growth.

BUDGETARY SYSTEMS

Budgetary Systems in Socialist Economies

National budgets in the former Soviet Union included the budgets of the central governments and subnational governments (provinces, municipalities, and prefectures).[17] The provincial and local budgets were prepared in conformity with the guidelines provided by the central ministry of finance, and the budgets so prepared were reviewed and consolidated by the central governments. The budgets also reflected extensive linkages between government and public enterprises. Traditionally, the state provided from its budget all the capital needed for the establishment of enterprises and the needed inputs, and bought the outputs. In return for the capital provided, the state demanded and received in turn, in addition to turnover taxes, a share of the profits as well as a share of depreciation reserves. The close links between the government budget and the enterprises resulted in a situation where transactions were conducted without any movement in cash. Taxes due were routinely adjusted against subsidies to be paid or capital to be transferred. In addition, the budget itself showed total revenues net of subsidies paid to enterprises. These practices were not conducive to transparent budgetary practices or to effective spending controls.

In addition, there was a proliferation of extrabudgetary funds created to provide a measure of managerial autonomy to budget units with own resources to ensure "a more efficient use of resources." These extrabudgetary funds grew in number and spawned a number of activities, and in some countries grew in size to a dimension equivalent to the size of the state budget such as in China. They tended to blur the distinction between what is basically a budgetary task of the government and the task of an enterprise.

Some aspects of the budgetary process of former centralized economies are worth highlighting.[18] First, general guidance was provided in the preparation of the budget as to the areas where investment was needed and the kind of production targets that were expected to be fulfilled. On this basis, the concerned agencies prepared a number of project proposals for review by the planning agency. The prices assumed for this exercise reflected the valuation of the officials. Second, while budgetary programs were reviewed, approved, and monitored by a central body, before final decisions were made, there was a substantial input from all concerned into what was included in the plan and the budget. During this stage there

---

17. This section draws on A. Premchand and L. Garamflavi, "Government Budget and Accounting Systems," in V. Tanzi, op. cit.

18. For a detailed discussion see Premchand and Garamfalvi, op. cit., pp. 274-280.

was room for bargaining at every level. Depending on the politics, the plan set the framework for the budgets or negotiated budgets set the basis for plans. Moreover, once the plans and budgets were approved, there was really a measure of flexibility given to executing agencies, subject, of course, to the compliance of various process controls. This operational freedom provided a relief from the high degree of centralization that was implicit in the process.

Finally, another aspect worth noting in the budgetary process was the role of the legislature and the role of the officials who prepared the budget. In most countries, the party congress played a key role but the way it exerted influence was different from the way legislatures in market economies exert powers. The party congress did not have taxing powers or specified roles in introducing and processing expenditure bills. But none of that could take place without the tacit approval of the party congress. Budget officials in this situation had an easy task inasmuch as everything is specified and macroeconomic stability was specified. Prices were fixed by the government and did not necessarily reflect market scarcities. It is this aspect which undergoes a total transformation as economies are opened and prices are fixed by the market. In this new environment, officials preparing the budget have to recognize the impact of the macroeconomic aspects of the budget and the impact of the budget on the economy. This requires making revenue forecasts and preparing contingency mechanisms to cope with changes in the economy.

The budgetary procedures of the centralized economies had the advantage of the relative abridgement of the payment process. The assignment of banks to each spending agency reduced the red tape and the numerous steps of verification associated with other budgetary systems. There were too many weak areas, however. The establishment of numerous extrabudgetary funds has tended to overshadow the importance of the budget. It was difficult to assess the impact of fiscal policy with contradictions arising in the approaches of the budget, on one hand, and extrabudgetary funds on the other. The strong role of bargaining in the budgetary process resulted in budgetary outcomes being different from estimates. The

biggest problem was the way in which the resource constraints were internalized in the various stages of the budgetary process. Calculations of requirements were made in terms of materials and agencies did not have to think of monetary costs (they were to be financed regardless of cost). In these circumstances, there was a practice to demonstrate a need for more resources, rather than to manage effectively the already available resources.

Necessary Budgetary Reforms in the Transition to Market Economies

A move to a market economy usually is accompanied by movement toward a system of political freedom and the establishment of democratic forms of government. Under a democracy the budgets have to be more transparent and accountable. The budget should be more transparent to ensure that funds are applied for the approved purposes. Transparency provides the legislative branch an opportunity to monitor the performance of the executive but should not be interpreted as an invitation for micro management by the legislature.

Accountability imposes additional tasks on the executive in that it has to ensure delivery of goods and services in an economic, efficient, and effective manner. There was little incentive for government departments in centrally planned economies to economize and there was little concern for the delivery of services. To be able to do this, it is imperative to formulate the budget in the context of a macroeconomic framework with an explicit recognition and assessment of the linkages of the budget and the economy. A realistic projection of government revenues has to be made and of the cost involved in delivering government services. Spending agencies need to be informed of the resource ceilings. Working with a macroeconomic framework would imply that resource allocation would no longer be a matter of ensuring increments, but downward adjustments too. The budgetary process needs to adapt itself to that significant change.

The budgetary institutions also would need to be changed in two other associated aspects. The extrabudgetary accounts have to be rationalized and incorporated into the budgets. The national budgets in centrally planned economies also included the budgets of the subnational governments, contributing to a good deal of overlap and frequent duplication in the efforts of central and subnational governments. There is a need to clearly define the respective roles, responsibilities, and jurisdictions of the various level of government in regard to revenues and expenditures (this, of course, is not only true for economies in transition). Ministries of finance and budget would need to monitor the implementation of budgets and ensure that macroeconomic policies are on track. For these purposes, the power of finance and budget ministries have to be increased. To institutionalize these changes and minimize the role of bargaining, it would be necessary to approve a new budgetary law. Accounting systems would need to be strengthened so as to ensure the preparation of comprehensive accounts and provide adequate cost information.

The changes advocated above will not be easy to implement and by necessity all the changes will not be able to be introduced at once. The strategy for introducing the changes will have to take into account financial and human resource shortages; the heterogeneous requirements of various users of budgetary systems; and the cost to proposed changes and their technological underpinnings. Organizational bottlenecks such as inertia, legal obstacles, efforts at self preservation, and protection of territorial turf will also need to be taken into account.

PUBLIC EXPENDITURE POLICY

The transition to a market economy of socialist economies has important implications for public expenditure policy because it requires, among other things, a redefining of the eventual role of the public sector vis-à-vis the private sector. In socialist economies the government intervened heavily in production, allocation, and distribution through the operation of the general budget, the public enterprises, and the fiscal functions of monetary authorities and financial intermediaries. Despite their large role, public sector financial operations were frequently subservient to the

quantity-based plans and were only a residual of the planning process for assuring, together with credit and cash plans, the consistency of financial balances at administratively determined prices.[19]

At least temporarily, the budget is likely to be burdened by former implicit subsidies that would become explicit as the reform proceeds. A successful program will require an adjustment in relative prices through domestic price liberalization, the move toward positive real interest rates, and an appropriate exchange rate policy. The mostly upward adjustment of real interest rates and exchange rates will affect those with net financial liabilities, including those with housing credits and foreign debt, that are likely to pressure with some success for budgetary subsidies.

Reforms to transform centrally planned economies into market economies compels the countries carrying out these reforms to reduce, or even eliminate, many government activities and to shift these functions (partly or fully) to the emerging private sector.

Reforms should be aimed at reducing public ownership and the scope of the budgetary intermediation, and at virtually eliminating traditional subsidies to household and enterprises. In doing this, reformers will face the problem that an analysis of public expenditure in economies in transition is severely hampered by distorted product and factor prices, including controlled product prices, nontransparent public-sector compensation systems, and unrealistic interest and exchange rates. These problems are compounded in the case of Cuba due to the existence of a dual monetary system where transactions are carried out in domestic currency and U.S. dollars.

At the same time it is important to remember that in a market economy, the public sector has an essential role to play. The general budget becomes a major instrument of macroeconomic policy. The government has to provide public goods and services that the private sector either does not provide or provides less-than-socially optimal quantities. In addition, the

---

19. See Ke-Young Chu and Robert Holzmann, "Public Expenditure: Policy Aspects," in Tanzi, op.cit.

government through public spending policies redistributes income between individuals, groups, and generations. Difficult policy questions will arise regarding to what extent, if any, there should be transitory budget support for private initiatives. The demand for low taxes will conflict with the demand for resources by the public sector to supply necessary public goods, frequently after years of neglect in their provision, such as in the case of Cuba.

Public expenditure policy has an important role to play during the transition period in reducing macroeconomic imbalances, increasing the efficiency of resource use, promoting sustained economic growth, and fostering social objectives. The absence of domestic financial markets has frequently precluded the possibility of domestic nonmonetary financing, while the possibilities of external financing are quite limited because of the existence of external payment arrears. To compound these problems the revenue performance is likely to weaken at the beginning of the process of transition as discussed above. All these factors point to the need to execute substantial budgetary spending cuts as a central element in securing the stabilization of the economy during the transition.

A strong case can be made for the elimination of many expenditure programs found in these countries on efficiency grounds. Prime candidates in this respect would be the large budgetary subsidies to consumers and enterprises. These cuts are bound to enhance allocative efficiency. It is frequently possible to reduce unduly large military expenditures. The role of the public sector as a guarantor of employment has been a major source of inefficiency and as the reform process advances it will have to be abandoned. At the same time the wage structure will have to change in the public sector with a more pronounced differences in the pay lines to account better for different skills.

Investment expenditures of enterprises will have to rely more on their own retained earnings and even on market financing. The privatization of these enterprises should reduce even further their dependence on the state budget. However, the difficult choices that will arise to the authorities between providing budgetary support to restructure state enterprises prior to privatization or to hand them over to domestic

and foreign investors at a very low value should not be underestimated.

To establish the basis for sustainable growth, public expenditure policy should emphasize public investment programs in human capital. Investment programs in physical infrastructure should be made in such a way as to maximize their complementary with private investment, while taking into account the possibility that private sector responses may not be fast enough. In framing public expenditure policy, the policy makers will need to take into account the need for the public sector to contribute to national savings given the usual limited foreign financing possibilities. There may be a role for public expenditures (or tax expenditure) to support private initiatives to compensate for market imperfections and uncertain business climate. There are likely to be demands for public resources to clean the balance sheet of banks and enterprises arising from the mismanagement and distortions created under central planning that would need to be addressed eventually.

The public sector will need to also be instrumental in protecting the poor and the environment. The traditional social programs (particularly pension, sickness, and family benefits) should be made more efficient and targeted to the poorest and more vulnerable. There will be a need to establish a social safety net program, not an easy thing to do with the budgetary constraints that are likely to exist. Another key area, frequently neglected in the central planned economies was the environment. Care will need to be taken to establish appropriate energy prices that will help to eliminate waste but there are likely to be some demands on the budget to clean the environment.

THE FISCAL REFORM IN CUBA

According to the CEPAL reports on the Cuban economy, fiscal policy in Cuba has aimed at two principal objectives in the last decade: first, to attain macroeconomic stability by stopping the inflationary spiral arising after the break-up of the economic relations with the former Soviet Union countries (that involved large levels of subsidies to the Cuban economy); and second, to implement a structural reform oriented to rationalize the productive activities and the functions of the state, as well as increasing the efficiency in the assignment of government resources.[20]

In this paper, the fiscal reform of Cuba in analyzed mainly from the perspective of the second objective. An important step to formalize the ongoing efforts appears have been taken in April 1999 when Decree-Law 192 (DL 192) on the Financial Administration of the State was approved. DL 192 replaced the Organic Law No. 29 of July 1980 that had established the budgetary framework and had become obsolete, especially after the appearance of new forms of property in the economy.

DL 192 is supposed to pursue the objectives of generating financial resources for the public sector in order to allow the implementation of government policies and programs, including those carry out through public entities and enterprises. The law is supposed to provide the basis for the development of information systems in a timely and reliable manner. To attain these objectives, the law defines the legal provisions for the budget, public credit, treasury operations, and government accounting. It also specifies that the existing tax legislation remains in effect.

The Tax Reform of 1994[21]

The Tax System Law (Law 73), passed in August 1994, modified both direct and indirect taxation. The provisions of this law are still in effect. As a result of this law, the profits of all enterprises (*personas jurídicas*) has been gradually made subject to the **corporate income tax** at a single rate of 35 percent. Prior to this law only mixed enterprises and private enterprises (*sociedades anónimas*) were subject to the income tax. There is a simplified system for smaller enterprises. The private enterprises, mixed enterprises and certain state entities were fully brought under the new corporate income tax regime between 1994 and 1995.[22] The incorporation of state enterprises (*paraestatales)* began in 1996.

According to CEPAL, corporate income tax receipts grew rapidly after 1994 and amounted to 1,132 million pesos, equivalent to 30 percent of direct taxes and 12 percent of tax revenue in 1998 (See Table A.13 of CEPAL (2000)).[23] About two-thirds of the corporate income tax in 1998 was accounted for by the 1,700 state enterprises incorporated into this tax regime. In the case of the state enterprises, their adoption of the income tax regime has been compensated by some tax exemptions, not only from the corporate income tax, but also from the tax obligations on the utilization of the labor force, and from import duties. No official estimate exist of the tax expenditure involved in these exemptions. In addition, there are a number of state enterprises that remain outside the corporate income tax regime because of their unprofitability. These are principally agricultural, textile, and shipbuilding companies. According to the CEPAL report, the objective of the authorities is to have all the enterprises subject to the corporate income tax in the year 2000.

Law 73 created the **personal income tax**, with a very progressive marginal tax rate schedule (5 percent for income up to 3,000 pesos and 50 percent marginal tax rate for income above 60,000 pesos). The tax base is supposed to cover salaries, interest income, dividends and foreign exchange earnings, but in practice this is not the case. As a transition measure, salaries in domestic currency are exempted, as are also the salaries of workers in "priority sectors." In addition,

20. *La Economía Cubana: Reformas Estructurales y Desempeño en los Noventa*, CEPAL, 1997 and 2000.

21. The description of the tax reform and of the evolution of the expenditure policy in Cuba are based on the material contained in the public finances chapter of CEPAL (2000).

22. Persons or companies who rent dwellings have been subject to this tax since 1997. In 1998 small sugar cane farmers, who before were subject to special regimes, and foreign companies, previously exempted from income tax, were made liable to it. In the case of the latter, the author is not sure whether this was a general decision or whether some foreign companies are still exempted of income taxes according to the original terms of their investment in Cuba.

23. Out of a total of 48.3 percent of GDP in state revenue in 1998 (compared with 62.6 percent of GDP in 1994), tax revenue accounted for 35.8 percent of GDP of which 21.4 percent was indirect tax revenue and 14.3 percent direct tax revenue (See Table A.14 of CEPAL (2000)).

the Cuban government retains most of the dollar wages of Cubans working for foreign enterprises, and it is not clear how these amounts are reported in the budget statistics, if at all. There are reports that the amount retained by the government can be as high as 94 percent, a rate that has to rank as one of the highest, if not the highest, income tax rates in the world.[24] Overall, according to official statistics, the personal income tax is mainly paid by self employed (cuenta propistas), and after 1996 also by professionals who have foreign income. In 1998, the personal income tax amounted to 275 million pesos or 3 percent of tax revenue. Two thirds of the personal income tax was paid by the self employed and 12.5 percent by small farmers.[25]

The amounts of advanced payments through the year demanded from the self-employed appear to have resulted in an unduly high burden that has halted the growth of the private sector in Cuba during the 1990s. Monthly minimum payments are set by law depending on the presumed income of economic activities, but these minimum payments can be increased by the municipal governments; altogether, the monthly minimum payments apparently were set at unrealistically high levels. For example, the Ministry of Finance and Prices increased the monthly payments of taxi drivers from 100 pesos in 1995 to 400 pesos in 1997. As a result, the number of registered self-employed declined from 208,000 to 160,000 in 1996, recovered somewhat to 172,000 in 1997, and remained at that level through July 1999.[26]

Law 73 also established a **social security contribution**. Enterprises pay 12 percent of the wage bill in social security contributions and retain 2 percent from the wages of workers to cover the cost of the social services they provide to their workers. Moreover, salaried workers contribute with the equivalent of 5 percent of their wages to the social security system.

However, there are also exemptions to the general rule regarding these contributions. Among the state enterprises, only workers of enterprises that are participating in a special program (sistema de perfeccionamiento empresarial) pay these contributions and only after their salaries have been revised in line with new salary scales.

In addition, Law 73 established that profitable enterprises pay a 25 percent **tax on the utilization of the labor force**, while the social security contribution is reduced to 14 percent. In the case of joint ventures with foreign investors a tax of 25 percent is only applied (14 percent of the contribution of the social security and an 11 percent rate of the tax on the utilization of the labor force).

Law 73 also modified **indirect taxes**. Before the passage of this law, the main revenue raiser was a turnover tax collected at the wholesale level (impuesto de circulación). The 1994 law established a new sales tax to be collected in the then-recently-created agricultural markets (mercados agropecuarios) and industrial fairs (mercados artesanales). The tax rate varies among regions: 5 percent in La Habana; 10 percent in the provincial capitals; and 15 percent in the rest of the country. The idea is to have the new sales tax replace the turnover tax. The sales tax is to be converted into an ad valorem tax with the decision of whether it is to be collected in one or various stages still to be made. However, no specific plans to do this exist yet and, not surprisingly, the government is moving cautiously on this area because the turnover tax and the sales tax together collected 2,784 million pesos in 1997, or about 30 percent of total tax revenue.[27]

There are **excise taxes** on tobacco and beverages that are becoming an important source of revenue since their creation in 1994 (2,292 million pesos in 1998

24. Fernão Lara Mesquita, a correspondent for the Brazilian newspaper *O Estado de Sao Paulo*, reported in the edition of July 17, 2000, that Cuban workers who are paid between $500 and $600 by foreign companies operating in Cuba only receive $30 or less, with the rest being kept by the government.

25. CEPAL (2000), p. 110.

26. CEPAL (2000), pp. 110-111.

27. CEPAL (2000), Table A.13.

Table 1.   Cuba: State Budget: Revenues and Expenditures: 1989, 1993-1999
(Millions of Pesos)

	1989[a]	1993	1994	1995	1996	1997	1998[b]	1999[c]
1. Total Revenues	12501	9516	12757	13043	12243	12204	12502	12470
1.1. Current revenues	12188	8196	10873	10720	11564	11574	12014	11970
1.1.1. Tax Revenue	6224	4950	7048	7974	7969	8574	9252	9481
1.1.1.1. Indirect Taxes	5547	3611	5595	6165	5513	5330	5543	5598
1.1.1.2. Direct Taxes	676	1339	1453	1808	2456	3244	3709	3883
1.1.2. Non Tax Revenue	5964	3246	3825	2746	3595	3000	2762	2489
1.2. Capital Revenue	313	1320	1884	2323	679	630	489	500
2. Total Expenditure	13904	14567	14178	13809	12814	12663	13062	13190
2.1. Current Expenditure	10844	12529	11495	12064	10770	10824	11481	11440
2.1.1. Budgeted Activities	7380	6298	6566	6510	6939	6808	7082	7648
2.1.2. Transfers to the entrepreneurial and cooperative sectors	3465	6168	4222	3096	3206	2954	2973	3142
2.1.3. Financial Operations	...	63	58	236	386	381	426	500
2.1.4. Extraordinary Expenditures	...	...	650	2222	239	681	1000	...
2.1.5. Reserves	...	...	...	...	...	...	...	150
2.2. Capital Expenditure	3060	2038	2683	1745	2043	1839	1581	1750
3. Current Balance	1344	-4333	-622	-1344	794	751	533	530
4. Fiscal Balance	-1404	-5051	-1421	-766	-571	-459	-560	-720

Source: CEPAL estimates based on information provided by the Ministry of Finance and Prices.

a.   The data for 1989 is not strictly comparable to the information for 1993-1998.
b.   Preliminary figures
c.   Budgeted in December 1998, before the salary increases granted in February 1999 in various sectors, particularly in health, education, judiciary and police.

Table 2.   Cuba: Structure of Fiscal Revenues: 1989, 1993-1999 *(In Percent)*

	1989[a]	1993	1994	1995	1996	1997	1998[b]	1999[c]
1. Total Revenue	100.0	100.0	100.0	100.0	100.0	100.0	100.0	100.0
1.1. Current revenue	97.5	86.1	85.2	82.2	94.5	94.8	96.1	96.0
1.1.1. Tax Revenue	49.8	52.0	55.2	61.1	65.1	70.3	74.0	76.0
1.1.1.1. Indirect Taxes	44.4	37.9	43.9	47.3	45.0	43.7	44.3	44.9
1.1.1.2. Direct Taxes	5.4	14.1	11.4	13.9	20.1	26.6	29.7	31.1
1.1.2. Non Tax Revenue	47.7	34.1	30.0	21.1	29.4	24.6	22.1	20.0
1.2. Capital Revenue	2.5	13.9	14.8	17.8	5.5	5.2	3.9	4.0

Source: CEPAL estimates based on the data in Table 1.

a.   The data for 1989 is not strictly comparable to those of 1993-1998 because of a change in the presentation.
b.   Preliminary estimates
c.   Budgeted in December 1998, before the February 1999 salary increases in various sectors, notably in health, education, judiciary and police.

or 25 percent of tax revenue). The **service tax** precedes the Law 73 and it is imposed on essentially two type of services: those provided by state restaurants and electricity supply (totaling about 5 percent of tax income).

Other taxes and duties are mostly import duties, followed by tolls (*peajes*) imposed mostly on airport use by tourists, and document taxes. Import duties apply to all imports, including those of the state. CEPAL (2000) reports that the maximum import duty was 40 percent in 1999 and that the arithmetic mean

of the import duties was 10.7 percent for most-favored-nation country imports and 12 percent in general. Import duties have declined as the import duty rates have been lowered in line with Cuba's commitments in the World Trade Organization and the stagnation in imports (370 million pesos in 1998).

The share of **nontax revenues** in total revenues has been declining in recent years (see Tables 1 and 2). In 1999 they are estimated to have accounted for 2,489 million pesos or 20 percent of total revenue, almost half of what they were in 1989. These revenues consist of dividend payments of state enterprises that pay income tax and the transfer of profits of state enterprises that are still not incorporated in the new tax system. Fines and other charges are also included. There are also charges for the use of state land paid by mixed enterprises, and royalties for the exploitation of mineral resources.

Overall, Cuba's revenue performance deteriorated during the 1990s, reflecting the experience of former Soviet Union countries during that period, except that in the case of Cuba the observed decline in revenues is probably more the result of the strong negative shock to economic activity produced by the loss of the Soviet subsidies, and less to efforts to move to a market economy. Between 1989 and 1993, total state revenues declined on average by 10 percent in real terms, in line with an average real GDP decline of 9 percent per year.[28] The decline was particularly pronounced in revenues of turnover taxes, profit contributions of state enterprises to the budget, and nontax revenues that are very sensitive to economic activity. In 1994, the tax revenues improved by over 40 percent in nominal terms (see Table 1) due to the introduction of excise taxes on tobacco, beer, liquor, and automobiles and the increase of public and import tariffs.

The gradual application of the Law 73 has increased the relative contribution of the private sector to tax collections. Counting both the nonstate enterprises and taxes paid by natural persons, this contribution rose from 6.7 percent of the total in 1995 to 11 percent in 1998. It was estimated to have increased by another 1 percent in 1999.[29]

Tax Administration Reforms

Improvements in tax administration were made in the second half of the 1990s, after the creation of the *Oficina Nacional de Administración Tributaria*

(ONAT). A first step has been to accelerate the registration of personal taxpayers and enterprises. The number of enterprises registered with the ONAT increased from 16,144 in 1996 to 20,805 in June 1999, the majority being state enterprises, budgetary agencies, and *Unidades Básicas de Producción Cooperativa* (UBPCs).[30] In addition, there were registered 1,152 agricultural cooperatives, 965 sociedades mercantiles cubanas, 706 commercial representations, 135 mixed enterprises and 47 sociedades mercantiles extranjeras. About 193,000 persons already have a tax identification number, out of a total of 362,385 taxpayers, of which 156,000 are self-employed (cuenta propistas),and 8,000 are persons who earn income by renting dwellings.

CEPAL (2000) reports that the tax forms have been revised and the control systems improved. Since 1998, taxes are collected in the currency that the revenues are generated.[31] From 1997 general tax audits are being emphasized that aim to verify the payment of all taxes in the visits to taxpayers. The authorities are apparently increasing the technical assistance in the area of fiscal accounting and tax code obligations to civil servants, but the ONAT has not been able to expand these services to the private sector. A unit to deal with large tax payers has also been formed in the ONAT.

The Budgetary Process in Cuba and Accounting Practices

The Cuban state budget consists of the consolidation of the central government budget, and the budgets of the agencies of the central government, provinces and municipalities.[32] First, the Council of Ministers establishes the priorities with the Economic Plan as background. Once the priorities are defined, the Ministry of Finance and Prices (MFP) issues norms for the preparation of the budget. About some 200

28. CEPAL (2000), pages 134-135.

29. CEPAL (2000), page 117.

30. CEPAL (2000), page 133.

31. It is not clear to the author whether the tax rates on dollar revenues are different from those on peso revenues.

32. For the period prior to the 1990s, see Jorge Pérez-López, *The Cuban State Budget: Concepts and Measurements*, North-South Center, University of Miami, Research Institute for Cuban Studies, 1992.

Table 3. Cuba: Structure of State Expenditures: 1989, 1993-1999 *(In Percent)*

	1989[a]	1993	1994	1995	1996	1997	1998[b]	1999[c]
1. Total Expenditure	100.0	100.0	100.0	100.0	100.0	100.0	100.0	100.0
1.1. Current Expenditure	78.0	86.0	81.1	87.4	84.1	85.5	87.9	86.7
1.1.1. Budgeted Activities	53.1	43.2	46.3	47.1	54.2	53.8	54.2	58.0
of which:	...	...	...	...	...	...	...	...
salaries	...	14.6	15.0	15.1	16.4	16.7	15.6	17.3
other expenditure	...	28.6	31.3	32.1	37.7	37.0	38.7	40.7
1.1.2. Transfer to the entrepreneurial and cooperative sectors	24.9	42.3	29.8	22.4	25.0	23.3	22.8	23.8
1.1.3. Financial Operations	...	0.4	0.4	1.7	3.0	3.0	3.3	3.8
1.1.4. Extraordinary Spending	...	...	4.6	16.1	1.9	5.4	7.7	...
1.1.5. Reserves	...	...	...	...	...	...	...	1.1
1.2. Capital Expenditure	22.0	14.0	18.9	12.6	15.9	14.5	12.1	13.3

Source: CEPAL estimates based on the data in Table 1.

a. The data for 1989 is not strictly comparable to those of 1993-1998 because of a change in the presentation.

b. Preliminary estimates

c. Budgeted in December 1998, before the February 1999 salary increases in various sectors, notably in health, education, judiciary and police.

budgets are prepared that are subsequently consolidated into the state budget. Decree Law 192 allows the MFP to modify the budgetary appropriation during the year as long as the total spending amount of the state budget is not affected.[33] Transfers from the central government to provinces are a function of the coefficient of participation of the provinces in the turnover tax, the profit tax, and the current transfers of public enterprises of the central government. The coefficients of participation are determined every year at the time of the preparation of the state budget and they are established taking into account the differences in economic and social development among the provinces. The provinces do not have taxing authority and their deficits are covered by budgetary transfers.

Reflecting the high degree of centralization in the Cuban economy, the central government accounted for 73 percent of total state spending in 1996.[34] According to CEPAL (2000), the high central government share in state spending is in large part due to the fact that the government accounts for 98 percent of the spending in state entrepreneurial activities (probably included in line 1.1.2, transfers to the entrepreneurial sector, in Table 3) and over 80 percent of investment spending. Meanwhile, subnational governments accounted in 1996 for 41 percent of current budgeted expenditure such as in primary and secondary education, municipal hospitals, and other health spending The central government accounted for 36 percent of current spending, and the social security administration for the remaining 23 percent.

CEPAL (2000) urges caution in analyzing these budgetary statistics because of the difficulties of distinguishing between the public and private sectors and deficiencies in public sector accounting. It is also not possible to distinguish clearly between central administration, the state enterprises and the financial sector which makes difficult to make estimates, for example, of general government spending. Until 1999, many enterprises carried out quasi-fiscal activities such as the provision of subsidies and services. The budget recognizes only a share of the cost of these free services through the provision of transfers, and, thus the cost of the provision of social benefits is underestimated in the budget For example, the sugar mills still provide free services to the workers whose financing is incorporated into the cost of production

33. CEPAL (2000), page 107.

34. No information beyond 1996 about the relative importance of the central government in state spending is available to the author at this time

of sugar mills. Another problem is that according to CEPAL (2000), the investment carried out by the enterprises is not accounted for in the state budget as part of investment. The state budget only takes into account the deficit of state enterprises which, in turn, are covered by government subsidies. Public enterprise investment has been growing and accounted for 30 percent of total investment contemplated in the economic plan.

The unclear lines of demarcation between the central administration and public enterprises is also manifested in that agencies of the central administration can finance part of their spending through entrepreneurial activities, although the authorization of this entrepreneurial spending is supposed to go through normal channels of approval. The most notorious case is that of the enterprises of the armed forces that have been given the opportunity to conduct business activities in key sectors such as tourism. This is also true in the sport and health sectors. This is an area of concern in Cuba and the authorities are apparently trying to increase the coverage of these activities in the budget. to better monitor them. Another problem in the accounting practices is that in the case of some budgetary units and public enterprises, revenue, spending and financing are not reported separately in a clear way. In the past, in some instances, only the deficits that could not be financed from internal and external sources were reported in the budget.

Up to now, the state deficit has been financed by central bank financing, apparently at no cost to the state. This creates another important distortion in the public sector accounts. No provision is included in the budget for interest payments, which is a serious omission of the resources used by the public sector. Not only are interest liabilities not recorded on account of the central bank credits, but neither are the loans in arrears to Paris Club creditors or to Russia (Russia acquired the Cuban debt at the time of the break up of the Soviet Union).[35] The existence of an overvalued currency and the administration of a foreign exchange budget by the central government produces implicit transfers between sectors in surplus in terms of foreign exchange and sectors in deficit, that are not well accounted for in the budget. The official exchange rate of US$1 equals 1 peso introduces a strong distortion in the accounting of the value of tradable goods and services in the budget.

DL 192 introduced significant modifications in public sector accounting. Transactions are to be registered on an accrual basis. In the state budget all revenues and expenditures are to be registered separately without any netting among them. The exception is the public enterprises that can report net revenues or net losses to the state budget. CEPAL (2000) reports that these new accounting practices are being adopted gradually and that the authorities expect to implement them for the 2000 budget. CEPAL (2000) also points to the need of reducing the earmarking of revenues.[36] These practices, as in other countries that use these arrangements, can distort resource allocation by increasing unnecessarily spending in certain areas without due regard to other budgetary priorities. Current examples of these are the highway tolls which are supposed to be used for road maintenance. Fifty percent of the airport tolls are to be used for the maintenance of the airports and the rest of the proceeds go to the central budget. To control these practices, DL 192 determines that revenues cannot be directed to specific spending without authorization of the Ministry of Finance and Prices, unless the resources come from specific financing operations or grants received for specific purposes.

Public Spending

CEPAL (2000) notes that the size of state spending in Cuba in terms of GDP has declined in recent years as a result of the increase in the size of the private sector (called the "segunda economía" in the report) and fiscal tightening. After reaching two thirds of GDP

---

35. For a discussion of the Cuban external debt see, Alberto Martínez-Piedra and Lorenzo Pérez, "External Debt Problems and the Principle of Solidarity: The Cuban Case," in *Cuba in Transition—Volume 6*, 1996.

36. CEPAL (2000), page119.

in 1989, and increasing to 88 percent in 1993, it declined steadily to about 50 percent in 1998. Table 3 shows that current spending accounted for about 87 percent of total spending during 1997-1997 in Cuba, while capital spending amounted to about 13 percent of total spending during these years, compared with 22 percent of the total in 1989.

Among current spending, budgeted expenditures, that encompass salaries and a wide range of public administration services (such as education, health, housing, social security,[37] defense, internal security, culture and sports), and transfers to enterprises and cooperatives are the two largest current spending categories, accounting for about 90 percent of total spending during 1997-1999. The relative size of salaries in total spending has risen to about 17.3 percent in 1999 from a level of 14.6 percent in 1993. Education, health, housing, and social security spending included in public administration spending are recorded in gross terms, but other activities such as defense, internal security and sports where the implementing agencies have their own sources of revenue are still recorded in net terms reflecting the accounting problems referred to above.

Total state spending declined from 70 percent of GDP in 1994 to 50 percent of GDP in 1998. Apparently, the Cuban government has tried to protect social spending during the period of fiscal tightening and, as a result their relative share in total spending rose, while those of defense and internal security lost ground. While spending in education, health, and social security only declined from 19.3 percent of GDP in 1994 to 17.6 percent of GDP in 1998, the contraction in real terms has, of course, been sharper.

Transfers to enterprises include those that are given to subsidize the impact of policy decisions (e.g. price subsidies) and those granted to cover operating losses of state enterprises. These transfers have declined from the equivalent of 42 percent of total spending in 1993 to about 24 percent in 1999. According to

CEPAL (2000) most of the decline has taken place in the transfers granted to cover operating losses of enterprises, while transfers to finance losses created by price subsidies have experienced relative growth. The operating losses of state enterprises increased dramatically from the period prior to the break-up of the Soviet Union up to 1993, when they reached a level equivalent to 33 percent of GDP.[38] After 1993, state enterprises were asked to prepare restructuring plans that apparently were successful in reducing the subsidies to only one fifth of what they were in 1993 by 1998. CEPAL (2000) warns rightly against making too much of a distinction between subsidies that are given to cover open price subsidies and those that are given to cover operating losses of enterprises. Relative prices are seriously distorted in Cuba and state and mixed enterprises cannot carry out foreign exchange transactions outside the official exchange market where the peso is sharply overvalued. In these circumstances, it is difficult to distinguish the reasons behind the losses of enterprises.

The third largest component of state spending, capital expenditure, also shows a relative decline during the 1990s, dropping from about 22 percent of total spending in 1989 to 12 percent of total spending in 1998. For 1999, there is a relative increase in the budgeted amount in capital spending of 10 percent in nominal terms that it is expected to be complemented also by an increase in investment in state enterprises whose investment is not included in Table 3. As noted above, accrued interest liabilities are not shown in the budget.

ASSESSING FISCAL POLICY REFORMS IN CUBA AND RECOMMENDATIONS FOR FURTHER ACTION

The Cuban government has taken important necessary steps to reform the fiscal policy regime to adjust the economy to the external shock that it suffered when the large Soviet subsidy to Cuba was eliminated and to begin integrating the Cuban economy into

---

37. Social security expenditure data apart from spending on old-age, disability, and survivors pensions included until very recently subsidies to enterprises to avoid the dismissal of redundant workers.

38. CEPAL (2000), p. 123.

the global economy. However, in most areas the steps taken appear to be timid and not adopted within a well thought out strategy. This experience mirrors that of several republics of the former Soviet Union, as noted above, but it is also a reflection of the fact that the Cuban government, contrary to the more successful republics of the former Soviet Union, has not made the decision to transform its socialist economy to a market based economy.

The results of the tax reform have been mixed if judged from the perspective of establishing a tax system that meets the revenue requirements; beginning to change the tax system toward a more appropriate structure for the longer run; and making the existing taxes more stable and transparent as well as incentive-enhancing and equity improving. The tax reform of 1994 arrested the revenue deterioration, particularly with the introduction of excise taxes. But most taxes suffer from arbitrarily narrow tax bases and, as noted by CEPAL (2000), from excessive exemptions that limit seriously their buoyancy.

In the case of the corporate income tax, state enterprises are only being made subject to the corporate income tax gradually and have been exempted from the payments of other taxes when they have been made subject to the payment of this tax. This is not a very transparent method and can be subject to abuses.[39] To be fair, the incorporation of the state enterprises into the tax system could not be made overnight, but the process seems to be taking too long, suggesting the possibility of arbitrary decisions. CEPAL (2000) argues that the generalized application of the income tax to corporations cannot be implemented until a financial reform is carried out. Presumably, the argument is that by exempting companies from the payment of income taxes, resources are maintained within the enterprises that can be used to make the necessary investments. Only after domestic financing resources are available to these enterprises, should they be made liable for paying income taxes. Undoubtedly, a financial system reform is necessary

in Cuba but aside from this, all enterprises in the country need to carry a fair share of the burden of revenue mobilization. State enterprises, in particular, should be made subject to a minimum profit tax as a minimum return on past state equity. Consideration may be given to reducing the top marginal tax rate of 35 percent, a rate that appears to be on the high side, particularly for a country with Cuba's level of development. Loss making enterprises should not be exempted a priori from the corporate income tax regime, and should be forced to become profitable or shut down. In this way, the spending of scarce resources without going through the discipline of approving them in the state budget (where the relative merits of such expenditure can be evaluated) will be avoided.

The marginal tax rates of the personal income tax are set at very high levels. International experience shows that this is counterproductive and encourages tax evasion. In addition, the fact that as a transition measure, salaries in domestic currency and the salaries of workers in priority sectors are exempted, has narrowed considerably the base for this tax. This conclusion may need to be qualified if the government retains a very high share of the dollar income of Cuban workers who work for foreign companies in Cuba and the revenues generated this way are not classified as income tax revenue. If this is the case, then the argument can be made that the income tax rates for the workers employed by foreign companies should be lowered and that these workers should receive the same treatment as other taxpayers on equity grounds. In general, it is clear that the current announced income tax rates are a strong disincentive for the entrepreneurial activity of cuenta propistas, limiting the dynamic role that this small, but key sector of the economy, can play. CEPAL (2000) notes that the government faces the difficult problem that the salary structure in the public sector is very low and that before the tax base of the personal income tax can be widened, the salary structure has to be revised. This undoubtedly is a difficult problem but it has more to

---

39. An area not discussed in this paper is that of the tax holidays given to foreign investors. Anecdotal evidence suggests that they have been excessive in Cuba.

do with spending priorities and the tax bases of the various taxes can be widened as part of a sweeping reform program that can include some salary increases.

As noted above, the main revenue raisers in Cuba are the turnover and the sales taxes (impuesto de circulación and impuesto de ventas). The announced policy is to convert the sales tax into a VAT that would substitute the impuesto de circulación. As discussed earlier, this is the most recommended consumption tax. At the present time, it does not appear that specific steps are being taken to adopt the VAT but given the stage of institutional development in Cuba, this is probably unavoidable. However, again care should be taken that the bases of existing indirect taxes are as wide as possible, and the tax rates should be converted to ad valorem rates if it has not been done already. In moving to a value added tax, the number of rates should be few and will need to be made uniform throughout the island to avoid creating distortions. Municipalities could be allowed to charge some sales tax, as well as property taxes, something that will require the eventual development of a cadastro.

The role of the tax on the utilization of the labor force and of the contribution to the social security would need to be reexamined. The current payroll taxes appear to be on the high side and to discourage the demand for labor. As other buoyant taxes are developed, it may be possible to reduce the rates of these taxes, while still addressing the very difficult problems of the social security system in Cuba.[40] The average import duty of Cuba, at around 11 percent, does not appear to be high, although as recommended by Gallagher,[41] consideration should be given to making all imports subject to a single rate to avoid distortions.

Not much information is available regarding the changes in tax administration to be able to assess how much progress has been made in improving tax administration practices. Necessary steps are being taken such as registering tax payers, but again the progress in this area is rather slow. The number of personal and corporate taxpayers registered so far in Cuba appear to be rather small given the size of the country. It is not known to what extend systems and procedures are being simplified and made more taxpayer friendly to facilitate the creation of a tax paying culture and permit the smooth processing of returns and payments. These are key steps that need to be taken. The creation of a large taxpayers unit is a positive step and will increase the returns on audits but the decision to do general tax audit to cover all taxes in visits to taxpayers can be questioned because the alternative of doing single-items audits would increase coverage of tax payers, while, at the same time, reducing the possibilities for corruption.

DL 192 takes important steps to reform and improve budgetary practices in Cuba. For example, as explained earlier, it calls for state budget revenues and expenditures to be registered separately without any netting among them and provides the legal means for reducing earmarking of revenues by determining that revenues cannot be directed to specific spending unless authorized by the Ministry of Finance and Prices. However, the information contained in CEPAL (2000) and discussed earlier shows that actual practices still have a low level of transparency and are not conducive to accountability by spending units. The carrying out of quasi-fiscal activities by state enterprises which go unreported, or the fact that deficits that obtain financing domestically or externally are not clearly reported in budget documents, reduce the transparency of public expenditure, and make it difficult to hold high accountability standards. Also, the

---

40. For analysis of the problems of the social security system in Cuba, see my paper "The Pension System of Cuba: The Current Situation and Implications of International Pension Reform Experiences for Addressing Cuba's Problems," in *Cuba in Transition—Volume 8*, 1998.

41. Mark Gallagher, "Some Ideas for Taxation during Cuba's Transition," in *Cuba in Transition—Volume 9*, 1999. Gallagher and René Costales, in commenting on Gallagher's paper, emphasize the importance of having transparent taxes, easy to collect, with few rates and exemptions. These recommendations go in the same direction as my own.

fact that parts of the central administration can finance its spending through entrepreneurial activities also goes against the intentions of improving the transparency in budgetary practices. These practices, as well as the high degree of earmarking of revenues, would need to be eliminated in order to move to a more modern approach to budget management. Making the earmarking of revenue subject to the authorization of the MFP would not appear to solve the problem because it would give too much discretion to the MFP.

It is not clear to the author to what extent the state budget is prepared within a realistic macroeconomic framework; the extent that the respective spending responsibilities of various levels of government are well delineated; and the extent that the spending units are informed of their resource ceilings and are held to them. Unless this is done in Cuba, the state budget would not be a very useful instrument for public administration. Finally, steps should be taken to start showing in the budget the cost of financing of state deficits by showing the accrued interest arising from the financing of the deficits, even if the deficits are financed by the central bank

Perhaps the area where the least progress has been made in reforming the fiscal regime in Cuba is public spending. Although according to CEPAL (2000), public spending in relation to GDP was down from 70 percent of GDP in 1994 to about 50 percent in

1998, this ratio is still too high for an economy that needs to open room for private sector initiative to attain higher levels of growth. For example, transfers to state enterprises still accounted for 24 percent of total state spending in 1999, a proportion that indicates a highly distorted economy.

For Cuba to start a more serious transition towards a market economy, it would need to start reducing public ownership in the economy and the scope of budgetary intermediation, and start cutting traditional socialist subsidies to households and enterprises more effectively. As discussed above, this does not mean that the public sector does not have a key role to play, particularly in the areas of investment in human capital, in social programs to protect the poor and the more vulnerable, and in programs to protect the environment. There are also likely to exist relatively valid demands to use public money to clean the balance sheet of certain enterprises whose performance suffered under the distortions created by the socialist regime before they are privatized. In addition, there may be a role for public expenditures to compensate for limited periods of time for market imperfections and uncertain business climate. However, given the need for the public sector to contribute to national savings and the limited financing possibilities available to Cuba, this type of assistance would have to be rather limited in framing public expenditure policy.

CUBA Y AMÉRICA LATINA: CONSIDERACIONES SOBRE EL NIVEL Y LA EVOLUCIÓN DEL ÍNDICE DE DESARROLLO HUMANO Y DEL GASTO SOCIAL EN LA DÉCADA DE LOS NOVENTA

Rolando H. Castañeda[1]

Si el gobierno de Castro no demuestra tener soluciones ni futuro para Cuba que permitan que los que estamos proponiendo alternativas, con el apoyo de nuestros hermanos del exilio y de lo que quizás es una mayoría silenciosa en el país, le demos lo que hasta ahora ellos no han permitido brindar a cabalidad.

—Entrevista a Félix Antonio Bonne Carcassés, René Gómez Manzano y Marta Beatriz Roque Cabello, *El Mercurio*, Santiago, 16 de julio del 2000, p A-6.

En general los ensayos presentados en las reuniones anteriores de ASCE han brindado poca atención al tema de las comparaciones de los índices sociales y del gasto social de Cuba y América Latina, así como al análisis de las políticas sociales de Cuba en educación, salud, vivienda y seguridad social, uno de los llamados logros de la revolución. Si bien algunos ensayos han comparado los resultados y el gasto social de Cuba con el de algunos países latinoamericanos a partir de los años sesenta (Castañeda, 1991; Alonso, Donate-Armada y Lago, 1994; Romeu, 1995) y otros ensayos han cubierto algunos sectores sociales en mayor o menor detalle (Alonso, Donate-Armada y Lago, 1994; Donate-Armada, 1994; y Pérez, 1998), no ha habido un tratamiento global y sistemático de estos temas y de su relación con el crecimiento económico del país. Este ensayo pretende dar un paso en esta dirección en las reuniones de ASCE.

Concretamente el ensayo compara el nivel y la evolución (los avances o retrocesos) del índice de desarrollo humano (IDH) y del gasto social real por habitante de América Latina y Cuba durante la década de los noventa, así como hace algunas consideraciones generales sobre la situación de los sectores sociales, el nivel de ingreso real de la población y la desigualdad de ingresos en Cuba en la década.

El ensayo hace referencia al IDH, que pondera los resultados del gasto social en educación y salud con el nivel de ingreso por habitante, para mostrar no sólo el acceso efectivo a los servicios sociales básicos sino también el nivel de ingreso que permite adquirir bienes y servicios para satisfacer el consumo requerido para una vida decorosa. El ensayo conceptualiza el gasto social, desde la perspectiva del desarrollo humano sostenible, o sea lo considera como inversión, dado que favorece las oportunidades para el desarrollo y mejoramiento del nivel y la calidad de vida de las personas al proporcionar, entre otros aspectos, acceso a los conocimientos y las herramientas necesarias

---

1. Las opiniones expresadas son de la exclusiva responsabilidad del autor y no reflejan sus vínculos institucionales. Se dedica este ensayo a Félix Antonio Bonne Carcassés, René Gómez Manzano, Vladimiro Roca Antúnez y Marta Beatriz Roque Cabello, autores de *La Patria es de Todos*, quienes fueron encarcelados en junio de 1997 y condenados por el "delito de opinión." Todavía Vladimiro Roca permanece en prisión, mientras sus colegas están en libertad provisional.

para su consolidación y actualización, a ambientes de salud, y a condiciones nutricionales adecuadas y habitacionales dignas y sanas.

El ensayo utiliza información estadística proveniente del Programa de Naciones Unidas sobre el Desarrollo (PNUD) y la Comisión Económica para América Latina y el Caribe (CEPAL), especialmente los Informes sobre Desarrollo Humano de 1990 y 1999 (PNUD, 1990 y 1999) y el estudio económico sobre Cuba de 1997 (CEPAL, 1998), su actualización del 2000 (CEPAL, 2000b) y el Informe del Panorama Social de 1998 (CEPAL, 1999a). El Informe de la CEPAL de 1998 adolece de contradicciones internas que han sido señaladas en otros ensayos en las reuniones de ASCE (Castañeda, 1998 y 1999; Mesa-Lago 1998). Ellas se refieren a la evaluación de la situación y políticas macroeconómicas en el período 1990-1996, que en general se consideran adecuadas y acertadas, mientras que la situación social se considera difícil y las políticas sociales insostenibles.

El ensayo está organizado en ocho secciones. La primera compara el IDH de Cuba y América Latina a principios y finales de la década de los noventa. La segunda contrasta el gasto social real por habitante de Cuba y América Latina en la década de los noventa. La tercera estima los gastos sociales de Cuba en US dólares. La cuarta discute la situación, características y tendencias de los principales componentes del gasto social, del ingreso por habitante y la desigualdad de los ingresos de Cuba en los noventa. La quinta compara la evolución económica de Cuba y América Latina en las décadas de los ochenta y noventa. La sexta hace una breve disgresión sobre las implicaciones de la ausencia de ayuda externa oficial, el embargo norteamericano y las remesas familiares a Cuba en la década de los noventa. La séptima comenta los desafíos que conllevan la modernización, la sostenibilidad del aumento, y la eficiencia interna y externa del gasto social para Cuba y América Latina. La octava presenta las conclusiones y las consideraciones finales del ensayo (¿se requiere más de lo mismo o algo diferente?).

EL ÍNDICE DE DESARROLLO HUMANO DE CUBA Y AMÉRICA LATINA EN LA DÉCADA DE LOS NOVENTA

El grado de desarrollo social de Cuba y de América Latina medido por el IDH, considera el impacto del acceso efectivo a los servicios sociales (más allá de problemas de calidad de los mismos), junto al ingreso que proporciona posibilidades de llevar una vida decorosa. Existen vínculos significativos y estrechos entre la satisfacción de las necesidades sociales básicas de los servicios sociales y el nivel de ingreso para superar la pobreza y la marginalidad. Se considera que los países con un IDH superior a 0.80 presentan un desarrollo humano alto, mientras que los restantes tienen un desarrollo humano medio o bajo. A su vez, dentro de los países de la región latinoamericana y caribeña hay diferencias importantes en el grado de desarrollo humano, pues los índices asumen valores en casi todo el rango de la categoría, mostrándose claramente la fuerte desigualdad existente entre los países que conforman la región.

Conceptualmente un bajo nivel de ingreso por habitante muestra una situación de carencias o privaciones, porque no se dispone de ingresos suficientes para satisfacer las necesidades materiales, resultado de la ausencia de oportunidades o herramientas suficientes para generar ingresos. La solución al problema de la pobreza involucra tanto políticas de desarrollo productivo y generación de empleo, como políticas de formación de capital humano con una perspectiva de mediano y largo plazos, y políticas sociales de carácter asistencial o compensatorio en el corto plazo.

El Informe de Desarrollo Humano de 1990 (PNUD, 1990), presentó un IDH de 0.877 para Cuba en 1987, o sea entre los países de desarrollo humano alto. Cuba ocupaba la séptima posición entre los países de la región, una posición absoluta y relativa más elevada que en la actualidad. Cuba tenía la segunda posición de esperanza de vida al nacer (74 años), la segunda de tasa de alfabetización de adultos (96%) y la décimo tercera en cuanto a niveles de producto por habitante (US$2,500), medido por la paridad de poder adquisitivo, superando el nivel de otros 7 países de la región: Nicaragua, República Dominicana, El

Cuadro 1. América Latina y el Caribe: Indice de Desarrollo Humano y sus Principales Componentes, 1990

Posición del País en el Indice de Desarrollo Humano en la Region	Esperanza de Vida al Nacer (años)	Tasa de Alfabetización de Adultos (%)	PIB Real por Habitante (ppa)[a]	Indice de Desarrollo Humano
1 Chile	72	98	4,862	0.931
2 Costa Rica	75	93	3,760	0.916
3 Uruguay	71	95	5,063	0.916
4 Argentina	71	96	4,647	0.910
5 Trinidad y Tobago	71	96	4,647	0.885
6 Panamá	72	89	4,009	0.883
7 Cuba	**74**	**96**	**2,500**	**0.877**
8 México	69	90	4,624	0.876
9 Venezuela	70	87	4,306	0.861
9 Jamaica	74	82	2,506	0.824
10 Colombia	65	88	3,524	0.801
11 Brasil	65	78	4,307	0.784
12 Ecuador	66	83	2,687	0.758
13 Perú	63	85	3,129	0.753
14 Nicaragua	64	88	2,209	0.743
15 Repúb. Dominicana	67	78	1,750	0.699
16 El Salvador	64	72	1,733	0,651
17 Guatemala	63	55	1,957	0.592
18 Honduras	65	59	1,119	0.437
19 Bolivia	54	75	1,380	0,548
20 Haití	55	38	775	0.356

Fuente: PNUD (1990, p. 134).

a. ppa: paridad del poder adquisitivo

Salvador, Guatemala, Honduras, Bolivia y Haití (ver Cuadro 1).

Según el Informe de Desarrollo Humano de 1999 (PNUD, 1999), Cuba tenía un IDH medio, de 0.765 en 1997, inferior al de 11 países de la región latinoamericana y del Caribe: Barbados (0.859), Bahamas, Chile, Argentina, Uruguay, Costa Rica, Trinidad y Tobago, Venezuela, Panamá, México y Colombia (0.768). Cuba tenía un IDH mayor al que le correspondería con base en su producto real por habitante (US$3,100), el cual también era inferior al de otros 9 países de la región: Brasil, Belice, Ecuador, Jamaica, Perú, República Dominicana, Paraguay, Guyana y Guatemala, lo que muestra la pobreza endémica del cubano en términos de ingreso en la región y establece dudas sobre la sostenibilidad de los avances sociales logrados (ver Cuadro 2). Cuba tiene un nivel de producto real por habitante mayor que sólo 5 países de la región: El Salvador, Bolivia, Honduras, Nicaragua y Haití.

En cuanto a los índices de resultados sociales, Cuba descendió en términos relativos; ahora ocupa la tercera posición en esperanza de vida al nacer (75.7 años), la sexta en tasa de alfabetización de adultos (95.9%) y la décima posición en tasa bruta de matriculación (72%). Estas posiciones todavía altas o medias en resultados sociales en la región, tal vez se expliquen por los efectos acumulativos rezagados del elevado gasto social por habitante, o inversión en capital humano, realizado por el país en la década de los ochenta.

Los dilemas de sustentabilidad surgen de las magras posibilidades de sostener una pesada estructura social, mientras la economía no recobra los ritmos históricos de expansión y en tanto no se pueda superar el estrangulamiento externo.

—CEPAL (1998, p. 381).

EL GASTO SOCIAL REAL POR HABITANTE DE AMÉRICA LATINA Y CUBA EN LA DÉCADA DE LOS NOVENTA

A continuación se analiza el nivel de los gastos sociales por habitante (educación, salud, seguridad social,

Cuadro 2. América Latina y el Caribe: Indices de Desarrollo Humano y sus Principales Componentes, 1997

Posición del País en el Indice de Desarrollo Humano de la Región	Esperanza de Vida al Nacer (años)	Tasa de Alfabetización de Adultos (%)	Tasa Bruta de Matriculación[a]	PIB Real por Habitante (ppa)[b]	Indice de Desarrollo Humano
1 Barbados	76.4	97.6	80	12,001	0.857
2 Bahamas	73.8	95.8	74	16,705	0.851
3 Chile	74.9	95.2	77	12,730	0.844
4 Argentina	72.9	96.5	79	10,300	0.827
5 Uruguay	73.9	97.5	77	9,200	0.826
6 Costa Rica	76.0	95.1	66	6,650	0.801
7 Trinidad y Tobago	73.8	97.8	66	6,840	0.797
8 Venezuela	72.4	92.0	67	8,860	0.792
9 Panamá	73.6	91.1	73	7,168	0.791
10 México	72.2	90.1	70	8,370	0.786
11 Colombia	70.4	90.9	71	6,810	0.768
12 Cuba	**75.7**	**95.9**	**72**	**3,100**	**0.765**
13 Ecuador	69.5	90.7	73	4,940	0.747
14 Brasil	66.8	84.0	80	6,480	0.739
15 Perú	68.3	88.7	78	4,680	0.739
16 Jamaica	74.8	85.5	63	3,440	0.734
17 Belice	74.7	75.0	72	4,300	0.732
18 Paraguay	69.6	92.4	64	3,980	0.730
19 República Dominicana	70.6	82.6	66	4,820	0.726
20 Guyana	64.4	98.1	64	3,210	0.701
21 El Salvador	69.1	77.0	64	2,880	0.674
22 Bolivia	61.4	83.6	70	2,880	0.652
23 Honduras	69.4	70.7	58	2,220	0.641
24 Guatemala	64.0	66.6	47	4,100	0.624
25 Nicaragua	67.9	63.4	63	1,997	0.616
26 Haití	53.7	45.8	24	1,270	0.430

Fuente: PNUD (1999, p. 134-137).

a. Ppa: paridad de poder adquisitivo

b. En primaria, secundaria y terciaria combinada.

vivienda, etc.) de América Latina y Cuba a finales de la década de los 90 como resultado de dos relaciones: el gasto social como proporción del producto interno bruto (PIB) y del PIB por habitante. El gasto social se refiere exclusivamente al gasto del sector público. Por ello, hay una subestimación del gasto social total de los países latinoamericanos, ya que excluye el gasto del sector privado.

En los 17 países analizados por la CEPAL en el Panorama Social de 1998 (CEPAL, 1999a), el promedio del gasto público social real por habitante ascendió a US$457 en 1996-1997, que contrasta con US$331 en 1990-1991, significando un aumento del 38% en el período, que equivale a una tasa anual de crecimiento real del 5.5% (ver Cuadro 3). Este incremento, orientado a atender la llamada deuda social acu-

mulada durante los años ochenta, fue superior al del PIB, de tal forma que el gasto social por habitante aumentó significativamente más que el producto por habitante en todos los países que mostraron crecimiento económico. Así el gasto social como proporción del PIB promedio pasó del 10.1% en 1990-1991 al 12.4% en 1996-1997.

Al respecto, la cuantía de los recursos públicos reales por habitante destinados a los sectores sociales aumentó en 14 de los 17 países analizados en los años noventa, mientras que en 2 países (Honduras y Nicaragua) se mantuvo más o menos en el mismo nivel durante el período y en Venezuela se redujo en un 6%. El gasto real aumentó en educación en 13 de 15 países, en salud y nutrición en 11 de 14 y en seguri-

Cuadro 3. América Latina (17 países): Tendencias y Niveles del Gasto Publico Gasto Social Real por Habitante, 1990-1997

Países[a]	Gasto social real por habitante (US dólares) de 1997		Variación período (%)	Tasa anual de variación del período	Gasto social en relación con el PIB		Gasto social en relación al gasto público total	
	1990-1991	1996-1997	1990-1991	1996-1997	1990-1991	1996-1997	1990-1991	1996-1997
Gasto social alto y medio-alto (promedio)	727	975	34.1	5.0	17.5	19.5	58.2	60.8
Argentina	1222	1570	28.6	4.3	17.7	17.9	62.2	65.1
Uruguay	929	1371	47.5	6.7	18.7	22.5	62.3	69.8
Brasil	821	951	15.8	2.5	19.0	19.8	59.5	59.1
Chile	451	725	60.5	8.2	13.0	14.1	60.8	65.9
Panamá	494	683	38.1	5.5	18.6	21.9	40.0	39.9
Costa Rica[b]	445	550	23.6	3.6	18.2	20.8	64.4	65.1
Gasto social medio (promedio)	267	353	32.3	4.8	7.9	10.5	35.1	43.4
Colombia	181	391	116.6	13.7	8.1	15.3	29.7	38.2
México[c]	283	352	24.5	3.7	6.5	7.8	41.6	52.9
Venezuela	338	317	(6.1)	- 1.0	9.0	8.4	33.9	39.0
Gasto social bajo (promedio)	59	109	83.9	10.7	5.3	7.7	30.3	38.4
Perú	5.1	169	229.5	22.0	2.3	5.8	16.7	40.9
Paraguay	55	148	166.8	17.8	3.0	7.9	39.9	47.1
El Salvador	87	147	69.7	9.2	5.4	7.7	21.9	26.5
Bolivia	55	119	118.1	13.9	6.0	12.0	25.8	44.2
República Dominicana	66	107	62.8	8.5	4.5	6.0	36.9	39.0
Guatemala	52	71	37.4	5.4	3.3	4.2	29.8	42.1
Honduras	59	58	(1.7)	-0.3	7.8	7.2	33.1	31.9
Nicaragua[d]	48	49	2.1	0.3	10.3	10.7	38.3	35.6
Promedio regional	331	457	38.0	5.5	10.1	12.4	41.0	47.2
Cuba (en CU$ a precios de 1997)[e]	632	466	-26.3	-5.0	22.5	21.1	—	—
Cuba (en CU$ a precios de 1997)[f]	624	549	-12.0	-1.4	21.7	23.0	—	—

Fuente: CEPAL (1999a, p 97) y Cuadro 5.

a. Los países se presentan en orden decreciente según el nivel de su presupuesto social durante el período 1996-1997.
b. Para el período 1996-1997 sólo pudieron considerarse las cifras correspondientes a 1996, debido a falta de información.
c. La cifra no incluye el gasto en vivienda en 1996-97. Si éste se considera, el gasto social real de dicho período se sitúa en torno de 446 dólares.
d. Para el período 1990-1991 sólo pudieron considerarse las cifras correspondientes a 1991, debido a problemas de hiperinflación durante el año 1990.
e. 1990-1991/1996-1997 a la tasa de cambio oficial.
f. 1990-1999 a la tasa de cambio oficial.

dad social en los 13 países sobre los que dispuso de información.

Existe un marcado grado de heterogeneidad en el gasto social por habitante en los países de América Latina. Los países de gasto social alto (Argentina, Uruguay y Brasil) tenían un nivel de gasto social por habitante de aproximadamente US$1,300 y los países de gasto social medio-alto (Chile, Panamá y Costa Rica) tenían un nivel de gasto por habitante de US$650 en 1996-1997. Estos 6 países tienen un gasto social por habitante mayor que Cuba, independientemente de la tasa de cambio que se utilice para convertir el PIB de Cuba de 1999 a US dólares.

Los países de gasto social real medio por habitante (Colombia, México y Venezuela) gastan un promedio de US$353 y los países de gasto social real bajo por habitante (Perú, Paraguay, El Salvador, Bolivia, Guatemala, República Dominicana, Honduras y Nicaragua) gastan un promedio de US$109. El gasto social bajo o muy bajo de algunos de estos países es consecuencia de las crisis políticas, económicas y sociales en muchos de ellos en los últimos 20 años. Los países que aumentaron el gasto social por habitante a una mayor tasa de crecimiento anual, fueron aquellos con un gasto social bajo, que alcanzó una tasa de crecimiento del 10.7% anual, aproximadamente el doble del promedio de los países de la región.

Cuadro 4. América Latina (17 paises): Factores Explicativos de la Variación de Gasto Social por Habitante entre 1990–1991 y 1996–1997 (en US dólares de 1997)

País	Variación del gasto social por habitante (en US$ de 1997)	Contribuciones a la variación del gasto social por habitante			
		Efectos evolución del PIB por habitante	Efectos evolución del gasto social respecto PIB	Efectos evolución del PIB por habitante (%)	Efectos evolución del gasto social respecto PIB (%)
Países con gasto social por habitante alto					
Argentina	349	338	11	96.85	3.15
Uruguay	441	211	230	47.85	52.15
Brasil	130	90	40	69.23	30.77
Promedio	307	213	94	71.31	28.69
Países con gasto social por habitante medio-alto					
Chile	273	214	59	78.39	21.61
Panamá	188	85	103	45.21	54.79
Costa Rica	105	39	66	37.14	62.86
Promedio	189	113	76	53.58	46.42
Países con gasto social por habitante medio					
Colombia	210	28	182	13.33	86.67
México	69	10	59	14.49	85.51
Venezuela	-21	-2	-19	9.52	90.48
Promedio	86	12	74	12.45	87.55
Países con gasto social por habitante bajo					
Perú	118	15	103	12.71	87.29
Paraguay	93	1	92	1.08	98.92
El Salvador	60	17	43	28.33	71.67
Bolivia	65	5	60	7.69	92.31
República Dominicana	41	14	27	34.15	65.85
Guatemala	19	4	15	21.05	78.95
Honduras	-1	3	-4	(300.00)	400.00
Nicaragua	1	-1	2	(100.00)	200.00
Promedio	50	7	42	14.65	85.35
Cuba 1990-91/1996-97	**-166**	**-156**	**-10**	**93.98**	**6.02**
Cuba 1990-1999	**-75**	**-81**	**6**	**-108.00**	**8.00**

Promedios no Ponderados

Fuente: CEPAL (1999a, p 115) y Cuadro 5.

Los aumentos del gasto social por habitante en la región señalados compensaron la disminución del gasto social por habitante registrado en tres cuartas partes de los países durante la década de los ochenta, por lo cual 12 de los 17 países, superaron en el bienio 1996-1997 el nivel de gastos alcanzado en 1980-1981. Las excepciones son Honduras, que mantuvo los niveles de los años ochenta, y el Salvador, Guatemala, Nicaragua y Venezuela, donde descendió.

De los países que tuvieron una mayor tasa de expansión del gasto social real por habitante (Bolivia, Chile, Colombia, El Salvador, Paraguay, Perú y República Dominicana) en los años noventa, sólo Chile debió esa expansión a la elevada tasa de crecimiento económico, mientras que en los otros países se debió principalmente al aumento del gasto social como proporción del PIB. Chile ha puesto un énfasis creciente en el mejoramiento de las condiciones macroeconómicas para superar la pobreza y mejorar el acceso a los servicios sociales básicos; para lo cual pretende altas y sostenidas tasas de crecimiento económico.

Con relación a los factores determinantes de la expansión del gasto social por habitante en la región, es pertinente indicar que el crecimiento económico explica el 71% del aumento de dicho gasto en los países con nivel de gasto social por habitante alto y el 54% en los países de gasto social medio en 1996-1997 (ver Cuadro 4). En estos países, el área social ya capta el 61% del gasto público total y no es fácil aumentarlo.

Esto sugiere que en estos países el margen es cada más escaso para elevar el nivel de gasto real social por habitante más allá del ritmo de crecimiento económico, relación que también parece ser válida para Cuba.

En cambio, en países con gastos sociales medio o bajo por habitante (Colombia, México, Bolivia, Guatemala, Paraguay y Perú), el factor predominante en la década de los noventa fue el incremento de la participación del gasto social en el PIB, que explica más del 80% del incremento logrado en la década. En su mayoría estos países de gasto social medio y bajo, todavía presentan cierta holgura para aumentar el gasto social por habitante, a un ritmo mayor que el PIB por habitante, otorgando una mayor prioridad al gasto social dentro del presupuesto nacional. Al respecto, entre los países donde más aumentó el gasto social como proporción del PIB en los años noventa están: Colombia (con 7.2 puntos porcentuales del PIB), Bolivia (con 6 puntos), Paraguay (con 4.9 puntos), y Perú (con 3.5 puntos).

Según la CEPAL (1999a), la consolidación democrática en la región ha incidido en la creciente prioridad otorgada al ámbito social. Varios de los países de la región emprendieron significativas reformas en educación, salud y seguridad social, muchas de ellas financiadas con recursos extra presupuestarios provenientes de préstamos de las instituciones financieras internacionales, que significaron aumentos en los gastos corrientes y de inversión, y se incorporaron posteriormente a los respectivos presupuestos nacionales. Los programas de reforma en la educación se concentraron en la educación básica y media, orientados a elevar la calidad y equidad de estos gastos de alta rentabilidad socioeconómica. Ellos incluyeron particularmente la capacitación y mejoras en los sueldos básicos de los docentes; el mejoramiento de la infraestructura física y tecnológica; la actualización de los métodos y los materiales de enseñanza; la descentralización de la gestión y la medición permanente de los resultados educacionales. La reforma de la seguridad social incluyó reajustes en las jubilaciones y pensiones orientadas a tener un gasto por habitante algo superior a los US$300 en Uruguay y entre US$100 y US$150 en Argentina, Brasil y Chile, así como a ampliar la cobertura.

Una preocupación de la CEPAL, es que el ritmo de crecimiento económico sufrió una significativa reducción del 6.4% en 1990-1995 al 3.3% en 1996-1997 y años posteriores, lo cual pone en peligro la continua expansión y aún la consolidación del gasto social por habitante en los países de la región. Según la CEPAL se requiere una tasa de crecimiento del 6% del PIB para reducir razonablemente los rezagos tecnológicos y sociales existentes (CEPAL, 2000a, p. 11).

El Gasto Social Real por Habitante de Cuba en la Década de los Noventa

El gasto social real por habitante de Cuba (a precios de 1997) fue de CU$549 en 1999 que contrasta con CU$624 en 1990 (ver Cuadro 5), y significó una reducción del 13% en el período 1990-1999, equivalente a una tasa de contracción anual del 1.4%. Dicha contracción fue menor que la del PIB por habitante, que fue del 17% en dicho período, ya que el gasto social como proporción del PIB aumentó del 21.7% en 1990 al 23.0% en 1999.

El gasto social real por habitante disminuyó de CU$624 en 1990 a CU$431 en 1995, pero después se recuperó a CU$549 en 1999. En educación se redujo de CU$223 en 1990 a CU$120 en 1995 y se recuperó a CU$158 en 1999; en salud disminuyó de CU$129 en 1990 a CU$98 en 1995 y se recobró a CU$134 en 1999; en seguridad social se redujo de CU$161 en 1990 a CU$141 en 1995 y se recuperó a CU$155 en 1999; y en vivienda y servicios comunales, se redujo de CU$53 en 1990 a CU$31 en 1993, aunque se recobró a CU$59 en 1999. Así, en el período 1990-1999, los gastos sociales reales por habitante se contrajeron significativamente más en educación (29%), cultura (39%) y deportes (29%), mientras que la reducción fue menor en seguridad social (4%). Sólo aumentaron en bienestar, salud, y vivienda y servicios comunales en 6%, 4% y 11%, respectivamente, pero aún en estas categorías mostraron reducciones hasta 1998.

El gasto social como proporción del PIB aumentó 21.7% en 1990 al 27.5% en 1993, uno de los peores años de la crisis económica, contribuyendo al significativo aumento del déficit fiscal de entonces; poste-

Cuadro 5. Cuba: Gastos Sociales Reales por Habitante, 1989–1999

Años	1989	1990	1991	1992	1993	1995	1996	1997	1998	1999
PIB en millones a precios corrientes	20795	20879	17554	16382	16617	23025	24481	24675	25863	27596
Deflactor (1981=100)	99.2	102.6	95.3	98.7	115.9	155.8	153.9	151.3	156.5	157.3
Deflactor (1997=100)	66	68	63	65	77	103	102	100	103	104
Población en miles	10577	10694	10793	10869	10940	10999	11028	11057	11086	11115
Gastos Sociales a precios corrientes (en CU$ millones)										
Educación	1651	1620	1504	1427	1385	1359	1421	1454	1510	1830
Salud	905	937	925	938	1077	1108	1190	1265	1345	1553
Seguridad social	1094	1164	1225	1348	1452	1594	1630	1636	1705	1786
Vivienda y servicios comunales	406	383	281	248	260	411	462	488	566	684
Cultura y arte	191	200	203	178	173	163	165	165	169	191
Bienestar	101	96	88	98	94	119	128	135	145	158
Deportes	116	124	126	122	125	125	114	109	104	141
Gastos Sociales Totales	4464	4524	4352	4359	4566	4879	5110	5252	5544	6343
Educación/PIB	0.079	0.078	0.086	0.087	0.083	0.059	0.058	0.059	0.058	0.066
Salud/PIB	0.044	0.045	0.053	0.057	0.065	0.048	0.049	0.051	0.052	0.056
Seguridad social/PIB	0.053	0.056	0.070	0.082	0.087	0.069	0.067	0.066	0.066	0.065
Vivienda y servicios comunales/PIB	0.020	0.018	0.016	0.015	0.016	0.018	0.019	0.020	0.022	0.025
Otros (cultura, bienestar y deportes)/PIB	0.020	0.020	0.024	0.024	0.024	0.018	0.017	0.017	0.016	0.018
Gastos Sociales/PIB	0.215	0.217	0.248	0.266	0.275	0.212	0.209	0.213	0.214	0.230
Gastos Sociales por Habitante (a precios corrientes)										
Educación	156	151	139	131	127	124	129	131	136	165
Salud	86	88	86	86	98	101	108	114	121	140
Seguridad social	103	109	113	124	133	145	148	148	154	161
Vivienda y servicios comunales	38	36	26	23	24	37	42	44	51	62
Cultura y arte	18	19	19	16	16	15	15	15	15	17
Bienestar	10	9	8	9	9	11	12	12	13	14
Deportes	11	12	12	11	11	11	10	10	9	13
Gastos Sociales Totales	422	423	403	401	417	444	463	475	500	570
Gastos Sociales Reales por Habitante (a precios de 1997)										
Educación	238	223	221	201	165	120	127	131	132	158
Salud	131	129	136	132	129	98	106	114	117	134
Seguridad social	158	161	180	190	173	141	145	148	149	155
Vivienda y servicios comunales	59	53	41	35	31	36	41	44	49	59
Cultura y arte	28	28	30	25	21	14	15	15	15	17
Bienestar	15	13	13	14	11	11	11	12	13	13
Deportes	17	17	19	17	15	11	10	10	9	12
Gastos Sociales Totales	644	624	640	615	545	431	456	475	483	549
Ingresos Seguridad Social	676	691	666	673	925	898	959	1071	1025	1115
Déficit Seguridad Social	418	474	559	676	527	696	671	565	680	671
Déficit Seg. Social/PIB	0.020	0.023	0.032	0.041	0.032	0.030	0.027	0.023	0.026	0.024

Fuente: CEPAL (1998, Cuadros A-1 y A-8; y 2000b, Cuadros 1 y 26-A).

riormente fluctuó alrededor del 21% en 1995-1998 y se expandió al 23% en 1999.

Una preocupación de la CEPAL (1998) es que la severa contracción económica y la debilidad del sector externo del país ponen en peligro el elevado gasto social por habitante de Cuba. Cuba se encuentra por arriba del promedio latinoamericano en el gasto social como proporción del PIB con un nivel del 23%, el mayor de la región, 85% superior al promedio latinoamericano; sin embargo, el PIB por habitante de

Cuba, aún a la tasa de cambio oficial, es menor a la mitad del promedio latinoamericano.

El Gasto Social Real por Habitante en Relación con el PIB y el PIB por Habitante

Si bien el nivel de gasto social como proporción del PIB de Cuba es muy elevado en comparación con los países latinoamericanos, a pesar de los esfuerzos que han venido haciendo los países de la región para aumentar esta relación en los años noventa, sólo es ligeramente mayor al de los 6 países de la región con mayor gasto social por habitante y era inferior a los de Uruguay (22.5%) y Panamá (21.9%) hasta 1998. En cambio el nivel del PIB por habitante de Cuba se redujo en la década de los 90, a pesar de su recuperación a partir de 1995, y está perdiendo importancia relativa con respecto a los otros países de la región, aún si se utiliza la tasa de cambio oficial para valorizar el PIB cubano en US dólares.

Los análisis tradicionales sobre el gasto social de Cuba y América Latina se han concentrado en el gasto social como proporción del PIB, que es una relación difícil de modificar a corto y mediano plazo en los países con alto nivel de gasto social como proporción del PIB, pues requiere de una reasignación de los recursos en el ámbito de la sociedad a favor del Estado y que los recursos captados se utilicen en el sector social, lo cual puede conllevar efectos negativos sobre la tasa de crecimiento del PIB. En cambio, dichos análisis han ignorado en general los cambios del PIB por habitante, que se ha modificado significativamente en la década de los noventa en la medida que las economías de la región han logrado crecer, mientras que la economía cubana se contrajo. Como se indicó, Chile ha logrado ocupar un lugar destacado en el gasto social por habitante en América Latina en los años noventa, mayor que el de Cuba, principalmente con base en el aumento del PIB por habitante asociado a su alta tasa de crecimiento económico a partir de 1984.

El efecto combinado de ambas relaciones en Cuba *vis-a-vis* la región, una ligeramente creciente y otra en franca declinación, explica porque el país que era considerado un paradigma social en la región por los elevados niveles de gasto social por habitante, haya ido perdiendo su atractivo entre los intelectuales y países de la región. Cuba vio reducir su gasto social por habitante no sólo en términos absolutos sino en relación con los otros países de la región debido a su significativa contracción económica en la década de los noventa.

UN ESTIMADO DEL GASTO SOCIAL DE CUBA EN US DÓLARES

El Cuadro 6 muestra que el gasto social real por habitante de Cuba expresado en US dólares, al utilizar una tasa de cambio que pondera los ingresos externos

del país a las tasas de cambio que éstos se obtienen (US$1=CU$4), está entre los países de bajo nivel de gasto social real por habitante en la región, pero el gasto social con respecto al PIB es muy superior al que le corresponde de acuerdo con su nivel de PIB por habitante, que sería cercano al 10%.

Cuadro 6. Gastos Sociales Reales por Habitante en US$ a una Tasa Cambio Ponderada de US$4

Años	1995	1996	1997	1998	1999
Educación	30	32	33	33	40
Salud	24	27	29	29	34
Seguridad Social	35	36	37	37	39
Vivienda y servicios comunales	9	10	11	12	15
Cultura y arte	4	4	4	4	4
Bienestar	3	3	3	3	3
Deportes	3	3	2	2	3
Gastos Totales	108	114	119	121	137

Fuente: Cuadro 5.

Al respecto, la tasa de cambio unificada de mercado para Cuba debería estar entre la tasa de cambio oficial de US$1 y la tasa de cambio "libre" administrada, que ha estado fluctuando alrededor de US$20 a partir de 1996. Ello supone que el proceso de unificación se haga ordenadamente con un déficit fiscal moderado, una política de salarios reales constantes para el sector público y las empresas públicas, una política monetario-crediticia neutral, y una tasa de cambio fija inicial que sirva de firme ancla al principio del proceso de estabilización.

Una manera gruesa y conservadora de estimar la tasa de cambio unificada de mercado, aunque no la única y menor que la que se debería utilizar como ancla al principio del proceso de estabilización, es ponderando el porcentaje de los ingresos externos que se obtienen a las dos tasas de cambio existentes. Así, todos los ingresos de Cuba, excepto las remesas familiares y otras transacciones similares que aparecen en las transferencias unilaterales, se realizan a la tasa de cambio oficial, entre ellas están: las exportaciones de bienes y servicios, la inversión directa y las donaciones. De esta forma aproximadamente el 85% de los ingresos externos de Cuba se obtienen a la tasa de cambio de US$1=CU$1 y el 15% restante a una tasa de cambio alrededor de US$1=CU$20. Al ponderar los ingresos externos totales de Cuba, se obtiene una tasa de cambio ponderada de aproximadamente US$1=CU$4 para cada uno de los años 1995 a 1999.

Así, al aplicar el estimado de la tasa unificada de mercado a los gastos sociales reales por habitante, Cuba pasa de tener gastos sociales por habitante medio-altos—menores, pero cercanos a los de Chile, Costa Rica y Panamá—a gastos sociales reales por habitante bajos del orden de US$137, similares a los de El Salvador, Paraguay, Bolivia y República Dominicana (ver Cuadro 3). También la proporción del gasto social en relación al PIB es casi el doble al que le que corresponde a países con ese nivel de ingreso real por habitante, que es del orden del 10% del PIB, y apoya la interpretación de que Cuba está sobreinvirtiendo en los sectores sociales.

> Lo anterior no significa que las estrategias hubiesen estado exentas de errores de concepción y aplicación.
>
> —CEPAL (1997, p. 359).

SITUACIÓN, CARACTERÍSTICAS Y TENDENCIAS DE LOS PRINCIPALES COMPONENTES DEL GASTO SOCIAL, DEL INGRESO POR HABITANTE Y LA DESIGUALDAD EN LOS INGRESOS DE CUBA EN LOS NOVENTA

Concurrente con lo que muestra la evolución del IDH en los años noventa y la reducción del gasto real por habitante señalada en la sección 2-B, que también es destacada por la CEPAL (1998, sección 4. D), ésta señala retrocesos significativos en los sectores de educación y vivienda, en los salarios reales y la igualdad de los ingresos lograda hasta 1990, así como la precariedad de los avances sociales.

Educación

"La dotación de recursos presupuestarios a la educación se redujo sustancialmente entre 1989 y 1996" (CEPAL 1998, p 369), con ello ha ocurrido una marcada disminución de la matrícula secundaria y universitaria, una reducción de los materiales y útiles escolares, y un estancamiento y desgaste de las instalaciones y el equipamiento educacionales. También se detuvo la ampliación de la educación preescolar. Aunque los índices de cobertura escolar de Cuba han disminuido, la calidad de la educación en términos

de repetición, completar el nivel educativo y los resultados de las pruebas académicas aún son elevados a nivel regional.

Los estudiantes matriculados (en miles) en escuelas medias disminuyeron de 1,073.1 en 1989 a 778.0 en 1997 y los estudiantes matriculados (en miles) en escuelas superiores de 242.4 en 1989 a 104.6 en 1997, o sea se produjeron reducciones del 37% y del 57%, respectivamente. En cambio los estudiantes en educación primaria (en miles) aumentaron en forma continua de 885.6 en 1989 a 1,044.6 en 1996, o sea un 18% (ver Cuadro 7).

Si bien "no se han cerrado escuelas, no obstante problemas muy críticos de mantenimiento de las instalaciones" (CEPAL, 1998, p 369) ni se redujo el salario monetario del personal docente y se aumentó en un 30% en 1998, esto conllevó una reducción del salario en términos reales se efectuaron reducciones en el suministro de útiles, textos y materiales, así como en la formación de capital, que "comienzan a reflejarse de manera muy desfavorable en los servicios" (CEPAL, 1998, p. 369). La repercusión ha sido significativa en los laboratorios y talleres, que se han utilizado más intensamente y carecen de piezas de repuestos y el equipamiento se ha ido deteriorando y acelerando su depreciación, con el consecuente retraso tecnológico y obsolescencia. Esto es preocupante cuando éstos se deberían ir adaptando y modernizando regular y sistemáticamente al cambiante entorno tecnológico mundial.

Lo señalado implica que se rechaza la apreciación de que se ha invertido mucho en educación en Cuba. Sin duda se puede invertir mejor en educación, pero el problema fundamental del país es que no se ha permitido que la economía crezca de acuerdo a su potencial, alentando el circulo virtuoso de que el crecimiento aprovecha el gasto en educación, lo que a su vez genera más crecimiento y requiere más gasto en educación.

Salud

El Informe Mundial de la Salud del 2000 muestra que los índices de desempeño de la salud y del nivel de salud de Cuba están entre las posiciones 33 y 39 entre 191 países, mientras que el nivel de respuesta

Cuadro 7. Cuba: Indicadores Socioeconómicos Seleccionados de CEPAL, 1989-1998

Indicadores	1989	1990	1991	1992	1993	1994	1995	1996	1997	1998	1999
1. Inversión bruta interna como % del PIB	25.0	25.0	14.9	6.9	4.8	4.9	6.5	7.4	8.2	8.7	8.9
2. Ahorro nacional bruto como % del PIB	9.9	11.1	4.7	3.4	3.6	3.7	4.4	5.9	4.7	5.4	Nd
3. Ahorro nacional bruto como % inversión interna bruta (rubros 2/1)	39.6	44.4	31.5	49.3	75.0	75.5	67.7	79.7	57.3	62.1	Nd
4. Déficit fiscal como % del PIB	6.7	9.4	21.4	29.7	30.4	7.0	3.3	2.3	1.9	2.2	2.2
5. Tasa de desempleo urbano				6.1	6.2	6.7	7.9	7.6	7.0	6.6	6.0
6. Tasa de desempleo equivalente	7.9	10.8	19.2	25.6	35.2	33.5	31.5	27.3	Nd	Nd	Nd
7. Productividad media por trabajador (en miles de CU$ (a precios de 1981)	4.43	4.29	3.89	3.58	3.12	3.21	3.27	3.52	3.54	3.56	3.75
8. Salario medio mensual (1990=100)	103.8	100.0	96.4	86.2	77.2	59.5	56.1	58.6	Nd	Nd	Nd
9. Tipo de cambio extraoficial	5	7	20	35	78	95	32.1	19.2	23	21	20
10. Remesas en US$ millones							537	630	670	700	725
11. Matrícula en educación primaria (en miles)	885.6	887.7	917.9	942.4	983.5	1107.8	1026.4	1044.6	Nd	Nd	Nd
12. Matrícula en educación secundaria (en miles)	1073.1	1002.3	912.2	819.7	752.8	674.2	702.6	710.6	778.0	Nd	Nd
13. Matrícula en educación terciaria (en miles)	242.4	242.2	224.6	198.5	165.8	140.8	122.3	111.6	104.6	Nd	Nd
14. Construcción de viviendas (en miles)	39.6	36.3	26.2	20.0	27.1	33.5	44.5	57.3	54.5	45.0	42.0
15. Médicos (en miles)	34.8	38.7	42.6	46.9	51.0	54.1	56.8	60.1	Nd	Nd	Nd
16. Camas de hospital (por mil habitantes)	7.4	7.4	7.5	7.5	7.4	7.5	7.5	7.4	7.4	Nd	Nd

Fuente: CEPAL (1998, Cuadros A.1, A.59 y A.60; 2000b, Cuadros 1-4, 15, 23 y 27; 1999c, Cuadros 20, 43 y 50).

Cuadro 8. Posición Internacional de Cuba en Indicadores de Salud Entre 191 Países

Logro de metas	
1. Nivel de salud (índice de expectativa de vida con plena salud)	33
2. Distribución de salud (índice de igualdad de sobrevivencia de vida de los niños)	41
3. Nivel de respuesta (dignidad, autonomía y confidencialidad, prontitud en la atención, etc.)	115-117
4. Distribución de la respuesta	98-100
5. Equidad de la contribución financiera	23-25
Logro global de metas (índice ponderado de 25% para 1, 2 y 5, y 12.5% para 3 y 4)	40
Gastos en salud (en dólares) por habitante	118
Desempeño del nivel de salud (resultados de salud en referencia a la norma)	36
Desempeño general del sistema de salud (resultados de salud con respecto a gastos de salud)	39

Fuente: World Health Report, 2000.

del sistema está entre las posiciones 115-117 y el gasto en salud (en dólares) por habitante a la tasa de cambio oficial está en la posición 118 (ver Cuadro 8).

Según la CEPAL (1998), Cuba avanzó en cuatro aspectos en los noventa: prevención y diagnóstico de las enfermedades, instalaciones hospitalarias, formación y disponibilidad de recursos profesionales y paraprofesionales, e investigación científica. Sin embargo, la escasez de divisas redujo la disponibilidad de medicinas[2] y ha "conducido a la utilización excesiva de los equipos existentes, con el consabido acortamiento de su vida útil" (CEPAL 1998, p 365), tampoco hubo ajustes en las remuneraciones nominales al personal médico hasta 1998, cuando se reajustó en un 30%, lo que determinó una reducción en las remuneraciones reales en el período.

Además, hay distorsiones y desproporciones desde el punto de vista de los factores empleados, así mientras hay mayores recursos humanos e instalaciones hospitalarias, hay una menor disponibilidad de medicinas convencionales y un deterioro en las condiciones habitacionales y sanitarias. Por ello el costo efectividad de los gastos hospitalarios y personal médico no parecen justificados por las diferencias de resultados de Cuba en comparación con otros países de América Latina como lo habían señalado Alonso, Donate-Armada y Lago (1994). La situación de la salud también se ve afectada por el sistema de racionamiento que no provee alimentos suficientes, y hay carencias de artí-

---

2. Según una misión de la American Association for World Health que recorrió hospitales y centros de salud cubanos en 1997, Cuba sólo tuvo acceso a 889 de los 1,297 medicamentos considerados imprescindibles. *El Mercurio,* 28 de junio de 2000, p.10.

culos básicos de higiene (tales como: jabón, papel higiénico, etc.), y de control de plagas (insecticidas, pesticidas, etc.). Una "cuestión central es la viabilidad y conveniencia de largo plazo de sostener un sector tecnológico de avanzada y excelencia en las condiciones económicas de Cuba" (CEPAL 1998, p 367).

Vivienda

En Cuba "se resienten déficit y atrasos muy significativos" en vivienda (CEPAL, 1998, p. 360). Aún desde el segundo quinquenio de los ochenta, antes de la crisis, la construcción de nuevas viviendas no alcanzaba a satisfacer la reposición de viviendas que superan su vida útil (CEPAL, 1998, p. 372). Durante todos los años de la década de los noventa, el número de nuevas viviendas fue inferior a las 60,000 anuales, número mínimo (conservador) requerido para reponer las viviendas que superan su vida útil (ver Cuadro 7). "Las consecuencias se reflejan en el hacinamiento y deterioro en las condiciones de vida", particularmente en la ciudad capital (CEPAL 1998, p 360), lo que está afectando negativamente las condiciones sanitarias y el nivel y calidad de vida.

El gasto real en viviendas y servicios comunales por habitante que es bajo (CU$59 en 1999) aumentó ligeramente, 11% en la década de los noventa (ver Cuadro 5). Las novelas costumbristas sobre Cuba, particularmente las de Zoé Valdés, destacan la precariedad de la vivienda al igual que lo muestran las películas recientes (p.e. Buenavista Social Club). Asimismo, el déficit de mantenimiento y reparación de la infraestructura de servicios sanitarios (agua y alcantarillado) y urbanos (recolección de desechos, limpieza de calles y control de plagas) refuerzan lo indicado.

Seguridad Social

El sistema de seguridad social vigente es de reparto, con edades de jubilación de 55 años para las mujeres y de 60 años para los hombres, y se ha utilizado como mecanismo de compensación social para enfrentar la crisis económica. La CEPAL indica que el nivel de seguridad social "en el producto no es sinónimo de alivio permanente a la pobreza" (CEPAL, 1998, p. 203). Para ello hay que "ligar en forma transparente beneficios y financiamiento" (CEPAL, 1998, p. 205). En el caso de Cuba "toda vez que los beneficios son independientes de las recaudaciones, no se cono-

ce "si son atribuibles a una previsión social mal diseñada o una política excesivamente generosa" (CEPAL, 1998, p. 206). En mi opinión, ambos conceptos son ciertos y el sistema requiere una reforma sustantiva, como lo han fundamentado Alonso, Donate-Armada y Lago (1994), Donate-Armada (1994) y Pérez (1998) en reuniones anteriores de ASCE.

Asimismo, la CEPAL considera que los gastos sociales y el sistema de previsión social se han convertido en una carga y exceden "la capacidad de la economía nacional" para sostenerlos (CEPAL, 1998, p. 59). Esta conclusión había sido expuesta en las reuniones anteriores de ASCE por Alonso, Donate-Armada y Lago (1994), Donate-Armada (1994) y Pérez (1998), y tiene serias implicaciones fiscales debido al cambio en la estructura demográfica de la población. El Cuadro 7 muestra que el déficit del sistema de seguridad social se ha mantenido alrededor del 2.5% del PIB en los últimos cuatro años, a pesar de la recuperación económica a partir de 1995.

Salario Real y Desigualdad del Ingreso

En términos de retrocesos sociales, la CEPAL muestra una marcada caída del salario real del 41% entre 1990 y 1996 (CEPAL, 1998, Cuadro A-1). Así, el salario mensual real de 1996 era el 58.6% de 1990 (ver Cuadro 7). Esto junto a una política de incentivos al trabajo y remuneraciones arbitraria, que sólo beneficia a un tercio de la población, ha aumentado la desigualdad en la distribución del ingreso, ha creado efectos perversos sobre los hábitos y la motivación al trabajo (CEPAL, 1998, p. 197) y sienta las bases materiales de mayores desigualdades sociales en el futuro al no brindar igualdad de oportunidades con todas sus contradicciones y tensiones. Como se dice popularmente en Cuba "ellos hacen como si me pagaran y yo hago como si trabajara."

La CEPAL señala que a mediados de los años ochenta "se habían eliminado la pobreza y la indigencia tanto en las zonas urbanas como rurales" (CEPAL, 1998, p. 37). Es probable que se hubiera eliminado la indigencia; sin embargo, definitivamente no se eliminó la pobreza, ya que la situación actual de la población es de bajos ingresos aún en el contexto latinoamericano en el cual Cuba ocupa una de las más bajas posiciones de la región.

La CEPAL (2000b) muestra con un índice simple que la productividad media por trabajador cayó en un 15.3% entre 1989 y 1999 (ver Cuadro 7), o sea la causa subyacente de la reducción del salario real y del empobrecimiento. Asimismo, calcula un nivel de desempleo equivalente al 27.3% en 1996 (ver Cuadro 7), debido al desempleo abierto, la caída en productividad y la menor participación de la población en la PEA. Estos dos indicadores fundamentan la pobreza endémica de los cubanos y la dificultad de superar rápidamente la situación existente.

> La viabilidad de la política social se facilitó por la singular y privilegiada relación que Cuba mantuvo con los países de la esfera socialista, en especial con la antigua URSS. Esa cooperación fue importante en los aspectos financieros, en el suministro de materiales y equipos, y en la asistencia técnica; también tuvo repercusiones significativas en aportar recursos que elevaron el bienestar de la población por arriba del que se disfruta en economías de similar y aun mayor nivel de ingreso.
>
> — CEPAL (1998, p. 359).

LA EVOLUCIÓN ECONÓMICA DE CUBA Y AMÉRICA LATINA EN LAS DÉCADAS DE LOS OCHENTA Y NOVENTA

Los países de América Latina y el Caribe mostraron una contracción del PIB real por habitante del 1% anual en 1981-1990. En cambio tuvieron una expansión del PIB real por habitante del 1.4% anual en 1991-1999 (ver Cuadro 9), debido al proceso de transformaciones institucionales y de políticas económicas para ser más competitivos internacionalmente e insertarse en la economía global, que en general les permitió no sólo recuperar sino también superar el nivel de gasto social real por habitante de principios de la década de los ochenta.

Por el contrario, Cuba mostró una expansión del PIB real por habitante del 2.8% anual en 1981-1990, la mayor de los países de área, cuando el país estuvo mayormente inmune a los efectos negativos de la segunda alza del precio del petróleo de 1979 y de la crisis de la deuda externa de la década de los ochenta,

gracias a la masiva ayuda externa soviética. Sin embargo, Cuba experimentó una contracción del PIB por habitante real del 2.6% anual en 1991-1999, que sólo fue superada por la contracción de Haití que alcanzó al 3.1% anual en 1991-1999. La disminución del PIB por habitante de Cuba en la década de los noventa estuvo determinada porque afrontó simultáneamente los efectos del libre comercio internacional, pagar los precios internacionales del petróleo (en ausencia del subsidio soviético por el azúcar), la moratoria de la deuda externa declarada en 1986 y el recrudecimiento del embargo norteamericano, sin haber realizado significativas transformaciones en su ineficiente organización productiva e institucional.

Como muestra el Cuadro 7, e independientemente de la recuperación de la economía en los años 1995-1999, Cuba no está efectuando la inversión fija bruta requerida ni tiene el ahorro nacional para alcanzar y mantener un crecimiento alto y sostenido en los próximos años, a fin de desarrollar nuevas actividades o añadirle valor agregado a las que desarrolla. La CEPAL (1998) reitera particularmente el deterioro de las instalaciones y el equipamiento vinculado con tres áreas básicas del gasto social: educación, salud y vivienda.

En resumen, las experiencias de Cuba y América Latina en las décadas de los ochenta y noventa, muestran claramente un fenómeno evidente: Cuando las economías crecen, y con ello se expande el PIB real por habitante, el gasto social real por habitante tiende a aumentar (por dos razones: aumenta el PIB y se puede expandir el gasto social con respecto al PIB) y cuando las economías se contraen el gasto social real por habitante tiende a disminuir. Por consiguiente, una forma de mejorar el IDH y lograr la expansión continua del gasto social real por habitante, es mantener un crecimiento alto y sostenido del PIB real por habitante. Esta ha sido la experiencia chilena a partir de 1984, país donde la estabilidad y el crecimiento económico han abierto posibilidades en términos de más puestos de trabajo y mejor remunerados para satisfacer el consumo de bienes y servicios y para mejorar la cobertura y la calidad de los servicios sociales que el Estado provee.

Cuadro 9. América Latina y El Caribe: Evolución del PIB por Habitante, 1981–1999

(en porcentajes, sobre la base de valores a precios de 1995)

	1991	1992	1993	1994	1995	1996	1997	1998	1999	1981-90	1991-99
América Latina y el Caribe[c]	2.0	1.4	2.1	3.5	- 0.6	2.0	3.7	0.4	-1.6[a]	- 1.0[b]	1.4
América Latina y el Caribe (excluye Brasil)[c]	3.7	3.5	1.5	2.8	2.6	2.4	4.6	1.6	- 2.0	...	1.7
Subtotal (19 países)[c]	**2.0**	**1.4**	**2.1**	**3.5**	**0.6**	**2.0**	**3.7**	**0.4**	**1.6**	**1.0**	**1.4**
Subtotal (19 países, excl. Brasil)[c]	**3.8**	**3.5**	**1.6**	**2.8**	**2.7**	**2.4**	**4.7**	**1.6**	**2.0**	**...**	**1.7**
Argentina	9.2	8.2	4.5	4.4	-4.1	4.1	6.6	2.6	-4.5	-2.1	3.3
Bolivia	2.9	-0.8	1.7	2.2	2.2	2.0	1.7	2.1	-1.3	-1.9	1.4
Brasil	-0.6	-1.8	3.0	4.7	2.7	1.4	2.4	-1.4	-0.9	-0.7	1.0
Chile	5.6	9.1	4.8	3.5	7.4	5.3	5.5	1.7	-2.7	1.3	4.4
Colombia[d]	0.0	2.1	3.2	4.0	3.2	0.1	0.7	-1.2	-6.9	1.6	0.5
Costa Rica	-0.9	3.7	2.5	1.1	-0.6	-3.2	0.8	3.0	5.0	-0.6	1.2
Cuba[e]	**-11.6**	**-11.8**	**-15.2**	**0.0**	**1.8**	**7.3**	**2.0**	**1.1**	**5.6**	**2.8**	**-2.6**
Ecuador	2.7	0.7	- 0.1	2.1	0.8	0.2	1.8	-0.9	-9.0	-0.9	-0.2
El Salvador	0.9	5.1	4.2	3.7	4.0	-0.3	2.0	1.1	0.3	-1.4	2.3
Guatemala	1.1	2.2	1.3	1.4	2.2	0.3	1.6	2.3	0.9	-1.6	1.5
Haiti	-2.0	-15.4	-4.0	-9.9	3.1	0.9	-0.4	1.3	0.4	-2.4	-3.1
Honduras	-0.4	2.7	4.0	-4.7	0.7	0.9	2.1	1.1	-4.5	-0.8	0.2
México	2.2	1.8	-0.1	2.8	-7.8	3.4	5.1	3.2	1.8	-0.3	1.3
Nicaragua	-3.1	- 2.1	-3.3	0.9	1.5	2.1	2.6	1.4	3.2	-3.9	0.3
Panamá	6.9	6.2	3.4	1.3	0.1	0.9	2.9	2.7	1.2	-0.7	2.8
Paraguay	-0.4	-1.1	1.3	0.4	1.7	1.6	-0.2	-3.2	-2.5	0.0	-0.6
Perú	0.6	-2.6	4.0	11.6	6.8	0.5	6.7	-1.6	1.0	-3.3	2.9
República Dominica	-1.2	4.3	0.0	2.4	2.7	4.9	5.3	4.2	5.3	0.2	3.1
Uruguay	2.2	6.6	2.4	4.7	-2.7	4.3	4.3	3.8	-3.2	-0.6	2.4
Venezuela	7.9	4.6	-2.7	- 5.8	3.7	2.5	4.4	-2.2	-8.8	-3.2	-0.3
Subtotal Caribe[f]	**0.9**	**0.1**	**0.3**	**2.4**	**1.7**	**2.4**	**1.0**	**0.9**	**2.3**	**0.9**	**1.1**
Antigua y Barbuda	2.1	0.3	4.3	5.5	-5.4	5.2	4.2	...	...	5.6	2.3[g]
Barbados	-3.8	-6.2	0.7	2.8	2.1	4.7	2.2	4.0	2.1	0.7	0.9
Belice	0.7	6.2	1.5	- 1.3	1.1	-1.8	1.7	1.3	...	1.9	0.8[h]
Dominica	2.6	3.0	2.2	2.1	2.3	2.9	2.7	3.5	...	4.8	2.7[h]
Granada	3.5	0.8	-1.3	3.2	2.8	2.8	4.3	4.5	...	4.7	2.6[h]
Guyana	9.5	10.4	2.1	16.5	1.5	8.2	5.1	2.3	0.7	3.4	5.6
Jamaica	-0.5	1.6	0.9	0.8	0.8	-1.2	- 3.0	-1.6	-1.9	1.1	-0.5
Saint Kifts y Nevis	3.0	3.7	5.7	6.1	3.7	5.8	7.2	1.7	...	7.0	4.6[h]
San Vicente y las Granadinas	0.7	5.8	1.5	- 3.5	6.8	0.8	2.3	4.5	...	5.5	2.3[h]
Santa Lucía	-3.3	5.9	-0.9	0.6	-0.6	-0.8	1.5	0.5	2.5	5.3	0.6
Suriname	3.8	-2.0	-8.7	- 4.3	-2.2	20.1	3.1	...	...	-0.7	1.1[g]
Trinidad y Tobago	2.7	-1.9	-1.9	3.3	3.4	3.4	2.6	2.7	6.3	-3.9	2.3

Fuente: Fuente: CEPAL,1999c

Los totales y subtotales, cuando corresponde, excluyen aquellos países para los que no se presenta información.

a. Estimación preliminar.

b. Calculadas sobre la base de cifras a precios constantes de 1990

c. Excluye Cuba.

d. Los valores para el período 1997-1999 fueron estimados por la CEPAL, en base a cifras provisionales proporcionadas por el Departamento Administrativo Nacional de Estadística (DANE).

e. Calculado sobre la base de moneda constante del país.

f. Calculado sobre la base de cifras expresadas a costo de factores.

g. Se refiere el período 1991-1997.

h. Se refiere al período 1991-1996.

Russia is regularly dispensed a drug which never cures but keeps the patient in a vegetative state. And the drug habit is growing … The roughly $20 billion pumped into the Russian budget over the last decade have, in fact, had no positive effect whatsoever.

— Boris Federov, "No More Help for Russia, Please" *The Wall Street Journal Europe*, June 8, 2000, p. 20.

UNA BREVE DISGRESIÓN SOBRE LAS IMPLICACIONES DE LA AUSENCIA DE LA AYUDA EXTERNA OFICIAL, EL EMBARGO NORTEAMERICANO Y LAS REMESAS FAMILIARES EN LA DÉCADA DE LOS NOVENTA

La CEPAL (1998) explica la contracción económica de Cuba en los noventa con base en dos factores negativos principales: (1) el embargo norteamericano y (2) la ausencia de financiamiento externo oficial. No obstante, también destaca el monto significativo de las remesas familiares y menciona la necesidad de que Cuba adopte medidas para restablecer el crecimiento económico. Como se comenta a continuación, la contracción económica de Cuba se debe a su política económica e institucional, y no a la ausencia de financiamiento externo oficial ni al embargo, el cual es compensado por las remesas familiares.

El embargo norteamericano, sin dudas, determina un costo y una pérdida del PIB real por habitante debido a los desvíos del comercio internacional, efecto que es similar a un aumento de los precios de petróleo. Sin embargo, en un momento que Cuba comercia y moviliza inversiones de todo el resto del mundo, no se puede atribuir la contracción económica del país al embargo norteamericano. Más importante que el costo del embargo es el de mantener la economía relativamente cerrada y con marcadas ineficiencias debido a una tasa de cambio artificial para la mayoría de las transacciones externas, asi como a otras marcadas distorsiones existentes (o sea el llamado "embargo interno").

Cuba dejó de recibir financiamiento externo oficial en 1990, después de varios años de una ayuda masiva de la antigua URSS en términos de precios diferenciados muy favorables para el comercio exterior y de préstamos externos para el desarrollo en términos con alto contenido concesional, así como de declaración de moratoria de la deuda externa en 1986. Sin embargo, el desarrollo económico no lo determina fundamentalmente el financiamiento externo oficial, porque ello sería dependencia y no asistencia. Esta es una condición facilitadora, pero no es necesaria para el desarrollo. Así varios países, entre ellos Cuba y Rusia, han utilizado el financiamiento oficial inapropiadamente por largos períodos como lo prueban los resultados económicos logrados, aumentando el consumo o desarrollando inversiones no rentables.[3] Por ello, la iniciativa de condonación de la deuda externa a los países pobres altamente endeudados (HIPC), se condiciona a que los países beneficiarios adopten medidas de transformaciones estructurales para superar los problemas fundamentales de desarrollo de forma que el nuevo financiamiento externo les permita realizar inversiones conducentes al desarrollo sostenible y a que puedan hacerle frente al nuevo servicio de la deuda externa, asi como que tengan programas sólidos de reducción de la pobreza; de lo contrario, se alientan comportamientos inapropiados. Cuba no califica en estos momentos para la ayuda externa oficial porque carece de un programa confiable de recuperación y transformación.

La ayuda externa soviética en forma de sobreprecios a las exportaciones de elevados volúmenes de azúcar y de bajos precios a las importaciones de elevados volúmenes de petróleo, determinó la llamada "enfermedad holandesa" para el país. Así, Cuba desarrolló una industria azucarera ineficiente, sobredimensionada y tecnológicamente obsoleta, mientras no desarrolló otros sectores con claras ventajas comparativas y se acostumbró a un consumo de petróleo excesivo, lo que ha contribuido significativamente a la ineficiencia global de la economía y de la cual el país aún no se

---

3. El reciente Informe Meltzer es muy crítico de ciertas formas de financiamiento externo oficial que no sólo han brindado malos préstamos sino que los han continuado ante malas políticas, fortaleciendo el argumento del riesgo moral. O sea, brindar ayuda sin transformaciones significativas alienta conducta inapropiadas.

ha recuperado. El Informe Meltzer señala varias formas en que la ayuda externa, aún la proveniente de los organismos financieros internacionales, suele hacer más daño que bien. En cambio, Chile utilizó apropiadamente la ayuda externa oficial en los años ochenta para realizar transformaciones económicas y sociales fundamentales, por lo que hoy día prácticamente no la requiere, o sea se "graduó" de ella.

Actualmente Cuba está recibiendo remesas familiares equivalentes a aproximadamente el 3% del PIB y que podrían significar cerca del 12% del PIB dependiendo de la tasa de cambio que se emplee para valorizar el PIB cubano:

En última instancia, el problema de la falta de desarrollo de la economía cubana se debe principalmente a su falta de competitividad internacional determinada por su ineficiente organización productiva e institucional y sus deficientes políticas económicas, y no al embargo y a la falta de acceso al financiamiento externo. Dado el bajo nivel del comercio internacional del país, el total de exportaciones e importaciones de bienes y servicios sólo alcanzan al 34% del PIB, la pérdida de ingreso determinada por la desviación del comercio internacional por el embargo es compensada por el elevado monto de las remesas familiares. Además, es difícil justificar la condonación total o parcial de la deuda externa y restablecer el financiamiento externo oficial, mientras Cuba no se haya comprometido con un programa serio, confiable y transparente de transformación de su economía para recuperarse, crecer y reinsertarse efectivamente en la economía global. Las autoridades cubanas aún no están conscientes de los beneficios del funcionamiento de los mercados y de la globalización en un mundo cada vez más interdependiente, como vehículos para impulsar el crecimiento y avanzar en la reducción de la pobreza endémica, si actúan proactivamente con seriedad y persistencia.

Yet progress can be achieved only if there is growth.

— Grzegorz W. Kolodko, (2000, p. 7).

LOS DESAFÍOS DE LA MODERNIZACIÓN, LA SOSTENIBILIDAD DEL AUMENTO, Y LA EFICIENCIA INTERNA Y EXTERNA DEL GASTO SOCIAL PARA CUBA Y AMÉRICA LATINA

En la actualidad la región enfrenta una economía internacional muy dinámica, competitiva, y con muchas áreas poco reguladas, liderada por la economía norteamericana en un crecimiento sostenido sin precedentes y un marcado cambio tecnológico aplicado a la actividad económica, en un entorno con otros cambios estructurales y cualitativos importantes. Entre estos últimos destacan la reducción de la tasa de crecimiento demográfica, una expectativa de vida cada vez mayor, cambios en los métodos de adquisición, acumulación y difusión de conocimientos, en el desarrollo de nuevas medicinas, y de nuevas técnicas de aprendizaje y de resolver problemas. Por ello. los requerimientos de los gastos sociales son diferentes a los de hace una década.

Por ejemplo, Chile ha incorporado a los estudiantes de educación pública media a la internet y está haciendo ingentes esfuerzos por incorporar también a todos los estudiantes de educación pública básica a la internet antes del año 2006, captando así la imaginación y energía de los chilenos que consideran que el acceso a la información, la tecnología, el conocimiento y al desarrollo para actuar con ellos potencian mejor a los estudiantes. Además, Chile está modificando sustancialmente la duración de la jornada escolar, los currículos y las metodologías de enseñanza, en especial de ciencias (matemáticas, física, química y biología).

Hay un consenso que considera que es muy importante lograr y mantener altos niveles de gastos en los sectores sociales, debido a que la inversión en capital humano es muy rentable socialmente e indispensable para una apropiada inserción internacional y combatir la pobreza. La Cumbre Mundial para el Desarrollo Social de Copenhagen de marzo de 1995, sostuvo que sería posible alcanzar la meta de cobertura universal de los servicios sociales básicos en todos y cada uno de los países en desarrollo si destinaban un 20% de los presupuestos públicos a los servicios sociales básicos. La iniciativa considera que la entrega de estos servicios es una de las maneras más eficientes y costo-efectivas de combatir las más extremas manifestaciones de la pobreza, y que se podría lograr el acceso universal a esos servicios en un plazo ambicioso, pero factible, mediante la reorientación de los recursos existentes, la movilización de nuevos recursos y el aumento de la eficacia en la entrega de servicios sociales básicos en función de costos, eficiencia y calidad.

Dado que los requerimientos de gastos sociales son significativos y mayores que los recursos disponibles, la región ha comenzado a prestar una creciente atención a la calidad de gestión orientada a resultados, a la eficiencia interna y externa de los gastos sociales en general y al costo efectividad de los gastos sociales en particular, o sea al porcentaje de aumento de los resultados específicos en relación con el porcentaje de aumento de los gastos sociales. Ello con el fin de racionalizar la asignación los recursos disponibles para que logren mayores resultados y respondan más flexible y apropiadamente al nuevo entorno.

Algunos países de la región, particularmente Chile, están reduciendo los gastos públicos directos en la inversión y mantenimiento en infraestructura de servicios públicos —tales como: energía eléctrica, gas, telefonía y telecomunicaciones, agua potable, alcantarillado, carreteras, aeropuertos, puertos, etc— mediante la privatización de estos servicios o mediante concesiones de los mismos, con el fin de liberar recursos públicos para canalizarlos a los sectores sociales, en especial para incorporar las nuevas tecnologías de la información. No obstante, como se indicó antes, en economías donde el porcentaje de los gastos sociales como proporción del PIB es ya elevado, la forma más expedita y sostenible de gastar más en lo social es expandiendo la economía y el PIB real por habitante. Por ello, la sostenibilidad de un mayor gasto social en el largo plazo depende fundamentalmente de un mayor producto por habitante.

También, la eficiencia externa o la relevancia efectiva respecto al entorno de los gastos sociales es muy importante; así en economías con elevados niveles de desempleo en ciertas profesiones u ocupaciones, se cuestionan la rentabilidad social de los gastos educativos en ellas. Por ejemplo, muchos universitarios y técnicos especializados en Cuba prefieren no ejercer sus profesiones porque están mal pagadas, muy reguladas y presentan superávits debido a la organización productiva e institucional del país, en cambio deciden ejercer otras actividades que están mejor pagadas y no están tan reguladas dada la organización vigente.

El aumento del gasto en educación en general depende en última instancia de si la economía está en expansión o no. En una economía en expansión, el gasto en educación es rentable, mientras que en una economía en contracción, el gasto educación puede considerarse excesivo. Sin embargo, en términos de las perspectivas de crecimiento de mediano y largo plazo de la economía cubana y de su reinserción a la economía internacional, es necesario mantener los gastos en educación a los niveles logrados anteriormente. De lo contrario se caería en el circulo vicioso de que porque la economía no crece no se justifica el gasto en educación, lo que contribuirá a que la economía no crezca en el futuro.

CONCLUSIONES Y CONSIDERACIONES FINALES (¿SE REQUIERE MÁS DE LO MISMO O ALGO DIFERENTE?)

El IDH de Cuba era de desarrollo humano alto y ocupaba la séptima posición de la región en 1987; en contraste en 1997, el IDH de Cuba era de desarrollo humano medio y ocupaba la duodécima posición de la región. En 1987 Cuba tenía la segunda esperanza de vida y la segunda tasa de alfabetización en la región. Los índices de resultados sociales de Cuba en 1997 habían descendido, pero todavía estaban entre los más elevados o medios de la región: la esperanza de vida era la tercera, la tasa de alfabetización de adultos era la sexta y la tasa bruta de matriculación era la décima. El PIB real por habitante que ya era bajo en 1987, ocupando la décimo tercera posición de 20 países de la región, ocupó la vigésima primera posición y sólo es mayor al de otros 5 países en 1997. Esta situación muestra la situación de empobrecimiento del cubano y establece dudas sobre la sustentabilidad de los logros sociales alcanzados.

El gasto social real por habitante de Cuba se redujo significativamente (12%) en la década de los noventa, asociado a la contracción económica que determinó que el PIB real por habitante sufriera una fuerte disminución (2.6% anual), la mayor de la región después de la de Haití. Por ello, la contracción de la economía cubana en la década de los noventa explica la totalidad del retroceso en el gasto social por habitante, el cual fue compensado parcialmente por el aumento en la proporción del gasto social en relación al PIB del 21.7% al 23.0%.

El crecimiento económico en los años noventa explica el 71% y el 54% del aumento del gasto social por habitante registrado en los países de la región con niveles altos y medio-altos de gasto social por habitante, respectivamente.

A una tasa de cambio ponderada realista (US\$1=CU\$4), los gastos sociales reales por habitante de Cuba pasan de niveles medio-altos en América Latina (ligeramente inferiores a los Costa Rica, Chile y Panamá) a niveles bajos (similares a los de El Salvador, Paraguay, Bolivia y República Dominicana) y en cualquier caso están por debajo del promedio de la región. Esto concuerda conque el producto real por habitante de Cuba, medido por la paridad del poder adquisitivo, es bajo en la región; la marcada contracción del número de estudiantes matriculados en educación secundaria y terciaria en 1990-1996, así como los modestos gastos en vivienda y servicios comunales, en reparación y mantenimiento de servicios sanitarios (agua potable y alcantarillado) y de servicios urbanos (recogida de desechos, control de plagas y limpieza de calles) en la década de los noventa.

Posiblemente los índices de resultados sociales altos y medios de Cuba reflejen los altos niveles de gastos sociales del país en la década de los ochenta y no la eficiencia del nivel de gastos sociales que realiza en la actualidad. Además, como señala la CEPAL (1998), dichos resultados reflejan un uso más intenso de las instalaciones y del equipamiento existentes, situación que no es realista ni deseable y que es insostenible en el largo plazo.

Es muy probable que en el futuro el IDH y el nivel de gasto social real por habitante de Cuba continúen disminuyendo su posición relativa en la región, al menos mientras el país no recupere su crecimiento económico y supere su autoinfligido estrangulamiento externo. Al respecto, Cuba requiere un proceso de crecimiento alto y sostenible que permita expandir y

mejorar la calidad de los servicios sociales básicos y los ingresos de la población para así mejorar el nivel y la calidad de vida, superar la pobreza endémica y brindar mayor igualdad de oportunidades a los ciudadanos. Adicionalmente, es imprescindible que Cuba modernice los gastos sociales en esta época de rápido cambio tecnológico mundial, en especial los referentes a instalaciones y equipamiento en tres áreas sociales básicas (educación, salud y vivienda) que influyen decisivamente en el nivel y la calidad de vida de los ciudadanos.

Los sectores sociales de Cuba presentan un conjunto de problemas y debilidades importantes que requieren ajustes mayores o reformas en las políticas sociales, entre los cuales se destacan los siguientes:

- El gasto real en educación por habitante se redujo marcadamente (un 29%) en 1990-1999, habiéndose reducido la matrícula en educación media y terciaria en un 27% y un 57%, respectivamente en 1989-1997. Se detuvo la expansión de la educación preescolar, hay carencia de materiales y útiles que afectan la calidad de los servicios prestados y el equipamiento y laboratorios no se reponen ni actualizan.

- El gasto real en salud por habitante aumentó un 4% en 1990-1999 en parte porque el sector ha sido capaz de financiar directamente sus necesidades de divisas. Los componentes de recursos humanos e infraestructura hospitalaria continuaron aumentando, mientras que los gastos en medicinas y equipamiento se redujeron, lo que plantea un problema de distorsiones y proporciones óptimas de factores para brindar los servicios requeridos a la población.

- El gasto real en vivienda y servicios comunales por habitante es muy bajo (CU\$59 en 1999) y enfrenta un abultado y creciente déficit habitacional acumulado por años, de aproximadamente un millón de viviendas, así como deterioradas condiciones sanitarias (mantenimiento, reparación e inversión en acueductos y alcantarillados) y servicios urbanos (recolección de desechos, limpieza de calles y control de plagas) con sus serias implicaciones para la salud.

- El gasto en seguridad social real por habitante disminuyó en un 4% en 1990-1999, cubriendo más personas aunque con menor ingreso real por jubilado. El sistema de seguridad social presenta un déficit del orden del 2.5% del PIB por su generosidad y porque se ha empleado como instrumento compensatorio para enfrentar la crisis económica de los noventa.

- Los ingresos reales por habitante sufrieron un severo retroceso en los años noventa, ya que el salario real promedio se redujo en un 41% en el período 1990-1996. Un índice simple de productividad media por empleado mostró una reducción del 15.3% en 1989-1999, la causa subyacente del empobrecimiento y la caída del ingreso real.

- La desigualdad en la distribución del ingreso de Cuba debe haber aumentado marcadamente en la década de los noventa, porque sólo cerca de un tercio de la población tiene acceso a los empleos mejor remunerados, asociados a las actividades de los bienes transables, y a los ingresos de las remesas del exterior.

- Adicionalmente a los problemas señalados de los sectores sociales, la modernización, la sostenibilidad del aumento, y la mejoría de la eficiencia interna y externa de los gastos sociales presentan marcados desafíos a las autoridades cubanas para enfrentar un mundo con importantes cambios tecnológicos y demográficos. Cuba está acumulando una importante deuda social. Es necesario superar la inmediatez, la rigidez, la reacción y los falsos dilemas. Se requiere algo diferente, ser más proactivos y no seguir brindando más de lo mismo.

BIBLIOGRAFIA

José F. Alonso, Ricardo Donate-Armada y Armando Lago," A First Aproximation Design of the Social Safety Net for a Democratic Cuba" en *Cuba in Transition—Volume 4*, Washington: Association for the Study of the Cuban Economy, 1994, pp 88-154.

Rolando H. Castañeda, "Una Opción por la Libertad, el Desarrollo y la Paz Social" en *Cuba in Transition—Volume 1*, Miami: Florida International University, 1991, pp 257-308.

Rolando H. Castañeda, "Apreciación y Análisis de los Aciertos y Mitos del Estudio de la CEPAL" en *Cuba in Transition—Volume 9*, Washington: Association for the Study of the Cuban Economy, 1998, pp 114-129.

Rolando H. Castañeda, "Cuba y los Antiguos Países Socialistas de Europa: La importancia de los Aspectos Institucionales y de Economía Política en la Transición del Socialismo a una Economía de Mercado" en *Cuba in Transition—Volume 9*, Washington: Association for the Study of the Cuban Economy, 1999, pp 224-243.

Comisión Económica para América Latina y el Caribe (CEPAL), *La Economía Cubana: Reformas estructurales y desempeño en los noventa*, México: Fondo de Cultura Económica, 1998.

Comisión Económica para América Latina y el Caribe (CEPAL), *Panorama Social de América Latina, 1998*, Santiago de Chile, 1999a.

Comisión Económica para América Latina y el Caribe (CEPAL), *Cuba: Evolución Económica durante 1998*, LC/MEX/L392, 24 de agosto de 1999b.

Comisión Económica para América Latina y el Caribe (CEPAL), *Indicadores Básicos de la Subregión Norte de América Latina y el Caribe*, LC/MEX/L387, 10 de agosto de 1999c.

Comisión Económica para América Latina y el Caribe (CEPAL), *La Brecha por La Equidad: una se-*

gunda evaluación, Santiago de Chile, 15 al 17 de mayo de 2000a.

Comisión Económica para América Latina y el Caribe (CEPAL), *Cuba: Evolución Económica durante 1999*, LC/MEX/L441 26 de julio de 2000b.

Ricardo Donate-Armada, "Cuban Social Security: A Preliminary Actuarial Analysis of Law #24 of Social Security" en *Cuba in Transition—Volume 4*, Washington: Association for the Study of the Cuban Economy, 1994, pp 155-173.

Grzegorz W. Kolodko, *From Shock to Therapy*, New York: Oxford University Press, 2000.

Carmelo Mesa Lago, "ECLAC's Report on the Cuban Economy in the 1990's" en *Cuba in Transition—Volume 8*, Washington: Association for the Study of the Cuban Economy, 1998, pp 130-133.

Lorenzo L. Pérez, "The Pension System of Cuba: The Current Situation and Implications of International Pension Reform Experiences for Addressing Cuba's Problems en *Cuba in Transition—Volume 8*, Washington: Association for the Study of the Cuban Economy, 1998, pp 520-534.

Programa de Naciones Unidas para el Desarrollo (PNUD), *Human Development Report*, 1990, New York: Oxford. University Press, 1990.

Programa de Naciones Unidas para el Desarrollo (PNUD), *Informe de Desarrollo Humano 1999*, Madrid, España: Mundi-Prensa Libros, S.A. 1999.

José Luis Romeu, "More on the Statistical Comparison on Cuban Socioeconomic Development" en *Cuba in Transition—Volume 5*, Washington: Association for the Study of the Cuban Economy, 1995, pp 293-301.

THE INTERNATIONALIZATION
OF COLLECTIVE BEHAVIOR: LESSONS FROM ELIAN

Benigno E. Aguirre

Despite the enormous economic crisis experienced by Cuba in the aftermath of the 1989 disappearance of the Soviet Union, the systems of social control in the island have been very effective in minimizing the number of people who participate in political protests, the number and variety of places in the society in which these overt political acts have occurred, and the institutions of civil society which would provide support for political alternatives. It has virtually eliminated all iconic dissident leaders and rendered very difficult all communication and coordination among members of dissident groups and publics. The system has also succeeded in reducing the degree of conceptual sophistication of the ideologies of resistance articulating the values and goals of the political dissidence, the knowledge of these ideologies among Cubans, their awareness of governmental abuse, and the ability of dissidents to claim ownership of the central constitutive historical experiences, beliefs, values and myths of the nation.

The above-mentioned list of successes is not due solely to the operation of formal social control mechanisms, despite their effectiveness. Instead, as is true to some extent in all societies (Boudon and Bourricaud, 1989, 331-333), they are to a significant although unknown extent the result of a broader effort to transform Cuba's society and culture on behalf of an ideology that justifies the continued political domination of the state by the present day regime.

In a comparative international context, Cuba is in a pre-transitional political stage in which civil society is undeveloped (O'Donnell et al., 1986; Munck, 1994;

Baloyra, 1993; Puerta, 1996). Cuba's political dynamics are very different from that of East Germany and Czechoslovakia in 1989, in which the worker brigades refused to back the police against the demonstrators (A. Oberschall, personal correspondence; see Dahrendorf, 1990). Absent in it are the political opportunities that come with the end of state repression, as in the case in Hungary and Poland during most of the communist period (Touring, 1983; Burrow and Lucks, 1992; Rothschild, 1993; for Russia see Duka et al., 1995; Yanitsky, 1993). In J. Kadar's Hungary the relative few that protested the political dictatorship were never a real threat to the state and were largely ignored by it (Szoboszlai, 1991; Gombar et al., 1994; Hanak, 1991, pp. 213-223). Kadar's government kept a close reign on the state security system, never allowing it to have operational autonomy. Poland's experience during the Solidarity period of the 1980s is also quite similar in its relative near absence of official terror (Staniszkis, 1984).

Cuba is also dissimilar from the post-1956 Hungarian state in that Hungary made a clear distinction between the political and the private spheres of life, respecting the latter (Burawoy and Lukacs, 1992). Another important difference is that membership in the Hungarian communist party became a form of participation that many believed could be used to change the system. And when the end came in 1989, after Russian foreign policy failed to reestablish control of Central and Eastern Europe, the party was at the vanguard of the transformation and one of the most important factors favoring the Hungarian transition to democracy. In contrast, the Cuban Communist Party (CCP) does not represent such options. The CCP continues to oppose political change (*Granma*, 1996; Amuchastegui, 1997; Darling, 1997a; *Cubanet*, 1997b) and leads its mobilized supporters and members of the secret police in very effective acts of repression.

The system of domination is most effective in destroying independent associations and dissident leaders. It is least effective in controlling the emergence of a generalized culture of opposition to the government and the occurrence of relatively unorganized collective protests. Paradoxically, the very activities of repressing people have the largely unintended effect of creating similarities of experiences and collective awareness among them. It has also transformed the culture of the neighborhood, making the neighborhood identity an important facilitator of mobilization as people react against official actions. And more importantly for my present purpose, it cannot determine entirely the outcome of political processes in the international system.

As a way of partial summary, the continuing, effective repression and neutralization of social movement organizations by the state security systems, the dominance of the state-directed culture, the relative lack of independent associations and civil society, and the division of the opposition regarding strategies and tactics, make relative non-institutionalized collective behavior the primary means that the people of Cuba use to demand changes in the political system. It is the thesis of this paper that there is a dire need to internationalize collective behavior in and out of Cuba.

In view of these assumed facts, recent events show the appropriateness of a general strategy of guided social change that, while continuing to sponsor and support organized collectivities clamoring for social and political change in Cuba, would also concentrate on the mobilization of the Cuban community outside Cuba and the creation and enhancement of links between these democratic forces and international organizations and fora that would support a culture of opposition in the island and peaceful social change. While the time is not ripe for the establish-

ment of a pluralistic, democratic political system in Cuba, it is possible to prepare now the foundations for such change in the future. This preparation will involve much greater integration of the constituents of Cuba's culture of opposition to the international community working against the Castro dictatorship and for peaceful political change in the island.

LESSONS FROM ELIAN

The aforementioned considerations serve as backdrop to the Elian episode. Elian as symbol and historical episode has taught and clarified for us a number of important matters.

First, it shows the continued power of the Cuban state to organize and choreograph demonstrations throughout the island. Despite the well-known, documented increase in popular discontent in the island, the state apparatus continues to have power to mobilize people and to create collective behavior events akin to mass theater in which political ritual is enacted. The government continues to dominate the public space. Moreover, even a cursory examination of the rhetorical aspects of the Elian episode reveals Fidel Castro's political style.

Distinguished scholars like Antonio Benítez Rojo have begun to dissect Castro's rhetoric, which can be best understood through the use of the metaphor of *melodrama*. The formal aspects of melodrama as a genre of theater are well understood (Hatlen, 1992). In it, the action is centered on a grave conflict. There are tremendous difficulties of various natures, such as physical impairments, economic and material differences and exploitations, dangers and moral sufferings. Key to melodrama is the life and death struggle between good and evil. There is a villain and a morally pure, vulnerable victim. And then there is the hero, weak in material resources but a giant in virtue. As a process, melodrama never explores the psychological underpinnings of human action. Rather, it is in the development of external conflicts among them and the predictable resolution favoring the weak over the strong, the good over the bad. There are no surprises or historical developments, no escape into other forms of resolution, for the end result of the struggle is assured.

255

A working hypothesis of a paper now in preparation is that melodrama provides a useful metaphor to understand the unchanging deep structure of Fidel Castro's public speeches during more than 40 years in power. Elian represents the extension and enactment of this melodramatic theater style so successfully used by Castro in his public speeches to the area of international politics. Just as in the speeches, Fidel is the hero of the Elian melodrama, responding to the clamoring for justice of the Cuban people. The "Cuban mafia" in Miami is the villain. The victims are the young child and the mother, coerced by an unfeeling and perverse second husband to undergo the dangerous sea travel and kidnap her child. Alive still is the loving father deprived of the love and company of his cherished son. Reason and justice will prevail. The wrong will be righted, for as in all melodrama the victory of good over evil is a given. This is the interpretation of events that the propaganda system has made to prevail in Cuba and that gains credence in the U.S. through the operation of the U.S. mass media and the cooperation of the executive branch of the U.S. Federal Government.

The Elian episode shows the unchallenged totalitarian control of the country and the undiminished genius of Fidel Castro in selecting from the seemingly disorganized events of daily life a symbol that is amenable to treatment as *simulacra* in Jean Baudrillard's meaning of the term (Horrocks and Jevtic, 1997). Elian as simulacra allows the Cuban state to claim to be the protector of family values, a claim that is arguable, debatable, for many would say that it has never been concerned with such matters, much less a defender of parental rights over children.

It would take too long to document this fact, reflected in many well known instances, from the documented unpunished murder by government agents of many children in the sinking of the "13th of March" tugboat in the bay of Havana in 1994 to the official policy prohibiting parents to immigrate with their teenage children. Indeed, the precedence of the socialist state over the rights of parents towards their children is a basic principle of Cuba's legal system. Cuba's official constitution (see *Granma*, September 22, 1992) does not give the family institutional pre-

cedence in the socialization of children. Instead the family is one of a number of institutions so charged, to wit: "The family, the school, state organs, and mass organizations have the duty to give special attention to the total formation (*formación integral*) of children and youth (Chapter V, Article 40)." Likewise, Cuba's "Code of the Child" (Sicre-Rivas, 1978) reflects the emphasis on politics as a key principle of childhood socialization:

- The communist formation of the young generation is a valued aspiration of the state, the family, the teachers, the political organizations, and the mass organizations that act in order to foster in youth the ideological values of communism (Article 3).

- Society and the state watch to ascertain that all persons who come in contact with the child, constitute an example of the development of his communist personality (Article 5).

- The state grants special attention to the teaching of Marxism-Leninism due to its importance in the ideological formation and political culture of young people (Article 33).

These principles are periodically enforced. Recently, Mr. José Enrique Rives Peña and his wife, Mrs. Debora Cento Perna, were sanctioned to detention by the courts in the City of Camagüey, accused by the teacher of their young boy of opposing his ideological indoctrination and not performing their ideological duties as parents (*Diario Las Americas*, 24 March 2000).

Despite these ascertainable facts, it is undoubtedly true that, in a political sense, in the minds of most Americans the reality of the case is superseded by its simulacra representation as articulated by Mr. Castro. The many who in recent years have argued for the enfeeblement of Mr. Castro with advancing age are proven wrong by the Elian episode. Whatever the mechanisms of execution of the decisions of the Cuban elite — and we know only imperfectly how the top leadership's will is put into practice — the Elian episode shows both, that the system works quite efficiently in pursuit of state policy, and that at its most general it is a policy guided by the melodramatic instinct so quintessential to Castro's style of politics. Elian shows us that it is a grave mistake to base programs and policies on the presumed growing senility of Mr. Castro. Even if one is keenly aware, as I am, of the many serious crimes committed by Mr. Castro and others in his inner circle, it is nevertheless indispensable to carry out clearheaded and dispassionate examinations of his successes and failures. Instead of demonizing or ridiculing him, the objective should be to show his mode of operation and the systems and culture created to ensure the continuity of his regime.

Second, the Elian incident shows both, the contemporary ability of the Cuban state to manipulate the mass media in the United States in the furtherance of its simulacra interpretation, and the changed nature of the ideological discourse of American elites in the post-1989 period.

The Cuban state's power of manipulation is partly due to the widespread practice by the U.S. mass media of *naïve realism*, at its basis an ethnocentric view of how the world operates, denoting the tendency by the mass media to interpret the world using concepts and theories that have wide currency in American society to interpret and explain how reality operates outside it. Thus, the widely accepted view in civilized societies, with ample precedence in Roman Law, that parents have privileged rights over their children, is used to justify the claims of Elian's father while ignoring the political realities of such claim, the long history of its violation in Castro's Cuba, and its disastrous effects on Elian's freedom.

It is also due to the assiduous monitoring and sanctioning by the Cuban state of the operation and reporting of the news in Cuba by foreign journalists, to include their proscription from the island if their reporting is seen as unfriendly to the government and the consequent self censorship that most often ensues. This is a very important matter that just now is beginning to receive sustained attention.

To my way of thinking, however, the power of the Cuban state to manipulate the coverage of the news by the U.S. mass media, most recently in its mass agitation efforts surrounding the Elian incident, is due

most importantly to the transformations that have occurred in the operation of the mass media in the United States particularly since World War II. For purpose of analysis, it is useful to think of the mass media in the United States as a non-totalitarian *propaganda system*. This is Noam Chomsky's celebrated and in my estimation well-founded criticism of the industry (Herman and Chomsky, 1988). To justify it, he points to what are empirically irrefutable facts: (1) The decline in investigative journalism and the dependence of the mass media on the state and established organizations and institutions for the sources of news, rendering them vulnerable to manipulations and the production of "news" by public relations; (2) The concentration of the news media into a few giant organizations and their organizational integration into larger economic multi-industry corporate conglomerates, so that what they report as news is very much impacted and mediated by the economic interests of other segments of the conglomerate of which they are part; (3) The dependence on corporate sponsors for advertising and funding for special reports, acting to curtail the treatment and substance of "sensitive" mass media programs in the United States.

It is clear to me that changes in the ownership and operations of the U.S. mass media makes a significant proportion of the reporting of the news about Cuba much more malleable to the interests of the U.S. and Cuban states and the political elites of both countries. To give two examples that can be derived from Chomsky's critical analysis: since increasingly the U.S. mass media depends on the state and on established institutions and organizations to source its items of news, U.S. reporters in Cuba accept the sourcing of the news by the Cuban state as a normal part of doing their business, for it is after all standard operating procedures. Or to give another example, the corporate integration of the U.S. mass media organizations into large economic conglomerates with interests in Cuba render understandable the consistently politically biased, anti-Cuban exile reporting of the news by entities such as CNN and ABC.

Third, and very much implicated with the situation just described is the peculiar, ongoing ideological transformation in the United States in the post-1989 period. A tremendous lesson from Elian is what it tells us about the definite decline of the ideology of anti-communism in vogue during the Cold War period as applied to Cuba. Many other events in the last ten years have anticipated the turn of events during Elian, but not any one of them have shown with such clarity the new ideological climate emerging in the United States.

In a paradoxical and unexpected way, the disappearance of the Soviet Union threatens the ideological justification of the anti-Castro community. The ideology of anti-communism widely in vogue in the United States during much of the post-1958 period, gave support to the claims of the exile community in its struggle for a free Cuba. This support is now largely gone. In its place, a new ideology is emerging in the US and elsewhere in the developed world that, while continuing to cultivate nationalistic xenophobia, lends support to the expansion of international capital. In the United States, symptomatic of this passing is the effective abandonment of the long standing policy of asylum and the rendering void of the promise engraved in The Statue of Liberty, and its replacement with penal systems under the aegis of the Immigration and Naturalization Service that are acknowledged by Amnesty International and other influential organizations as constituting grave violations of human rights (Wilch, 2000).

Obviously, there are many variations and dimensions to this new ideology, often termed neo-liberalism, that should not be downplayed, such as the protection of the environment and human rights. Nevertheless, it would be a mistake not to emphasize that the search for profit drives the emergence of the new ideology, particularly in the case of Cuba. In it, calculations of possible profits in an invigorated Cuban market and perceived present-day competitive disadvantages to European corporate interests go a long way in explaining the motivations of American political and economic elites. In light of these changes, the Cuban exile community's continued use of the anti-communist ideology to justify its struggle against the Castro brothers is increasingly seen as anachronistic and reactionary by large segments of the American public, a public manipulated by the

propaganda that nowadays masquerades as news of Cuba in the United States.

The continuation of the anti-communist ideology and the continued absence of mobilization of the Cuban community in exile would mean that the ongoing ideological transformations will make the lifting of the U.S. embargo and sustained efforts in the United States to improve relationship with the Cuban government, even to the point of reestablishing diplomatic relations, a logical outcome during the next ten years irrespective of the national political party in power in the United States. Of course, it may be argued that the tremendous lack of isomorphism existing between the ethical dimensions of the emerging ideology of neo-liberalism and the Cuban government's persistent and grave violation of human rights would prevent such an outcome. I do not believe so. U.S. foreign policy in the 20th century is full of this sort of contradiction. Importantly, if and when it happens, it will be done in such a way so as to further the interest of the Castro-led Cuban elite in power. Ironically, to the surprise of most people in the United States and elsewhere that have a superficial understanding of political dynamics in Cuba, the greatest obstacle for these events to occur in the short term is not the U.S. but the Cuban government. Still, the increasing abandonment in the United States of a system of values that proclaimed freedom as its greatest hope for mankind means that in the new ideological dispensation increasingly dominant in the United States, "practical" considerations reign and accommodation with the Castro regime should be expected that would dispel its chronic fears of rapprochement.

Fourth, another important lesson that can be derived from the Elian episode is that it showed the continued vitality of the anti-Castro feeling among the vast majority of Cubans in the United States and elsewhere outside Cuba and the willingness of Cubans throughout the country to express their dismay at the actions of the federal government. Despite the systematic and overwhelming downplaying and misrepresentations of the community's actions by the American mass media, the show of support by the Cuban community in the United States for the

Gonzalez family, their massive protest strike in South Florida, their boycott of schools, their demonstrations in most major cities throughout the country, are unparalleled in the annals of the exile.

For years, social scientists at Florida International University and elsewhere argued that the culture of the exile community was changing and that the new generations were less militant, more willing to come to terms with Castro's political domination. Fidel Castro himself started to use the epithet "mafia" to signify the presumed remaining extremists, the small segment of the Cuban exiles still opposed to his government. Yet, the collective behavior of Cubans in the United States during the Elian episode shows all such thinking to be incorrect in some very important ways.

This theme of generational transformation is wrong because it ignored the power of family socialization and political indoctrination into an anti-totalitarian point of view. It is a socialization experience based not only on the direct observations by young Cubans of how people live in freedom, but also of the pain of their parents, their longing for their homeland, the collective sufferings of a nation, their struggles as a minority group in the United States, their pride, their hard work, their love for freedom. In a myriad ways, through witnessing the ongoing life-and-death struggle of escapees at sea, socialization into the language, the music, the norms and values, the rights and wrongs of being Cuban, children from Cuban families with no immediate experience of Cuba become Cuban. The community reproduces itself. It is obviously changed by births and deaths, for these children are in some very important ways socialized differently than their parents and grandparents. Yet, as Elian showed us, the political passion against Castro's government remain.

LOOKING TO THE FUTURE

If the foregoing analysis is correct, certain things need to be done at this juncture to improve the chances of peaceful change and the establishment of democracy in Cuba.

First and foremost, there is a dire need for the political leadership in the Cuban community to recognize the lessons from Elian and act accordingly. Clearly, Elian showed that the community must change its anti-communist ideological stance in ways that would make it more palatable to the larger American society. This change will demand inspired leadership. There are things that facilitate it. The socialist-inspired dream of the Cuban revolution died many years ago. What exists now is a dictatorship of a minority of the population over the majority under the aegis of the Cuban Communist Party.

This emphasis on the totalitarianism of the political system has gained us friends in Europe and elsewhere in the past and should be stressed in the future. The exile community needs to broadcast this message with renewed vigor. It is on the matter of violation of civil rights, the brutality of the social control systems, the absence of a multiparty political system, the destruction of the environment by government directives and programs, the racism and sexism and homophobia of the Cuban political system, the use of semi-slave labor in Cuba by foreign corporations that operate in the island, that our chances to mobilize world opinion in favor of democratic social change in Cuba are maximized.

Second, Elian also showed us the need for the increased practice of civil protest by Cubans in the United States. The 1990s saw the beginning of such practices in South Florida, but they must be increased and perfected. Saul D. Alinsky's justly famous book, *Rules for Radicals: A Practical Primer for Realistic Radicals* (1989), should become forced reading for every aspiring community leader and organizer, for the time is ripe for the mobilization of the community. There is a tremendous reservoir of spiritual and material resources in it that could be obtained for mobilization in the struggle against Castro if the right strategy and tactics are put in place, and Alinsky's monograph is the best place that I know of for guidance as to how to do it. For example, it is conceivable that boycotts against products of companies in the industrial conglomerates to which key U.S. mass media organizations belong that consistently misrepresent the Cuban community could be used to exert pressure on them to change their reporting practices and make them more objective.

Similarly, boycotts and other acts of protest could be organized against international corporations that use semi-slave labor in Cuba.

I cannot think of a more important remaining matter to prepare for a political transition in Cuba than the organization of the exile community and its integration to the dissidence, the Catholic Church, other segments of the emerging civil society, and other unorganized manifestations of alternative culture in the island. Clearly, the organization of the community and its participation in civil disobedience outside Cuba must be guided overwhelmingly if not solely by the expressed needs of the people of Cuba in Cuba. In other words, the struggle should not be directed primarily to change U.S. society or to improve the living conditions of Cubans in the United States but rather to change practices in the United States and elsewhere to facilitate the coming of freedom to Cuba. Obviously, from a tactical point of view, the ideal situations that should be selected to bring about mobilization and the civil disobedience of Cubans in the United States and elsewhere will combine the grievances of Cubans generated by their living in these societies with the aspirations and needs of Cubans in the island.

Third, Elian reminded us about the sociological truism that people do not live in an unmediated world. Rather, they live in the world that they construct symbolically. And in the battle of symbols that Elian brought about the exile community lost. Elian showed us that in the future war of symbols we must choose our battles much more carefully than we did in Elian and we must go against the majority of the U.S. mass media and the propaganda it spreads. The only way to counter these effects is to use better propaganda. Thus, there is an immediate, dire need to systematically present a different view of the Cuban community to the rest of the country and to the Cuban people in the island. It is for this reason that all efforts must be made to improve the technical capability and programmatic sustainability of *Radio Martí*. The function of *Radio Martí* in bringing about information to the Cuban people is a critical part of any effort against the present day regime. The same is true of other smaller radio stations that operate as

parts of specific transnational movement organizations, such as *La Voz del CID*. There is also a very important need to create institutionalized means to systematically counter the anti Cuban exile propaganda in the United States.

More broadly, every effort should be made to improve communication and interaction between the people of Cuba and the rest of the world and in designing new mechanisms whereby such goal is maximized. The recent opposition in Miami to artistic groups from Cuba is a tactical error. It must be discontinued. Despite its anti-Castro rationale, in fact such collective protests run contrary to the needed improvement. True artists are always the creators of new styles and new ways of thinking, the harbingers of change. To oppose art and to curtail it is to commit moral suicide.

Similarly, irrespective of differences in political credo, all democratic forces willing to respect and abide in the future by the results of elections in a multiparty political system in Cuba must be financially supported and encouraged by the exile community. The recent difficulties of *Cubanet* created by the withdrawal of financial assistance by the U.S. federal government, and the continuing financial difficulties of important journals like *Disidente*, must not be allowed to continue. Instead, the community's resources must be mobilized to support these and other similar efforts to broadcast the situation of Cuba throughout the world. Again, it is totally unimportant as a basis for collective action what fellow Cubans may believe should be the precise form of government in a future Cuba. As long as they believe and respect democratic ideals, the desirability of free elections, and the need for a multiple party political system, they should receive support and assistance by the mobilized community.

Fourth, in the sociology of social movements there is the truism that organizational efforts that combine both public and private goods often work best. We need to think of ways of combining the maximization of both private and public goals. For example, at the present time an important private goal of many Cuban families is to send dollars to their relatives in Cuba. Indeed, foreign remittances are the most important source of hard currency for the Castro government and a very lucrative business (Alfonso, 2000). Still, however, there is a need to create a corporation, perhaps a not-for-profit entity, that would do the transferring of these funds and that also would, from its earnings, give grants to improve the quality of life of communities in Cuba, or would give financial support to organizations in Cuba and in the United States with an interest in furthering progressive peaceful social change in the island. In the post-embargo period, this and other types of activities would become possible and an activity for radicals in the spirit of Alinsky, with obvious benefits for the people of Cuba.

Fifth, Elian also revealed as few other times before it the relationship between national boundaries and national politics in the case of Cuba. True in the past and increasingly so in the future, anti-hegemonic political collective action by Cubans in and out of Cuba is not a national but an international process. As is the case in other social movements in the United States and elsewhere (McCarthy and Zald, 1977), events in Cuba and South Florida often coincide with political sensitivities and agendas of agencies and organizations that are distant from the place of action. Distal political participatory events occur as reflections of events elsewhere. This is a key reality embodied by Elian that all community leaders and organizers must attend to in the future.

The international nature of politics is maximized by the new means of electronic communication. Despite many attempts, the system of government control and repression has been incapable of stopping dissidents' use of the new electronic means of communication and their forging relationship with international associations. There is a very effective censorship of the Internet inside Cuba. Nevertheless, the new electronic means of communication are playing a key part in energizing and transforming the organizations and affinity groups that are part of Cuba's culture of opposition. They have also proven very important in informing the world about unplanned collective protests such as the August 5, 1994 protest in Havana.

In Cuba, while most people do not have access to the Internet, they have access to the recently improved international telephone services. Increasingly, they also have organizational representatives and cooperating organizational affiliates and representatives outside Cuba that have access to the Internet. They are key sources of organizational resources that must be strengthened (not unrelatedly, the e-mail addresses of members of Amnesty International's Urgent Action Network are distributed outside Cuba among supporters of the Cuban organizations to facilitate their appeals to AI for help).

Examples abound. A few years ago the Partido Acción Nacionalista (Nationalist Action Party) had three representatives in Miami and Costa Rica (*Cubanet*, 1997a). Movimiento Humanista Evolucionario Cubano (Cuban Evolutionary Humanist Movement) circulates its telephone, e-mail address (MHEC@compuserve.com) and home page in the Web (http://ourworld.compuserve.com/homepages/mhec), as does Hermanos al Rescate (Brothers to the Rescue, http://www.hermanos.org) and Partido Demócrata Cristiano de Cuba (Christian Democratic Party of Cuba, http://www.pdc-cuba.org), to mention three well-known organizations operating in Cuba and elsewhere. A number of organized members of the culture of opposition act as clearing houses of information on the action of state security and other events in the island. Among them are the Cuban Information Center, the Bureau of Independent Journalists, and the Information Bureau of the Human Rights Movement in Cuba. Once contacted via telephone, these transnational organizational resources broadcast their needs, experiences and information to other Cubans via radio as well as to members of the international community. Using this simple communication system, independent journalists in Cuba devoid of access to the Internet, facsimile machines or office equipment other than antiquated typewriters practice their profession. Likewise, individual Cuban citizens report events and state actions.

News about events affecting a community, group, or person travels around the world before neighbors hear about it. Despite the distance, nowadays they are much more likely to hear about it than in the past. An excellent example of this process is the convocation by the "Comité Cubano Pro Derechos Humanos" (Committee for Human Rights) of the population in the municipalities of Güines, Nueva Paz, Nicolás de Bari, Güira de Melena, and others in the Mayabeque region in the Province of Havana, to attend a religious rally in the Chapel of Santa Barbara, in the City of Güines, on December 4, 1991, to pray for the democratization of the country. Cuban activists sent the invitation to Cuban Catholic priests in Miami, Florida. The priests were asked to broadcast it to Cuba through Radio Martí, La Voz del CID, and the Voz de la Fundación.

State actions are known that in the past were unknown by most people. This includes rumors of political infighting within the Cuban Communist Party and among the highest authorities of the government as well as knowledge of political mobilizations (LAT 92-188; LAT 92-146). The new electronic system also makes it possible, for example, for interested persons outside Cuba to double-check with their contacts in Havana the truthfulness of reports circulating outside Cuba of bombings of public buildings and have the information divulged worldwide in a matter of hours after the initiation of the request. Recently, at least one independent journalist advertised his services to the public; and in an unusual twist, an underground activist actively being searched for by state security used the system to ask for international protection before his capture. It also makes it possible for people to communicate to the general public information on the abuses done by individual agents of state security, the names of the victims and the likely place of their imprisonment in the island.

The dependence of organized members of Cuba's opposition on transnational organizational partners existed prior to 1989. What is new in the post-1989 period is the enormous power of the Internet to broadcast their appeal and to mobilize their constituencies outside Cuba. Its impact on Cuba and on the Cuban community in Europe and the United States is hard to overestimate. The new electronic system neutralizes governmental secrecy, improves the accuracy and timeliness of the ongoing monitoring of the Cuban state and helps people evaluate their interpretations of events and coordinate their actions.

These examples argue for the existence of a transnational political dynamic. The collective actions that occur in Cuba and among Cubans in South Florida, Puerto Rico, and other communities of the Cuban Diaspora must be understood in light of this recently emergent transnational political reality that is facilitated in large part by the new means of mass communication. The strengthening of transnational organizational links should be a priority for community organizing.

The importance of these processes and mechanisms is obvious. Irrespective of their political credo, every effort should be made by the community to help independent journalists in Cuba as well as the organizations and social movement affiliates that actively broadcast and monitor the situation inside the island.

Elian is thus challenge and promise. Challenge to abandon the wrong policies and beliefs of the past. Promise in that it shows what we are capable of doing to help our brothers and sisters. In this effort a spirit of inclusiveness must pervade our actions. Even democratic communists and socialists must be encouraged. In some respects, they have been among the most victimized.

REFERENCES

Alfonso, Pablo. 2000. "Reconocen la importancia de remesas familiares." *El Nuevo Herald*, 15 de marzo.

Alinsky, Saul D. 1989. *Rules for Radicals: A Practical Primer for Realistic Radicals.* New York: Vintage Books.

Alinsky, Saul D. 1991. *Reveille for Radicals.* Vintage Books.

Amuchastegui, Domingo. 1994. "Rioting on the Malecon: Castro's Response." *Cubanews,* vol. 2 (September): 9.

Amuchastegui, Domingo. 1995a. "Election Analysis: State Wins but Opposition Trend Emerges." *Cubanews,* vol. 3 (9): 8.

Amuchastegui, Domingo. 1995b. "Authorities Brace for Vote." *Cubanews,* (July): 10.

Amuchastegui, Domingo. 1997. "Discipline, Corruption Issues for Party Congress." *Cubanews,* (June): 6.

Baloyra, E. 1993. "Socialist Transitions and Prospects for Change in Cuba." Pp. 38-66 in E. A. Baloyra and J. A. Morris, editors. *Conflict and Change in Cuba.* Albuquerque: University of New Mexico Press.

Burawoy, M. and J. Lukacs. 1992. *The Radiant Past: Ideology and Reality in Hungary's Road to Capitalism.* Chicago: The University of Chicago Press.

Cubanet. 1997a. "Entrevista a Aguileo Cancio Chong, presidente de Partido Acción Nacionalista." 16 Junio.

Cubanet. 1997b. "Falsos debates de documento partidista en Cuba." 5 Julio.

Boudon, R. and F. Bourricaud. 1989. *A Critical Dictionary of Sociology.* Chicago: University of Chicago Press.

Dahrendorf, R. 1990. *Reflections on the Revolution in Europe.* New York: Random House.

Darling, J. 1997a. "Documento del PCC mantiene modelo estalinista." *El Nuevo Herald,* 25 de Mayo.

Gombar, C., E. Hankiss, L. Lengyel, G. Varnai. 1994. Editors. *Balance, the Hungarian Government, 1990-1994.* Budapest: Korridor Books.

Granma. 1996. "El trabajo del Partido en la actual coyuntura," 15 Agosto.

Hanak, P., editor. 1991. *The Corvina History of Hungary.* Budapest: Corvina Books.

Hatlen, Theodore W. 1992. *Orientation to the Theater.* New Jersey: Englewood Cliffs.

Herman, E. S. and N. Chomsky. 1988. *Manufacturing Consent.* New York: Pantheon Books.

Horrocks, C. and Z. Jevtic. 1997. *Introducing Baudrillard.* New York: Totem Books.

LAT 92-146. 1992. "Reports of anti government mobilization denied." July 28.

LAT 92-188. 1992. "Aldana's future to be decided shortly." September 28.

McCarthy, J. D. 1995. "Mobilizing Structures: Constraints and Opportunities in Adopting, Adapting and Inventing." In McAdam, D., J. D. McCarthy and M. Zald, *Comparative Perspectives on Social Movements: Opportunities, Mobilizing Structures and Cultural Framings.* New York: Cambridge University Press.

McCarthy, J. D. and M. N. Zald. 1977. "Resource Mobilization and Social Movements: A Partial Theory." *American Sociological Review,* Vol. 82 (6): 1212-1241.

Munck, G. L. 1994. "Democratic Transitions in Comparative Perspective." *Comparative Politics,* Vol. 26 (3): 355-375.

O'Donnell, Guillermo and P. C. Schmitter. 1986. *Transitions from Authoritarian Rule. Tentative Conclusions about Uncertain Democracies.* Baltimore: The John Hopkins University Press.

Puerta, Ricardo. 1995. *Sociedad Civil y el Futuro de Cuba.* Coral Gables, Florida: Coordinadora Social Demócrata de Cuba.

Puerta, Ricardo. 1996. "Sociedad civil en Cuba." Pp. 1-57 in R. Puerta and M. Donate Armada, *Ensayos Políticos.* Coral Gables, Florida, Coordinadora Demócrata de Cuba.

Rothschild, J. 1993. *Return to Diversity: A Political History of East Central Europe Since World War II.* New York: Oxford University Press.

Sicre-Rivas, Alfredo A. 1978. *Codigo de la niñez y la juventud.* La Habana, Cuba: Instituto Cubano del Libro, segunda edición.

Staniszkis, Jadwiga. 1984. *Poland's Self-Limiting Revolution.* Princeton, New Jersey: Princeton University Press.

Szoboszlai, G. (Ed.). 1991. *Democracy and Political Transformation: Theories and East-Central Euro-*

pean Realities. Budapest: Hungarian Political Science Association.

Wilch, Matthew. 2000. "Detect, detain, deter, deport." *Refugees,* volume 2 (119): 14-21.

Yanitsky, O. 1993. *Russian Environmentalism: Leading Figures, Facts, Opinions.* Moscow: Mezhdunarodnyje Otnoshenija Publishing House.

THE LAST WAVE: CUBA'S CONTEMPORARY EXODUS — POLITICAL OR ECONOMIC IMMIGRANTS?

Silvia Pedraza[1]

The Cuban exodus is now over 41 years old and has brought close to a million Cuban immigrants to American soil — about 12 percent of the Cuban population. That exodus harbors distinct waves of immigrants, alike only in their final rejection of Cuba. The focus of this paper is on the exodus of Cubans in the nineties during what Castro himself called "*el período especial*" — the special period that resulted when the collapse of communism in the Soviet Union and Eastern Europe meant the end of the Soviet subsidy that Cuba had received for nearly 30 years. This research is part of a larger research project on the Cuban exodus and the Cuban revolution that began on the heels of the revolutionary transformation of Cuban society in 1959 and that, while intermittent, has never ceased and is ongoing still in the present. The goal of my research is to capture the processes of political disaffection of participants in this major historical drama, emphasizing the contrasts along the four major waves of the exodus not only in their social characteristics but also in their attitudes as members of different political generations.

To establish the characteristics of this last wave, however, I often need to contrast it to earlier waves. Hence, I will first briefly depict the differences between the 4 major waves of the exodus.

Each of the 4 major waves of the Cuban exodus has been characterized by a very different social composi-

tion with respect to their social class, race, education, gender and family composition, and values — differences that resulted from the changing phases of the Cuban revolution. They render the Cuban community in the U.S. today an extremely heterogeneous one, not only in terms of the dramatic contrasts in their social characteristics but also in terms of their processes of political disaffection as what E. F. Kunz (1973) called "vintages" — "refugee groups that are distinct in character, background, and avowed political faith" (p. 137).

WAVES OF MIGRATION

Nelson Amaro and Alejandro Portes (1972) portrayed the different phases of the Cuban political immigration as changing over time with the exiles' principal motivation for their decision to leave. With the unfolding of the Cuban revolution, they argued, over the years "those who wait" gave way to "those who escape," and they to "those who search." To update their analysis, I added "those who hope" and "those who despair" (Pedraza 1996).

The immigrants of the first wave (1959-1962) were Cuba's elite: executives and owners of firms, big merchants, sugar mill owners, cattlemen, representatives of foreign companies, and professionals. They left Cuba when the revolution overturned the old social order through measures such as the nationalization of American industry and agrarian reform laws, and the

---

1. This research project was supported by the American Sociological Association's Fund for the Advancement of the Discipline (1995-96) and by the University of Michigan's Horace H. Rackham School of Graduate Studies' Faculty Grant and Fellowship (1997-99).

United States severed all ties. "Those who wait" characterized these first refugees that came imagining that exile would be temporary, waiting for American help to overthrow Cuba's new government. After the fiasco of the exiles' Bay of Pigs invasion (April 1961), the exodus doubled and "those who escape" constituted the second phase. Castro called them counter-revolutionaries — *gusanos* (worms).

The second wave of migration (1965-1974) arrived through the air bridge which resulted when the United States and Cuba negotiated the orderly departure of Cubans. "Those who search" characterized this wave of migration that Alejandro Portes, Juan Clark, and Robert Bach (1977) studied, a wave that was largely composed of *la petite bourgeoisie*: cooks, gardeners, domestics, street vendors, barbers, hairdressers, taxi drivers, and small merchants who left Cuba when Castro launched a new "revolutionary offensive" in Cuba, confiscating over 55,000 small businesses (Mesa-Lago 1978).

With the economic transition to socialism effected, in the 1970s the Cuban government cast the shape of the political system — an institutionalization during which Cuba took on the features of Eastern European communism. The old idealism and romanticism of the 1960s gave way to what Carmelo Mesa-Lago (1978) called pragmatism. In 1978, a Dialogue took place between the Cuban government and the Cuban community in exile as a result of which the Cuban government agreed to the release of political prisoners and to promote the reunification of families by allowing Cubans in the U. S. to visit their families in Cuba. Those visits were partly responsible for the third wave — the chaotic flotilla exodus from the harbor of Mariel in 1980. Towards the end of the outflow, this wave included Cuba's social undesirables, many of whom had been in prison (whether they were political prisoners, were common prisoners who had committed real crimes, or had only challenged the state). Castro called them *escoria* (scum).

The most salient characteristic of the *Marielitos* was their youth (most were young men single or without their families) and the visibly higher proportion of Blacks than ever. As Robert Bach's (1981/82) studies of the *Marielitos* highlighted, this last exodus was overwhelmingly working class, mostly composed of blue-collar workers. Along with them came a significant number of young intellectuals (the most famous of which was Reinaldo Arenas), who recognized themselves as belonging to a political generation that they themselves called *la generación del Mariel* (the Mariel generation), and went on to found several journals. "Those who hope" might well characterize this wave.

Recently, the fourth wave of the Cuban exodus to the United States developed (it began around 1985 and deepened in the nineties). Cuba's economic crisis reached new depths when communism collapsed in the Soviet Union. Cuba's enormous dependence on the Soviet Union (cf. Mesa-Lago 1994) meant that when the latter disappeared, it brought about an economic crisis of such severity that Castro himself declared this a "*período especial*" — a special period that was to have been temporary, but coupled with the United States' tightening of the embargo in 1992, have made abject need and hunger a daily reality for Cubans. Indeed, Cubans became so desperate that they began leaving on *balsas* (rafts, tires, makeshift vessels) that drifted on the ocean, risking death due to starvation, dehydration, drowning, or sharks. Over 34,000 left just in the summer of 1994. "Those who despair" constituted this last wave of migration.

While the émigrés of the first two waves were those that became politically disaffected in the process of the transition from a democratic, capitalist society to a communist society, the *Marielitos* as well as the recent émigrés are those that, especially the young, became politically disaffected from the only society they ever knew — Cuba in communism. As such, they are the children of communism. At stake very often are different political generations. As defined by Karl Mannheim (1952), a political generation is constituted by individuals of approximately the same age who shared, in their coming of age (roughly the young adult years of 18-25), certain historical experiences that shaped their political outlook. For example, in the early sixties the dramatic social changes taking place in Cuba were those associated with the transition from capitalism to communism, while in the early eighties the enormous changes taking place in Cuba reflected the debates then raging within the communist world — *glassnost* and *perestroika*. Young people who lived through such distinctly different stages of the history of Cuba and the revolution constitute different political generations.

While the exodus of Cubans have been studied from the point of view of the social and demographic characteristics of the various waves, it has hardly been studied from the point of view of the political attitudes of the émigrés. This is ironic for a community that defined itself as being in *exile*, and where — both in the island and outside of Cuba — participants in this major drama thought of themselves as belonging to different political communities.

POLITICAL COMMUNITIES

Living the revolution inside the island, joining the exodus that left the island, living *el exilio* (the exile) in Miami, being imprisoned for their political activities in Cuba, and being active in the dissident movement within Cuba entailed becoming a part of or exiting political communities that defined themselves against one another.

Those who chose to stay in Cuba integrated to the revolution ascended in social status but suffered the emotional loss of their family who left, though at times they also rejected and repudiated them. Those who chose the path of exile and left Cuba suffered not only the material loss of property and status but also the emotional loss of their memories and the community of peers with whom they had once shared their childhood, adolescence, or old age. Those who joined the dissident movement (that eventually emerged in Cuba as an organized political force in the mid 1980s) found themselves repudiated and shunned by even the most intimate of family and friends. As declared dissidents, they experienced an isolation that was both social — becoming pariahs within their own country — and often also physical and mental — when they suffered imprisonment. Those who chose the path of exile had been profoundly alienated while in Cuba; once in Miami, some again found themselves alienated, now from the oppressive conservatism of *el exilio* — victims of a double alienation, possibly, a double exile.

In short, the revolution and the exodus were deeply intertwined not only as historical and political processes but also as cognitive and emotional processes. Mistrust, fear, betrayal, isolation, humiliation, denunciation were part and parcel of the lives of Cubans as they lived through a historical and political process that forced them, over and over again, to define and redefine themselves, to side with one political community against another.

To date, this attitudinal, emotional, and experiential dimension of the Cuban revolution and exodus had not been explored. Using the distinction developed by Albert O. Hirschman (1970) in *Exit, Voice, or Loyalty*, over a period of about 2 and a half years, I conducted 100 in-depth, semi-structured interviews with people who were representative of the four major waves of the Cuban exodus and who were also protagonists of what are now four major political communities.

As I see it, the four major political communities that developed overtime are: the supporters who never wavered and became highly integrated to the revolution (*loyalty*); those who remained in Cuba but uninvolved in the political process (*neglect*); the exiles who rejected it and joined the Miami political community (*exit*); and the dissidents who, living their criticism within, both support the revolution and reject it (*voice*). While cross-sectionally all of these communities exist at present, overtime people also left one to join another.

My interviews were guided by the concepts of "vintages," political disaffection, and political generations, concepts that help to capture the changes in political attitudes across time, for the same person, and across social groups at the same historical moment. A central hypothesis of this research is that the critical experiences that promoted their processes of political disaffection — by which I mean the loss of faith and trust in government and cause — will vary quite markedly across the major waves of migration, not only because of their varying social composition (social class, race, age, gender) but also because they represent different political "vintages" — refugee groups that are distinct in character, background, and avowed political faith because they lived through and experienced very different stages of the revolution.

METHODOLOGY

The interviews were conducted not only in Miami — where the bulk of them were conducted, since Cubans see Miami as "the capital of the Cuban exile" — but also in New York (the Bronx, Manhattan, and Brooklyn, which are very different social worlds), in New Jersey (Union City, Patterson, and Elizabeth, the communities that used to comprise the second largest Cuban community in the U.S.), and in places where sizable communities of Cubans in exile exist, such as Chicago, Los Angeles, Texas, Puerto Rico, and Spain, as well as among Cubans who live surrounded by only a few Cubans. This geographic spread represents the major Cuban communities of settlement.

In selecting the respondents, I chose to interview persons who were representative of the known social and demographic characteristics that typified each of the four major waves of the Cuban exodus. In addition, since I had a number of hypotheses regarding the nature of political participation in general, and specifically in communist societies, I chose both persons who were active politically and those who were not — in Cuba, and in *el exilio*. In addition, I chose to include a wide range of political expression — from Left to Right, so to speak, which in the Cuban community is known as *los intransigentes, los moderados,* and *los dialogueros* (the intransigents, the moderates, and those who seek to dialogue). This is clearly a form of what Anselm Strauss (1987) called "theoretical sampling."

I also want to stress that the 100 interviews that I conducted in total are the 100 persons that I sat down to tape their interview on their life experiences. In a more informal manner, I interviewed easily three times that number of persons, as the result of the substantial participant observation that I engaged in the various Cuban communities over a four year span, as I grew to know the Cuban community from a multitude of vantage points. That field work, participant observation, was the foundation for this research effort. As a result, the community itself more

often than not identified who I should interview to represent the particular political community they knew well — "You should talk to such and such." I also entered the community in many different ways — through the rich, through the poor, through hospitals, schools, organizations, apartment buildings, and the like.

Contrary to what is known as snowball sampling, I never took more than one suggestion for another interview from each respondent, so as not to tap into that person's social network too much. Nonetheless, Cuba is a small island, and at the time of the revolution, most people who were well educated in the private schools that existed then, knew one another; most dissidents who joined the formal organizations of the dissident movement that sprang in the late 80s knew one another, and the like. Hence, one often taps into networks, yet my effort to enter the community through many different ways was an effort to minimize this.

Moreover, it is important to stress that because the Cuban revolution and exodus to this day remain a very live issue — not one in the past, but still in the present — and a highly politicized one on both sides, where people are often afraid to speak the truth in public, these were interviews that could not have been conducted in the absence of a trust relationship. Hence, I either developed a trust relationship with the subject of my interviews myself — as I did by first reaching out to them via letter, including some of my previous writings on this topic, and letting them know why I wanted to interview them — or someone else lent me theirs: "You talk to Silvia as if you were talking to me," a trusted friend often said to my potential interviewee. Without the trust we developed, much of what people told me would not have been told. Of the 100 interviews I thus collected, 32 were with Cubans who emigrated during the special period, interviews on which I base this paper. Because the number is small, my emphasis is not on the numbers but on the range of political expression these latest *émigrés* represent. Since this wave of the exodus is still ongoing, we cannot yet characterize its definitive social and demographic characteristics (e.g., the *balseros* (rafters) have recently given way to the *lancheros* (boatmen) and the latter clearly have a great deal more money than the former). But it is possible that this latest wave may yet be the most heterogeneous to date.

The typical interview, taped, took from 4 to 6 hours, although some took two days (some people had lived 9 lives!). To preserve anonymity and confidentiality, all names and other identifying information were changed when requested, although many people chose to be interviewed under their own name. The respondents were of all races; men and women; young and old. Many were professionals — a doctor, a journalist, a lawyer, University professors, a biotechnician, a priest, a physicist, a government technocrat, some of whom had participated in international missions overseas; and University students, including some that Castro himself called *gusanos rojos* (red worms) because they left while studying in the Soviet Union, and a student that represented what are now called *los quedaditos* (those who stayed) who left while on a trip taken abroad to study or work.

My interviews also included many artists and intellectuals — a painter, one who worked in film and theater, a gifted musician. They also included working class Cubans who lived in the city — one who worked in the tourist industry, another in the tobacco industry, and in construction, as well as a *guajiro* from the countryside who worked in a sugar mill. The interviews encompassed Cubans who left in a myriad of ways — who crossed the Rio Grande as *mojados* (wetbacks), as Mexicans have always done, as *balseros* (rafters), "*balseros aéreos*" (who came by plane because they had more money, but otherwise were very similar to the *balseros*), those who lived in the tent city of Guantanamo Bay for about a year and a half; and those who left Cuba to study abroad (in Italy, France, and Russia) and never returned to Cuba, or returned to then leave again. They included Cubans who formerly were active members of the dissident movement, as well as those who did their best to stay out of politics altogether, and those rebels who landed in prison for their political activism or simply because they challenged the state.

My interviews also included Cubans of all races and ethnicities — White Cubans, Black Cubans, Mulatos, Chinese Cubans, Cuban Jews, Cubans of Lebanese ancestry. And they included Cubans of all religious persuasions — Catholic, Protestant, and Jewish Cubans, a *Santero* (a priest in the *Santería* religion, the syncretic blend of Catholicism and West African religious beliefs now widely spread in Cuba), and some who grew up in Cuba without any religious instruction, as atheists who, as one of them put it to me, wish they knew how to pray, but did not.

Thus, rather than seek statistical representation, which in a small sample would fail to include Cubans in small numbers, such as Cuban Jews, Chinese Cubans, and the like, I sought to represent Cubans as social types. In a small sample, admittedly, this means that they all have the same weight, but they better represent the full gamut of what it means to be Cuban.

In addition, I often interviewed members of the same family, so as to better explore the issue of family dynamics, which interested me. However, if they made the decision to leave Cuba as a family decision, I counted them as just 1 interview; while if they made the decision to leave as separate individuals, and thereafter met and married, I counted them as 2 interviews. Hence, my 100 interviews include many more than 100 persons. The interviews themselves took place in either the person's home or their office, so that I could also grow to understand them in the social context where they lived or worked. This also allowed me to occasionally point to photographs, paintings, and the like, as a way of discussing the issues the interviews deal with. Because the interviews had a great deal of depth to them, often times they provided both of us with a friendship, so that I remained in touch with many of the people I interviewed. That also allowed me to see their reaction at later times to other events, to hear things that were said outside the context of the interview but that pertained to the issues at hand. Even more, when I traveled I often met the remainder of the family or close friends that had been left behind in Cuba, or who now lived in Houston or Spain. Hence, the interviews themselves ran very deep and a great deal of the social context of people's lives also surrounded them.

RESULTS

Because the Cuban revolution is now very old — 41 years old — the generational differences in experiences and attitudes between those who made the revolution and felt affirmed by it — were its protagonists — and their children — who only inherited its problems — are profound, resulting in very different motivations for the exodus.

César Mata, a surgeon who was greatly respected in Cuba, left at the age of 47, primarily due to family reunification reasons. He wanted to be reunited with his daughter, who sailed away in a stolen boat with her boyfriend. This is not to say that Mata had no political differences with the society in which he lived; rather, that he had adjusted to those and carved a life in Cuba that gave him satisfaction. In the beginning, his identification with the revolution had been very profound. Two of his uncles had fought together with Frank País, in the uprising of the 30th of November, 1956, in support of the arrival of Fidel Castro aboard the yacht *Granma* to Cuba. When the revolution triumphed in 1959, he had been rather young, only 12 years old, but he had felt it in a very personal way, because family members had died fighting against Batista.

However, he pointed out, while his family was composed of many committed revolutionaries, they were not communists because communism had nothing to do with the revolution when it was initially fought. His identification, therefore, like that of his family and most who actually fought and risked their lives in the revolution, was with being a *revolucionario* (revolutionary), not with being a communist. Therefore, as the revolution progressively took the course of communism, his doubts increased and he increasingly felt that he had to convince himself that the truth lay with Fidel and communism, as he tried to justify policies, such as the October Missile Crisis, that he felt were wrong. And yet he lived within the system, as he put it: as a *miliciano*, who guarded against possible invasions; as an *alfabetizador*, who went to the rural areas to teach the peasants to read and write; as a participant in public acts that revolved

around the government and sang the International; as a *becado*, on a fellowship who attended military schools and who went to the countryside 9 times to cut sugar cane while studying medicine.

He ceased being a revolutionary progressively. In the beginning, he said, he had been a 100 percent *revolucionario*; but after the "civil war," as he called it, that culminated in Playa Girón (Bay of Pigs), and especially after the October Missile Crisis, which he felt glad the Americans had won, he felt that he was only 50 percent *revolucionario*. The Cuban revolution was consolidated and the effervescence of the early years — what could be called the revolutionary moment properly speaking — was over with. Then began a new stage that, with the aid of the Soviet Union, was very stable for many years. Cuba was part of the communist bloc, that comprised nearly half of mankind, social inequality was not very great, and those who remained behind — after most of their circle of friends left — had to adjust to life as it was and lead a normal life.

He himself put all his energy and talents into becoming a good doctor and became a surgeon, and he took pride in helping to create the first coronary unit within a hospital in Cuba, only the second in Latin America. Doctors came from everywhere in the world, he said, to see what Cuba had done in public health. Today, he said, to concentrate on creating something of value in Cuba through your work is no longer possible; in the *special period* the aim has become to survive — any way possible.

In Cuba, he said, people had three options: they could leave the country, in whatever way; they could become integrated to the revolution, whether or not they really believed in it, and climb with it professionally, as far as it took them; and they could do what the vast majority did, they could remain as passive observers, concentrating only on their work and their family. He himself had chosen the second option; his father, also a doctor, who to this day lives in Cuba, the third. Because he had chosen to adjust himself to the reality of Cuba in communism, the impact of the fall of the Berlin wall and Eastern European communism was decisive because, he said, it made it clear that one no longer had to adjust to life under communism and, in addition, that life would no longer be worth living in Cuba. César described himself as an economic immigrant because, he said, he had adjusted to life in Cuba for many years, including its lack of liberty, he had succeeded in his medical profession, and lived as well as he could there, but he sought to leave to reunite with his daughter and to be able to help his parents back in Cuba. While he worked as a doctor in the U.S., he was not able to regain the medical prestige that had been his in Cuba, and after a few years he left the medical profession altogether, carving a new career for himself as he developed and imported a Cuban/Dominican tobacco (the seed was Cuban, as was the labor, though grown in Dominican soil) that he labeled "César."

Likewise, Tomás Medina had also lived well and adjusted to life in Cuba. He was educated in the United States as a young man in the 1950s, and came from a family that had quickly gone from being poor to being very rich in Cuba — from going places by bus to being driven by a chauffeur, he remembered — and whose father had, at the beginning of the revolution, held a high post in a ministry. However, his father was viscerally anti-communist and had helped many people in Cuba leave in the early years, securing passports for them, until he himself was imprisoned. As a result, Tomás himself was never fully a believer in the revolution. He had, however, risen "as high as is possible," he said, "when you are not a Party militant, come from a bourgeois family, and have close family in the United States" due to his hard work as a well-qualified economist that was involved in economic planning in Cuba. He had also never wanted to leave Cuba, especially since he knew first-hand the problem of race in the U. S. and he himself was Mulato. As a member of the *tecnocracia*, in Cuba he had lived well in a penthouse overlooking the *Malecón*, had traveled throughout the world representing Cuba, and had no real economic problems. But his family problems loomed large. For his sons threatened to leave the country on a *balsa*, risking death. Tomás, therefore, made the choice to desert in 1996, at the age of 59, while working overseas on a foreign mission, thinking he would later be able to bring his children and wife.

Younger Cubans, however, who perhaps had not yet had the time to work out a modus vivendi, often had more purely political motives in their experience. For example, Oscar Aguirre and Natalia Goderich (the names here are real), a young married couple with 3 beautiful children, were both students in the Soviet Union who eventually became what Castro called *gusanos rojos* (red worms) when they failed to return to Cuba. Natalia is the daughter of a Russian mother, who taught Russian history to students who were going to study in Russia, and a Cuban father, while Oscar is all Cuban. Both were born in 1966, and grew up, therefore, fully within the revolution, without ever having known the old society nor what César Mata called "the effervescence" of the revolutionary moment.

In the years when they were reaching adulthood, both were studying in Russia — as were approximately 10,000 other Cuban students. But they arrived there at a time when young Russians their age were living, very fully, the processes of change that we came to know as *perestroika* and *glassnost*. Oscar himself had grown up around family who thought that Cuba was nothing other than a disaster: "We were always *gusanos*," he said. Natalia, by contrast, grew up surrounded by family who were true believers in communism, as she herself had been, until they grew disillusioned. Her father, who had been an economist working with the central planning board, the arbitrary use of power in the case of General Ochoa had been "the drop that made the cup overflow." In Natalia's case, her love for Oscar had been decisive, coupled with her experience in Russia when they went there to study and live for 8 years. Suddenly, due to *glassnost*, there was no longer censure and all the literature in the world was available for them to read and to consider on their own. Moreover, Russian students were deeply engaged in this process and the dorms where they lived were hotbeds of discussion that would last late into the night.

After the first two years studying in the Soviet Union, Oscar and Natalia married and were able to move to married student housing, away also from the ideological control most Cuban students were under then, and close to students from many other countries. Worried that the Cuban students would catch the flame of *perestroika*, Cuba sent some representatives to explain to the students that Cuba's process was different, not a *perestroika*, but a process of rectification of errors. But the Cuban students had already begun to discuss quite freely, and had openly debated the extent to which in Cuba there was a personality cult. Ultimately, Oscar's open criticisms regarding the extent to which Cubans are not allowed to speak freely, to travel, to be masters of themselves, cost him the end of his career, for he was only one semester short of graduating with excellent grades when he was "expelled at the request of the Cuban embassy," as his transcript reads. Natalia was saved from a similar fate because she could remain there on her Russian passport and because she also had the backing of her Dean, "a man of new ideas," as she put it.

Oscar went to Germany and actually witnessed the fall of the Berlin Wall, after which he returned to Russia and told Natalia that they would not be returning to Cuba. She finished studying while he cared for their first child and worked at whatever he could, as a barman for a couple of years, and they went on to found the *Unión Cubana*, to help the over 100 other young Cubans in their situation who had become illegal and could neither return to Cuba nor gain political asylum in Russia. Eventually, they were able to come to the United States in 1993, thanks to Jorge Mas Canosa's "Program Exodus." They were then 27 years old, young enough to remake their lives and have 2 more beautiful children and have her parents join them. Yet with the weight of a large family to be responsible for, Oscar never finished studying metallurgical engineering. He makes a good living as a self-employed electrician, while Natalia first taught Russian and Spanish and now teaches high school Physics.

The experience of studying in Russia during the years of *glassnost* and *perestroika* changed the way of looking at the world — what Max Weber called the *weltanschaung* — for many Cuban students. Not all, however, became *gusanos rojos*. Some returned to Cuba, like Heriberto Leyva (name is real) who had gone to Russia to study Philosophy. In Cuba, he had been a member of the *UJC* (*Unión de Jóvenes Comunistas*) and had always attained the very best grades, as he did again in the Soviet Union. But while there he underwent a deep attitudinal change as he "began to breathe the air of freedom" and began a process of change in his consciousness as he started "to open myself up to the changes that were taking place there." It was he that, in the students' debates, had underscored that in Cuba what people were living was a personality cult.

He returned to Cuba with the idea that he would go on to promote peaceful, democratic change within Cuba itself. He then joined with Radamés García de la Vega and Néstor Lobaina, who had founded the *Movimiento Cubano de Jóvenes por la Democracia* (Cuban Youth Movement for Democracy), and developed a political and social project called *La Universidad sin Fronteras* (University without Borders) that aimed to democratize the University and to make it accessible to all Cubans, irrespective of their political beliefs — rather than the *consigna "la Universidad es para los revolucionarios"* (the University is for the revolutionaries), as Fidel Castro himself had long ago declared. Early in 1996, they had presented the project to 5 state organizations (Ministerio de Educación Superior, Ministerio de Justicia, Dirección Nacional de la Federación de Estudiantes Universitarios, Ministerio de Relaciones Exteriores, el Consejo de Estado) and in 2 weeks' time they were arrested and imprisoned on the charges of enemy propaganda, illicit association, and provocation to transgress the law. While they were in prison, Fidel himself gave them a reply when he went to the University of Havana and asked the students there: "Is it not true that the University will continue to be for those who are revolutionaries?" to which the students replied, "*Sí*, Fidel."

They were freed on the condition that they leave the country or the capital. So they left for Oriente, and resumed their political activism there. Two months later, Radamés and Néstor were again arrested, while Heriberto escaped. Eventually, Radamés left the prison and lived under domiciliary arrest in Palma Soriano, while Néstor was in Baracoa. Nonetheless, early in 1997 together they wrote the document called "*La*

Carta Cívica Universitaria" and they again sent it to the official government organizations, denouncing their treatment and asking for a plebiscite or referendum in the Universities so that the faculty and students could decide for themselves whether they agreed with their project of academic freedom, and at the same time they wrote a letter to China, in solidarity with the Chinese dissident Wang Dan that also worked for a pro-democracy university movement. Soon they were once again in jail, where they remained until their names were included in a list of political prisoners whose freedom the Pope requested during his visit to Cuba in 1998.

While in these experiences I have just told, the political motives for the emigration reigned supreme, for many people who left Cuba in the 1990s — perhaps most — politics and economics are deeply intertwined. For example, at 26, Olguita Gómez never thought that she and her husband would ever leave Cuba. But they arrived in 1994. A pretty and vivacious young woman, her adolescence had been carefree, with much partying and dancing. As smart as she was pretty, always the best student in her class, in the early eighties, Olguita had won a trip to the Soviet Union, where she spent a month touring the country together with her teachers. Though finding the Soviet Union somewhat colorless, in comparison to Cuba, she firmly believed that communism was a good system until its collapse in the Soviet Union ushered in Cuba both an economic crisis and a crisis of disbelief. "They had told us that communism was a good system," she said, "but then we could see that it wasn't."

Georgina Mestre's story shows the impact of the economic conditions as well as the profound generational differences in experiences and attitudes that now exist in Cuba between those who made the revolution and felt affirmed by it — were its protagonists — and their children — who only inherited its problems. Georgina is a tall, impeccably well-mannered and lovely woman who left Cuba when she was 30 years old for Venezuela under the guise of a marriage by proxy to a Venezuelan citizen, as did her real husband. She was born in the Soviet Union while both her parents finished their college education there.

She described her father, a convinced communist to this day, as being very grateful to the revolution because, coming from a very humble family — his own father had made and sold brooms — the revolution had made it possible for him to study and to become "someone," to have a career. Her mother's social origins were also very humble, as her grandmother ran a boarding house to supplement her husband's meager seasonal earnings cutting sugar cane.

Georgina's father was only 14 years old when the revolution triumphed, so he had been too young to fight for it, but he and his wife enthusiastically became integrated to the *Jóvenes Rebeldes* (Rebel Youth). Moreover, the government had given him a nice house, a car, enabled him to travel — things he thought he could not have otherwise obtained and enabled him to become middle class, a professional, and manager of several major industries involved in machinery. This experience, coupled with his studying in the Soviet Union together with his wife, had made Georgina's parents fervent believers in the revolution, unwavering to this day. "My father and I respect one another," she said, "respect each other's beliefs." Still, in his letters he would invariably find a way of pointing to the accomplishments of the revolution — and whatever was wrong with Cuba he would always blame on the U.S. embargo.

Georgina herself, however, underwent a process of profound political disaffection that — as was usually told to me by most people I interviewed — was gradual and cumulative, "until one day you suddenly see it differently," she said, but it comes about gradually. In the 1970s, when the economic inequality that began to characterize Cuba during the *special period* had not yet arisen, and Georgina herself was in her teens, there was also no freedom of expression, no civil liberties, but since in her circle of family and friends at that time she knew no one who thought differently, she did not miss them. Wherever she turned, the *consignas* on the billboards, the radio, television, read "¡Viva Fidel!" or "¡Patria o Muerte!" (Fatherland or Death!). And in the pre-University years, she took a leading organizing role in the FEEM (Federación Estudiantil de Enseñanza Media).

The change in her attitudes began to come about in the mid to late 1980s when she began studying electrical engineering at the CUJAE (Instituto Politécnico Juan Antonio Echevarría), where she met people of all persuasions. Although she became a member of the UJC (Unión de Jóvenes Comunistas — the Young Communists), and she remained convinced, she began to exchange opinions and to discuss with people who were not in favor of the revolution. These students' parents had tried to leave Cuba, and had suffered a great deal there — because they had been political prisoners or because they had been the objects of violent *actos de repudio* (repudiation acts) when they tried to leave during the Mariel exodus. "Then they began to explain all that to me," she said, "and I began to know a world that I had not known existed." She herself had participated in those *actos de repudio* when she was only 11 years old in her school and her teachers and principals had given her tomatoes and eggs to throw at those who were trying to leave through the port of Mariel. Like all the young girls then, she sang and danced the insults of *gusanos* and *escoria*, not understanding why those people wanted to leave, simply following what she was told: that they were counterrevolutionaries and bad people. She never heard anything good being said about capitalist societies, but only about the seamy side of the poverty and inequality that reigned there. To her, the fundamental tenet of socialism was equality. And her new friends at the University also pointed out that not everyone in Cuban society was equal — that the party elite and their children had many privileges others lacked. "When I met people whose opinions were different, I realized for the first time what freedom of expression meant." And she also learned that some people had been jailed only because their opinions were different.

She transferred to the University of Havana to pursue law as a career, and soon began to chafe under the excessive control there, when the leaders of the UJC would tally whether or not their members had attended certain political activities, such as the May 1 Parade o a meeting to shout in support of Fidel. Up until then she had thought the CDR (Committees for the Defense of the Revolution) were intended for neighbors to get together and solve their problems, such as the need to paint the building they lived in, but then she began to realize that the purpose of the CDR was to exercise control over persons. In addition, Cubans who had left and lived elsewhere began to arrive: "Everyone had someone," she said, "an uncle, a grandfather, some relative. And we could then see all the material things that were possible, and we did not have them." And then, at the end of the 1980s, the communist world in Eastern Europe collapsed. In Cuba, she stressed, people began to speak more freely. And she realized that the equality she had thought was so critical was not so equal after all: "The equality that existed was among all of us who were poor — we were all poor," but not among the upper class of the political leaders: "they had everything and lived well, living in the huge mansions that they took over from those who left, the rich who left."

Moreover, when she began studying law, she tried to hold an open discussion in the classroom regarding why Cubans who wanted to form another political party were not allowed to do so, and the professor and other students insisted that she should not express herself in that manner since Fidel had said that these people were nothing other than a "grupúsculo" (a tiny group, labeled with contempt) maintained by the Cuban American National Foundation whose intent was only to sabotage the revolution. And then she fell in love with a young man who was a dissident. At first they fought a lot, because their points of view were different, but they always came back together. And as a result of her love for him, a new world opened up for her in Cuba — that of the dissidents — that she had not known existed. "And then he began to change me," she underscored. Though this boyfriend was not the man she would later love and marry, his impact on her feelings and attitudes was decisive. Indeed, most people I interviewed showed the impact of the political commitments of those they loved deeply and admired — whether a boyfriend, father, sister, or friend — on their own.

Thereafter, the economic problems in the 1990s dealt yet another blow to the profound process of political disaffection she had already undergone. For her husband worked as a doctor in the tourist industry and, therefore, he had access to dollars. In addition, his family in the U. S., regularly sent remittances. Thus, very soon, she began to live a life very different from that of her sister and family, who had no access to the dollar economy that had grown side by side with the economic problems in Cuba, and began to belong to a new social class that has grown in Cuba in the last decade, in contrast with the poverty in which the vast majority of Cubans live, including most of Cuba's professionals. This new social class that has emerged is rather ostentatious in its economic behavior and, though hardly supportive of the government, is mostly apolitical. Georgina and her husband had a car, could travel to the beautiful tourist spots of Varadero and Soroa, threw a birthday party for their one-year-old with a clown, *piñata* favors for the children, beer, pop, and cake for the adults. She and her husband also ate well and would invite the rest of her family to eat a nice dinner with them every Saturday — often the only time of the week her family ate meat. In my apartment building, she said, they began calling us *los millonarios* (the millionaires). That, however, eventually also became a reason to leave since they began to fear for her husband's safety, as they were becoming *señalados* (noted). "It was the economic problems that opened up the eyes of the people," she underscored.

Today, Georgina works in an old folks' home in Los Angeles, trying to learn English while she cares for an old man in a wheel chair, care that she gives with a lot of affection while also being a mother to a 4-year-old. She hopes that she can in the future study another career than law. While corresponding with her father — whom she still admires since, as she said, he never harmed anyone nor was opportunistic — they both try to avoid a political confrontation, though they each tell the other what is good about the system in Cuba and in the United States.

Juan López's story is also instructive regarding how the political and economic are deeply intertwined for many people in Cuba in the 1990s. In the summer of 1994, at the age of 29, he finally succeeded in his attempt — for the third time — to leave Cuba as a *balsero*. By training an engineer, he loved working in a sugar mill in the Cuban countryside in Camagüey.

So much so, that when he first arrived to Tampa, he tried to find work in a sugar mill in northern Florida, where "everything was green for miles, covered by sugar cane, and where you could smell the burnt sugar smell" that filled his senses with delight. Unsuccessful in this venture, he began working as a security guard in a high rise condominium.

After working in Cuba in the sugar mill, López spent two years working with Gran Caribe hotels, in the tourist industry, and he happened to be in Havana during the "*5 de Agosto*" (5th of August) riots that took place in Centro Habana in the summer of 1994, moment that caught him running away from the police who were indiscriminately beating people to stop the protest. While his parents and grandparents had never been in favor of the revolution, he himself had been born within it, been educated by it, and studied overseas as a result. Hence, for him the experience of working in the tourist industry had been decisive, for there he had been able to see up close the double standard that exists in Cuba today for foreigners versus Cubans, that everything was for the tourists, the foreigners, while Cubans themselves had no access to that lifestyle and were quite literally kept out of the hotels they could not enter. He recalled Nicolás Guillén's poem that said that prior to the revolution he could not enter the hotels because he was Black. Now, Juan said, you cannot enter because you are Cuban, period. Asked whether he thought that people such as himself left Cuba predominantly because of the economic problems, he replied: "That really is the question for a *balsero*, isn't it?" And he went on to add: "It was the economic problems, yes. But they were the economic problems of *that* political system."

CONCLUSION

In conclusion, my interviews tell me that among Cuba's most recent émigrés, some Cubans left motivated by family reunification considerations above all because they had already made an adjustment to living in Cuba "as is" and carved out a satisfactory life for themselves until their children, who had not developed any such *modus vivendi* "pushed' them to leave. Some Cubans also left for purely political reasons — they left irrespective of the economic conditions in the island, and would have done so in times of plenty, because to them the central issue was the Cuban government's systematic violations of civil liberties and human rights. And some Cubans left because for them, the political and the economic were profoundly intertwined — the bulk of my interviews. For them, the profound economic problems Cubans lived through in the nineties led to their political disaffection.

REFERENCES

Aguilar León, Luis E. 1972 [1958]. *Cuba: Conciencia y Revolución*. Zaragoza, España: Ediciones Universal.

Amaro, Nelson, and Alejandro Portes. 1972. "Una Sociología del Exilio: Situación de los Grupos Cubanos en los Estados Unidos." *Aportes* 23: 6-24.

Bach, Robert, Jennifer B. Bach, and Timothy Triplett. 1981/1982. "The Flotilla 'Entrants': Latest and Most Controversial." *Cuban Studies* 11/12: 29-48.

Domínguez, Jorge I. 1978. *Cuba: Order and Revolution*. Cambridge, MA: Belknap Press.

Hirschman, Albert O. 1970. *Exit, Voice, and Loyalty*. Cambridge: Harvard University Press.

Horowitz, Irving Louis, ed. 1995. *Cuban Communism*. New Brunswick, N. J.: Transaction.

Kunz, E. F. 1981. "Exile and Resettlement: Refugee Theory." *International Migration Review* 15: 42-51.

Kunz, E. F. 1973. "The Refugee in Flight: Kinetic Models and Forms of Displacement." *International Migration Review* 7: 125-46.

Lee, Everett S. 1966. "A Theory of Migration." *Demography* 3: 47-57.

Mannheim, Karl. 1952. *Essays in the Sociology of Knowledge*. New York: Oxford University Press.

Mesa-Lago, Carmelo. 1994. "Will Cuba's Economic Reforms Work?" *The Miami Herald*, 2 January.

Mesa-Lago, Carmelo. 1978. *Cuba in the 1970s: Pragmatism and Institutionalization*. Albuquerque: University of New Mexico Press.

Pedraza-Bailey, Silvia. 1990. "Immigration Research: A Conceptual Map." *Social Science History* 14 (Spring 1990): 43-68.

Pedraza, Silvia. 1996. "Cuba's Refugees: Manifold Migrations." In *Origins and Destinies: Immigration, Race, and Ethnicity in America*, eds. Silvia Pedraza and Rubén G. Rumbaut. Belmont, CA: Wadsworth.

Portes, Alejandro, and Robert L. Bach. 1985. *Latin Journey: Cuban and Mexican Immigrants in the United States*. Los Angeles: University of California Press.

Portes, Alejandro, Juan M. Clark, and Robert L. Bach. 1977. "The New Wave: A Statistical Profile of Recent Cuban Exiles to the United States." *Cuban Studies* 7: 1-32.

Rose, Peter I. 1981. "Some Thoughts about Refugees and the Descendants of Theseus." *International Migration Review* 15: 8-15.

Strauss, Anselm L. 1987. *Qualitative Analysis for Social Scientists*. Cambridge University Press.

Zald, Mayer N. 1991. "Sociology as a Discipline: Quasi-Science and Quasi-Humanities." *The American Sociologist* 22: 165-87.

Zeitlin, Maurice. 1966. "Political Generations in the Cuban Working Class." *American Journal of Sociology* 71: 493-508.

MODELS OF DEVELOPMENT AND GLOBALIZATION IN CUBA

Nelson Amaro

A model is a simplification of reality by which specific characteristics are taken out of their context for analytical purposes. Globalization is a recent process that is linking societies beyond the nation-state's limits through massive ways of consumption, communications, capital and credit management that supersede former borders and pervade political, social and cultural spheres. At least one author thinks that "development" as such was a world goal until the seventies; nowadays, this project has left behind this vision and globalization has taken its place (McMichael 1996).

The Cuban Revolution has not had a unique development model throughout its existence. This paper will outline four development models that the revolutionary elite has pursued. Each model has had its own characteristics along the same dimensions: ideological justifications, main strategic sector for growth, emphasis on social investment and quality of life, nature of the economic units, external relations with other countries and interactions with the institutional framework. Finally, on the basis of this evidence, an analysis will be made of the most recent development model and the globalization process.

THE INDEPENDENT PATH MODEL, 1959-62

The euphoria of the Cuban revolution's triumph brought new ideas. They circulated among the bulk of the population even before the former regime was overthrown. They were along the line of similar ideas expressed by social democrats elsewhere in Latin America and the world. For this reason, personalities such as José Figueres in Costa Rica, Rómulo Betancourt in Venezuela and Mexican leaders welcomed the Cuban Revolution as if it were one of their own. The new political discourse embraced democracy as opposed to traditional dictatorships, which were witnessing their disappearance in Latin America, and especially in the Caribbean. Another tenet was honesty in public affairs as opposed to the corruption shown by past regimes.

In terms of economic philosophy, they supported the main assumptions of the Economic Comission for Latin America (ECLA) — import substitution and industrialization as the focal points for further autonomy from undesirable external powers and greater independence. Land should be put to work and peasants should have access to markets, generating a new consumption power that in turn would energize industrial growth, the engine for real development.

The ideological justification described above increasingly became more radical during this period. Soon the social democratic ideals were abandoned together with democracy and, in practice, ECLA's advice began to resemble a conservative approach. Nevertheless, the need for an industrial "push" remained in force. The way agriculture had been managed in the past, relying only on sugar, was rejected. The presence of Ernesto Guevara as the Minister of Industries, and the earmarking of more than one hundred thousand hectares of land formerly planted with sugar cane to new crops, demonstrated a willingness on the part of the revolutionary elite to put their beliefs into practice. Above all, the premise of independence from external powers, mainly and almost uniquely from the United States, became a prevailing priority for the revolutionary elite.

The Cuban Revolution promised the millenium to the people. During this period, the attainment of a better quality of life was paramount. This need provided the justification for the radical measures taken. The selfishness of the politicians and propertied class of the past was emphasized while massive literacy campaigns, the "Sixth Grade Battle," the opening of universities to the people, and the universal right to health and housing were constantly invoked. Many goods and services were instantly distributed to those that remained loyal or simply stayed in Cuba, while the upper and middle classes left the island. Even some urban workers felt alienated by these radical measures. Houses that belonged to the people that left the island were distributed to others. This way the revolution touched hundreds of thousands of citizens and provided a strong economic force and vested interest for the Revolutionary Defense Commitees (Comités de Defensa de la Revolución, CDRs) in urban areas.

During the 1959-62 period, 37% of the land was expropriated and turned into "Cooperatives" and "People's Farms"; 85% of the industries became government enterprises; 80% of construction firms were taken over by the government; 92% of the transportation sector went into the state's hands; 52% of retail trade was nationalized; and 100% of activities in the wholesale and foreign trade, banking and education sectors fell under government control (Mesa-Lago 1971, p. 283).

External trade was shifted between 1960 and 1961 from the United States and other non-socialist countries to the USSRR and socialist countries. Thus, around 80% of Cuba's external trade was conducted with United States and other non-socialist countries in 1960; between 1961 and 1962 around 70-80% of trade became oriented toward the USSR and the socialist countries (Baklanoff 1971, pp. 260-261). This was without doubt a remarkable achievement for the period.

A crucial element for the institutional setting to respond to these radical changes was the kind of leadership Fidel Castro exercised vis-a-vis the revolutionary and mass organizations and the state. This period was overwhelmingly charismatic. The new regime was able to extirpate any organized opposition and became free to implement its own unilateral project for the development of the island. The "July 26 Movement," the political organization led by Castro, that galvanized the opposition against Batista, played no role during the period. On the contrary, many leaders that were part of the movement were discredited, persecuted, jailed or became exiles when they were perceived as joining the opposition. The remaining revolutionary forces, such as "Segundo Frente del Escambray," followed the same path and even some of their "Comandantes" were sent to the firing squad. The revolutionary student movement "Directorio Revolucionario Estudiantil," remained quiet and remarkably collaborative despite some exceptional cases that resulted in indivuals winding up in jail or in revolutionary organizations in exile.

The lack of legal opposition forces, the successful containment of revolutionaries belonging to different organizations and mild opposition to collaboration from political organizations that had certain autonomy, such as Directorio Revolucionario, paved the way for Fidel Castro to exercise his charismatic qualities. Television appearances of many hours became a formidable instrument for a direct relationship with the masses. Since 1960, the population was inserted in a network of mass organizations such as the Federación de Mujeres Cubanas, la Asociación de Jóvenes Rebeldes, "Pioneros," Comités de Defensa de la Revolución, "Con la Cruz y por la Patria," etc. Simultaneously, the state was freed from elements belonging to former governments and played into the hands of the new revolutionary elite whose commanding officer was Fidel Castro. All of these forces, were put to work for the development model of an accelerated industrial society capable of eradicating poverty and making Cuba an independent country.

THE RETURN TO AGRICULTURE AND SUGAR, 1963-70

This model may be subdivided in two stages that extend from 1963 to 1966 and from 1966 to 1970, as Carmelo Mesa-Lago (1979, pp. 20-27) has suggested. The first stage witnessed the first attempt to model Cuba after the Soviet Union in a coherent and integrated way, while the second again introduced a radical independent movement in the political sphere and in the domestic economy, but without altering fundamentally the economic dependence on the Soviet Union. Finally, there is a two-year period (1968-70) in which close relations with the Soviet Union again take place, preparing the scenario for a different model in the seventies. A constant is the emphasis on sugar and agriculture. For this reason this model may be depicted as having ambivalent political purposes, with sweeping changes in relation to the USSR. Initially it goes in the direction of closeness to the USSR, then it takes a radical independent path and finally returns to the original trend.

The shift from the development model of 1959-62 is marked by a paradigmatic event: the signing of a commercial treaty between Cuba and the USSR that launched a new stage for the goals of the revolutionary elite. This event was preceded by a long discussion within the higher revolutionary circles about Cuba's industry as an engine of economic growth and a vehicle for enhancing the quality of life promised by the Cuban Revolution's leaders. The scenario at the end of 1962 was not promising: sugar production had significantly diminished and food rationing, adopted as a provisional measure, seemed to become a permanent measure affecting the quality of life of the Cuban people.

The disorganization of the state meant that it was not able to cope with its new massive responsibilities. A symbol of this disarray was the arrival at Cuban ports of whole industrial plants ready to be assembled that government officials could not put into operation. The "star" of Ernesto Guevara, the promoter and defender of rapid industrialization policies, began to decline significantly. Suddenly, he was dismissed from all his responsibilities and he moved his base of operations to Africa in search of new endeavors. Sugar ceased to be the symbol of "imperialist" influence and the dream of a Cuba free of the influence of the United States and the USSR was left behind. Sugar, according to the new discourse, was in fact the basis for such independence. It was the skill that Cuba knew well and could share in a socialist division of labor. A schedule for delivery of Cuban sugar to the USSR contained within the bilateral commercial treaty with the USSR would require that Cuba produce ten million tons of sugar by the 1970 harvest.

A new development model was installed. Agriculture — and not industry — was the pivot for reaching the millenium. Sugar was the product that would provide the basis for prosperity in the long term. Nevertheless this shift was a pragmatic concession made by the revolutionary elite. The goal was economic autonomy within the framework of socialist triumph elsewhere in the world. However, the new revolutionary regime was lacking credentials in the socialist world, with COMECON, the economic organization formed by the USSR and European socialist allies, not giving a seat to Cuba during this period. Vietnam was the main challenger to U.S. hegemony in a polarized world.

The pursuit of agricultural development with the support of the USSR did not contradict the global policy of weakening the United States in its backyard. Domestically these changes needed an iron hand, a new revolutionary awareness, in one word, "a New Man." Economic stimuli could not be offered. Instead of relying on military means to force people to give their extra effort to accomplish revolutionary goals, "conciencia" (consciousness) was needed. In this context, the ideological elaboration of Guevara regarding the importance of "subjective factors" in the revolutionary struggle was relevant. Guevara could have had this scenario in mind considering that the direct confrontation with the United States had been exhausted after the missile crisis. The USSR would not mind much this approach, except for the complaints of their traditional allies, the network of communist parties in Latin America.

This contradiction was already solved in Cuba after the trial and death sentence of Marcos Rodríguez (1964), a Communist Party affiliate and confidant of Batista's repressive forces. His cooperation with the Batista government led to the loss of life of well known student leaders during the revolutionary struggle. In addition, the denunciation by the revolutionary elite of the "microfaction" (1968) that sent Anibal Escalante, a prominent "old guard" Communist leader, to confinement in a collective farm, proved that no intermediaries were needed between Fidel Castro and the USSR.

The revolutionary regime and Fidel Castro himself fought for this representation and won it. Another Communist Party different from the one that emanated from the Cuban Revolution was not permissible. After all, the Communist "Old Guard" were Batista's allies in the 1940s and they did not participate in the Sierra Maestra's struggle until the very end. The minimization of the old Communist Party provided the basis for the Cuban revolution's leadership in the rest of Latin America. Guevara's adventure in Bolivia would have been unthinkable without a satisfactory solution of this contradiction within Cuba.[1] The call for a revolution in the continent belonged to this new generation that was in search of a new party rather than an established one with an aging leadership. This contradiction, however, confronted Guevara in Bolivia, when the Bolivian Communist Party questioned his credentials to lead the revolution in that country. Nevertheless, during this period, reacting to the discredit and exclusion of its traditional Communist Party allies, the USSR partially cut its oil exports to Cuba, a warning that alerted the revolutionary elite with respect to the fragility of their relations.

During the first years of the revolution, economic units followed centralized management techniques derived from similar experiences in the USSR. By 1963, a second agrarian reform put 70% of agriculture under state control. Adding to the first wave of expropriations, 95% of industry, 98% of construction, 95% of transportation and 75% of retail trade were under the control of government ministries. These measures added to the total control that already existed over wholesale and foreign trade, banking and education. Soon, the revolutionary elite realized that they needed greater centralization and less technocratic management and measures (1965). Economic units were literally put under each Minister's command. Finally, virtually the entire economy was put under the state's control (1968) with the excep-

tion of the 30% of agriculture that remained in private hands.

Increasingly, economic units were managed without any relationship to the market, departing considerably from the Soviet model and other socialist experiences. On the contrary, emphasis on "conciencia" were reminiscent of the Chinese's "great leap forward" at a moment when tensions between the USSR and China were paramount. Castro's dismissed any doubt about a possible alliance straining their relationship with the Chinese in 1966. During this period, around 75% of exports-imports were already being conducted with the socialist world, a figure that remained remarkably stable until the crisis of the nineties.

Moral stimuli, "conciencia," the deliberate effort to make man-hours of work the measurement unit of the economy rather than money became the priority for the revolutionary process. The government started to provide free services in transportation and communications (including free telephone calls). The goal was to improve the quality of life of the people now and not sacrifice it for the sake of accumulation. Castro sounded optimistic: "We will build communism in one generation."

These efforts, however were not accompanied by economic successes. Sugar exports were below the figures agreed in the commercial treaty signed in 1963 and the accumulated export deficit grew each year thereafter. Allocation of resources was made without concern about criteria of efficiency. Efforts to export the revolution ended with the death of Ernesto Guevara in Bolivia. In 1968, the differences with the model agreed with the USSR came to an end: the invasion of Czechoslovakia by the USSR gave the opportunity to reverse course. It was fully supported by the Cuban revolutionary elite and then, domestically, the sugar "Ten Million Ton Campaign" was launched, symbolizing that the old revolutionaries were beginning to understand "Realpolitik."

---

1. A good account of the tensions during this period may be seen in González (1971).

Despite the efforts to build technical and autonomous institutions and economic units at the beginning of the period, the relationship between the revolutionary elite, the state, the party and mass organizations showed a clear direct relation between Fidel Castro followed by his loyal comrades and the masses without any other intermediation. This charismatic order, based on Fidel Castro, intensified to tremendous proportions in the mid-sixties despite the formation of a political party, the so-called "Partido Unido de la Revolución Socialista (PURS)," which grouped the main revolutionary organizations in the struggled against Batista.

The only purpose of the PURS apparently was to check the ambitions of the "old guard" of the Communist Party to become the intermediary between the revolutionary elite and the USSR. The identification of the top positions of the state apparatus with the revolutionary elite was complete and at the end of the period there were no differences among the revolutionary elite, the state, the diminished political party and the mass organizations. The top leadership circulated horizontally among all these entities. Above them, Fidel Castro presided over the most minute details.

PRAGMATIC DEVELOPMENT AND GEOPOLITICS, 1970-86[2]

The period between 1968 and the 1970 provided a link for the implementation of the new model. Sugar would not be the basis for growth at the expense of the rest of the economy, according to the new ideology. More important was the modernization of the economy and its place in the context of the socialist world with which Cuba had relations. The domestic political system should not constitute a grouping of institutions with the same purpose. The building of a political system that differentiated among state, political party, mass organizations, the revolutionary elite and "the Maximum Leader" was needed. The latter should give rise to an institutionalization of the revolution.

Institutions, not men, were the goals of this period. There were deliberate efforts to separate out administrators from the Party. The brand new Cuban Communist Party celebrated its first Congress in 1975 and approved the SDPE (Sistema de Dirección y Planificación de la Economía, Economic Management and Planning System). The SDPE would be based on "objective economic laws" and consider market mechanisms such as earnings, credit, interests, rational prices, budgets, and economic calculus, especially regarding firms' self-financing, taxes and transactions among state enterprises. Firms would also enjoy a relative independence, e.g., to hire its work force, seek loans, make investment decisions, establish accounting systems and seek earnings (Mesa-Lago 1979, pp. 69-70). Work norms were again implemented at the firm level. There was a return to long term planning together with emphasis on the training of managers, who were forced to learn the new technology with warnings that failure to do so may bring firing and rotation of personnel.

Moreover, material incentives were introduced to reward economic performance and criticism leveled at the "voluntarism" that was practiced in the context of the application of the former model. As a result, voluntary labor declined considerably, absenteeism was checked and increases in productivity sought. New and more specialized ranks were introduced in the armed forces, which were also reduced in size. Meanwhile, the older, voluntary militias started to disappear. All these changes were made in the midst of self-criticisms on the part of the revolutionary elite and Fidel Castro regarding "the mistakes of the past" based on voluntarism and subjectivity.

A moderate reduction in capital accumulation and an increase in consumption improved the quality of life of the people. During this period, Cuba enjoyed moderate economic growth and was able to keep active social policies. Cuba's performance in this regard looks more outstanding when compared to the rest of Latin America, which engaged in massive borrowing that created a huge external debt and later on in-

---

2. I acknowledge that in this section I borrow liberally from Mesa-Lago (1979), especially pp. 20-27.

duced structural adjustments of their economies and considerable reductions of their social expenditures by the end of the seventies and well into the eighties (the so-called "lost decade").

Although times series differ, especially for the period 1960-64, the magnitude of the outburst of the economy between 1970-75 — around 7.5% according to Mesa-Lago (1987) and 10% for Madrid-Aris (1997) — and for 1980-84 — 5.7% for Madrid-Aris (1997) — seems to be well established. Other authors show lower growth in the sixties, around 2.25% for Madrid Aris (1997) and 2.3% for Mesa-Lago (1987) for 1960-70; around 3.4% for Madrid-Aris (1997) and 4% for Mesa-Lago (1987) for 1975-80; and 1.3% for Madrid-Aris (1997) for 1985-88.

Summarizing, it is possible to conclude that economic growth in Cuba from 1960 to 1980 was average in the context of Latin America growth (around 4%). It was better than Latin America's during the "lost decade," but trailed the 5.3% median growth rate of the Newly Industrialized Countries (NICs) (Singh 1998, p. 250).[3] In any event, the extraordinary external conditions that prevailed during this period makes the Cuban model almost impossible to replicate — attempts to do so in Chile and Nicaragua ended in failure.

This period witnessed the close alignment of the Cuban economy with the rest of the socialist world. This is what makes the Cuban experience unique. At the beginning of the seventies (1972), Cuba obtained a seat in COMECON; this put the USSR in a position similar to that held by the United States vis-à-vis pre-revolutionary Cuba, even in details such as the share of foreign trade conducted with the island and the preferencial sugar paid to Cuba. In addition, the external aid given to Cuba during the period exceeded any amount provided to any developing country in the world in a similar situation. Between 1970-80, Castro made 4 visits to the USSR and Brezhnev made one visit to Cuba.

Never again would Cuba enjoy such levels of preference. Judging from the outcomes at the end of the eighties, probably never had the revolutionary elite faced more hidden resistance to their goals. Complaints about "irrational investments by the USSR in tropical revolutionaries" that were unheard in earlier periods began to be aired. The caution of the USSR with respect to the help given to the "Sandinistas" in Nicaragua was the consequence of this internal criticism of over-generous aid to Cuba. Overall, one wonders how it was possible for the critics to accept such generosity when Cuban goals in the social area aimed to elevate social indicators beyond those enjoyed internally in the USSR.

An examination of social indicators as a measurement of quality of life, originating from different sources, shows that the Cuban regime during this period made significant inroads in the areas of employment, education, health and social security. Nevertheless, these achievements were made at a great cost for the overall economy and its sustained growth, as the process of capital accumulation and the investment rate show. A more thorough study of these advancements makes evident a heavily subsidized labor, social and consumption sector. Comparisons with Chile and Costa Rica, countries with different ideologies (Pinochet in Chile and democratically-elected leaders in Costa Rica), regarding education and health show comparable advancements under different conditions. Thus, technology may be more important than ideological framework in such advances.

The advances made during this period would have been impossible without a close political agreement between the USSR and Cuba. The model did not resemble the thesis of "socialist development in one country" as the Stalinist period may show, although certain domestic similarities may be highlighted. Castro complained about criticisms made by the Latin American left regarding his concern for development and the abandonment of the "permanent revolution" beyond Cuba's borders in the area. He justified his pursuit of development as also revolu-

---

3. This is also the conclusion of Ernesto Hernández-Catá (1999) regarding NICs.

tionary, but this ingredient was not the main characteristic of the period.

The way the revolutionary elite played geopolitics at the global level constituted the defining trait of this period. The strategy meant that weak foreign spots, allied or potentially allied, were occupied by ten of thousands of Cuban military, doctors, teachers and other personnel. This was the result of commitments made at the beginning of the seventies. Packenham (1987, p. 136) says about this period:

> In short, the military has been by far the most "dynamic" sector of the Cuban economy for at least a decade. The Soviets have paid most of the economic costs in this sector…Many commentators maintain that Cuba's foreign policy reflects Cuba's own interests. However, it is not plausible a country of Cuba's size, location, and precarious economy would, in its own interests, have 70,000 troops and military advisers in 23 countries around the world, mostly in Africa and the Middle East.

Institutionally, a good effort was made to separate out state administrators from the party and even from the armed forces. Nevertheless, the interplay of Castro's charismatic personality, mass organizations, the state and the party was difficult to overcome. Among the most interested in the rule of law were the former Communist Party members — the "old guard" — who had seen many of their peers taken to trial and condemned publicly. They, more than anyone else, could benefit from "socialist legality." The Constitution that was approved in 1976 established a government structure similar to the USSR. Within the central administration, there was separation of the legislative and executive functions (previously concentrated on the Prime Minister's Cabinet). The Communist Party began to have an importance it did not have in the past.

The same happened with mass organizations. The workers' movement witnessed a revival through elections at the local level, union reorganization and periodic national meetings. There was also pressure to integrate the agricultural private sector into the state, following the practice in Eastern Europe. In addition, the youth movement, through the Communist Youth Union (UJC), received special attention to

strengthen its capacity to cope with students abandoning school and with any rejection of accepted practices through rebellious behavior. The same applied to culture and intellectuals, seeking to gain the affiliation of writers, journalists, visitors from Western intellectual circles and judges in national literature contests.

Nevertheless, though one may observe a greater sophistication and diversification in the formal power structure, this period could not erase the pervasive influence of Fidel Castro in all affairs. Elite horizontal circulation intensified among the inner circle at the top of party, state, armed forces and mass organizations. Castro dedicated a large amount of time to war games in distant countries and geopolitics. Any sense of crisis, however, immediately brought him to the fore. The most critical situation came around 1986, after Mikhail Gorbachev became general secretary of the Communists Party of the USSR. This resulted in a new situation that unexpectedly challenged the URRS-Cuba agenda. For the first time, a generation that did not live through the Russian Revolution was in power in the USSR. For the first time, Castro had to face a generation of leaders in the USSR that were younger than he. His political instincts told him that this was change was capable of jeopardizing the honeymoon Cuba enjoyed with the USSR for fifteen years. Winds of change began to blow again and a new model began to emerge.

RECTIFICATION OF ERRORS AND THE SPECIAL PERIOD MODEL, 1986-TO DATE

The fact that the model we are describing starts in 1986 may raise doubt regarding the link between the "Special Period" and the previous events. From our perspective, they are part of the same underlying trend: the revolutionary elite's search for formulas to cope with the new agenda put forward by the USSR. The events that began in 1986 were a prelude to the fall of the Berlin Wall in 1989 and the demise of Marxist-Leninist regimes in the USSR and Eastern European countries.

The justification for beginning "la rectificación de errores y tendencias negativas" in 1986 was the disgust of the revolutionary elite with the effects of SDPE for 10 years. This line, however, was the official version told to the Cuban public. Underlying this official rhetoric was a concern about the alliance between Cuba and the USSR and the decline of Soviet geopolitical influence in Central America, Africa and the Middle East. Consequently, Cuban international missions declined. The SDPE, the Soviet and Eastern European model adapted to Cuban realities, became the "scapegoat" of all evils in Cuba.

There was criticism of inequalities brought about by market mechanisms permitted within the SDPE. Peasant, artisan and housing markets — where producers and consumers freely came to buy and sell their products — were eliminated. The disappearance of voluntary labor was regarded as negative and such practice was reinstated. Similarly, the importance that had been given to technocratic approaches over political considerations was deemed to have become a source of deviations that should be corrected. All organizations were called upon to discuss ways in which they could "rectify" ideological and practical incongruences of the system installed in the seventies.

The ethical drive, however, was not a return to the 1966-68 period, but moral stimuli was praised over the materialistic approaches attempted by those that allegedly did not understand the Revolution's high moral goals. Corruption was particularly attacked as well as profiteering from the "black market" using state's resources. Ernesto Guevara's figure was resurrected but without the intensity of the past. Thousands of meetings to drum up support for the new campaign were held throughout Cuba for several months.

All accounts of economic performance during this period show that the economic growth rate declined when compared with the former period (Castañeda and Montalván 1996, p. 222). Jorge Pérez-López (1998, p. 225) mentions that there was a recession that intensified in the 1990s. The return to old banners did not work as expected. Economic problems worsened instead of being rectified.

What looked like a temporary reform cycle, perhaps to consolidate the bargaining position of the Cuban revolutionary elite with respect to the changes taking place in the USSR, became a permanent farewell due to the political changes and transitions to capitalism experienced by the former allies in COMECON. The impact of the breakdown in economic relations differs according to different authors, but without any doubt Cuban economic activity declined between 39 and 50% in the 1990-93 period (Pérez-López 1998, pp. 226-7 and CEPAL 1997, p. 626).

The real magnitude of the debacle probably will never be known, but the disappearance of COMECON made transparent the subsidies given to Cuba. Preferential sugar prices disappeared and sugar trade was transacted at world prices as was also oil. When the Fourth Congress of the Cuban Communist Party met in 1991, most expected drastic changes in the direction of democratization and economic liberalization. This was not the case although the government subsequently relinquished control of some aspects of the economy and encouraged some private activity. The most important measures were the allowance of joint ventures with foreign investment operating outside the official economy and the liberalization — to certain extent and without completely losing control — of certain corporations, especially those engaged in foreign trade. In addition, the government proceed to give more independence to the farm sector, legalized the use of dollars by Cuban citizens and made self-employment legal.

In addition to these defensive measures, the "Special Period" forced the revolutionary elite to make an extraordinary effort in tourism. Tourists visiting Cuba have risen from a little more than 400 thousand in 1990 to 1,440 thousand in 1998, almost a four-fold increase, making this activity the main source of foreign exchange (US$1.8 billion). Other efforts in nickel exploitation and oil production are either volatile or not significant enough to make an impact on the crisis.

This new model brought some economic revival to the embattled Cuban economy. By all accounts, the years 1994-99 witnessed positive economic growth but indicators showed some volatility. From 1994 to 1996, GDP growth rates were 0.4, 2.5 and 7.8%, respectively. It appears, then, that the success reached this last year and the confidence that the Cuban economy had reached bottom in 1993, made the drive toward further changes fade somewhat between 1997 and 1998. According to official data, 1999 witnessed again a strong recovery, 6.2% according to official sources, which has been challenged (Castañeda 1999 and Maybarduk 1999).

The historic levels reached by Cuba in social expenditures and social indicators suffered with the economic decline though there has been a conscious attempt on the part of the revolutionary elite to maintain these levels.[4] The CEPAL study showed that real salaries dropped 41.4% compared to 1989. State budget expenditures in education declined 46% from 1989 to 1996. Salaries of teachers maintained their levels, but severe cuts have been made in expenditures on supplies and text books as well as in capital formation. Laboratories and workshops that need equipment and materials have suffered together with students housing to which food and transportation have been difficult to provide. This situation has affected all levels of education, but to a greater extent higher education, especially careers such as biology, chemistry and veterinary science where considerable equipment and investment is required.

According to CEPAL, the Cuban government expanded and kept satisfactory levels of public health until 1989. Since then, imports to support this sector began to suffer. Assistance received from COMECON countries stopped, and the allocation of foreign exchange to purchase medicines, equipment, medical instruments and so on declined from US$237 million in 1989 to only US$66 million in 1993. It increased again from 1994 to 1996 (US$90, US$108 and US$126 million, respectively). Self-financing through medicine exports, remittances from Cuban medical doctors outside Cuba, attention to international patients, etc., only reached 15% of the needed resources.

Regarding public health, the CEPAL study concluded that massive preventive measures taken by the government before the crisis has allowed Cuba to maintain the historic public health levels and at the same time has supported austerity measures and reorganizations made as a result of the crisis. Nevertheless, the pressure on the available capacity is such that it is foreseen as shortening the life span of needed health equipment. Assistance given by the European Union and non-governmental organizations has also eased the situation.

Housing has never been a sector about which the government can feel proud. Despite reforms introduced in 1985, the housing situation has tended to worsen. The same can be said of community services related to housing. The CEPAL study noted that during the Special Period, difficulties in the public water and drainage systems were severe. Garbage collection has also deteriorated. Some "cuentapropistas" (small, private entrepreneurs) have started to provide some of these services.

Finally, the culture sector has been more successful than recreation, physical education and sports in attracting financing from abroad for its activities. The CEPAL study, however, sees difficulties in the future related to imports. Sports, like culture, faces the dilemma of commercializing activities abroad to raise foreign exchange, and raises doubts about genuine "amauterism." The equilibrium is precarious at present.

Cuba today faces an institutional crisis that has been brought by the same measures that are being used to defend the system. The elitist inner circle has closed ranks around the charismatic personality of Fidel Castro, whose age calls for a clear picture of a successor. Nevertheless, this subject is not touched and each time the question is asked of Castro, he answers that there are permanent institutions in the island formed throughout the last forty years that will take care of the matter. The armed forces have raised their status during the Special Period, and many officers are carrying out their official duties being directors of firms related to foreign trade. Privileges attached to these posts have increased the differences between these managers and the bulk of the population.

---

4. The situation described below has been taken from CEPAL 1997, pp. 359-82.

State technocrats that were successful during the decade when the SDPE was implemented are kept at a distance by the revolutionary elite. The opening of a dollar area around tourism and the priority given to certain strategic firms may have created wide differences depending on where a person works. Loyalty is preferred over expertise. The debate over the future of the island has intensified and polarized. The sudden dismissal of Foreign Minister Roberto Robaina is proof of this statement. The cautious approach of the liberalization measures, which slowed down in 1996, must have created further discussion on how to exit the critical situation.

A serious analysis of the alternatives Cuba has for overcoming the Special Period raises important questions. Cuba has no hard currency to engage in significant trade with Western countries. Former socialist countries are part of the problem and hardly can provide solutions at present. China does not appear to be a significant and viable partner to accompany Cuba in this endeavor.

The critical situation described above surprised Cuba while it had the same old charismatic order in place. The state apparatus called to face this situation appears fragmented. The reward system tends to be concentrated on certain economic sectors and in the hands of people loyal to Fidel Castro and the revolutionary elite. Mass organizations play a lesser role than in the past except when they need to mobilize the population on issues such as the Elian case or more recently on the "Adjustment Law" and the embargo. This kind of mobilization tends to strengthen the link between the charismatic leader and the mass organizations directly, without any intermediary. This is the model that Fidel Castro has used in the past in times of crisis. Intermediary organizations such as the Communist Party or the state are a disturbance. This is an element that does not help in seeking solutions that could give Cuba a pathway to the twenty-first century.

GLOBALIZATION AND DEVELOPMENT MODELS

It is difficult to place a definite time when globalization began. Ferrer (1998, pp. 198-9) believes that it may be traced back to the travel made by Vasco de Gama opening the way to the East. Is Cuba isolated or it is suffering the globalization impact as it follows different development alternatives? Domínguez (1987, pp. 647-50) says:

> Cuban foreign policy has always been global out of both necessity and principle. In the early 1960s, U.S. policy sought to enlist the assistance of other countries to isolate and overthrow the Cuban government. Survival of revolutionary rule required the sear for support everywhere; this is the foundation of Cuban Soviet relations….Cuba's entry into the Nonaligned Movement in 1961 and its continued membership throughout that decade was consistent with the need for global support…The Cuban government's foreign policy is global also because of the ideological commitments of its leadership…These are not parochial revolutionaries…Cuba's global policies spring also from an analysis of the shifts in the so-called "correlation of forces"…A final aspect of Cuba's global policies is its assessment of the relative opportunities and efficacy of assistance to revolutionaries the world over.

Thus, we have to conclude that despite all the isolation that can be cited, in at least one area — foreign policy — Cuba has been global. Another question is the development policies followed in the described models. The development model between 1970 and 1985 was the most integrated with the outside world, although it was framed within the most intense "Cold War" mentality. During this period, Cuba acted as a complement of global Soviet policies all over the world. During the second development model, the vision of Guevara weakening U.S. imperialism by opening other fronts in Latin America and selecting a location in Bolivia capable of extending revolutionary warfare to Argentina and Peru, also contributed to this global trend.

Of all the development models followed, the present one seems the most isolationist one. There are no international missions. Cuba is not integrated into the Western world and its links with the developing world are tenuous and without dynamism. The small economic diversification Cuba developed during forty years now constitutes a hindrance for expanding its relationships with other countries.

Cuba has not developed economic platforms in a large scale as China has done. China has attracted massive investments from countries that ideologically are far apart, as Hong Kong and Taiwan. The Cuban enclave in Miami, on the contrary, is regarded as a visceral enemy. Still, tourism, the most dynamic sector of the current Cuban economy seems to have global ingredients. Nickel and oil can be discarded because their contribution to the overall economy is not significant.

Tourism, however, finds enormous obstacles to really globalize the island. Tourism enterprises are not able to hire labor freely in the island. A complicated government system provides the labor requested and corporations pay salaries to the government; the government in turn pays the workers after taking a significant share. Spanish and Canadian corporations are competing for the potential earnings of this sector. Recently, small margins seem to be discouraging tourism investments due to conditions put forward by the Cuban government (Maybarduk 1999, p. 2). These multinational corporation have firms all over the world and may shift their geographical interests if conditions worsen for them, a negative aspect that is part of the globalization process. Only by presenting competitive advantages to foreign investors may Cuba overcome this tendency. There is no political will yet that may encourage this trend but if the Cuban government decides to do so, tourism is the best candidate to start with.

CONCLUSIONS

This paper has distinguished four development models pursued by Cuba since the victory of the revolution. Ideological justifications for each model have changed from one period to the other to come back again to the same discourse. This has been a tireless exercise throughout time. Moral stimuli displaced other justifications at the end of the sixties only to appear again more than twenty years later to justify the Rectification Process and the Special Period. The most efficient model was the one executed between 1970 and 1986. It provided the economic base for more ambitious goals but it was aborted when a new elite emerged in the USSR, breaking the close alliance enjoyed by Cuba for more than fifteen years.

Voluntary labor, mass mobilizations, emphasis on moral stimuli, and charismatic relationships that prevailed between 1966 and 1970 and between 1986 and 1990, had a bad economic record. The same happened in China with "The Great Leap Forward" and "The Cultural Revolution." During these times, idealism is invoked and heroic deeds are praised. Loyalty and revolutionary fervor are considered worthy for the people to practice. Dissident forces are excluded and mass mobilizations become part of ordinary life. Economic activities decline as a result. At present, during the Special Period, these calls are beginning to be more frequent since the Elian case became a rallying point for the revolutionary elite. If these mobilizations become frequent, negative economic effects may interfere with planned goals.

What comes up clearly is the current isolation of Cuba from the world economy. Political and economic relationships with other countries have become difficult given the present economic model. Politically, the regime is vulnerable to campaigns undertaken elsewhere to press for a government with greater respect for human rights, a greater emphasis on democratic principles and procedures and a more tolerant policy toward dissidence and opposition. The majority of countries condition help on democracy, political concessions and liberalization of the economy. In addition, the Cuban government has very little to offer and has no hard currency to back up its intentions.

The Cuban government saw the transition in the former socialist world as a withdrawal from revolutionary ideals. "Glasnost" and "Perestroika" are regarded as ideas that precipitated this failure. For this reason, they are excluded from the revolutionary agenda. In taking such a stand, however, Cuba becomes more excluded and isolated in a world that becomes more global. The global strategy of the seventies and eighties worked for Cuba, but the world has changed and Cuba has to find its place in this new world. The advice given by Juan Pablo II is relevant: "Cuba has to open itself to the world, and the world has to open itself to Cuba." Otherwise, the current development model could result in a tragic end.

BIBLIOGRAPHY

Baklanoff, Erik N. "International Economic Relations." In Carmelo Mesa-Lago, editor, *Revolutionary Change in Cuba*. Pittsburgh: University of Pittsburgh Press, 1971, 251-27

Castañeda, Rolando H. "Cuba y los Antiguos Países Socalistas de Europa: La Importancia de los Aspectos Institucionales y de Economía Política en la Transición del Socialismo a una Economía de Mercado." *Cuba in Transition—Volume 9*. Washington: Association for the Study of the Cuban Economy, 1999, 224-43.

Castañeda, Rolando H. and George Plinio Montalván. "Cinco Areas de Acción Estratégicas para Lograr el Milagro Económico Cubano: Una Rápida Recuperación con un Alto y Sustentable Crecimiento con Equidad e Inclusión Social." *Cuba in Transition—Volume 6* Washington: Association for the Study of the Cuban Economy, 1996, 219-33.

Comisión Económica para América Latina y el Caribe. *La Economía Cubana. Reformas Estructurales y Desempeño en los Noventa*. México, Naciones Unidas/CEPAL, 1997.

Domínguez, Jorge I. "Limitations and Consequences of Cuban Military Policies in Africa." In Irving L. Horowitz, editor, *Cuban Communism*, Sixth Edition. New Jersey: Transaction Inc.,1987, 645-81.

Ferrer, Aldo. "Desarrollo y Subdesarollo en un Mundo Global." In Louis Emmerij and José Núñez del Arco, editors, *El Desarrollo Económico y Social en los Umbrales del Siglo XXI*. Washington: Banco Interamericano de Desarrollo, 1998, 198-208.

Gonzalez, Edward. "Relationship with the Soviet Union." In Carmelo Mesa-Lago, editor, *Revolutionary Change in Cuba*. Pittsburgh: University of Pittsburgh Press, 1971, 81-104 .

Hernández-Catá, Ernesto. "Globalization, Transition and the Outlook for the Cuban Economy." In *Cuba in Transition—Volume 9*. Washington: Association for the Study of the Cuban Economy, 1999, 217-223.

Madrid-Aris, Manuel. "Growth and Technological Change in Cuba." In *Cuba in Transition—Volume 7*. Washington: Association for the Study of the Cuban Economy, 1997, 216-28.

Maybarduk, Gary H. "The State of the Cuban Economy 1998-1999." In *Cuba in Transition—Volume 9*. Washington: Association for the Study of the Cuban Economy, 1999, 1-11.

McMichael, Phillip. *Development and Social Change*. Beverly Hills, California: Sage, 1996.

Mesa-Lago, Carmelo. "Economic Policies and Growth." In Mesa-Lago, editor, *Revolutionary Change in Cuba*. Pittsburgh: University of Pittsburgh Press, 1971, 277-338.

Mesa-Lago, Carmelo. *Dialéctica de la revolución cubana: Del idealismo carismático al pragmatismo institucionalista* Madrid: Editorial Playor, 1979.

Mesa-Lago, Carmelo. "Cuba's Centrally Planned Economy: an Equity Tradeoff for Growth." In Irving L. Horowitz, editor, *Cuban Communism*. Sixth Edition. New Jersey: Transaction Inc., 1987.

Packenham, Robert A. "Cuba and the USSR since 1959." In Irving L. Horowitz, editor, *Cuban Communism*, Sixth Edition. New Jersey: Transaction Inc., 1987, 109-39.

Pérez-López, Jorge. "Cuba's Socialist Economy: The Mid-1990s." In Irving L. Horowitz, editor, *Cuban Communism*, Ninth Edition. New Jersey: Transaction Inc., 1998, 225-56.

Singh, Ajit. "Oriente se Equipara con Occidente: Perspectiva del Desarrollo Económico de Asia y Enseñanzas para América Latina." In Louis Emmerij and José Nuñez del Arco, editors, *El Desarrollo Económico y Social en los Umbrales del Siglo XXI*. Washington: Banco Interamericano de Desarrollo, 1998, 247-92.

WINNERS AND LOSERS IN RESTORING OLD HAVANA

Joseph L. Scarpaci, Jr.

The socialist leadership seeks to remedy the tattered fabric of Havana's built environment by drawing on a comparative advantage: tourism. Since 1959, tourism had never been a leading economic sector. Fidel Castro had often vowed that Cuba would not become an island of bourgeoisie-catering bartenders and chambermaids as did other Caribbean nations (Eckstein 1977). Accordingly, in 1975, just 25,000 nonmilitary foreigners visited Cuba, while in the year 2000, the figure should approach two million (Scarpaci 1998a). Following UNESCO's recognition of Havana as a World Heritage Site, few planners, architects, and politicians imagined that in just seven years, the USSR would disband, and Cuba's economy would enter a tailspin. In the uncanny fashion that the revolutionary leadership views opportunity in times of crisis (Codrescu 1999), attention was again cast on *Habana Vieja*, the city's original gateway to the world.

This essay examines the revitalization of Habana Vieja and the role played by Habaguanex, S.A (incorporated) in that process. It also considers how that firm works with international financiers in both joint-venture arrangements and the symbolism of restoring the old city. Revitalization refers to the general physical and socioeconomic enhancement of a designated built environment. In the United States and Canada, revitalization frequently entails public-private partnerships. In Habana Vieja, the process depends mainly on joint-venture deals or direct intervention by Habaguanex, S.A. A state company headed by the City Historian, Habaguanex oversees public works, historic preservation, and refurbishing older buildings since the early 1990s. Its budget comes from hard-currency operations in tourism, general retailing, restaurants and bars. Elsewhere, I have argued that historic preservation has unleashed gentrification in Habana Vieja (Scarpaci forthcoming; 1998a; 1998b). In U.S., Canadian and Western European cities, the "gentry class" tends to be better educated and more affluent than local residents, but are usually of the same nationality (Ley 1996). While in many Latin American cities street vendors irritate gentrifiers (Jones and Varley 1994; 1999), this is not a problem in Cuba. In Cuba, the gentrifiers[1] are a transient group made up of foreign tourists or business people from Canada, Western Europe, and Latin America. I aim to situate the process of historic preservation in a broader context of geography of heritage, to which we turn in the following section.

A GEOGRAPHY OF HERITAGE: WHOSE PAST, WHOSE MEMORY?

The study of landscapes of the past is fundamentally a geographic inquiry because of the concern over location and the social, economic and political forces that give shape to those places. Heritage means using the past as an economic resource for the present. Historic places allow nation states to create national

---

1. Though there may be a very small gentry class of artisans and "hustlers" living in Old Havana, they lack the kind of purchasing power required to enter the dollar-driven foreign housing market. Even if they could, they cannot legally purchase new construction under current law.

identity, forge ideologies and to "ground" abstract notions into tangible forms (Hobsbawm 1990; Hall 1995; Woolf 1996). The desire to preserve relics of past environments is frequently tied to influential elites. However, the tension created over what is to be preserved, and whose collective memory should be celebrated, is often ignored in official public circles. A bewildering array of places and objects can determine the issues used in legitimizing power structures (Graham, Ashworth and Turnbridge 2000).

Significantly, the many ways these landscapes are created is not unique to either market or centrally planned economies. Economic place images even drive the present construction boom in the United States. Walt Disney Corporation created Celebration, Florida —a planned community— as a theme to embrace the pre-automobile era that characterizes Disney's Main Street boulevard at Disney World. Not so many years ago, Eastern European and Soviet public housing brandished banal high-rise housing units to impose a stamp of equality on all its citizens. Geographer David Lowenthal argues that the built environment, especially reconstructions of the past, give familiarity and guidance to present-day generations. At the same time, heritage in the form of historic preservation can legitimize the history of local people, as well as invoke negative images of the past (Lowenthal 1985). In an era of rapid and affordable travel for the middle classes, heritage is becoming a driving force in international tourism. Hewison captures this globalizing trend by arguing that heritage is manufactured like a commodity, "which nobody seems able to define, but which everyone is eager to sell" (Hewison 1987, 9). If heritage tourism is commodified, then, a further layer of tension is grafted onto local communities in developing nations where the need for hard currency conflicts with local residents. What sets historic preservation apart in Old Havana versus the rest of the nation is that aside from a few museums, most of the built environment that is being restored marks a time during the Republican and colonial eras when Cuba was deeply exploited. It is ironic, then, that those relics of bygone era are noteworthy in a centrally planned economy. This reconstruction is not free of tension, and Cuba's

economic quagmire reflects that tension as noted below.

A STAR IS BORN

Habaguanex grew out of calamity. In June 1993, an architect from the National Center for Conservation, Restoration, and Museum Science (CENCRM) had been escorting Jonathan Glancey, a journalist from the London tabloid, *The Independent*, through Habana Vieja. Along the walking tour, the Cuban architect pointed out buildings around Old Square (*Plaza Vieja*), a district full of grand old *casas-almacenes* that served as 19th century houses and warehouses (Segre, 1995; Segre et al. 1997, Chapter 2). As the journalist paused to photograph a turn-of-the-century structure that was undergoing renovation, the building suddenly collapsed. Recent rains had saturated the crushed-rock materials (*mampostería*). Apparently, a load-bearing column gave way.

The British media reveled in the remarkable photographs. They underscored the physical decay of Habana Vieja. The story became syndicated and its comments were newsworthy: "No one died in the collapse of Plaza Vieja…Neither, remarkably, was anyone killed later than evening when a second building imploded on the Malecón [the seaside promenade]." As one Cuban architect aptly described the relationship between environment and colonial architecture: "In this weather (86 degrees, 100 percent humidity and frequent storms)…we can expect there to be several more collapses" (Glancey, 1993).

I believe that the creation of Habaguanex, by the Council of State through Law Decree 143-93 shortly after the Plaza Vieja incident, was not a coincidence. The company is part of the Office of the City Historian, headed up by historian Eusebio Leal Spengler. Habaguanex assumed legal right to operate restaurants, museums, gift shops, and hotels that other state agencies (CIMEX, Gran Caribe, Horizontes, Havanatur, and Rumbos) had managed. As part builder-developer and part tourism promoter, Habaguanex[2] claims on its web site that there is "intense and happy nightlife [in Habana Vieja] that creates in cafeterias and restaurants, open 24 hours, a festive and bohemian ambience of quality and pleasure" (Habaguanex, S.A., www.habaguanex.com).

The Office of the City Historian designed and implements the Master Plan for Old Havana's Revitalization that manages land use and investment priorities for the 214-hectare and 242 blocks of Habana Vieja. The area includes some 4,000 buildings, of which just under a quarter (900) possess heritage value. Development projects concentrate heavily in the northeast corner of Habana Vieja, around the Plaza de Armas, Plaza de San Francisco, the cruise ship terminal, and Plaza Vieja. Eusebio Leal recently told an economist of the U.S. International Trade Commission—an independent nonpartisan federal agency—about the effect the embargo has on Habana Vieja and, in turn, Habaguanex operations. "You would see cruise ships full of American tourists arriving here," remarked Leal. "We would be able to buy more cheaply the materials needed to renovate…old buildings" (Snow 2000). However, it is unclear how much of such revenues might accrue directly to the residents, versus sustaining the socialist establishment. Nonetheless, if "sustainability" is a term debated widely around the world (Dyck 1998), in Habana Vieja it has surely come to mean self-financing (Grogg 1999).

Habaguanex is a unique public entity. It is one of the few Cuban companies in post-1959 Cuba to manage dollar-operated facilities but not have to remit profits to the main legislative body, the National Assembly. Nor must it arrange joint venture deals for historic preservation through the Ministry of Foreign Investments (MINVEC) as do all other public entities. Instead, it negotiates historic preservation and new construction projects directly with foreign capitalists. Its fiscal autonomy and decentralized decision-mak-

ing ability are unique in socialist Cuba. From a design and planning perspective, its principal duties allow the firm to use profits to refurbish the UNESCO district. Elsewhere in Cuba, the general tenets of the Foreign Investment Act of 1995 stipulate the conditions under which joint ventures must operate.[3] Habaguanex, though, has much autonomy.

This legal framework spells good news for historic preservationists and more than a few European and Canadian tourists. However, one question rarely posed is: What about the residents of Habana Vieja? As Diane Barthel (1996) has argued, authenticity in historic preservation projects is an elusive goal because social classes have different allegiances to the built environment. The tensions between architectural authenticity and social actors —politicians, tourists, investors, and local residents— fashion the collective memory of places. Habana Vieja, like other historic centers, beckons the question: Whose history and collective memory will be forged under Habaguanex's charge?

Habaguanex's primary responsibility is to generate dollars. In 1995, it generated $5 million USD in gross revenues. Its 1997 figures were estimated to be greater than $10 million. In early 1999, the figure stood close to $40 million and by the year 2002, Habaguanex revenues should approach $200 million (Burr 1999, 73). Habaguanex CEO Eusebio Leal stated that investment in Habana Vieja in 1999 exceeded the previous four years combined. Moreover, the firm employed 3,000 construction workers in 163 restoration projects, not all of them joint-ventures (Leal 1999). Although it employs 3,000 construction workers—many of whom reside in Habana Vieja—the economic multipliers for local residents

---

2. According to Burr (1999), the company was launched in 1994 with just $20,000 in state financing. Today it runs four hotels (including the four-star Santa Isabel, and the Ambos Mundos (Hemingway's old haunt), 13 restaurants, 13 cafeterias, 10 open-air bars, 22 shops, a bakery, nine markets and a pastry shop). By 2004, the company is expected to have 25 hotels under construction or in operation.

3. On September 5, 1995, the National Assembly of People's Power of the Republic of Cuba passed Law No. 77/95 of Foreign Investment which superseded Decree Law No. 50, passed in 1982. For an English-language discussion of the act and related commentaries, see Conas (1995).

are limited. Because it is a commercial enterprise,[4] it has a different legal relationship to the residents of Habana Vieja than, say, the Ministry of Housing does. Through its Cuban building partner Fénix (Phoenix) and its real-estate agency, Aurea, the company engages in ambitious construction projects in the old city. To be sure, not since American businesses set up banks and corporations there between 1902 (the formal end of U.S. military occupation) and 1920 (the year of the "dance of the millions," a year when world market prices for sugar sky-rocketed) has their been such a flurry of construction activity (Weiss 1950; Llanes 1993).

Several Habaguanex interventions are noteworthy. These include the restoration of buildings on the Plaza de Armas, Plaza de la Catedral, and Ambos Mundos Hotel (where Ernest Hemingway resided). Another major project is the renovation of the former stock market of Havana (Lonja de Comercio) on San Francisco Square, facing the new Italian-financed renovation of the ocean terminal at Sierra Maestra docks. The Lonja de Comercio project relied on Spanish investment capital for approximately $12 million USD. Intervention in the building's interior entailed relocating the front stairway to the back of the building, installing two pairs of elevators, updating office space for new technology (FAX and Ethernet connections), building a café and post office on the ground floor, and constructing a dark-glass encased floor on the roof.[5] Adjacent buildings surrounding San Francisco Square include another post office, a money exchange house, an upscale tea shop and restaurant, and the Italian clothing chain, Benetton. To many local residents it is a great irony that an $85 pair of jeans, equivalent to a half year's earnings for an average Cuban worker, is sold in a socialist city where many basic needs are unsatisfied (Nickel

1990). However, just like the planning and design strategies of the Republican era that aimed to forge a good impression on visitors who gazed out from the rails of steamers coming into Havana Bay (Schwartz 1997), Habaguanex wants to make sure that San Francisco Square "impresses" cruise ship passengers as they spill into streets of Habana Vieja. What waterfront visitors do not count on, however, is the foul stench of Havana Bay. It is one of the most heavily contaminated bodies of water in the Caribbean, receiving several hundred tons of organic material and oil products daily (Díaz-Briquets and Pérez-López 2000, 245-247).

HABAGUANEX AND JOINT VENTURES

Habaguanex competes indirectly for foreign investors and partners with other Cuban tourism companies such as Gran Caribe, Horizontes, and Cubanacán. Like other Cuban firms, Habaguanex allows partners to enjoy the right of owning a majority of shares in enterprises the government has prioritized. Tourism is the main sector that has received joint-venture support, absorbing more than half of all investments in the 1990s (Peters 1999). Inherent in these joint-venture deals is the ability for the foreign counterparts to freely repatriate profits. They are also exempt from certain custom duties, taxation on salaries for foreigners, and strikes, but may avail themselves to special Cuban-government services (architectural and legal) and related benefits (Mesa-Lago 1998, 181). As many authors have noted (Werlau 1998; Jatar-Hausmann 1999, 125), the number of declared joint ventures versus those that actually deliver goods or services varies.

Thus far, I have argued that unique historical circumstances have earned Habaguanex, S.A. considerable autonomy in its operations. Because of the sym-

---

4. The U.S. based real-estate company and franchise RE/MAX, is now operating in Cuba. In May 1999, its WWW site home page had registered more than 100,000 hits. Enticingly, the opening lines state: "The purchase of Real Estate in Cuba is now a reality! Condos, Homes, Office Space and more. Probably the most anxiously awaited real estate opportunity in the Americas. Hundreds of units have already been sold to astute buyers." These units, however, are mostly in Miramar and the Monte Barreto complex in the western suburbs. See http://www.realestatecuba.com/.

5. A black glass wall envelopes the roof (*azotea*) of the original structure. It is a modern design that stands out several blocks away and contrasts with the sober turn-of-the-century façade. A radio station and communication operations are located behind the black glass. Unaccompanied foreigners cannot enter this area. Located at the eastern edge of Havana Bay, the view is exceptional.

bolism inherent in Habana Vieja, and the bad public relations that resulted from the 1993 building collapse, Habaguanex has been able to move very quickly in carrying out its work. However, like all Cuban companies, we cannot review financial statements and balance sheets about the firm's annual performances. Therefore, I will turn to other secondary data sources that identify how Habaguanex has entered working relationships with foreign partners. I will use the example of two hotels: one under construction (Hotel Saratoga) and one completed (Parque Central) as examples of Habaguanex's special relationship with foreign firms.

Hotel Saratoga

The Hotel Saratoga stands at the extension of the Malecón, just southeast of the Capitolio building, and in front of the Fuente de India and Parque de la Fraternidad. This building is located in the Republican core of the city, as are Centro Asturiano, Hotel Telégrafo, and Hotel Parque Central. The facility has been undergoing redevelopment since 1998. It is financed by a British-Lebanese consortium, and corresponds to the "economic association" type of joint venture (Burr 1999). Habaguanex is in charge of approving the technical dimensions of the project because the hotel lies in the UNESCO-designated site.[6]

Habaguanex directs the reconstruction of the Hotel Saratoga through Fénix, its construction branch. It employs what I call a "gut and preserve" approach. Basically, this entails stabilizing the façade of the building and hollowing out (demolishing) the rest of the structure. The Republican-era "shell" of the early 20th century building stands, while a new 21st core will rise behind the "skin."

Not all Habaguanex-refurbished buildings are gutted this way. Santa Teresa, Ambos Mundos, and Hotel Florida are renovation sites that were not "hollowed"

out in the gut-and-preserve fashion of the Hotel Saratoga. The gut-and-preserve approach is conducive to sites that are very large (more than 80 rooms) or whose infrastructure is dilapidated and would require considerable time and expense to bring up to contemporary standards. My sense, though, is that the gut-and-preserve approach is simply quicker than the more laborious and tedious type of historic preservation. In the end, dollar-generating abilities come on line more quickly for the state using gut-and-preserve.

Parque Central

Remuneration terms make joint ventures attractive for non-Cuban financiers. It would seem that Article 33.4, Chapter XI, Labor System, of Law 77, the Foreign Investment Act, is the most deleterious to Cuban architects and engineers. The article mandates that "payments to Cuban workers…are made in national currency which must be obtained beforehand from convertible currency." This is the well-known clause that pays Cubans about one-twentieth of what their foreign counterparts earn in dollars, or what said Cubans would receive if they were paid in convertible currencies. The justification for paying Cubans in local currency is that their education was paid for by the state, and that they continue to receive free health care and pay little for housing. My impression is that most Cuban professionals who work in the construction of or operation of hotels that were arranged through Habaguanex joint-ventures believe that this is a ruse; they expect more than a little bag of soap at the end of the month. Instead, a cash payment in dollars would appear to be commonplace as well as sharing quality meals and beverages with the foreign counterparts on a regular basis.[7] One vignette from the Parque Central illustrates the importance of this remuneration (Box 1).

---

6. Habaguanex's clout in the city and nation has risen and its sphere of influence is not just confined the UNESCO World Heritage Site of HabanaVieja. In late 1999, Habaguanex was granted restoration control of Ricardo Porro's splendid complex, Escuela de Bellas Artes, located in the western suburb of Cubanacán. The "decision" to allow Habaguanex to direct the renovation of Porro's 1962 design was made at the highest levels: the Council of State. This is the first large-scale foray by Habaguanex into a project outside the old city. More than a few architects and restoration experts within the Ministries of Culture and Education have expressed displeasure at Habaguanex's growing sphere of influence.

7. This is one of two claims I make in this paper that I base on 23 trips and five and half months of field research.

Box 1.   Tomás Obrapía[a]

Tomás graduated from the José Antonio Echeverría Polytechnic University with a degree in civil engineering in the mid-1980s. After a brief stint with the Ministry of Construction in the late 1980s, he was laid off in the early years of the Special Period. After several years of un-, under-, and multi-employment in tasks ranging from illegal auto mechanic, taxi driver (*botero*), and tourist guide, he was hired by the Golden Tulip management company in 1997. His familiarity with spreadsheets landed him a job in the accounting department.

For the first 18 months he worked as an assistant to the head accountant on the day shift. Then, in late 1998, he had an opportunity to work as an auditor on the night shift, one of several upper-level positions available to Cubans. His task is important, as he must provide a check on eight cash registers from as many departments throughout the hotel (two bars; swimming pool-bar-café; main bar; two restaurants; and two gift shops). Discrepancies between receipts and cash as well as matching charges with the proper guestrooms are his most important responsibility. He is the first line of resolution between any of the eight departments and the top-line management (Dutch personnel). In the morning, he prepares an Excel file with the previous day's tallies for his European boss.

Half of his $875 dollar monthly salary reaches him in pesos; the other half, of course, is directed to the state. After his third month as the chief night accountant, he began receiving $80 USD under the table. As of June 2000, he was receiving an additional $25. "It is to be expected," he explained. "I've proven my worth and I can weed out any underreporting or low-level petty-cash theft if it continues over time." When asked if he thought that the full $875 USD should rightfully come his way, he told me: "Of course. But I cannot complain. Maybe over time things will change." He then proceeded to tell me woeful tales of his siblings and how hard it is for them to etch out a living based on their meager peso salary. "Golden Tulip knows I am reliable. I clear thousands of dollars for them daily." In addition, he eats breakfasts most every morning in the main tourist restaurant. "With that banquet of a breakfast, I'm good all day, and that helps at home with the *libreta*. Sometimes they have luncheons for us in the back restaurant or in the lobby-bar, and occasionally we can bring our wives. …Joseíto," he laughed, "I really cannot complain! *Tú sabes bien que estoy resolviendo!*"

a.   A pseudonym.

Historic preservation in the old city also creates tension between foreign investors (who tend to favor turnkey hotel and construction operations and who prefer architects from their countries), versus Cuban professionals. One case in point is the Dutch-operated (Golden Tulip) Parque Central located on the park of that same name. In the mid-1990s, Cuban architects submitted numerous designs for Parque Central Hotel at the west-central edge of Habana Vieja. In the end, a feasibility and design project submitted by a Spanish outfit, allegedly for half a million-dollar fee, won the design competition. One Cuban architect remarked, "With that kind of money, dozens of local architects could have received a stipend for two-months of work while they were

completing their *Parque Central* submissions. It would have given them money to buy drafting materials too. And I bet we could have come up with a project just as good as the Spanish one, if not better" (Personal communication, October 9,1999). Such foreign investment control over the use of design professionals smacks of an earlier, pre-Revolutionary era when local talent and projects were crowded out by foreign influences (Rigau 1994).

By striving towards a uniform, Spanish-colonial setting, Habana Vieja's uniqueness will dissipate.[8] Socialist planning in the old city cannot commodify the colonial city fast enough. As Cuban architect and urbanist Mario Coyula (1999, 158) stated recently in the reputable Cuban journal, *Revista Bimestre Cubana de la Sociedad Económica de Amigos del País*:

> Another problem is carrying out high-standard hotel and housing projects by foreign architects. Every great city needs architectural works from different countries, but they should be first-rate architects who can enrich the city with relevant projects that can situate the city on the universal cultural map, [the architects should not be] just anonymous servants to investors who at times are rapacious and uncultured. Nonetheless, many of the recent foreign projects are far from this goal of excellence. Why allow this, when some Cuban architects are better than some of the imported ones? Why pay hundreds of thousands of dollars for irrelevant projects? Why don't we use the normal procedure used on all important projects around the world: that its, hold a design competition and let the best one win? With such a procedure, Havana would also win (my translation).

There are, then, voices of reason.

DISCUSSION: WINNERS AND LOSERS

One hears often among design professionals, architects, and planners that there are no "young urban professionals" residing in Habana Vieja.[9] This feature attests to the revolutionary view of the socialist city that is defined by an absence of "young Cuban Americans"[10] of the Miami ilk. Most residents of Habana Vieja displaced by historic preservation must relocate in Habana del Este, across the bay on the eastern side of the city (Table 1). This is the site of some of the first public housing projects in the 1960s. Many habaneros consider it unattractive because of its poor sites and services, public transportation problems, and badly maintained grounds (Hamberg 1994). Although no official data exist, I estimate that Habaguanex has displaced at least 200 residents. How can displaced local residents be justified in socialist Cuba?

In the meantime, ordinary citizens wait for improvements in their residences as this uneven development manifests itself at different geographic scales of analysis. Nationwide, nearly half a million workers have been downsized from state jobs since 1990. Those who have not retired seek employment among the new self-employed, *cuentapropistas*, who amount to about 150,000 workers in a nation of 11 million. On average, they earn as much as 3.5 times state workers. Many self-employed work in the old quarters of Havana (Peters and Scarpaci 1998).

As noted above, the state built new housing in the early 1960s to accommodate those displaced from eradicated settlements because one in twenty Havana households lived in squatter settlements. Habana Vieja absorbed a sizeable share of relocated squatters. One building in particular represents what has happened elsewhere in the old city. On the northeastern corner of the square rests a stately apartment complex built in 1904. Much of the ornate plasterwork and some of the balconies have fallen off the six-story apartment building over the years. By the late 1960s, the former single-family apartments had become homes to several families. Crowding compounded the interior deterioration. In 1996, a joint venture

---

8. When Parque Central opened its doors in 1998, though, only a small corner facade withstood the wrecking ball. A swimming pool graces the top floor, but it is on the ninth and not sixth story as originally specified. In addition, the traditional Havana colonnaded walkways are considerably taller than others in the vicinity. See Violetta and Scarpaci (1999).

9. Although Yuppies are not present, there is concern among urban planners and architects about a "what if" scenario should Cuban-Americans in Miami suddenly appear in Old Havana. In that case, the YUCAS (Young Urban Cuban Americans) would likely find much real estate to their liking. Other concerns about a potential onslaught of Florida influences include the "Miamification" (high-rise waterfront construction), "Disneyification" (contrived cultural spaces) "McDonaldization" (chain retailing onslaught) of Havana, or "Cancunization" (Caribbean high-density waterfront development). These points of reflection exceed the scope of this essay. For a consideration of them, see the home page and related links of Cuban-American architect Andrés Duany and his partner and wife, Elizabeth Plater-Zyberk, at http://www.dpz-architects.com. It is noteworthy that despite the highly polemical debate about Cuban-Americans desires for transforming Havana, there is strong agreement that it should not become another Miami (e.g., turning its back to the sea, becoming a highly automobile-reliant metropolis, and other maladies of late 20th century suburban sprawl). See Kunstler (1996) for a succinct review.

10. For a hypothetical discussion of how Havana might have looked had the revolution not occurred see Segre at al., 1997:324-26.

Table 1.   Winner and Losers in Habaguanex's Collaboration with Joint-Ventures

Direct		Indirect	
Winners	**Losers**	**Winners**	**Losers**
International heritage admirers; world patrimony; UNESCO	Residents of Habana Vieja whose opportunity costs include forgone residential improvements	Some segments of the international tourist market who are unfamiliar with the nature of renovation	Cubans, especially dark-skinned ones, who are denied access from certain tourist facilities
Cuban government: Symbolism[a] of restored buildings and construction cranes over the old city[b]	Displaced residents who are relocated to Alamar, Habana del Este, and other 'remote' suburban enclaves	Commercial sex workers ←——————→	Commercial sex workers
Selected neighborhoods (San Isidro, Belén) whose infrastructure (water, sewage, power lines improve) because of joint-venture investment	Adjacent neighborhoods of Atarés, Regla, Centro Habana, and others which badly need refurbished	Selected architects and engineers who are able to practice their trades with Habaguanex	Cubans who identify tourism as a path to sustainable development; internal 'brain drain' of other professionals seeking work in Habana Vieja's tourist realm
Foreign investors turn profits because of low wages and salaries paid to Cuban workers	Cuban workers	Retired "maestros" who teach young apprentices their building and art trades (carpentry, masonry, stained glass, plaster)	Skilled professionals who have no say in the redevelopment of the old city; denied a chance to practice their skills & training
Foreign architects & engineers	Cuban architects & engineers	Tourism police, cuentrapropistas, jineteros working in old city[c]	Residents of Habana Vieja inundated with tourists

a.   See King (1990) for an insightful discussion of the role of symbolism, power and architecture.

b.   See Violetta and Scarpaci (1999) for a summary of this process in the old city.

c.   See Elinson (1999) for an excellent review of street hustlers in Havana and their impact on civil society.

Italian-Cuban project began renovating the structure into condominiums. Future occupants will be foreign business people working in Cuba, not residents of Habana Vieja. Foreigners will rent the apartments from Habaguanex and will pay in dollars, not pesos. The adjacent Plaza Vieja has been restored with an expensive ornate Italian-marble fountain[11] in the center of the plaza, and the perimeter of the plaza is framed by metal spheres to prevent vehicular traffic.

Officials[12] at Habaguanex justify such building renovation, civic beautification, and residential displacement. In the end, the preservation of a collective, so-

cialist order will be ensured since social property remains the *sine qua non* of the Cuban Revolution. Habaguanex and the socialist leadership are, in the words of one company official "in [the preservation business] for the long haul."[13] These and related examples are just a few anecdotes surrounding the many winners and losers surrounding Habaguanex's foray into accommodating foreign investors (Table 1).

CONCLUSIONS

Habaguanex, S.A., the restoration company in Old Havana, operates in a unique political and economic

11.   I have heard that the Carrera-marble piece cost half a million dollars.

12.   Eusebio Leal Spengler has requested payments to Habaguanex for his interviews, approximately $1,000 USD per conversation. Generally, only prominent journalists or politicians can speak with him. This information comes from personal communication between the author and journalists from the *Dallas Morning News, Times-Picayune, Ft. Lauderdale Sun-Sentinel, Condé Nest Travel,* and *U.S. News and World Report.*

13.   I had these interviews with two administrators of Habaguanex on March 6, 9, and 10, 1998.

environment that has given it special abilities in attracting foreign investors. This paper has attempted to identify the merits and detriments of the firm's behavior within the logic of the socialist system. In many ways, a post-Soviet era of downsizing and foreign investment in tourism has made tourism a viable option in a socialist Cuba that once refused to create another island of bartenders and chambermaids. To be sure, foreign investment exacerbates household income differentials but, for some workers like Tomás Obrapía, it is a survival mechanism. As Gunn observed (1993, 15):

> present conditions in Cuba suggest that while rising foreign investment is undermining Castro's power in several important ways, this subversive effect is balanced by other sociological results of foreign investment that actually consolidate the system…That balance could easily change, however. If investment rises faster and spreads further [sic] from the tourism enclaves…then the class of privileged workers will grow, and the contrast with the hardships of their neighbors employed in state enterprises will become more evident.

Seven years after her observation, such contrasts are even more striking, especially in Habana Vieja. Income disparity and the contrast of housing stock between tourist facilities and locals call attention to a long-standing debate in socialist planning about moral versus material incentives (Zhao 1995; Rohter 1995; Szlenyi 1982).

Habaguanex will continue to serve as the redevelopment engine of Habana Vieja. The approval by both houses in the U.S. Congress that permit the sale of food to Cuba may allow some of the Habaguanex and joint-venture facilities in Habana Vieja to lower their costs, but that is likely to be a small benefit. Objectively, we still must question the nature of historic preservation in Habana Vieja. While it is true that "Cuban officials…have toned down their socialist rhetoric to make overtures to entrepreneurs overseas" (Jatar-Hausmann 1999, 128), salvaging the urban heritage is an easier sale because of the seemingly apolitical appeal of safeguarding an element of past culture and architectural design. One need only walk through Havana and see the numerous restoration

projects donated gratis to appreciate this powerful allure. This free contribution (mainly from Spanish and Italian architectural societies) of money, materials, and technical skills also makes Habaguanex unique in its relationship with foreign economic associations; Canada's Sherrittt International Corporation does not donate nickel-mining machinery and Spain's Sol Meliá will not give hotel furniture for goodwill only.

Michael Edwards, the former Civil Society Specialist of the World Bank, argues that globally the past 50 years have been characterized by corporate and state meddling in the lives of the poor. He contends that the next 50 years should witness co-operation as the dominant discourse in development circles. "The changing global context makes co-operation both more necessary and more possible. There has never been a better time to pursue the vision of a more co-operative world" (Edwards, 1999, 23). Restructuring in Habana Vieja unfolds without consulting local residents even though some Cuban planners and social scientists encourage such collaboration in Habana Vieja (Collado et al. 1996; Dávalos and Velázquez 1996). Furthermore, neither tourism nor revitalization develops at the grassroots, despite Cuba's intent on using mass organizations to further the goals of the revolution (cf. Arnold 1999). Habaguanex guides this restructuring and enters into agreements with foreign partners to facilitate a limited process of capital accumulation not unlike revitalization projects in Baltimore and other U.S. cities (Smith 1979; Smith 1987; Smith and Feagin 1987; Harvey 1985; Holcomb and Beauregard 1982). Cooperation with civil society is not part of joint-venture operations in Cuba.

Only Habaguanex can bring Habana Vieja into the new millennium and avoid the kinds of economic and social exclusion that urban revitalization and restructuring create in historic districts outside Cuba. Voices of concern about the joint-venture frenzy, which brings both bad design to the city and excludes Cuban professionals from gainful employment, will be drowned out by the stampede of investors to the UNESCO site. In that case, there can be no winners.

REFERENCES

Arnold A, 1999, *Democracy in Cuba and the 1997-98 Elections* (Editorial José Martí, Havana).

Barthel D, 1996, *Historic Preservation: Collective Memory and Historical Identify* (Rutgers University Press, New Brunswick, NJ).

Burr C, 1999, "Capitalism: Cuban Style," *Fortune*, March 1 (International Edition) 72-74.

Codrescu A, 1999, *Ay, Cuba! A Socio-Erotic Journey* (St. Martin's Press, New York).

Collado R, Mauri S, Coipel M, 1996, "Revitalización urbana, desarrollo social y participación. La experiencia en el barrio San Isidro" (Urban revitalization, social development and participation. The experience in San Isidro neighborhood) In Dávalos R, Vázquez A, Eds. *Participación social. Desarrollo urbano y comunitario* (Social participation. Urban and community development) (Universidad de La Habana, Havana) 106-118.

Conas 1995, *Foreign Investment Act of Cuba* (Havana, Conas).

Coyula, M, 1999, "Arquitectura y ciudad en la cultura cubana," *Revista Bimestre Cubana de la Sociedad Económica de Amigos del País* 86:155-160.

Dávalos, R, Vázquez, A, 1996, *Participación social. Desarrollo urbano y comunitario* (Social participation. Urban and community development) (Universidad de La Habana, Havana).

Díaz-Briquets, S, and Pérez-López, J, 2000, *Conquering Nature: The Environmental Legacy of Socialism in Cuba* (University of Pittsburgh Press, Pittsburgh).

Dyck, R, 1998, "Integrated planning and sustainability theory for local benefit," *Local Environments* 3:27-41.

Eckstein S, 1977, "The debourgeoisement of Cuban cities." In I.L. Horowitz, Ed., *Cuban Communism* (Transaction Books, New Brunswick, NJ) 443-474.

Edwards M, 1999, *Future Positive: International co-operation in the 21st century* (Earthscan Publications Ltd, London).

Elinson H, 1999, "Cuba's Jineteros: Youth Culture and Revolutionary Ideology." *Cuba Briefing Paper Series* 20, Georgetown University: Center for Latin American Studies, The Caribbean Project.

Glancey J, 1993, "Architecture Page: Walls came tumbling down," *The Independent* (London), October 20.

Graham, B, Ashworth, JE, and Tunbridge, JE, 2000, *A Geography of Heritage* (Arnold, London).

Grogg, P, 1999, Ciudades de America Latina: Habana Vieja, una ciudad para vivir mejor, August 2, InterPress Service, Third World News Agency, Montevideo, Uruguay.

Gunn, G, 1993, "The sociological impact of rising foreign investment." *Cuba Briefing Papers Series* No. 1 (Georgetown University, Washington, D.C.).

Habaguanex, S.A. URL http://www.habaguanex.com.

Hall, S, 1995, "New cultures for old." In Massey, D, and Jess, P, (eds) *A Place in the World? Place, Cultures and Globalization* (Open University/Oxford University Press) 175-214.

Hamberg J, 1994, "The dynamics of Cuban housing policy," unpublished PhD dissertation, Columbia University.

Harvey D, 1985, *The Urbanization of capital* (Johns Hopkins University Press, Baltimore and London).

Hewison, R, 1987, *The Heritage Industry: Britain in a Climate of Decline* (Methuen, London).

Hobsbawm, E J, 1990, *Nations and Nationalism since 1789: Programme, Myth, Reality* (Cambridge University Press, Cambridge).

Holcomb H.B, Beauregard R, 1982, *Urban Revitalization* (Association of American Geographers, Washington, D.C.).

IPS (InterPress Third Wold News Agency) 1999, "Cuba: Disminuirá construcción de vivendas," (Cuba: Will decrease housing construction) Report posted on http://www.ips.org, Dated February 23.

Jatar-Hausmann, J, 1999, *The Cuban Way: Capitalism, Communism and Confrontation* (Kamarian, West Hartford, CT).

Jones G A, Varley A, 1994, "The contest for the city center: buildings versus people," *Bulletin of Latin American Research* 13:247-265.

Jones G A, Varley A, 1999, "The reconquest of the historic centre: Urban conservation and gentrification in Puebla, Mexico," *Environment and Planning* 31:1547-1566.

King A, 1990, "Architecture, capital and the globalization of culture," *Theory, Culture & Society* 7:397-411.

Kunstler J H, 1996, *Home From Nowhere* (New York, Simon and Schuster/Touchstone Books).

Leal E, 1999. Opening remarks, plenary session, the Fourth International Conference on Cultural Heritage and Historic Preservation, Ministry of Culture, National Center for Restoration, Conservation, and Museum Science (CENCREM) October 12, Spanish language presentation audio-recorded and transcribed by the author.

Ley D, 1996, *The New Middle Class and the Remaking of the Central City* (Oxford University Press, Oxford and New York).

Llanes L. 1993. 1898-1921. *Apuntes para una historia sobre los constructores cubanos* (Notes for a history of Cuban builders) (Editorial Letras Cubanas, Havana).

Lowenthal, D, 1985, *The Past is a Foreign Country* (Cambridge University Press, Cambridge).

Mesa-Lago, C, 1998, "Cuba's economic policies and strategies for the 1990s." In J. Suchlicki and I.L.

Horowitz (Eds.) *Cuban Communism* (Transaction, New Brunswick NJ) 177-203.

Nickel A, 1990, "El casco histórico de La Habana: La situación de vivienda y los conceptos de renovación urbana en La Habana," *Revista Geográfica* 112:75-90.

Peters, P, 1999, *A Different Kind of Workplace: Foreign Investment in Cuba* (Alexis de Tocqueville Institute, Arlington, VA).

Peters, P, Scarpaci J, 1998, *Cuban entrepreneurs: Five years of small-scale capitalism* (Alexis de Tocqueville Institute, Arlington, VA).

Rigau J, 1994, "No longer islands: Dissemination of Architecture Ideas in the Hispanic Carribean, 1890-1930," *The Journal of Decorative and Propaganda Arts* 20:237-251.

Rohter R, 1995, "In Cuba, Army takes on party jobs, and may be only thing that works." *The New York Times*, June 8, p. A-12.

Scarpaci J L, 1998a. "The changing face of Cuban socialism: Tourism and planning in the post-socialist era," In (D. Keeling and J. Wiley, eds.), *CLAG_Yearbook* (University of Texas Press, Austin) 87-110.

Scarpaci, J.L. 1998b, "Tourism planning during Cuba's 'Special Period,'" In (F. Costa, R. Kent, A. Dutt, and A. Noble, eds.), *Regional Planning and Development Practices and Policies* (Ashgate Publishing Ltd, Aldershot, UK) 225-244.

Schwartz R, 1997, *Pleasure Island: Tourism and Temptation in Cuba* (University of Nebraska Press, Lincoln).

Segre R, 1995 *La Plaza de Armas de La Habana. Sinfonía urbana inconclusa* (Havana's Arms Square: An unfinished urban symphony) (Editorial Arte y Literatura, Havana).

Segre R, Coyula M, Scarpaci JL, 1997, *Havana: Two Faces of the Antillean Metropolis* (Wiley, Chichester, UK).

Smith M, Feagin J R, 1987, *The Capitalist City* (Basil Blackwell, Oxford and New York).

Smith N, 1979, "Toward a theory of gentrification: A back-to-the-city movement by capital, not by people," *Journal of the American Planning Association* 45:538-548.

Smith N, 1987, "Of yuppies and housing: Gentrification, social restructuring and the urban dream," *Environment and Planning D: Society and Space* 5:151-179.

Snow, A, 2000, "Economists evaluate embargo impact," Associated Press (AP-NY-07-21-00 2249EDT), July 21.

Szlenyi, I, 1982, *Urban Inequities under State Socialism* (Oxford University Press, Oxford).

Violetta B, Scarpaci, J L, "1999 Havana construction boom in old city," *CubaNews*, December, (Target Research Group Washington, D.C.) 4.

Werlau, M, 1998, "Update on foreign investment in Cuba for 1997-98 and focus on the energy sector." *Cuba in Transition—Volume 8* (Association for the Study of the Cuban Economy, Washington, D.C.).

Weiss J, 1950, *Medio siglo de arquitectura cubana* (Half a century of Cuban architecture) (Universidad de La Habana, Havana).

Woolf, S, 1996, *Nationalism in Europe, 1815 to the Present: A Reader* (Routledge, London).

Zhao H, 1995, "The dual-structured land market in Shenzhen City, China," *Regional Development Studies* (Tokyo Institute of Technology) 1: 17-29.

TOWARD BEST BUSINESS PRACTICES
FOR FOREIGN INVESTORS IN CUBA

Ambassador Anthony C.E. Quainton[1]

At a time when consumer awareness is rising and responsible corporate policies are gaining international attention, the National Policy Association (NPA) is focusing on best business practices for foreign investors in the Republic of Cuba.

The concept of promoting human rights through the private sector is, of course, not new. Private sector adherence to the McBride Principles resulted in the establishment of fair labor practices in Northern Ireland. The Sullivan Principles, issued in 1977, ultimately contributed to the downfall of apartheid in South Africa.

As one of the nation's principal nonpartisan, nonprofit organizations conducting informed dialogue and independent research on major economic and social problems, NPA first took up the issue of worker rights in Cuba in 1997 under the auspices of its North American Committee, a group of senior business and labor leaders from Canada, Mexico and the United States. With the collective effort of an international working group, the National Policy Association is now working to persuade current and future investors in Cuba to adopt voluntary best business practices and to use their leverage with the Cuban government to promote worker rights.

WORKER RIGHTS IN CUBA

Although the Republic of Cuba has ratified ILO Conventions 87 (Freedom of Association and Protection of the Right to Organize) and 98 (Right to Organize and Collective Bargaining) and Cuba's constitution guarantees the freedom of association and assembly, Cuba's record with regard to worker rights is the worst in the Western Hemisphere. Worker rights are severely constrained, as the officially sponsored Central de Trabajadores de Cuba (CTC) is the only legitimate association of workers under Cuba's labor code.

The CTC is a confederation of state-run, state-sanctioned labor unions. Cuban labor expert Efrén Córdova describes the CTC:

> The CTC is not a legitimate workers' organization, but an appendage of the government and the Communist Party. It has never been a forum for open discussion, criticism, proposals, or alternatives to the official line. At none of it meetings have demands ever been proposed or complaints lodged; it only serves as a sound box for the regime's demands and a transmission belt for political watchwords and production plans.[2]

Because the CTC is mandated to promote the "struggle for the defense of Socialism and its princi-

---

1. This paper was prepared with substantial assistance of Kaylin Bailey, International Program Associate at the National Policy Association. Ms. Bailey directs the NPA Working Group on worker rights and best business practices in Cuba. NPA is a nonprofit, nonpartisan organization conducting dialogue and independent research on major economic and social problems facing the United States.

2. Córdova, Efrén. "Labor Conditions in Revolutionary Cuba," in *Modern Slavery: Labor Conditions in Cuba*. ICCAS Occasional Paper Series, University of Miami. April 2000.

ples," CTC members must be members of the Cuban Communist Party. This factor, in itself, narrows the scope of workers' rights in Cuba; it allows workers the "freedom" to be part of the government-run union, or to remain unrepresented. In the normal sense of the word, labor is not free. Overall, these conditions have caused great concern among human rights organizations and socially responsible businesses alike.

The labor structure in Cuba presents many problems for the Cuban worker. The government repeatedly ignores requests from independent worker groups for legalization. Because workers are deprived of the freedom of association, they lack a forum for collective bargaining in both public and private sectors. Foreign investors are required to hire workers through a government agency, screening workers according to their *expedientes laborales* and often noting political affiliation as a criteria for employment. Jobs in the private sector, which have better pay and benefits than state sector jobs, are usually reserved for "good revolutionaries." The indirect payment system, which requires foreign investors to pay employees through the sieve of government hands, results in an actual wage in pesos of between five and ten percent of the original dollar amount paid by the company. Many foreign investors in Cuba recognize that the indirect payment system leaves most workers struggling for the means to buy basic necessities. These companies often provide Cuban workers with a small basket, or *jabita*, of soap, toothpaste, fruit, vegetables or dry goods in an attempt to compensate their tiny wages. While the distribution of *jabitas* is a small positive step on the part of foreign investors, a more fair system or direct payment to workers would eliminate this need.

THE NPA WORKER RIGHTS AND BEST BUSINESS PRACTICES IN CUBA PROJECT

In July 1997, the National Policy Association's North American Committee (NAC), an association of business, labor and academic leaders from the United States, Canada and Mexico, issued "Principles for Private Sector Involvement in Cuba." The Principles proposed by the NAC include: a safe and healthy workplace, fair employment practices, direct

employment of workers, the right of workers to organize and bargain collectively, a workplace which allows for freedom of expression, and the strengthening of legal processes in Cuba. The NAC Principles are similar to the more elaborate Arcos Principles, named after one of Cuba's leading human rights activists, Gustavo Arcos.

The NAC's interest in the role of the private sector in Cuba arose from its belief that the private sector could and should seek to advance the three member countries' commitment to democracy, human rights, and the betterment of the lives of the Cuban people.

In response to the challenge of promoting worker rights in a country whose very structure impedes those rights, the National Policy Association received a $225,000 grant in October 1999 from the United States Agency for International Development to promote worker rights and best business practices.

CUBA WORKING GROUP AND VOLUNTARY INVESTMENT PRINCIPLES

Under this project, NPA has formed an international private sector-working group. Each organization contributes its unique perspective on the issue of worker rights. Its members are not by any means homogeneous and they hold differing views about Cuba. The working group is comprised of the following business, labor and human rights groups from Europe, Canada, Mexico and the United States:

- AFL-CIO American Center for International Labor Solidarity (ACILS)
- American Chamber of Commerce of Cuba in the United States (AmCham Cuba)
- Consejo Mexicano de Comercio Exterior (COMCE)
- The Conference Board of Canada
- Florida International University
- Instituto Tecnológico Autónomo de México (ITAM)
- National Policy Association
- Pax Christi Netherlands

- Prince of Wales Business Leaders Forum

- United States Chamber of Commerce

- US Cuba Business Council

- Confederation of Netherlands Industry and Employers (VNO-NCW).

The Cuba Working Group has agreed on an updated set of principles for private sector investment in Cuba. The Working Group agreed to urge businesses investing in Cuba to voluntarily adopt socially-responsible and internationally accepted business practices in their activities in Cuba. While constrained by the laws and regulations in force in Cuba, foreign companies should endeavor to respect internationally recognized principles, such as those embodied in the Arcos and NAC Principles, and to advocate changes in laws and regulations where adherence to these principles is not currently possible. Most of these principles apply to other countries as well, and the Working Group has urged all companies to conduct their worldwide operations with these principles in mind.

Principles for Private Sector Investment in Cuba

The international private sector has a vital role to play in promoting open, free market institutions and adherence to universal standards of human rights. The International Working Group on Best Business Practices in Cuba has made clear that socially responsible business practices can help foster human rights and, ultimately, a more productive workforce. They have urged businesses investing in Cuba to adopt socially-responsible business practices in their activities in Cuba. They also recognize that the situation in Cuba is dynamic, and that the challenges facing private sector involvement in Cuba are many. While operating in a manner consistent with current laws and regulations in force in Cuba, companies should endeavor to respect fundamental worker rights principles and advocate changes in laws and regulations where adherence to these principles is not currently possible.

Based upon the Arcos Principles (1994) and the North American Committee Principles (1997), as well as the Sullivan, McBride, and other socially-re-

sponsible principles that have served as a catalyst for progress in non-democratic societies, the Working Group has encouraged the private sector to voluntarily adopt the following basic principles:

- Respect workers' right to organize freely in the workplace and to choose a union to represent them in negotiations with management, in accordance with ILO Conventions 87 and 98;

- Maintain a corporate culture that respects free expression consistent with legitimate business concerns, and does not condone political coercion in the workplace;

- Work to gain the right to recruit, contract, pay and promote workers directly, not through government intermediaries;

- Employ socially responsible employment practices, including the avoidance of child and forced labor and discrimination based on race, gender, national origin, religious beliefs, or political beliefs or affiliation, in accordance with ILO Convention 111;

- Provide a safe and healthy workplace, consistent with the principles of sustainable development;

- Support the strengthening of legal procedures, encouraging respect for due process, human rights, and the international conventions of which Cuba is a signatory.

The Cuban government has a critical need for hard currency. As a result of the recent slight openings in Cuba's economy, foreign investors meet a significant part of that need. Many members of the Working Group believe that, while the Cuban people have a very limited voice in the protection of their fundamental human rights, those companies that choose to invest in Cuba can use their financial power to promote these rights.

CUBA WORKING GROUP AND OTHER ACTIVITIES

The NPA Cuba project hosted an international conference on worker rights and best business practices in Cuba in June 2000 in Mexico City. Mexican investors have shown great interest in the project, and more than 70 participants from Mexico, the United States and Canada registered for the conference. The main focus of the event was to increase awareness about the current labor situation for foreign investors in Cuba. A variety of speakers endorsed the Working Group Principles, indicating that responsible private sector involvement can be an effective means for the promotion of democracy and human rights. Conference presenters included Gare Smith (Attorney at Law, Foley Hoag & Eliot); Howard Sullivan (Global Sullivan Principles and son of Rev. Leon Sullivan); Ambassador Otto Reich (President, US Cuba Business Council); Benjamin Davis (Americas Coordinator, American Center for International Labor Solidarity); Francisco León (Senior Fellow, Institute for European-Latin American Relations); and Pedro Pérez Castro (Secretary of International Relations, Solidarity of Cuban Workers).

In accordance with Section 109 of the *Cuban Freedom and Democratic Solidarity (LIBERTAD) Act*, the Working Group is actively working to make contact with independent or so-called "dissident" groups on the island, and to the extent possible disseminate translated materials about worker rights to Cuban nationals. Though the Working Group is primarily building these contacts through organizations such as the Solidarity of Cuban Workers (STC), based in Caracas, Venezuela, members are planning a visit to Cuba in late summer 2000 to solidify relationships and to learn more about Cuba's independent labor movement and to establish direct contact with foreign investors on the island.

AMERICAN INVESTORS

The United States Congress is currently reviewing the U.S. embargo against Cuba. U.S. law clearly states that American business is prohibited from investing in Cuba until a democratic transition has taken place. It is clear, however, that at some point in the future American business will reenter Cuba. While the National Policy Association's efforts are primarily focused on Mexican, Canadian and European investors, we believe that it is vital to involve U.S. companies in our efforts. The Principles for Private Sector Investment in Cuba are relevant now and will be in the future.

CONCLUSIONS

We can be under no illusions about the difficulty of effecting change in Cuba. The International Labor Organization has no real power to enforce international labor law, although it can publicize labor rights abuses as a means to effect change. Castro's refusal to grant basic human rights or to adopt economic measures that would benefit the Cuban people (instead of the regime) suggest that publicizing abuses, although necessary, will not in and of itself be a sufficient tactic with the Cuban government.

Instead, we must work from the bottom up to encourage business, labor and human rights groups to work together to support and encourage the organization of genuinely independent groups within Cuba. One approach is to work with foreign investors already on the island to promote change. The development of a free and independent labor movement is an essential first step toward genuine democracy and human rights for all.

ECONOMIC REFORMS AND
SOCIAL CONTRADICTIONS IN CUBA

Charles Trumbull[1]

Cuba is a land of contradictions. People have no money, but no one goes hungry. Buildings are crumbling, yet Havana is one of the most beautiful cities in the world. It rains when the sun is shining, and the streets are full of antique cars that should have died years ago. Cubans continue to risk their lives at sea trying to reach Miami on handmade rafts, yet people on the island seem to survive somehow. Life does not appear to follow an orderly pattern, yet everything seems to move along.

The Cuban economy and economic reforms are just as difficult to understand. The economy shrank by 40% in the early 1990s, following the collapse of the USSR. The United States has tightened the embargo on Cuba, making it even more difficult for Cuba to acquire food, technology, and investment capital from abroad. However, Cuba's economy is slowly recovering and Fidel Castro seems to be as in control over it as ever.

Over the past decade Castro has instituted reforms that seem to move Cuba towards a market economy. Although Cuba is still very much a socialist country, economic necessity has forced Castro to allow many previously-banned activities, such as foreign invest-

ment, the use of dollars, and most importantly, self-employment. Still, Castro adamantly denounces the evils of capitalism and insists on Cuba's resolve to stay the socialist course.

This paper will examine the inherent contradictions that the newly-authorized reforms cause within Cuba's ideological socialist state. It will show that even though the economy is improving, Castro's economic policies and fear of capitalist reform cost the Cuban economy billions of dollars annually. Finally, the paper will examine the possibility of co-existence of capitalism and socialism within Cuba.

The paper comprises six sections: crisis period, economic reforms, economic success, immediate problems, long-term problems, and the future of Cuba. The paper as a whole presents an overview and analysis of the events precipitating the current economic and social situation and their potential implications for Cuba's future.

CRISIS PERIOD[2]

Although the USSR did not officially withdraw its support until September 12, 1991, the Cuban economic crisis was precipitated by cutbacks in trade and subsidies from the USSR in 1989. In the period from 1989 to 1993, Cuba's GDP fell, according to

---

1. This paper is based on a research trip to Havana during the winter of 1999. The research was sponsored, and funded by, Darmouth College. I would like to acknowledge David Becker, Larry Corwin, Jorge Pérez-López and Matías Travieso-Díaz for their valuable comments on earlier drafts. Remaining errors are mine.

2. The crisis experienced by Cuba upon the downfall of the Soviet Bloc is well described in the literature and will only be summarized here. The reader is referred to, e.g., *Cuba After the Cold War*, edited by Carmelo Mesa-Lago, 1993, for additional details.

different sources, between 35 and 40%.[3] Imports fell, due to the end of preferential trading with the USSR, by 75%. Employment declined from 4.4 million to 4.1 million, and real wages fell almost 40% in urban areas. Consequently, personal consumption declined by 15% each year until 1994 (Pérez-López, 1995:126-135). The problems created by the crisis were exacerbated by immense foreign debt, which greatly limited Cuba's ability to secure financing for trade and investment activities.[4] Cuba has expressed willingness to negotiate debt payments, but claims it will not be able to pay off debts without receiving fresh loans first.

Another element of the crisis is that Cuba's physical infrastructure is obsolete. For example, Cuba is stuck with Soviet Bloc machinery and technology that are impossible to repair because they were manufactured with parts incompatible with modern day, Western made parts. Cuba desperately needs capital to modernize its factories, mines, sugar mills, hospitals, and other potential sources of hard currency. However, because of its foreign debt as well as its terms for joint ventures and lack of management experience, Cuba has been unable to secure loans or to attract substantial amounts of foreign investment.

This economic crisis prompted the government to institute in the early 1990s certain reforms that altered the economy and the prevailing social ideals. The first and most drastic measure was a strict rationing of energy and food items. In 1990, Castro announced a shortfall of 3.3 million tons of oil, about a third of annual consumption. To deal with these shortages, Castro reduced gas and oil deliveries by 50% to the state sector and 30% to the private sector, reduced the number of public buses, imported 1.2 million bicycles from China, temporarily shut down several cement, nickel, and textile factories, and implemented a series of electrical blackouts throughout the country (Pérez-López, 1995: 136-142). Castro also implemented a *programa alimenta-*

rio whose aim was to conserve food supplies while increasing internal production. Food rations were cut in half and thousands of workers were removed from bureaucratic jobs to help in the harvests of coffee, sugar and other staples.

FOUR MAJOR ECONOMIC REFORMS

Having halted the economic crash by cutting consumption and reducing public expenditures, Castro initiated changes in the middle of 1993 meant to bring the country out of the crisis. Although some of these reforms appeared at the time to be pushing Cuba towards a market economy, it is clear now that they were meant to maintain socialism rather than serve as the first steps of a transition to a market-oriented economy. While some members of the government, and numerous economists in and outside of Cuba, advocate further reforms such as those that have proven successful in China and Vietnam, most members of the Communist Party, including Castro, see those countries as having abandoned socialism, which the Cuban government is not prepared to do.

The four major economic reforms instituted by Castro in 1993 are: (1) liberalization of foreign investment; (2) breakup of state farms and creation of farmers' markets; (3) dollarization of the economy; and (4) legalization of self-employment. These reforms have resulted in some economic growth and appear to be pulling Cuba out of its crisis, though GDP is still well below 1989 levels. However, they clash ideologically with socialism and are not structurally consistent with capitalism. Most importantly, they have created a variety of contradictions that threaten to undermine communist control and undo the successes of socialism.

To understand these contradictions, it is necessary to briefly analyze the four reforms. The four reforms are inherently connected and thus should be studied together rather than viewed as separate entities. Likewise, it is impossible to attribute any social contradiction solely to a single reform. For example, Castro

---

3. The period of economic crisis has often been referred to by Fidel Castro as *el período especial en tiempo de paz.*

4. In 1990, Cuba's debt reached $7.3 billion (Mesa-Lago, 1993: 201). It has reached on the order of $12 billion (principal and interest), not counting outstanding—and contested—debt to Russia as successor state to the Soviet Union.

likes to denounce the liberalization of self-employment since it has had the most visible economically beneficial effect, especially for those individuals who have found ways to work independently of the state. However, without the increase of tourism due to foreign investment, and the dollarization of the economy, self-employment would not have been as economically successful as it has been.

Foreign Investment

Not being able to trade sugar at subsidized prices, Cuba was forced to find new ways to obtain foreign currency. However, Cuba does not have the resources or capital to build up its tourism, nickel, or biomedical technology industries, and thus was forced to invite foreign investment in joint ventures with the government. Although foreign investment was legalized in 1982, it wasn't until the 1990s that many sectors of the economy were open to investment. Although Cuba is still considered a risky country to invest in, it has given several legal rights to foreign investors, including, among others:

1. Joint ventures are guaranteed autonomy and can freely choose their boards of directors, establish prices, define the nature of their products, etc. (although there are frequently contractual time limits for these rights). The right to hold property, within certain limits, is guaranteed for foreign investors;

2. Joint ventures are able to transfer earnings abroad in convertible currency;

3. Joint ventures are subject only to a 30% tax on profits and a 25% tax on the payroll of Cuban citizens.

Despite Cuba not being included in the top 100 safest countries to invest in, it has attracted over 300 joint ventures, of which about 200 are with smaller businesses. In addition, fourteen U.S. companies, including AT&T and Coca-Cola, have signed contracts to invest in Cuba once the U.S. embargo is lifted (Pérez Villanueva, 1998: 26).

By 1998 Cuba had attracted $1,756,900,000 in foreign investments, with another $4 billion committed or in discussion. Although last year the Minister of Labor and Social Security reported that only 3-4% of Cuba's 4.5 million workers are employed by foreign firms, investment has sparked production and growth in several important sectors of Cuba's economy. For example, nickel production with the aid of Canadian firm, Sherritt International, has grown 44% above 1989 levels reaching 68,000 tons. Likewise, oil production has increased by 150% since 1991.[5]

The majority of foreign investment is focused on the nickel, petroleum, biotechnology, and tourism industries. It is tourism, though, that is expected to make the greatest contribution to the economy. The tourism sector in Cuba, which had been small prior to 1990, has grown at an astounding 20% annually since 1993, compared to the regional average of only 6-7%, putting tourism as the top source for foreign currency. In 1997, the government reported that tourists spent $1.54 billion on air travel, accommodations, national products, and food. Additionally, millions of dollars were spent in the emerging second economy (the legal economy that is heavily controlled by the state but runs primarily according to free market rules) in *paladares,* apartments, taxis, souvenir sellers, etc. In 1998, an estimated 2 million tourists traveled to Cuba, and by 2010 the Cuban government expects to attract up to 10 million foreigners to the island who will spend $5 billion (Godínez, 1998: 51).

Sol Meliá, a large Spanish hotel firm, has led the way with 11 hotels in Cuba offering 3568 rooms. The investment has been lucrative for Sol Meliá; while it only has 4% of its hotels located in Cuba, they represent almost 10% of the company's earnings. Sol Meliá employs 21,000 Cubans while its Cuban partner, Cubanacán, employs an additional 20,000 (Godínez, 1998:53-58). With the recent addition of Meliá Cohiba in Havana, the only hotel on the island

---

5. However, domestic production still accounts for only 17% of the national consumption and Cuba spends $1.2 billion per year to import oil (Werlau, 1998:204-208).

that rivals the elegance of the Hotel Nacional, Sol Meliá is in an excellent position to continue to benefit from the expected tourist explosion on the island. It is important to remember, however, that while Sol Meliá manages these hotels, it only invested and owns 33.5% of them. By Cuban law no foreign firm can own more than 50%. Thus, Cubanacán invested 50% along with an additional investment of 16.5% by private Spanish investors. Although the investment has been profitable for Sol Meliá, these restrictions on ownership discourage some potential investors.

Agricultural Reform

In addition to having to compete in a world market for goods, Cuba faced an agricultural crisis that demanded immediate reform. Because of the inefficiency of large state farms, Cuba has had problems producing enough food to feed its 11 million inhabitants and has relied on a rationing system to supply the basic necessities. After 1990, the government was forced to cut the already meager food rations in half, thus causing major public discontent while sending prices on the black market soaring.

Castro took two main steps to increase agricultural output: (1) he broke up state farms into agricultural cooperatives; and (2) he created farmers' markets to sell off part of agricultural production. The large, inefficient state farms were broken into smaller cooperatives. Although these cooperatives (UBPCs) existed before 1993, they employed only about 1.5% of the working population. As of 1996, 10.5% of the working population belonged to a UBPC and 67% of agricultural land was farmed by non-state workers (Fernández Tabío, 1998: 2-5). UBPC farmers are given more freedom than state farmers and their salary is contingent on the amount harvested. UBPCs have drastically increased food production in Cuba. In 1996, UBPC Amistad Cuba Laos, a co-op studied by Fred Royce, produced 59.2 metric tons of sugar cane/hectare, compared to the state farm average of 32.5 tons/hectare. The standard of living in UBPCs is higher than on state farms. Co-op workers were paid an equivalent of 14,282 pesos/year in cash and food products (Royce, Messina, and Alvarez, 1997:461-467). The national average for state workers is around 2500 pesos/year. Although the UBPCs are not as liberal as many reformists pushed for (the farmers are still told what crops to produce and they have to sell a set amount to the state) their creation is regarded as a step forward, albeit one motivated by the need for economic reform.

In September 1994, Castro announced the opening of the *mercados agropecuarios* (MAs), a market where farmers could sell surplus goods to the Cuban people. Cooperative farmers were assigned an *acopio*, i.e., a set amount of products that they had to sell to the state at a fixed price. Whatever they harvested beyond their *acopio* contract they were able to sell in the farmers' market.[6]

The MAs have been a major success. Within a year of their legalization almost 300 MAs had been formed across the country. Currently, over 25% of the nation's food supply is sold through these markets (Espinosa, 1996: 63). This is a high number considering that farmers are only allowed to sell crops in the MAs after they have produced and sold to the state the set amount required . Thus, since any surplus crop can be sold at the MA, there is a large incentive to produce more than what is required by the state. The government has also benefited. Income earned by food vendors is taxable, thus providing the government with additional revenue. MAs also soak up a small portion of the workers cut from their jobs between 1990-93, and limit the growth of the black market, which is not taxed by the government. In addition, the MAs boost food production and provide a wider range of products to the Cuban people.[7] This said, only an estimated 20% of the population have the money to purchase goods on the market and until recently many people complained about unreason-

---

6. Castro had been adamantly opposed to farmers' markets, and after legalizing them in the early 1980s, shut them down later, saying, "The liquidation of the MLC's (farmers' market) is the beginning of the end of the weeds that are the remnants of capitalism" (Espinosa, 1996: 57). Yet in 1994, he reopened these markets in response to public demand, in a victory of economic necessity over socialist ideology.

ably high prices. Regardless of these complaints, the MAs are always crowded from 7AM until 4PM, and stands are almost always empty by the end of the day.

Dollarization

Since dollar transactions commonly took place on the streets before 1993, the legalization of foreign currency was more of a decriminalization than a legalization. Dollars fueled the black market for years before their legalization in 1993.[8] Still, the dollarization of the economy has had the most profound effect on Cuba and has pumped millions of dollars into Cuba's government. As I discuss later, this reform also clashes with socialist ideals more than any other reform, and evidence of the problems that dollars cause in Cuba is everywhere. This reform shows another shift in the government's policy from ideology to economics.

The reason to legalize dollars was simple. Cubans receive hundreds of millions of dollars in remittances from relatives living in the United States. In 1993, when possession of dollars was a criminal offense, an estimated $250 million was sent from the United States to relatives in Cuba. By 1997, that figure reportedly grew to over $700 million (Mesa-Lago, 1998: 22). With the legalization of the dollar, and greater circulation of this currency, the government has been able to capture the majority of this cash flow. Last year sales in dollar stores reached $1 billion.[9]

With the increase of tourists, remittances, and the emerging middle-class Cubans, the demand for more consumer products and food prompted the government to build hundreds of new stores, malls, fast food restaurants, night clubs, etc that cater to those that hold dollars. A dual economy arose almost overnight with the legalization of the dollar, and there is a marked difference between Cubans with dollars and those without.

Self-employment

In 1993, the Cuban government legalized self-employment in 140 occupations and, in 1995, reinstated *paladares* (small restaurants located in the proprietor's house) and permitted professionals to engage in self-employment in fields other than those in which they were trained. This reform is clearly the most market-oriented reform, and has drastically changed the way many Cubans work and live (Peters, 1997: 2).

The decision to liberalize self-employment was made due to economic necessity and, once again, contrary to past decisions by Castro. Without the $5 billion a year subsidies from the USSR, Cuba could no longer afford to employ 4.4 million workers in large, inefficient state industries. Thus, employment declined to 4.1 million workers, with 300,000 unemployed. Self-employment has virtually filled this void, with between 200,000 and 300,000 people registered for legal self-employment in 1996. In that year, including farmers, 23% of the work force was not employed by the state. This is a drastic change compared to the 1989 level of 5% (Fernández Tabío, 1997). Self-employment has also precipitated the formation of a tax system, and the government collects millions of dollars annually from these taxes. Despite these economic benefits to the state, the government has been shutting down self-employed workers, raising their taxes, and harassing individuals that are becoming successful. In fact, official self-employment fell over the past few years to between 150,000 and 200,000.[10] Additionally, the number of legal *pala-*

---

7. I, for example, shopped in the MA to find spearmint leaves to make *mojitos*, a Cuban drink made famous by Hemingway, for my host family. Spearmint leaves are not a necessity, and before the creation of the MA this mint would be almost impossible to find, making *mojitos* a drink enjoyed almost entirely by tourists.

8. In 1993 the dollar was selling for between 125 and 140 pesos, six or seven times the official exchange rate now, 22 pesos to the dollar. The Cuban government makes it easy to trade in dollars for pesos but very uneconomical to trade in pesos for dollars.

9. Castro has instituted several measures to capture dollars. Several years ago the national bank issued a convertible currency that is guaranteed to hold the same value as the dollar. Thus, many government dollar stores will make transactions in convertible currency. The government can hold most of the dollars to use for foreign trade while the convertible currency is used for internal transactions.

10. As discussed below, almost every Cuban relies on some form of clandestine self-employment.

dares, which are popular with tourists because they serve authentic home-cooked Cuban food, has dropped from a couple hundred to around 25.[11] The government has been especially strict on *paladares* because they divert tourist money away from state-run restaurants and in to the hands of individuals.

Even with the recent decline of self-employed workers it is impossible not to notice the impact that self-employment has on Havana and the rest of the country. Every block hosts ice cream sellers, taxi drivers, snack stands, mechanics, plumbers, barbers, etc. Illegal activity flourishes as well. Every morning people rang my doorbell selling eggs, air fresheners, chicken, lobster, and appliances.[12] Their prices were usually well below the market price. Much of the food consumed by Cubans comes from these illegal transactions. CD's, rum, and tobacco can also be easily purchased on the street.

I spoke with many *cuentapropistas*, and several of them agreed to share with me the details of their business, taxes, profits, ambitions, and way of life. These four cases are common stories and represent the lives of thousands of Cubans.

Bike Taxi Driver: David moved to Havana about 5 years ago without a job and without much money. He bought his first bicycle taxi shortly after arriving, spending all of his savings. A year later, he was able to buy a nicer bike for $125. At the beginning of each year he pays $102 for his license to be self-employed. This annual tax also covers his insurance. Every month he has to pay an additional $24 and at the end of the year he has to pay income tax if he makes over a certain amount.

David works six days a week to support his wife and child. For most rides he charges $4 to $5 and he serves as a guide for $10/hr. (However, to fellow Cubans, he is willing to give rides for much less.) David spends most of his time in front of the Hotel Nacional with five other bike taxi drivers. Some days he doesn't give a single ride. Other days, he can give as many as seven. David makes up to $150 a month after taxes, which is about ten times what he could make working for the state. David is part of the emerging middle class of Cubans. He can afford to go to bars with his co-workers, buy clothes in dollar stores, and live in a nicer part of Havana. His entrepreneurial ethic is clear, as he works up to 80 hours a week.

Peanut Seller: Peanut sellers swarm the *Malecón* (the oceanfront walkway), movie theaters, and restaurants. I spoke with an old woman that sold peanuts outside my apartment. She is retired and sells peanuts everyday to supplement her 50 peso/month pension (about $2.50) from the government. She has to support her 33-year-old son who is mentally retarded and cannot work, although he does receive a small pension and free medicine.

Every day she fills 34 packets of peanuts, which she will sell for 1 peso each. She has to buy two pounds of peanuts at 9 pesos/lb in order to fill these 34 packets. Thus, if she sells all her packets, her daily profit is 16 pesos, or 80 cents. Although this seems like a small income, assuming that she sells all her peanuts every day, she would make close to 500 pesos a month, twice the average salary of state workers. One afternoon she told me, "We didn't have much luck with Batista. I was very poor. But then the revolution came and helped us, taught us. What can you do but accept it? Step by step, a little money here, there. We get by alright." Talking to many Cubans I heard a similar sentiment over and over.

Room or Apartment Renter: These are generally the wealthiest of all the self-employed, and supply large revenues for the government. Most people rent out rooms at $15-$30 a night. These are people who had large houses or apartments before the revolution and were able to keep their houses after 1959 because they were on favorable terms with the Castro administration. My host family, with whom I stayed for a

---

11. It is obvious, from the numerous individuals that approached me in the streets asking if I'd like some home cooked food, that many of the *paladares* that were shut down by the government continue to operate on the black market.

12. A good friend that invited me over for dinner bought eight pounds of lobster at $1.50/lb, $4 to $5 below the market price.

month, lives in a relatively affluent section of Havana, about 5 minutes to downtown. They rent out two rooms at a time, each with air conditioning and a private bathroom. Guests pay $20-$25 and have access to the phone, laundry, balcony, and kitchen.

While looking for a place to stay I spoke with another very nice family in a different barrio of Havana. The mother of the family, "Carmen," a former government employee now in charge of the operation, pays $500/month in taxes for the two rooms she rents in addition to an income tax at the end of each year, which adds another $500. If she reported her entire income, the tax would be much greater, but no one in Cuba reports what he or she actually makes. Although a guest would pay around $900/month to stay in one of her rooms, she only reports receiving $500. This is a very common practice and many apartment renters do not even register with the government and lease rooms clandestinely. Carmen has developed an extensive clientele from all over the world that rent a room from her whenever they travel to Cuba, usually for business. However, during the slow months there is pressure to fill the rooms in order to meet the $500 tax, which is assessed regardless of earnings.

Apartment renting is the most lucrative form of self-employment and many of the families that are in this business would be considered upper class. Their monthly income from leasing rooms is usually over $500 and can be as high as $1000 after taxes. This money affords them the luxury of having products such as TVs, VCRs, clothes, CD players, etc. that can only be bought in dollar stores. Still, they would never be considered rich by U.S. standards. In Cuba, there is only a handful of truly wealthy people.

Food Vendor: Government salaries make it almost impossible to survive. The majority of the people resort to another way of making money, legally or illegally, in addition to their normal job. It actually seems strange that people even show up for their official job, but there are many benefits from working for the State: all workers are fed breakfast and lunch, receive a salary, and through good work can receive bonuses or incentive packages. The biggest reason to work, however, is access to supplies and goods that

can be sold on the black market. Gas station workers sell gas covertly, tobacco rollers sell cigars to tourists, and butchers sell meat after work. Many of these goods are stolen and represent a huge loss to the state.

When two young women came to my door one morning trying to sell chickens, I spoke to them about their operation. "Clara" works in a tobacco factory and earns 156 pesos/month ($8). "Mercedes" is a student of economics but does not believe that she will be able to find a professional job after graduation. "I just study for fun. I know that after I graduate I will have to look for a job in a factory or state company. I won't be an economist. There aren't enough jobs." Clara works Monday through Friday from 7AM to 4PM and then meets up with Mercedes to sell chickens door to door.

Both girls told me that it is impossible to live on less than $20 a month, so they each have to earn an extra $10/month on the second economy just to get by. Clara says that she buys chicken at 13 pesos/lb from a supplier who works at a chicken factory. The two young women sell the chickens door to door for $5 per chicken and thus earn about $1.50 for each chicken. Furthermore, they are able to convert pesos to dollars by buying the chickens in pesos and selling in dollars. Chicken is generally a luxury food in Cuba, and thus only the people with access to dollars can afford this food item more than once a month. The girls usually sell 10 chickens a week and make about six dollars each. I asked why they don't sell chickens full time; Mercedes answered that it was illegal to do what they were doing. If they only do it part time, to survive, the police will often look away. Everyone in Cuba, even the families of the police, depends on and realizes the importance of the black market.

ECONOMIC SUCCESS

The four economic reforms described above have helped Cuba's economy. Cuba's GDP grew by 7% in 1996, 2.5% in 1997 (Mesa-Lago 1998: 22), 1.5% in 1998, and the government claims 6% in 1999. The value of the peso has stabilized against the dollar and the standard of living is improving.

Some reformists in Cuba argue that Cuba should look to China and Vietnam for a new economic model, but Castro refuses this more extensive liberalization. Cuba is stuck trying to hold on to a failing socialist system by instituting limited market reforms. However, socialism and capitalism cannot be mixed together easily. Socialist ideals crumble, while capitalist markets are held back by high taxes, regulations, and Castro's rhetoric against success. Thus, Castro has exchanged economic problems for social and ideological problems. The future will prove whether Castro can balance these two different ideologies, whether the new equivocal reforms will be abandoned, or whether the Leninist/Marxist regime will crumble.

IMMEDIATE PROBLEMS

Several problems became clearly evident shortly after the initiation of the reforms. Among the most serious was an increase in crime, drugs, and prostitution. With state workers earning $15 a month, many Cubans looked to earn a quick dollar by ripping off tourists, dealing marijuana, or selling their own bodies. Several teenagers approached me selling "ganja" for two dollars a joint. According to them it was safe to smoke pot in private houses. The next day I read in the newspaper that a man was sentenced to eight years in prison for the possession of a few joints. Prostitution is a more lucrative business. The first-class prostitutes sell themselves for $50 a night. Although many of these prostitutes work primarily for foreign tourists, it is not uncommon for a Cuban man to solicit sex from prostitutes, although at a lower rate. Many of the women that I spoke to moved to Havana a couple of years ago. They plan to prostitute themselves for several years, save up a lot of money, and move back to their original towns. Gay prostitution is equally as evident and quite open. While standing on a corner on La Rampa I was confused for a prostitute and offered $50 for a "quickie." I politely turned him down.

Since 1996, the government has taken several steps to combat these "evils of capitalism." Six thousand policemen were added to Havana's district in 1997-99 (Fernández Tabío, 1999). Drug trafficking and pimping became punishable by death. Prostitutes were cleared from many tourist areas. Castro also instituted laws to protect tourists from scam artists known as *jineteros*. (This word carries bad connotation as it is also used to refer to sex traders.) Loitering is now illegal. Children must be accompanied by adults while walking the streets, and most Cuban citizens are not allowed in tourist destinations including hotels, Varadero beach, and certain restaurants.

For the first time since 1959 distinct economic classes have emerged. Workers in the private sector can earn one hundred times what state workers, who are still the great majority, earn. With the increase of wealth of a portion of Cuban citizens, a high demand for consumer products has emerged. Among Cuba's "middle" and "upper" classes, government dollar stores have been extremely popular. Last year sales reached $1 billion. This number is significant for several reasons. First, it shows that citizens have more access to dollars than previously thought. In 1997, about $700 million in remittances were sent to Cuban families. Thus, Cubans must have earned an additional $300 million from tourism, the only other source of dollars into the mainstream economy. Second, $1 billion in sales shows the propensity of Cubans to spend almost all their liquidity. With interest rates at 2-3%, there is not much incentive to save, and Cubans highly value products such as TVs, VCRs, radios, and kitchen appliances (Maybarduk, 1999: 5).

Polarization of wealth is a major concern for Castro because it is contrary to the traditional socialist belief that dictates that people should work only for the good of the country. Such a sudden and wide difference in wealth among the Cuban population has caused the increase in crime. Cubans who are worse off after these reforms are unaccustomed to seeing their neighbors with more material wealth. Inequality leads to crime. This polarization of wealth has also disillusioned many people who had remained loyal to the Revolution. People that have worked for years to support the socialist ideas are suddenly seeing themselves worse off than their fellow citizens that have engaged in capitalist endeavors. As one man, an officer in the military, told me, "I have dedicated my whole life to the Revolution. Now I see that it is all for nothing; my life has been for nothing." I was surprised to hear this candid response.

Dual Economy

Cuba operates with two distinct economies, a dollar economy and a peso one. Dollars can buy peso products and dollar products, but pesos can only buy peso products. Only domestically made products are sold for pesos. Thus, Cubans who only earn pesos have little purchasing power. After purchasing the month's rations of food, a peso earner can afford some state-subsidized luxuries such as ice cream (3 pesos), cinema tickets (1 peso), and beer, (3-8 pesos). Cubans also depend on the sea for food and entertainment. Every dawn and sunset fisherman crowd the *Malecón* casting lines to catch fish for dinner. In the water children spear fish and catch lobsters and other shellfish. During the day they float on old tire inner-tubes or pieces of styrofoam.

The large majority of Cubans earn at least several dollars a month doing odd jobs or selling things on the black market. Most Cubans claim that one needs about $25/month to survive. This means that almost all Cubans have to gain about $10 a month to supplement the average salary of $13/month. The population with regular access to dollars (more than $15/month), an estimated 55%, have substantially more purchasing power than the 45% of Cubans with limited dollars (Rivera, 1998: 110). There is a clear distinction between these two groups of people and walking around Cuba they reminded me of Dr. Seuss's star bellied snitches and plain bellied snitches. The two groups eat in different restaurants, shop in separate stores, drink different beer, and wear different clothes. Almost every item has a different brand, one for dollars and one for pesos. Beer, for example, can be bought in bottles for 8 pesos. The bottled beer is called "Polar" and is acceptable to drink as long as it is cold. Beer can also be bought in cans for 85 cents of a dollar. "Cristal," "Bucanero," and "Mayabee" are all brands of canned beer and are preferable to those who can afford it. Thus, it is easy to determine which people fall into the dollar category and which fall into the peso category by the brand of beer that they drink. If a deepening of social class lines continues, it could lead to greater animosity in the future.

It is important, however, to recognize the role of subsidies in the Cuban economy. If one earns a hundred times more than another does, it does not mean that he/she is a hundred times richer. Because of food and clothing subsidies, peso earners can buy products that are worth far more than the price they pay. However, each citizen can only buy a set amount of these products. Thus, the average state workers' real income is more than $12. After one buys the subsidized products, the purchasing power of the peso and dollar goes way down. Even for Cubans that make dollars, it is almost impossible to buy a car, eat out often, or buy many imported products.

LONG TERM PROBLEMS

Theft from the State is a major problem in Cuba. Most items that are available on the black market are stolen from state stores, factories, and companies. The liberalization of self-employment did not cause this theft, but encouraged it by spurring the internal economy and raising demand for consumer products. In grocery store parking lots vendors sell stolen meat, cheese, and vegetables for less than they can be bought in the store. Gasoline is sold at half price by private vendors that steal it from the state.

The presence of an extensive black market in Latin American countries is not uncommon. Black market activity in Mexico, for instance, represents 30% of the country's GDP. Black markets usually arise in countries with high taxes, strong government intervention in economic activity, and large bureaucracies. Whenever the market cannot function freely, black markets arise. Cuba's black market is similar to those in other countries and could be controlled by economic reforms.

Cuba's first economy is completely controlled by the government. Many consumer products are reserved solely for exports and are either sold only in dollars or priced above the national market price in pesos. Chicken, beef and lobster, for example, are mainly reserved for tourists who are willing to pay high prices in dollars. Thus, Cubans are forced to pay exorbitant prices for these foods. Castro's goal is to discourage domestic demand for these products and sell them to foreigners for hard currency. Since there are few other producers of these foods besides the state, the local demand is met for these foods by the black market. Workers steal chickens and lobsters and sell them door to door like the two young women that I spoke with outside of my house. This is a risky way to earn a living, and Castro has cracked down on these "traitors of the Revolution" by dealing out long jail sentences. Even with the threat of imprisonment, vendors sell their products at below state prices, an unusual outcome for black markets where prices are usually higher than market prices.

In Cuba, however, the problem is not that the supply of products is too low, but that the things produced are reserved for foreigners. Chickens are not difficult to raise and in many other Latin American countries are common and easy to purchase. In Cuba, where it is no tougher to raise chickens, their price is substantially higher (because they are reserved for tourists) while the demand is equal to that in any other country. Thus the black market supplies chickens to families willing to pay about $1.50/lb. The legalization of small businesses would increase the supply of chickens and other products to the Cuban population while still allowing the government to sell chickens at high prices to tourists in government run restaurants.

Castro might argue that small businesses would divert products away from the external sector and to the domestic economy. This probably would not happen because the production curve would shift with the emergence of small businesses that are more efficient and have economic incentive to produce more chickens. Thus, chicken production would increase in two ways: theft from the state would decrease and production of chickens on the local scale would increase and be more efficient.

Castro is opposed to any individual success and heavily taxes all private enterprise in an attempt to distribute wealth evenly. This policy has several negative effects on the Cuban government and on the Cuban people. High tax rates reduce the revenue that the government collects because high rates discourage economic activity (the so-called Laffer Curve effect). That is, as rates rise economic activity falls. At some point, once the rate is sufficiently high, the resulting fall in economic activity reduces revenue by as much as the increased revenue on the remaining economic activity. If tax rates are raised further, then production falls and thus profit and tax revenue fall as well.

Castro imposes a set monthly tax on all private enterprise. Apartment renters, for instance, pay $250/month regardless of their profit. Most apartment renters rarely have more than a 50-75% occupancy rate. If a private apartment renter leases a room at $25/night for 20 nights a month then he will gross $500. Thus, the set tax would be 50% of revenue, not profit. Clearly, this occupation can be risky. If one fails to lease out the room more than ten nights a month, at the fairly high price of $25, he will lose money.

High taxes also create an entry barrier for many Cubans wanting to become self-employed. Imagine the case of a state worker who wants to buy a bicycle taxi and a license to operate it as a *cuentapropista*. The start-up cost would be $125 for the bike, $102 for the yearly tax that covers insurance, and $24 for the first month's tax. This totals $251 or 21 months salary for an average state worker. To further hinder entrepreneurs, it is almost impossible to get loans from the bank. Thus, only Cubans who receive remittances from abroad, or have access to dollars from other sources, are able to enter the private market. This furthers the polarization of wealth.

Many Cubans who have limited access to dollars find ways to avoid these taxes and still work in the second economy. Some simply operate illegally. This is obviously risky, and many Cubans are thrown in jail every year for this illegal activity. The majority of Cubans, dollars or no dollars, find ways to avoid paying the full tax. Cubans who have a reliable source of dollars can afford to pay most of the taxes and reduce the risk of imprisonment, but Cubans who live primarily off of pesos are forced to find ways to evade the brunt of the taxes imposed on self-employment. This can be done in several ways, and Cubans are very creative.

The easiest way to dodge taxes is to register for a low tax form of self-employment and then operate a different business. Joseph Scarpaci in his article, "The Emerging Food and Paladar Market in Havana," describes a *paladar* owner, "Rosa," who is licensed to make and sell candy in her home (1995, 76-84). Selling candy is not a very lucrative business, and thus the taxes are not very substantial. Rosa proceeds to operate a *paladar* in her living room and even illegally employs other Cubans at various times to help cook or run errands. The license to sell candy allows her to explain the constant stream of people that flow through her house, and also explain her supply of oil, flour, milk, and sugar, if inspectors were to ask. Rosa also makes sure to be on good terms with the local CDR representative. If Rosa were forced to pay the full tax on *paladar* owners, she would probably not be able to afford the cost of business.

Many Cubans who do register their actual occupation do not report their full earnings. In addition to monthly taxes, the government also has instituted an income tax to limit any monetary success. However, since Castro is forced to rely on self-reporting of income, no one reports what he/she makes. A Canadian tourist I spoke with told me that the woman with whom he stayed reported that he paid her $15/night instead of the $30 that he gave her. She was worried that he would not approve of this action and said, "Nick, if I tell the government what I actually make, they will eat it all up with taxes. Already, at the end of the year I have to pay around $500 in income tax. I am supposed to pay another $500, but we just can't afford it." He assured her that he would do the same.

I bought a painting at the artisan market in the historic section of Cuba. After bargaining with the vendor, "Carlos," I got the price down to $70. We talked about the taxes on artists. Artists have recently been given more freedom than any other types of self-employed workers. Larry Corwin, an officer at the U.S. Interest Section jokes, "the thing that I like best about Cuba is that the artists are rich and the lawyers are poor." Although this may be true, taxes are heavy on artists too. One difference is that artists

don't have to pay a monthly fee to be artists. They are only taxed on what they sell. Carlos explained that he sells the artist's work and makes a 15% commission on everything that he sells. Also, the artist has to pay 30% of the price of the paintings to the state to rent the stand in the artists' market. Then, he has to pay 20% to the state as income tax. Thus, if the artist and the vendor report what they sell, the artist makes 35% of the selling price of the painting. For a $70 painting, the artist would make $25. Carlos, however, told me that they report the paintings' value at half of what they actually sell it for. The painting that I bought they reported selling for $40, so they pay 50% of $40 to the state and are left with the remaining $50.

By forcing Cubans to dodge taxes and participate in the black market, Castro has made criminals out of the majority of Cubans. In a land where national pride plays such an important role, this can be extremely detrimental. Since the Revolution, Castro has relied on anti American sentiment and national pride to justify many of the sacrifices that he asks his country to make. He declares that Cuba is for Cubans. Propaganda appears on hundreds of billboards across Havana: "Creemos en Fidel," "Tenemos y Tendremos Socialismo," and my favorite billboard located in front of the U.S. Interest Section, "Señores Imperialistas: ¡No les tenemos absolutamente ningún miedo!" Fidel constantly tries to convince people that they must give up ideas of personal wealth in order to benefit the country, and they must not give in to capitalism or they will all be slaves to the United States.[13] In a socialist system where incentives to work are not always apparent, Castro uses exhortations to encourage the people to work.

However, by making average, hard working citizens into criminals, Castro is creating a large split between the people and the government. No longer is the government seen as the provider for the people; it is

---

13. Ernesto Betancourt writes in "Potential Impact of the Helms/Burton Act": "His (Castro's) rise to national leadership and international acclaim was based to a great extent on his becoming the embodiment of Cuban nationalist sentiment. The failure of the regime and the disaster it has entailed for the Cuban people in no way reduce the nationalist cravings Castro so effectively mobilized in support for his leadership role. In fact, in the fear of return to American domination, it is one of the emotional forces he still uses to rally his followers around him, especially within the armed forces" (1995, 412).

now something to be feared and robbed. National pride is falling. In the 1960s, the majority of refugees were upper-class businessmen, professionals, and landowners who fled after Castro confiscated most private property. Now, however, Cubans of all socio-economic classes are taking to rafts. A woman, from whom I bought fruit every day, asked me if I knew any older males in the United States who would like to marry for convenience. She says that she would make an excellent housewife. People constantly dream of leaving the island for Miami, Texas, or LA, and it is understandable. Who feels pride for a government that criminalizes its people? Thus, Castro is losing one of his largest political assets.

It is also difficult to support a leader who goes out of his way to crush the successful. Castro claims that it is important to divide the wealth equally; no one can be richer than his neighbor. However, in Cuba there is little wealth, and Castro makes it hard to accumulate more. Most Cubans support some of the ideas of the Revolution, but many are beginning to realize that Castro is hurting the country. In 1994, Castro shut down *paladares* because they were becoming too successful. In 1995 he was forced to re-open them. In 1986, Castro closed the MLCs (mercados libres campesinos), contrary to public support for the MLCs, because these farmers were making too much money. After the food crisis, Castro legalized the new farmers' markets now called *mercados agropecuarios* (Espinosa, 1996:58-63). In 1995, Castro announced that he would lay off half a million state workers to make state firms more efficient. He was forced to abandon this plan in 1996 because the private sector could not absorb these laid-off workers, in large part because of a 300% increase in the cost of business permits (Mesa-Lago, 1998). Castro prefers to employ half a million redundant state workers than to let the private sector grow. These reversals of laws make Castro look foolish and without any political platform for the good of the people. They also undermine the validity of other laws that Castro imposes.

Castro's police force regularly terrorizes individuals who attempt to earn a living apart from the state. Larry Corwin, of the U.S. Interest Section, told me that his neighbor, a retired man who had to support

two grandchildren, was thrown in jail for the weekend because he washed Larry's car for $2.50 every week. I spoke with a crippled man who was regularly put in jail for the night because he washed cars for a couple pesos each in front of the Hotel Nacional.

Castro does have a legitimate fear that Cubans will become successful. Independently wealthy citizens in Cuba would pose several problems for the government. First, they would create pockets of power that are independent from the state. Currently, Castro's reign is not in jeopardy because there is no one who can oppose him. All political leaders are in the Communist party. Second, people with money care more about how they are governed and taxed. Revolutions rarely occur in countries where the people are totally oppressed. The United States for example, prior to 1776, was one of the wealthiest colonies in the world. Additionally, taxes paid to England were not greater than any other colony. Yet, the revolution started because Americans took a great interest in how they were taxed and whether they were taxed unfairly. Jack Greene writes in *An Uneasy Connection* that by 1773, the colonies had developed an economic and social elite, and had drastically increased the wealth and size of the colonies over the previous ten years. According to Greene, the revolution was caused by the economic elite and fueled by the growing middle-class (1973: 60). Cuba has yet to develop an economic elite independent from the Communist party, and Castro knows that economic power leads to political power.

Perhaps the biggest contradiction in Cuba today is the purpose of its current economic/political model. Castro claims that Cuba must preserve socialism and fight U.S. imperialism at all costs; socialism will preserve Cuba for the Cuban people. Anyone who has been to Cuba recently knows that the island is controlled less by the Cuban people than it ever was before the Revolution. Cubans are not allowed in many of the hotels that cater to tourists. Cubans must have special permission to travel to Varadero beach. Cubans cannot freely move to Havana because of the overpopulation of the city, nor can they leave the country without permission from the government. Citizens must carry identification at all times and are constantly stopped and harassed by the police. My friend, Kramer, was stopped on average twice a day while he was with me because the police thought that he was bothering me, especially since he is black and I am white. Once, after being questioned by the police, Kramer said, "Charlie, you could walk up to me and break my nose and while I am on the ground bleeding the police would take me to jail and apologize to you for your swollen knuckles."

Foreigners have complete reign in Cuba and walk around on a red carpet while Cubans are made to feel second rate. This has an immense effect on nationalism, but results directly from Castro's policy. Since he refuses to allow the internal economy to grow, the dollars that the government needs must come from foreigners. One reason that Cuba has so many tourists is its competitive advantage over other Latin American countries in crime. Tourists can walk around at almost all hours of the night without feeling any physical danger. Tourists stay in nice hotels at comparatively cheap rates (the Hotel Nacional a five star hotel charges about $100/night), eat at fancy restaurants, go to the beach, and drink exotic drinks, while most Cubans live a controlled and restricted life. It seems impossible that before 1959 the situation could have favored Americans over Cubans any more then it does now.

By suffocating the internal economy, Castro limits the multiplier effect that foreign investment can have on the local economy. This multiplier effect is the domestic business that develops in response to foreign investment. Andy Isserman, an economist at the University of Illinois, estimates that the multiplier effect in third world countries can be as high as twice the amount of foreign investment. For example, Sol Meliá invests ten million dollars into a new hotel in Havana. In an open economy, Sol Meliá would hire construction workers, artists, managers, chefs, and buy local products and materials. With this $10 million spurring the local economy, the demand for products would rise, and growth would occur to match this new demand. In Cuba, however, Sol Meliá is forced to buy many of the products needed for construction and management from Spain. Additionally, the $10 million investment is soaked up by

the state, which uses it to import oil, food, and medical supplies. Thus, the $10 million is almost immediately diverted away from the Cuban economy and any potential growth is thwarted. Nicolás Crespo, in his article "Back to the Future: Cuban Tourism in 2007," estimates that in 1997, Cuba lost $1.9 billion in the tourism sector alone, due to its economic policy. Crespo used Puerto Rico's multiplier effect in making this estimate, an island with an open economy (1998: 42-43). Thus, by 2010, with the $5 billion dollars that is expected from tourists, Castro's restrictive economic policy would cost Cuba over $6 billion.

Consider an actual example. Sherritt International operates a nickel mine in Cuba. Cuban law prohibits foreign companies from hiring Cuban citizens, so Sherritt contracts 10,000 workers through Castro. Sherritt pays Castro $10,000 a year for each worker. Castro then pays each worker in Cuban pesos the equivalent of $120 per year. So, Castro takes about 90% of the salaries paid by Sherritt and redirects it to other purposes. If Castro let foreign companies directly hire Cuban workers, then the Cuban economy would be boosted by the increase of dollars in the economy, consumer demand would rise, and producers would produce more to meet this demand. The only downfall of permitting companies to directly hire Cubans would be that the workers would not make $10,000 a year. At first, since so many Cubans would be willing to work for even $200 a year, companies would be able to employ workers at extremely low salaries. However, as workers developed unions, the right to negotiate directly with their employers and the government instituted a minimum wage, salaries would begin to rise.

CUBA'S FUTURE

I do not believe that anyone can predict what will happen in Cuba over the next decade. The U.S. government is worried that with the death of Castro over a million Cubans could take to the seas to get to the United States. "The United States remains committed to promoting a peaceful transition to democracy and forestalling a mass migration exodus that would endanger the lives of migrants and safety of our nation" (White House press release, May 1997). Several officials that I spoke with in the U.S. Interest Section believe that up to 1.5 million people might attempt to leave Cuba for the United States when Castro dies.

Although I do agree that many Cubans may try to flee Cuba with the death of Castro, I am not so sure that Cuba will turn to a free market economy with the death of Castro. Currently, there is no one outside of the Communist Party that can oppose Castro. Anyone that has any money is associated with the Party, and most dissidents now live in the United States. Those next in line to succeed Castro (Carlos Lage, Ricardo Alarcón, and Raúl Castro) are devout communists and support the ideals of the Revolution. I cannot say that Cuba will not open up within the next decade, but I believe that it will be a slower process than some think and hope.

If no further economic reforms are made I believe that Cuba will once again enter an economic crisis. Currently, Cuba depends too much on its tourism industry. Although it has been growing rapidly, there is no guarantee that this growth is sustainable. Sol Meliá, for instance, reports low return rates (about 10%). For many tourists, Cuba is a place they want to see once, to witness life in one of the last socialist countries. Without access to Cuba by Americans, it may be difficult for Castro to reach tourist levels (10 million by 2010) that the government predicts (Godínez, 1998:53-57).

Cuba will also continue to decline as a leader in health care and education. Thousands of professionals — doctors, lawyers, professors, and managers — are quitting their state jobs to join the private sector. The woman I stayed with used to work for the state as an editor of national statistics. She traveled to several other socialist countries and had a graduate degree. Five years ago she quit her job that paid 350 pesos/month to rent out two rooms in her apartment. She now makes over a hundred times what she made working for the state. I spoke with a taxi driver who used to be a captain of a trading ship that sailed around the world. Three years ago, while he was at port in Canada, he bought a used car and became a taxi driver. Cuba is suffering a huge social loss from these professionals that have received thousands of

dollars worth of education who quit to do mundane jobs that earn significantly more money.

Finally, I believe that thousands of Cubans will continue to flee to the United States. National pride is declining, and the U.S. is thought of as the land of dreams, where one can make as much money as he is willing to work for. Unless Castro is willing to make some changes, he will be governing a sinking ship. The four major economic reforms that I have discussed only managed to slow the leak, but they do not come close to keeping the boat afloat.

I believe, however, that Castro can reform the economy while avoiding complete transformation to a market economy. I think that Castro could move to an economy much like that of Denmark or Sweden. These countries basically have free markets (the governments still run the large communication and transportation companies), but provide large safety nets for their citizens. Of course, these welfare programs are expensive, but a sound economy would add more money to fund these programs. An economy similar to Denmark's would be successful in Cuba while protecting against some of the inherent problems of capitalism. To accomplish this, Castro first has to legalize small business. Small businesses would increase production, lower prices, and supply more tax revenue to the state. Furthermore, they would soak up the unemployed workers that have been laid-off from inefficient state companies.

Castro has to reduce taxes. Since the government provides many services to the Cuban people for free, it is understandable that the government has to collect a large amount of revenue. High taxes, however, is not the best way to maximize revenue. Denmark provides many of the same services to its citizens but only taxes 40% of income. Cuba could have a similar tax structure; this would encourage workers to produce efficiently, while still providing the money that the government needs.

Finally, Castro has to allow foreign companies to hire and pay Cubans directly. It is more efficient to let Cubans decide how to spend their own money and maximize utility, rather than have the government decide how to allocate these funds. If each Cuban could spend the money that he rightfully earned, then Cuba would see goods and services being distributed to the people that value them the most. More importantly, permitting companies to hire Cubans would increase the multiplier effect, noted above. This multiplier effect could add several billion dollars annually as foreign investment continues to grow.

I was living in Costa Rica when I first traveled to Cuba three years ago. I fell in love with the island and was amazed at the cleanliness of the streets, the lack of homelessness, and the kindness and spirit of the people. Havana was a vast contrast to San José, Costa Rica, where the streets are lined with trash, people beg for money on the streets, and crime is an increasing problem. Initially, I supported Castro and his attempt to provide for the entire Cuban population. I viewed socialism as different than capitalism but not necessarily inferior.

This summer, however, I came to see the situation very differently. I still applaud the advances that Castro has made in education and health care, although I realize that this was fairly easy to accomplish while Cuba was living off of the USSR. Now, I see Castro as a dictator that cares more about preserving power and socialism than the welfare of his people.

The Cuban people are the country's most valuable natural resource and Castro is forcing them to live in relatively impoverished conditions. He is precipitating a decline in national spirit and forcing thousands of people to leave their beloved homeland. Cuba is like an adolescent boy, struggling to get its freedom and identity from his controlling parents. Soon, however, Castro will no longer be able to control the Cuban people, and like the boy, the people will not tolerate these restrictions on growth and prosperity.

REFERENCES

Bethel, Leslie. *Cuba: A Short History.* New York: Cambridge University Press, 1993.

Blasier, Cole. "The End of the Soviet-Cuban Partnership," in Carmelo Mesa-Lago (ed.) *Cuba After the Cold War.* Pittsburgh: University of Pittsburgh Press, 1993.

Commercial Data International. *Country Review, Cuba-1999.*

Crespo, Nicolás. "Back to the Future: Cuban Tourism in the Year 2007." *Cuba in Transition—Vvolume 8.* Washington: Association for the Study of the Cuban Economy, 1998.

Espinosa, Juan Carlos. "Market Redux: The Politics of the Farmers' Market in Cuba." *Cuba in Transition—Volume 5.* Washington: Association for the Study of the Cuban Economy, 1995.

Fernández Tabío, Luis René. "La Dolarización y la Segunda Economía." Havana: University of Havana, 1999.

Godínez, Félix. "Cuba's Tourism Industry: Sol Meliá, A Case Study." *Cuba in Transition—Volume 8.* Washington: Association for the Study of the Cuban Economy, 1998.

Kozak, Michael. "The Prospects for a Peaceful Transition in Cuba." Remarks made at the Dallas Morning News Conference on Cuba in Evolution, 1998.

Locay, Luis. "Towards a Market Economy or Tinkering with Socialism?" In Pérez-López and Travieso-Díaz (eds,) *Perspectives on Cuban Economic Reforms.* Tempe: Arizona State University Press, 1998.

Maybarduk, Gary. "Measures not Taken—A Future Full of Problems." *Cuba in Transition—Volume*

319

9. Washington: Association for the Study of the Cuban Economy, 1999.

Mesa-Lago, Carmelo. "The Economic Effects on Cuba of the Downfall of Socialism," in Mesa-Lago (ed.) *Cuba After the Cold War*. Pittsburgh: University of Pittsburgh Press, 1993.

Mesa-Lago, Carmelo. "Cuba's Economic Policies and Strategies for Confronting the Crisis," in Mesa-Lago (ed.) *Cuba After the Cold War*. Pittsburgh: University of Pittsburgh Press, 1993.

Mesa-Lago, Carmelo. "The Cuban Economy in 1997-98." *Cuba in Transition—Volume 8*. Washington: Association for the Study of the Cuban Economy, 1998.

Pérez-López, Jorge. *Cuba's Second Economy*. New Brunswick: Transaction Publishers, 1995.

Pérez-López, Jorge. "Economic Reforms in a Comparative Perspective," in Pérez-López and Travieso-Díaz (eds.) *Perspectives on Cuban Economic Reforms*. Tempe: Arizona State University Press, 1998.

Pérez Villanueva, Omar. "Cuba's Economic Reforms: An Overview," in Pérez-López and Travieso-Díaz (eds.) *Perspectives on Cuban Economic*

Reforms. Tempe: University of Arizona State University Press, 1998.

Peters, Phillip. *Islands of Enterprise: Cuba's Emerging Small Business Sector*. Arlington, VA: Alexis de Tocqueville Institution, 1997.

Royce, Frederick, Willaim Messina and José Alvarez. "An Empirical Study of Income and Performance Incentives on a Sugarcane CPA." *Cuba in Transition—Volume 7*. Washington: Association for the Study of the Cuban Economy, 1997.

Scarpaci, Joseph. "The Emerging Food and Paladar Market in Havana." *Cuba in Transition—Volume 5*. Washington: Association for the Study of the Cuban Economy, 1995.

Smith, Kirby, and Hugo Llorens. "Renaissance and Decay." *Cuba in Transition—Volume 8*. Washington: Association for the Study of the Cuban Economy, 1998.

Werlau, María. "Update on Foreign Investment in Cuba 1997-1998 and Focus on the Energy Sector." *Cuba in Transition—Volume 8*. Washington: Association for the Study of the Cuban Economy, 1998.

LAST RESORT OR BRIDGE TO THE FUTURE? TOURISM AND WORKERS IN CUBA'S SECOND ECONOMY

Ted Henken[1]

It's good the competence this has brought. It's good that these markets and self-employment have taught people a little bit of capitalism…But we have to think of how to do things correctly…Some [of these self-employed] earn more in a day than our honored teachers earn in a month.

— Fidel Castro (Peters 1997: 5)

[I]nformality is so widely present under existing forms of *state socialism* that any inquiry into the actual economic, social, political, and even cultural processes of the supposedly "centrally planned economies" is bound to be misspecified unless it takes into consideration the socialist informal sector

— (Portes and Borocz 1988: 17).

As part of a month-long preliminary study of Cuba's tourism industry carried out in August 1999, I traveled to the island's renowned international resort beach town of Varadero. Unable to stay with my intended hosts due to their fear of being fined for lodging a foreigner, I had to look elsewhere for hospitality. A waiter in a nearby restaurant generously offered to help me find a place to stay. Like a man on a mission, he led me to six different homes, and although renting private rooms is illegal in Varadero (unlike in other areas of Cuba where licenses are available), I quickly discovered that many local families do indeed rent to tourists, despite the risks. To my surprise, my

Cuban entrepreneur hosts also ran a private seafood restaurant out of what was to become my bedroom. They were even then in the process of expanding their operation by adding a second floor to their home, all without any effort to conceal these activities from their neighbors or the local housing inspectors. Eventually, I would learn that even the "friendly" waiter was actually paid a $5 per-day commission for "services rendered."

Three central questions immediately arose from this and other similar experiences throughout Cuba that, thus far, have not been answered by the available literature on Cuban tourism or on the island's "second economy."[2] First, is self-employment (*trabajo por cuenta propia* — TPCP) a desperate last resort or a constructive bridge to an unsure future for the Cubans who engage in it? Second, how is work as a licensed self-employed worker *(cuenta propista* — CP) different from clandestine private economic activity? Third, how do the Cuban government's strict regulations and high taxes affect the CP sector, and what is the intent behind these seemingly illogical and counterproductive restrictions? Beginning with the assumption that both tourism and self-employment will continue to play central roles in the Cuban economy in the foreseeable future, this paper explores the consequences of self-employment in the tourism in-

1. The author would like to acknowledge a grant from the Cuban Studies Institute of Tulane University which enabled him to carry out this research. An earlier version of this paper was presented in March at the LASA 2000 meeting in Miami, Florida.

2. See the section 'Theoretical Discussion' below for a definition and differentiation between Cuba's "second economy" and the more commonly used "informal economy."

321

dustry. As Castro inadvertently hints at above: What kinds and levels of "competence" has the introduction of micro-enterprises and self-employment — the "little bit of capitalism" — brought to socialist Cuba? How does licensed self-employment differ from clandestine work? And, what are the practical effects of the government's strict regulations and licensing requirements?

TOURISM AND THE SECOND ECONOMY: PAST AND PRESENT

Tourism is nothing new to the island of Cuba. Prior to the 1959 revolution, Cuba was easily the most popular Caribbean get-away for American tourists. Following the revolution, however, the island's place as an important tourist destination was abruptly reversed. After a brief period of equivocation about what to do with Havana's extensive tourism infrastructure, the ideology of the revolution came to scapegoat tourism, implicating it as a bankrupt industry that subordinated the island's economy and political system to the whims of foreigners (Schwartz 1997). The best example of the conversion of tourist facilities from foreign to Cuban use is the famous *Havana Hilton* which first opened its doors in March 1958, just months before the triumph of the revolution. Its revolutionary name, *Hotel Habana Libre*, survived as a proud symbol of Cuban sovereignty until the late 1990s, when the French hotel group Tryp, which now collects 50 percent of its profits, tellingly re-christened it the *Hotel Habana Libre Tryp*.

Any understanding of the current Cuban reality, of course, must begin with the changes the collapse of the Soviet Union and the subsequent imposition of the "special period" have brought to the island. During the years 1989-1993, foreign trade declined by 92 percent and the island's Global Social Product (similar to the GDP measure) fell an estimated 40-50 percent, displacing nearly 20 percent of the island's labor force. Finally, the minimum wage shrunk to an astounding $2 a month in real buying power, with monthly pensions worth just over $1 on the black market (Mesa-Lago 1994). Reacting to these macroeconomic shocks, President Fidel Castro declared a "special period in peacetime" to begin on August 30, 1990. However, the significant changes in the Cuban

economy were not intended to begin a "transition" toward a capitalist economy. Instead, changes were explicitly aimed at enabling survival, preserving socialism, and "saving the revolution." As if under siege of war, Cubans were forced to make major sacrifices such as experiencing severe energy shortages, a massive reduction in public transportation, the expansion of food rationing, and the disappearance of many basic products. Cuba's touted social services were negatively affected as vital medical and school supplies became virtually non-existent. Cuban industry and exports also declined; the essential sugar crop dropped by half from 8.4 million tons in 1990 to a mere 4.2 million three years later. The island was forced to look to other areas to bring in foreign exchange.

A principal area of economic growth arising from the needs of the special period has been tourism. Tourism has rapidly become the island's number one "export," recently pulling ahead of both sugar and hard-currency remittances. Tourist visits to the island have grown from a mere 300,000 in 1989 to an estimated 1.7 million in 1999, and the number of hotel rooms jumped from 5,000 in 1987 to over 30,000 in 1999. Two million tourists are expected by the end of 2000, an estimate that does not include the tremendous effect an end to the U.S. travel ban would have on the number of foreign visitors. Ironically, the defiant nation that had once scoffed at foreign investment from the capitalist West, is now forced to compete vigorously for hard-currency investment and aggressively seek out partners for joint-ventures in tourism projects. "Who would have thought," Castro asked in the summer of 1993, "that we, so doctrinaire, we who fought foreign investment, would one day view foreign investment as an urgent need?" (Pérez 1995: 404).

Though not entirely new on the Cuban scene, Cuba's second economy has also expanded significantly during the last decade. In fact, there is a consensus among government officials, analysts on the island, and scholars abroad that as the official, first economy has entered a major crisis since the early 1990s, the unregulated, second economy has exploded in scope and size (Pérez-López 1995). An indicator of the growing economic importance of Cuba's second economy is the government's attempts to legalize and incorporate it into the official, first economy. For example, on the 40th anniversary of his attack on Moncada in July 1993, President Castro legalized over 100 kinds of self-employment, depenalized the holding of foreign currency, re-opened farmers' markets, cut subsidies to many state-run companies, and laid off thousands of workers (Peters 1997: 1-2).

The growth in the size of the official "self-employed" sector during the special period has been traced by a number of researchers (Peters and Scarpaci 1998; Jatar-Hausmann 1999; Smith 1999). According to them, the number of licensed self-employed workers grew from 70,000 in December of 1993 (just months after it was legalized) to 140,000 in May of 1994 (Smith 1999: 49). The unofficial government policy of alternately encouraging, repressing, and regulating the self-employed sector has produced significant fluctuations in its size and composition since 1994. Though the sector reached its zenith in January of 1996 with 209,606 licensed operators, it has shrunk considerably (20%) thereafter due primarily to the institution of a quota-based, personal income tax later that same year. For example, by April of 1997 official numbers of the self-employed sector had dropped to 180,919, falling further to 165,438 by April of 1998 (Peters 1997; Jatar-Hausmann 1999).

Peters and Scarpaci (1998) have described the short life of the CP sector in Cuba as having passed through two phases since it was legalized in 1993. First, from 1993 until 1995 the sector was characterized by lax enforcement and no personal income tax. This lack of enforcement was likely due to the fact that during these years, the most difficult ones of the special period, the Cuban state had to count on the private sector to pick up the slack, providing the necessary goods and services that the state could not. The second phase began in 1996 when Cuba's first private income tax in 37 years was instituted and regulation and enforcement were strengthened. New

and more strictly enforced regulations since 1996 include a prohibition against partnerships and non-family employees, a restriction on the size and foods served in *paladares* (no beef or shellfish), restricting private taxis from picking up foreigners or any passengers at hotels or airports, and a restriction against university graduates from becoming self-employed in their field of expertise. Finally, starting in the summer of 1997, private home-stays (*casas particulares*), which had been in semi-clandestine operation since the early 1990s, were added to the list of occupations which required a license and the payment of a fixed monthly minimum tax (*cuota fija mínima* — CFM).[3]

THEORETICAL DISCUSSION

As recently as 1981 theoretical discussions about and distinctions between the "informal," "underground," and "second" economies were still tentative and largely inconclusive. Since its origin in Keith Hart's study of small-scale business in Ghana in 1972 (ILO 1991), all that could be consistently agreed upon was that the "informal sector" was a phenomenon peculiar to less developed countries (LDCs) (Portes and Walton 1981). Contradicting this preliminary conclusion, however, Portes led a multi-country comparative study of the informal economy (Portes, Castells and Benton 1989; de Soto 1989), updating the definition of the informal economy and delineating a number of its common characteristics across different world regions (see also Portes and Borocz 1988; Sik 1992; Los 1990). They found that such a phenomenon exists to different degrees not only in LDCs but also in advanced capitalist economies of the West and in centrally planned economies (CPEs). Effectively, this landmark study "revealed the global scope of what was originally thought to be an exclusively Third World phenomenon" (Portes, Castells and Benton 1989: 2). Furthermore, Portes and his colleagues found that the informal economy seemed to have increased significantly in size and scope since the early 1970s, and their study challenged the common presumption that the only economy worthy of sustained and systematic study was that reflected in official statistics.

---

3. See Peters and Scarpaci (1998) for further information on the growth of self-employment in Cuba during the 1990s.

Despite a number of major disagreements among scholars about the particular causes and entrepreneurial potential of unregulated economic activity, there is consensus on a few of its central characteristics. First, most scholars subscribe to the definition employed by Portes, which characterized informal activity as "the unregulated production of otherwise licit goods and services" (Portes, Castells and Benton 1989: 15). Second, rejecting common negative assumptions about unregulated activity, Portes, Castells and Benton (1989) also agree that the informal economy is not simply the set of different activities performed by destitute or "marginal" individuals in order to survive. Third, strong evidence has been found in many different contexts indicating that the informal economy is in fact intimately linked to the official economy, each comprising different sectors in the same interdependent economic system.

Fourth, despite important exceptions, labor in the informal economy tends to be "downgraded." In other words, workers in this sector can expect lower rewards and protections than they would normally receive if formally employed, a characteristic that leads to the systematic use of undocumented, ethnic-minority, female, and child labor in the informal sector. Finally, the informal sector is commonly characterized by a government attitude of tolerance despite its illegal or unregulated nature. This ironic acquiescence can be understood as a government strategy intended to address inefficiencies and periodic crises such as unemployment in the regulated economy. With specific reference to centrally planned economies (CPEs), Pérez-López has noted the inherent links between the official and "second" economies, observing that "the second economy aris[es] as a result, and address[es] the failures of, the official economy" (1995: 25).

Grossman began giving systematic scholarly attention to the unregulated economic activity common in CPEs as early as 1977, with a seminal article on what he then termed the "second economy" of the Soviet Union. In that article, Grossman set down a working definition of the "second economy" as those productive activities which meet at least one of the two following criteria: (1) they are to a large extent

carried out in knowing violation of existing laws, and/or (2) they are directly engaged in for private gain (Grossman 1977: 25; Pérez-López 1995: 13). Thus, the key difference between the "informal" economy as it exists in underdeveloped regions of the third world, and the "second" economy as applied to CPEs is one of legality vs. control. In other words, the "second economy" expands the concept of informality to include not only economic activity that is illegal or unregulated by the state, but also all profit-driven activities (legal or not) which by definition contradict the socialist ideal. In her collection of essays on the second economy in socialist states, Maria Los (1990) echoes this ideological definition: "the second economy includes all areas of economic activity which are officially viewed as being inconsistent with the ideologically sanctioned dominant mode of economic organisation" (1990: 2). Therefore, this ideological criteria would specifically include formally legal but ideologically suspicious activities such as licensed self-employment, an important distinction for the Cuban second economy where licensed *cuentapropistas* struggle alongside clandestine self-employed workers. Echoing both Los and Pérez-López, Jatar-Hausmann has appropriately termed the ambivalent position of licensed self-employed workers in 1990s Cuba: "legal but not legitimate" (1999).

The Hungarian economist Endre Sik (1992) has looked specifically at the transformations of the second economy within his own country as it undergoes a transition from a centrally planned to a market economy. While not attributing the transition itself to the growth of the second economy, Sik does grant that the impact of the second economy on the transition has been considerable. He has found that while the second economy "lubricated the wheels" of the state-run sector, it also distorted its functioning (1992: 170) by implicating all levels and sectors of the first economy in routinized illegality and corruption. A whole society engaged in short-term profit maximization had the unintended consequence of creating a nationwide sub-culture of favor networks[4] and loopholes that has made difficult the formation of an efficient, responsible, tax-paying workforce in a market economy. According to Sik, Hungarian workers learned to distrust the system and looked at state-imposed controls with hostility, while they developed mutual trust and support amongst themselves. However, Sik maintains that the existence of a well-developed second economy in Hungary did allow for a relatively non-violent transition. In essence, these workers had developed valuable social networks, accumulated capital, and made significant investments to the extent that come a transition, "they had more to lose than their chains" (1992: 173).

Building on this fresh yet tentative research on second economies around the world, Pérez-López (1995) has applied the concept of the "second economy" directly to the Cuban case during the "special period." Like Grossman (1977) and Los (1990) before him, Pérez-López makes the important observation that the critical criterion in his own definition of Cuba's second economy is "control" rather than "legality." In other words, he understands the second economy concept as appropriate for Cuba because it includes "all those economic activities which are inconsistent with the dominant ideology that shapes the official ("first") economy" (1995: 14), not simply those which have been officially outlawed. Furthermore, Pérez-López contends that the "second" economy concept fits the Cuban context better than that of mere "informality" since in Cuba the rise in individual entrepreneurial activity takes place in a political context where societal gain is preferred over private gain. Therefore, he also distinguishes the second economy from the somewhat broader concept of the informal economy as it captures "all forms of deviations from the model of a socialist command economy" (1995: 13).[5] It is this particular understanding of the second economy that I employ in my study of Cuba.

THE SURVEY

In order to better focus the study and have a means of comparative analysis with which to approach the research questions outlined above, qualitative research was carried out in three somewhat intercon-

nected areas of the "informal tourism economy" that seem to be the most lucrative, dynamic, and sizeable: (1) lodging (*casas particulares*); (2) small-scale, privately run restaurants (*paladares*); and (3) transportation (*taxis particulares*).

Because of efforts during the last decade by the Cuban government to incorporate clandestine self-employment into the official economy, many *cuentapropistas* now serve tourists legally with government licenses and must pay monthly income taxes. Thus, in looking at workers in the second economy, both those CPs who pay taxes and those who work illegally without the benefit of a government license were included in the study. Though some anecdotal information was collected in other sites throughout the island, this study was carried out primarily in Havana, where licenses are theoretically available, where self-employment is wide-spread, and where foreign tourists are concentrated (interviews were conducted in the municipalities of *Habana Vieja*, *Centro Habana*, *Plaza*, and *Playa*). More specifically, building on initial interviews and observations collected in August 1999, this paper is based on 30 in-depth interviews conducted during July 2000, with the proprietors of ten private home-stays, ten *paladares*, and ten taxis. The homes, restaurants, and taxis were strategically selected in order to compare licensed self-employed workers with their unlicensed (clandestine) counterparts.

Following interview research done in Cuba by other investigators (Peters and Scarpaci 1998; Jatar-Hausmann 1999; Smith 1999; Holgado-Fernández 2000), the subjects for this study were selected in a casual, snowball method. Potential subjects were identified through observation and, on many occasions, through referrals by other self-employed individuals. I generally met with and interviewed the self-employed individuals in their place of business (usually their own homes), explaining that I was a researcher interested in the growth of Cuba's private

---

4. In Cuba, this system of personal networks, *palancas* (levers), has acquired the appropriately sardonic name, *sociolismo*, a *socio* being the Cuban equivalent of "friend" or "associate."

5. See Michalowski and Zatz 1990 for a significantly different assessment of Cuba's second economy before the advent of the "special period."

sector and how it interacted with the tourism economy.

The interviews normally took between 30 and 90 minutes to complete; the first part was usually dedicated to explaining the research project and gaining the trust of the subject. Though many respondents were quite guarded in their responses and most asked that their names not be used, no one refused to participate in the survey.

The survey consisted of demographic questions about the age, gender, race, and licensing status of the self-employed individual. The individual's education and work history, including the amount of time they had been self-employed, were discussed first. To this was added the hours and earnings in their previous (and for some concurrent) state salaried jobs and their current self-employed activity. Use of employees, amount and type of expenses (including taxes), input sources, and primary customers were also included. CPs were asked to comment on the best and worst aspects of being self-employed, and to specifically list what they saw as the major obstacles and restrictions to the growth of their enterprise. Finally, respondents were asked about their own as well as the more widespread use of commissions (paid to middlemen) and bribes (paid to inspectors and/or police).[6]

CUBA'S SECOND ECONOMY: BETWEEN REPRESSION AND LEGALIZATION

During many of my interviews with CPs in Cuba, I was met with the following explanation of the island's second economy: "En Cuba todo es prohibido, pero todo se hace," (in Cuba everything is prohibited, but everything is done); another version of this same quip goes, "En Cuba lo que no es prohibido, es obligatorio" (in Cuba that which is not prohibited is obligatory). Thus, while a significant segment of Cuba's underground economy has been legalized and incorporated into the official economy through fees, taxes, and licensing requirements, much self-employed activity remains beyond government control and many Cuban entrepreneurs opt not to seek out a legal license for their clandestine activity.

While legalizing formerly unregulated economic activity allows the government to reduce inequalities through taxes and fees (revenue theoretically shared with the population at large), such a strategy also allows the government to track CPs and control their activities more effectively. Furthermore, legalization allows the government to benefit financially from economically significant transactions that once took place beyond its reach (even if a less onerous tax system would likely bring the government much more revenue). Finally, licensed CPs are easily targeted when the state decides, as it periodically has in the past, that such activity should be restricted or eliminated altogether. My own and other studies (Peters and Scarpaci 1998) have found that many clandes-

---

6. It goes without saying that doing sociological research in today's Cuba poses special challenges for any researcher, native or foreign. Added to this is the piece of advice given me by a respected Cuban sociologist, "Be careful and skeptical, we Cubans have a tendency to exaggerate the truth or tell you what we think you want to hear." Recognizing these very real stumbling blocks, however, does not mean that meaningful sociological research is impossible in Cuba. Cuban researchers benefit from a deep and personal knowledge of the setting, language, and culture. They have knowledge of and special access to data sources, key informants, and the research environment. However, given the politically charged atmosphere characteristic of the island, Cuban subjects are unlikely to trust their fellow Cuban researchers with their secrets — especially if the focus is on 'delicate' matters like self-employment. There is a palpable fear that the researcher, being Cuban, may share the information with the state or inadvertently expose the subjects. Foreign researchers, on the other hand, are much less likely to have a personal knowledge of the setting, culture, or language. Furthermore, their access to data, informants, and the research environment is much more limited. However, in my experience Cubans are much more likely to open up and show their "true face" to a foreigner than to a fellow Cuban. Ironically, as I was surprised to find again and again in my interviews, the common Cuban use of the *doble moral* (two faces) makes little sense when interacting with someone who is not part of the society or subject to its rules. Added to this is a deep desire for many stressed self-employed individuals to vent, getting their frustrations "off their chest" (*desahogarse*), a process whereby a foreign researcher acts as a kind of confessor. Finally, many Cuban CPs expressed a desire to teach foreigners about the reality of Cuban society, counteracting both the negative or simplistic image Cuba may have abroad as well as their own government's propaganda.

tine CPs have decided to postpone applying for a state license precisely because they fear such an open declaration would make them potential targets in future capitalist purges.

Another distinct possibility behind the license requirements for CPs is that their aim is simply to prohibit such activity by taxing it at such a high level as to make it unprofitable. In my interviews, many clandestine CPs who rent out rooms to foreigners justified their reluctance to obtain a license by explaining that doing so would be prohibitively expensive. One frustrated Havana resident who periodically rents out a spare bedroom in her home explained that she would have to pay a $100 USD registration fee coupled with a $250 USD monthly rental tax to the government regardless of occupancy. She argued that she would have to dedicate herself to finding renters on a full-time basis in order to have enough occupants just to break even. Thus, along with many other Cubans, she has decided to occasionally rent out her apartment clandestinely, avoiding what she considers an exorbitant and prohibitive tax.

Ironically, it is not simply clandestine CPs who operate outside the law. Again and again in my interviews, I discovered that the CP license was used in practice as a cover, protecting its holder from suspicion while he or she engaged in many money-earning activities not included in their license. One licensed CP in Santiago whom I interviewed described her fear at not having enough residents to pay the $200 monthly tax required of renters in that city. She has come to have to rely on middle-men (whom she pays $5 per day) to bring her renters from the train station in order to keep her residence full during the low season. Also, she has resorted to illegally serving meals to her guests at extra cost in order to augment her income, enabling her to pay the monthly tax. Licensed CPs have developed a host of ingenious strategies or *trampas* in order to ensure that they are able to pay their tax at the end of each month and still make a profit. For example, one common strategy is to sub-

stantially underreport one's income, making the year-end, progressive tax on earnings as low as possible. Among my sample, this strategy seems to be employed most by taxi drivers and renters as they can easily underreport the amount each clients actually pays, while the *paladar* operators are less able to use this tactic since their sales receipts are more easily tracked.

In the private housing sector, a common tactic used to ensure sufficient income is renting more rooms than one's license allows. For example, one renter I interviewed routinely uses a second room in his home when the official one was occupied. He even has a special arrangement with his next-door neighbors to house guests in their home when both of his rooms are full. A further strategy used by nearly all renters is that of serving food to guests without declaring it part of their business (which would push their monthly tax up by 20 percent).[7] Finally, a strategy commonly used by nearly all self-employed individuals in the housing and *paladar* sectors is that of utilizing various friends and connections in order to bring in more revenue and serve their customers better. For example, many CPs hire non-household and non-family employees to aid them in their daily tasks. Others commonly pay commissions to middlemen to bring in clients. Ironically, many private taxi drivers (commonly called *boteros* in today's Cuba) play the double role of driver and middleman since they are both mobile and knowledgeable about the available private markets.

According to a number of those interviewed, government restrictions and licensing requirements function as a "Sword of Damocles" that the state can hold over their heads. Laws are enforced when enforcement is in the state's interest, yet these laws need not be enforced if the population can be intimidated into policing itself. Some of the more insightful CPs explained this seemingly illogical government policy of alternating legalization and increased restriction on self-employment as a government policy of retaining

---

7. Likewise, some *paladar* owners offered the option of lodging to their customers obviously without a license since legally there is no possibility of engaging in two self-employed activities at the same time.

absolute control over economic activity on the island. These Cubans reasoned that the government would allow only that level of independent economic activity that would address scarcities and inefficiencies in the first economy, yet restrict activities when they began to threaten centralized control. This, however, is still an open question. The previous experiences of the CPEs of Eastern Europe indicate that a government cannot absolutely and indefinitely control second economy activity. While government policies of benign neglect and limited legalization of the second economy can grease the rusty wheel of a centrally planned economy in the short run (allowing individuals to "resolve" their many consumption problems and ironically enable the short-term continuance of the system as a whole), in the long run such activities have been known to pose a significant threat to top-down control of both the economy and polity.

THE FINDINGS

This section of the paper is organized around two of the three self-employment sectors focused in the research: *casas particulares* and *paladares*.[8] Furthermore, each of the two following subsections will attempt to share tentative answers to the three central research questions outlined in the introduction. First, what are the socioeconomic effects that this new kind of private economic activity brings to the island and to the individuals who engage in it? Second, what is the relative size, incentive structure, and profitability of licensed/regulated informal activity vs. unlicensed/unregulated activity? And third, what is the purpose of state regulation, licensing requirements, and taxes for the legal sector of the informal economy? These findings are admittedly preliminary. The interview data collected still needs to be analyzed and systematized in a more coherent fashion. For this reason, I will here supplement my analysis with descriptions (as well as a few quotations) of a number of instructive cases of self-employed workers.

Casas Particulares

Socioeconomic Effects: Unlike most other licensed self-employment in Cuba, renting rooms in private homes only came under state regulation in the summer of 1997. Prior to that, those who engaged in this type of activity did so in a kind a "no man's land," as one respondent put it. Though the tax system for private homes is very similar to that applied to other areas of self-employment, it has a few unique features. First, the amount of one's monthly tax is based largely on one's location relative to Havana's primary tourist hotels. For example, a renter in *La Rampa* area of *Vedado* must pay a $250 monthly tax, while the monthly tax is just $100 for most residents of *Centro Habana* and other parts of Plaza. Second, self-employed renters must pay a year-end percentage of their earnings after deducting 10 percent for expenses and the total year's payments in the monthly CFM tax. Therefore, unlike many of the *paladar* proprietors in my sample who are able to avoid the year-end tax altogether based on their high monthly payments, private home-stays must pay an extra tax at the end of the year based on their *after* tax earnings. Third, private home renters seem to be the most vulnerable to fluctuations in the tourist economy since the vast majority of their customers are foreigners (not necessarily the case with *paladar* owners and taxi drivers). These special characteristics have the result of pushing many potentially legal renters underground and pressuring those with licenses to cheat in order to survive.

For example, Luis, a young college graduate who lives with his mother and sister on the outskirts of Havana, stressed the fact that the renting strategy (without a license) has only been a manner of supplementing the family's meager combined income of 400 Cuban pesos, not a scheme to get rich. He pointed out the fact that all CPs have been targeted/criticized unjustly by the government as some kind of *lumpen* that live off of others. While he readily admitted that there were many who had gotten rich un-

---

8. Self-employed taxi drivers will be left out of this discussion due to a lack of sufficient time with which to analyze and interpret the data collected. However, impressions would indicate that despite being of more humble origins, on average private taxi drivers share many of the same complaints of their self-employed counterparts in the housing and restaurant sectors.

justly through the diversion of goods and stealing from state warehouses, he argued that CPs worked hard for their earnings, many times much harder than those with state jobs (where "we pretend to work, you pretend to pay us" is sometimes the most accurate motto). "It hasn't been a marvel, it's only been a way to survive," is how he summed it up. Magda, a licensed renter echoed Luis' comments, saying, "I'll always have enough if I save my money during the good months," she reasoned. "I make enough to live with honor and feed my family, but not enough to buy a car. After you deduct the $100 tax each month, there is enough left to live, but without luxury. We can sometimes go out to a restaurant paying in Cuban pesos. I can't imagine how other renters survive who have to pay taxes of $250 per month or higher."

When asked if he could change one thing about the tax system, a third licensed renter named Oscar responded, "Taxes should be based on occupancy and income and not on a quota system. The Cuban economy is not one that gives incentive to capital as in the United States. It is designed to do just the opposite — discourage it." Given these many restrictions, however, Oscar does admit that he still fares better than others and has a disposable income. As an example of the very slow growth of the sector and difficulty of saving or investing much money, he shared that he has been saving part of his earnings each month ($50 USD) for the past five years in order to buy a car. He explained that he wants to buy a diesel powered American car that has a price tag of $6,000. The car would allow him to take his family on outings to the beach once in a while. He concluded by reiterating that no one is in the housing business to make it rich. According to him, most go into the CP sector to ensure their economic survival, and possibly to have a little bit of disposal income: "Thanks to this, I am alive," he explained. "Without this I'd be a dead man".

Licensed vs. Clandestine Renters: While one would like to use the licensed/unlicensed demarcation as the central distinguishing element in analyzing rental activity, it remains to be seen if there is any real sociological difference between the two. My impression is that the licensed renters charge more, rent more often and intensively, and dedicate more time and effort to renting as their principal economic activity than do their unlicensed counterparts. This seems to be so because of the very high government fixed minimum monthly tax (CFM) that must be paid by those with licenses, regardless of occupancy. In other words, these licensed renters must pay between $100 and $250 (which changes depending upon location in the city/country) per month for the right to rent out one room of their homes, regardless of whether they have clients or not. Of course, this tax grows substantially if one wants to declare more rooms for rent or serve food to the renters. Furthermore, clandestine workers seem to treat their rental activity as a secondary activity (even if it is primary in terms of the amount of income it generates), while few licensed renters can avoid to be casual or lax about it due to the quota tax system.

Another tentative lesson from my interviews is, as one respondent put it: "We all cheat a little" (*Todos hacen su trampita*). In other words, while the legal distinction between licensed and unlicensed CPs is important, it is not absolute by any means. Actually, Miguel, a former renter who is interested in returning to the fold, said that he was unable to make enough to pay the tax the first time around due to his honesty and strictness in following the law. If he is able to get his license reissued (which seems doubtful given the government's refusal of issuing many CP licenses), he was clear in stating that this time "I will do what it takes" to stay in business. Thus, while clandestine CPs operate totally outside the law, even licensed CPs make a large part of their earnings (the range was between 10% and 75% in my interviews) by practicing "creative bookkeeping" and bending the self-employment rules. In this way, the CP license becomes more a protective façade, used to mask host of activities either not allowed or not specifically licensed. It is not merely a legalizing mechanism that separates the law-abiding citizens from supposed delinquents.

Ironically, one renter had originally printed up business cards that read, "Room for Rent — Specialist in Food Service" (*Rento Habitación — Especialista en*

Gastronomía). He explained to me that due to his special talents in the kitchen, he had originally intended to serve food to his guests. However, he found this to be both too costly for tax purposes and too time consuming. Thus, he only occasionally serves food to his guests, charging them a few dollars for each meal, yet still has no authorization to do so. While his cards were clear in stating that he only had one room for rent, another licensed renter gave me a handful of business cards openly declaring *"Habitaciones Doña Amelia,"* the use of the plural indicating that she did rent more than one of her many rooms in an old, outwardly crumbling mansion in Vedado (even if she admitted to paying tax on just one of the rooms). The truly ironic aspect of her business cards, however, was the fact that they were double sided. While one side assured the holder of a comfortable and agreeable stay, the reverse side declared, "Dr. Amelia Betancur — Specialist in Traditional Medicine" (*Dra. Amelia Betancur — Especialista en Medicina Tradicional*).

The Purpose of Regulation: In explaining the intent behind the state's strict regulation of the private housing sector, Miguel, a university professor (once a licensed renter) who is currently looking to return to the self-employed fold shared these comments:

The tax is designed to drown the client, not to make money for the government or share the wealth with the people. If profit were the government's intention, they would lower the tax and make a lot more money because everyone would have an incentive to sign up. The strict and ridiculous laws and taxes have the effect of pushing people underground and causing those with licenses to cheat. The law as it stands only benefits the larger entities (usually owned by ex-ministers, ex-military, or ex-members of the central committee). These people have large homes with many rooms and can earn enough to stay afloat by declaring one or two yet renting many more. The little guy is pushed out of the picture or must live in fear of not earning enough to pay the tax.

Joaquín, also a university professor, who has clandestinely rented a spare room in his home for years saw the state's approach to the self-employed sector in much the same way. He argued, "The tax is designed to push them all out of business, because the tax and inspections and police are so high and strict. Everyone who rents illegally would legalize themselves if the tax were based on how much they earned and not a monthly quota." When asked why the government did not just close down the CP sector if it really did not accept it ideologically, Joaquín argued, "The government is concerned about its image. It doesn't want to be seen as ruling it out, but would prefer to let it die on its own. It can do this through high taxes and restrictions, as well as catching CPs in illegality." He added the caveat, "Of course, it's not a matter of them being delinquents, but based on the fact that there is not another way for them to make money. They don't choose to be illegal."

A recent article from Cuba's fledgling independent press estimated that as many as 35% of Cuba's tourists stay in private homes and that an estimated 200,000 tourists had lodged in such homes in the first six months of 1999. The article indicated that Cuban authorities are becoming concerned about the loss of tourism revenue to the second economy and reason that they cannot adequately "protect" tourists who stay in private homes. It is worth asking whether the government also wants to "protect" Cubans from the "corrupting" influences increased exposure to foreigners may bring. The article also quoted a government official who indicated that rising levels of bribery and corruption are also worrying regulators of self-employment activities, "There is a limited confidence in the capacity of government inspectors to resist the bribes of the proprietors" (Zúñiga 1999a). In my own research into the private housing market, only two respondents admitted to giving bribes to government inspectors. However, most of the others admitted that it was a fairly widespread practice. One respondent mentioned that of the three different types of inspectors (housing, immigration, and tax) the immigration inspectors were the "least bribable" being members of the military. A number of respondents agreed that inspections were most common toward the end of the year, hinting that they came in search of extra cash for the holidays. Sandra, a former licensed renter now living in Miami, openly admitted to paying bribes on a regular basis. She even stated that some housing inspectors played the secondary role of middle-man, occasionally showing up at her home with foreign tourists in tow, searching for their own commissions.

Restaurantes Particulares (*Paladares*)

Socioeconomic Effects: As compared with the proprietors of *casas particulares*, *paladar* owners express a much deeper frustration with government restrictions. My interviews with them reflect a steep rise in government taxes over the last five years, in one case rising from 2,500 Cuban pesos per month, to 5,000 after the first two years of operation, and then to 10,000 per month by the fifth year. Also, according to my sample of *paladar* proprietors, the government has closed off the issuance of new licenses for private restaurants, not yet the case for *casas particulares*. One advantage that *paladares* have over those active in the housing market is that they need not rely exclusively on foreigners for their clientele. Instead, most of the *paladares* in my sample have a mixed (if predominantly foreign) clientele, especially those more affordable ones that charge in Cuban pesos. Furthermore, possibly as a result of increased government vigilance, clandestine (unlicensed) *paladares* were much more difficult to locate than was clandestine housing. Finally, given the large number of *paladares* which have been forced to close their doors in the last few years and the constant struggle in which the remaining ones must engage to stay in business, I would conclude that the economic effects of the existence of private restaurants is negligible.

When asked what it was he likes best about being a *cuentapropista*, Baudelio, a middle-aged former university professor who runs a *paladar* in the *La Rampa* area, was quick with a laundry list of benefits to working for one's self. First, he mentioned that he is able to work at home. Second, he argued that he has more money and he can do with it as he pleases, investing it in ways that he decides and thinks best. Third, though he works long hours and is ultimately responsible for every aspect of the business, he said that he has the ability to work when he likes and take off when he decides. In other words, he enjoys being independent, saying, "Here, I'm my own boss." Finally, he argued that being a *cuentapropista* enables him to ensure his family's well being. He even argued

that this strategy should help the state out since, "If the family flourishes there is less to worry about for the state." Of course, even though he saw this as an ideal, he knew that the state does not see his work in that way. "What I do," he understood, "is contrary to the system of the country." When asked to elaborate, Baudelio mentioned that beyond the capitalist nature of his enterprise, in the past any association with foreigners was seen as suspect. Now, however, his business runs mainly due to his contact with foreigners and he sees himself as "restructuring relations with foreigners" through his many international contacts.

Licensed vs. Clandestine Paladares: Though she has struggled with appeals for two years in order to have her business license reinstated, Blanca, a middle-aged retired economist who ran a financially successful *paladar* for almost four years, seemed almost resigned to the fact that she will never get permission to open back up again. When I asked her why another member of her family didn't get a new license, she explained that the government has stopped issuing licenses for new *paladares*. She sarcastically, almost bitterly, explained to me the government's official "política" on the closure of *paladares*. "It's not the intention of the government to close them down. If you follow the law, you will have no problem" she repeated while smirking and rolling her eyes. "If you get fined and closed down you have no one to blame but yourself," she ironically explained. According to her, then, the government strategy is very wise, if also quite devious and hypocritical. Those who get closed down can be labeled criminals, cheats, or even the infamous *lumpen*, while those who remain are that much more wary about violating the law. What could be seen as a structural imbalance or flaw in the economic system, is instead interpreted for the public by the government-controlled media as the result of a few criminal, or capitalist "bourgeois" elements trying to cheat an otherwise smooth, egalitarian socioeconomic system. The sword of Damocles can be hung over the heads of those who remain, while the government can claim to simply be enforcing the law when it revokes the licenses of those who cheat the system. Furthermore, when *paladares* turn in their licenses "voluntarily" after finding that they can not make profit enough to pay their monthly taxes, the government can claim that they gave capitalism a chance and that it failed. Their hands remain clean.

An interview I had done with a formerly licensed *paladar* owner in *Habana Vieja* named Carlos who voluntary gave up his license illustrates Blanca's arguments well. I only had to ask a few questions of him before he was off describing and explaining for me the many trials of running a *paladar* in Cuba. Overall, his general attitude was one of frustration with all the government's taxes and regulations. He gave me many justifications for his giving up his license about a year ago and reopening just a few weeks later without one. Besides avoiding the $900 per month tax that he had to pay as a licensed *paladar*, he explained that working underground allowed him to avoid harassment from inspectors who would periodically come by to enforce the many "repressive" regulations placed on private restaurants. He reminded me that *paladares* could not serve either lobster or beef and that the state limited the number of chairs they could have. In addition to this, he complained that it was nearly impossible to obtain all of his inputs (food) from the state suppliers. He explained that most tourists do not want the same pork and rice that they can get in their countries, but instead come to Cuba in order to try some of the island's great seafood. He also explained that the typical *paladar* clientele were the less wealthy, more adventurous types who were in search of a more authentic Cuban experience than could be found in the typical state restaurant. Furthermore, he argued that he was not stealing anything from anyone but only working honestly to make it in a country with very few options.

Said Carlos: "If you ask me to work without pay today, fine. I can sacrifice a day, I'm with you. But don't ask me the same tomorrow. Tomorrow I will want a reward." He also commented that the government needs to find a balance between reward and sacrifice, even if for its own benefit and long-term survival because it cannot expect the population to live through the special period without resorting to new means of generating private income. He argued that if the government does not provide an escape valve, allowing people the room and flexibility to resolve their economic problems, frustration could grow to a boiling point — and explode — threatening the existence of the system itself.

The Purpose of Regulation: When compared to private home-stays, *paladares* seem to be under much more pressure from government inspectors to close their doors. For example, a recent closed-door meeting of the Communist Party and the Assembly of People's Power focused on Havana's *paladares*. It seems party officials are increasingly worried about the fierce competition these eating establishments are posing for state run and tourism restaurants. Official numbers from 1999 cited in the article place the city's food service and tourist restaurants at 12,416, while there are only 466 legally recognized *paladares*. Officials cited an increase in legal violations where restaurateurs have served prohibited products (beef and seafood) and charged patrons in dollars without government permission. Proprietors have also been accused of hiring employees outside their immediate family and expanding their operations beyond the legal limit of 12 patrons. Cuban law stipulates that *paladares* should be strictly family businesses with maximum seating of just 12 patrons. Furthermore, they are authorized to charge only in *moneda nacional* (national currency) unless they have obtained a specific license to charge in dollars, with the condition that all taxes are also paid to the government in dollars (Zúñiga 1999b).

Whether the motivation behind government restriction of *paladares* is reducing competition or doing away with an ideologically anachronistic form of business in a supposedly socialist context, my interviewees certainly expressed anxiety at the constant inspections and strict laws. For example, during my interview with Baudelio, he noted that he has been in business for four years and seven months and that his is one of the few remaining *paladares* in the Plaza municipality. He estimated that a year and a half ago (December 1998) there were as many as 2,500 *paladares* while now there are no more than 16 or 17 in his municipality (Plaza).[9] He hinted that these *paladares* did not go out of business due to lack of business, exclaiming, "They sold a lot" (*¡Vendían!*). Instead, he explained that they have been pushed out of business by rising government taxes and by "other methods." In other words, according to him the government has been looking for excuses to close down these *paladares* and hygiene and/or regulation violations are only some of their many justifications. "They look for excuses," was the way Baudelio put it.

When asked to describe the biggest obstacles he faced in running his business, Baudelio did not hesitate to answer that government inspectors are his biggest headache. According to him, they do not come to visit exactly to "inspect," but "with full intention to find negative things" (*con plena intención de encontrar cosas malas*). Furthermore, he openly and convincingly argued that the government's intent was plainly one of doing away with the *paladar* sector, saying, "It is clear that their intention is to close down the *paladares*" (*Queda claro que su intención es de cerrar los paladares*). Furthermore, he made the observation that the inspectors are even give closure goals or quotas. "Back when the repression began," he explained, "they had goals to close 2 or 3 *paladares* a month." Recently however, "they are trying to close down as many as 20 to 30 each month." When asked what were some of the methods used to trip up the *paladar* owners, he said that the inspectors might focus on an insignificant item like a bottle of oil or a salt shaker. They ask for proof of how it was obtained and must be shown both the receipt from the cash register as well as the hand-written, itemized receipt (*factura*). If either of these is missing, a fine of 1,500 Cuban pesos can result and the business license can be revoked. Finally, Baudelio mentioned that after the "opening" (*apertura*) of 1994, the state has gradually but inexorably moved to restrict, repress, and do away with the *paladar* sector of the CP economy. According to him, besides the strict regulations, high taxes, and steep fines, the government recently froze all requests for new *paladares*.

Elena, another licensed *paladar* proprietor, echoed many of Baudelio's complaints. For example, when asked what she would change about the tax law if given the chance, she argued that she and the other mi-

cro-entrepreneurs had no real complaint against having to pay their fair share of taxes. In fact, she explained that she would gladly pay her taxes if they were based on her income and not derived from a quota system. Also, she took issue with what she saw a ridiculous restrictions such as forcing her to obtain all her inputs through state stores in dollars. She complained that there were no wholesale stores where CPs could go for supplies. "They should set up a market where the self-employed can make purchases," she argued. Finally, she saw as illogical and repressive the entire existing system of taxes and incentives. "The government doesn't permit many things," she explained. "They give you fines. They are always showing up looking for a receipt for our purchases." She concluded, "It is obvious that the objective is to close down (*cerrar*) not to encourage (*crecer*) the business of the self-employed." In other words, instead of facilitating the growth of the CP sector from which the government could benefit financially through increased revenue and tax compliance, Elena feels that the government's current regulations act as a disincentive to potential CPs driving them or keeping them underground where they pay no taxes and earn little money for themselves or the state. According to her, however, when the government represses the sector through fines and taxes no one discontinues working, they simply give up their licenses and continue to work clandestinely, as is confirmed in Carlos' case.

CONCLUSION

Lessons from other Latin American contexts about the role of the informal economy and the second economy in the CPEs of Eastern Europe suggest that these sectors can produce entrepreneurial development, individual mobility, micro-enterprise growth, and even pressure for larger systemic change. Such findings make study of Cuba's second economy an important indicator of social change. However, the conclusions about the second economy garnered from other national contexts have not been consis-

---

9. Later he reiterated these numbers, changing the second figure to "between 30 and 40 *paladares* left." Such "exaggerated" numbers were corrected by a young Cuban scholar who has done research on the CP economy. However, she did echo the general spirit of his criticism confirming that the number of private restaurants has shrunk considerably over the past 18 months.

tent or generalizable. Simultaneously bemoaned as a "last resort" and celebrated as the "bridge to the future," Cuba's second economy has not yet been subjected to the rigorous, in-country study required before this debate can be resolved. The possibility remains that state restrictions will so debilitate and discourage the self-employed sector that there may be little left to study in the future. Despite this possibility, this research project has sought to begin just such a process. The transitional experiences of the formerly socialist countries of Eastern Europe indicate that the contradictions of Cuba's second economy could lead to greater conflict and socioeconomic inequality during a future transition to a market economy. However, these experience also teach us that a thriving second economy can act as a brake on the growth of chaos during a transition, giving citizens an incentive to protect their investments.

Returning to the first of my original research questions: What are the socioeconomic effects that this new kind of private economic activity brings to the island and to the individuals who engage in it? Are selfishness, rugged individualism, and inequality the fruits produced in these new islands of capitalism? Does activity in the second economy socialize its participants in tax evasion, criminality, and "anti-social" behavior? Does the government-run tourism economy suffer "unfair competition" from these clandestine or semi-clandestine operations, which actively and unapologetically place private profit over the public good? Or are self-employed Cubans developing entrepreneurial skills and attitudes? Are they creating jobs and other backward linkages that help the larger economy? And are they building up capital, creating the backbone of a small-business sector, enabling the establishment of private investment and credit systems, and laying the groundwork for a more stable, diversified, and more fully "Cuban" economy?

My research indicates that those who engage in informal economic activity are not among the most desperate of Cubans. Though licensed CPs as a rule have more capital and make more in terms of profit than their clandestine counterparts, neither group seems to be choosing the self-employment option out of desperation. Instead, they are consciously investing

the little material capital and the enormous inventive talent they have in order to "live a little better". However, even if many CPs are making many times more in the second economy than they made in the first in Cuban pesos, this comparison has increasingly lost its meaning and force over the last five years since nearly everyone needs access to dollar income over and above the peso salary to insure sheer survival. Therefore, to say that these CPs earn substantially more than in the past, does not mean that these Cubans are becoming a new wealthy class. Instead, this is a group of people who are able to survive and live more comfortably than others, with a bit of disposal income. On average, the CPs work much longer and harder than state employed Cubans and produce more for themselves and for the country. They are as far from an "idle rich,"parasite, or lumpen class as can be imagined. However, despite the key role CPs play in sustaining many households, they currently do not present an economic or political challenge to the state, especially due to the continued existence of innumerable restrictions and sanctions on their growth.

What do my findings say about the relative size, incentive structure, and profitability of licensed/regulated informal activity vs. unlicensed/unregulated activity? Is there a sociological difference between licensed and unlicensed second economy activity? The Cuban government clearly categorizes them in two different legal camps, but ideologically they both cut against the ideal of a socialist (state-run and centrally-planned) economy. My findings are clear in uncovering that while some CPs may be legal, none are seen by the Cuban government as ideologically legitimate. Furthermore, existing state regulations systematically drive potential CPs into clandestine activity, or force those with licenses to routinely violate the law in order to keep those licenses. It would seem that the government could profit much more from CP activity by lowering taxes and/or tying them to earnings, than it currently does. How then do we understand a seemingly illogical policy of extremely high and prohibitive taxes?

The Cuban government has never seen the self-employed sector as more than a stop-gap measure, employed during the economic crisis with the ironic purpose of "saving socialism." The government never intended its economic adjustments to be the beginning of any "transition." Nor has the government ever described the private sector as a good thing. Instead, it is consistently portrayed as a necessary evil in the short-term. Thus, with a relative economic recovery underway, we should not be surprised to find the government slowly, yet inexorably "choking the sector to death" (in the words of one interviewee) with increasingly draconian laws. The government policy toward the self-employment sector cannot be explained from a purely economic point of view. Instead, restrictions derive from a demonstrated desire to retain absolute political control which is likely to be threatened by the growth of a private sector, however small. Thus, licensing requirements and taxes on the self-employed are not intended as a redistribution of newly acquired wealth nor as a measure aimed at countering the island's growing inequality. Instead, the stringent taxes, fees, and regulations are designed to make private enterprise so costly that it becomes all but impossible for the self-employed to accumulate private wealth.

One question I will leave open-ended is whether the Cuban government can go back to a more orthodox version of a centrally planned economy. The government seems to have both the political power and the political will to do so. It may find, however, that the self-employed sector has become too extensive and rooted in the family economy (and in national economy through multiplier effects) to easily do away with it. Though remittances and tourism have grown substantially over the last decade, it is doubtful that they alone would be able to compensate for the elimination of Cuba's extensive self-employed sector. Furthermore, as one interviewee commented, "No one is an idiot" (*nadie es tonto*), and it is well known that the government would be shooting itself in the foot by eliminating a sector of the economy that fills a gap which the government has not succeeded in addressing alone.

BIBLIOGRAPHY

Grossman, Gregory. "The Second Economy of the USSR," pp. 245-269, in *The Underground Economy in the United States and Abroad.* Vito Tanzi, ed. Lexington: Lexington Books, 1977.

Holgado-Fernández, Isabel. *¡No es fácil!: mujeres cubanas y la crisis revolucionaria.* Barcelona: Icaria editorial, s.a., 2000.

International Labour Office (ILO). *The Dilemma of the Informal Sector.* Geneva: ILO, 1991.

Jatar-Hausmann, Ana Julia. *The Cuban Way: Communism, Capitalism, and Confrontation.* West Hartford, CT: Kumarian Press, 1999.

Los, Maria, ed. *The Second Economy in Marxist States.* London: Macmillan, 1990.

Mesa-Lago, Carmelo. *Are economic reforms driving Cuba to the market?* Miami: North-South Center, University of Miami, 1994.

Michalowski, Raymond J., and Marjorie S. Zatz. "The Cuban Second Economy in Perspective," pp. 101-21 in *The Second Economy in Marxist States.* Maria Los, ed. London: Macmillan, 1990.

Pérez, Louis, Jr. *Cuba: Between Reform and Revolution* (second edition). New York: Oxford, 1995.

Pérez-López, Jorge F. *Cuba's Second Economy: From Behind the Scenes to Center Stage.* New Brunswick: Transaction, 1995.

Peters, Phillip. "Islands of Enterprise: Cuba's Emerging Small Business Sector," (14 pp.) *Alexis de Tocqueville Institution* (http://adti.net/html_files/cuba/curpteml.htm), 1997.

Peters, Phillip, and Joseph L. Scarpaci. "Cuba's New Entrepreneurs: Five Years of Small-Scale Capitalism," (20 pp.) *Alexis de Toqueville Institution* (http://adti.net/html_files/cuba/TCP-SAVE.htm), 1998.

Portes, Alejandro, and Jozsef Borocz. "The Informal Sector under Capitalism and State Socialism: A Preliminary Comparison." *Social Justice* 15 (Fall/Winter 1988): 17-28.

Portes, Alejandro, Manuel Castells, and Lauren A. Benton, eds. *The Informal Economy: Studies in Advanced and Less Developed Countries.* Baltimore: The Johns Hopkins University Press, 1989.

Portes, Alejandro, Carlos Dore-Cabral, and Patricia Landolt. *The Urban Caribbean: Transition to the New Global Economy.* Baltimore: The Johns Hopkins University Press, 1997.

Portes, Alejandro, and John Walton. *Labor, Class, and the International System.* New York: Academic Press, 1981.

Schwartz, Rosalie. *Pleasure Island: Tourism and Temptation in Cuba.* Lincoln: University of Nebraska Press, 1997.

Sik, Endre. "From the Second to the Informal Economy." *Journal of Public Policy* 12, no.2 (1992): 153-75.

Smith, Benjamin. "Self-Employment in Cuba: A Street-Level View." *Cuba in Transition—Volume 9.* Washington: Association for the Study of the Cuban Economy, 1999.

Soto, Hernando de. *The Other Path: The Invisible Revolution in the Third World.* New York: Harper and Row Publishers, 1989.

Zúñiga, Jesús. "Preocupación por alojamiento de turistas en casas particulares," CubaNet News, September 10, 1999; www.cubanet.org/CNews/y99/sep99/10a2.htm.

Zúñiga, Jesús. "Paladares amargan la vida de restaurantes estatales," CubaNet News, September 6, 1999; www.cubanet.org/CNews/y99/sep99/06a3.htm.

CUBA'S TRADE POLICY AFTER CASTRO

Sidney Weintraub

I was invited to talk because I am reasonably well versed in U.S. and international trade policy, and not because I am an expert on Cuba. My focus, as suggested, will be on the post-Castro period. Put differently, I was asked to speculate because none of us knows what the political or economic structure will be at that time.

THE CURRENT TRADE CONTEXT

It is useful to first set forth some of the main trade policy developments taking place in the United States, in the Western Hemisphere, and in the world so that developments in Cuba can be put into context. These include the following:

- Omitting Cuba and a few other countries, the U.S. market is highly open to imports and this fact, coupled with the high U.S. economic growth rate of recent years, is sucking in goods and services in amounts never before experienced. The U.S. current account deficit is estimated to reach $420 billion this calendar year.

- Economic integration in the Western Hemisphere is moving forward at a pace unprecedented in the modern era. There are active integration agreements — free trade areas (FTAs) or customs unions (CUs) — in the Caribbean, Central America, the Andes, the Southern part of South America, and the mother of them all, NAFTA. In addition, FTAs cut across hemispheric sub-regions, such as those of Mexico with almost every country in sight, plus Canada and Chile, and Mercosur flirting with the Andean countries

- A provisional FTA between Mexico and the European Union (EU) went into effect on July 1, 2000, and Mexico is discussing an FTA with Singapore and is even talking with Japan about this — although trade progress with Japan is typically made slowly and deliberately.

- The negotiators looking toward a Free Trade Area of the Americas (FTAA) will have a preliminary text of the agreement, undoubtedly full of brackets to indicate points still in contention, by the end of this year. The deadline for concluding an FTAA, as agreed among the 34 participating nations, is 2005. The principal impediment to concluding this agreement is the lack of fast-track authority from the U.S. Congress to the president and this is certain to become an issue in the new administration. If fast-track authority is granted, the FTAA negotiators will be able to move to the end-game of reaching specific deals.

- The European Union (EU) continues its preferential treatment for imports from countries in Asia, Africa, and the Caribbean.

- Asian countries, those from Southeast and Northeast Asia, are discussing how to move toward free trade. Australia and New Zealand have free trade with each other.

- Finally, even though the ministerial meeting of the World Trade Organization (WTO) collapsed in disarray in Seattle late last year, global trade negotiations continue in agriculture and services, and the attempt to begin a comprehensive trade round is certain to be renewed.

The foregoing listing is by no means complete. My point, nevertheless, should be clear. Countries all over the world are negotiating preferential trade arrangements regionally, subregionally, cross-regionally. Efforts are simultaneously under way to revive global, nonpreferential trade negotiations. The EU is enlarging beyond the current 15 to include former socialist countries of Eastern Europe. China will shortly become a member of the WTO. So, too, will Russia and many of the other states of the former Soviet Union. Vietnam just signed a trade agreement with the United States under which Vietnam will open its market to imports of goods and services and in return receive most-favored-nation trade treatment (now called normal trading relations) from the United States.

Where is Cuba? It is outside all the main trade initiatives going on in the world, except in the most tenuous way with the Association of Caribbean States. This isolation is not completely Cuba's fault. After all, the United States does maintain an embargo against most trade with Cuba. However, Cuba also isolates itself. It does this by the nature of its socialist structure, the uncertainty of its judicial process, and the unpredictability of its regulations. China remains a dictatorial, communist country politically, but its internal economic policies are light years ahead of Cuba's in the sense of encouraging market initiatives. Cuba will never prosper as a trading nation if its internal economic procedures remain unchanged. It is by now inevitable that Cuba will be forced to play catch-up with its neighbors in the hemisphere — and the sooner this process begins, the less arduous it is likely to be for the Cuban population.

THE PROCESS OF TRANSITION

There are signs, still tentative, still partial, still inadequate, that a transition is taking place in Cuba's thinking about trade. Similarly, there are indications that the United States is beginning to think about the transition, even though Castro remains on the scene.

The transition in Cuban trade and related policies to which I refer is better known to all of you who follow this matter more closely than I do. The actions include decriminalizing the holdings of hard currencies by Cubans; opening foreign currency exchange houses; introducing a convertible peso; expanding the scope for foreign investment; creating export processing zones; permitting foreign banking within Cuba; ending the state monopoly for carrying out foreign trade; and publishing statistics on economic relations with the rest of the world more fully (although not completely so, to be sure) than had been the case earlier. Many of these changes took place after the breakdown of the trade and aid relations with the Soviet Union and the Council for Mutual Economic Assistance. These changes by no means have brought Cuba into the mainstream of modern trading relations, but they do represent the beginnings of a transition. The transition is most unlikely to reach the logical conclusion of a market economy while Castro remains in power, but what is happening may facilitate the movement to market processes after his departure.

Changes in U.S. economic policy toward Cuba also have been taking place. These include the legalization of remittances from the United States, greater tolerance of visits to Cuba by U.S. citizens, and legislation in Congress to permit more sales of foodstuffs and medicines to Cuba. The prohibition against providing credit to facilitate these sales may make the initiative inoperable in light of Cuba's high external indebtedness, but both those who support and those who oppose such sales are probably correct that transitions happen one step at a time.

Each individual action taken by itself is limited in scope. What is more important in a policy sense is the accumulation of measures intended to broaden U.S. economic relations with Cuba — cautiously, to be sure. This, I think, is evidence of misgiving by many in the Congress about continuation of past policy. I don't know fully what is stimulating these changes in U.S. sentiment, whether the lobbying by U.S. agricultural export interests, the anomaly of giving permanent normal trading relations (PNTR) to China but not to Cuba, the attention devoted to the Elián González case, and the frustration with a unilateral trade embargo that has lasted so long even as Castro remains in power — or, more likely, all of these together.

My purpose here is not to take a position on U.S. policy toward Cuba, but rather to state my impression that many U.S. lawmakers and senior officials in the executive branch are already thinking about the transition to a post-Castro Cuba and wondering whether this would be smoother if some economic transitions begin now.

There are substantial reasons for treating China differently from Cuba. China is vastly more populous and the potential market much more significant. China took the initiative to open deeper economic relations with the United States out of a desire to develop a more competitive economy. But China is not the only country that is being treated differently from Cuba. Normal trade relations are soon to begin with Vietnam. Talks between the United States and North Korea, the archetype closed society, are taking place and it would not surprise me if this led to more open trading relations.

In each of these cases — China and Vietnam in particular — the argument made by U.S. supporters of economic engagement is that the stirrings of a market economy will promote corollary political changes. I do not wish to push this argument too far. Democracy exists *only* in market economies, but markets do not by themselves assure democracy. I certainly do not wish to push the market/democracy connection in Cuba while Castro remains in power, but this surely will be a key consideration once he is gone.

Perhaps the most interesting country to examine for the interplay between market economics, trade, and political change is Mexico. It is next door to the United States, as is Cuba. Mexico's politics cannot be compared with Cuba's (or with politics in China or Vietnam for that matter). Mexico has long had an authoritarian regime, but not a repressive dictatorship in the Cuban mold. Mexico, however, was hardly a democratic nation as the West defines democracy. Despite this, the United States (and Canada) joined with Mexico in NAFTA. Mexican trade has since skyrocketed such that it is now the seventh most important trading entity in the world (counting the EU as one entity). And, just last month, on July 2, Mexico went through a democratic transformation

by toppling the party that had been in power for 71 years. The economic transformation in Mexico was by no means the sole reason for the political transformation that occurred — but it surely contributed significantly to this progression.

LOOKING AHEAD

One of the papers presented at your meeting last year, that by Ernesto Hernández-Catá, dealt systematically with the kinds of issues I am addressing here — the transition and the effects of globalization on the Cuban economy. His informed guess was that the transition to a market economy in Cuba can take place relatively rapidly. I agree. Hernández-Catá had two caveats: the need for peace in Cuba; and sound economic policies. I accept this. Learning to shift from a constricted, inward-looking, controlled economy, whether of the type that exists in Cuba or, say, the Ukraine, to one that can thrive in a globalized world structure, is not simple. I am convinced, however, that Cuba is better situated to make this transition than was the Ukraine. This has much to do with neighborhood.

Outside influences come to Cuba mostly from the Western world. Castro has been in power for a long time, but it is unlikely that he has erased all the earlier cultural conditioning. The countries in the former Soviet Bloc that fared best, the Czech Republic and the Baltic states, for example, had comparable Western influences before Stalin. The states that made up the former Soviet Union had fewer Western influences and their conditioning from the harsh Soviet system penetrated more deeply in their thinking — into their souls. It will take repression to hold back Cuban initiative once Castro leaves the scene.

The other reason for my guarded optimism is that if Cubans can avoid internal conflict after Castro departs, much investment there is likely to come from the United States. The Ukraine did not have as prosperous an exile community right next door to help in the transition. Instead, it had the more or less bankrupt Russia as a neighbor.

The central issue of the current debate on U.S. policy toward Cuba is whether the movement toward a peaceful post-Castro structure is better facilitated by beginning a modest transition now or by retaining a thoroughly hard-line policy until Castro dies. I will not tackle this question head on. One reason for this is that I am less informed than all of you about how the Cubans in the streets of Havana and other cities think. Yet, I believe it is fair to say that one reason for the change in U.S. congressional sentiment is the conviction that increased economic engagement now is more likely to deter later strife in Cuba than waiting until Castro dies before engaging.

This is a particularly strong motivation of those who favor eased regulations to allow U.S. citizens to travel to Cuba. Cuba's tourism earnings are likely to grow in the future in light of the U.S. action. If Cuba erupts in internal conflict after Castro's death, tourism will surely decline to the detriment of many Cubans. Is this a good argument, that vested interests in growing tourism earnings will dampen the ardor for internal conflict once Castro dies? What I can say in answering this question is that it is an important part of the case that is made by those who favor beginning the U.S. economic policy transition now — to temper the temptation for violence after Castro departs the scene.

Jorge Pérez-López presented an informative paper two years ago on Cuba's external sector in the 1990s. I benefited considerably in understanding Cuba's trade picture from reading this publication. Cuba, based on data from the U.S. Directorate of Intelligence, is not much of a trading nation. Its total trade in 1998 — for the whole year — was roughly $5 billion. This is less than five days of current two-way U.S. trade with Canada, and about 10 days of current U.S. trade with Mexico. Cuba had a merchandise trade deficit in 1998 of more than $1.5 billion.

These data are not representative of what Cuban trade could be under different circumstances. If Cuba were prepared to join the global structure after Castro's death, some of the following actions would be necessary:

A rapprochement would be needed with the United States, the natural market for Cuba, as it is for Canada, Mexico, and just about all the other countries in the Caribbean Basin.

Such a rapprochement would also stimulate U.S. investment in Cuba for exports of manufactures, such as biotech products, fruits and vegetables, and services. It is unlikely that sugar, still Cuba's most important export by value, will ever regain its former position in the U.S. market. It is unlikely that Cuba, if it were incorporated into the global economy, would want sugar to dominate its exports.

Cuba's exports to countries in the Western Hemisphere, other than Canada, are low. There are limits to the potential of hemispheric markets for Cuba — other than to Canada and the United States — but Cuba has not even begun to approach these limits. A globalized Cuba would surely want to participate in regional and subregional economic integration arrangements.

Cuba's biggest market is still Russia — for sugar. Canada takes mining products, as does the Netherlands (nickel) for re-export to other destinations. These are attractive markets for Cuba based on its current trading structure, but they would be dwarfed quickly if Cuba were able to enter the U.S. market. This would particularly be the case if free trade in the Americas were achieved, and if Cuba were part of this process.

The countries that have made most foreign direct investment in Cuba (as of May 1998, based on Pérez-López) are Canada, Mexico, Italy, Spain, and other European countries. The total as of that date was less than $2 billion. Investment from the United States could quickly overtake other sources, assuming rapprochement and the establishment of a system in Cuba friendly to foreign investment.

CONCLUDING REMARKS

Cuba attracts much attention in the world, largely because of U.S. policy and the irresistible attraction this provides for some countries to make a political statement of a foreign policy independent of U.S. hegemony. This is particularly the case for Canada and Mexico. As beneficial as actions of these and other countries have been for propping up the Cuban economy following the alteration of the relationship with the former Soviet Union, they cannot provide the basis for meaningful economic development in

Cuba. Given its small population, Cuba cannot prosper without more intensive trade. And the most promising countries for thriving Cuban trade in goods and services are in its own neighborhood — especially the United States.

Cuba is almost surely not equipped to move immediately from its largely controlled economy to competing in the global market. Cubans do not have mastery of most modern technology and the country's communications network will need updating. Current producers under the closed system will want protection against more competitive imports, at least for a time. There is no safety net for those Cubans who will be made redundant by moving to a market structure and something will have to be devised.

Despite these problems, there undoubtedly will be many Cubans — perhaps a majority, at least among those who have had experience with the outside world — who will see the need for change in order to bring Cuba into the mainstream of world economic activity. Global engagement offers a potentially bright economic future for Cubans to replace the constrained economy that has prevailed under Castro. The conflict will be between Cubans who think this way — who think the way most Czechs, Poles, Hungarians thought once freed of the Soviet yoke — and those who will want to retain the political-economic dominance of the state as it existed under Castro. My view is that Cuba, if it is to prosper in the post-Castro period, has to join the modern trading world. I don't know how many Cubans share this judgment. That is a key question whose answer we may discover in the not too distant future.

EDUCATION'S CONTRIBUTION TO ECONOMIC GROWTH IN CUBA

Manuel E. Madrid-Aris[1]

The main problem faced by government is allocating scarce resources across competing activities and sectors. The choice between alternative investments, such as education versus physical infrastructure, depends on society's objectives, which are represented by governmental decisions, and on the comparison of costs and future benefits of an investment. Since economists treat education as an investment, it is therefore important to estimate its benefits in the form of contribution to economic growth and/or its rate of return.[2]

Education represents both consumption and investment. Education is valued for its immediate as well as for its future benefits. Since the distribution of educational investment affects future income distribution, equity plays an important role in educational investment decisions. Different societies give different weight to the objectives of efficiency and equity in analyzing educational investment. In general, centrally planned economies placed a higher weight on equity grounds in defining their educational policy investment than capitalist economies.

This paper follows up and complements my previous publications related to sources of economic growth in Cuba (Madrid-Aris, 1997, 1998) in the sense that the growth accounting or sources of growth analysis

is extended by creating a labor quality index to determine the contribution of education to economic growth. This paper has two goals. The first one is to provide a very brief descriptive analysis of the historical pattern of factor accumulation (physical investment and human capital creation), social investment, and human capital creation in Cuba. The second is to determine education's contribution to economic growth.

The paper is organized as follows. The first section provides a brief review of the historical patterns of Cuban growth, factor accumulation, and human capital for the period 1962-1988. The second section contains a brief review of different methodologies normally used to estimate education's contribution to economic growth. The next section contains the estimation of education's contribution to economic growth using Denison-type growth accounting methodology. The final section contains the conclusions.

CUBAN FACTOR ACCUMULATION AND LABOR FORCE STRUCTURE
Cuban Growth and Investment Indicators
Table 1 presents a summary of Cuba's main macroeconomic indicators and of Soviet assistance received by Cuba during the period 1960-1988.

1. I would like to express my deepest appreciation to Rodrigo García for his helpful research assistance. The views expressed, opinions and conclusions reached in this paper are those of the author, and do not necessarily reflect those of the institutions with which the author is affiliated.

2. For an excellent review of international rates of return to education, see Psacharopoulus (1972, 1985, 1994).

Table 1. Macroeconomic Indicators

Period	Economic growth (%)	Income per capita growth	Investment as share of GMP	Total Soviet assistance as share of GMP[a]	Exports as share of GMP	Imports as share of GMP
1960-1964	1.9	-0.2	0.14	0.08	0.15	0.19
1965-1969	3.6	1.7	0.19	0.07	0.14	0.21
1970-1974	10.0	8.2	0.17	0.07	0.18	0.23
1975-1979	3.4	2.2	0.28	0.18	0.34	0.40
1980-1984	5.7	5.1	0.30	0.33	0.44	0.52
1985-1988	1.3	0.3	0.31	n.a.	0.40	0.60
Average	4.4	3.2	0.23	0.15	0.28	0.36

Note: Economic growth has been estimated with Gross Material Product (GMP) since statistics of Gross Social Product (GSP) are not as accurate as GMP (See Mesa-Lago and Pérez-López, *World Bank Staff Working Paper Number 770*, 1985).

Source: Rodríguez (1990), Brundenius (1984), Mesa-Lago and Pérez-López (1985), CIA-Directorate of Intelligence (1984, 1989), Comité Estatal de Estadísticas (CEE)-*Anuario Estadístico de Cuba*, several years, and author's estimates.

a.   Total Soviet Assistance includes Soviet trade subsidies (sugar, petroleum and nickel) plus development aid (for further details, see, Central Intelligence Agency (CIA), Directorate of Intelligence, 1984, p. 40 and 1989, p. 39).

Cuba's gross material product (GMP)[3] grew at an average annual rate of 4.4% and per capita income increased at an average rate of 3.2% during this period. Cuba greatly increased the rate of investment, which went from 15% of GMP in 1960 to 30% in 1988. Data from Table 1 shows that between 1960 and 1964, there was no increase in income per capita. Meanwhile, during the period 1965-1988 income per capita increased at a considerable rate. Table 1 also shows that Soviet assistance increased considerably over this time. During the period 1960-64, Soviet assistance was on average only 7% of GMP, but it increased to a level of 33% of GMP for the period 1980-1984. The amount of Soviet assistance was larger than the investments realized by the Cuban government for the period 1980-1984. In other words, during this period, it could be assumed that most of the investments realized by the Cuban government were realized by using capital received from Soviet assistance.[4] Therefore, it could be inferred that the Cuban economy was losing its saving capacity.

Note that the highest rate of economic growth (10%) was achieved in the period 1970-1974. Ironically,

during this period the Cuban investment rate was low (17%) and even decreased from 19% to 17%. Additionally, the lowest rate of economic growth (1.3%) was during the period 1985-1988, when the highest rate of investment (31%) was observed. Looking at these figures, it seems that the Cuban economy was not able to absorb in an efficient way such a high level of investment.[5] If the rate of investment exceeds the country's technical, human and institutional capacity to allocate it in an efficient way, most of the investment goes to poorly managed projects. Hence, investment is not very productive and depreciates. In sum, it can be concluded that during the 1980s, investment was not allocated as efficiently as during the 1970s.

National Income and Social Investment

Table 2 shows that social investment increased considerably over the period 1960-1987. In 1960, investment in education was only 3.2% of total national income and increased to a level of 13.1% in 1987. Investment in health represented only 2.0% of national income in 1960 and it increased to a level of 6.6% of national income by 1987.

3. The Cuban accounting system is different from the western concept of Gross National Product (GNP). Cuba uses the Soviet system of Global Social Product (GSP) and Gross Material Product (GMP), which is also called "gross product." For further explanation of the Cuban national income accounting system, see Brundenius (1984), pp. 19-40, Mesa-Lago and Pérez-López (1985).

4. Note that in a centrally planned economy like Cuba, investment is mainly realized by the government since there are no opportunities for private enterprises or for private investment. Therefore, private income is spent mostly in consumption.

5. Miguel Figueras, the former Director of Planning of the Cuban Ministry of Industry, supports this view. For further details, see Figueras (1994).

Table 2. National Income and Social Investment (Education and Health)

Year	In Millions of Current Pesos (C$)			In Percentage (%)		
	Value of national income	Investment in education	Investment in health	Investment in education as % of national income	Investment in education as % of GMP[a]	Investment in health as % of national income
1960	2,625.5	83.7	51.3	3.2	3.3	2.0
1965	3,888.2	260.4	148.9	6.7	7.0	3.8
1970	3,517.6	351.1	216.4	10.0	10.4	6.2
1975	8,112.6	808.5	304.2	10.0	10.4	3.8
1980	9,853.1	1,340.8	440.2	13.6	14.1	4.5
1987	12,202.2	1,600.0	810.2	13.1	13.6	6.6

Source: Rodriguez (1990), pp. 218 and 293.

a.   Figures estimated by the author considering an aggregated depreciation rate of 4%.

Table 3. Student Enrollment by Level of Education (per 1,000 habitants)

Year	Primary education	Secondary education	Higher education	Other education	Total enrollment
1958	104.9	11.8	3.8	0	120.5
1970	193.4	24.9	4.1	32.4	254.8
1975	205.2	57.1	9.0	31.3	302.6
1980	164.2	110.0	15.7	6.8	296.7
1985	116.8	110.0	23.2	2.0	252.0

Note: For Cuba, secondary education includes technical schools. Other types of education include the worker farm educational program developed after the revolution.

Source: Madrid-Aris (1998).

Labor Force, and Human Capital[6]

Table 3 contains data on enrollment per 1,000 habitants by educational levels in Cuba between 1958 and 1985.

Cuba considerably increased the rate of enrollment during the period 1959-1988. The data show that human capital accumulation was quite rapid during the last 35 years. Without looking at economic variables, such as the amount invested in education and the return on human capital creation, it could be concluded that the Cuban government was successful in achieving a very high rate of enrollment during this period.

As Table 4 shows, the share of those with only primary education in Cuba was large initially, but it decreased considerably between 1960 and 1986. In addition, there was a uniform increase in university-educated workers, which will have an important ef-

fect on the calculation of the growth of the labor quality component.

Summary of Factors' Contribution to Economic Growth

Table 5 shows the factors' contribution to Cuban economic growth for the period 1963-1998, estimated without considering quality adjustment factor for the labor force.

Previous tables show that for the agricultural sector, the average total factor productivity (TFP) growth is negative (-1.5%), and the contribution of TFP to output is negative (-56%) during the period of 1963-1988. In the industrial sector, at least the average TFP growth is positive, but it was moderate (0.6%), and its contribution to economic growth was very low (12%). In sum, the Cuban government's interventionist policy during 1975-1988 was accompanied by very low TFP performance. Previous results

---

6. Human capital investment is a concept widely used by economists, meaning the process of improving the quality of the labor force. Thus, human capital is referred to as the level of education of the labor force. This improvement of the labor force quality is basically achieved by education and training (Becker, 1963).

Table 4. Labor Force Composition by Educational Level in Selected Years as Percentage of Total Labor Force (%)

Country	Year	Illiteracy	Primary education	Secondary education	University education	Unspecified
Colombia	1950	37.7	54.8	5.4	1.1	1.0
	1960	27.1	63.7	6.1	.8	2.3
	1970	4.5	56.6	30.6	8.6	0.0
Chile	1950	n.a	77.4	20.2	2.3	.1
	1960	n.a	75.1	22.3	2.6	0.0
	1970	8.3	52.2	31.5	3.3	4.7
Brazil	1950	48.3	44.0	6.6	1.1	0.0
	1960	41.5	50.5	6.8	1.2	0.0
	1970	28.3	58.1	11.7	1.9	0.0
Cuba	1960		63.7[a]	34.3	2.1	0.0
	1970		56.3[a]	40.7	3.0	0.0
	1980		37.6[a]	57.5	4.9	0.0
	1982		36.4[a]	57.7	5.9	0.0
	1986		24.3[a]	67.7	8.0	0.0
	1996		17.3[a]	70.0	12.7	0.0

Source: Cuban figures estimated by the author. Figures from other Latin American countries, from Elias (1992), p. 92.

a.   This figure includes illiteracy and primary education.

Table 5. Factors' Contribution to Cuban Aggregated and Sectoral Economic Growth (%)

	Contribution of Factors (as % of economic growth)								
	All Productive Sectors			Agriculture			Industry		
Period	Labor	Capital	TFP	Labor	Capital	TFP	Labor	Capital	TFP
1963-1970	25	53	22 (1.0)	30	120	-50 (-1.9)	18	56	26 (1.4)
1971-1980	17	70	13 (0.8)	12	132	-44 (-1.2)	19	67	14 (0.7)
1981-1988	38	99	-37 (-1.2)	27	158	-85 (-1.5)	36	73	-9 (-0.4)
AVERAGE	26	70	4 (0.2)	23	133	-56 (-1.5)	23	65	12 (0.6)

Note: Value of total factor productivity (TFP) growth is in parenthesis.

Source: Madrid-Aris (2000).

show that the industrial sector, which had a lower rate of investment, had the higher TFP growth and contribution to economic growth. TFP analysis results show that Cuba's growth during 1963-1988 was almost entirely the result of capital accumulation rather than productivity gains. Decreasing TFP growth through the 1970s and 1980s, with increasing amount of subsidies received from Soviet Union during the same period, seem to suggest that Soviet dependency created inefficiency in Cuba.

This seems ironic, because Cuba's centrally planned development strategy was oriented toward getting resources from agriculture to develop the industrial sector. But, in reality, agriculture was a big consumer of resources, especially capital, without any positive result. Results show that governmental creation of institutional mechanisms to deal with inefficiencies

may not always be an efficient way to force technological change. Cuba's decreasing TFP growth under factor accumulation is a confirmation of the low level of technical and allocative efficiency of a centrally planned system. Results from this research and other analyses of centrally planned economies (Nishimizu and Robinson, 1984) confirm that the lack of allocative and technical efficiency is a common pattern of centrally planned economies as a result of lack of competition and incentives.

MEASURING EDUCATION'S CONTRIBUTION TO ECONOMIC GROWTH

The concept of investment in human capital and its relationship with productivity and economic growth dates back to the time of Adam Smith and the early classical economists. The empirical literature on education's contribution to economic growth began in

1960. This was mainly triggered by the need for understanding the role of education in economic growth. The most often cited works in this field are Schultz (1961), Denison (1962, 1967), Psacharopoulos (1972) and Nadiri (1972). By the 1980s, there was renewed interest in this field. Thus, in this period the most influential works are those developed by Hicks (1980), Wheeler (1980), and Psacharopoulus (1984).

With respect to methodologies to estimate education's contribution to economic growth, some researchers have used growth accounting or productivity indexes (Denison, 1967; Selowsky, 1969), production functions (Grichiles, 1970), and other growth equations (Harberger and Selowsky, 1966). Denison and Schultz were the pioneers in measuring the contribution of education to economic growth. While different methodologies have been used to estimate education's contribution to economic growth, the two most commonly used[7] are: (1) the labor quality adjustment growth accounting, or Denison-type of growth accounting (Denison, 1967); and (2) the rate of return to human capital (Schultz-type of growth accounting). With respect to the specification of the education variables, the number of years of schooling of the labor force in relation to the wage differentials of the labor force by different levels of education is frequently used (Denison), or the amount of capital invested in education in conjunction with the rate of return on that capital (Schultz).

The starting point of the Denison estimation is the Solow (1957) methodology for growth accounting, based on an aggregate production function implicitly considering neutral technical progress. Thus:

$$Y_t = A(t)f(K_t, L_t) \qquad (1)$$

The Denison-type of growth accounting methodology normally applied to estimate labor's contribution to economic growth is based on analyzing the effect of quality of the labor force due to education. In other words, in Denison's methodology not only gross capital and labor are considered as in Solow's methodology, but factors (labor and capital) are adjusted by quality. Normally, different factors for estimating the quality of labor can be considered, such as education, age and gender of labor force, hours of work, and unemployment. Thus, the contribution is based on how much the quality of the labor force contributes to the "residual" or to the total factor productivity growth. The Denison-type of growth accounting can also distinguish between different kind of educated labor within the production function. Normally, the disaggregation is done into different categories — no education, primary, secondary or higher education.[8]

Denison used the wage differentials of labor with different schooling levels as weights in order to measure the quality of labor. Thus, the Denison type of growth accounting production function adjusted for quality of labor takes the form:

$$Y_t = f(K_t, L_t, \sum_s L_s * (W_s - W_{s-1})) \qquad (2)$$

In equation (2), the index s represent the different schooling levels of the labor force and W represents the average wage of the educational category. Denison (1967) estimated that 23% of the rate of growth of output in the United States between 1930 and 1960 was due to increases in education of labor force. Denison also estimated that the corresponding share 1950-1962 was 15%.

It is important to note that Denison-type growth accounting, as commonly applied without considering the maintenance component[9] of a growing labor force, could result in an underestimation of the contribution of education to economic growth (Selowsky, 1969). Selowsky (1969), using a Denison type of growth accounting considering the mainte-

---

7. For a more detailed review of these two methodologies, see Psacharopoulos (1973), pp. 111-118.

8. For an empirical application to Latin American countries, see Elias (1992), pp. 71-99.

9. Maintenance component is the effort entailed in maintaining constant the relative distribution of the labor force by years of schooling. For further details, see Selowsky (1969).

nance component, determined that education's contribution to economic growth in the United States for the period 1940-1965 was 21%, in Mexico approximately 11% and in Chile approximately 24%.

Schultz introduced the concept of rental value of education in growth accounting. In this methodology, investment in education is introduced into the traditional methodology by distinguishing two kind of capital: human capital and physical capital. Another way is by distinguishing several non-homogenous inputs based on educational levels.[10] Thus, the Schultz type of production function is:

$$Y_t = f(K_t, L_t, r*K_{edu})$$ (3)

Where K_{edu} is the educational capital stock in the economy and r is the rate of return on the educational capital. Thus, the product $r*K_{edu}$, is the measure of the educational factor of production that contributes to output. Thus, the Schultz-type calculation of the contribution of education to economic growth is made by estimating the factor rentals (rate of return to human capital times educational investment). The difficulty of this approach is that it requires the estimation of the stock of educational capital in the economy and the rate of return on that capital. Obviously, the estimation of these two variables is a very large task. In most cases it is impossible to estimate them as result of the lack of data, especially for less developed countries (LDCs).

It is known that growth accounting and residuals are not a good tool for explaining the process of economic growth as result of the exogenity of technical progress. The important issue is to determine what are the variables that could explain the residuals. Although the residuals approach lost ground, especially with the development of the new growth theory, economists have not yet agreed on what is the proper way to measure the contribution of education to economic growth.

ESTIMATING EDUCATION'S CONTRIBUTION TO ECONOMIC GROWTH FOR THE CUBAN ECONOMY

For the purpose of estimating education's contribution to economic growth in Cuba, the traditional Denison-type method of calculation will be applied.

Denison Methodology

According to the Denison-type of growth-accounting methodology, the rate of change of the quality component of the labor force as result of education captures the effect of education's` contribution to economic growth. According to this methodology, the rate of change of the quality component is equal to the weighted average of the changes in the share of each kind of labor with respect to the average wage for the labor force as a whole. The weights are represented by the wages structure for different educational levels of labor with respect to the average wage of the total labor force.[11] Thus, the basic aggregate production function with quality adjustment factor can be expressed as follows:

$$Y_t = f(K_t, L_t, Q_t)$$ (4)

where Qt is the quality of labor force. The growth accounting equation (discrete approximation) can be expressed as follows:

$$\frac{\Delta Y}{Y} = \alpha_k * \frac{\Delta K}{K} + \alpha_l * \frac{\Delta L}{L} + \alpha_l * \frac{\Delta Q}{Q} + TFP$$ (5)

where the relative change in an index of the quality of the labor force due to education is defined as follows:

$$\frac{AQ}{Q} = \sum_i \frac{w_i}{W} * \frac{L_i}{L}$$ (6)

In equation (6), the index i represents the different years of schooling of the labor force or educational level. In our specific case, the index i represents the educational level attained by the labor force.

---

10. For further details, see Schultz (1963), Psacharopoulus and Hinchliffe (1973, pp. 20-34)

11. If there is no change in the level of education of the labor force, the rate of change of the quality of the labor force will be zero. If there are changes in favor of the groups with higher relative wages (university graduates), the quality of the labor will increase.

Table 6.   Relative Wages by Level of Education (*wi/W*)

| Country | Year | Relative Wages by Educational Level Attained | | |
		Primary Education	Secondary Education	University Education
Colombia	1965	0.916	1.394	1.455
	1967	0.560	1.120	n.a
Chile	1960	0.598	1.862	4.717
	1965	0.708	1.376	5.233
Brazil	1960	1.088	2.020	3.960
	1969	0.814	1.340	3.545
Cuba[a]	1970-1980	0.80	1.25	1.70

Source: Cuban figures estimated by the author; other Latin Countries from Elias (1992, p. 92).

a.   Estimated based on employment categories (workers, administrative, manager, *dirigentes*).

For the purpose of estimating the index of the quality of labor force, each component of labor corresponds to a well-defined educational category (primary, secondary and university) as shown in Table 4. In other words, it is assumed that education is one of the most important factors determining labor income. The educational component could be defined in a way that covers formal schooling and informal education (e.g., on the job training). However, only formal education is considered in our analysis.

Results

It can be argued that growth accounting implicitly assumes perfect competition of labor markets, i.e., that the marginal product of labor equals wages. If labor markets are not competitive, as is the case in Cuba,[12] then relative wages across different levels of education are not necessarily a good measure of the relative productivity at different level of education of workers, unless the government sets the wages according to some productivity rule. If the wages are not a reliable measure of productivity, it may be preferable to measure the effect of education on physical measure of output, rather than using wage differentials. Another alternative is to use shadow wage rates, instead of actual wage rates, to estimate the labor quality index for the growth accounting estimation. In the analysis presented here, a sensitivity analysis is conducted using shadow wage rates from Brazil. Table 6 shows the relative wages by level of education in Cuba and other Latin American countries.

Computing the labor quality component requires the data on labor force composition presented in Table 4 as well as on relative wages by level of education (Table 6). The quality of the labor force is due to education and is obtained by multiplying the rate of change of different educational categories or change in the labor composition by the relative wage of that category. Normally, earnings differentials have been adjusted by a common factor that ranges from 0.4 to 0.6. This adjustment tries to reflect that only a small part of the higher income should be attributed to schooling, the rest being due to others socioeconomic factors. In our case, no adjustment factor has been considered.

In many cases, when this methodology is applied to LDCs, there is only one year of wage earning differentials or relative wages by categories (data presented in Table 6). One way to solve this problem is simply to use these one-year figures for all other years. This has been the approach used in all the country studies in which such information on relative wages is missing (Denison, 1967; Selowsky, 1969; Elias, 1992). Thus, using the data from Table 4 and Table 6, three different indexes for rate of change in quality of the labor force have been estimated (Table 7).

As shown in Table 7, labor quality indexes using shadow wage differential from Colombia and Brazil have been estimated for comparative purposes. Using shadow wages from Colombia, the labor quality index estimated is lower than the one using the Cuban wages. Applying the factor estimated with the Co-

---

12. In Cuba wages are set by central planners instead of define by labor market competitive forces.

Table 7. Annual Growth Rate of the Labor Quality Index due to Education (ΔQ/Q)

Period	Results based on Cuban relative wages (%)	Results based on relative wages from Colombia (%)	Results based on relative wages from Brazil (%)
1963-1970	0.37	0.35	0.58
1971-1980	1.16	1.13	1.75
1981-1988	0.83	0.71	1.63
1963-1988	0.75	0.70	1.26

Source: Based on data from Tables 5 and 6.

Table 8. Education's Contribution to Economic Growth (as % of GMP)

	All productive sectors	Agricultural sector	Industrial sector
1963-1970	3.8 (5.9)	4.4 (6.8)	2.8 (4.4)
1971-1980	8.6 (12.5)	16.9 (23.6)	8.6 (12.5)
1981-1988	10.7 (19.1)	18.9 (31.3)	8.0 (13.1)
AVERAGE (63-88)	7.3 (11.6)	11.4 (17.7)	5.7 (9.7)

Note: Figures in parenthesis are the contribution of education to growth based on quality index with Brazilian shadow wage differentials.

lombian wages to Cuba, the contribution of education to economic growth will be lower than using the index based on Cuban wages. Hence, the contribution of education to growth will be estimated with the Cuban index and the index estimated using shadow wages from Brazil. The annual growth rate of the labor quality index due to education estimated increases over time until 1980 as a result of changes favoring the groups with higher relative wages (university graduates). The rate of growth of the Cuban quality index increases from 0.37% for 1963-1970 to 1.16% for 1970-1980, then it decreases to 0.83% for the period 1980-1988.

Table 8 shows the contribution of education to economic growth estimated for the all productive sectors as well as for the agricultural and industrial sectors. Estimated figures presented in Table 8 assume that the quality of labor has increased at the sectoral level at the same rate as for the overall economy.

The percentage contribution varies in part because of the different growth rates of output in the different periods for the different sectors (see Table 1). However, the main characteristic is the rising trend of this contribution. The important feature of these increases with regard to the education's contribution to economic growth over the years is the increased index of the quality of the labor force (ΔQ/Q) complemented with the decreasing TFP growth. The increase in the rate of growth of the quality factor is mainly due to the rate of acceleration of the number of workers

with a high level of education as a percentage of the total labor force (see Table 4). Obviously, this acceleration can not be expected in the future since most of the illiteracy has been eliminated, as Cuba has already achieved a very high rate of primary and secondary education.

CONCLUSIONS

Our research shows that education's contribution to Cuban economic growth overall has increased over the years from 1963 to 1988. The increases in education's contribution to economic growth over the years resulted from the increased index of the quality of the labor force (ΔQ/Q) due to a more educated labor force and the decrease of TFP growth.

The highest contribution of education to economic growth can be found in the agricultural sector (11.4%). This high contribution is due to the low overall productivity of this sector (see Table 5). The lowest contribution of education to economic growth is in industrial sector (5.7%), since this sector has grown based on more productivity gains than on labor gains. In other words, due to the assumption of neutrality of technical progress (exogenity) common in the growth accounting production function, the higher the technological change, the lower the expected contribution of education to economic growth.

In general, education's contribution to economic growth in Cuba can be considered low compared with other studies applied to less developed countries (Selowsky, 1969). This low level of contribution can be explained based on factor contributions to growth (Table 5), which show that Cuba's growth during 1963-1988 was almost entirely the result of capital accumulation — which contributed 70% to economic growth — rather than productivity and labor gains.

The low contribution of education to Cuban economic growth estimated from the simple empirical work conducted for this paper, complemented with the investment pattern on education (see Table 2), seem to suggest that the educational resource allocation policies adopted by Cuba's centrally planned system seemed to have been aimed more at equity goals rather than efficiency goals.

REFERENCES

Barro, Robert. "Economic Growth in a Cross Section of Countries," *Quarterly Journal of Economics,* pp. 407-444, 1991.

Barro, R., and Xavier Sala-i-Martin. *Economic Growth.* New York: McGraw Hill Press, 1995.

Becker, Gary. *Human Capital: A Theoretical and Empirical Analysis with Special Reference to Education.* Chicago: University of Chicago Press, 1963.

Central Intelligence Agency (CIA), Directorate of Intelligence. *The Cuban Economy: A Statistical Review.* Washington, 1984, 1989.

Comité Estatal de Estadísticas (CEE). *Anuario Estadístico de Cuba,* several years

Denison, E. "United States Economic Growth," *Journal of Business,* 35, 357-394, 1962.

Denison, E. *Why Growth Rates Differ: Post-War Experience in Nine Countries.* Washington: Brookings Institution Press, 1967.

Denison, E. *Trends in American Economic Growth, 1929-1982.* Washington, Brookings Institution Press, 1985.

Elias, Victor. *Sources of Growth: A Study of Seven Latin American Economies.* San Francisco: ICS Press, 1992.

Figueras, Miguel. *Aspectos Estructurales de la Economía Cubana.* La Habana: Editorial de Ciencias Sociales, 1994.

Harberger, Arnold. "A Vision of the Growth Process," *American Economic Review,* Vol. 88, No. 1, pp. 1-31, March 1998.

Hicks, N. "Economic Growth and Human Resources," *World Bank Staff Working Paper,* No 408, Washington, 1982.

Jiménez, Georgina. *Hablemos de Educación: Recopilación de Artículos, Comentarios y Reportajes sobre Educación.* La Habana: Editorial Pueblo y Educación, 1985.

Jorgenson, Dale, Frank M. Gollop, and Barbara M. Fraumeni. *Productivity and U.S. Economic Growth.* Cambridge: Harvard University Press, 1987.

Kim, J.I., and Lawrence Lau. "Economic Growth of the East Asian Newly Industrializing Countries," *Journal of the Japanese and International Economics,* 235-271, 1994.

Krugman, Paul. "The Myth of Asia's Miracle," *Foreign Affairs,* Nov/Dec, pp. 62-78, 1994.

Madrid-Aris, Manuel. "Growth and Technological Change in Cuba," in *Cuba in Transition—Volume 7.* Washington: Association for the Study of the Cuban Economy, 1997.

Madrid-Aris, Manuel. "Investment, Human Capital, and Technological Change: Evidence from Cuba and its Implications for Growth Models," in *Cuba in Transition—Volume 8.* Washington:

Association for the Study of the Cuban Economy, pp. 465-481, 1998.

Madrid-Aris, Manuel. "The Tyranny of Numbers, Linear Models or Central Planning: Confronting Cuban and Singaporean Factor Accumulation and Technological Change," working paper, 2000.

Mesa-Lago, Carmelo. *The Economy of Socialist Cuba: A Two Decade Appraisal.* Albuquerque: University of New Mexico Press, 1981.

Mesa-Lago, Carmelo and Jorge Pérez-López, "A Study of Cuba's Material Product System, its Conversion to the System of National Accounts, and Estimation of GDP per Capita and Growth Rates," *World Bank Staff Working Papers*, Number 770, Washington, 1985.

Mincer, Jacob. *Schooling, Experience and Earnings.* New York: Columbia University Press, 1974.

Pérez-López, Jorge. *Measuring Cuban Economic Performance.* Austin: University of Texas Press, 1987.

Poznanski, K. "The Environment for Technological Change in Centrally Planned Economies," *World Bank Staff Working Papers,* No. 718, Washington, 1985.

Psacharopoulos, George. "Measuring the Marginal Contribution of Education to Economic Growth," *Economic Development and Cultural Change*, Vol. 20, No. 4, pp. 641-658, July 1972.

Psacharopoulos, George. *Economics of Education: Research and Studies.* New York: Pergamon Press, 1987.

Psacharopoulos, George. *Returns on Education.* San Francisco: Jossy Bass-Elsevier, 1973.

Psacharopoulos, George. "Returns to Investment in Education: A Global Update," *World Development,* 22(9):1325-134, 1994.

Psacharopoulos, George and Maureen Woodhall. *Education for Developmet: An Analysis of Investment Choices.* New York: Oxford University Press, 1985.

Rodríguez, José Luis. *Estrategia del Desarrollo Económico de Cuba.* La Habana: Editorial de Ciencias Sociales, 1990.

Romer, Paul. "Endogenous Technical Change," *Journal of Political Economy,* 98, S71-S102, 1990.

Schultz, T. W. "Investing in Human Capital," *American Economic Review*, March 1961.

Schultz, T. W. *The Economic Value of Education.* New York: Columbia University Press, 1963.

Schultz, T. Paul. "Education Investment and Return." In *Handbook of Development Economics*, eds. H. Chenery and T.N. Srinivasan, eds, Chapter 13. New York: North Holland, 1988.

Solow, Robert. "A Contribution to the Theory of Economic Growth," *Quarterly Journal of Economics*, 70, 65-94, 1956.

Solow, Robert. "Technical Change and the Aggregate Production Function," *Review of Economic and Statistics*, 39, 312-320, 1957.

Solow, Robert. "Investment and Technical Progress." In *Mathematical Methods in the Social Sciences.* Edited by Kenneth J. Arrow, Samuel Karbin and Patrick Suppes. Stanford University Press, 1959.

Wheeler, D. "Human Resource Development and Economic Growth in LDC's: A Simulation Model," *World Bank Staff Working Paper*, No 407, Washington, 1980.

World Bank. *World Development Report.* New York: Oxford University Press, 1990

Zimbalist, Andrew. "Cuban Industrial Growth, 1965-1984," *World Development*, Vol. 15, No 1, 83-93, 1987.

A COMPARISON OF CUBA'S TOURISM INDUSTY WITH THE DOMINICAN REPUBLIC AND CANCÚN, 1988-1999

Nicolas Crespo and Charles Suddaby

In order to evaluate the potential for increased tourism to Cuba, it is important to consider its performance in the context of other competitive destinations of a similar nature. In this paper, we compare the past and present performance of Cuba to both the Dominican Republic and to Cancún. Puerto Rico, with its Spanish heritage, has been omitted from this comparison because of its direct relationship with the United States and its inherent ability to attract large numbers of U.S. visitors.

Cuba is the largest island in the region, comprising almost 111,000 sq km in a land mass that stretches 1,250 km from end to end. There is a population base of approximately 11 million people, of which about 75% resides in urban areas including Havana (over 2 million people), Santiago de Cuba (390,000 people) and Camagüey (280,000 people).

The Dominican Republic is located to the east of Haiti, which together comprise the island of Hispaniola. The country has an area of 48,000 sq km and a population of about 7.4 million people. While smaller than Cuba in both geographic size and population, the country's tourism industry exceeds that of Cuba in the number of arrivals and in room supply, largely the result of the longer term that tourism has been a key economic generator as well as the existence of the U.S. market as a major demand generator.

Cancún, a planned resort area within Quintana Roo, Mexico, and not a distinct country or island, is not compared either in size or population base.

TOURISM ARRIVALS

The graph below illustrates the number of tourist arrivals in Cuba, the Dominican Republic and Cancún for the period 1988 to 1999. As shown in the graph, tourism arrivals in each of the three destination areas is very significant, with the combined number of visitors representing a total of 2.3 million visitors in 1988, or 20% of the regional total. By 1999, the three destinations recorded 7.1 million visitors, or 36% of the total Caribbean visitation.

Cuba's re-entry into world tourism occurred in 1988, with 309,000 visitors being recorded. In 1999, it had grown to 1.6 million, representing a compound average annual increase of 16.1%. Cuba has also increased its share of the Caribbean market, from 2.7% in 1988 to about 8% in 1999. Cancún, which has been a popular destination for about 25 years, had 838,000 visitors in 1988, representing 7.3% of the Caribbean market. This volume had increased to 2.8 million in 1999, representing a compound growth rate of 11.6% annually and giving Cancún 14.3% of the regional market. The Dominican Republic, with 1.1 million visitors in 1988 and 2.6 million last year, recorded a growth rate of 8.2% annually over this same period. The Dominican Republic increased its share of the Caribbean tourism market from 9.6% in 1988 to 13% in 1999.

The dramatic rise in popularity of these destinations is primarily attributable to their targeting of, and ability to attract, mass tourism. The development of numerous large hotels in a fairly confined area in Cancún created a critical mass that quickly gained

Figure 1. Tourism Arrivals in Cuba, Cancún and Dominican Republic — 1988 to 1999

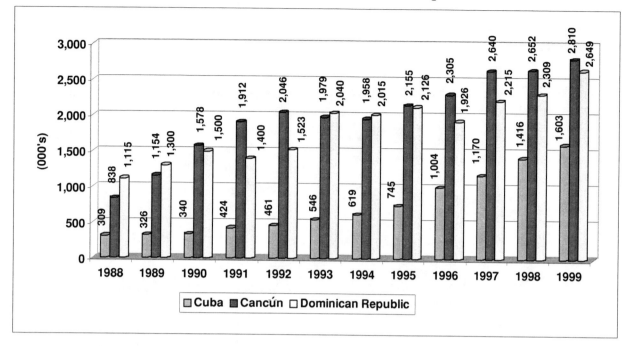

recognition in foreign markets. The rapid growth in tourism occurred in the late 1980s and early 1990s with the volume of arrivals jumping from 838,000 in 1988 to 1.6 million in 1990 and 1.9 million in 1991. Over the next few years, the rate of growth slowed, before surging ahead again in 1996 through 1999.

The Dominican Republic was the next entrant into the tourism markets, although its later entry was compensated for by rapid early growth in popularity. By 1988, the country was already receiving 1.1 million visitors, but then growth slowed over the next few years (volumes fluctuated from 1.5 million in 1990 to 1.4 million in 1991 and 1.5 million in 1992). In 1993, growth rates picked up again for two years, before stagnating at approximately 2.0 million visitors for the next four years. In 1997, 1998 and 1999, growth started to move forward again quite strongly, with 1999 being higher by almost 15% over the previous year.

Cuba was the latest of the three destinations to focus on tourism, rekindling its tourism industry in the late 1980s. In 1988, the first year that the country effectively reopened to international markets, there were 309,000 visitors. Growth rates averaged over 13% annually through 1995, but have since grown

stronger. Tourism volumes increased by 35% in 1996, 16% in 1997, 21% in 1998 and 13% in 1999.

HOTEL ROOMS
Cuba

Cuba's hotel supply, as applied to "international quality" hotels, grew from about 10,000 rooms in 1988 to 32,300 in 1999, representing an average annual increase of over 11%. Over the same period, arrivals in Cuba grew by 16%, raising the average market occupancy from about 55% in the initial years to just over 60% today.

Of the total supply, just over 10,000 hotel rooms are located in Havana, while about 11,000 are in Varadero. Other important nodes of hotel supply are the Jardines del Rey region (2,900 rooms), Santa Lucía, Guardalavaca, Cienfuegos, Trinidad, Santiago de Cuba and Cayo Largo.

Of Cuba's 189 hotels, the Ministry of Tourism classifies 50 properties as being 5-star hotels; 60 properties as 4-star; 66 properties as 3-star; and 13 other properties. The rating of hotels in Cuba is generally higher than recognized elsewhere in the world, and these categories should be reduced by one star to truly meet international standards. A further important aspect of Cuban tourism is its diversity and the relative importance that has been placed on promoting this diversity. In addition to the traditional "sun, sea and sand" market, Cuba has established other categories of tourism experience:

- Water-based experiences. Diving, boating and fishing are common, and they are also promoted in the applicable destinations.

- Cultural tourism. Encouraging visitors to travel throughout the country to observe cultural events and facilities including museums, art galleries, historical sites, music and dance (the ballet in Havana is widely considered to be of a quality only slightly less than the world-renowned Bolshoi in Russia).

- Hunting. Cuba actively promotes hunting in its forests and mountainous areas.

- Medical tourism. Cuba has established a reputation for certain medical and therapeutic treatments, at costs significantly lower than in North America, Europe and Eastern Europe. The country has a network of hospitals, clinics and spas targeted toward foreign visitors, with dedicated hotel facilities.

Dominican Republic

The Dominican Republic has by far the largest inventory of hotel rooms among the three destinations, with almost 50,000 of the total 106,487 rooms in the combined markets. The supply of rooms has increased at an average annual rate of almost 11% over the eleven-year period 1988-99, higher than the 8% growth in tourism arrivals. The room supply in the Dominican Republic is generally located within 5 recognized tourism zones: Punta Cana and Bavaro Beach; Santo Domingo; Boca Chica/Juan Dolio/La Romana; Puerto Plata; and Samaná.

- Punta Cana and Bavaro Beach are located on the northeast shore, in the eastern sector of the country. They boast 50 km of beaches and an ex-

tensive range of tourism infrastructure including an international airport which is 20 km from the main hotel supply. Punta Cana and Bavaro Beach have approximately 17,110 hotel rooms, including the 2,000-room Bavaro Beach Resort.

- Santo Domingo, the capital of the country and the largest and most important city, has 5,364 rooms, including Boca Chica and Juan Dolio. La Romana, located near the eastern end of the country but on the south shore, has another 1,444 rooms, including the well-known Casa de Campo resort.

- Puerto Plata, on the north shore, west of Punta Cana, has approximately 1,014 rooms.

- Samaná in the northeast area, has 1,761 rooms.

The Dominican Republic's tourism offering has many similarities to Cuba's, with a substantial land mass, wide variety of beach areas, colonial heritage and a fairly recent entry into the tourism markets. At the same time, much of the image of tourism in the Dominican Republic is of "all inclusive"[1] beach resorts with inexpensive package prices. While this image is substantially a reality, with an estimated 88% of the total hotel supply falling into the all inclusive category, the Dominican Republic has started to move beyond this stage with an increasing selection of high quality traditional and all inclusive resorts. Particular examples of the more upscale product include Casa de Campo (with rates from US$250 to US$300 per night European Plan) and a few smaller, boutique-type products.

Cancún

Cancún first entered the tourism markets in 1974 with just one hotel; it now has more than 24,000 rooms along a stretch of 14 miles of beach area. In 1988, Cancún had 11,891 hotel rooms, and there was a fairly rapid increase in supply over the next few years before the level of new construction activity

---

1. "All inclusive" is a modality of the hospitality industry where clients pre-pay a fixed amount for one or two weeks of accommodation including food, beverages, entertainment and gratuities and, frequently, air and ground transportation. Payment is generally made to a travel agent or "wholesaler" who then pays the hotel for its services. The traveler usually flies on a chartered aircraft rather than on a scheduled flight.

slowed in 1991. From 1991 to 1995, the number of rooms grew by only 920, or 5%. Supply growth increased again in the ensuing years, although the rate of growth has remained low. With 24,564 rooms today, Cancún has experienced an average annual increase in supply of just under 7%, while tourism arrivals over the same period grew by almost 12%.

A review of the hotel supply in Cancún indicates it is typically comprised of larger, relatively upscale products. The hotels are effectively located in three key areas — Cancún Island (the main concentration of hotels along the eastern shore of Cancún Island), Punta Cancún (the western shore of Cancún Island) and Cancún City.

- Cancún Island contains approximately 18,000 of the total rooms, in approximately 60 properties. The hotels typically range in size from 40 units to as many as just under 1,000 in the Oasis Cancún. The quality also ranges from economy, to 5-star, with hotels such as the Ritz Carlton and Coral Beach representing the upscale product.

- The Punta Cancún area, associated with the Convention Centre and located just east of the downtown area, has about 4,000 rooms within 20 hotels. Major properties in this area include the Hyatt Regency Cancún, Camino Real Cancún and Fiesta Americana Coral Beach. Many of the hotels in this area are larger, upscale products catering to the convention delegates and more discerning leisure travelers.

- The Cancún City area, with about 2,000 rooms, is mostly comprised of smaller, lower quality properties, although well-known brand names such as Holiday Inn and Novotel are present.

All-inclusive packages are an integral part of tourism to Cuba and the Dominican Republic, while relatively few of the hotels in Cancún offered this category of vacation until the last 10 years or so. Today, new construction of hotel properties with this mode of marketing is proceeding at a rapid pace. In addition, the large inventory of hotels, proximity to downtown Cancún, and large volumes of visitors has given rise to a well developed tourism infrastructure including plenty of freestanding restaurants, bars, nightclubs and retail stores.

HOTEL PERFORMANCE
Cuba
Cuba's 32,300 hotel rooms achieved an average market occupancy of 62.6% in 1999. A review of individual market segments shows Varadero with the highest average occupancy, about 74%, while Havana operated at an average of 62%. Other beach areas performed less well, with the Jardines del Rey region operating at 61% occupancy, Cayo Largo at 60%, and Santa María (located north of Camagüey) at 59%.

The average length of stay in Cuba is 7.8 days, down from just under 10 days in 1993. The reduced length of stay is attributable to the increased number of flights, particularly scheduled airlines, and the increased number of short-term visits to Havana. The average expenditure, per tourist, is $1,200, down from $1,300 in 1997 and $1,500 in 1995.

Dominican Republic
The Dominican Republic's 50,793 rooms (as of June 30, 2000) achieved an average market occupancy of 71.1% in 1999. The occupancy in the resort hotels differs significantly from the Santo Domingo hotels in that the latter operated at 67.3% occupancy while the resort properties reached 72.3%. However, the total annual Revenue per Available Room (RevPAR) in Santo Domingo, at $34,880, is far superior to the annual RevPAR in the resorts of the rest of the country, which reached $14,887. The 57% difference in this performance measure is the result of the all-inclusive marketing mode applied in most of the resort properties.

Cancún
Cancún's almost 25,000 hotel rooms operated at average market occupancy of 79% in 1999, down from 88% a year earlier (based on 21,802 rooms) and 81% in 1997 (21,381 rooms). The hotels in the All Inclusive category outperformed the overall market, reaching occupancy levels 5 to 6 percentage points higher than the overall market. Occupancy levels tend to follow very traditional Caribbean markets, with strong occupancy in the northern hemisphere's win-

ter months, and lowest occupancy in the October through December period. Of particular note in Cancún is the popularity of this destination in the June-August period, with the average hotel occupancy being in the mid-80% range, higher than in the normally peak winter months. The increased occupancy is partially the result of strong European visitation, but is mostly attributable to visits by Mexican nationals on vacation.

The average room rate for Cancún was $99.82 in 1999, down from $101.54 the year before although this lower rate is the result of changes in the exchange rate. The average rate actually increased from 935.18 pesos in 1998 to 943.35 pesos in 1999.

SOURCE MARKETS

Cuba

Whereas Canada is the most important single source country for visitors to Cuba, with about 276,000 visitors in 1999, Europe, as a region, delivered 55% of the country's total foreign travelers. In 1999, just over 880,000 Europeans went to Cuba, up from about 170,000 in 1990. Within Europe, Italy and Germany are the most important countries, with 161,000 and 182,000 visitors respectively in 1999. Tourism from Italy appears to have stagnated for the time being, with fewer visitors now than in 1996-98, when approximately 200,000 Italians went to Cuba. Spain is the fourth most important country, delivering 146,000 tourists in 1999, or 9% of the total. Following Spain was France with 123,000, England with 85,000 and Mexico with 70,000. Other countries are emerging as important source markets for Cuba, with tour groups from Japan, China and other Asian countries starting to show stronger presence.

Dominican Republic

Europe also represents a critically important source of visitors to the Dominican Republic, with about 46% of the total 2,649,418 visitors in 1999, or slightly more than 1.2 million visitors. Germany is the largest source of tourism arrivals from Europe, generating 453,000 tourists, or 17% of the total; Spain and Italy both generated about 137,000 visitors, representing 5% of all visitors each. The North American market is the second largest group, with

about 717,000 visitors, of which 500,000 visitors, or 20% of the country's total foreign arrivals, were from the United States. Of note in the Dominican Republic is the fact that of the total 2.6 million visitors, half a million, or 19% if the total, were Dominican Republic nationals who currently reside abroad and visit their native country.

Cancún

Cancún received 2.8 million visitors in 1999, of which 54% originated in the United States, making this market by far the most important, although the absolute number of American arrivals has not changed significantly over the last three years. Next in numbers are Mexican nationals, which accounted for 28% of all tourists to the area last year, reaching almost 750,000 visitors. The volume of tourists from within Mexico appears to be the fastest growing segment in recent years, having increased by 35% from 550,000 in 1997 to last year's volume of 750,000. Europeans accounted for 11% of total arrivals (15% of foreign arrivals), reaching 317,000 tourists, followed by South America with 108,000, Canada with 90,000 and other countries with 24,000.

While the total number of visitors has increased from 1,454,433 in 1997 to 2,818,488 last year, there has been no increase in numbers from other countries or from Canada. Furthermore, the number of visitors from South America has declined by almost half, from 201,000 in 1997 to 109,000 last year. The real growth in arrivals has therefore come from the European market (10% increase in the two years), Mexicans (35% growth) and the United States (5% growth).

FUTURE EXPECTATIONS

It would appear as if the greatest growth potential among the three destinations rests with Cuba, although the future is necessarily tied to political and economic conditions and, to a certain extent, upon attitudes in both the United States and Cuba. In the event that the political environment changes for the negative in Cuba, or should investment attitudes by foreign parties take a different direction, then it is almost certain that Cuba's tourism industry growth will also be affected.

In order to explain why Cuba is likely to see the strongest growth, let us consider the destinations individually and examine the factors that could influence their performance.

Cancún

Cancún has been extremely successful at establishing itself as one of the premier resort destinations in the Caribbean. With almost 25,000 hotel rooms, many of which are of very high quality, and a year-round occupancy level that has consistently been in the low 70% to mid 80% range for many years, the area has clearly had a positive impact on the Mexican economy. The destination offers a wide selection of excellent hotels, convention facilities, numerous restaurants, bars and retail outlets, as well as access through an international airport located close by.

However, in looking to the future, it must be remembered that Cancún is somewhat of an isolated area, with little tourism diversity outside of the "sun, sea and sand" experience (including water-based activities) or visits to nearby Mayan ruins. There is not a lot of cultural tourism or health tourism, while ecotourism remains somewhat of a gray area. Most importantly, however, is the high concentration of hotels in a relatively limited space. The development of hotel after hotel along the eastern and northern shores of Cancún Island will limit supply increases to infilling of isolated land parcels suitable for hotels. Land along the coast, to the north and to the south of the existing development area, is being cleared and prepared for new development, and a virtually endless number of new hotels could likely be added. However, it is also likely that the mere "sameness" of the extended destination area will detract from its appeal, while infrastructure and labor issues could also slow expansion.

Considering the current inventory of almost 25,000 hotel rooms, and the reasonably limited increase in supply over the last 10 years compared to the other two destinations, it is unlikely that Cancún's expansion potential over the next 10 years will amount to much more than 5,000 to 10,000 rooms.

Dominican Republic

The Dominican Republic has extensive tourism growth potential, due in part to the large size of the country, its diverse tourism product offerings, and the availability of new development areas.

The country boasts of having over 200 miles of first-class beaches, as well as rainforests, mountains, and numerous historic towns and villages scattered throughout the coastal and inland areas.

Tourism growth has been impressive, with the number of tourism arrivals increasing by 8.2% annually over the last 11 years, and the market share of Caribbean tourism growing from 9.6% to 13.0% over the same period. The Dominican Republic now has 2.6 million visitors annually, slightly below the 2.8 million recorded by Cancún but above the 2.1 foreign visitors to Cancún (i.e., not counting the over 750,000 Mexican tourists).

The hotel supply is primarily categorized as "all inclusive" beach resorts targeted at the middle market. As indicated previously, 88% of the total national inventory of hotel rooms is classified as "all inclusive"; most are also located in the beach resort areas of Punta Cana, Puerto Plata, Samaná and other similar areas. A review of price quotes among many of the hotels throughout these areas indicate typical low season rates, including room, meals, beverages and certain entertainment and recreational activities ranging from $50 to $100 per person, increasing to between $110 and $150 per person during the peak season (for 4-star accommodations).

The Dominican Republic has benefited from strong demand form the European market, while another 580,000 of the country's 2.6 million visitors came from the United States. While growth from all market sources is expected, the key will be continued demand from Europe and the United States coupled with stronger growth from South America and other countries — this largely depends upon the continued improvements in economic conditions in these areas.

There have been large numbers of new rooms added throughout the last 10 years, with almost 11,000 alone in the last 2 years, and almost 21,000 or more than 40% in the last 5 years. Additional supply has been a combination of national development and investment from foreign corporations including Sol Meliá, Iberostar, Club Med and Jack Tar. Future growth is expected to be quite strong, focusing on more "all inclusive" hotels, and some traditional non-inclusive properties in both beach and inland areas where they can be supported by other commercial developments.

The future growth in the Dominican Republic is also somewhat tied to the future of Cuba. In the event that travel restrictions between the United States and Cuba are lifted, it is likely that the surge in interest in Cuba by the U.S. market will detract from travel to the Dominican Republic. On the assumption that these restrictions remain in place, it is likely that there will be between 15,000 and 25,000 new rooms built in the Dominican Republic within the next 10 years.

Cuba

Cuba had become the fifth most popular tourism destination in the Caribbean region by 1998, following behind Puerto Rico, Cancún, the Dominican Republic and the Bahamas, just 10 years after re-entering the tourism market. Between 1994 and 1998, Cuba recorded the highest rate of growth in tourism arrivals of all Caribbean countries, with an increase of 129%; for the other large destinations, the corresponding growth rates were 31% for the Dominican Republic, 2% for the Bahamas by 2%, 12% by Jamaica and 11% for Puerto Rico.

The very strong growth rates have been achieved as a result of the country's ability to provide a large inventory of hotel rooms, several airports capable of accommodating wide-bodied aircraft, and a wide range of tourism products. The majority of the hotel inventory was, and continues to be, of average quality. The need to attract large numbers of tourists, the lack of professional staff, a mediocre quality food product and other similar issues forced the industry to target the less discerning traveler — this inevitably meant the mass market, which prefers package pricing. The growth in this market has provided the country with primary recognition as an inexpensive, all-inclusive destination.

Within the past 5 years or so, introduction of new hotel concepts through joint ventures with foreign parties has allowed Cuba to begin changing this image. New traditional hotel developments in both beach resort and urban areas have generally been of a much better quality, with names such as Meliá, Novotel and Golden Tulip appearing. Also, the success of the SuperClubs Varadero hotel has initiated further discussions with this company to partner in other projects elsewhere in the country.

There are numerous new development projects in various stages of development, although the majority are still in the preliminary study and financial evaluation stages. Based on discussions with Ministry of Tourism representatives and other Cuban officials, we estimate there to be about 10,000 rooms presently under serious consideration for development (with formal announcements having been made). There are also numerous other projects in the early stages of review and planning.

The government has announced plans to develop as many as 172,500 rooms by 2010, effectively requiring the construction of an average of 14,000 new rooms every year. This very aggressive rate of expansion assumes all U.S. travel and trade restrictions will be lifted and over $22 billion will be available for investment in hotels alone, with much of this coming from U.S. and other foreign corporations. Based on current conditions, it would appear that the travel limitations between the U.S. and Cuba are likely to remain in place for at least another year or so, suggesting that the number of new rooms in the short term will be less than 14,000 per annum. Conversely, it suggests that over the mid to longer term, the rate of addition will need to surpass by a large number the 14,000 average, having to reach 20,000 or more.

As indicated previously, Cuba has improved its share of the Caribbean market from only 2.7% in 1988 to 8% in 1999. The growth in tourism arrivals is likely to slow in the upcoming years, being unable to maintain the torrid rate of the last 10 years. With a rate of growth of, say, 13% annually for the next 5 years, the number of arrivals would increase to 3.3 million by 2005. If Caribbean tourism grew at the same rate as in the past 10 years, it would reach 31.3 million arrivals in 2005, and Cuba would hold a 10.5% market share. If occupancy levels, average length of stay and number of guests per occupied room were not to change, Cuba would require a total of 66,000 rooms, or the addition of 33,700 over the level today. This initially appears to be reasonably realistic, except when considering the actual level of increase over the last 5 years has only been a total of 9,000 rooms and the process from initial consideration of a project through construction tends to be quite slow. With this in mind, we estimate there will likely be between 10,000 and 15,000 new rooms added over the next 5 to 7 years.

While the number of new accommodations for foreigners is likely to be less than expected by the government, the quality is expected to be far superior to what is generally available today. We expect the introduction of timeshare and resort villages will begin to change to typical Cuban hotel image, and while all inclusive destinations will continue to be crucial components of tourism travel, we also expect to see several new commercial hotels in major urban centres, particularly Havana.

SUMMARY

In summary, we believe there are similarities in these three very important Caribbean destinations:

- All are islands, even Cancún in Mexico's Yucatán Peninsula;

- they are all located in the Caribbean Sea, in the same latitude, the same climate, same natural attractions and colonial heritage, the same language, and similar racial mix (with the exception of Cancún with its indigenous Mayan roots);

- They have experienced similar natural disasters, such as hurricanes;

- Each recently began significant tourism development efforts that led them to their present successful positions in the Caribbean;

- The governments of the three destinations support tourism activity in their countries at varied levels of financial commitment;

- They are competitors primarily in the "all inclusive" market segment.

But there are also differences:

- Two of the islands are emerging democracies while the third is not;

- Two of the islands entered the tourism activity primarily by design of private entrepreneurs with different degrees of support by their respective governments. The third island isolated itself from world tourism until such time as the demise of the Soviet Union and its economic support compelled this country to begin development of a tourism infrastructure almost as a means of survival;

- As the tourism industry matured in two of the destinations, government support concentrated on the promotion of the destination in cooperation and support of private sector initiative. In the third destination, the government is the owner/developer and utilizes from 40% to 60% of the available national resources to create and support tourism activity. Only foreign private sector organizations are allowed to participate while local citizens are excluded;

- Local citizens frequent tourism establishments, sometimes representing a high percentage of the demand, in two of the destinations, while in the third they are not even permitted to enter those establishments;

- Since its inception, Cancún cultivated the U.S. market as its principal source of demand for room accommodations. In general, Dominican Republic hotels, mostly owned and operated by European interests, did not pay much attention to the U.S. market until recently when more upscale properties were developed to satisfy this market. Cuba followed the Dominican Republic in targeting the same sources of demand for hotel rooms but cannot access the lucrative U.S. market except at a minimal level.

To conclude, Cuba's extraordinary effort in developing a tourism infrastructure and reasonable success in attracting a growing number of visitors, suggests that the economic "embargo" from the United States has not precluded the island from achieving its present position in the Caribbean tourism market. While this issue is argued by both sides for internal and external political reasons, there is little doubt that Cuba would further benefit from a share of the U.S. market's enormous source of potential visitors.

CUBAN TOURISM DURING THE SPECIAL PERIOD

María Dolores Espino

In 1990, in an attempt to deal with the devastating impact the collapse of the Soviet bloc inflicted on the Cuban economy, Cuban authorities announced the start of "the special period in time of peace," an economic adjustment program. The following year the Fourth Communist Party Congress ratified the program and spelled out its main components: (a) a food (*Plan Alimentario*) and energy import substitution program; (b) the promotion of key traditional exports, such as sugar, as well as new exports, in particular tourism and biotechnology; (c) the encouragement of foreign capital; and (d) some decentralization and moderate reforms in the management of enterprises (Ritter 1994). Earmarked as a key sector, international tourism was to be promoted as "an important source of revenue for economic development."

Ten years have passed since "the special period" was announced and many changes have occurred in the island. Economic reforms have gone further than the hardliners of the Fourth Party Congress envisioned, but have fallen well short of what economists (both inside and outside the island) deem necessary. Performance of the non-sugar agriculture sector remains dismal. Sugar lost its predominance in Cuba's economy and in the 1990s, the sugar industry experienced the lowest annual production figures of the second half of the century. Hopes and expectations about the biotech industry proved illusory. Foreign investment has been erratic and has fallen short of expectations. Tourism, on the other hand, registered a strong performance throughout the decade and is no doubt the star of the "special period."

At the First Annual Meeting of the Association for the Study of the Cuban Economy (ASCE), I presented a paper titled "International Tourism in Cuba: An Economic Development Strategy?" In that paper, and in subsequent articles (Espino 1993; 1994), I documented the performance of the tourist industry in the 1980s and early 1990s and estimated the sector's impact on the Cuban economy. In this paper I will update the analysis to 1999, focusing on the ten years that encompass the special period. The paper is divided into three parts: the first part traces the development of the industry; the second part presents and analyzes indicators of tourist activity in the island; and the third part estimates the economic impact of international tourism on Cuba. The paper ends with some concluding remarks.

DEVELOPMENT AND PERFORMANCE OF INTERNATIONAL TOURISM

Tourism in pre-1959 Cuba was a major industry and a primary source of hard currency and employment. In 1957, 347,508 foreigners visited Cuba (Truslow 1950; Grupo Cubano de Investigaciones Económicas 1963; Martín Fernández 1988) and tourist receipts amounted to 62.1 million pesos. In that year, hard currency earnings from tourism were greater than those from the tobacco industry and were only surpassed by earnings from the sugar industry (Banco Nacional de Cuba, 1960b, 1960c). During the 1950s, Cuba's share of the Caribbean tourism market ranged between 18 and 21 percent (Espino 1994; 1993; 1991) and most visitors to the island were from the United States.

During the late 1950s, the Cuban tourist boom was accompanied by increased foreign interest in the sector and ties to American organized crime (Schwartz 1997). Cuba became known as the gambling, sex and pleasure capital of the world. While the demise of the tourist industry in the early years of the Revolution has been attributed to the U.S. embargo and the industry's ties to "the evils of capitalism" (Martín Fernández 1988; Leal 1990; Villalba Garrido 1993), others offer a different vision, arguing that during the first year of the Revolution the government attempted to embrace the tourist industry, but failed (Schwartz 1997):

> In spite of prodigious efforts, the tourist business succumbed to uncertainty, inconvenience and unpleasantness (p. 202). ... People stopped going to Cuba because the island no longer was a pleasure to viisit. Vacationers wanted to relax, and they had their choice of sunny beaches and gambling casinos elsewhere in the Caribbean. Escalating antagonism over the issues of sovereignty, property, and ideology threatened and then ruptured U.S.-Cuban relations. By the time Castro nationalized U.S. property in October of 1960, most North Americans already had scratched Cuba off their list off desirable travel destinations (p. 203).

International tourism all but disappeared from the island. During the 1960s and 1970s no major investment in tourism was undertaken. The vast tourism infrastructure built up during the pre-revolutionary years was left for the use of Cuban citizens and international guests from socialist and other friendly nations, or simply abandoned. Some sixteen hotels were closed down and hotel capacity was reduced by 50 percent (Ayala Castro 1991, p. 15).

After years of neglect, the government timidly started to promote international tourism in the mid-1970s. Visitors from non-socialist nations started trickling back. In 1974, 8,400 visitors from capitalist countries visited Cuba. In 1976, recognizing Cuba's comparative advantage as a vacation spot and the potential benefits to be derived from international tourism, the Cuban government created the Instituto Nacional de Turismo (INTUR). INTUR became the agency primarily responsible for developing policy for both national and international tourism, as well as

for collecting data on tourist arrivals and tourist receipts.

The late 1970s also saw an increase in the island's imports from Western nations and growth in the hard currency trade deficit. Cuba's hard currency debt grew in tune with the trade deficit. By 1982, debt obligations to the West were estimated at $3 billion, and in August of that year the Banco Nacional de Cuba announced its inability to meet debt repayment obligations and called for a debt rescheduling (Turits 1987, p. 165).

It the midst of this external sector crisis, in February 1982 Cuba enacted Law Decree No. 50, which allowed restricted foreign investment in the island for the first time since the triumph of the Revolution. Under Law Decree No. 50, mixed operations with up to 49 percent foreign ownership were allowed to operate in Cuba (Pérez-López 1985).

It is clear that one of the main objectives of the joint venture law was to open up the tourism industry to foreign capital. The decree established significantly more favorable provisions for foreign investment in tourism than for other industries. In particular, joint ventures in tourism could be exempt from taxes and other licenses and subject to less regulation. Additionally, foreign managers of joint ventures in international tourism were allowed to lease Cuban installations and to hire Cuban workers directly. Foreign capital in the tourism industry was deemed necessary not only to finance development of the tourism infrastructure but also as a means to transfer managerial know-how and as a marketing tool. In reference to the role of foreign capital in the development of the tourism industry Castro himself has stated:

> ...lots of opportunities are emerging. Important opportunities, very important opportunities! That is in the form of mixed enterprises, due to the fact that tourism is a very special endeavor, it is not nickel, it is not sugar, it is not the manufacturing industry; there exist international organizations that possess capital, and possess, on top of that, experience and, above all, possess the tourist markets (Castro 1988).

By the mid-1980s, the external sector crisis had intensified. Soviet subsidies in the form of oil re-exports, which had since the 1970's contributed to finance Cuba's trade deficit (Pérez-López 1988), started to disappear. In 1986, Cuba defaulted on its hard currency debt. The Cuban government, in sharp contrast to trends in the Soviet Union, at the time experimenting with glasnost and perestroika, embarked in a counter-reform, idealistic economic development program named the "Rectification of Errors and Negative Tendencies" (Mesa-Lago 2000). Along with the abolishment of free farmers markets, a return to moral incentives and the elimination of many of the market-based reforms made during the late 1970s and early 1980s, the rectification process added emphasis on the development of the international tourism industry.

A new development strategy was based on a food program with unrealistic targets that optimistically foresaw that in five years the island would be self-sufficient in food and generate a surplus for export; biotechnology was also promoted as a source of exports and to make Cuba a world power in that field; the only sensible development strategy was the expansion of foreign tourism enclaves (Mesa-Lago 2000, p.11).

To accommodate this expansion of foreign tourism, Cuba turned to foreign investment in earnest. In 1987, another tourism development agency, Cubanacán, S.A., was created. The main task assigned to Cubanacán was the attraction of foreign capital. In 1990, two hotels constructed and operated under joint venture agreements opened their doors in Varadero (Espino 1994): the Sol Palmeras Hotel, a joint venture between Cubanacán and the Spanish conglomerate Grupo Sol; and the Tuxpán Hotel, a joint venture between Cubanacán and German interests, managed by the German company LTI International Hotels (Cabrera 1991). Also by 1990 a smaller corporation, Gaviota, S.A., with ties to the military, operated in Cuba and engaged in joint ventures with foreign capital (Espino 1994).

The rectification process created a marked dichotomy in the Cuban economy. In the words of a researcher:

> Cuba's rejection of market-oriented economic reforms, at the same time that it steps up promotion of

incoming foreign investment, has given rise to a curious phenomenon: the proliferation of economic enclaves subject to capitalist rules—"islands of capitalism"—within a centrally planned economy—"an ocean of socialism" (Pérez-López 1994, p.190).

The Cuban leadership, aware of the dichotomy, justified the priority of international tourism on the basis of its ability to be the generator of the much needed hard currency. The success of the industry depended on foreign capital, which was viewed as a necessary evil. Rectification, the return to the revolutionary ideals, was to provide the "immunization" needed to combat any possible contamination from capitalist evils:

> To engage tourism with such low defenses (*prior to Rectification*) …because the defenses were being lowered, there were no antibodies, we had a sort of AIDS. The technocrats and bureaucrats suffered from and transmitted a sort of ideological AIDS, something like AIDS that was destroying our revolutionary defenses. Now that we are strengthening our defenses, can we succeed or not? Or are we going to let them buy us for four dollars?

> Or is it that anyone can come and buy us for four dollars and corrupt us? With our defenses well strengthened, as we are strengthening them now, and with the capacity of our people, their integrity, their virtues, I am sure that we will be able to be good hosts to as many tourists as are necessary (Castro 1987).

To further isolate international tourism from Cuban society, tourism was to be promoted in enclaves where, as much as possible, tourists would be segregated from Cuban society. The growing dichotomy was not lost on the average Cuban citizen, and the government tourism policy soon began to be referred to as "tourism apartheid." But the official policy did not succeed in immunizing society from the "evils" of international tourism. By 1990, while it was still illegal for Cuban citizens to hold foreign currency, there existed a de facto dollarization of the Cuban economy, crime had increased, and prostitutes (*jineteras*), were rampant in the streets of Havana.

The late 1980s saw a rapid expansion of the international tourism sector. Tourist arrivals from capitalist nations increased from 101.5 thousand in 1982 to

310.3 thousands in 1990, while gross revenues from tourism increased from $61.1 million in 1982 to $310 million in 1990. In spite of the impressive performance of the international tourism sector, in 1986 the Cuban economy entered a deep crisis from which it has yet to emerge. The disappearance of the socialist bloc and Soviet subsidies, as well as the counter-reform policies of rectification, caused the worst economic downturn of Cuba's history (Mesa-Lago 2000; Roca 1991; Ritter 1988). As has been mentioned above, in an attempt to address the crisis, Cuban authorities announced, in 1990, the start of "the special period in time of peace," an economic adjustment program. The following year the Fourth Communist Party Congress ratified the plan and spelled out its main components previously alluded to, including (a) a food (*Plan Alimentario*) and energy import substitution program; (b) the promotion of key traditional exports, such as sugar, as well as new exports, in particular tourism and biotechnology; (c) the encouragement of foreign capital; and (d) some decentralization and moderate reforms in the management of enterprises (Ritter 1994).

During the early years of the special period, Cuban authorities concentrated on expanding the export sector (Mesa-Lago 2000). Rapidly becoming Cuba's main export industry, tourism was to play a key role. In 1992 the Cuban Constitution was amended. The changes included the recognition and protection of private foreign property, an inducement to attract more foreign capital. By 1993 deteriorating economic conditions forced the Cuban government to embark on a number of market reforms (Mesa-Lago 2000). In 1993 the dollar was decriminalized.

In 1994, as part of an overall government restructuring pursuant to Decree-Law 147, a Ministry of Tourism was created and Intur and Cubanacán were broken up into a number of separate entities. The new Ministry of Tourism (MINTUR) was to oversee the nation's "Tourism System," which is made up of several state-run and quasi-independent entities, including: Hoteles Cubanacán S.A., Gran Caribe, Horizontes, Gaviota, Islazul, Habaguanex, Las Terrazas, Cubatur, Transtur, Turarte, Cubamar, Caracol, Rumbos and Puertasol (MINTUR 2000). MINTUR

is charged with the elaboration of policy for the sector and overseeing its application by the entities that make up the System. MINTUR's present objectives include:

- the design and production of more efficient tourism marketing programs;

- diversification and increased competitiveness of tourist supply;

- refurbishing and expansion of the stock of hotels;

- increase of economic efficiency within the Tourism System

- develop, as far as possible, information and communication systems;

- attract more foreign capital for tourism development; and

- prepare tourism development plans until the year 2010

INDICATORS OF INTERNATIONAL TOURISM ACTIVITY

The most reliable indicator of international tourism activity is the number of foreign travelers arriving in a given country. Though the tourism industry uses various definitions of what constitutes a traveler or a tourist, the international community has accepted a standard definition recommended by the United Nations Conference on International Travel (World Tourism Organization 1981). The United Nation defines a visitor as "any person visiting a country other than that in which he has his usual place of residence, for any reason other than following an occupation remunerated from within the country visited." Visitors are classified as either tourists or excursionists.

A *tourist* is defined as a visitor staying at least twenty four hours in the country visited whose purpose in making the journey can be classified as (a) leisure (recreation, holiday, health, study, religion, or sport); (b) business; (c) family; (d) mission; or (e) meeting.

An *excursionist* or day visitor is a visitor staying less than twenty-four hours, such as a sea cruise traveler.

Table 1. International Arrivals to Cuba *(in thousands)*

Year	Total arrivals		Tourists		Excursionists	
	Number	Growth rate	Number	Growth rate	Number	Growth rate
1982	150.7					
1983	174.1	16%				
1984	218.3	25%				
1985	243	11%	238		5	
1986	281.9	16%	276	16%	5.9	18%
1987	293.9	4%	282	2%	11.9	102%
1988	309.2	5%	298	6%	11.2	-6%
1989	326.3	6%	314	5%	12.3	10%
1990	340.3	4%	327	4%	13.3	8%
1991	424	25%	418	28%	6	-55%
1992	460.6	9%	455	9%	5.6	-7%
1993	544.1	18%	544	20%	0.1	-98%
1994	617.3	13%	617	13%	0.3	200%
1995	745.5	21%	742	20%	3.5	1067%
1996	1004.3	35%	999	35%	5.3	51%
1997	1170.1	17%	1153	15%	17.1	223%
1998	1415.8	21%	1390	21%	25.8	51%
1999	1602.8	13%	1561	12%	41.8	62%

Source: World Tourism Organization.

In accord with international guidelines, the Cuban government collects data on international visitors. One series is compiled by the Dirección de Immigración y Extranjería and includes all arrivals at the border. This series is published by the World Tourism Organization and by the Caribbean Tourism Organization. MINTUR also compiles data on visitors who arrive in the country through travel agencies and/or who stay in international tourism accommodations.

All sources point to the rapid growth of international visitors in the 1990s. In 1999, for example, 1,602,791 visitors arrived in Cuba, almost five times as many as the 326,300 that visited in 1989. Growth rates during the 1990s, which averaged approximately 18 percent per annum, outpaced those of the 1980s, which averaged about 12 percent per annum. Arrivals seem to have accelerated in the later part of the decade, growing at an average annual rate of 21.2% annual increase since 1995, compared to an annual average of 13.8% in the early 1990s (see Table 1).

The vast majority of visitors to Cuba in the 1990s have been tourists, that is, visitors who stayed in the island for longer than twenty-four hours. Very few excursionists visited the island during this period, for

example only 41.8 thousand in 1999, although their number increased rapidly during the end of the 1990s (see Table 1). The percentage of excursionists among all visitors in 1999, 2.6, percent, was lower than the 3.8 percent recorded in the late 1980s and early 1990s. The tourist/excursionist breakdown that prevails in Cuba in the 1990s is quite different from that in pre-revolutionary Cuba and from the pattern in most of the Caribbean. During the 1950s, a major portion of the tourists traveling to Cuba were excursionists: 90,000 in 1958, 22 percent of total foreign arrivals. The low number of excursionists today can be attributed to the island's exclusion from the sea-cruise industry as a consequence of the U.S. trade embargo.

Cuba's share of Caribbean tourism increased during the 1990s, from an average of 3 percent during the 1980s to about 8.9 percent in 1998 (see Table 2). Cuba's share, however, is still less than half of what it was during the 1950s. It is unlikely that Cuba's share of the Caribbean tourism market will reach pre-revolutionary levels as long as the U.S. trade embargo and travel restrictions remains in effect. First, U.S. citizens are prohibited from traveling to Cuba for pleasure. This denies Cuba access to the U.S. travel market, though the U.S. is its "natural partner." The

United States is, in fact, the principal source of tourists to the Caribbean area, though its predominance in the Caribbean market has been declining. In 1998, the U.S. supplied 48 percent of all visitors to the Caribbean, down from around 60% during the 1980s (Espino 1994). Second, as long as the embargo remains in place, Cuba will continue to be left out of the lucrative Caribbean sea-cruise industry. The U.S. embargo prohibits cruises based in the U.S. from including Cuba in their itineraries.

Table 2.   Cuba's Share of the Caribbean International Tourism Market

	Visitors to Cuba (thousands)	Visitors to the Caribbean (thousands)	Cuba/Caribbean (%)
1989	326.3	10772	3%
1990	340.3	11411	3%
1991	424	11382	4%
1992	460.6	11764	4%
1993	544.1	12850	4%
1994	617.3	13699	5%
1995	745.5	14051	5%
1996	1004.3	14355	7%
1997	1170.1	15293	8%
1998	1415.8	15955	9%
1999	1602.8		

Source: Author's calculation from World Tourism Organization data.

U.S. policy restricting pleasure and business travel to Cuba has forced Cuba to seek alternative markets. During the 1990s, Canada generated the largest number of tourists visiting Cuba. In 1999, 276,346 Canadians tourists traveled to the island, 17% of the total number of visitors that year. During 1999, 55 percent of all tourist arrivals in Cuba were Europeans, with Germany, Italy and Spain the largest European suppliers of tourists to Cuba. In 1999, 182,159 Germans, 160,843 Italians and 146,978 Spaniards visited Cuba as tourists; together these three European countries accounted for 20% of all visitors to Cuba in 1999 (Table 3).

In the 1990s, Cuba was able to profit from a strong general growth in European travel to the Caribbean region, although its performance with regard to attracting tourists from individual countries was spotty. Cuba's share of total European tourists to the Caribbean increased from 10 percent in 1989 to 16

percent in 1997; however, Cuba's share of the German Caribbean travel market has steadily declined from an average of 38 percent in the late 1980s, to an average of 29 percent in the early 1990s and to an average of 20 percent in the late 1990s. Cuba seems to be also losing market share for Spanish tourists to the Caribbean; Cuba's share averaged 60 percent in the late 1980s, increased to 81 percent in the early 1990s, but fell to 58 percent in the late 1990s and to 50 percent in 1999. With regard to its three largest European suppliers of tourists, only with respect to Italy has Cuba been able to increase its share of the Caribbean market, from average of 33 percent in the late 1980s to 51 percent in the late 1990s.

Cuba has been able to compensate for lost of market share among its top suppliers by diversifying to other European countries. In recent years Cuba has been attracting an increasing share of tourists from France and the U.K and the Netherlands, who traditionally have preferred to vacation in their former Caribbean colonies. Among Latin American countries, Mexico, Argentina, Colombia, Venezuela and Chile are the major suppliers of tourists to Cuba. Among these, only with respect to Colombia has Cuba been able to increase its share of the Caribbean market (Table 4).

In spite of travel restrictions, the U.S. remains a major supplier of visitors to Cuba. While the WTO statistics shows that 62,345 visitors from the United States arrived in Cuba in 1999 (see Table 3), Cuban officials have alluded that this figure represents visitors considered as U.S. citizens and that in addition, "over 100,000" Cuban-Americans visited the island (Rice 2000). Others have estimate that 153,000 U.S. citizens legally visited the island in 1999, while an additional 28,000 traveled in violation of U.S. law (Amberg 2000). Combining both categories makes the United States at least the third largest supplier of visitors to Cuba, rivaling Germany for second place.

Investment in Cuba's Tourism Infrastructure

Since the mid-1980s, Cuba has targeted the international tourism infrastructure as a priority investment area. Rooms available for international tourism doubled during the 1990s, from the 12.9 thousand in 1990 to an estimated 32.3 thousand in 1999 (Table

Table 3. International Visitors to Cuba by Country of Origin *(in thousands)*

	1990	1991	1992	1993	1994	1995	1996	1997	1998	1999
Canada	74.4	81.1	94.1	114.8	109.7	143.5	162.8	169.7	215.8	276.3
Germany	59.5	63.9	58.1	63.2	61.0	57.5	80.2	86.5	149.0	182.2
Italy	16.9	24.9	39.8	49.2	66.4	114.8	192.3	200.2	186.7	160.8
Spain	33.9	40.7	49.8	54.1	62.2	89.5	118.0	116.6	140.4	147.0
France	8.2	9.9	13.2	23.4	33.9	34.3	62.7	93.9	101.6	123.6
United Kingdom	2.6	3.2			25.4	19.6	28.1	46.2	64.3	85.8
Mexico	34.5	48.8	44.6	56.3	49.4	32.1	37.2	52.7	61.6	71.0
United States	7.4	11.2	10.1	14.7	17.9	20.7	27.1	35.0	46.8	62.3
Argentina	5.5	16.2	19.5	19.3	36.4	32.6	31.3	41.5	47.6	42.6
Switzerland	3.8	2.8	3.1	3.9	7.0	6.0	10.1	14.0	21.1	26.1
Portugal	0.8	1.7	1.7	2.4	4.3	10.6	14.5	13.4	18.6	25.5
Netherlands	0.4	2.1			15.1	12.6	14.0	12.4	17.3	22.4
Belgium	0.3	2.1	2.5	4.4	4.3	4.4	6.0	10.7	18.0	20.1
Austria	7.6	14.8			7.3	5.8	5.4	6.1	12.0	16.1
Colombia	0.9	1.4	2.3	4.0	7.3	21.0	25.3	28.7	20.7	15.6
Venezuela	17.3	10.3	11.4	14.4	9.0	8.6	8.2	8.6	10.0	12.7
Chile	0.1	3.8	6.8	7.5	6.8	13.7	12.4	13.6	12.9	12.0
Russian Federation					9.0	8.2	9.1	11.4	11.7	11.2
Sweden	1.0	0.9	1.1	1.1	0.8	1.2	3.9	8.4	12.6	9.3
Japan	1.3	1.2	1.4	1.6	1.8	1.8	2.5	3.6	4.4	4.4

Source: World Tourism Organization.

Table 4. Cuba's Share of Tourists to the Caribbean from Selected Markets *(percentages)*

	1985-89	1990-94	1995-99
Canada	9	16	25
Germany	38	29	20
Italy	33	32	51
Spain	60	81	58
France	3	3	12
United Kingdom	1	1	7
Mexico	69	72	71
United States	0	0	1
Argentina	91	44	32
Switzerland	13	9	25
Portugal	37	56	80
Netherlands	3	2	11
Belgium	24	27	24
Austria			21
Colombia	7	10	32
Venezuela	8	9	6
Chile	0	54	47
Russian Fed.			93
Sweden	11	5	22
Japan	11	5	14

Source: Author's calculation From World Tourism Organization data.

Table 5. Tourist Accommodations *(Rooms)*

	1989	1990	1992	1994	1999
Varadero	3291	4134	6534	7151	11245
La Habana	3395	3122	7055	7223	9850
Santiago de Cuba	276	276	2117	1611	
Total	13541	15151	22561	23254	32260

Source: Instituto Nacional de Turismo (INTUR); Caribbean Tourism Organization, *Caribbean Tourism Report 1994*; and Ministerio de Turismo, at www.cubagov.cu.

Santiago de Cuba, "costa sur central" and Los Canarreos (MINTUR 2000).

Despite efforts at diversifying the supply of tourim facilities, the majority of hotel rooms — 66 percent — are still concentrated in Ciudad Habana and Varadero. Of the 9,006 new hotel rooms added since 1994, 2,627 were added in Habana and 4,094 in Varadero. Varadero's share of total rooms in the island increased from 31 percent in 1994 to 35 percent in 1999.

Presently, 189 hotels operate in Cuba (MINTUR 2000). Most independent research agree that the quality mix of these hotels is lower than of others in competing Caribbean destinations, though they have been improving (Godínez 1998). In 1998, only 7.1 percent of hotels in Cuba had a quality rating of five

5). Cuba's tourism development plans calls for an ambitious expansion of rooms in eight priority geographic areas: La Habana, Varadero, Jardines del Rey, Norte de Camagüey, "litoral norte holguinero,"

stars; 30 percent of four stars; and 66 percent were ranked as either 2 or 3 stars (Godínez 1998, p.69). Official sources claim that new construction and expansions have improved this product mix, and that currently 64% of all rooms are in four and five stars hotels.

The expansion of hotel capacity in the 1990s occurred in spite of low occupancy rates. Hotel occupancy has fluctuated during the second half of the 1990s from 54 percent in 1997, to 61.2 percent in 1998, and down to 56.5 in 1999 (CEPAL 1999; CTO 2000). During 1999, occupancy rates averaged under 50 percent from May to October and were at their highest during February, when they reached 74.5 percent (CTO 2000).

In spite of this excess capacity, plans for new construction are driven by a forecast of 5 to 7 million tourists by the year 2010 (Rice 2000; Pérez-Mok and García 2000). To accommodate these tourists, Cuba plans to add 50,961 to 88,519 new hotel rooms in the island. A contingency forecast foreseeing the lifting of the U.S. embargo and travel restrictions to Cuba, would bring in an additional 5 million tourists and create the need for 136,321 new rooms (Fletcher 2000; Pérez-Mok and García 2000).

Fulfillment of these ambitious expansion plans hinges to a large extent on Cuba's ability to attract foreign investment to finance hotel and motel construction. At the start of the year 2000, Cuba's Tourism Ministry claimed that 900 million dollars of foreign capital had been invested in the industry through 26 joint venture firms (MINTUR 2000); 25 of these were identified as hotel joint ventures. Fifty of the island's 189 hotels, with 15,390 rooms, are operated by foreign firms.

The fastest growing region in terms of new construction and foreign investment is the Jardines del Rey and the area in the north coast of Cuba, stretching from the town of Caibarién in the province of Villa Clara to the province of Camagüey. The area encompasses a number of barrier islands, including Cayo Coco, Cayo Santa María and Cayo Guillermo (MINTUR 2000; Fletcher 2000).

THE ECONOMIC IMPACT OF INTERNATIONAL TOURISM ON CUBA

The economic importance of international tourism lies in its ability to generate benefits for the host country. Tourism can improve the balance of payments, generate government revenue, enhance income, create jobs and promote economic growth and development.

International Tourism Receipts

International tourism receipts are defined by the WTO as follows:

> expenditures of international inbound visitors, including their payments to national carriers for international transport; this should also include any other prepayments made for goods and services received in the destination country (WTO 1995).

For statistical and analytical purposes it is recommended that receipts be broken down into at least seven broad levels of tourist expenditures. These include:

- Package travel, package holidays and package tours.
- Accommodation.
- Food and drinks.
- Transport.
- Recreation, culture and sporting activities.
- Shopping.
- Other.

Unlike international arrivals, which are relatively easy to account for, receipts from international visitors are hard to measure. Though attempts are being made to standardize the methodology countries around the world use to estimate these receipts, estimating techniques vary from country to country. This makes a meaningful comparison of visitors receipts across countries difficult.

In the case of Cuba, analysis of visitors receipts is complicated by a number of factors. First, data on two distinct series of receipts are collected and reported by Cuba (Martín Fernández 1988). The first series reports visitors' expenditures on lodging, food, entertainment, travel within the country and the like, but following recommendations of the International Monetary Fund (IMF) for the treatment of tourist receipts in the balance of payments, excludes international travel fares. The second series is much broader and refers to gross revenues; it includes receipts from activities related to international tourism, such as international communications and aviation. These two series are often reported interchangeably, leading to confusion and at times overestimates (or underestimates) of growth rate when the gross revenue series is compared to the expenditures series.

Secondly, I suspect that both the coverage and methodology used to estimate the tourist receipts series have changed significantly from the late 1980s, when INTUR was the only player in the tourism sector, through the 1990s with the diversification of tourism agencies and the creation of MINTUR, increased participation of foreign capital, the decriminalization of dollar holding, and the increased participation of foreign capital in the industry. In recent years both official sources and international agencies have been publishing what seem to be historically revised series (see Table 6).

Table 6. Receipts and Gross Revenue From Tourism (million dollars)

| | Receipts | | Gross Revenue | |
	Value	Growth rate	Value	Growth rate
1990	243			
1991	387	59%		
1992	443	14%	567	
1993	636	44%	720	27%
1994	763	20%	850	18%
1995	977	28%	1100	29%
1996	1185	21%	1333	21%
1997	1354	14%	1543	16%
1998	1571	16%	1816	18%
1999	1714	9%		

Source: World Tourism Organization and Mintur

Both of the revised series indicate strong growth in international tourism receipts during the 1990s. Visitors expenditures (WTO receipts series) grew from $443 million in 1992 to $1,714 million in 1999. Gross revenues from tourism were reported at $567 million in 1992 and increased to $1,816 million in 1998. From 1992 to 1995, tourism receipts grew at a

faster rate than arrivals; this is reflected in average receipts per visitor, which increased from $962 in 1990 to $1,300 in 1995 (see Table 7). Since 1995, however, average receipts per visitor have been declining and stood at $1,069 in 1999. The fluctuations in the average receipts per visitor series might be due to a number of factors, among them change in expenditures per tourist, increases/decreases in prices and inconsistencies in the tourism receipt series.

Tourism Receipts and Cuba's Balance of Payments

Because international tourism represents the consumption of domestic goods and services by foreigners, it is considered an export activity. A country's tourist exports are recorded for the most part in the services (or invisible) category of the balance of payments accounts. Of the major expenditure categories, only in the shopping category are some of the expenditures considered goods and not services. While estimated and recorded separately, all components of tourism receipts, including international fares accruing to the country, should be recorded as credits in the balance of payment accounts. The impact of tourist receipts on the balance of payments is one of the important economic benefits derived from international tourism.

The importance of tourist receipts in Cuba's balance of payments has increased steadily in the 1980s and 1990s. In 1987, tourism receipts were Cuba's third largest source of hard currency, excluding oil re-exports (Banco Nacional de Cuba 1988, p. 10). In 1994, tourist exports surpassed sugar exports, making international tourism the top export industry in Cuba.

Table 8 compares Cuba's tourist receipts to total exports of goods and services. Since 1994, export earnings from tourism have been, on average, about 39 percent of total hard currency earnings; in 1998 the ratio of gross revenues to total goods and services exports was 43 percent, compared to 22 percent in 1992. Gross revenue from tourism made up 66 percent of Cuba's service export in 1998, making tourism by far the most important source of service exports in the island. In 1998, gross revenues from

Table 7. Visitors and Receipts

	1990	1991	1992	1993	1994	1995	1996	1997	1998	1999
Visitors (thousands)	340.3	424	460.6	544.1	617.3	745.5	1004.3	1170.1	1415.8	1602.8
Receipts (million dollars)	243	387	443	636	763	977	1185	1345	1571	1714
Average receipts (dollars)	714	913	962	1169	1236	1311	1180	1149	1110	1069

Source: Author's calculation from WTO data.

Table 8. Cuba's International Trade in Goods and Services *(million pesos)*

	1990	1991	1992	1993	1994	1995	1996	1997	1998
Total	5940	3563	2522	1968	2542	2926	3707	3882	4182
Merchandise exports total	5415	2980	1779	1137	1381	1507	1866	1823	1444
Services exports total	526	584	742	832	1160	1419	1841	2059	2738
Gross revenues from tourism	243	387	567	720	850	1100	1350	1500	1800
Gross revenue from tourism as a % of total revenue from goods and services exports	4	11	22	37	33	38	36	39	43
Gross revenues from tourism as a % of merchandise exports	4	13	32	63	62	73	72	82	125
Gross revenues from tourism as a % of services exports	46	66	76	87	73	78	73	73	66

Source: Author's calculation from CEPAL.

tourism exceeded total merchandise exports. The importance of tourism in Cuba's balance of payments reflects, to a large extent, the poor performance of Cuba's other export industries.

Gross receipts from tourism measures the contribution of tourism to the overall balance of payments. However, when assessing the contribution of export industries to the generation of foreign exchange, a more accurate measure would be net earnings, that is, gross earnings minus the associated imports required to generate these earnings. In tourism the latter is known as the import component, and includes such items as: the cost of imported goods and services used by tourists; the foreign exchange cost of capital investment; payments that leave Cuba in the form of profits, interest payments royalties, management fees, payment to foreign travel agents, and so on; and the cost of overseas training of service personnel.

It is hard to ascertain the exact value of Cuba's tourist import component. In 1990, a Cuban source citing INTUR studies reported that between 23.0 and 64.9 percent of the cost of providing goods and services used by tourists and up to 50 percent of the cost of capital investment in the tourism sector was in hard currency (Canovas Rada 1990, p. 5). Another Cuban researcher calculated that the import component was, on average, between 30 and 38 percent (Ayala Castro 1991, p. 23). In 1996, a Cuban official

was cited in *Granma*, stating that $500 million in imports had been required in the tourism sector (Lee 1998). Since tourist gross revenue for that year reported at $1,350 million, the tourist import component can be estimated at 37 percent. For that same year, the import component for the total export sector had been cited at 54 percent (Lee 1997).

Reducing the import component in tourism and in the rest of the export sector has been stated as one of the goals of Cuban economic policies. In spite of efforts made towards this goal, only modest improvements have been reported (Ministerio de Economía y Planificación 2000).

International Tourism and Government Revenues

A major economic benefit of international tourism is that it generates government revenues. Direct and indirect revenues derived from tourism include aircraft landing fees, airport departure taxes, hotel occupancy taxes, sales tax on tourist purchases, import duties on goods and services used by tourists, corporate taxes and profit repatriation taxes and other licenses and fees.

Revenues generated by international tourism allows the host nation to export a portion of its tax burden. The portion of government revenues contributed by foreign visitors in Caribbean countries is estimated to be quite high, ranging from 20 percent in Saint Lucia to 62 percent in the Bahamas (Caribbean Tourist Research and Development Centre 1987, p. 11).

It is hard to ascertain the impact of tourism on government revenues in Cuba. While the bulk of tourism goods and services are supplied by governmental entities or foreign interests, the market reforms of the mid-1990s created a small private sector that supplies services to tourism. Four sources of government revenues from tourism can then be identified: (a) those derived from official entities providing tourism services; (b) those derived from taxes, licenses and fees imposed on foreign corporations; (c) revenues derived from taxes, licenses and fees on the private sector supplying goods and services to the tourism industry; and (d) taxes and fees paid directly by tourists.

The logical method for estimating total government revenues from tourism generated by official entities would be net revenues from tourism (gross revenue minus the import component). From this, however, one would have to subtract the domestic cost of supplying tourist goods and services. Official figures on gross revenue, however, seem to include tourist revenues from the other three sources, though it is impossible to ascertain what exactly is included.

The actual portion of the state budget that is financed by revenues generated by international tourism is also hard to estimate. It is probably a substantial proportion, and one of the primary benefits of tourism to Cuba. In 1994 it was reported that a third of net revenues from tourism were used for healthcare and education.

International Tourism's
Impact on Income and Employment
Spending by tourists directly injects foreign funds into the local economy, creating income and employment for those who sell their goods and services to tourists. The tourism industry in Cuba directly employed 81,000 workers in 1998 (see Table 9). This represents 2% of the Cuban labor force. This percentage has remained constant since 1996, the first year for which such data are available.

Tourist spending has more than a direct impact, however. Those who gain income from it in turn

Table 9. Total Employment and Direct Employment from Tourism (*in thousands*)

	1996	1997	1998
Total employment	3626.7	3705.2	3753.6
Tourism direct employment	64	70.9	81
Tourism direct employment/ total employment (%)	2	2	2

Source: Pérez-Mok and García; ONE.

purchase other goods and services. As spending circulates through the economy, a multiplier effect is created, generating more income and jobs.

The total impact of tourist spending on the local economy is a combination of direct and indirect (induced) effects. It is calculated by multiplying tourist expenditures by a tourist income and/or employment multiplier. The value of the multiplier depends on the portion of income that leaks out of the local economy at each round of circulation. These leakages include payments for import of raw materials, rent and profits paid to nonresidents, and savings by residents. The larger and more diversified the economy in question, the lower the leakages and the larger the value of the multiplier (Espino 1994).

Estimated values of the tourist income multiplier for small island economies in the Caribbean range from 0.58 for the British Virgin Islands to 1.58 for Jamaica; for other Caribbean island nations the estimated tourist income multipliers are: Cayman Islands, 0.65; Bahamas, 0.78; Antigua, 0.88; Bermuda, 1.03; and Dominica, 1.20 (Archer 1982). The differences in these estimates result, in part, from different methodologies underlying their calculation.

Making a number of assumptions, the value of the tourism multiplier for Cuba has been estimated to be in the range of 0.74 to 0.84, one of the lowest values in the literature (Espino, 1994). This low value results primarily from Cuba's high propensity to import from both tourism receipts and income as a whole. The current value of the Cuban tourism multiplier remains low. Though a small reduction has been reported in the import component of the economy at large and of the tourism sector, these are more than counter-balanced by leakages due to taxes.

The expansionary effect of the multiplier is also affected by supply constraints. The multiplier concept rests on the premise that demand stimulates supply, but the Cuban economy, in spite of the market reforms of the mid-1990s, does not facilitate this process. The multiplier effect for tourist expenditures is further curtailed by continuing government policies designed to keep the tourism sector separate from the Cuban economy. The total impact of tourism expenditures on the Cuban economy is probably not much larger than the direct income and employment that these expenditures create.

CONCLUDING REMARKS

The analysis of the Cuban tourism sector during the special period does not change significantly the conclusions reached almost a decade ago. While Cuba's tourism sector will continue to post strong growth, strong growth in an export sector will not by itself promote economic growth and development in an entire nation (Bryden 1973; Griffith 1989).

The primary economic benefit that Cuba currently derives from tourism is that it generates hard currency and revenues to finance both foreign and domestic deficits. This seems to be the main motivation behind Cuba's tourism policy. The economic impact of tourism on the island's national income and employment is still very small, both in absolute terms and in relation to the size of the national economy. This is due to two factors: (1) the low value of the tourism income multiplier; and (2) constraints on supply.

If international tourism is to become a vehicle for Cuba's future economic development, it must first become a leading generator of income and employment. For this to happen, in turn, the value of the tourism multiplier must increase—that is, Cuba must reduce its imports in all sectors. Moreover, effective linkages must be established with other sectors of the Cuban economy, in particular agriculture, services, and retailing. This entails both abandoning the enclave mode and engaging in further market liberalization.

The current policy of keeping the tourism sector separate from the rest of the economy hinders both the expansionary effect of the income multiplier and discourages linkages between tourism and other industries. The absence of free markets further constraints the multiplier effect. Unless government policy changes, Cuba will continue to forgo the potential economic benefits from international tourism.

REFERENCES

Amberg, Jay. 2000. "Cuban Tourist Industry Outpaces Sugar and Tobacco Economy." *Bloomberg Lifestyle.* June 6.

Archer, B. H. 1982. "The Value of Multipliers and Their Policy Implications." *Tourism Management* 3, no. 4.

Ayala Castro, Héctor. 1991. "Notas Sobre el Turismo." Serie de Estudios Sobre la Economía Cubana, Universidad de la Habana. (June).

Banco Nacional de Cuba. 1960a. *Informe Económico.* Havana.

Banco Nacional de Cuba. 1960b. *Memoria 1958-1959.* Havana.

Banco Nacional de Cuba. 1960c. *Programa de Desarrollo Económico.* Informe no. 4, Havana.

Bryden, J. 1973. *Tourism and Development: A Case Study of the Commonwealth Caribbean.* New York: Cambridge University Press.

Cabrera, Carlos. 1991. "A Challenging 12 Months." *Granma Weekly Review,* January 13.

Canovas Rada, Iveliz. 1990. "Evaluación de la Eficiencia Económica de los Polos Turísticos." *Planificación Fisica/Cuba*, no.1.

Caribbean Tourism Organization (CTO). Various years. *Caribbean Tourism Statistical Report*. Barbados.

Caribbean Tourism Research and Development Centre (CTRC). 1987. *The Contribution of Tourism to Economic Growth and Development in the Caribbean*. (October).

Castro, Fidel. 1987. "Discurso pronunciado en la clausura de la asamblea provincial del partido de Ciudad Habana." Havana (November 28).

CEPAL. 1999. *Cuba: Evolución Económica Durante 1998*.

Espino, María Dolores. 1992. "International Tourism in Cuba: An Economic Development Strategy?" In *Cuba in Transition*, pp. 193-220. Miami: Florida International University.

Espino, María Dolores. 1993. "Tourism In Cuba: A Development Strategy for the 1990s?" *Cuban Studies* 23.

Espino, María Dolores. 1994. "Tourism In Cuba: A Development Strategy for the 1990s?" In *Cuba at the Crossroads*, edited by Jorge F. Pérez-López. Gainesville, FL: University Press of Florida.

Fletcher, Pascal. 2000. "Cuba's tourism still booming." *Financial Times*. May 17.

Godínez, Félix B. 1998. "Cuba's Tourist Industry: Sol Meliá and Varadero As Case Studies." Unpublished Masters Thesis. St. Anthony's College, Oxford, May.

Griffith, Wiston. 1989. "Tourism in the Commonwealth Caribbean: A Case Study." In *The Troubled and Troubling Caribbean*, edited by Roy Glasgon and Winston Langley. Lewiston, N.Y.: Edwin Mellen Press.

Grupo Cubano de Investigaciones Económicas. 1963. *Un estudio sobre Cuba*. Coral Gables, FL: University of Miami Press.

Leal, María M. 1990. "El turismo y su aporte a la economia mundial." Paper presented at the WAPTT/AMFORT Conference, Havana (November).

Lee, Susana. 1997. "Imprescindible mayor eficiencia en el manejo de los recursos en divisas." *Granma*, September 10.

Lee, Susana. 1998. "En Cuba mas de 340 asociaciones económicas con capital extranjero." *Granma*.

Martín Fernández, Ramón. 1988. "El turismo y su desarollo" *Economía y Desarrollo*, no. 5.

Mesa- Lago, Carmelo. 2000. "Economic-Ideological Cycles in Socialist Cuba: 1959-1998." Paper Presented at the XXII International Congress of the Latin American Studies Association (LASA). Miami, FL

Ministerio de Economía y Planificación. 2000. http://www.cubagov.cu/

Ministerio del Turismo (MINTUR). 2000. http://www.cubagov.cu/

Pérez-López, Jorge F. 1985. *The 1982 Cuban Joint Venture Law: Context, Assessment and Prospect*. Institute of International Studies, University of Miami, July.

Pérez-López, Jorge F. 1994. "Islands of Capitalism in an Ocean of Socialism: Joint Ventures in Cuba's Development Strategy." In *Cuba at the Crossroads*, edited by Jorge F. Pérez-López. Gainsville, FL: University Press of Florida.

Pérez Mok, Moisés and Alfredo García. 2000. "Reformas Económicas en Cuba: Retos, Posibilidades y Perspectivas." Paper Presented at the XXII International Congress of the Latin American Studies Association (LASA). Miami, FL.

Rice, John. 2000. "More than 160,000 U.S. visitors to Cuba last year despite restrictions, Cuba says." *Sun Sentinel*, April, 13

Ritter, A. R. M. 1988. "Cuba's Convertible Currency Debt Problem." *CEPAL Review* 36 (December): 117-40.

Ritter, A. R. M. 1994. "Cuba's Economic Strategy and Alternative Futures." In *Cuba at the Crossroads*, edited by Jorge F. Pérez-López. Gainsville, FL: University Press of Florida.

Roca, Sergio G. 1991. "Cuba y la nueva economía internacional: Tiempos duros, deciciones difíciles." Paper presented at the Latin American Studies Association meeting, Washington, DC. (April).

Truslow, Adam Francis. 1950. *Economic and Technical Mission to Cuba.* Washington, D. C.: International Bank for Reconstruction and Development.

Turits, Richards. 1987. "Trade, Debt, and the Cuban Economy" In *Cuba's Socialist Economy: Towards the 1990s,* edited by Andrew Zimbalist. Boulder: Lynne Rienner Publishers.

World Tourism Organization (WTO). 1981. *Technical Handbook on the Collection and Presentation of Domestic and International Tourist Statistics.* Madrid.

World Tourism Organization (WTO). 1995. *Collection of Tourism Expenditure Statistics.* Madrid.

Schwartz, Rosalie. 1997. *Pleasure Island: Tourism and Temptation in Cuba.* Lincoln, NE: University of Nebraska Press.

TELECOMMUNICATIONS AND POWER SECTOR REFORMS IN LATIN AMERICA: LESSONS LEARNED

Juan A. B. Belt[1]

The first country in Latin America to implement far-reaching economic reforms was Chile, which began the process in 1975.[2] Other countries followed after the debt crisis of the 1980s, and today almost every country in the region has implemented stabilization programs, liberalized trade and privatized large numbers of state-owned enterprises. Stabilization programs succeeded in reducing inflation markedly, and much greater emphasis has been given to market solutions. On the political side, there has been a steady move towards democratization that can be best exemplified by the election in Mexico of June 2000, where the opposition candidate won the presidency after seven decades of one-party rule.

Cuba, meantime, continues to follow fairly orthodox Marxist economic policies, there is no democracy and basic human rights are not respected. While other counties in Latin America are beginning to enjoy the benefits of more liberal economic and political systems, Cuba languishes in a low-level equilibrium and tourism and family remittances are the only areas that show some dynamism.

The founders of the Association for the Study of the Cuban Economy (ASCE), some of whom had been involved in supporting transition processes in the former Soviet Union and in Eastern and Central European countries, believed that some of these transition processes had not benefited from the lessons learned in other areas of the world. Of course, a transition from a communist regime to a liberal political and economic regime was unprecedented. Nevertheless, the founders of ASCE believed that the experience of countries undergoing reforms, for example in Latin America, could be a source of useful lessons in a political and economic transition in Cuba.[3]

The purpose of this paper is to describe the important reforms in the telecommunications and power sector carried out in several countries in Latin America that could be applicable to a transition in Cuba.[4] A logical question would be to ask why bother to speculate on such a thing, as Cuba seems farther from implementing liberalizing reforms than ten years ago, when ASCE was founded. An answer would be to quote George Bernard Shaw, when he said: "You see things as they are and ask, 'Why?' I dream of things as they never were and ask, "Why not?'"

---

1. The opinions expressed in this paper are the author's, and they do not necessarily reflect the points of view of the Inter-American Development Bank.

2. Some countries implemented reform efforts before. These included Chile under President Alesssandri (1958-61), Brazil under Minister Campos (mid-1960s) and Argentina under Minister Krieger Vasena (mid-1960s). However, these reform efforts did not attempt to reduce the role of the state in society.

3. Conversation with Joaquín Pujol.

4. The paper gives more emphasis to telecommunications, as that is the sector where the greatest innovations have taken place.

RATIONALE FOR STATE INTERVENTION IN THE TELECOMMUNICATIONS AND POWER SECTORS

The telecommunications and power sectors have often been viewed as natural monopolies, as they exhibit economies of scale and scope, network externalities, and economies of density. The sectors are also characterized by large, sector specific, sunk investments, i.e. investment with a minimum value in alternative uses. Additionally, telecommunications and electricity services are consumed directly by a large proportion of the population, which has a relatively inelastic demand for those services. As a result of these characteristics, it is generally concluded that there is a case of market failure and that there should be some type of government intervention in the telecommunications and electricity sectors.

Two common solutions to the monopoly problem were usually offered: state ownership, which characterized Latin America up to the 1990s, and private ownership with rate-of-return regulation, which has characterized the United States. Both solutions face problems. Government ownership is often highly inefficient, and the problems are well known, so there is not a need to discuss this at length. The problems of private ownership with regulation are discussed in the next section.

PROBLEMS ASSOCIATED WITH REGULATION OF MONOPOLIES

A good regulatory framework for monopolies should have two primary objectives. First, it should protect society from the monopoly power of firms, and second, it should protect private firms from the capricious and sometimes confiscatory behavior of the state. If this last objective is not met, investment incentives could be reduced or even eliminated. A copious literature has been developed in the United States on the reasons why it is difficult to achieve both objectives. These reasons are discussed briefly below.

Time Inconsistency of Economic Policy

In the case where there is discretionary regulation by the state, before a private firm invests, the best strategy for the government would be to agree on a rate that would give a strong incentive for investment. The optimal policy, however, could change after the investment is made, as the politicians may wish to reduce the rates (or let them be eroded by inflation). By reducing the real rate, politicians increase their popularity with consumers, who are always more numerous than investors, and they increase the probability of being re-elected, something that they may value more highly than social welfare.

Regulatory Capture

As has been amply discussed by George Stigler, regulators are often captured by the regulated enterprises, promoting the interests of the firms instead of the common good.[5]

Averch-Johnson Effect

Even if regulators attempt to protect the interests of society, it is possible that they do not have sufficient information to determine what kind of actions they should demand from the regulated firms. Fairly commonly, regulators adjust rates to reflect full costs of production, but it is difficult for them to determine if the costs reflect the maximum level of internal efficiency possible. If the regulator uses a rate of return under the real cost of capital to the firm, rate of return regulation can result in excessive employment in a bias towards capital intensive production.[6] If the rate of return is lower than the real cost of capital, underinvestment will result.

As discussed above, the regulators may not have sufficient information nor the proper incentives to promote efficiency. If they are captured by the regulated, consumers will pay higher prices. More commonly in Latin America, government opportunism has prevailed, and there was a tendency to "expropriate" the assets of the telecommunications and electricity enterprises through a reduction in real rates which often resulted in a decapitalization of the firms and a

---

5. George Stigler, "The Theory of Economic Regulation," *Bell Journal of Economics*, 1971.

6. H. Averch and L. Johnson, "Behavior of the Firm under Regulatory Constraint," *American Economic Review*, 1992.

reduction in the quality of services. Once this deterioration occurred, the companies were often nationalized.

In summary, one may conclude that the solutions to the problem of market failure, government ownership, or private ownership accompanied by traditional (rate of return) regulation, also have significant problems. To avoid these problems, some countries have devised regulatory frameworks that minimize state intervention and give much greater emphasis to measures to encourage competition. The rest of the paper discusses the pioneering reforms implemented in the telecommunications and power sector in several countries in Latin America.

PRINCIPLES GUIDING MODERN TELECOMMUNICATIONS AND POWER SECTOR REGULATION

A good regulatory framework should achieve the following objectives:

- Credibility with investors.

- Flexibility to adjust when fundamental changes take place, such as the deployment of new technology.

- Protection of consumer from monopoly power.

- Low cost for the government and for the regulated firms.

- Provision of incentives for allocative and internal efficiency.

Important technology changes as well as regulatory innovation have permitted some countries to implement very modern regulatory frameworks that minimize some of the problems associated with the traditional forms of regulation (rate-of-return regulation) and that meet some of the objectives outlined in the preceding paragraph.

Technological changes have affected both the telecommunications and power sectors. The main technological change affecting telecommunications regulatory schemes has been the development of technologies for the provision of local telephone service. Television cable can be upgraded to provide telephone service, and here are now several options for mobile and fixed wireless telephony. The costs of wireless solutions are declining rapidly so that they are now cheaper than wired solutions at densities of less than 250 subscribers per square kilometer, and the unit costs of wireless are declining steadily.[7]

In the power sector, technological innovation has had a more limited effect. Essentially, the development of gas turbine technology has reduced the economies of scale of generation and reductions in transmission losses have increased the effective size of markets.

Individuals formulating innovative regulatory frameworks in Latin America were inspired by the U.S. literature on problems of traditional regulation. Essentially, these individuals endeavored to devise regulatory frameworks designed to minimize regulatory discretionality and to give a greater role to competition. These modern regulatory frameworks rely more on competitive market forces and concentrate regulatory action on "essential facilities."

The essential facilities doctrine has a long history in the United States. For a facility to be considered essential it must have the following characteristics:

- It must be impossible or enormously costly to build an alternative facility.

- The facility must be necessary to enable a competitor to provide services in the relevant market.

- Providing access must be feasible.

The frameworks promote competition of the following types:

- Competition in the market by reducing or eliminating legal barriers to entry.

- Reduction of other barriers to entry and exit, thus increasing contestability.

---

7. See Peter Smith, *End of the Line for the Local Loop Monopoly?*, World Bank, December 1995, and Peter W. Huber, Michael K. Kellog and John Thorne, *The Geodesic Network II: 1993 Report on Competition in the Telephone Industry.*

- Promotion of competition for the market through concessions for the provision of services which are monopolistic, or to enter where resources are fixed such as a specific band of the radio spectrum).

- Yardstick competition (comparison with costs and quality of similar firms in other markets).

- Competitive joint ventures or clubs (joint ownership of segment of sector with monopoly characteristics, such as the joint ownership of the wholesale electricity market facilities by energy distribution companies in the U.K., or the joint ownership by all main market agents and government of the power dispatch center in Argentina).

TELECOMMUNICATIONS SECTOR REFORMS

Countries that have implemented modern regulatory frameworks include the United States, Chile, New Zealand and Australia. The U.S., with the breakup of AT&T in 1982, encouraged competition in long distance, and the Telecommunications Act of 1996 is trying to foment competition in local telephony, with limited success. Chile totally deregulated the telecommunications sector but this resulted in years of interconnection-related lawsuits. A second set of reforms required that disputes be resolved through arbitration rather than litigation, and the regulator now establishes interconnection charges based on long run incremental average costs. As a result of the later reforms, there is now competition for local telephony, and a very competitive market for long distance services has evolved. As a the result, Chile now has long distance rates that are probably the lowest in the world (roughly equivalent to U.S. rates). New Zealand eliminated all telecommunications regulation, relying instead on generic anti-trust legislation. Interconnection disputes arose, and these have delayed the development of competition. Australia, having apparently learned form the New Zealand ex-

perience, explicitly established the right to interconnection in the Telecommunications Act of 1991.

El Salvador and Guatemala enacted almost identical legislation in October, 1996, establishing very modern regulatory frameworks for electricity and telecommunications. These frameworks reflect the lessons learned from the reforms in the United States, Chile, New Zealand and Australia. Reform efforts in El Salvador and Guatemala received USAID support.[8]

The laws of El Salvador and Guatemala follow the same principles. These are:

- Main focus is the promotion of competition.

- Different aspects of regulation, such as dispute resolution and management of the spectrum, are largely "privatized."

- The regulatory body has very limited discretionary authority.

- Mechanisms were established to provide direct subsidies, thus eliminating cross subsidies, as cross subsidies would be incompatible with the competitive model being implemented.

Laws in Guatemala and El Salvador promote facilities based competition, forced leasing of unbundled network elements, and resale of services.

The right of a commercial network to interconnect to another commercial network to terminate calls or to get a call from a customer is absolutely necessary to permit facilities-based competition in telecommunications. In the presence of positive network externalities, the incumbent would have tremendous power to keep potential entrants out. The connection must be offered at all feasible levels, and at costs representing the long run average incremental cost (LRAIC). If disputes arise on interconnection, or access to other essential facilities, an alternative mechanism for dispute resolution has been devised, and is discussed below. Connection charges have to be reg-

---

8. Some of the discussion that follows is based on Juan A. B. Belt, "Telecommunications Reform to Promote Efficiency and Private Sector Participation: The Cases of El Salvador and Guatemala," USAID Economists Working Paper Number 10, June 1999.

istered with the regulator, and become the equivalent of unbundeable tariffs. That is, the rates are made are public, and are available to any other party on the same basis. Other essential facilities include signaling, (technical information needed for connection of different networks), automatic caller identification (necessary for billing calls from another network), access to telephone listing data as well as the right to include listings in the white pages of another network.

Interconnection alone merely allows a customer in a network to route traffic to another network but does not go far enough to give customers the right to choose a particular network or service. Equal access is another key element. For example, a network may demand that one of their clients dial 20 digits before they can access another long distance carrier. Dialing parity, i.e. that all networks can be accessed under similar terms, is an important aspect of the promotion of competition. Similarly, number portability, the ability of a client changing networks to keep the same number, something which is mandated in El Salvador and Guatemala, is another important provision to encourage competition. The numbering plan will be administered by the regulator in Guatemala and El Salvador, thus helping to ensure a more level playing field. A temporary measure was included in Guatemala and El Salvador prohibiting presubscription to long distance services for a period of two years in order to foment competition.

Unbundled access at reasonable rates is a temporary measure, with a duration of three years.[9] It requires the incumbent to offer entrants basic network elements separately, and at cost (including a return to capital). This is an important provision to increase the contestability of the market, as it converts fixed entry costs into variable costs, thus also reducing or even eliminating exit costs. With unbundling a firm that is trying to enter service in a given area can lease facilities (sunk costs) from the incumbent without having to make new investments. For example, a TV cable company could lease switches and ports from the incumbent, and provide dial tone to a client using its own TV cable network. Similarly, a firm with switching equipment could use the local loops of the incumbent. As both Guatemala and El Salvador want to give incentives for network expansion, unbundling will only last for the three years following the enactment of the laws (laws were enacted in October 1996). The alternate dispute resolution mechanism discussed below will be used to solve conflicts related to the unbundling requirement.

The laws of Guatemala and El Salvador contain an innovative alternate dispute resolution mechanism, something that was devised after the experience of Chile and New Zealand, where litigation through the justice system related to access to essential facilities delayed the onset of competition in those countries. In Guatemala, the alternative dispute resolution mechanism is as follows:

When an operator requires access to essential resources of another network, it will send a request with copy to the Superintendency. Parties have the duty to negotiate and have a period of 40 workdays to reach an agreement; but the period for negotiations can be extended by mutual agreement of the parties. If no agreement can be reached, the parties would submit to the Superintendency an analysis of the points of divergence. If one of the parties does not present a final offer on any point of dispute, the Superintendency would be obliged to resolve it in favor of the other party.

After the Superintendency has received the positions of the parties in dispute, the use of a private sector expert arbitrator ("perito") would be mandated. The party denying access will receive from the Superintendency a list of all qualified arbitrators, and will choose three names from that list. The list with three names would then be submitted to the party requesting access, and it would then choose one "arbitrator" to provide expert analysis to assist in the resolution of the dispute.

9. The reason this measure is temporary is that the Government would like to encourage in the future an increase in facilities-based competition. The U.S. Telecommunications Act of 1996 also mandates unbundling until the FCC considers it is not necessary to promote competition.

The law establishes well-defined standards for arbitration that must be used by the arbitrators in the resolution of disputes. In conflicts related to fees for the use of essential resources the arbitrator must ensure that the requestor pay for the use of the network the long run average incremental cost (LRAIC) of an efficient firm. The law specifies the costs that can be included in the calculations as well as a detailed methodology to estimate the cost of capital. The arbitrator follows final rule arbitration and must base his decision on which offer is closer to the LRAIC. In the case of technical disputes, the arbitrator must adhere to the standards of the International Telecommunications Union, the standards of regional telecommunications organizations, and the standards of regional telecommunications professional associations.

Radio spectrum management has been privatized to a large extent, and it is here where the laws of Guatemala and El Salvador have been most innovative. The laws establish negotiable rights for the use of the spectrum ("derecho de usufructo"). These titles constitute private property, and can be sold, leased, and mortgaged. They can also be fragmented vertically (if new technology allows a more intensive use of a given band), geographically, and in time.

All transactions of "derechos de usufructo" have to be registered in the Telecommunications Registry, which forms part of the Superintendency. The law specifies the information that must be contained. In the case of Guatemala, titles are granted for periods of 15 years, and can be renewed if a request is submitted between 200 and 120 days of the expiration date. The only reason for not granting a renewal would be if it could be proven that the particular portion of the spectrum was not used at all during the period of ownership of the title. In the case of El Salvador, the titles are for 20 years, but at that time they would be auctioned again; an owner of a band of the spectrum can initiate the auction process before the 20 years expire, and can then share in the proceeds of the auction on a present value basis.

In both countries, a title is assigned to any person that requests it, and the Superintendency is obliged to respond to requests within three days. The Super-

intendency is obliged to award use of the spectrum and a title unless it is impossible, for technical reasons, to define that portion of the spectrum. If other parties are interested in that portion of the spectrum, then a public auction for that portion of the spectrum must be carried out. These auctions are carried out by the Superintendency and are supervised by reputable firms of external auditors. The title is awarded to the highest bidder.

The competition model being implemented in El Salvador and Guatemala makes it very difficult if not impossible to continue with the system of cross subsidies. In order to promote service in low-income areas, both countries established mechanisms to provide direct subsidies for telephone service expansion in those areas. The legislation in Guatemala establishes the Fund for Telecommunications Development. The purpose of the fund is to subsidize telecommunications services in low-income areas, and is financed from 70% of the proceeds of auctions of the spectrum, up to a maximum of US$ 5 million. Firms wishing to use the resources from the fund would submit bids for covering an area, and the firm that can do it at the lowest cost wins. A similar fund was established in El Salvador, but it also covers rural electrification, and is financed from the national budget, as the Constitution of El Salvador does not permit the earmarking of revenues.

Both countries established regulatory agencies. In Guatemala, there are separate regulatory agencies for telecommunications and energy, while in El Salvador they were combined. The regulatory agency of Guatemala is the Superintendency of Telecommunications. The Economic Cabinet proposes the candidate for the office of Superintendent, who is appointed by the President for an indefinite period, i.e. serves at the pleasure of the President. Expenditures of the Superintendency are financed mainly from a proportion of the proceeds of auctions of the spectrum. Originally, the plan was to make the Superintendency more independent of the Executive, but to create an independent agency it is necessary to have two thirds of the votes in the Legislative Assembly, and the administration was unable to muster this support.

In El Salvador, the General Superintendency of Energy and Telecommunications (SIGET) was created initially with more independence, as the Superintendent was named for a fixed term of seven years, and could not be removed from office except under very well defined circumstances. Unfortunately, this was later modified, and the Superintendent now does not have a fixed tenure.

The laws of Guatemala and El Salvador contain a provision termed "administrative silence." Basically, if a request made to the regulator is not resolved within prescribed periods of time, it is automatically resolved in favor of the requestor. The laws also establish well-defined time limits for many of the activities of the regulator.

The results of these innovative reforms in El Salvador and Guatemala have been outstanding. The number of service providers in both counties increased sharply. In each of the two countries, the number of basic telephone service providers increased from one to seven, and the number of cellular providers increased from one to three, and in both counties a fourth cellular provider has bought spectrum.

The number of users also increased sharply in both countries with respect to the period before the reforms were initiated. Basic telephony users increased from 350,000 to 800,000 in El Salvador and from 250,000 to 600,000 in Guatemala. Cellular subscribers increased from 24,000 to 350,000 in El Salvador and from 30,000 to 250,000 in Guatemala.

While the prices of local telephone services were increased, there were very sharp declines in the prices of long distance and cellular telephony. Long distance rates declined from US$1.80 a minute in both countries to about US$0.15 in El Salvador and to US$0.30 in Guatemala. Cellular rates also declined sharply, by 70% in El Salvador and by more than 50% in Guatemala.

POWER SECTOR REFORMS

Power sector reforms began in Chile, ahead of the England and Wales reform, and the process was long. In 1979, the state-owned power enterprises were corporatized, i.e., forced to operate more like private entities. In 1980, tariffs were adjusted to reflect long run marginal costs, rates for large clients were liberalized, and independent cost centers were established. In 1982 ENDESA, the largest state-owned power company was registered as an open stock company and was compelled to go to the capital markets for financing, thus eliminating the "soft budget constraint" that it enjoyed until then. Divestiture of ENDESA and its subsidiaries took place in 1987, almost ten years after the process started.

The regulatory framework developed in Chile is known as the "Chilean model." Its main characteristics were:

- Monopoly franchise was eliminated.

- Generation (except hydro) was deregulated.

- Wheeling (transport of electricity) was mandated and wheeling rates were regulated.

- A private entity, owned by the generators, was in charge of dispatch.

- Dispatch was based on marginal costs declared by the generators and audited by the regulator.

- Rates for small clients were based on the sum of the cost of generation plus the cost of transmission plus the "value added for distribution" (VAD). The regulator determines the VAD based on the costs of an efficient firm.

A majority of countries in Latin America has implemented power sector reforms similar to the ones in Chile. These reforms, however, these reforms were carried out significantly faster, and some improvements were made on the Chilean model.

Main improvements made by Argentina on the Chilean model include:

- Firms cannot participate in more than one of the three market segments (generation, transmission and distribution).

- The dispatch center is owned jointly by distribution, generation and transmission companies; government; and large users.

- The maximum generation by one enterprise is 10% of the national market.

The results of the Argentine reforms have been outstanding. Almost all state-owned enterprises were privatized, and total proceeds from privatization reached US$ 7.8 billion. New generating plants with a total capacity of 4,000 MW were built at a cost of US$1.2 billion. As these new plants are fired by natural gas, the new energy is "greener." Labor productivity has increased in generation, transmission and distribution. In generation, number of workers per MW of installed capacity declined from 1.0 to 0.33. The main transmission company reduced the number of workers from 150 to 70. In distribution, the number of workers per 1,000 clients declined from 4.0 to 1.5. More importantly, the wholesale price of electricity declined by 50%, from US$0.05 per kWh to US$0.025.[10]

While the "Argentine model" has had some very positive results, some important issues remain. The most significant concerns the expansion of transmission capacity, where some delays have been encountered as a result of the difficulty of establishing wheeling rates with adequate incentives. Another issue, prevalent in most countries in Latin America, is whether the wholesale market should move to a commodity type market, where generators bid on any price, as is the case in the so called second generation electricity markets such as California.

LESSONS LEARNED
- The far-reaching reforms of the power and telecommunications sector in Latin America have demonstrated that efficient regulatory frameworks can be implemented. The very favorable results achieved in the power sector in Argentina and the telecommunications sector in El Salvador and Guatemala, demonstrate this.

- Technological changes in telecommunications, such as wireless telephony, make it easier to introduce competition in telecommunications than in the power sector.

- Alternate dispute resolution mechanisms can play an important role, particularly is resolving disputes related to the terms of access to essential facilities.

- Regardless of the regulatory framework, rent-seeking behavior will continue. Measures to enhance the independence and autonomy of regulatory agencies should continue to be emphasized.

- In telecommunications, the management of the spectrum is of the greatest importance, as wireless technologies offer an important channel to bring competition.

- Lessons learned are useful but "models" can not be copied in their entirety.

- Cuba, in comparison to the rest of Latin America, has lost several decades by not adopting a more liberal economic and political system. Cuba can, however, benefit from the lessons of other countries in the region in several areas, including power and telecommunications.

---

10. Some of this decline is the result of the improvement in the efficiency of gas fired turbines.

A DISCUSSION ON INSTITUTIONAL RESEARCH FOR A TRANSITIONAL CUBA

Jorge Luis Romeu[1]

It is generally accepted that research, in all of its diverse modalities, is an excellent indicator of the socioeconomic level of a nation, as well as of its future direction. It is also evident that, since research is deeply rooted in the society in which it is engrained, it also reflects its values and modus operandi. As Cuba will surely experiment, some time in the future, substantive changes in its social and political framework (a transition to pluralism), it is important to take a serious look at this important facet of its intellectual life. Hence, we proceed within our now established line of work at previous ASCE meetings (Romeu 1995, 1998, 1999). We examine the history and the existing modes of institutional research in Cuba and present some ideas on how this needs to evolve, once a transition to pluralism occurs in the country, in order to maintain its current levels in an open society.

We analyze Cuban research currently carried out in institutions, academia and government. We believe that the problems and needs for reforming such research activity, after the transition, are not very different from those we have already signaled in our paper on reforming the (higher) education system (Romeu 1998). The causes, and the consequences, of both of these intellectual activities remain the same under the current Cuban political system.

As in our previous work, we propose here some specific courses of actions. These proposals are part of the ongoing dialogue that ASCE maintains regarding Cuba's future. Unfortunately, in this important debate, Cubans inside the island, prevented by Castro's government, can barely participate. We are all very much aware of this problem. Hence, we want to underline, right from the outset, that our conclusions and recommendations are only intended to enrich this truncated dialogue on Cuba's future —and never to impose our point of view on our colleagues inside Cuba. We welcome dialogue, which is one of the main ingredients of society; one that Cuba has thoroughly missed during these last forty two years of history and that is at the root of all of its current problems. We long for the participation of our now silenced brothers. But it will eventually come. And, at that time, all our contributions will be available in the ASCE proceedings.

In the remaining of this paper we provide some topical background and context by discussing different research models and by giving some examples of their applications in different countries. We then give an overview of the history of Cuban research until the present days. Next we compare the current Cuban research model with that of a well-known organization in an open society, the American Statistical Association (ASA), pointing out advantages and disad-

1. The concepts expressed in this paper represent the opinions of the author and not necessarily those of IIT Research Institute or the other Institutions with which the author is affiliated. The author greatefully acknowledges the helpful comments and suggestions of Professor Benigno Aguirre, of Texas A&M University, the discussant of the paper.

vantages. We finally propose specific actions for organizing and adapting the current Cuban research model for the pluralistic and open society toward which Cuba will transition.

RESEARCH ACTIVITY AND ITS MODELS

Research, sometimes also called "scholarship" in academic circles, is the set of activities that leads to new discovery, or to the expansion of the existing knowledge base. Following Boyer (1990), we consider four types of research or scholarship: discovery, application, synthesis and teaching (Chamberlain 1993).

Scholarship of discovery, also known as "basic research," leads to the development of new principles, new methods, theories, etc. It is the most conceptual type and usually takes place in isolated labs or cubicles, in the heart of the "ivory tower." It is also extremely important because it is the basis of all new developments. One example is the invention of the transistor, in Bell Labs.

Scholarship of application, also known as "applied research," takes the findings of basic research, finds purpose for it, refines it and turns it into practical applications that we can all use: The development of TVs, radios, computers, and so on, using the transistor, constitute some examples.

Scholarship of synthesis produces quality reviews of past work, integration of research results from various disciplines, technology transfer, etc. It takes pure and applied research results and puts them in a broader perspective, weaves them together and converts them into multidisciplinary topics. It is usually undertaken in academic institutions and in "think tanks."

Scholarship of teaching, which is less recognized and glamorous than the three previous ones but not less important, occurs in undergraduate classrooms and consists in preparing future generations of researchers, by including them in inquiries of small—but important—topics. The consequences of caterpillar migrations on certain plants, or of the application of technology to the learning of statistics, are some examples of this type of research (Burke 1986).

In addition to these four types of research, we have different models of research structure, what may be called the decentralized, centralized, mixed and anarchic models.

The **decentralized** model is prevalent in the United States and other highly developed countries. Research of the four above-mentioned types is undertaken by all sorts of institutions: private, public, commercial, non-profit. At the university, faculty is required to undertake research as part of their obligations and hence become part-time researchers. Full-time researchers work at independent (e.g., RAND), industrial (e.g., DuPont) and government labs, both military (e.g., Air Force Research Laboratory) and civil (e.g., Oak Ridge). There is no direct government control. However, oversight and direction is provided through certain official organizations (the National Science Foundation or the Academy of Sciences) and mechanisms (government grants, amounting to US$75 Billion, invested annually in all sorts of research activity). In addition, independent research is also supported by grants from private foundations and professional organizations.

The **centralized** model existed in the former USSR and other socialist countries and in Cuba. Research here is directly and openly managed and supported by the State. Government labs and research organizations hire, fire, promote and transfer all research personnel. They select research topics and evaluate and disseminate their results. Instead of open competition for grant money, that fosters ingenuity, universities and research centers depend on government subsidies and budgets. This also constitutes a form of patronage that disincentives innovation and reduces independence.

The **mixed model**, a combination of the two above-described ones, fosters cohabitation of both state and private research in nations with strong, but democratic central governments. France has the Centre National pour la Recherche Scientifique (CNRS) and Mexico the Consejo Nacional de Ciencia y Techología (CONACyT), institutions that carry out or advance the official research policy. But there also exist many private research centers, in industry and academe, which prosper and work independently of any government supervision or interference.

Finally, there is what we will call the **anarchic** model, prevalent in underdeveloped countries. There, little research is undertaken. And whatever research is done, by a small group of pioneers, is conducted in universities, stations, primitive labs and research facilities, with little if any support or recognition and with meager budgets. Many Latin American countries fall within this latter category.

This author considers that research in Cuba, before 1959, followed the anarchic model. It was, in most part, reasearch of the applications, synthesis and teaching types, with few exceptions of scholarship of discovery, and mostly done in government agricultural stations and at the university. After 1959, by paying a huge social, political and economic price, this model changed to a centralized one and basic research grew considerably, especially in certain areas such as biotechnology.

HISTORY OF CUBAN RESEARCH

The origins of Cuban research activities are closely linked to two institutions: the University of Havana (1728) and the Sociedad Económica de Amigos del País (Santiago, 1788; Havana, 1792). The Cuban Academy of Sciences came later (1861) as the result of the work of researchers from these two institutions, especially of Cuban physician Dr. Tomas Romay ("La Academia" 1996; *La Enciclopedia*, 1974).[2] Since little can be learned in isolation, in the next paragraphs we compare the history of the development of research in Cuba and in the United States and, in particular, the history of the U.S. and Cuban Academies of Sciences (CAS) and their related institutions.

Harvard, the first U.S. university, was founded in 1636. In the XVIII Century, intellectuals such as Franklin, in the United States, and Arango, Poey and Romay, in Cuba, undertook research on their own.

The first U.S. scientific institution, comparable to the Cuban Sociedad Económica, was the American Association for the Advancement of Science (AAAS), founded in 1848.[3] The U.S. National Academy of Sciences (NAS) was founded in 1863, during (and to help in the effort of) the Civil War.[4] All these Cuban and U.S. scientific societies languished throughout the second half of the XIX Century. Their main contributions consisted in periodically gathering the best scientific minds and encouraging and publishing the first research papers discussing national issues of scientific interest.

At the onset of the XX Century these scientific institutions in both countries lost many of their members to the professional societies that they encouraged and had helped create. In Cuba, relevant scientists such as Drs. Finlay, Albarrán and de la Torre were members of the CAS. Their research was a "tour de force" while, in the United States, their counterparts enjoyed industry's research resources. But NAS, AAAS and CAS functioned more as clubs, where researchers met and exchanged information, than as sponsoring or coordinating organizations. Their time for such proactive roles had not arrived.

In the second half of the XX Century, as a result of World War II in the United States and of the 1959 revolution in Cuba, things changed. Both Academy of Sciences acquired proactive roles in encouraging, sponsoring, directing or reviewing research, either directly (Cuba) or through their government links (e.g. through the National Research Council, created by NAS in 1916, to help advance scientific research during the war and later the National Science Foundation). In a decentralized way in the United States, and in a centralized one in Cuba, a national scientific policy was finally initiated and directed, using the Academy of Sciences and their network of scientific organizations.

After 1959, CAS became an active instrument of the government scientific policy. It received substantial

---

2. Academia de Ciencias de Cuba, http://www2.cuba.cu.

3. American Society for the Advancement of Science, http://www.aaas.org.

4. National Academy of Sciences, http://www.nas.edu.

subsidies and created numerous Institutes where government sponsored research was undertaken. CAS became a de facto government agency. In 1976, CAS was established as a National Institute and, in 1980, its Director held ministerial rank. At this time, CAS literally managed all scientific and technical research in Cuba. In 1996, CAS was restructured and started becoming again an honorary and scientific institution (rather than a government agency). After 1998, CAS is again coordinating all university and other institutional Cuban research, which was its original function. It also holds the official function of representing all Cuban research organizations abroad.

The best way to illustrate the extent of the organization and functions of the CAS is to present a partial list of all the institutes that CAS directs and, to a point, controls (see Appendix 1). We can see how most science and humanities areas are included in the CAS list of organizations. But the consequences of having such high degree of control on the entire research activity is far reaching. Cuba is a country where over 90% of the population is employed by the state (including those working for CAS organizations). In addition, the media and all levels of education are under government control and ownership. There is only one legal political party with a strong hierarchical organization, with President Castro and his brother on the top. Under this configuration, the current structure of CAS can only strengthen the country's concentration of personal power.

For comparison, we present the organizational structure of an alternative research model: the American Statistical Association (ASA), an open U.S. professional society with 15,000 members worldwide, founded in the 1850s. ASA operates on a voluntary basis, and is run by unpaid officers elected through secret ballot, who serve fixed terms providing leadership and offering professional growth to all ASA members. A list of ASA Committees is presented in Appendix 2.

The ASA recruits its officers from within its members, through annual elections. Its officers do not de-

pend economically on the ASA or the U.S. government.[5] CAS meanwhile selects its officers by following (as with everything else in Cuba) a highly politicized process. These officers become state employees and remain as such for an undetermined period of time (as opposed to fixed terms). High level officers of CAS receive special privileges, not available to the average Cuban researchers — let alone Cuban citizens. These include travelling abroad, attending official functions for foreign researchers, and the use of cars, computers and other modern devices. It is not unreasonable to suggest that fear of losing such special government privileges plays an important role in these CAS officers' decisions.

ADVANTAGES AND DISADVANTAGES

In the previous section we described several research models and structures. Each combination model-structure has advantages and disadvantages. They function and serve the society in which they are inserted. Advantages and disadvantages are, therefore, subjective. In an effort to overcome this difficulty we call "general" those characteristics for which a consensus assessment is reached by a large number of researchers. For example, many researchers will agree that the anarchic model of research is the least efficient of all, for very little research of importance is able to come out from such poorly endowed and supported model at a very high human cost.

More difficult is to agree on the comparative merits of the other three models. For example, centralized models provide researchers with support, recognition and economic stability, which is lacking under the anarchic mode, as long as their government sponsors are happy with their work and personal behavior. But research topics and results (as well as personal researchers' activities) should advance — or at least not harm — the government goals. Does this make it a better or worse model?

To a certain point, the same could be said of any other research model. For example, we have recently found out that substantial adverse research results were suppressed by the tobacco industry in the Unit-

---

5. American Statistical Association, http://www.amstat.org.

ed States. But in an open, civil society it is more likely that objectivity finally prevails. In addition, in such a system, researchers can move from one research environment to another if they disagree with their politics or if their interests are not advanced, much more easily than in a closed society, like Cuba's. Finally, there are more "donors" (foundations) both private and public (Ford, Rockefeller, NSF, NIH, etc.). The likelihood of finding alternative sponsors is larger in an open, civil society than in a one-party, state-controlled society.

Hence, we will propose several research-related problems where, in abstracto, the specific research model selected plays a decisive role. These include having the opportunity to work on specific research problems, obtain support to undertake one's proposed research, assemble the qualified research team, secure the host lab or institution and find an adequate scientific forum to disseminate and verify one's research results. The manner in which all these research issues are resolved is highly dependent on the research model under which research operates.

We will illustrate the situation with a recent real example. In Cuba, four independent, up to then unknown colleagues, wrote a research paper on Cuban socioeconomic problems titled *The Fatherland Belongs to All*. We all know their names, for the four have been made honorary members of ASCE. Their research paper discussed and documented important aspects of the recent history of our country. When these four researchers were ready to release their paper, they were arrested, tried, and sentenced to several years in jail. After much international protest, three of them were released on parole. The fourth one, Mr. Vladimiro Roca, is still in prison.

Without reaching the above example extremes, the average Cuban researcher faces a level of scrutiny (on his research topic, research associates, results) way above that of his peers almost everywhere in the pluralistic world. We know of the high levels that Cuban scientific research has reached in some areas such as biotechnology. We can only conjecture the levels it could have reached, were Cuba an open society where anyone — independent of political ideology,

religion, etc. — were provided an opportunity to do research, or to acquire the knowledge to do research.

In addition to the major issues illustrated above, there are also several other problems. They include the lack of access to specialized and advanced training, to current publications, to research resources (labs, computers, libraries, internet), to technical research assistance, to exposure to foreign researchers and to their interaction. In a centralized model such as Cuba, access to these resources is conditioned on the researcher's government allegiance.

A centralized system nurtures government "patronage." Researchers who are committed to the government are likely to advance faster — and those who are not, can be penalized and held back. Thus, the centralized model advances the current goals of Cuban society, because it is a closed, government controlled one. As it opens up, via a transition to pluralism, the centralized model will become useless and obsolete and will have to change to one where research results and knowledge (and not allegiance to the government) constitute the criteria for recognition, reward and support.

PROPOSAL FOR FUTURE CUBAN INSTITUTIONAL RESEARCH

There is a common theme between institutional research and Cuban education. In our earlier papers (Romeu 1998 and 1999) we talked about modifying the educational system that already exists, so it can work in the new Cuban society, instead of "throwing out the baby with the bath water." The fundamental disease of the current Cuban society is its asphyxiating state control and patronage. As Cuba transitions to an open society, there will be neither room for nor need for the existing CAS control and patronage mechanisms. The real control of all elements of society, including the education and research activities, will logically pass on to the "civil society."

Hence, we propose three measures for the organization and support of all research activities. With the transition process, Cuba will move from a statist, pyramidal, highly controlled society into a pluralistic and decentralized one. And CAS should become, accordingly, a director and a catalyst for research.

These three measures are important to prevent Cuba from going back to the pre-1959 "anarchic research" model while, at the same time, moving out of the centralized one. Cuban society will have to select between the mixed and the decentralized research models to determine which model will suit it best. The three measures are:

- All research should be developed and directed through open processes. CAS officers should be either directly elected or at least scrutinized by peer professional organizations and publicly elected authorities. The new role of the CAS should not be to control research but to stimulate and evaluate it, through open and efficient professional organizations, as it occurs in open societies. Through such open process, the type of research work to encourage and support should be selected, based on the experiences and successes of the past and on the economic possibilities that such research can bring to the Cuban economy and nation.

- There must exist funds to support research activities and they should come from those who benefit mostly from it: Cuban society as a whole. The funds may include contributions from private foundations as well as contributions (through taxes and government spending) from the industrial and agricultural sectors. The main problems of the pre-1959 anarchic model were lack of funds and of organization to support research. After 1959, this lack of research support was traded-off for lack of freedoms and economic discrimination. We want to improve on the current Cuban situation by opening the research activity to all — not just to substitute one form of

discrimination by another. This can't be achieved if there is lack of adequate economic resources for education and research.

- There are currently many honest and well-prepared officers and researchers working in Cuban research institutions and the CAS. They have acquired valuable experience that can continue to serve Cuban science and technology. It is not difficult to differentiate a true scientist (or academician or researcher) from an *apparatchik* (the case of Mrs. Ceaucescu in Romania, is a recent classical example). Careful evaluation of professional dossiers is in order to accomplish this task.

CONCLUSIONS

Traditionally, drastic political changes in Cuba (e.g., the revolutions of 1933 and 1959) have replaced entire rosters of people from the previous administration by new and often inexperienced ones, without doing any evaluation. The principle was: every person who worked with the previous administration had "collaborated," was guilty by association and should go. This approach disrupted the continuity in the processes of our nation's life. It also created a false sentiment of social "advancement" and a belief that only through revolution, could the younger generations find a place at the "banquet table." Such inefficient remedy only transitorily resolved Cuba's chronic problems of unemployment and lack of social mobility, without attacking its root causes. It is important to avoid such costly approach in the future. When the transition takes hold and political change occurs in Cuba, we propose to salvage the good, modify the questionable, discard the bad, and move on with the business of rebuilding our nation in peace.

BIBLIOGRAPHY

Boyer, E. L. *Scholarship Reconsidered: Priorities of the Professorate—A Special Report of the Carnegie Foundation for the Advancement of Teaching.* Princeton: Princeton University Press, 1990.

Burke, J. C. "Teaching, Research and Service: An integrated view." Speech to the SUNY Faculty Senate. SUNY-Fredonia. September 30, 1986.

Chamberlain, S. C. "Research in the Student-Centered Research University." *Engineering & C.S. Newsletter.* Syracuse University. Spring 1993.

La Enciclopedia de Cuba: Historia. Editor: Vicente Baez. Editorial Playor, Madrid. 1974.

"La Academia de Ciencias en Cuba: 135 años de reflexión y promoción en la ciencia y la sociedad." *Revista Cubana de Medicina Tropical* 48(3): 147-148, Septiembre-Diciembre, 1996.

Romeu, J. L. "More on the Statistical Comparison of Cuban Socioeconomic Development." *Cuba in Transition—Volume 5.* Washington: Association for the Study of the Cuban Economy, 1995.

Romeu, J. L. "A Project for Faculty Development in a Transitional Cuba." *Cuba in Transition—Volume 8.* Washington: Association for the Study of the Cuban Economy, 1998.

Romeu, J. L. "Un Proyecto para la Formación de Profesionales Internacionales Para Una Cuba en Transicion." *Cuba in Transition—Volume 9.* Washington: Associaition for the Study of the Cuban Economy, 1999.

APPENDIX 1
Instituciones Aceptadas Como Auspiciadoras de la Academia de Ciencias de Cuba

1. Universidad de la Habana
2. Centro de Ingeniería Genética y Biotecnología
3. Instituto de Medicina Tropical "Pedro Kourí"
4. Instituto de Investigaciones del Transporte
5. Instituto de Historia de Cuba
6. Instituto de Investigaciones Hortícolas "Liliana Dimitrova"
7. Instituto Nacional de Angiología y Cirugía Vascular
8. Instituto de Hematología E Inmunología
9. Instituto de Ecología y Sistemática
10. Instituto Superior Politécnico "José A. Echevarría"
11. Instituto Nacional de Oncología y Radiobiología
12. Centro de Investigaciones Pesqueras
13. Centro de Investigaciones de la Economía Mundial
14. Instituto Nacional de Higiene, Epidemiología y Microbiología
15. Centro Internacional de Restauración Neurológica
16. Instituto de Investigaciones de Cítricos
17. Instituto de Investigaciones para la Industria Alimenticia
18. Instituto Cubano de Investigaciones de los Derivados de la Caña de Azúcar
19. Centro de Investigaciones del Petróleo
20. Centro de Estudios de Historia de la Ciencia y la Tecnología
21. Estación Experimental de Pastos "Indio Hatuey"
22. Centro de Investigaciones Psicológicas y Sociológicas
23. Centro Nacional de Sanidad Agropecuaria
24. Instituto de Geografía Tropical
25. Hospital Psiquiátrico de la Habana
26. Instituto de Investigaciones del Arroz
27. Universidad de Matanzas
28. Instituto Superior de Ciencias Agropecuarias de la Habana
29. Centro Nacional de Investigaciones Científicas
30. Centro de Inmunología Molecular
31. Instituto de Matemática Cibernética y Física
32. Instituto de Meteorología
33. Instituto de Investigaciones Fundamentales en Agricultura Tropical
34. Universidad de Pinar Del Río
35. Instituto de Geología y Paleontología
36. Instituto Cubano de Investigaciones Azucareras
37. Instituto de Investigaciones de Metrología
38. Instituto de Investigaciones Avícolas
39. Instituto de Investigaciones Forestales
40. Instituto Central de Ciencias Pedagógicas
41. Centro de Desarrollo de Equipos E Instrumentos Científicos
42. Instituto de Investigaciones Porcinas
43. Centro de Antropología
44. Instituto Central de Investigación Digital
45. Centro de Investigaciones Metalúrgicas
46. Instituto de Filosofía
47. Hospital "Frank País"
48. Instituto de Neurología y Neurocirugía
49. U.i.p. de la Celulosa Del Bagazo "Cuba 9"
50. Instituto de Literatura y Lingüística
51. Centro de Investigaciones para la Industria Minero-metalúrgica
52. Instituto de Investigaciones Económicas
53. Instituto Nacional de Endocrinología
54. Instituto de Materiales y Reactivos de la Universidad de la Habana
55. Instituto de Investigaciones en Viandas Tropicales

56. Instituto Nacional de Investigaciones de la Caña de Azúcar
57. Instituto Nacional de Ciencia Agrícola
58. Instituto de Investigaciones de Sanidad Vegetal
59. Instituto de Geofísica y Astronomía
60. Universidad de Oriente
61. Universidad Central de las Villas
62. Hospital Clínico-quirúrgico "Hermanos Ameijeiras"
63. Instituto de Cardiología y Cirugía Cardiovascular
64. Centro de Investigaciones Científicas de la Defensa Civil "Labori "
65. Sociedad Económica de Amigos Del País
66. Sociedad Cubana de Historia de la Ciencia y la Tecnología
67. Centro de Química Farmacéutica
68. Instituto de Ciencia Animal
69. Centro Técnico para el Desarrollo de los Materiales de Construcción
70. Centro de Investigaciones Marinas de la Universidad de la Habana
71. Centro de Estudios Demográficos de la Universidad de la Habana
72. Centro de Bioplantas de la Universidad de Ciego de Ávila
73. Instituto Superior Pedagógico "Juan Marinello"
74. Centro de Investigación para el Mejoramiento Animal (Cima)
75. Centro de Estudios Aplicados al Desarrollo Nuclear
76. Instituto "Finlay"
77. Instituto de Suelos
78. Centro de Investigaciones en Microelectrónica del Ispjae
79. Instituto Superior Pedagógico "Capitán Silverio Blanco Núñez"
80. Instituto Superior Pedagógico "Frank País García"
81. Centro de Investigaciones Hidráulicas Del Ispjae
82. Jardín Botánico Nacional
83. Consejo Científico de las Fuerzas Armadas Revolucionarias
84. Instituto de Nefrología
85. Instituto Técnico Militar
86. Academia de las Fuerzas Armadas Revolucionarias
87. Sociedad Cubana de Química
88. Asociación de Pedagogos de Cuba
89. Sociedad Meteorológica de Cuba
90. Sociedad Cubana para la Promoción de las Fuentes Renovables de Energía
91. Sociedad Cubana de Geografía
92. Sociedad Espeleológica de Cuba
93. Archivo Nacional de Cuba
94. Consejo Asesor Provincial de Ciencia y Tecnica de Villa Clara
95. Consejo Asesor Provincial de Ciencia y Tecnica de Pinar del Rio
96. Centro de Investigación y Desarrollo de la Cultura Juan Marinello
97. Instituto de Nutrición E Higiene de los Alimentos
98. Instituto Superior de Ciencias y Tecnología Nucleares
99. Instituto Superior Pedagógico Félix Varela
100. Centro de Investigación y Desarrollo Técnico Del Ministerio Del Interior
101. Centro de Inmunoensayo
102. Centro de Investigaciones D'economía Internacional; Universidad Habana
103. Sociedad Cubana de Investigaciones Filosóficas
104. Sociedad Cubana de Botánica

APPENDIX 2
Publicly Held Offices of the American Statistical Association

- ASA Board of Directors
- Council of Sections Gov Board
- Council of Chapters Governing Board (COCGB)
- Biopharmaceutical Section
- Business and Economic Statistics Section
- Council of Sections
- Section on Bayesian Statistical Science
- Section on Government Statistics
- Section on Nonparametric Statistics
- Section on Physical and Engineering Sciences
- Section on Quality and Productivity
- Section on Risk Analysis
- Section on Statistical Computing
- Section on Statistical Consulting
- Section on Statistical Education
- Section on Statistical Graphics
- Section on Statistics and Marketing
- Section on Statistics and the Environment
- Section on Statistics in Epidemiology
- Section on Statistics in Sports
- Section on Survey Research Methods
- Section on Teaching of Statistics in Health Sciences
- Social Statistics Section
- Alabama Chapter (C057)
- Arizona Chapter (C061)
- (......all States.......)

- Utah Chapter (C038)
- Washington Statistical Society (C002)
- ASA NCTM Joint Comm on Curriculum in Stats and Probability
- ASA Task Force on Electronic Journals
- ASA-MAA Joint Comm on Undergraduate Statistics
- Advisory Committee on Continuing Education
- Advisory Committee on Quantitative Literacy
- Budget Committee of the Board of Directors
- Census Advisory Committee
- Committee of Representatives to Aaas
- Committee on ASA Archives and Historical Materials
- Committee on Applied Statisticians
- Committee on Award of Outstanding Statistical Application
- Committee on Career Development

- Committee on Electronic Communications
- Committee on Energy Statistics
- Committee on Gay and Lesbian Concerns in Statistics
- Committee on International Relations in Statistics
- Committee on Scientific Freedom and Human Rights
- Committee on Women in Statistics
- Current Index to Statistics Management Committee
- Management Review Committee of the Board of Directors
- Planning Committee of the Board of Directors
- Radiation and Health Steering Committee
- Scientific and Public Affairs Advisory Committee
- Technometrics Management Committee
- Web Editorial Board

CUBAN FLORA, ENDOPHYTIC AND OTHER, AS A POTENTIAL SOURCE OF BIOACTIVE COMPOUNDS: TWO TECHNICAL APPROACHES TO BIOACTIVE COMPOUND DISCOVERY

Larry S. Daley

This paper addresses technical approaches potentially useful to bioprospecting in Cuba. Previously we addressed the matter in a more general way, discussing the reasons why Cuba is a potentially rich source of bioactive materials of plant origin (Daley, 1997). Definitions of some terms used in the paper are given below in a box.

The approaches discussed here are intended only for a post-Castro Cuba. Thus it is hoped to avoid the personal and political dangers inherent with working with the present Cuban regime, the unworkable Marxist policies, the micro-management and bungling bureaucracies that have done so much to wreck the Cuban economy, and the doubtful ethical compromises that such a collaboration would entail.

The search for bioactive, especially medicinal, plants has occurred over many millennia. Many plants provide effective medicines (Klein, 1979). These medicines include quinine, digitalis, precursor compounds for birth control pills, Taxol® (Wani *et al.*, 1971; Stierle *et al.* 1993; Hoffman, *et al.*, 1998; Hoffman, 2000), and many others.

The historic importance of these bioactive substances should not be underestimated. Quinine for example was essential to the effectiveness of the Mambí armies of Cuban independence. On December 6, 1896, Mambí General Calixto García, writing from La Ensenada between the Cauto River and the city of Bayamo asks for "quinine, much quinine and small pox vaccine because the fever (malaria) and smallpox

are causing heavy losses among the Mambí" (free translation from Casasus, 1962, p. 210).

There is no doubt that many useful bioactive compounds are found in plants and that many of these remain to be discovered. The difficulty is finding bioactive compounds for specific uses among the vast numbers of species, and even vaster numbers of plant germplasm accessions. This is the process of discovery and this is what we address here.

This paper, less general than the previous presentation (Daley, 1997), will discuss in the Cuban context, two specific examples of approaches to bioactive compound discovery: (1) following leads from folk medicine in Cucurbitales using an enzymological approach; and (2) mass spectroscopic screening of crude extracts.

FOLLOWING LEADS FROM FOLK MEDICINE

One approach is to follow the folk medicine leads with rigorous scientific investigations. This is now a common approach and a good number of sources collate these folk remedies (e.g., Robineau, 1991; Schultes and Raffauf, 1990).

Hermano (Brother) León (1974, pp. 154-155) describes a plant loved in my childhood, called in the vernacular as **cundeamor**. Its scientific name is *Momordica charantia* L. And it grows on a delicate vine with five or more lobed leaves on chicken wire fences and the like through out the tropics, including Cuba.

Box 1.   Definitions

Bioactive compounds are those biochemicals found in living things which induce or otherwise produce biological activities in the same and/or different organisms.

Endophytic flora are those organisms that live in plants. These are often fungi or bacteria that cause no harm to their plant host and frequently produce bioactive materials of use to the host.

Bioprospecting is the search for new bioactive materials or new sources of known materials.

Plant germplasm accessions. Plants, even of the same species, are not identical. Individual plants within a species have small but significant differences. This is made apparent considering cultivated plants such as different kinds (cloned varieties) of apples, mangoes etc. These differences extend to less readily apparent traits such as disease resistance. For instance only some banana accessions (here clones) are susceptible to Panama disease (*Fusarium oxysporium* Schl. F. sp. *cubense*). This is the reason why Cuba could not readily produce the once predominant commercial banana variety "Gros Michel"; thus Cuba was never a "Banana Republic." Now this disease is limited to only a few banana accessions (here clones) and outside the genus to a few species (Holliday, 1980 pp. 170-173). And this is also why the rumors of crop danger from a putative coca pathogen are essentially without foundation.

In times gone by we as children ate the little yellow orange three ridged fruit as we passed by in the hot, dusty, afternoons of Oriente province. The good monk Hermano León describes its properties thus:

> Los frutos de esta especie y la siguiente (*M. balsamina* L.) son comestibles, cocidos o curados; la pulpa es dulce y comida por los niños y algunas aves. Las hojas y los frutos se usan como aperitivo, **vermicida** (my emphasis), y emenagogo; el cocimiento de las hojas se usa contra enfermedades del hígado, la colitis, y los cálculos renales.

The cundeamor belongs to the order Cucurbitales, and the family Cucurbitaceae. This is very interesting, since some time ago my laboratory was involved in a project seeking insecticidal, fungicidal, and bactericidal proteins that are harmless to man. We were concentrating research on a group of proteins called thionins (Daley and Theriot. 1987; Daley, Daley and Theriot, 1983).

Thionins are a group of fungicidal, insecticidal and bactericidal proteins (e.g., Daley *et al.*, 1983; Daley and Theriot, 1987; Bohlman and Apel, 1991; Reuber T. L., *et al.*, 1998; Oh Boung-Jun *et al.*, 1999). Thionin are small proteins (4-5 kilo-Daltons), and thus coded for by shorter DNA sequences (e.g., Schrader and Apel, 1991; Stefania, O., *et al.*, 1997).

Thionins from different plants have different activities against different pests and pathogens, as a consequence of different amino acid sequences and thus are made in each plant species from different DNA sequences. It would seem that every plant species has one or more unique thionins, e.g., wheat which has three distinct ancestors has three distinct thionins. This is an advantage that makes thionins useful for bioengineering.

Different thionins have different levels of activity (Daley and Theriot, 1987). 'Mild mannered' thionins like those found in corn (maize) do not seem to attack anything. Aggressive thionins like viscotoxins may have been used by cavemen as arrow poisons to kill megafauna (Daley *et al.*, 1983).

Thionins are useful for bioengineering plant resistance to pests and pathogens: (a) because since thionins are proteins (Bohlman and Apel, 1991), they can be readily coded into DNA of other organisms (e.g., Broglie *et al.* 1991; Reuber T. L., *et al.* 1998). This is more difficult to do with bioactive compounds that are not proteins. And (b) because thionins attack a wide range of pests and pathogens.

Although thionins, including phoratoxin and viscotoxins, can be toxic to insects, bacteria and fungi, many are found in foods we eat such as bread (Bohlman and Apel, 1991). Barley thionin has already been put into tobacco, adding thionin codes to the DNA of this plant, where it inhibits *Pseudomonas syringae* (Carmona *et al*, 1993).

There is great interest in such proteins that kill or inhibit pathogens that cause plant disease, because proteins can be bioengineered in ways that can protect crops without spraying. Thus thionins can be fungicides, which kill late blight (*Phytophthora infestans*) on potato leaf tissue more effectively than the chemical fungicide Ridomil (Wilson, 1953; Molina *et al.*, 1993) (See Table 1).

Table 1. *In vivo* **activity of thionins against** *Phytophthora infestans*

Compound	% inhibition (at 0.04 mM active ingredient)
Wheat alpha-1-thionin	64%
Wheat alpha-2-thionin	60%
Barley alpha-thionin	100%
Barley beta-thionin	100%
Ridomil	86% (or less)

Source: Adapted from Molina, *et al.*, 1993.

The motivation for such research is that now it is practical to move proteins from one plant to another to help improve crop value and crop defense. Thionins are ideal for this purpose and frequently used because their small size facilitates incorporation into the genome of other plants. Regulatory problems are minimized because thionins are already found in such foods as wheat and barley flour (e.g., Astwood *et al.*, 2000). Thionins found in food don't harm us because they are proteins and we digest them.

An effective pest or disease fighting protein moved into and activated in a crop plant can be very useful because the farmer does not have to spray it. The active material is already there, it stays there even if it rains, or even if the fields are too muddy to get the sprayer in. It is there before the insect or the disease reaches the plant. Thus pests and pathogens do not spread readily.

We found that there are thionins that when fed (insects have very different digestive processes than hu-

mans) can inhibit growth of coleoptera insects (Jeknic and Daley, unpublished). Thus these thionins could be put to such uses as incorporation into cherry rootstocks to inhibit soil invertebrates such as root weevils (Daley, 1994-1995). Since many tree crops have separate and genetically distinct rootstock, it might well be possible to put even the very toxic viscotoxin into rootstocks resistant to root weevil, and where one would not expect that the toxin would reach the upper, crop bearing, part of the tree.

Some time ago we found that a thionin (phoratoxin) from American mistletoe was the best to stop beetle larvae from growing. In Europe, a colleague (Zoran Jeknic) once told me, the seeds of Cucurbitaceae are also used to treat intestinal worms. Following this lead, the next year we found a more effective thionin-like protein from a common cucubit (Jeknic *et al.*, unpublished).

Bioengineering, is not Star Trek stuff. It is real. There are already a number of DNA-transformed plant products on the market and more are coming. These products include, among others:

- Flavr Savr tomatoes

- herbicide resistant cotton

- herbicide resistant turf

- insect resistant BT cotton

- virus resistant melons, tobacco, potato, papayas, etc.

- petunia color maize gene pelargonanin

- fungal resistant tobacco, potato

- senescence resistant carnation, chrysanthemum.

The Cuban Connection for Thionins

Now that practical things can be done with thionins from diverse plants, especially food plants, we can seek them in Cuba. As mentioned above cundeamor (*Momordica charantia* and *M. balsamina*) are introduced species in Cuba and thus its germplasm, would be expected to vary less (Sánchez *et al.*, 1988). Consequently one would expect to find very little variation in cundeamor thionins in Cuba.

However, a good number of unique native Cucurbitaceae of a number of genera are found throughout Cuba (Alain, 1962; Bromide, 1991). These grow widely and since they are exposed year round to Cuba's numerous insects, selection pressure for insecticidal thionins can be expected to have achieved results. These plants often grow on abandoned ground, manigua and sao and thus present conditions of agricultural abandonment in Cuba would be expected to favor the spread of these species.

MASS SPECTROSCOPIC SCREENING OF CRUDE EXTRACTS

Paclitaxel (active ingredient in Taxol®, Bristol Myers Squibb) was once thought found only in yews. However, in our research in Oregon, we found Taxol in hazelnut trees (hazel, *Corylus avellana*) (Hoffman, *et al.*, 1998; Hoffman 2000). Paclitaxel, one of several Texans commonly found in yew (especially Pacific yew *Taxus brevifolia*, Wani *et al.*, 1971), is approved to treat ovarian cancers, breast cancers, Copses sarcoma and non-small-cell lung cancer. It is also in clinical trial for treatment of several other cancers (Hoffman, 2000).

Complete laboratory synthesis of Paclitaxel is too complex for commercial use. Commercial Taxol is made by derivitizing related compounds from related yews. The presence of such a compound in so distant a genera as (*Corylus*), which as an Angiosperm is as far from the yew (a Gymnosperm) as perhaps we humans are distant from turtles, suggests that Taxol may be found in many more species than is already known at present.

Not only that but Taxol is also found made by the endophytic flora of within the hazel as well as the tree itself (Hoffman, 2000). This places the evolutionary distance between sources of Taxol as far or further than between humans and bacteria. Yet, this is not an unknown situation as the plant "hormone" gibberellin has the same wide distribution between plants and fungi.

What this means is that it is logical to find Taxol in widely unrelated plants and endophytic flora. The function of Taxol in plants it not known; however despite the fact that it is also made by fungi, Taxol has some anti-fungal properties (e.g., Hoffman, 2000). Both the yew and the hazel are humid area trees. These theoretical considerations suggest that high levels of Taxol will be found in plants from humid areas. Thus, searches for Taxol producing plants and endophytes should logically start in humid areas of high plant diversity and unique flora. Cuban flora is quite unique (e.g., Daley, 1997) and much of Cuba is humid (see following map taken from Borhidi, 1991). And the phytopathology of the Antilles (Cook, 1939) bears witness to the abundant fungal flora of the area.

One advantage of hazel for this use is that such a tree, unlike the yew, is fast growing and not endangered, and its direct product is Taxol. The tropical equiva-

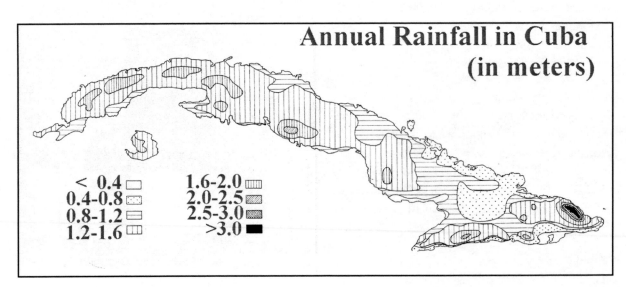

Annual Rainfall in Cuba (in meters)

< 0.4   1.6-2.0
0.4-0.8 2.0-2.5
0.8-1.2 2.5-3.0
1.2-1.6 >3.0

lent of the hazel for this use would be expected to have the same advantages; since growing crops for secondary metabolites is much less expensive and allows greater production than in vitro techniques.

However, to date hazel Taxol yields are about 1/10 that of yew. Any tropical tree that exceeds this initial yield would be expected to be useful now as the Taxol patent expires and this $1 billion-grossing product is expected to "go generic."

An additional factor that favors a new source of Taxol, despite preliminary low yield data, is that traditionally new crop yields increase as data from studies designed to increase the yield come in. Increasing yield is usually done by breeding and cultivation techniques; as in Oregon mint and hop crops, and, in pre-Castro Cuba, sugar.

Theories to increase secondary metabolites vary. In our experience Gingko metabolite production increases as fertilizers promote fast growth. However, other metabolites increase in response to stress. An expert, Gary Strobel (personal communication, 2000) suggests that damp conditions, which favor fungal diseases, may enhance Taxol, a known antifungal bioagent, production to fight fungi. Experiments on this matter are underway in my laboratory.

Cuba Connection

Thus it is conceivable, were an appropriate species found, that a tree crop of Taxol in Cuba could bring in income in excess of historic maximal sugar profits. However, a small useful crop would seem more likely.

EXPERIMENTAL

In the incredible progress of the United States, the saying that "G-d is in the details," is of paramount importance. Such things as the curved handle of the U.S. designed axe, which is said to increase the tree felling efficiency as much as two or more fold, compared to the European straight handled axe, made possible the rapid expansion to the West. In the Cuban context, prior to the present government, much of the island's wildly successful agriculture depended on tiny details of wisely directed effort, such as wider spacing plantings in the cane fields which allowed ratooning (multiple successive yearly harvests from a

single planting). Failure to attend to, and wisely apply, such technical details is a hallmark of the failure of present-day Cuban agriculture.

Attention to details is also true in bioprospecting, where economy of effort to achieve results is essential. And thus methods are also of paramount importance. What follows in this "experimental" section is my contribution to this matter. However, it is wise to keep in mind that these methods found here are starting points, not completed technologies and that their application will vary widely with the particular use.

Thionins Preparation

One cannot buy thionins; one must prepare them oneself. However, standard biochemical purification methods for thionins, such as chromatography, yield limited amounts of thionins; this limits the amount of materials available for activity testing.

To get around this problem we found a better way to prepare thionins. We stopped working with the usual-size scientific equipment and went to industrial sized equipment. For instance, we got a pickup load of mistletoe and, using ultrafiltration filters with about 200 times the through-put of our old lab equipment, we proceeded to prepare gram amounts of phoratoxin.

We extract thionins in large batches using the traditional dilute sulfuric acid/solvent method (Bohlman and Apel, 1991), then purify and concentrate with our new ultrafiltration method. To determine purity we use a new electrophoretic method (Zoran Jeknic, unpublished) since these small molecular weight (about 5,000 Daltons, that is 5 kilo-Daltons) proteins are lipophilic (fat loving) and positively charged and thus do not commonly appear on most electrophoretic gels (Daley and Theriot, 1987)

Taxol Determination by HPLC

Ground plant material is shaken with methanol, solvent removed under reduced pressure and more water added. The aqueous mixture is extracted with hexane (discarded). The more non-polar components remaining will be removed by solid phase extraction on C-18 Sep-Pak cartridges (Millipore). Components rinsed from the cartridges with methanol are separated by HPLC (reverse-phase column Curosil B, Phenomenex, Hoffman *et al.*, 1998). Mass spectroscopy (same reference) is used to verify HPLC peaks.

Taxol Determination from Crude Extracts by Mass Spectroscopy

We came upon this method, and found Taxol in hazel (Hoffman *et. al.,* 1998, and unpublished), by accident while we were screening hazel accessions (different clones) for biochemical indicators of Eastern Filbert Blight, a disease of that nut-crop tree.

Our approach was quite simple: we cut twigs (about 100 g) from each of the accessions tested, placed them in a mason jar in methanol (total volume approximately 0.97 L), and left the sealed jars for two months. Then the jars were opened, the twigs removed, the methanol solution filtered; adding three

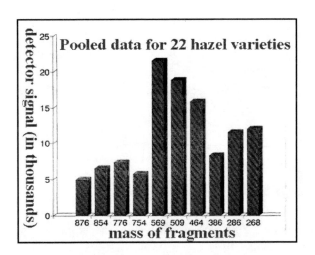

washes of methanol the pooled methanol was allowed to evaporate. Water (250 ml) was added to residue. Conductivity and pH of solution was measured with hand held devices. Twenty grams of mixed bed resin (HN high capacity Barnstead/Thermolyne, D8901 taken from cartridge) were added to mixture and conductivity and pH re-measured. The pH and the conductivity dropped somewhat, the former from a pH of 3.8 or less to approximately 3.5-2.7, and the conductivity from 6-15 mhos to 4-5 mhos. This aqueous solution was lyophilized (freeze-dried at low temperature). Yield was about 0.5 to 2 g, depending on variety and sample.

The Mass Spectrometer used was a Kratos MS 50 T-C (Manchester, England). For these experiments we used a gentle mass spectroscopic method, generally called fast particle bombardment (FAB) when used to examine neutral molecules or less commonly secondary ion mass spectrometry (SIME) when used with charged particles. The bombardment was done with a cesium ion "gun" and the negative ions examined. Samples (0.5 g) were dissolved in 1.5 ml of 2:1 methanol:dimethylformamide. The instrument was set at negative mode, mass/charge range 2100 to 120 at 30 sec per decade. Mass resolution was 2000 (at 2000 mass charge ratio can distinguish between ions differing by one mass charge unit). The metric used was thioglycerol/glycerol 2:1.

The figure is a summary identifying mass peaks for one year's data for 22 hazel varieties.

REFERENCES

Alain, Hermano (Brother, Frère) (Dr. E. E. Liogier). 1962. Flora de Cuba. Tomo V. Editorial Universitaria, Universidad de Puerto Rico, Rio Piedras.

Astwood J., Tran Kairong. Liang Jihong, R. Goodman, H. Sampson. 2000. Digestibility and allergenicity of gamma-thionin from wheat flour. Journal of Allergy & Clinical Immunology. 105(1 part 2). Jan., 2000.

Bohlman, H. and K. Apel. 1991. Thionins. Annu. Rev. Plant Physiol. Plant Mol. Biol. 42:227-240.

Borhidi, A(ttila). 1991. Phytogeography and Vegetation Ecology of Cuba. Akademiai Kiado, Budapest (English translation).

Broglie, K. *et al.* 1991. Transgenic plants with enhanced resistance to the fungal pathogen *Rhizoctonia solani*. Science 254:1194-1197.

Carmona, M. J., A. Molina, J. A. Fernández, J. J. López-Fando and F. García-Olmedo. 1993. Expression of the alpha-thionin gene from barley in tobacco confers enhanced resistance to bacterial pathogens. Plant J. 3:457-462.

Casasus, J. J. E. 1962. Calixto García (El Estratega) Second Edition corrected and considerably amplified, published by the Office of the Historian of Havana.

Cook M. T. 1939. Enfermedades de las plantas económicas de las Antillas. Monografía de la Universidad de Puerto Rico Serie B. Ciencias Físicas y Biológicas Número 4.

Daley, L. 1997. Bioprospecting in a post-Castro Cuba. Cuba in Transition—Volume 7: 382-394.

Daley, L. 1994-1995. Test thionin kill on Sweet Cherry strains of *Pseudomonas syringae* Project Report to (Oregon State University) Agricultural Research Foundation.

Daley, L. S. and L. J. Theriot. 1987. Proteins-similar to purothionin from tomato (*Lycopersicum esculenta*), mango (*Mangifera indica*), papaya (*Carica papaya*) and walnut (*Juglans regia*). Purification, protein redox activity, and effect upon proteolytic activity. J. Agric. Food Chem. 35: 680-687.

Daley, L. S., N. S. Daley, and L. J. Theriot. 1983. Did mistletoe kill Balder or was it the chemistry of viscotoxins? Review of chemical properties and evaluation of probability. Hexagon 74: 87-90.

Hoffman, Angela. 2000. Poster at American Chemical Society Meeting, San Francisco, April 2000.

Hoffman, A., W. Khan, J. Worapong, G. Strobel, D. Griffin, B. Arbogast, D. Barofsky, R. B. Boone, L. Ning, P. Zheng, L. Daley. 1998. Bioprospecting for Taxol in angiosperm plant extracts: Using high performance liquid chromatography-thermospray mass spectrometry to detect the anti-cancer agent and its related metabolites in filbert trees. Spectroscopy 13:22-32.

Holliday, P. 1980. Fungus diseases of tropical crops. Dover Publications, New York pp. 170-173.

León, Hermano. 1974. Flora de Cuba. Lubrecht Cramer, 2317 pp.

Frere Marie-Victorin, Frere Leon. Itineraries Botaniques Dans L'ile De Cuba. 2 volumes. 1942-1944

McClure, T. D., K. H. Schram and M. L. J. Reimer. 1992. The mass spectroscopy of Taxol. Amer. Soc. Mass Spectroscopy 3: 672-679.

Molina, A., P. A. Goy, A. Fraile, R. Sánchez-Monge, F. García-Olmedo. 1993. Inhibition of bacterial and fungal plant pathogens by thionins of types I and II. Plant Science 92:169-177.

Oh Boung-Jun, Ko Moon Kyung, I. Kostenyuk, Shin Byongchul, and Kim Kwang Sang. 1999. Co-expression of a defensin gene and a thionin-like gene via different signal transduction pathways in pepper and *Colletotrichum gloeosporioides* interactions. Plant Molecular Biology. 41(3) 313-319

Reuber T L., Plotnikova J. M., Dewdney J., Rogers E. E., Wood W., Ausubel F. M. 1998. Correlation of defense gene induction defects with powdery mildew susceptibility in *Arabidopsis* enhanced disease susceptibility mutants. Plant Journal. 16(4) 473-485.

Robineau, L. 1990 (ed.) Towards a Caribbean Pharmacopoeia. Endo Caribe UNAH, Santo Domingo.

Sánchez, E. E., R. A. Menéndez, L. S. Daley, R. B. Boone, O. L. Jahn and P. B. Lombard. 1988. Characterization of quince (*Cydonia*) cultivars using gradient polyacrylamide gel electrophoresis. J. Environ. Hort. 6: 53-59.

Schultes, R. E. and R. F. Raffauf. 1990. The healing forest. Medicinal and toxic plants of the Northwest Amazonia. Dioscorides Press, Portland Oregon.

Schrader G. and Apel K. 1991. Isolation and characterization of complementary DNAs Encoding viscotoxins of mistletoe *Viscum album*. European Journal of Biochemistry 198 (3). pp. 549-554.

Stefania, O., S. Andrea, G. Matteo, U. Konrad, P. Piero. 1997. Amino acid sequence, S-S bridge arrangement and distribution in plant tissues of thionins from *Viscum album*. Biological Chemistry. 378(9). 1997. 989-996.

Stierle, A, G. Strobeland, D. Stierle. 1993. Taxol and taxane production by *Taxomyces andreanae*, and endophytic fungus of pacific yew. Science 260: 214-216.

Wani, M. C., W. H. Taylor, M. E. Wall, P. Coggon, A. T McPhail. 1971. Plant anti-tumor agents. VI. The isolation and structure of Taxol, A novel anti-leukemic and anti-tumor agent from *Taxus brevifolia*. J. Am. Chem. Soc. 93:2325-2327.

Wilson, E. E. 1953. In Plant Disease the Yearbook of Agriculture. United States Dept. Agric., Washington D.C. pp. 722-729.

A CONSTITUTIONAL FRAMEWORK FOR A FREE CUBA

Alfred G. Cuzán[1]

This essay proposes a framework of a mixed constitution for a free Cuba. By "free" I mean a republican, i.e., representative regime where the government is the product of competitive elections and the population enjoys judicially safeguarded political and civil rights.[2] By "mixed" I mean one that, in keeping with Aristotle's advice, incorporates several competing political principles or values in one coherent arrangement.[3] Finally, by "constitution," I do not mean simply a document, which can swiftly decay into dead letter. Rather, I have in mind what Sartori calls the "living" or "material" constitution, i.e., the "the actual configuration of the system."[4] It is a structure or pattern of political power that is aimed at here, one

that, however, is expected to emerge from a set of enforceable rules specified in the constitutional text.

Two theoretical assumptions underlie this essay. One is that political institutions matter.[5] That is, the constitutional allocation of authority across offices of the state and the rules for electing or appointing public officials and limiting and staggering terms of office structure political incentives and constraints in a predictable manner. Different arrangements make a qualitative difference on how well democracy works.[6] The other is that, particularly at founding moments in a nation's history,[7] people can purposefully design their own institutions, that they are not "forever destined to depend for their political constitutions on accident and force," but are "really capable" "of es-

---

1. A number of scholars read the first draft of the paper and gave me the benefit of their comments and encouragement, or their criticism. Although nearly all of them disagree strongly with at least one element in this framework, they deserve my thanks, even as they are exempt from responsibility for any errors of fact or insufficient political sagacity on my part. They are: Charles W. Anderson, Juan del Aguila, Mark P. Jones, Arend Lijphart, Juan L. López, Carlos Alberto Montaner, David Myers, Mario Rivera, James A. Robinson, and Mauricio Solaún.

2. See Freedom House, *Freedom in the World, The Annual Survey of Political Rights & Civil Liberties, 1997-1998,* New Brunswick: Transaction Publishers, 1998.

3. Aristotle, *The Politics,* Cambridge: Cambridge University Press, 1988, 94-95. Edmund Burke was another champion of a mixed constitution, one, however, that grows organically, so as "to unite into a consistent whole the various anomalies and contending principles that are found in the minds and affairs of men." See his *Reflections on the Revolution in France,* New York: Viking Penguin, 1969, 281.

4. Giovanni Sartori, *Comparative Constitutional Engineering. An Inquiry into Structures, Incentives and Outcomes,* New York University Press, 1994, 202.

5. The contrary assumption, that "constitutions do not matter, that free societies result from societal pluralism far more than from constitutional contrivance" is dismissed as "the behavioral absurdity" by Sartori, *Comparative Constitutional Engineering,* 200.

6. See, in particular, Arend Lijphart, *Patterns of Democracy. Government Forms and Performance in Thirty-Six Countries,* Yale University Press, 1999; Matthew Soberg Shugart and John M. Carey, *Presidents and Assemblies. Constitutional Design and Electoral Dynamics,* Cambridge University Press, 1992.

7. On the significance of founding moments, see Seymour Martin Lipset, *Continental Divide. The Values and Institutions of the United States and Canada,* New York: Routledge, 1990.

tablishing good government from reflection and choice."[8]

This is not to deny Alexis de Tocqueville's conclusion that culture is more important than the laws in making democracy work. Assessing that "American legislation, taken as a whole, is extremely well adapted to the genius of the people and the nature of the country which it is intended to govern," de Tocqueville went on to note that "American laws are therefore good, and to them must be attributed a large portion of the success that attends the government of democracy in America; but I do not believe them to be the principal cause of that success[;] . . . their effect is inferior to that produced by the customs of the people."[9] However, that at any given moment laws place second, after customs, in determining the success of democracy is no reason to give them short shrift. In planning for a free Cuba, one should aim at the very best set of institutions suggested by contemporary political research so as to make the most of that "large portion" of democratic success which is attributable to them. Moreover, one should not assume that political culture is frozen. It itself is subject to gradual modification by institutions. As Lijphart observes, the Swiss did not always have a consensual political culture, having been embroiled in several civil wars. Although it takes time for institutions envisioned in a constitution or laws to take root in and modify the political culture,[10] and although they usually take a life of their own, evolving in ways not entirely anticipated by those who begot them, it is supposed that, like the characteristics of domesticated animals and plants, the way a country conducts its political life is subject to human manipulation.[11]

In crafting a constitution, then, one would be well advised to consider recent empirical findings of the "neo-institutionalist" school of political science, particularly the work of Lijphart on two types of democ-

racy and Shugart and Carey on presidentialism. Lijphart compares the operation and performance of what he calls majoritarian and consensual democracies in thirty-six countries. The former concentrate political authority at the national level, where it is exercised by a prime minister whose party's legislative majority in a single or dominant lower house of parliament is disproportionate to its actual share of the popular vote. This is most likely to occur when legislators are elected from single-member districts according to a first-past-the-post rule, under which the candidate with the most votes, even a simple plurality, wins. In majoritarian democracy, the judiciary, as well as other institutions such as the central bank, play a subordinate role to the legislature, which can amend and interpret the constitution more or less at will, limited only by tradition, public opinion, and its own self-restraint. In turn, parliament is dominated by the prime minister and his cabinet, who are leaders of the majority party. Other parties are relegated to playing the role of opposition. The United Kingdom is the model of majoritarian democracy.[12]

By contrast, in consensual democracy authority is separated horizontally across branches of government and divided vertically between national and sub-national levels according to a relatively rigid (i.e., difficult to amend) written constitution, under which ordinary laws are subject to judicial review, as in the United States. Vertically, sub-national units enjoy a great deal of legislative and fiscal autonomy either in a federal or a decentralized unitary regime. Horizontally, a legislature that is independent or not dominated by the executive is divided between two chambers relatively equal in authority, each elected by different rules and for different lengths of term. Where the executive is a creature of parliament, it is normally composed of members of a coalition cabinet in which several parties are represented. This arrangement is usually the result of proportional repre-

---

8. Alexander Hamilton, "Number I," in Isaac Kramnick, (Ed.), *The Federalist Papers*, New York: Penguin Putnam Inc., 1987, p. 87.

9. Alexis de Tocqueville, *Democracy in America*, New York: Everyman's Library, 1972, 321.

10. Robert D. Putnam, *Making Democracy Work. Civic Traditions in Modern Italy*, Princeton: Princeton University Press, 1993, pp. 58-60.

11. A supposition as old as Plato's *Republic*, running through the works of Aristotle, Locke, Rousseau, Burke, de Tocqueville, and Mill, down to the "neo-institutionalists"of today.

12. For a positive assessment of this form, see Quentin L. Quade, "Democracies-To-Be: Getting it Right the First Time," *Freedom at Issue*, 1990, 113, 4-7.

sentation in legislative elections. Where the executive and the legislature are elected separately, as in the United States or France, it is not unusual for each to be controlled by a different party, a circumstance necessitating inter-party "cohabitation," as the French call it. This involves having to compromise on major issues and, in some cases, working out a *de facto* grand coalition spanning the two branches of government. Other institutions, like the judiciary and central bank, enjoy a great deal of autonomy from both the legislature and the executive. Switzerland is the prototype of a consensual regime.[13]

When comparing the two forms of democracy on a series of performance measures Lijphart found that, although tied on most indicators, where a difference between the two types was discernible with the usual statistical tools, it was invariably in favor of the consensual variety. Of particular importance was this regime's relative superiority at reducing political violence and representing the interests and values articulated by minority parties, a factor that contributes to legitimating the regime. Thus, Lijphart concludes that "the consensus option is the more attractive option for countries designing their first democratic constitutions or contemplating democratic reform." He recommends, therefore, that "[d]ivided power institutions—strong federalism, strong bicameralism, rigid amendment rules, judicial review, and independent central banks . . . be prescribed by means of constitutional stipulations and provisions in central bank charters."[14]

Lijphart recognizes that certain features of consensual democracy are not easily transplanted across regions.

(For example, in Latin America, where presidentialism has long been the norm, parliamentarism is unlikely to be adopted, or if adopted to survive.[15]) Also, he realizes that "consensus democracy may not be able to take root and thrive unless it is supported by a consensual political culture."[16] Yet, the latter obstacle is not insurmountable because the relation between culture and institutions is reciprocal: "although a consensual culture may lead to the adoption of consensus institutions, these institutions also have the potential of making an initially adversarial culture less adversarial and more consensual."[17]

For their part, casting a skeptical glance at the academic consensus against presidentialism forged, *inter alia*, by Linz and Stepan,[18] Shugart and Carey find that the survival of this type of democracy depends on the actual distribution of authority between congress and president, on the one hand, and the party system, on the other, which are a function of the constitution and electoral rules, respectively.[19] They argue that the performance of presidentialism varies according to the relative powers vested in president and congress, their respective controls over cabinet formation and survival, and the number and internal cohesion of parties represented in the legislature. Presidential systems which centralize authority in the executive are the most vulnerable to breakdown. Where the president is granted legislative powers such as a strong veto, exclusive prerogative to submit bills over certain policy areas, strategic initiative over the budget, and rule by decree, and where he has authority to go over the heads of congress by calling a popular referendum to enact his program into law, executive-legislative relations tend to deteriorate to

---

13. Lijphart, *Patterns of Democracy*, Chapters 2-3 and 14-17.

14. *Ibid.*, 302. Lijphart's analysis and recommendations, particularly electing the legislature by proportional representation and organizing coalition cabinets, has not gone unchallenged. See the "debate" between him and his critics published in *Journal of Democracy*, 1991, 2 (3): Guy Lardeyret, "The Problem with PR," 30-35; Quentin L. Quade, "PR and Democratic Statecraft," 36-41; Arend Lijphart, "Double-Checking the Evidence," 42-48. See also Sartori, *Comparative Constitutional Engineering*, 70-74, 129.

15. Shugart and Carey point out that there has not been a single instance of a country exchanging a presidential system for a parliamentary one, although changes in the reverse direction have occurred. See *Presidents and Assemblies*, 3.

16. Lijphart, *Patterns of Democracy*, 306.

17. *Ibid.*, 307.

18. Juan Linz, "The Perils of Presidentialism," *Journal of Democracy*, 1990, 1 (1), 51-70; Alfred Stepan, "Constitutional Frameworks and Democratic Consolidation," *World Politics*, 1993, 46 (1), 1-22.

19. See, also, Scott Mainwaring and Matthew Soberg Shugart (Eds.), *Presidentialism and Democracy in Latin America*, Cambridge University Press, 1997, especially Chapters 1 and 11 and, by the same authors, "Juan Linz, Presidentialism, and Democracy," *Comparative Politics*, 1997, 29 (4): 449-472.

the point where the risks of regime breakdown become unacceptably high. By contrast, the longest-lived presidential democracies are those where the constitution contemplates a president whose role in the making of laws is marginal at best.[20] Costa Rica, the oldest continuous democracy in Latin America, is a case in point.

Another problematic type is what they call the "presidential-parliamentary" regime, one of shared authority over the cabinet, with the president being free to appoint and dismiss but the parliament able to censure and force the resignation of ministers. This form of government, plagued by "'confusion' over to whom the cabinet is responsible, is a recipe for dangerous cabinet instability. This is especially true where one branch alone names the cabinet to begin with."[21] In a confirmatory study of 14 Latin American countries over a ten year period, Jones, too, found that "the legislature's possession of the power to censure government's ministers results in an increased level of executive-legislative conflict."[22] As we shall see, this was a feature of the Cuban Constitution of 1940.

Another variable associated with the viability of presidentialism is the party system. A situation where the president faces a multi-party congress in which his own partisans constitute a distinct minority, with the opposition thwarting his every move, is all too likely to result in systemic "immobilism." Either the president becomes impotent or, to break the deadlock, resorts to extra- or unconstitutional measures.[23] Either

outcome imperils the survival of democracy. On the other hand, where the president's party, though a minority in the congress, controls anywhere from over a third to just under half of the seats, his bargaining position is much improved, and this is conducive to compromise across party lines.[24]

This last condition is facilitated if the number of effective parties in congress is less than four, an outcome associated with the rules for electing the president, as well as the electoral cycle.[25] Where the president is elected by a simple or qualified plurality[26] the number of effective parties represented in the legislature is smaller than if the leading candidate is required to win an absolute majority in the first round. Also, even if the congress is elected by proportional representation, when presidential and legislative elections are held concurrently the number of effective parties in the legislature is generally smaller than when they take place separately. Both outcomes are the result of the net centripetal effect which the presidential election has on that for congress. In light of these findings, Shugart and Carey suggest that the president be elected by less than an absolute majority of the vote and that elections for both branches be held simultaneously, a recommendation in which Jones concurs.[27]

In the remainder of this essay, I draw on these two streams of research to design a framework for crafting a constitution for a free Cuba. My purpose is not to expound on all the elements that go into a constitution. Rather, I limit myself to sketching what, according to Sartori, should be its "core and center-

---

20. Shugart and Carey, *Presidents and Assemblies*, 154-161.

21. *Ibid.*, 130.

22. Mark P. Jones, *Electoral Laws and the Survival of Presidential Democracies*, Notre Dame: University of Notre Dame Press, 1995, 52.

23. Along these lines, see Scott Mainwaring, "Presidentialism, Multipartism, and Democracy. The Difficult Combination," *Comparative Political Studies*, 1993, 26 (2), 198-228. But see Timothy J. Power and Mark J. Gasiorowski, "Institutional Design and Democratic Consolidation in the Third World," *Comparative Political Studies*, 1997, 30 (2), 123-155. In a study of over 50 Third World transitions to democracy since the 1930s, they find no empirical support for the "difficult combination" hypothesis (or, for that matter, the "perils of presidentialism" thesis). However, their rules for selecting cases and for declaring democracy to be consolidated differ from those of most other studies.

24. For parallel findings in Latin American countries, see Jones, *Electoral Laws*, 50.

25. Jones believes that in presidential systems a two party system is "desirable." *Ibid.*, 10.

26. E.g., in Costa Rica the leading candidate need win only 40 percent of the vote to avoid a run-off.

27. Shugart and Carey also suggest that the parties be moderately disciplined, a condition facilitated by closed party lists. However, Jones found that closed party lists are associated with executive-legislative conflict. See, respectively, *Presidents and Assemblies*, 205 and *Electoral Laws*, 52.

piece," i.e., a "frame of government."[28] That means a plan for partitioning authority horizontally, across branches of the national government, and vertically, among levels of government, specifying qualifications for office, election or appointment rules, and length and staggering of terms for each office. Much of what follows is rather conventional, incorporating as it does variations of constitutional formulas of long usage, either in the United States or, as in the case of the supreme electoral tribunal, Costa Rica. However, I do offer a few innovations that, as far as I know, have not been tried elsewhere.

I begin with a brief discussion of the last democratic constitution of Cuba, that of 1940, paying particular attention to what I consider to have been its principal structural weaknesses. Next, I lay out my proposal. Then I analyze it in light of the literature discussed above, and compare and contrast its most salient features to those of the 1940 Constitution.

THE CONSTITUTION OF 1940

The Cuban Constitution of 1940, the product of an assembly elected for the purpose in which every political current, including that of the communists, participated, though short-lived, having been in effect a mere twelve years, soon attained mythic status among generations of Cubans.[29] Its legitimacy was such that, when Fulgencio Batista's 1952 *coup d'etat* rendered it de facto inoperable, "its restoration soon developed into the rallying cry of the opposition movement."[30] In 1955, having emerged triumphant in a single-candidate "election" arranged the previous year, even the dictator himself felt compelled to de-

clare that the constitution was again in effect. Following Batista's flight four years later, Fidel Castro initially pretended only to have had it amended, even though from the very beginning his regime was in clear violation of its most basic provisions, such as proscription of the death penalty, prohibition of expropriation of property except for matters of public utility or interest, and then only after judicially-adjudicated compensation, independent courts, elections for legislative and executive offices, and amendment procedures. Today, nearly half a century after its disemboweling by Batista and betrayal by Castro, there are those who argue not only that restoration of the 1940 Constitution should be the first order of business of a post-Castro provisional government but that, it never having been abrogated, the 1940 Constitution remains in effect (in some sort of legal limbo, I suppose).[31]

Institutionally, the 1940 Constitution attempted to do the very thing which Shugart and Carey believe one should avoid, i.e., construct a "presidential-parliamentary" republic.[32] It provided for separate but concurrent elections of a president and a bicameral congress, all to a four-year term, with half the lower house elected every two years. The president was free to appoint and dismiss members of his cabinet, but these, including a prime minister, were responsible to the congress. Either house could interpellate and censure ministers individually or the cabinet as a whole, upon which vote of no confidence they were required to resign. The president, however, was free to reappoint them to another portfolio.

28. Sartori, *Comparative Constitutional Engineering*, 198.

29. René Gómez Manzano, "Constitución y Cambio Democrático en Cuba," *Cuba in Transition—Volume 7*, 1997, 395-414; Néstor Carbonell Cortina, "La Constitución de 1940: Simbolismo y Vigencia," *Cuba in Transition—Volume 7*, 1997, 415-421.

30. Marifeli Pérez-Stable, *The Cuban Revolution. Origins, Course, and Legacy*, Second Edition, New York: Oxford University Press, 1999, 9.

31. José D. Acosta, "El Marco Jurídico-Institucional de un Gobierno Provisional de Unidad Nacional en Cuba," *Cuba in Transition—Volume 2*, 1992, 61-84.

32. I have relied on Spanish and English versions of the text of the 1940 Constitution. For the former, see Mariano Sánchez Roca, *Leyes Civiles de Cuba y su Jurisprudencia*, Vol. I, La Habana, Editorial Lex, 1951, 1-100 and, for the latter, Amos J. Peaslee, *Constitutions of Nations*, Volume I, Concord, NH: The Rumford Press, 1950, 526-594. For the motivations of the drafters, and how well the system actually worked in practice, see William S. Stokes, "The Cuban Parliamentary System in Action, 1940-1947," *The Journal of Politics*, 1949, 11 (2), 335-364; Hugh Thomas, *Cuba or The Pursuit of Freedom*, Updated Edition, New York: De Capo Press, 1998, 691-789; Charles D. Ameringer, *The Cuban Democratic Experience. The Auténtico Years, 1944-1952*, Gainesville: University Press of Florida, 2000.

As diagnosed by Shugart and Carey, this recipe was, indeed, problematic.[33] Too much scarce congressional energy (and it was scarce, absenteeism being rampant) was spent in a tug of war with the president over his ministers. On one occasion, the congress censured the Minister of Commerce, whereupon President Ramón Grau San Martín made manifest his contempt of the legislature by promoting him to head Foreign Relations, an action that left the opposition frustrated and bitter. A contemporary analyst noted that "dangerous friction between executive and legislative branches in the years 1945-1947 presage further deterioration in the chances of ultimate successful operation unless both branches cooperate earnestly to give meaning to the Constitution."[34] But the problem was not only that of a lack of good will on the part of political adversaries, which was undoubtedly in short supply, with demagogic scandal-mongering and irresponsible oppositionism the order of the day, but also structural, the consequence of a "confused" division of authority between the president and the congress over the cabinet.[35]

Two other structural problems in the 1940 Constitution are worth mentioning. One, shared with many others in Latin America, prohibited the immediate reelection of the president, but allowed him to run again after two terms had elapsed. One can expect such a rule to have two effects. One, in his first term the president will cause some political capital to be spent by adherents and detractors alike over a scheme to amend the constitution to allow him to run for reelection. Two, if this stratagem fails, following the

end of his term the former president will not abandon the spotlight completely, but from time to time will call attention to himself, hoping for a comeback. Nor he will let go the reins of his political party.[36]

This appears to have happened in the case of President Grau San Martín, elected in 1944. First, he intrigued to amend the constitution. That went nowhere, it having met with opposition even from within his own party, the Auténticos. So, after vacating the presidential palace he lost no time in criticizing his successor, Carlos Prío Socarrás, a former protégé, expressing regret at having "made" him president and characterizing him as an "unfaithful disciple."[37] That set the two men at loggerheads. For his part, Batista, who had won a senate seat in 1948, and was eligible for election to the presidency in 1952, entered the race. A May 1951 survey showed him trailing badly, with only 20 percent of respondents favoring his candidacy. Less than a year later the Auténticos still outnumbered Batista's party two to one among registered voters.[38] Three months before the election, Batista staged a coup.

If it is a mistake to prohibit presidential reelection—and I believe it is—the error is only compounded by allowing the president to try again after sitting out one or two terms. Better to limit the president to one sole term, as is done in Costa Rica, than having him waiting in the wings until he is eligible to run again. However, even this does not solve the problem because, during his one and only term, the president

---

33. This is not to deny that extra-constitutional factors played at least as important a role in the demise of Cuban democracy. The appeasement of political gangsters by both Grau and Prío was a particularly nefarious practice. See Ameringer, *The Cuban Democratic Experience.*

34. Stokes, "The Cuban Parliamentary System," 362.

35. Something pointedly denied by Carbonell, who concludes that "los fallos de nuestro sistema semiparlamentario . . . no fueron realmente orgánicos, sino funcionales—producto de viejas corruptelas y de hábitos presidencialistas arraigados. Esos fallos son superables, a mi juicio, con una buena dosis de democracia, experiencia, y probidad." Carbonell, "La Constitución de 1940," 421.

36. Recent examples of newly-elected presidents who made it a priority to change the constitution to allow their reelection are Menem in Argentina, Cardoso in Brazil, and Fujimori in Perú. For its part, Venezuela offers two examples of former presidents who, bent upon making a come-back, prevented their parties's renewal: APRA's Andrés Pérez and COPEI's Rafael Caldera. These two men bear at least some responsibility for the decline of their respective parties, an erosion which paved the way for the populist demagogue Hugo Chávez to sweep the political slate clean.

37. Ameringer, *The Cuban Democratic Experience,* 77-78.

38. *Ibid.,* 153, 162.

still has the incentive to scheme to change the constitution so that he can run for reelection.[39]

The last organic problem in the 1940 Constitution I will take up has to do with the organization of provinces. It provided for the election of a governor, but not of a provincial assembly. Rather, a provincial council, made up of all the mayors of the province, was to exercise the legislative power. It was given authority to draw up a budget, to be financed by assessing each member municipality a quota in proportion to its revenues. In this aspect, the provincial government resembled a confederal arrangement. Not having read any studies of their operations, I have no empirical knowledge how the provincial governments worked in practice. However, my guess is that they were plagued by collective action and free-rider problems that are the bane of confederations, i.e., indifference on the part of many of their members, great difficulty in getting them to agree to undertake projects of common interest, and many municipalities falling in arrears with their financial obligations.

That said, and without minimizing the seriousness of these organic flaws, the Cuban Constitution of 1940 amounted to an earnest attempt to decentralize authority in a manner that is consistent with consensual democracy. Specifically, it provided for a bi-cameral congress, judicial review, an electoral tribunal administered by the judiciary, a Tribunal de Cuentas (a national inspector of accounts charged with auditing the books of all government entities), and municipal autonomy. At a time when most of Latin America and Europe was under the thrall of one dictatorship or another or rent by political conflict, this was no mean feat. As Thomas puts it, "The new Constitution was one of the most serious political achievements of the Cubans, and it was achieved as a result of an unusual degree of cooperation between the different politicians."[40]

A PROPOSED CONSTITUTIONAL FRAMEWORK[41]

In this section, I present a constitutional framework for a free Cuba that builds on the good structural features of the Constitution of 1940 while fixing its organic defects. I begin with a set of working assumptions. First, that in Cuba, as elsewhere in Latin America, it would be futile to attempt to introduce a parliamentary system. The constitution will be presidential. Second, that the Cuban state will be unitary, not federal.[42] And third, that the new republican regime will restore the six historic provinces of Pinar del Río, La Habana, Matanzas, Las Villas, Ca-

39. True, now that it does not have to accommodate José Figueres (elected first in 1953 and then again in 1970), Costa Rica is free of that problem. But there the tradition of one-term presidents has taken such deep roots that presidents see no mileage in taking it on.

40. Thomas, *Cuba*, 720.

41. For earlier papers published by ASCE that address many of the issues dealt with here, see, in addition to those already cited, the following: Néstor E. Cruz, "Legal Issues Raised by the Transition: Cuba from Marxism to Democracy, 199?-200?," *Cuba in Transition—Volume 2*, 1992, 51-60; Jorge Salazar-Carrillo, "The Case for an Independent Central Bank," *Cuba in Transition—Volume 4*, 1994, 77-79; Matías F. Travieso-Díaz and Steven R. Escobar, "Overview of Required Changes in Cuba's Laws and Legal Institutions During its Transition to a Free-Market Democracy," *Cuba in Transition—Volume 4*, 1994, 262-291; Luis L. Ubierna and Juan J. Ondarza, "Proyecto Constitucional: República Federal de Cuba," *Cuba in Transition—Volume 4*, 1994, 330-349; Néstor E. Cruz, "Legal Policy for a Free Cuba: Lessons from the Civil Law," *Cuba in Transition—Volume 5*, 1995, 191-194; Rebeca Sánchez-Roig, "Cuban Constitutionalism and Rights: An Overview of the Constitutions of 1901 and 1940," *Cuba in Transition—Volume 6*, 1996, 390-397; Alberto Luzárraga, "El Tribunal Constitucional y su Organización: Una Propuesta de Reforma," *Cuba in Transition—Volume 7*, 1997, 422-426; Lorenzo L. Pérez, "Comentarios Sobre el Artículo XVII Sobre Hacienda Pública de la Constitución de 1940 de Cuba," *Cuba in Transition—Volume 7*, 1997, 427-429.

42. These two assumptions are contrary to those posited by Ubierna and Ondarza, who propose a constitution for a federal, parliamentary government evidently modeled after that of the German Federal Republic. See their "Proyecto Constitucional: República Federal de Cuba."

magüey, and Oriente.[43] This would be desirable for a number of reasons, not least that these units would be large enough, in area or population, to support strong regional governments that, collectively, would function as an effective counterpoise to the national level. A related advantage derived from their size is that, if the provinces were made coterminous with electoral districts, these would be of sufficient magnitude to reduce the probability of electoral disproportionality.[44]

In a unitary republic, it is meet to begin with the national government. Here authority is to be partitioned into overlapping branches, legislative, executive, and judicial. The legislative power, including the power to tax and spend, would be vested in a bicameral congress, composed of a lower house (cámara de representantes) and a senate. To be eligible for election, candidates for the lower house would be at least 25 years old, and for the senate 30. The cámara would consist of one member per 50,000 inhabitants, but in no case fewer than 199 representatives, elected for a three-year term according to a system of proportional representation requiring parties to cross a five percent threshold. The electoral units would be the provinces, with a number of representatives allocated to each in proportion to their total population. The senate would consist of 36 members, six from each province, elected at large, for a six-year term. The terms would be staggered so that every year one-sixth of the senators, one per province, would be up for reelection.[45] Should no candidate for the senate win 40 percent plus one of the vote, a run-off would be held between the two top vote-getters.

Legislation could originate in either the cámara or the senate, except for expenditure and revenue bills, which would have to be voted out of the lower house first. In both chambers, a majority of the membership would constitute a quorum. To be enacted into law, a bill would have to be approved by both houses. Differences between the two versions of the same bill would have to be ironed out in conference. A three-fifths vote in both chambers would override the president's veto. Additional congressional checks on executive power would be divided between the two houses as follows. All appointments (but not their dismissal) to the president's cabinet would need approval by the cámara, while appointments to the courts and autonomous agencies (more about these below), as well as ambassadorships, and promotion of military officers to the rank of general (and their equivalent in the air force, navy, other armed services, and national police), would require confirmation by the senate. Also, all treaties with foreign nations would need senate ratification by a three-fifths vote of those present.

The executive power would be vested in a president, elected in a nation-wide popular vote for a three-year term. To be eligible for election, a candidate would have to be at least 40 years old. The president would be eligible for reelection two more times, either sequentially or after a break, for a maximum tenure in office of nine years. Should no candidate receive a minimum 40 percent plus one of the vote, a run-off would be held between the two top vote-getters. The president would be charged with "faithfully executing the laws," act as commander in chief of the armed forces, be responsible for conducting foreign

---

43. An assumption not shared by Gómez Manzano. His list of all the "most obvious objections" to a restoration of the 1940 Constitution just as it was when buried by Batista begins with the following: "Contiene la enumeración de las antiguas seis provincias, lo cual—como es lógico—no se ajusta a la realidad cubana de hoy" ("Constitución y Cambio Democrático en Cuba," 409). But this begs the question on whose authority Fidel Castro dismembered and mangled the country, breaking up the six provinces into more than twice their number. In my judgment, just as in Russia one of the first things that was done after the demise of the Soviet Union was for old cities like St. Petersburg to recover their venerable names, so in Cuba one of the first orders of business after the Castro regime has finally expired is to restore the sexpartite division of the Island. Of course, the new constitution, like that of 1940, should include a provision for provincial subdivision, but something that is to be done not arbitrarily, as the Castro regime did, but with the consent of their elected representatives and that of congress.

44. Lijphart, *Patterns of Democracy*, p. 150.

45. Should the present subdivision be retained, the number of senators elected from each province would be reduced to three and their terms staggered so that one would come up for reelection every other year.

affairs with the advice and consent of the senate, and subject to senate confirmation, make appointments to his cabinet, ambassadorships, the courts, and the autonomous agencies, and grant promotions to military officers.

On the other hand, the president's legislative power would be limited to a moderate veto (congress could override with a three-fifths vote in both houses), which must be cast within ten working days of congress having sent him a bill. He would not have line-item veto authority: any bill would have to be vetoed in its entirety or not at all. Concerning "pocket" vetoes, this would be discouraged by the following rule: any bill sent to the president fewer than ten days before the congress adjourns, which he neither signs nor vetoes, becomes law if, within three months of the new session of congress, it passes both houses by simple majority vote. The president would be explicitly prohibited from issuing decrees except for the express purpose of implementing a law or judicial decision, regulating a statute as provided for by congress, or arranging the internal administration of the executive branch, narrowly conceived, and then again never contrary to law. In other words, "the authority of the executive to establish laws in lieu of action by the assembly"[46] would be nil.

As for the budget, the president would be required to submit a proposal nine months before the start of the new fiscal year, but it would be up to the congress to decide what, if any, of the president's plan to adopt in one or more revenue and expenditure bills. Neither would the congress have to wait for the presi-dent's budget to consider revenue and appropriations bills. This would reduce the executive's strategic advantage over fiscal policy, an advantage derivative from his having the budgetary initiative, as is the case in many countries,[47] including the 1940 Cuban Constitution.

The judicial power would be vested in the courts, to consist of ordinary tribunals,[48] capped by a supreme court, and one constitutional court. The supreme court would be the final court of appeals in law and equity in civil and criminal cases. Questions regarding the constitutionality of any law, decree, ordinance, or regulation issued by any level of government would fall under the jurisdiction of the constitutional court. Appointments to these two bodies would be made by the president, subject to senate confirmation. To be eligible, candidates would be required to have a law degree from any accredited university in the world and be at least 45 years of age. There would be a mandatory retirement age of 70. Both courts would consist of ten members, nine associate justices and a chief justice. Except for the chief justice, whose appointment would extend until retirement, the term of office would be nine years, renewable once. In both the supreme and constitutional court, the chief justice would chair meetings and would have voice but no vote except to break a tie. All judicial appointments would be staggered so that one-third of the membership would be up for reappointment every three years.[49]

A number of autonomous agencies would be charged with administering a range of public responsibilities.

---

46. John M. Carey and Matthew Soberg Shugart, *Executive Decree Authority*, Cambridge University Press, 1998, 9. They note that "The boundaries of executive discretion, if any, are established by the constitution." *Ibid.*, 14.

47. Shugart and Carey, *Presidents and Assemblies*, 139.

48. I leave open the qualifications, mode of appointment, and length of term of trial and appeals courts. Like other civil law systems, e.g., present-day France and Portugal, the 1940 Cuban Constitution provided for a sort of judicial civil service, admission to which was by competitive examinations. I am agnostic as to whether this system should be replicated in the new constitution.

49. These specifications are a composite drawn from several actual models. According to McWhinney, "By a sort of common consensus among constitutionalists, in various, widely differing legal systems, the norm seems to have emerged that a final tribunal should be composed of eight or nine members." Also, appointing judges to the highest magistracy of the nation not for life but for a fixed term, "with or without right of renewal of the term, seems more in tune with contemporary constitutionalism and constitutional trends in it." Edward McWhinney, *Supreme Courts and Judicial Law-Making: Constitutional Tribunals and Constitutional Review*, Dordrecht: Martinus Nijhoff Publishers, 1986, 36, 63. In the Cuban Constitution of 1940 (as in the United States), the president nominates and the senate confirms lifetime appointments to the highest court. The French constitutional court consists of nine judges, appointed for nine years, staggered so that one-third is replaced every three years. In the International Court of Justice, the same applies, except that reappointment is possible. In Japan, the mandatory retirement age is 70. There, as in France, judges are normally appointed in their sixties.

The following would have constitutional standing: an electoral tribunal, a *Tribunal de Cuentas*, the central bank, and university boards of trustees. The electoral tribunal would be charged with voter registration, administering elections, certifying winners, and apportioning seats to parties according to the proportional representation formula specified by law or provincial or local charters. The *Tribunal de Cuentas* would be charged with auditing government accounts at all levels, national ones annually and provincial and local ones at least biennially, something it would either do itself or contract out to CPA firms, reporting its findings to congress and making them available to the press and the public. The central bank would be charged with safeguarding the value of the currency so that it is not eroded by inflation. University boards of trustees would set policy, appoint top administrators and generally oversee the operations of national universities. Except for the supreme electoral tribunal, these agencies would each be governed by a nine-member board appointed by the president with the consent of the senate, for staggered, nine-year terms, with one-third of the membership renewable every three years, with reappointment possible for another term, sequentially or after a break. For its part, the supreme electoral tribunal would be governed by a nine-member board appointed by the constitutional court for the same length of term and schedule for staggering appointments as those applicable to itself. The congress would be free to create additional autonomous agencies.

Below the national government, there would be provincial governments and municipalities. These would have legislative and fiscal autonomy, subject to the following constraints. On the revenue side, taxes over exports and imports would be the exclusive prerogative of the national government, and in taxing (and regulating) industry and commerce, provincial and local governments would be prohibited from discriminating between items produced or sold within their jurisdictions and those without. On the expenditure side, the national government could mandate provinces or local governments to provide for schools, water and sewers, public health, environmental protection, and other items the neglect of which at the regional or local level would have adverse national impact. To ensure at least minimal compliance with national mandates, provincial or local officials who ignore or flatly refuse to carry them out would be subject to civil suits and liable to judicially-imposed fines.[50] However, one would expect that the national government would rather rely on a fiscal carrot, offering grants-in-aid and similar subsidies to persuade recalcitrant provincial or local governments to comply. Another means would be for the senate to hold hearings on the state of public services in jurisdictions that are grossly under-performing, something which would attract unfavorable publicity and, presumably, negative electoral consequences for the officials responsible.

Other than that, provinces and municipalities would be free to levy taxes on property, income, sales or consumption, charge user fees for any service, and borrow money by issuing bonds, subject only to such regulations as are deemed necessary to guarantee transparency in all their financial transactions and to pay off creditors in case of default.[51] Similarly, over and beyond that required to fulfill national mandates, provinces and municipalities would be free to spend their revenues for any purpose that finds favor with the voters. All provincial and municipal accounts would be subject to at least biennial auditing by the Tribunal de Cuentas or by CPA firms contracted by it for the purpose.

Provincial governments would consist of an elected assembly, which would exercise legislative power, and an elected governor charged with executing the

---

50. Alexis de Tocqueville showed how in early 19th century New England local governments would be brought into compliance with state laws not through a hierarchy of administration but by judicial action. See *Democracy in America*, 70-79.

51. The fiscal power of provinces and municipalities would be subject to several political checks, including those exercised at the voting booth and, perhaps most importantly, by businesses and residents who would "vote with their feet," changing place of residence in response to high taxes, bloated budgets, and otherwise irresponsible fiscal management .

laws. Half of the assembly would be elected from single-member districts and the other half at large by proportional representation subject to a five percent threshold. Legislative districts would be drawn following the contours of municipal boundaries. Several municipalities of few inhabitants could be combined into one district, and one populous municipality divided into two or more districts, but in no case would a district be drawn with parts of two or more municipalities. Both branches would be elected simultaneously for a three-year term. All municipalities would be governed by a council or commission (elected by proportional representation, at large, or from districts, or some combination of the three) and either an elected mayor or an administrator appointed by and responsible to the council. Within these constraints, each province would be free to draw up a charter to govern its own affairs, subject to approval by referendum of the residents of the province, on the one hand, and by the national senate, on the other. Similarly, each municipality would draw up its own charter subject to approval, on the one hand by its residents and, on the other, by the corresponding provincial assembly. The charters might include a provision for provincial and local courts, respectively, with jurisdiction over their own legislation or ordinances, or either or both levels may opt to rely on the ordinary national tribunals to interpret and adjudicate their own laws, regulations, or ordinances. In either case, all decisions made by provincial and local tribunals would be appealable to the national judiciary.

The electoral calendar would follow a three-year cycle, to wit: the president, the entire cámara, and one-sixth of the senate would be elected one year; provincial governors and assemblies, and one sixth of the senators the next; and all municipal councils and mayors, and one sixth of the senate, the following year.[52] Thus, there would be an election every year.

To amend the constitution, two options would be available. One, initiated "from above," would be by a two-thirds vote of both houses of congress, followed by a popular referendum, with a two-thirds margin required for enactment. The other, initiated "from below," would be for two-thirds of the provincial assemblies, each by a two-thirds vote, to endorse an identically worded proposed amendment, followed by a popular referendum at the next election, with a two-thirds vote required for enactment. A transitory provision would stipulate that, twelve years after the adoption of the new constitution, the people, by a simple majority of those turning out in a referendum, would decide whether to maintain the schedule of annual elections laid out here or thenceforth to hold elections at all levels concurrently every three years. If this amendment were adopted, senate terms would be staggered so that half its membership would be renewed every three years.

ANALYSIS AND JUSTIFICATION

Although it does not fit it perfectly, several of the principal elements of the proposed constitution match those of a consensual type. These are: a legislature not dominated by the executive; a bicameral national congress, with the branches roughly equal in authority, elected according to different rules and for varying lengths of term; proportional representation in the lower house of congress, whose members are elected from districts of relatively large magnitude; equal representation of the provinces in the senate; an independent constitutional court to which a relatively rigid constitution is entrusted; an independent central bank; additional autonomous agencies; and vertical decentralization, with elected provincial and local governments.

Several features are sufficiently unusual or controversial as to require justification: the electoral calendar, the mode for electing and staggering terms of the senate, the three-year term for all elected offices ex-

---

52. To begin the cycle, upon adoption of the constitution elections for all offices would be held simultaneously. This would be followed by new elections for provincial governments and one-sixth of the senate the next year and for local governments and one-sixth of the senate the year after that. Thus, initially, only the president and the cámara would enjoy a full term. Also, upon first being elected, all senators, meeting by province, would draw lots for the initial length of term, which would range from one to six years. A similar method would allocate length of terms to the initial appointments to the courts and the autonomous agencies.

cept the senate, and presidential re-election. Taking them in order, frequent elections are desirable for a number of reasons. For one thing, elections function as the linchpin of a republican regime, the pivot on which government policy moves in response to public opinion. By staggering the terms of different offices in the manner proposed here, Cubans would vote annually according to a three-year cycle, thus infusing government at all levels (for all elected officials would monitor election results to measure changes in public opinion) with a healthy dose of popular input. Second, after half a century of dictatorship (or more, depending on the time left to the Castro regime), Cubans need to acquire, in relatively short order, the habits and skills of republicanism. Annual elections would speed up the learning process.[53] Third, frequent elections hold out hope to the losers of any one contest of victory in the next. They are much more likely to accept defeat gracefully, something that contributes to legitimating the regime, if, having lost at one level, they can look forward to a new election at another level shortly thereafter. Thus, a losing presidential candidate can seek election to the senate or as governor of his province the following year. Similarly with those who fail to win a seat in the lower house of the national congress: provincial and local elections in the next two years can yield a consolation prize. Also, having separate elections at each level would strengthen provincial and local autonomy, reducing the effect of extraneous issues on campaigns at these levels.

A senate with fewer members than the number provided for in the 1940 Constitution, elected for longer, staggered terms so that one senator per province (one sixth of the total) comes up for renewal every year needs defending. First, the size, length of term, and schedule of senatorial elections are all meant to endow this body with sufficient authority, prestige, and independence, and the individual senators with enough stature, so as to make the office an attractive alternative to the presidency. Extraordinary individuals whose hunger for political recognition cannot be easily satiated but for whom the presidency is an improbable attainment, as it must be for most, should find that the senate provides an adequate outlet for their ambitions. In turn, these would be harnessed for the public good, turned into checks on the inordinate pretensions on the part of an overweening executive and, more positively, into overseers of the long-term interests of the people, particularly when it comes to the prudence of the executive's foreign policy, the readiness of the armed forces, the effectiveness at combating crime and the respect shown for civil rights by the national police, the kind of justice meted out in the courts, the quality of higher education, the soundness of public finances and the performance of the economy, all areas governed or regulated by institutions to which presidential appointments require senate concurrence.

As to senate terms being staggered so that one-sixth or one per province is renewed every year, this would amount, in effect, to electing senators from single-member districts. This would tend to reduce the number of effective parties represented in that chamber, something which as we have seen facilitates the operation of a presidential system. Moreover, to the extent that they develop, senatorial coattails would contribute to reducing the number of parties in the provincial assemblies. Also, at large elections would allow for extraordinary persons who have distinguished themselves in other walks of life and have not previously been involved in internal party politics to make an independent run. Such potential competition from independents would help prevent political parties from taking the voters for granted. In short, the senate as conceived here would be a prestigious body, worthy of the cravings for distinction on the part of spirited men, which would lend necessary ballast to the ship of state and function as an effective

---

53. Be it noted that Taiwan, whose transition to democracy has been one of the smoothest on record, has held an average of one election per year for one office or another for a decade. See James A. Robinson (in participation with Deborah A. Brown and Eric P. Moon), *Appraising Steps in Democratization. Taiwan Elections, 1986-2000*, Pensacola, FL: The University of West Florida, 2000.

counterpoise to the executive even as it remains uniquely in tune with public opinion.[54]

It may be objected that having senatorial elections every year will interfere with the process of government. One might surmise that the president and his party, on the one hand, and opposition parties represented in the upper house, on the other, would be at constant loggerheads, seeking maximum electoral advantage from every disagreement or confrontation over policy. Engaged in a permanent electoral campaign, they would be less likely to compromise over issues that divide them. The plausibility of such a hypothesis led me to ask Mark P. Jones to see if he could find a relationship between election year and executive-legislative conflict in his data set. He graciously agreed to my request, and reported the results by e-mail: "There was no statistically significant difference in the level of executive-legislative conflict between election years and non-election years for the analysis population of Latin American democracies during the 1980s and 1990s."[55] This finding cannot be viewed as anything but tentative. Only experience can demonstrate whether annual elections for the senate would complicate relations between the president and the senate. Nevertheless, it is at least reassuring to know that the test came out negative, that empirical evidence on executive-legislative conflict in Latin America does not lend ready support to what is otherwise an entirely plausible hypothesis.

A three-year term for all elected offices except the senate is short by world standards and goes against the grain of Latin American practice. As far as I know, only Australia, New Zealand, and Sweden have tried it. By contrast, two-thirds of Latin American countries have adopted a five-year or longer presidential term. Yet, the advantages of a three-year term are manifest. Focusing on the presidency in particular,[56] if the incumbent makes wrong decisions,

and loses public support, the nation is not saddled with an unpopular and hence weak executive for long. Also, if congress and the president reach an impasse, the stalemate will be short-lived, thus reducing the risk of the government becoming mired in chronic "immobilism," one of the potential pitfalls of presidential regimes. Furthermore, requiring even a good president to be endorsed by the voters within three years of his having been elected would contribute to his keeping in mind where the source of his authority lies. Instilling humility into presidents, who tend to be short on this virtue, would be desirable.

A last advantage of a three-year term is that it reduces the cost of presidential reelection. That this is a sensitive subject in Cuban history is evident from the extremely difficult procedure which the 1940 Constitution stipulates before the clause prohibiting presidential reelection can be changed. Twice in the nation's history a revolt broke out when the incumbent president attempted reelection or to extend his term of office. The traditional Cuban aversion to *continuismo* cannot but have become stronger after more than four decades of Castroism. Nevertheless, for the reasons I gave when discussing the Constitution of 1940, I believe that, on balance, it is more prudent to allow reelection than to proscribe it. By limiting the presidential term to three years, and keeping in mind that the proposed framework contemplates both a reduction of the president's powers relative to the congress and autonomous agencies *and* a senate worthy of political ambition, presidential reelection should be less threatening to the opposition. Lastly, to allow presidential reelection is not to guarantee it. Nothing is more likely to deflate the pretensions of presidents and would-be presidents than an occasional defeat of one of their number in his bid for reelection.

54. On the "necessity of a well-constructed senate," see James Madison, "Number LXII" and "Number LXIII," in Kramnick, *The Federalist Papers*, 364-375. Also, be it noted that one of the criticisms that Burke leveled against the French revolutionaries was that they had made no provision for a senate. See *Reflections on the Revolution in France*, 316.

55. Mark P. Jones, personal communication, October 3, 2000.

56. Mainwaring and Shugart suggest the possibility of a three-year term for the president. See their *Presidentialism and Democracy in Latin America*, 38.

The analysis of the proposed framework would not be complete without a systematic comparison of its key provisions with those of the Constitution of 1940. This is shown in the Appendix. There are parallels as well as differences between the two designs. Taking the former first: like the 1940 Constitution, the proposed framework calls for a presidential, bicameral, and unitary regime. It provides for separation of powers and checks and balances between the executive and legislative branches, judicial review, a supreme electoral tribunal beyond executive or legislative control, an independent *Tribunal de Cuentas*, provincial governments, and municipal autonomy. Both are difficult to amend. Thus, in form, the two designs are very similar.

Substantively, however, the proposed framework is more consensual, taking the horizontal separation and vertical division of powers much farther than the 1940 Constitution. The most important departures from the 1940 Constitution are the following. First, the features characteristic of the "presidential-parliamentary" constitutional type are done away with in favor or a pure presidential regime, one where the survival of the cabinet is independent of the legislature. Second, the president is elected by a qualified plurality vote for a three-year term, with reelection for up to two more terms permitted. Third, the lower house of congress is also elected, concurrently with

the president, for a three-year term while the senate is elected for a six-year term, staggered so that every year one senator per province is elected. Fourth, such functions as judicial review, the administration of elections, and a central bank, all contemplated in the 1940 Constitution, are placed in separate, specialized, autonomous institutions. Fifth, a full-fledged provincial government—with an elected assembly and an elected governor—is provided for, and both provincial and municipal governments are granted greater autonomy. Finally, appointments to the supreme and constitutional courts would not be for life but for fixed, renewable terms.[57]

CONCLUSION

The constitutional framework proposed in this paper is intended to promote the establishment and development of a presidential democracy in post-Castro Cuba which, although necessarily majoritarian in some aspects, incorporates many elements associated with consensual democracy. In form, the design parallels the Cuban Constitution of 1940 in most respects, an attribute that should enhance its palatability. Substantively, the proposed framework perfects the better features found in the 1940 document while remedying its structural flaws. It is hoped that this proposal will contribute to discussion and debate pursuant to the crafting of constitutions in general and, especially, of a *magna carta* for a free Cuba.

---

57. This should provide a check on the contemporary trend, witnessed not only in the United States but in many places around the world, of judges arrogating to themselves legislative and even administrative powers which in a republican regime are or should be the prerogative of elected officials. See C. Neal Tate and Torbjörn Vallinder (Eds.), *The Global Expansion of Judicial Power*, New York: New York University Press, 1995.

Appendix 1. Suggested Framework Compared to 1940 Cuban Constitution on Selected Items

Item	Cuban Constitution of 1940	Suggested Framework
Regime	unitary, presidential, bi-cameral	unitary, presidential, bicameral
Congress: mode of election	lower house elected from each of six provinces, one per 35,000 inhabitants, for four-year staggered terms, one-half renewed every two years; candidates must be at least 21 years of age	lower house elected from each of six provinces, one per 50,000 inhabitants, for a three-year term, by proportional representation, with minimum threshold set at five percent of the vote; candidates must be 25 years of age
	upper house composed of nine senators from each of six provinces, for a total of 54, elected on same day, for a four-year term; candidates must be at least 30 years old; minority parties allowed representation [subsequently interpreted by the electoral code so that six senators went to the majority party and three to minority parties]	upper house composed of six senators from each of six provinces, for a total of 36, for staggered, six-year terms, one senator elected from each province every year; candidates must be at least 30 years old
Congress: length of session	the congress will meet twice a year for no less than 60 days at a time nor more than 140 days in total	the congress will determine the frequency and length of its sessions, but in no case will meet less than half the calendar year
Congress: power of impeach-ment	lower house has power to impeach the president by a vote of 2/3 of its membership; trial conducted in the senate, joined by members of the supreme court, and presided by its chief justice [with verdict reached presumably by majority vote]	lower house has power to impeach the president by 3/5 vote; trial conducted in the senate, chief justice of the supreme court presiding, with 2/3 vote required for conviction
Congress: vote of no confidence	either house, by a vote of an absolute majority of its membership, may register a vote of no-confidence in a cabinet minister or the whole cabinet, which requires immediate resignation by one or all, as the case may be	
Congress: power of lower house	has priority in discussion and approval of the budget of the nation	all revenue and spending bills must be voted out of this chamber first; approves presidential appointments to the cabinet
Congress: power of the senate	approves heads of diplomatic missions and treaties with other nations negotiated by the president; approves all appointments to the Supreme Court and the Tribunal of Accounts	approves presidential appointments of heads of diplomatic missions, other ambassadors, and treaties with other nations negotiated by the president; approves all appointments to the Supreme Court, the Constitutional Court, the Supreme Electoral Tribunal, the Tribunal of Accounts, the Central Bank, university boards of regents, other autonomous institutions established by law; and promotions in rank to general or its equivalent
Congress: overriding veto	by 2/3 vote of both houses	by 3/5 vote of both houses

Appendix 1. Suggested Framework Compared to 1940 Cuban Constitution on Selected Items (continued)

Item	Cuban Constitution of 1940	Suggested Framework
President: mode of election	elected by the provinces for a four-year term, the candidate receiving a plurality in a province being credited with a number of provincial votes equal to the total of senators and representatives to be elected from that province, the candidate receiving the largest number of provincial votes being elected; immediate reelection not allowed; to run again, a president must sit out two consecutive terms; candidates must be at least 35 years old	elected by the nation at large for a three-year term; if no candidate receives at least 40 percent plus one of the vote, a run-off is held between the two top vote-getters in the first round; reelection allowed consecutively or after a break for a maximum number of three terms in office; candidates must be at least 40 years old
President: legislative power	may introduce bills in congress; can veto bills; "pocket" veto is not allowed: if the congress will adjourn less than ten days after submitting a bill to the president, and he intends to veto it, he must communicate to the congress his intentions within 48 hours, so that the congress may stay in session and vote to override; if the president does not inform the congress, the bill becomes law without his signature	can veto bills subject to override by congress; line-item veto not allowed, the president must veto entire bill or not at all; neither is "pocket" veto permissible: any bill sent to the president less than ten days before the congress adjourns, which he neither signs nor vetoes, becomes law if, within three months of the new session of congress, it passes both houses by simple majority vote.
President: decree powers	to issue decrees and orders advisable for the purpose of executing the laws and for whatever is pertinent to the government and administration of the State, without in any case contravening what is established by law	to issue decrees and orders only for the purpose of executing laws duly enacted by congress, to implement judicial rulings, and what concerns the internal administration of the executive branch, narrowly construed, without in any case contravening what is established by law
President: budget power	sixty days before it is due to take effect, he presents the house with a budget; the congress may not increase funding of any of existing services beyond what is planned by the executive; nor may it abolish any "permanent" tax without enacting another in its place or reducing expenditures proportionately	the president is required to submit a proposed budget nine months before the start of the new fiscal year, but it is up to the congress to decide what, if any, of the president's plan to adopt in one or more revenue and expenditure bills; there are no restrictions on congressional authority to increase or decrease taxes or expenditures
Cabinet	president "freely" appoints and removes members of the cabinet, including a prime minister who represents the government to congress; the cabinet is responsible to congress, and members of the cabinet, individually and collectively, are subject to a vote of no confidence by either house of congress, which requires their resignation; members of congress may serve in the cabinet, and vote in their respective chambers	president appoints, with approval of the lower house, members of the cabinet, and is free to remove them; no member of congress may serve in the cabinet without resigning his seat first

Appendix 1. Suggested Framework Compared to 1940 Cuban Constitution on Selected Items (continued)

Item	Cuban Constitution of 1940	Suggested Framework
Supreme Court: mode of appointment	members of the court appointed by the president f rom a list of three names proposed by an electoral college appointed for the purpose by the supreme court, the president, and the law faculty of the University of Havana; chief justice and chiefs of sections shall be appointed by the president on proposal of the full bench of the supreme court with approval of the senate	appointed by the president with the approval of the senate
Supreme Court: qualifying age and length of term	must be 40 years old, appointed for life	must be 50 years old, appointed by president with senate approval; nine members appointed for staggered terms of nine years, with reappointment possible for another term (plus a chief justice, who is appointed for life); mandatory retirement at 70
Constitutional Court	supreme court doubles as constitutional court in one of its sections	a separate institution, appointed in the same manner and length of term as the supreme court
Supreme Electoral Tribunal	composed of three justices of the supreme court and two from the Havana court of appeals, named for a period of four years by the full bench of their respective courts	a separate institution, governed by a nine-member board appointed by the constitutional court for the same length of term and rules for staggering appointments as those applicable to itself
Tribunal of Accounts	composed of seven members, four attorneys and three accountants (or business professors); the supreme court appoints two of the lawyer members, the president and senate one lawyer and one accountant each, and the university council one accountant or professor of business; appointed for a term of eight years; lawyers must be 40 years old and accountants 35	composed of nine members, six certified public accountants or university professors of business and three attorneys, appointed by the president with approval of the senate, for staggered terms of nine years, with reappointment possible for another term, for a maximum length of service of 18 years; must be 40 years old
Central Bank	a National Bank of Cuba will be established; at the time of its creation, the State may require that existing banks contribute to its capital; those who comply with this requirement will be represented in its board of directors	a central bank is charged with safeguarding the value of the currency so that it is not eroded by inflation; it will be governed by a nine-member board appointed by the president with the consent of the senate, for staggered, nine-year terms, with one third of the membership renewable every three years, with reappointment possible for another term, for a maximum length of tenure of 18 years; must be 40 years old

Appendix 1. Suggested Framework Compared to 1940 Cuban Constitution on Selected Items (continued)

Item	Cuban Constitution of 1940	Suggested Framework
Provincial government	an elected governor and a provincial council composed of all the mayors of the province; fiscal powers are subject to conditions, such as, in certain cases, approval by the *Tribunal de Cuentas* or popular referendum	an elected governor and an elected assembly, elected concurrently for a three-year term; each province will draw up its own governing charter, subject to approval by the senate; complete fiscal autonomy, except for periodic audits by the *Tribunal de Cuentas*, laws designed to insure financial transparency and protect creditors in case of default, and prohibition of taxes levied on imports, exports, or taxes and regulations that discriminate between products produced or sold within and those without the province; provincial elections held on a year different from that of any other level (except the senate)
Local government	the municipality is an autonomous entity; it can draw up its own charter, as long as it fits one of three possible models (commission, council-manager or mayor-council) subject to approval by referendum; fiscal powers are subject to restrictions similar to those imposed on the provinces; municipal elections will be held on a day different from that of general elections	the municipality is an autonomous entity; it can draw up its own charter subject to approval by the provincial assembly; complete fiscal autonomy, except for the same restrictions applicable to the provinces; elections held on a year different from that of any other level (except the senate)
Constitutional amendment	two ways to enact most reforms to the constitution: (a) by petition from at least 100,000 voters, whereupon the congress will meet in joint session and within thirty days convoke the election of a constituent assembly or a referendum; (b) by congressional initiative, by petition from at least one-fourth of the joint membership of congress, whereupon it takes a 2/3 vote of congress, meeting jointly, during three sessions in a row; certain reforms, such as one negating national sovereignty, or removing prohibition against reelection or extending the term of office are even more difficult to pass	two ways to enact constitutional amendments: (a) "from above": a two-thirds vote of both houses of congress, followed by a popular referendum, with a two-thirds margin required for enactment; (b) "from below": two-thirds of the provincial assemblies endorse a proposed amendment by a two-thirds vote of their respective memberships, followed by a popular referendum, with two-thirds vote required for enactment

MICROECONOMIC INTERMEDIATION AND SECTORAL INTEGRATION IN A MARKET TRANSITION

Mario A. Rivera

Market transition theory has developed ever more nuanced methodologies for the analysis of institutional change in an economy at meso- and micro-levels of analysis. Relying on several of these contemporary analytical methods, this paper will discuss obstacles to, and suggest preliminarily some theoretical and empirical approaches to the study of, the extent of causal influence of levels of sectoral integration on market transitions. This will be undertaken with reference to the interaction in Cuba of (1) tightly-structured, exclusive, and corporatized military-run enterprises with (2) more loosely-bound managerial and entrepreneurial networks in foreign investment and trade sectors and (3) relatively tenuous social and economic networks tracing the outlines of the second economy. Specifically, an examination of incentive structures and operative rules affecting integration or synchronization across these economic sectors will suggest that there are major, and persistent, constraints against a significant transition to the market.

From an institutional perspective, economic development depends on integrative institutional linkages functioning in such a way that growth in one sector impels growth in other sectors. At times working at cross-purposes, since the mid- to late nineties, the Cuban government has promoted tourism, export, and foreign investment while severely limiting the development of financial and information infrastructures, and it has allowed very differently endowed military- and civilian-managed enterprises to advance in parallel. In short, it has taken contradictory policy initiatives that would appear to stymie the stated goals of economic restructuring, if only because of the severe disarticulation of the economy.

One scenario for market liberalization in Cuba might be that the eventual "thickening" of markets in either the second economy or in sectors open to the global economy will outweigh the distorting influences of military-run and other state-run enterprises. Of particular interest would be identification of enabling conditions which might "tip" the organization, membership, and functioning of firms in these economic sectors in a market direction. However, this study will concentrate on questioning the extent of enabling conditions for marketization, particularly the lack of market coordination mechanisms—such as factor markets—across economic sectors. Put another way, Cuba does not meet the criteria of an "emerging market economy" (EME), nor is in prospect of doing so, if an EME is defined by the acceleration of economic development through (1) policy mechanisms favoring economic liberalization and (2) the creation of institutions of law favoring a free and adequately integrated market such as property rights, contract protections, and employment laws favoring independent contracting of labor (Hoskisson, et al., 2000).

In a much-studied process which has received extensive attention in ASCE works and elsewhere, the Cuban government began in 1993 to introduce limited measures toward economic liberalization, legalizing certain kinds of foreign investment, joint venture, and private microenterprise, as well as legalizing the dollar. It thus sought to create demand abroad for

Cuban products and Cuban tourism, and generally to obtain hard currency, while attending to growing domestic demand that far outstrips an increasingly marginal rationing system. By the end of the 1990s, if its claims are accepted, many of these economic tactics had worked for the regime, if only to the point of bringing Cuba out of extreme economic recession and "reinserting" it, though precariously, in the global economy. There is no evidence, however, that these measures amount to a fundamental movement toward economic restructuring. To the contrary, the testimony of the Cuban leadership, notably Fidel Castro's, plainly exhibits a deep-seated antagonism toward profound, expansive, or enduring economic reform.

Three of the market-pegged devices which may have had the greatest impact are interrelated, and all betray serious limitations owing to institutional insufficiencies, as well as to self-defeating policy mechanisms that are conditioned by the imperatives of central control. These are: (1) the development and vigorous implementation of varied forms of joint ventures with foreign investors in key sectors such as tourism and telecommunications, often under the managerial direction of the military (the Revolutionary Armed Forces and the Union of Military Industries); (2) the creation of cadres of entrepreneurial managers made responsible for generating business for firms in tourism and other sectors, especially hard-currency foreign investment (reportedly with a 70 percent to 30 percent overall split between civilian and military managers); and (3) the development in various ministries of novel ways to promote Cuban exports, from tourism to cigars, sugar, nickel, and biotechnology, an endeavor tied in part to global marketing strategies relying on the Internet and World Wide Web. However, the unpredictability of applicable rules—their frequent modification in the foreign investment type of venture, as in the "own-account" sector—has produced or exacerbated market segmentation. Market coordination—i.e., the synchronization of information exchange and transaction streams across market sectors—is thereby significantly impeded.

SECTORAL LINKS AND POLITICAL CONTROL

Without a loosening of political control, Cuba cannot enjoy the movement found in other developing nations toward supply, subcontracting, financing, production, and marketing networks, nor toward the expansion of market intermediation, e.g., of factor markets in the distribution and reselling of finished products or in the contracting of labor. Central economic controls preclude the self-organizing development of markets and limit the reach and effectiveness of manufacturing, extractive industry, export, foreign investment, tourism, and service sector initiatives. While state agencies are being turned into corporate and joint stock enterprises, the persistence of subsidies, the privileged economic role of the military, and the growing leverage of foreign investors make for a significant distance between unequally-endowed enterprise sectors. The pervasive compartmentalization of economic actors and sectors precludes the generative tension between the second and formal economies that can arise in late state socialism (Gábor, 1994). Banking is similarly compartmentalized or segmented, under the purview of the state as owner, regulator, provider, and borrower, with insufficient controls and insufficient flexibility to respond to capital needs in domestic markets.

There is a problematic assumption in the literature on the Cuban transition of a dynamic linkage between the second, or "own-account," economy and the state-controlled economy (including both state enterprises of the traditional sort and military-run ones in agriculture and tourism, as well as joint ventures in the foreign sector). However, there is little functional connection between these economic sectors: as already suggested, there is virtually no freely-devised economic intermediation, such as that which is provided by "middlemen" and suppliers, who are deemed "parasites" and legally prohibited. There is little or no subcontracting with the second or informal economy, again as a matter of legal proscription; nor, therefore, is it possible to create vertical integration through the myriad manufacturing, supply, or service networks that are commonly found in other transitional economies. Labor markets are similarly stunted, as distortions abound in the contracting of labor and in employment law. In the tourist and other foreign investment sectors, for instance, employment of Cuban nationals by foreign firms is from state-provided Party lists, while in the "own-account" sector, employment is putatively limited to family members, and entire categories of professionals and state functionaries are excluded from self-employment in various ways.

The expediency, inconsistency, arbitrariness, and severity with which own-account economic activity is regulated represents a severe pull against the kind of economic relations that would allow the larger, state-run economy (especially in its foreign investment and tourism operations) and the second and informal economies to strengthen one another, literally to complement and inform one another. While market forces and values may appear pervasive, there is little real prospect for the autonomous development of markets, and less yet for a fundamental alteration of the state's mode of intervention in the economy such as might allow functional integration across state-controlled and partially-marketized sectors. That the Cuban leadership seems little concerned with the establishment of reliable procedural and substantive rules for either politics or commerce is consistent with the thesis that basic reform is unlikely. Periodic "rectifications" and the uncertainty they create also militate against liberalization and liberal-democratic values. Economic liberalization is *not* moving apace in Cuba, in the sense of fundamental and integrated restructuring of the economy in a market direction, and in the sense of institutional transformation in the direction of property rights and contract law regimes.

NETWORKS AS INCIPIENT INSTITUTIONS AFFECTING ECONOMIC COSTS

The overweening exercise of political control in Cuba has tended to thwart the full development of essential market institutions such as commercial, property, and labor law, even to the limited extent that these have taken shape in China and Vietnam, which have served as models for the Cuban government. Coupled with American sanctions, this creates a climate of uncertainty that deters both foreign and domestic investment and inhibits entrepreneurial activity at all levels. There is a lack, therefore, of a com-

plementary relation between institutions of the market, such as those permitting freedom to contract and to employ labor. The argument from institutional economics is that the interaction of institutions and firms is generated by the imperfections of markets, as these institutions provide the stable rules and protections that permit reliance on contracts and other commercial transactions, thereby reducing uncertainty and transaction costs. Institutional protections for commerce also permit the development of enduring economic strategies by firms and by inter-firm coalitions.

Network analysis is gaining prominence in economics on the premise that it is precisely in circumstances of fundamental uncertainty that enterprises seek strategic alliances, conducting business cooperatively as well as competitively in pursuit of common goals, operating at the conjunction of the organizational and the personal. Such alliances are functionally interdependent, basing their operations on the control of activities, resources, and knowledge. Networks are defined structurally by actual and latent relations, and by their horizontal or vertical position across firms. Government can engage in coproduction activities with and otherwise support such networks, if it affords them enough autonomy. The development of autonomous networks in commerce is a requisite part of the institutional development of markets, i.e., of the emergence of institutions with a functional and dynamic interrelation to markets.

In a similar vein, managerial networks can develop as managers' interactions within or across sectors (e.g., tourism, trade, and shipping) settle into predictable, social-exchange forms of governance or coordination, which gain structural "embeddedness" in the course of complex exchanges under conditions of uncertainty. Network structures are characterized by an institutionality of process rather than hierarchy, particularly in a society and economy like Cuba's, where there is little difference between managerial or inter-firm relations and interpersonal relations. Cuba's is a relational rather than individualistic culture (Earp, 1996) so that entrepreneurial and managerial nets consist mainly of interpersonal ties and reciprocal exchanges even when the institutions involved are well-developed. Network structures involve an identity-type of relation, i.e., relationships where social status predominates, whether based on school or family ties, social or political standing, or provenance (e.g., coming from the same town or neighborhood). Cuba's second economy is similarly based on cross-cutting family and social networks, and, if unfettered, it could provide a basis for the development and integration of markets in various sectors.

The argument of the network literature is that institutional development based on the increasing embeddedness of process (of social resources and production and commercial transactions) is positive, on the assumption that network ties reduce transaction costs, noise, friction, and uncertainty in economic activity. Moreover, they do so without resorting to hierarchy or bureaucracy, so that the vitality of process supersedes the restraint of structure—a characteristic feature, incidentally, of informal economies. Social and human capital then become a function of brokerage activities, as key individuals (managers, entrepreneurs, middlemen, and other boundary-spanners) facilitate transactions on the basis of interpersonal ties, obligations, and tactical alliances. The economic value of networks is a function of their requisite complexity along with traits like flexibility and maneuverability.

Transaction cost economics suggests that the cost of interorganizational transactions—which by definition "bridge" dyadic processes such as investment and allocation, production and marketing, and policy formulation and implementation—should be minimized, often by the choice of institutional frameworks and mechanisms through which the transactions are played out. The organizational form that is chosen is important, and no less important is the ability to test and select from a variety of institutional formations, since no one form is *a priori* best suited. One option is to incorporate transactions into a single firm, either literally or through various forms of vertical integration, including subcontracting. Another is a bilateral exchange relation between a pool of organizations and another, like a supplier, which enjoys singular economies of scale.

Resort to contracts is typically costly, while transactions based largely on trust stand to be the least expensive, be they intrafirm arrangements based on internal processes and controls or interorganizational ones which exclude other actors because of exclusive access to assets or resources. Integration within a single firm is most predictable, since network partners may cease to act in the common interest if environmental conditions change unexpectedly. The magnitude of costs in transaction networks may be gauged by the "connection density" of critical elements of the collective project, by the degree of dependency among critical activities and activity sequences, by the frequency of these interactions, by the uncertainty involved, and by the exclusivity of access to vital assets. Such assets include not only fiscal resources but also technologies, business processes, and structured strategic opportunities which serve as incentives to keep organizational partners on board.

The critical correlate is that certain institutional forms are deemed to be best suited to the minimization of costs, even though organizational actors may not be aware at the moment of engaging partners or of transacting business which form may work best in theory. It is through the lived experience of collaboration that the best institutional arrangements emerge and that norms of trust and fidelity come into play. Transaction costs economics assumes that organizations or firms are able to experiment with different institutional formations, entering into specific ones at times of their own choosing, in a sequence chosen for maximal competitive advantage, with partners of their own predilection (Miles and Snow, 1996).

There are some early signs of the development of more autonomous management practices in parastatal firms and in strategic partnerships with foreign investors in Cuba, given a move toward the liberalization and decentralization of trade relations and commerce, and it is here that one might look for managerial networks and inter-firm partnerships. It must be remarked, however, that while individual managers are given not only the freedom but also the responsibility to find business, especially with foreign partners, contracting and the fashioning of inter-firm arrangements still involves the scrutiny and approval or veto authority of state ministries, under legal dispositions that are subject to change at whim. While imports and exports were until recently entirely a matter of state control, now any manager of a tourist enterprise or one producing for export may make arrangements for commercial transactions directly, although these initiatives are often limited to the first investment or procurement decisions.

It is in these endeavors that greater reliance on autonomous associations or partnerships among managers, suppliers, and investors may come to the fore, in inter-firm entrepreneurial networks. It must be noted once again, however, that what could be promising avenues for networking, specifically subcontracting and supply and service networks engaging the own-account economy, continue to be prohibited in Cuba, and this reality renders Cuba an exception to the norm in both the "informal economy" and network economics literature. There continues to be in Cuba a sharp divide between the state-controlled economy and the own-account sector, with little communion between the two. Moreover, there is a great deal of collusive behavior and entrenchment of privilege among those positioned in the so-called "external sector," and a high incidence of outright corruption in the insterstices of this sector. According to Hoskisson, et al. (2000), rent-seeking behavior by incumbents contributes to the maintenance of core rigidities in a transitional economy like Cuba's. There is, therefore, a potential drawback to networks, in that players may collude to resist change, especially change in the formal and informal rules governing access to networks, in the absence of strong competitive pressures and reliable institutional restraints.

COMPUTER AND INFORMATION NETWORKS AND GLOBAL REINSERTION

In ascertaining the extent of economic liberalization in Cuba, it may be warranted to consider computer connectivity as an instance. Computer connectivity, including access to the Internet and World Wide Web, is often taken to be a critical factor in economic liberalization in Cuba and elsewhere. As this writer and coauthor Nelson Valdés indicated in "The Political Economy of the Internet in Cuba," presented at the 1999 ASCE annual conference, Cuba is well connected to the Internet and Web, particularly with regard to the international projection of its products, tourism, and commercial scientific research, with numerous, often sophisticated websites. This effort is key to its attempts at reinsertion in the international economy.

There is also great interest among Cubans in electronic mail and the Internet, and although there is rapid growth in domestic connectivity that might allow the development of electronic commerce, official access for individuals to the Internet is restricted in favor of connectivity for national research institutions, ministries, and commercial ventures. An example of the latter is Cubanet, which serves more than thirty joint-venture and tourism-oriented enterprises, offering them access to other commercial services abroad. Another example is Coral Container Lines—an enterprise involved in the shipping of containers to and from Cuba which operates an extensive private/local network.

Cuban banks serving domestic and international commerce have developed secure messaging and office transaction processing software packages, and bank automation has witnessed substantial increases in automation and internal networking, though not yet much external connectivity. The tourist sector has its own network administered by the Electronics for Tourism Group (Grupo de Electrónica para el Turismo), which serves all tourist chains in the country. The Islazul tourism chain, for example, is linking over forty of its hotels to the Internet. A complex of twenty schools of hotel operation and tourism across Cuba is networked by email. In Camagüey province, this network is part of a limited city network that channels electronic mail among a number of institutional users, including the school of tourism, the University of Camagüey, the medical school's site for the national "Infomed" network, a sugar mill center, and a software company.

In general, there is much more email connectivity across Cuba than Internet connections and access, but the island's commercial presence on the Internet is impressive nonetheless, particularly in tourism. For example, the State tourism firm Cubanacán rents automobiles, the Gran Caribe hotel chain offers reservations, and Artex offers a website for compact discs of Cuban music all via the Internet. A stated aim of the Cuban government is to involve erstwhile Cuban entrepreneurs as well as state enterprises in international electronic commerce, by both encouraging interest in it as a novelty and rendering its use a more or less routine part of the marketing of Cuban enterprises. However, individual Internet accounts are still forbidden by law and only obtain through surreptitious access, including *subrosa* dealings with operators of state-approved institutional sites. Entrepreneurial efforts using the net are therefore a legal as well as practical impossibility, and there is little prospect for the use of information networks as links for commerce.

The economic implications of the Internet—exactly how it will affect various markets or the uses to which it can be put—are only beginning to be understood. There is general agreement, however, that the Internet's effects on markets and on job creation (and subtraction) will be enormous in both developed and developing nations, and that it can transform the modes and processes of production, contracting, and marketing wherever its commercial use is widespread.

Two basic views of the Internet seem to dominate its discussion in the United States and Europe. On the one hand, it is understood physically as the connection among installed computers, allowing access to the information available on them. On the other hand, it is regarded spatially as a place or complex of places to frequent, for political, commercial, entertainment, and many other informational and communications purposes, tantamount in some treatments to a civic space and in others to a marketplace. Each concept carries its own assumptions about the economic role and possibilities of the Internet, and each has a particular set of political and public policy premises as well. In one instance, the role of information technology in the economy may be cast as that of a publicly regulated infrastructure, a public good that government provides and maintains. From the second perspective, it is a public arena, and the policy questions are in the main legal, having to do with jurisdiction and regulatory scope. In both cases, the institutional scaffolding of telecommunications and electronic commerce in policy, regulation, and law is of paramount importance.

The Internet is thus cast as both a commercial and political space allowing considerable freedom of entry, transaction, collaboration, and discourse. What is not countenanced in these debates, oriented as they are to the realities of developed or emerging market economies, is a governmental position that would prohibit individual and entrepreneurial access to the Internet and Web. In Cuba, because of concern over propaganda and over "undesirable" cultural influences from abroad, individual accounts are forbidden—although they would be beyond the means of most ordinary citizens if in fact permitted. While parastatals and state-sanctioned commercial ventures generally have access to the Internet and Web, most electronic commerce opportunities which might arise from individual entrepreneurship are excluded. Therefore, just as there is evidence of repressed consumer demand in the economy, there are many indications of repressed demand for access to computing and to information networks. When the prospects for undesirable political influence through information networks are drastically reduced, the possibilities for commercial and political interaction through them are also dimmed. Ironically, there is then virtually no role left for the state in the active promotion and regulation of information networks toward these ends.

THE ROLE OF THE MILITARY: GLOBALIZATION AND MARKET INTEGRATION

Cuba's military, though it has a prominent managerial role in the tourist sector through enterprises such as the firm Gaviota, is in a position to advance the cause of the country's reinsertion in the global economy relying, in part, on international marketing efforts. However, its limited technical capacity in this area, along with conflicts inherent in its dual aims of national defense and economic development, have sidelined the military with respect to information policy. Military direction of manufacturing, commercial, and service sector, especially tourist, enterprises has relied on close circles of old-line (largely Sierra-era) friendships at the helm.

The Armed Forces Ministry finds it difficult, prohibitively costly in both economic and political terms, to include nonmilitary managers and technocrats in their endeavors, or to go beyond the relatively static quality-control principles and mechanisms of their own managerial training (although, ironically enough, the FAR are transmitting their Total Quality Management and like practices to state enterprises through a much-vaunted program of "Perfeccionamiento Empresarial," or "Managerial Improvement").

The requirement for political clearances in a context of erratic economic policy renders such dynamism impossible for the Cuban Armed Forces, notwithstanding their relative institutional depth and sophistication, or their success in managerial endeavors since the mid-eighties. It is a maxim of transaction costs economics that the larger the group, the lesser its rents and privileges, and the greater the costs of organization and reorganization. There are great practical difficulties involved for Cuban military officers engaged in the managerial control of manufacturing and service firms to open their administrative apparatus to other actors. However, the overriding obstacles are those of state control over the extent, pace, and manner of FAR economic activity.

THEORETICAL FOUNDATIONS
AND A RESEARCH AGENDA

Whatever part of the Cuban economy one examines, there appears to be little cross-penetration of economic sectors and relatively little in the way of entrepreneurial initiative; in short, little evidence of a thoroughgoing transition to the market. An economic transition toward the market cannot occur without the development of autonomous and capable institutions, nor can it be sustained without the institutional capacity to combine and recombine in new organizational forms. The extent of articulation among economic actors, their combinatorial potential, and the freedom to align and realign strategically are the principal measures of marketization, for those national transitions in which the adaptation and readaptation of institutions is critical. Among emerging

market economies, socialist countries undergoing transition have evidenced the greatest need for fundamental institutional changes.

From an institutional perspective, economic development depends on integrative institutional linkages functioning in such a way that growth in one sector impels growth in other sectors. In Cuba, agriculture in recent years may have filled this generative role, through the dismantling of state farms and the developing of military-run farms as well as cooperatives. "Liberalization" of agriculture has proceeded in tandem with other, sometimes contradictory, economic and policy developments. As previously indicated, the Cuban government has promoted tourism, export, and foreign investment while severely limiting the development of (and access to) financial and information resources, and it has allowed military- and civilian-controlled managerial enterprises to advance in parallel but not through mutual engagement. Just as, in agriculture, farmer's markets, cooperatives, and the military farms are kept isolated.

The deliberate segmentation of the Cuban economy, along with the continual promulgation of new rules of the game for the owners of own-account enterprises ("cuentapropistas"), would appear to frustrate the stated goals of economic restructuring. The outcome is a kind of conditional openness akin to certain aspects of the Soviet transition of the late 1980s, and the prospects are no better (from a regime perspective) for the success of limited and inconsistent engagement with the global economy and polity.

Political and economic institutions are systemic responses to failures in societal capacity to process information through rational decision processes. They are "stopping rules" or "stopping devices" which bind otherwise intractable information challenges. Boisot and Child (1997) treat institutions as adaptive systems which have to match and respond to the complexity of demands from their pertinent environment, and they do so through a number of reductive means which include abstraction and diffusion of information through organizational repertoires and standard procedures, through cross-coupling across institutional boundaries, and through codification mechanisms which include the regulatory function of government. The complexity-handling modes of action in institutions generally aim at complexity reduction—efforts to comprehend and act on complex demands on the institutional system—and complexity absorption, typically through the generation of decisional and strategic-action options, risk-hedging strategies, and through alliances, coalitions, and networks.

Micropolitical institutional devices are prone to capture by rent-seeking groups or elites; the microfoundations of institutional forms are the province of the new institutional economics. Macropolitically, one may observe coalition-building behavior which aims at consolidating such gains; this is the province of political macroeconomics. At either level, opportunism (rent-seeking) makes for market coordination failures, specifically failures of timing and synchronization ties to the insufficiency or lack of availability of factors of production, assets or inputs. Brown (2000, p. 10) ties these institutional elements to network theory and the concept of social capital:

> These macrosocial regimes may: 1) determine the types and amounts of resources available ... over time; 2) describe with whom actors may forge ties, thus bounding and structuring [actual and incipient networks]; 3) legitimate and regulate transactions; 4) construct and implement sanctions in response to violations of the [given] regulatory system; 5) describe and regulate social status within the network; 6) construct the motivations underlying network transactions; [and] 7) construct and regulate competition between different networks.

These types of institutional embeddedness, Brown continues, are here framed with reference to a loop of *macro-to-meso* and *macro-to-macro* causation. Brown cites Portes and Landolt (1996) as suggesting that "networks whose membership is bounded by particularism can also constitute [what Adam Smith termed] conspiracies against the public, in that network resources are reserved to in-group members while access is denied to the general public (Brown, 2000, p. 10). *Macro-to-micro* causation can be traced to the ways that macrostructural regimes shape individual motivations for wealth, power, and opportunistic action, while *meso-to-micro* causal movement may be

exemplified by the way that regulatory measures are devised protectively by elites in response to threats by rivals, often rivals acting through collusive networks. At any of these levels, or in any of the possible combinations of level-to-level causation, transaction costs, defined for our purposes as "the costs associated with the transfer, capture, and protection of [ownership]" (Barzel, 1997, p. 4) and, more generally, information costs and costs of exchange, increase proportionately with the increasing fixity of economic control regimes.

In the Soviet case, it has been argued (Braguinsky, 1999, p. 3) that the collapse of the USSR, of the communist system, was largely caused by "the preceding collapse of hierarchical ownership rights." The departure from totalitarianism in Russia "presents a case of an 'entirely internal and spontaneous' transition [due less to exogenous forces than to] ... a large-scale transfer of de facto property rights (defined as residual control rights) [occurring] from the top political leadership and bureaucrats to coalitions comprised of [state-owned enterprise] management, middle-rank *nomenklatura* officials, and the barons of the so-called 'parallel economy.'" In short, the insider-coalitions changed, and with them, in both the pre- and post-socialist transition periods, transaction costs increased dramatically, accounting in large part for the gross inefficiencies of the Russian economy. In the Cuban case, while there have been some shifts in institutional power (for instance, the ascendancy of the FAR over the Interior Ministry after the Ochoa affair, which presaged a crucial politico-economic role for the military, particularly in trade and tourism), market mechanisms have fallen far short of restructuring relations around control rights as here defined.

While functioning networks are assumed to reduce transaction costs by means of trust, with social sanctions that reduce the gains than may be gleaned from opportunistic behavior, the struggle between insiders and outsiders, or conflictive transfer of de-facto property rights from one group or coalition to another, is usually very costly in exchange costs measures. Moreover, after such transfers of power, the new insiders must operate without the benefit of previously extant mechanisms of control, including both formal and informal mechanisms of regulatory control. Again, this is the case in Russia today. Such transitions are characterized by very high information and transaction costs until the development or reconfiguration of institutional regimes consistent with (favoring) new elite coalitions. In the Cuban case, however, there is little evidence of even this flawed kind of transfer of control rights or of any fundamental economic shift toward the market.

March-Poquet (2000) suggests areas of Cuba's economic transition where research could seek promising structural linkages between sectors. One is the functioning of the UBPCs—Basic Units of Cooperating Production—in agriculture which, if allowed "to overcome the operational [and regulatory] handicaps that limit their production growth, [could render rationing] unnecessary," and which, "with the current farming markets would generate an articulated food market nationally" (p. 105). However, he adds, such an articulation does not obtain yet. Other possibilities include linkages between dollar-only retail outlets and Cuban domestic producers of goods (rather than just imported goods), or between cuentapropista craft producers and sellers and their state counterparts. March-Poquet reports recent evidence that some economic intermediation may be allowed (though by state-owned companies), and specifically that

> the development of direct contracts between companies is to be promoted in a way that will enable them to agree [to] the terms for the exchange of goods and services freely. The intention has also been announced to develop a business sector to act as an intermediary in trade. ... The increase in the number of intermediate distribution companies trading raw materials and equipment, together with greater freedom [for] company supply policy, could be the origin of a future domestic market in intermediate goods and services (p.105).

March-Poquet concludes that in these areas of possible transition and in others (including free trade zones, telecommunications investments, the evolution of a quasi-private-ownership model in foreign direct investment generally) "... attempts are at an early stage and assessing their potential scope is risky" (p. 105). The dualities of controlled and relatively marketized elements of the economy seem much more entrenched than they were in the former Soviet Union before its collapse in 1991, or in the countries of Eastern Europe now undergoing postsocialist transitions. Other, more strictly political obstacles have been noted by other commentators, including this writer's earlier published research on Cuba: notably, the absence of civil institutions with any real autonomy, the absence of a political culture of democratic tolerance, and the absence of "social capital" on the basis of trust and reciprocity. It would appear that the depth of the Cuban transition has been overestimated by many analysts and commentators, largely because the premise of dynamic interaction, of causal linkage, between the state-controlled and market-oriented sectors of the economy has yet to be empirically justified.

CONCLUDING REMARKS: DIRECTIONS FOR FUTURE RESEARCH

Future research building on this study will incorporate consideration of advances in information theory that may shed light on the requirements for a market transition out of socialism, in view of the informational complexity of market interactions. It is anticipated that the Austrian economists, especially Mises and Hayek, will help make sense of the issues of information-generation and the use of knowledge in market systems, and therefore help elucidate the obstacles to marketization in the Cuban case. Of particular interest will be the problems associated with the generation of market information when economic sectors are both insufficiently autonomous and insufficiently integrated.

Gunning (1997) describes how Ludwig von Mises might have traced costs for an entrepreneur from a particular market for a first-order good to markets for higher-order goods in a way that highlights information processes and subjective valuations. The cost of producing a consumer good is seen to consist largely of the prices of the marketable factors of production needed to produce the good. In market economies, prices for these factors of production are set in factor markets through competitive bidding by entrepreneurs. Entrepreneurs are willing to marginally outbid each other when they anticipate that the object factor—labor, inputs, or finished goods—when combined with other, complementary factors, could earn them a profit. The net effect is prototypical of competitive markets: factors become available in supplies sufficient to meet demand, which lowers costs, while competitive bidding raises factor prices selectively, making for greater adequacy in compensation for labor and other factors of production.

If one entrepreneur wishes to gain control of a factor, such as labor, now used by another, the cost of that factor will rise beyond marginal-utility calculations on the basis of the *subjective valuations* of the entrepreneur bidding for it, on considerations of its complementarity with other factors of production—for instance, the value of an experienced webmaster to an enterprise wishing to project itself onto the Internet. Economic agents must closely follow changes in factor prices, and their opportunistic actions in processing and acting upon their assessments of market signals in turn alter those markets. They are processors and generators of information while altering, often in the positive directions just described, the operation of factor markets. However, the salutary effects of bidding in factor markets obviously presuppose the existence of both entrepreneurs and factor markets, as well as their operation across firms and across economic sectors. Neither of these conditions obtains in Cuba, and therefore synergies across markets are absent as well. Economic initiative and factors of production are constrained within state-determined boundaries, such as those delimiting the military-run tourist, manufacturing, and agricultural sector, the *sui generis* rules binding the foreign investment and own-account sectors respectively, and range and character of control rights pertaining to each economic sector.

Additionally, there can be no independent middlemen or suppliers in the distribution of intermediary goods or finished products, nor labor markets cutting across sectors, precluding therefore the emergence of agents as appraisers and makers of prices and costs. The synchronizing or coordinating role of intermediary agents operating in factor markets is therefore precluded, and the segmentation, isolation, and divergent development of markets, such as they are, continues apace.

This concluding discussion may recall Hayek's critique of socialist central planning. For Hayek, the question was "whether planning is to be done centrally, by one authority for the whole economic system," or effected by "many separate persons" on the basis of local information and local knowledge as individuals strive "to fit their plans in with those of others" (Hayek, 1945, p. 521). This perspective implicates the middlemen and brokers whose economic role in large part is to determine which factors of production are undervalued or underutilized. It also argues for the development and integration of markets for the sake of a more targeted and effective use of all of the material and human resources of society.

REFERENCES

Barzel, Yoram (1997). *Economic Analysis of Property Rights*. Second Edition. Cambridge: Cambridge University Press.

Boisot, Max and John Child (1997). "Organizations as Adaptive Systems in Complex Environments: The Case for China." WP 23-97, Judge Institute Working Paper Series. Available at: http:// www.jims.cam.ac.uk/research/working_papers/abstract_97/9723.html.

Braguinsky, Serguey (1999). "On 'Coasian Economics' and 'The Economics of Coase'—Ownership, Firms Governance and Transaction Costs in the Transition to a Market Economy." Monograph, Yokohama City University, Yokohama, Japan.

Brown, Thomas Ford (2000). *Theoretical Perspectives on Social Capital*. Available at: http://jhunix.hcf.jhu.edu/~tombrown/Econsoc/soccap.html.

Earp, F. (1996). "Transactions, circuits, and identity: Proposing a conceptual network." *Journal of Economic Issues* 30: 407-412.

Gábor, I. (1994). "Modernity or a new type of duality?: The second economy today." In J. Mátyás Kováks (Ed.), *Transition to Capitalism?: The Legacy of Communism in Eastern Europe*. New Brunswick: Transaction Books.

Gunning, J. Patrick (1997). "Ludwig von Mises's Transformation of the Austrian Theory of Value and Cost." *History of Economics Review* (26).

Hayek, F. A. (1945). "The use of knowledge in society." *American Economic Review* 35: 19-30.

Hoskisson, Robert E.; Eden, Lorraine; Chung, Ming; and Mike Wright (2000). "Strategy in Emerging Economies." *Academy of Management Journal* 43 (3): 249-268.

March-Poquet, José (2001). "What Type of Transition is Cuba Undergoing?" *Post-Communist Economies* 12 (1).

Miles, R. E. and Snow, C. C. (1996). "Organizations: new concepts and new forms." In P. J. Buckley and J. Michie (Eds.), *Firms, Organizations and Contracts* (pp. 429-441). London: Oxford.

Portes, Alejandro and Patricia Landolt (1996). "The Downside of Social Capital." *The American Prospect* 26, May-June: 18-21.

Rius, Andrés (1997). "Preface to a Computational Economic Theory of Democracy." CEF Conference paper, Computation and Economic Theory, Stanford University. Available at: http://bucky.stanford.edu/cef97/abstracts/rius.htm.

SOLDIERS AND BUSINESSMEN:
THE FAR DURING THE SPECIAL PERIOD

Armando F. Mastrapa III

Cuba's economic crisis began as a result of the collapse of the Soviet Union and an inefficient management of the economy. This crisis brought uncertainty to the survivability of the Revolution. Soviet subsidies to the Cuban economy could no longer be counted on by the Castro regime. A new focus on economic methods and techniques to sustain the Revolution were being examined by the *Fuerzas Armadas Revolucionarias* (Revolutionary Armed Forces — FAR). In latter part of the 1980s,[1] Defense Minister Raúl Castro sent a team of FAR officers to Europe to study Western techniques of economic management and production. The FAR were gradually assuming the responsibility of guiding the economy in its most difficult of times. The collapse of the Soviet Union ushered in a "Special Period in Time of Peace" as the supreme leader Fidel Castro used the term to signify the economic hardship of the system which called for a new initiative to solve the crisis.

The purpose of this essay is to analyze the FAR's involvement in addressing Cuba's economic crisis. The first part will look at the "special period" and its cause. The second part will review the FAR's management and strategy to address the crisis, e.g., the creation and implementation of *perfeccionamiento empresarial* and the last part will examine the armed forces control of the Cuban economy's two important sectors — tourism and sugar.

SPECIAL PERIOD

Cuba's economic crisis of the early 1990s created concern in the leadership for the survival of the regime. Speculation on the country's total economic collapse surfaced yet the regime saw in the FAR the opportunity to affect the economy's performance by employing new organizational management strategies and techniques.

Fidel Castro, the Commander-In-Chief, made a public pronouncement in January, 1990 forewarning the severe effect that the economic crisis would have on the Cuban populace. He stated,

> What does the special period in time of peace mean? That the economic problems would be so serious — because of relations with the countries of Eastern Europe or because of factors or processes in the Soviet Union — that our country would face a situation in which obtaining supplies would be very difficult. Bear in mind that all of our fuel imports come from the USSR and think about what it could mean if such imports were reduced by a third or by one half because of supply difficulties in the USSR or even if they were reduced to zero, a situation that would be equivalent to what we call the special period in time of war…It would not be so grave in time of peace because there would be some possibilities of exports and imports in that scenario.[2]

---

1. See Jorge I. Domínguez, "Cuba in the 1980s," *Foreign Affairs*, Vol. 65, No. 1 (1986), pp. 118-135, for an assessment of the 1980s.

2. "Período Especial," Ministerio de las Fuerzas Armadas Revolucionarias (MINFAR), (June 29, 2000), <http://www.cubagob.cu/otras_info/minfar/periodo_especial.html>, (translation by the author).

Two underlying factors caused the economic crisis — first, the cut off of external aid and second an inefficient economic model. Jorge Pérez-López points out that "the underlying causes of the crisis are the well known inefficiencies of centrally planned economies, compounded by distortions created by massive inflows of resources from the socialist bloc and the obstinacy of the leadership to undertake the political and economic reforms necessary to overcome the crisis."[3] The "special period" forced a reexamination of the Cuban government's economic policies and opened the way for the FAR to tackle the crisis by employing Western-styled business initiatives.

PERFECCIONAMIENTO EMPRESARIAL

Before the economic crisis of the 1990s, the Cuban government was examining new methods to make the economy more efficient and productive. The FAR were given the charge of taking control and administering enterprises so that they would implement organizational order to their function and production.

Army Corps General and Minister of the Revolutionary Armed Forces Raúl Castro saw the need to train his top officer corps in management techniques to run enterprises that would in effect be case studies and, depending on their success, would later be transferred to the civilian sectors of the economy. Prior to the collapse of the Eastern European socialist economies, Raúl Castro sent his top officers to Western Europe to train in business methods and practices so that they would later be able to apply them to the Cuban economy. Among those management experts studied were Peter F. Drucker, the late W. Edwards Deming and John P. Kotter.

In his book, *Management: Tasks, Responsibilities, Practices*, Peter Drucker addresses the policies and practices to accomplish managerial tasks. He states, "the manager always has to administer. He has to manage and improve what already exists and is already known. But he also has to be an entrepreneur. He has to redirect resources from areas of low or diminishing results to areas of high or increasing results. He has to slough off yesterday and to render obsolete what already exists and is already known. He has to create tomorrow."[4] Meanwhile W. Edwards Deming viewed with importance the concepts of quality and innovation. He articulated the view that "quality is improved in three ways: through innovation in design of a product or a service, through innovation in processes, and through improvement of existing processes. Hard work will not ensure quality. Best efforts will not ensure quality, and neither will gadgets, computers or investment in machinery. A necessary ingredient for improvement of quality is the application of profound knowledge we have in abundance. We must learn to use it."[5] And John P. Kotter guides the critical stages of leadership by changing the process of how organizations do business. Kotter believes that "transforming an organization is the ultimate test of leadership, but understanding the change process is essential to many aspects of a leader's job. Two skills in particular — building coalitions and creating a vision — are especially relevant to our times."[6]

The concepts and instructions of these management experts were the guiding strategy for FAR officers who applied their methods to the entrepreneurial environment. As Army General Reinaldo Muñoz López states, "we have trained our officials with a broader

---

3. Jorge F. Pérez-López, "The Cuban Economic Crisis of the 1990s and the External Sector," in *Cuba in Transition—Volume 8* (Washington: Association for the Study of the Cuban Economy, 1998).

4. Peter F. Drucker, *Management: Tasks, Responsibilities, Practices* (New York: Harper Business, 1993), p. 45.

5. W. Edwards Deming, "Quality and the Required Style of Management: The Need for Change," *The Journal for Quality and Participation* (1988). <http://deming.eng.clemson.edu/pub/den/files/reqstyle.txt>.

6. John P. Kotter, "Winning at Change," *Leader to Leader*, no. 10 (Fall 1998), <http://www.pfdf.org/leadersbook/L2L/fall1998/kotter.html>.

profile, with a much greater understanding of the role of the economy in defense."[7]

Cuba's armed forces implemented their own management technique by creating *perfeccionamiento empresarial* (business improvement). By adapting the West's management methods of business, the FAR began to put into practice their own homegrown business model. *Perfeccionamiento empresarial*'s main objective is to "increase maximum competition and efficiency of the base power, and establish the politics, principals and procedures that propel the development of the initiative, creativity and the responsibility of all managers and workers."[8]

The Business System of the FAR and the Department of Economic Affairs of the Ministry of Revolutionary Armed Forces (MINFAR) oversee the business enterprises directed by the FAR. Under the direction of officers like Brigadier General Luis Pérez Róspide who headed the *Unión de la Industria Militar* (Military Industries Union — UIM), and Colonel Armando Pérez Betancourt, who is Secretary of the Grupo Gubernamental de Perfeccionamiento Empresarial, the FAR shifted their management experiences into policy action.

The first application of the new management techniques was in the Military Industries Union, a powerful conglomerate of 12 enterprises throughout Cuba. UIM has the "mission to assure the repair of arms and the technology present in land, air, and naval units of the Revolutionary Armed Forces (FAR) as well as their periodic modernization, in accord with advances in technological development worldwide. It also controls a number of factories destined for production of light armament for infantry, ammunition, mines and other diverse outputs. It also develops important production that is commercialized in the in-

ternational and national markets."[9] Not only is the UIM involved with the production of military goods, but also it is also into biotechnology, sugar mills and manufacturing pharmaceutical products. "In 1994, the Military Industries Union produced 58 million pesos worth of goods, striving to achieve the principle of financial self-sufficiency. The Union's policies have enabled the FAR to satisfy a large number of its needs and successfully produce for the civilian sector."[10] Thus, the Union's success served as a blueprint for transferring managerial and organizational methods and practices to the civilian sectors of the economy.

MILITARIZATION OF THE ECONOMY

The marginal success of the Military Industries Union gave FAR officers the necessary experience to oversee two important sectors of the economy: sugar and tourism. By placing the FAR in charge of these sectors of Cuba's economy, the regime assured success to its survivability. In militarizing the management process and modernization of these sectors, the FAR ensured its own economic well being and that of the regime.

Domingo Amuchastegui contends that the FAR "are not militarizing the sectors and institutions to which they have expanded; it is not the regimentation of industries, services or agriculture, but its modernization according to certain models and standards perfectly comparable to those of *fordism*, including direct incentives. Their language is not that of *manu militari*, but of costs and benefits, of necessary layoffs, of responding to market demands of mathematical models, and relying on principles of financial engineering, of computerized systems and complex telecommunications, and not in giving orders or

---

7. America's Defense Monitor, "The Cuban Military: An Economic Force," Video Transcript (January 16, 2000).

8. "Bases generales del perfeccionamiento empresarial," *Opciones: Semanario Financiero, Comercial y Turístico*, no. 46, Año V (Noviembre 15, 1998), <http://www.opciones.cubaweb.cu/en39/wanda.html>.

9. "Industria Militar," Ministerio de las Fuerzas Armadas Revolucionarias (MINFAR), (June 29, 2000), <http://www.cubagob.cu/otras_info/minfar/industria/industria_militar.htm>.

10. Havana Cuba Vision Network, "Military Industries Increase Items for Civilian Sector," in FBIS-LAT-95-071 (12 April 1995), <http://wnc.fedworld.gov>.

resorting to extra-economic coercion."[11] This modernization of models and standards places an order of improved performance of the slowly recovering sectors of the economy.

In recent years, the sugar industry has suffered great losses. Minister of Sugar Nelson Torres was replaced in 1997 by Division General Ulises Rosales del Toro. This move by the regime was seen as a militarization of the Cuban economy. Jamie Suchlicki comments that "the sector is producing such poor results that there were no other alternatives. It is in part the militarization of the Cuban economy."[12] Sugar production was at its lowest level in well over 50 years. For the 1997 and 1998 harvests, total production was between 3.1 and 3.2 million metric tons, while exports are believed to have reached 2.4 million tons. For the 1998/1999 harvest, the Cuban government is reporting production in the order of 3.6 million tons. It is estimated that for the 2000 harvest, production will rise to 4.5 million tons.[13]

However, the most lucrative sector of the Cuban economy and for the FAR has been tourism. In 1999, Cuba had 1.6 million visitors and during the first seven months of 2000, there were 1 million visitors.[14] One of the key enterprises in the tourist sector is Gaviota, S.A., dedicated to promoting and commercializing its vast network of services to international tourism. Controlling Gaviota are active and former FAR officers. Gaviota operates and controls the following enterprises: Hoteles Gaviota, Gaviota Tour, Arcoiris, Marinas Gaviota, Via (auto rentals), Transgaviota (helicopter and small aircraft rentals), Tiendas Gaviota, Parques Naturales Gaviota, Inversiones Gaviota and Commercial Gaviota. At the end of 1998, Gaviota with 7% of existing rooms in the country, was able to capture in its hotels 10% of the island's visitors.[15]

Administering these enterprises and sectors are important players within the FAR command; among them is Division General Julio Casas Regueiro, who directs the Gaviota Tourism Group and is a *raulista*.[16] Frank Mora best sums up the success of military involvement in these enterprises: "rather than this new economic mission contributing to discontent within the FAR, it has offered many active and retired officers the means of protecting themselves from the economic crisis. Not only does the new economic role help ensure the institutional survival of the FAR during the 'special period,' but it allows many of its high- and middle-ranking officers to take advantage of emerging and lucrative opportunities in these areas. This partially alleviated the problem of morale and conflict in the military."[17] By providing these officers with a financial stake in the economic successes of these enterprises, the regime has assured their loyalty, institutional economic self-sufficiency and a direct link between their economic well being and the survival of the Revolution.

Therefore, the Armed Force's participation in economic activities has been beneficial to the regime as it provides a significant source of revenue from tourism

11. Domingo Amuchastegui, "Cuba's Armed Forces: Power and Reforms," in *Cuba in Transition—Volume 9* (Washington: Association for the Study of the Cuban Economy, 1999), p. 112.

12. Rui Ferreira, "Designación de militar genera debate entre expertos," *El Nuevo Herald Digital* (October 26, 1997).

13. Gary H. Maybarduk, "The State of the Cuban Economy 1998-1999," in *Cuba in Transition—Volume 9* (Washington: Association for the Study of the Cuban Economy, 1999), pp. 2-3; Pablo Alfonso, "Las 'mentiras encuadernadas' del Ministro de Azúcar," *El Nuevo Herald Digital* (Julio 23, 2000).

14. Directorio Turístico de Cuba, "Alcanza Cuba el millión de turistas en el 2000," (Julio 24, 2000), <http://www.dtcuba.com/esp/news/turismo/240700_T4.asp>.

15. "Grupo Gaviota," *El Nuevo Herald Digital* (Junio 13, 1999).

16. Raul Castro appointed key supporters loyal to him, thus consolidating his control over the FAR. For an assessment of the civilian control of the FAR see Frank O. Mora, "From Fidelismo to Raulismo: Civilian Control of the Military in Cuba," *Problems of Post Communism*, vol. 46, no. 2 (March-April 1999), pp. 25-38.

17. *Ibid.*

as well as the enrichment of the officer corps, which creates loyalty to the hierarchy.[18]

CONCLUSION

The "special period" brought the FAR a new mission of active management of important economic sectors. The days of foreign campaigns have been replaced with domestic organizational leadership and direction of enterprises.

By adopting Western style management and organizational techniques, the FAR first began its business operation with the Military Industries Union (UIM) and later created its own business improvement model — *perfeccionamiento empresarial.* The success of the UIM was a catalyst to expand into the key economic sectors of the Cuban economy: sugar and tourism. Utilizing the concepts of modernized methods of management and organizational structure, the FAR retooled economic socialist theory with a quasi-capitalist styled one.

The modest success of these economic sectors under FAR control does not resolve the major problem that the Cuban economy faces. The inefficiencies of centrally planned economies remains Cuba's major economic hurdle to modernization and the FAR's management of just two sectors does not sustain the failures of an economy based on this model.

Key officers involved in the FAR's enterprises are loyal to Raúl Castro and their entrepreneurial successes are linked to the survivability of the regime. They are experienced business leaders who have a vested self and institutional interest in asserting control over the important sectors of the Cuban economy. They have built an economic power-base that will be important during the post-Castro transition period. Combined with their institutional power, they will be key actors in a transitional period. However, the risk that the FAR officers face is that a sole focus on entrepreneurial success that provides a high standard of living for them will erode military readiness and order and foster new loyalties that can be inimical to their interests.

---

18. Armando F. Mastrapa III, "Evolution, Transition and the Cuban Revolutionary Armed Forces," in *Cuba in Transition—Volume 9* (Washington: Association for the Study of the Cuban Economy, 1999), p. 117.

FAR: MASTERING REFORMS

Domingo Amuchastegui

More than 15 years ago, something very important began to take shape. The *Fuerzas Armadas Revolucionarias* (FAR) began to restructure their industries and services. Such changes became to be known as *perfeccionamiento empresarial* (managerial improvement). No one paid too much attention to this development at the time despite of its tremendous importance. Nowadays, and especially after the V Congress of the Cuban Communist Party (PCC), held in October of 1997, when *perfeccionamiento empresarial* was adopted as the Party official policy to guide the full restructuring of the Cuban state economic system, it has become a must for a clear understanding of the latter and the current dynamics of reforms in Cuba.

Before entering into a discussion on *perfeccionamiento*, it is important to clarify the reasons why in the early 1980s the FAR embarked on a process that departed so radically from the existing policies and institutions. Let us outline some of the reasons behind such a decision.

First, Soviet-Cuban relations were entering an increasingly conflicting stage, which began in the late 1970s, the last years of the Brezhnev era. A chain of dramatic clashes with Soviet policies and actions characterized bilateral relations since then. Cuban unilateral actions in Angola (1975) and Ethiopia (1977) caused great concern and displeased the Soviet leadership. The Soviets even tried to stop Cuba's initial involvement in Ethiopia. In Angola, as in the past, they supported the *fraccionistas* and their armed uprising against Neto, who was being supported by the Cuban forces. Clashes over the support of the

Sandinistas and other guerrilla movements in Central America, in open opposition to Soviet policies, was another major source of conflict.

By 1979 two events came to aggravate bilateral relations. One was the failure of Cuban leaders to make the Soviet leadership accept their views and approaches regarding the dangers of the Reagan option and the impact of the Santa Fe program. Subsequently, the Soviets denied any possibility for additional commitments regarding defense and security, including requests for large increases in military supplies, particularly with updated technology; Moscow made it clear that security arrangements would have to adjust to the new and changing circumstances and Soviet leaders increasingly challenged Cuban views and actions. Soviet reactions on issues such as the submarine base at Cienfuegos and the subsequent deployment of Cuban submarines near U.S. targets, the incidents over the supply of MiG 23s, among others, were additional episodes perceived in the eyes of the Cuban leaders as dangerous signs of a potential sell-out. Cuban demands and pressures found blunt and unwavering Soviet rebuttals. These strained relations had an enormous impact on the Cuban leaders, who felt a growing sense of unreliability and insecurity about their Soviet allies as never before.

At the time, Cuba's international position had been boosted by its chairmanship of the Non-Aligned Movement (NAM), an achievement not appreciated by Moscow. The Soviets did not hesitate or consult with their Cuban allies on the decision to invade Afghanistan, a NAM member country. Fidel Castro felt humiliated, outraged and, once again, frustrated almost as much as during the days of the Missile Crisis. Forced to support — at least publicly — the Soviet invasion of Afghanistan, he took special care in conveying to the Soviet leadership his strongest condemnation and total disagreement with such action. At the same time, he shared these views with close associates and several Third World leaders.

Second, Soviet economic and military cooperation was seriously questioned and all kinds of uncertainties flourished among Cuban leaders. The repeated visits of to Havana of Nikolai Baibakov, Chairman of the Soviet Central Planning Agency, *GOSPLAN*, pointed to a *cul-de-sac* in relations and some key important economic projects in Cuba could not be properly implemented. The days of a second Soviet economic and oil embargo, as in 1965-1968, was perceived as a serious possibility.

And third, among Cuban experts dealing with Soviet/COMECOM affairs there was a growing perception that the economic decline in Cuba's foreign allies was reaching new and unprecedented heights — although no one predicted an imminent collapse — and that this was going to have a very negative impact over relations with Cuba.

Later on, in the course of the first half of the 1980s, relations would get even worse. Events in Central America and Granada had Soviet and Cuban policies clashing again and again. And military coordination with Moscow over Angola was cancelled completely.

This is the context in which the Cuban leaders began to seek new ways and alternatives. This is the context in which Fidel Castro took several key decisions:

- his overture to the Cuban-American community as a permanent component of Cuba's economic and political security; the orchestrating of the Mariel boatlift; and engaging in secret talks with representatives of the Reagan administration;

- the adoption and proclamation of the strategic policy of *Guerra de Todo el Pueblo* (All People's War);

- the creation of the *Milicias de Tropas Territoriales, MTT* (Militia Territorial Troops) and the acceptance of a special Vietnamese advisory for

such purposes, in opposition to Soviet advice; and

- the accelerated dismantling of the *Sistema de Dirección y Planificación de la Economía* (SDPE), the overall economic management and planning system sponsored by the Soviet Union.

These decisions confirmed the crisis of the Soviet-Cuban alliance, a crisis that did not result from the coming into power of Gorbachev — it simply culminated during Gorbachev's tenure — or from the collapse of the Berlin Wall.

It is in this context that *perfeccionamiento empresarial* is born: the prototype of a new economic system, implying a total restructuring of the economic, institutional, social, and, eventually, of the existing political system. The task of developing and implementing *perfeccionamiento* was not entrusted to the *Junta Central de Planificación* (a dying institution at that time), the Economic Department of the Central Committee of the Cuban Communist Party, the School of Economics of the University of Havana, or any other Cuban think-tank specialized in economic affairs. Instead, the FAR is the institution entrusted with this project. Why the FAR? Within the existing power structure the FAR provided important advantages:

- The highest degree of legitimacy in terms of historical background, performance, efficiency, control, honesty, prestige, dedication, loyalty, trustworthiness, popularity, representation/promotion of blacks, and real authority.

- The highest degree of reliability to meet the complexities and challenges of the drastic changes, something that was, and continues to be, perceived as entailing very high risks in terms of national security (*"defensa de la Revolución,"* is the equivalent concept in Cuban rhetoric) considering the changes in the nature of the system, the emerging social tensions, and the implications of close association with foreign capital/technology/influence.

- The best infrastructure, within Cuban standards, in every field (resources, reserves, transport, communications, financial accountability, management, and others) together with a highly qualified structure of professional personnel and cadres.

Mastering the reforms associated with *perfeccionamiento* has become the biggest and most difficult battle ever to be waged by the FAR, seeking to achieve survival and continuity.

HOW DID IT COME ABOUT?

The growing sense that the whole economic system had to be redefined and restructured was already very much in the minds of Fidel Castro and his brother Raúl by the early 1980s, but with very different perceptions and perspectives. While Fidel Castro was still considering various options and unrealistic projects, his brother Raúl focused on the need to experiment with one specific and coherent system, more in line with the major trends in the real world. Fidel Castro, while eager to dismantle the SDPE (some called it Baibakov's pet project), was absolutely reluctant to Raúl's project and ideas and had no alternative solution of his own. The ultimate compromise was to let Raúl experiment with his project, but only within the confines of the FAR.

By 1984-85 everything was ready to start the project. The enterprise chosen to begin the experiment was the huge "Ernesto Ché Guevara" industrial plant in Manicaragua, one of the key industries of the *Unión de la Industria Militar*. The team of planners, executives, and administrators (later in 1986 known as *Grupo de Perfeccionamiento Empresarial*, whose executive secretary was and continues to be Engineer Colonel Armando Pérez Betancourt), mostly composed of engineers and economists, were under the supervision of Division General Julio Casas Regueiro, who reported to Raúl Castro. Gradually, it expanded to all of the *Unión de la Industria Militar* (industries, services, and finance) and its 230 enterprises. By 1987, the slogan that the FAR was the laboratory for economic organization and leadership was becoming very popular among military leaders. To realize how subversive the experiment was, we must realize that a special authorization had to be issued by the government to allow the FAR to violate, ignore, bypass, more than 100 norms, codes, and regulations of the existing system.

Within 5 years, *perfeccionamiento* was already being applied within the FAR. Close to 40 percent (some 27,000 workers, technicians, and professionals) of the FAR civilian workforce (a key component within the military industries) was laid-off, while the gradual reduction of the armed forces reached 50 percent of its 1980 level. The incredible paradox in 1991 was that while the country was crumbling, virtually in shambles, the FAR were doing pretty well in a comparative sense.

The question then was: why not expand the experiment to the rest of the country? The answer was neither economic nor technical — it was essentially political. The internal pressures on Fidel Castro to move ahead and swiftly with reforms had caused serious internal clashes within the Cuban leadership. Men who had had the courage to advocate for urgent changes since the mid-1980s had been dismissed from the Politburo — like Julio Camacho Aguilera and Sergio del Valle. Juan Almeida was on the verge of a major confrontation with Fidel. And last, but not least, his own brother, Raúl, had had another major confrontation with his older brother on the same grounds as the others. Carlos Aldana and other low-level members of the Politburo were also in favor of changes, but Fidel Castro could not tolerate anything along such a line. It all smelled to him of *perestroika* and *glasnost,* and the consequences were too evident: *el desmerangamiento,* as he called it, meaning the crumbling of the systems in Easter Europe and the Soviet Union. He was unwilling to take any risk that could place in jeopardy his domestic control. And for Fidel Castro, expanding *perfeccionamiento* outside of the FAR and into the rest of the country could have very risky consequences.

It was only after the popular demonstrations and clashes in Cojímar-Regla in the summer of 1993 and in Havana in August of 1994, that Fidel Castro began yielding to the enormous pressures from within. It was only then that the imperative for reforms began to gain momentum, but even then any attempt to adopt *perfeccionamiento* as a general policy was rejected. His concession was that a small number of key enterprises (telecommunications, mining, beverages, rubber, energy, fisheries, and others) could adopt the new system on an experimental basis. Finally, a group of 100 enterprises carefully selected began preparing for the different steps and stages. A combination of increased domestic and international pressures plus encouraging good experimental results finally led, 12 years later, to the doption by the V Congress of the Cuban Communist Party of *perfeccionamiento* as a general economic strategy.

By 1999, approximately 900 enterprises (close to 30 percent of the existing industries in the country) were involved in implementing the early stages of *perfeccionamiento*. The group of 100 enterprises that began to implement *perfeccionamiento* has moved ahead rather successfully; 45 of them have been approved to continue on the path of implementation on the basis of their diagnoses, reliable accounting systems, and other previous studies, and 22 others have fulfilled the requirements for step one.

Currently — as of June 2000 — 1,419 out of a grand total of more than 3,000 enterprises are already involved in the early stages of the *perfeccionamiento*. They employ approximately 810,000 workers. The process is moving ahead cautiously, looking for reliable results, beginning with the diagnoses. For example, in one very sensitive and important province like Santiago de Cuba there were 72 enterprises already involved in the different steps in conducting the diagnoses, but only 4 have been approved to move ahead to the next stage.

The slow and cautious implementation of *perfeccionamiento* is currently subject to various pressures: from worker's unions, provincial and local administrators, collapsing industries, tensions derived from unemployment, need to expand to other areas, growing private sector, increased foreign investment, international sources. These pressures are likely to play a role in accelerating and expanding *perfeccionamiento*.

SOURCES AND LEADERSHIP

What are the sources and experiences guiding *perfeccionamiento*? Some who favor comparative studies will say that it is an ill-conceived, and too late, mixture of economic reforms from Hungary and Yugoslavia with a touch of Leiberman's legacy of Soviet re-

formists under Khruschev. In my humble opinion they are missing the current context and a clear understanding of the Cuban "big picture."

Others will argue that *perfeccionamiento* is inspired by the Chinese or even the Burmese paths, suggesting a more conservative, fragmented, approach to reforms. To some extent the arguments may be valid, but they are still far from real, local dynamics.

The Chinese pattern has had considerable influence; after all it preserves a certain flavor of nostalgia associated with socialist and communist past experiences. And Cuban leaders travelling to China — as part of the ritual of their host — are regularly taken to see and learn from Shenzhen. Zhu Rongji and his advisers are well known to Cuban leaders and executives. When Raúl Castro went to China, he spent long hours talking to Zhu (something that was not reflected in the Cuban press) and invited his main adviser to travel to Cuba (something that Fidel did not do when he visited China). This famous adviser went to Cuba, caused a tremendous impact, talked to leaders and executives for many hours and days, but there was one person who refused to do so, except for a brief and formal reception: Fidel Castro. This shows, once more, the different approaches, attitudes, and inclinations that coexist inside the Cuban leadership, and that Fidel Castro is, as always, the less enthusiastic person regarding the Chinese approach and this helps to curtail and prevent, to a considerable extent, the influence of the Chinese model. But this should not mislead us to underestimate China's enormous importance for the Cuban leadership. This importance is not so much as a model but as a practical alliance in terms of cooperation, trade, technology, military supplies and cooperation, and the political and diplomatic support that China can lend as a big power and a permanent member of the U.N. Security Council.

What is then the theoretical and practical basis of *perfeccionamiento*? The best economists in the European Union, the United States, Canada, Latin America, and Japan. Their views translated, duplicated, circulated, from hand to hand, through lectures, workshops, and seminars. These views are all over the place together with IDB and ECLAC studies and lectures from experts from the IMF and the World Bank, going back to the early 1980s, when U.S. experts began lecturing Cuban leaders under the sponsorship of the Ford Foundation and other U.S. institutions. This is the cultural and theoretical environment of the *Grupo Gubernamental para el Perfeccionamiento Empresarial*, the actual guiding and supervisory institution, and the kind of information and knowledge it disseminates. Its ideas are being debated at seminars and in publications of the ANEC (*Asociacion Nacional de Economistas Cubanos*, National Association of Cuban Economists), within the Cuban "think tanks" (*centros de estudios*), the School of Economics, and others. Marxism? It is acceptable as part of a certain legacy that it contains and for some methodological value. Nationalism? Yes, very much so, and more deeply entrenched.

The other important question concerns leadership. I am not referring to Fidel Castro, Raúl Castro, and others from the "old guard," but to the thousands of executives, managers, advisers, counselors, that is, the professional elite. Are they conducting this process with the old manuals from the Soviet Union? Hundreds and thousands of them have been retrained and retooled in many of the best universities and economic institutions of the Western Hemisphere, the European Union, and Japan over the last 10 years. Knowledge, culture, values, attitudes, even the current operational language, have changed considerably. They speak in terms of markets, of costs and benefits, of statistics and prices, of mathematical modeling and financial engineering, and even of stock markets. These professionals are the real leadership of the *perfeccionamiento*.

Allow me to use a metaphor : When Zhou and Deng were fighting against Mao and his supporters, where was Zhou Rongji? When the Four Modernizations were proclaimed in China, there were all sorts of objections, but nevertheless they cleared the way and helped history evolve. Where was Zhou Rongji if not somewhere along the line? This sense of history might help to understand the current dynamics of the Cuban experience beyond any other wishful thinking in terms of transition scenarios, at least for the foreseeable future.

GUIDING FORCE OR MILITARIZATION?

Perfeccionamiento has led to a considerable increase of the direct share of power in the hands of the FAR or former FAR leaders. A brief overview of the institutions and enterprises that are under the direct control, supervision or influence of the FAR provides ample evidence on this point:

- Ministry of the Sugar Industry (Division General Ulises Rosales del Toro, former Chief of Staff of the FAR, and a Politburo member).

- Ministry of Fisheries and Merchant Marine (Ship Captain/Colonel Orlando Rodríguez Romay, "the youngest colonel in the FAR" in the 1980s, member of the Central Committee).

- Ministry of Transport and Ports (Colonel Alvaro Pérez Morales).

- Cuban Civil Aviation Corporation, Sociedad Anónima, CACSA (Division General Rogelio Acevedo, member of the Central Committee).

- National Institute of State Reserves (Brigadier General Moisés Sio Wong).

- *Plan Turquino-Manatí,* a huge developmental plan covering some 20 municipalities, approximately 20 percent of the Cuban territory, in the Cuban mountain ranges and the Ciénaga de Zapata, where a large portion of the Ejército Juvenil del Trabajo is concentrated.

- *Banca Metropolitana* (Metropolitan Bank), a banking institution created 5 years ago.

- *Habanos S.A.,* an enterprise in charge of international marketing of Cuban tobacco/cigars/cigarettes. When created in the early 1990s, headed by Colonel Linares from the FAR; due to Linares' health problems, Colonel Oscar Basulto took over.

- *Gaviota S.A.,* Cuba's fastest growing tourist enterprise since 1992 in association with Spanish, German, French, and Jamaican capital. One of FAR's "pet" projects.

- *Grupo de Electrónica de Cuba,* formally a part of the Ministry of Steel, Mechanical Industry, and

Electronics, known as SIME, but very much autonomous under the direction of *Comandante de la Revolución* Ramiro Valdés Menéndez, a former Politburo/Central Committee member and former Minister of the Interior. The backbone of this *Grupo* is COPEXTEL, specialized in telecom.

• CIMEX, the First Cuban corporation to operate as a *Sociedad Anónima*. Created in 1979 under the control of the Ministry of Interior to engage in foreign trade of goods and services through 17 holding companies under its control; since 1989 under FAR jurisdiction.

• CUBANACAN, established in the early 1980s following the same pattern as CIMEX; currently has 10 companies focused on tourism and works very closely with CIMEX.

• *TECNOTEC,* an importer/exporter of high tech for civilian and military purposes.

• GeoCuba Entrepreneurial Group, which deals with policies and transactions connected with land concessions/leasing, related to mining, tourism, agriculture and real estate.

• Industrial Military Union, consisting of 12 major industries/services and 16 factories and bases throughout the country encompassing 230 facilities. Now closely associated with the most prosperous emergent sectors of the state economy. Headed by Colonel Luis Bernal León.

• Ministry of Information Technology and Communications. For more than 20 years it was in the hands of the FAR. Under Brigadier General Silvano Colás, the Ministry was refurbished in the mid 1990s and ETECSA — an important joint venture with Italian corporation STET — was founded. Recently, General Colás returned to the FAR and a famous civilian technocrat, Engineer Ignacio González Planas, the man who "rescued" SIME in the 1990s, was appointed Minister. Moreover, all information technology functions were transferred from SIME to a newly redesigned ministry under the name of Communications and Information Technology. It re-

mains to be seen if Colás' replacement was routine or a move to involve more civilians at high levels. In any case, FAR influence over Communications and IT is considered to be high.

• Citrus, both agriculture and industrial processing, an important sector of the economy controlled by the military with Israeli enterprise BM Group.

• Export-Processing Zones (EPZ)-Free Trade Zones (FTZ), under CIMEX (HAVANA IN BOND, in the Berroa Valley, in the outskirts of the capital city of Havana) and ALMACENES UNIVERSALES S.A. in El Chico (outskirts of Havana), and the city ports of Mariel and Cienfuegos.

• The State Commission for *Perfeccionamiento Empresarial,* where Colonel Pérez Betancourt plays a key role.

• Ideological Department of the Central Committee, Colonel Rolando Alfonso Borges, former second-in-command of the Central Political Directorate at the General Staff.

By every possible standard, this is well beyond the "lion's share" of the nation's economy. But it is not only this apparently disproportionate share that is relevant in understanding the FAR's place and role in mastering reforms. Their role in the policymaking process is not simply determined — and wrongly perceived — by how many high-ranking officers we find in the Central Committee and even in the Politburo (compared with earlier years, they have reached today their lowest level of numerical representation), but by the overwhelming centrality of the FAR in every single area of policymaking. We may wrongly perceive the Politburo as the only source of policymaking or look at the Council of Ministers as another major source, but the truth is that frequent policy designs and recommendations can play a more influential and decisive role than those coming from other quarters in the Party or the Government.

A similar pattern is connected with the Consejos de Defensa of the three armies, whose deliberations, concerns, and suggestions are extremely important.

Research and analyses conducted by the National Defense College in the 1990s are similarly important compared with other research centers. Looking at names, Julio Casas Regueiro, Leonardo Andollo, Luis Pérez Róspide, Armando Pérez Betancourt or Eladio Fernández Cívico (all of them key players from the FAR) are more crucial today to real policymaking in Cuba than many civilian ministers or brilliant civilian economists like Pedro Monreal, Julio Carranza, Osvaldo Martínez or even José Luis Rodríguez.

Should *perfeccionamiento* be perceived as a process of militarization, as was the failed experience of the late 1960s? Not at all. They are not militarizing the sectors and institutions to which they have expanded. They do not uphold a command economy — quite the opposite. It is not the regimentation of industries, services or agriculture, without an economic rationale. On the contrary, their language and tools are not those of *manu militari* or extra-economic coercion, but of costs and benefits and direct incentives, of eliminating subsidies and implementing massive lay-offs when necessary, of strict and transparent accountability, of responding to market demands and meeting each client's needs. It is by no means giving orders or resorting to direct pressures of any kind but responding to financial principles and updated technology.

This is not Prussian *militarization*, Russian *war communism*, a Pol Pot-type design or the rigid schemes of the Burmese military. These are not the whims and improvisations of Fidel Castro as in the past. This is a political elite, with or without a uniform, highly unified, fighting for its survival, recovery, and continuity. It is not a segment of society or the state known as "the military," isolated in its drills and barracks. It is a group learning to master new systems and spaces in which they can insert themselves once they retire, and that will meet as well the expectations of the generations and segments of the population that are still loyal to the existing power structure.

PERFECCIONAMIENTO... WHAT IS IT ALL ABOUT?

Perfeccionamiento is the closest approximation to a capitalist-type of organization within the current conflicting trends and pace of reforms in Cuba. It brings down the old bureaucratic, rigidly centralized and chaotic system and all of its foundations, with the sole exception of the state nature of property. But even the latter is being actually and potentially undermined and diluted to varying degrees by legal redefinitions like corporations, entrepreneurial holding companies, sociedades anónimas (share companies), and even sociedades mercantiles de carácter privado, propiedad del Estado cubano, as well as different forms of association with foreign companies in Cuba and abroad. It may be considered and discussed as a peculiar experience of privatizing the Cuban state.

An interesting perspective on this issue is provided by the prestigious IRELA (Instituto de Relaciones Europeo-Latinoamericanas), an institution actively supported by the European Union, in a document issued in 1999:

> Aunque no se autorizara la creación de empresas privadas (referring to the V Congress of the Cuban Communist Party), éstas podrían emerger a largo plazo como resultado del proyecto de "perfeccionamiento empresarial": en agosto de 1998 se eligieron 103 empresas para imponer un nuevo modelo piloto de gestión descentralizada orientada hacia la economía de mercado. Durante 1999 se incluirán otras 700 empresas en el experimento. Según esta reforma, la dirección de las empresas tiene un mayor nivel de independencia, ya no rinden cuentas ante los Ministerios, no producen según un plan quinquenal, ofrecen incentivos laborales y funcionan bajo los criterios de la economía de mercado (se permite la bancarrota). Según algunos expertos cubanos, si la reforma se lleva a cabo en estos términos, surgirán a largo plazo empresas privadas *de facto*.[1]

The implementation of perfeccionamiento is not a bureaucratic decision by which certain enterprises join the process: there is no jumping on the bandwagon or being a free-rider. Every enterprise must

---

1. IRELA, *40 años de revolución en Cuba: ¿Transición hacia dónde?*, Dossier 68, Madrid, Mayo 1999, p. 23.

start by doing away with their old foundations among them: centralization, central budgeting, production plans that totally disregard costs, planning based on material balances rather than on costs, lack of internal accounting systems and accounts payable and receivable systems, reliable statistics, inflated payrolls, huge inventories, subsidies, low levels of productivity, producing on the basis of a plan and not taking into consideration the specific needs of clients, low quality standards. Making this dramatic change is step one, the so-called diagnosis stage. Those who fail step one are in serious trouble and, eventually, will be out of the game.

It is only after successfully negotiating step one that enterprises will be evaluated to determine if they qualify to be admitted into *perfeccionamiento*. Once inside the system, they will have to meet a number of additional requirements to be granted the full benefits of achieving, and remaining within, *perfeccionamiento*, meaning that they have reached full decentralization and autonomy in every aspect; that they are on their own; that the whole production process of production will be placed entirely in their hands, from their supplies of raw materials down to the operation of their accounts in *pesos* and hard currency, their loans and payments; that they will be able to define or change production lines, upgrade technology and research, increase quality, productivity, and competetiveness, become profitable and make money; that they will be able to conduct their businesses with foreign partners in the country and abroad, going into the Internet with their websites, and distribute incentives and other social benefits.

For those not meeting the standards, the ultimate outcome will be closing down. This is a course of action that has been gaining momentum lately as several key government officials have raised, repeatedly, the possibility of closing down industries, including a considerable number of sugar mills, if they do not meet standards within two-years time at the most, arguing that those not meeting the standards cannot go living at the expense of others' achievements and financial viability.

Another important step being sought by *perfeccionamiento* is what has been described as *redimensiona-miento*, meaning essentially the downsizing of big enterprises and factories (those with more than 500, 1000 or even 3000-4000 workers. This *gigantismo* — as it has been described — is being tackled by a process of *redimensionamiento* which entails downsizing into small units, with less than 300 to 500 workers, and redefining productive profiles. It is believed that rationalization, technological upgrading, investment, control, and efficiency can flow more smoothly through the smaller enterprises.

Competitiveness is another key element. Government officials have stated clearly that there will be no protection given to Cuban products sold in the *mercado en frontera* (the dollar market in Cuba). Domestic producers of sea food, beverages, citrus, steel, cement, biotech products, pharmaceuticals, medical services, tourism, software, appliances, and others, will survive, compete, and succeed only on the basis of their costs, quality standards, and competitiveness *vis-à-vis* foreign products and services. Cuban electric fans competing *en frontera* with similar products from Japan, Korea or China or Cuban sea food competing in the EU markets, they have to meet the international standards without any protectionist interference, including subsidies.

Perfeccionamiento is not an isolated policy in the industrial sector; it potentially encompasses the entire economy, including services (tourism, banking, commerce), agriculture, and research, scientific and technological activities. Step by step, in a very cautious way, some times in virtual slow motion reflecting the contradictions at the leadership level, the pieces of the puzzle begin to fit. Cuba's reinsertion into Western markets; the reform of the banking system; the new investment law; the free zones; and a whole new body of legislation, principles, norms, and rules. These innovations are intended to reshape or shape the system to allow *perfeccionamiento* to work effectively.

PRELIMINARY CONCLUSIONS

On a national scale, we can argue that the *perfeccionamiento* is still a very recent experience (excluding their 12 years of isolation within the military), being implemented for less than two years and only five enterprises have completed the process. In many ways much of its development and long-term consequences remain to be seen. Objections? Yes, many. Conflicts and contradictions over its implementation? Millions of them, of course. Just one example: Let us all be aware that every step forward for *perfeccionamiento* will mean — as it has been proven already — tens of thousands of lay-offs and redundant workers that take time to relocate and readjust. Will the government risk it? It seems it is willing to do so, even in the sugar industry, where only the fittest will survive.

Is *perfeccionamiento* working? It seems to be working pretty well so far given the Cuban context. *Perfeccionamiento* is not something cosmetic or superficial. It is irreversible and it is not just a temporary thing. Will it deepen its scope? It is something unavoidable and it will be looked upon in the future as one of the turning points of the Cuban Revolution. Furthermore, my preliminary assessment suggests that it will have an impact over the next 10-20 years in transforming the Cuban polity and in shaping a very different transition, with very different outcomes, than those expected or suggested by many experts.

FAR, INC.

José Antonio Font

I was very appreciative when I was asked to participate in this session on the military in the economy of Cuba. Not only I am reconnected to the passion of my childhood — I collected toy soldiers — but now focused on a topic that requires mastering since, in most peoples' estimation, the Cuban Armed Forces will most likely play the determinant role in achieving the long term consolidation of the regime along the lines of the Chinese model, or in allowing and husbanding a transition to political democracy and market economy.

My comments will concentrate on Dr. Armando Mastrapa's contribution, entitled *Soldiers and Businessmen: The FAR During the Special Period.* I will, however, refer to and make use of Mr. Amuchastegui's paper entitled *Cuba's Armed Forces: Power and Reforms,* which was presented at last year's ASCE session.

Dr. Mastrapa's purpose is to "analyze the FAR's involvement in addressing Cuba's economic crisis." He believes that the "special period" forced an examination of the Cuban Government's economic policies and opened the way for the FAR to tackle the crisis by employing Western-styled business initiatives. In this connection, Mastrapa alerts us to the fact that even before the economic collapse of the early 1990s, Raul Castro had already sent his top officers to train in techniques promoted by management experts such as Peter Drucker, Edwards Deming and John P. Kotter. The purpose of this initiative, according to Dr. Mastrapa, was to train a cadre of military managers able to run enterprises in the civilian sectors of the economy.

He then very fleetingly tells us about the FAR's own homegrown business model — p*erfeccionamiento empresarial* — whose main objective is to "increase maximum competition and efficiency of the base power, and establish the politics, principles and procedures that propel the development of the initiative, creativity and responsibility of all bosses and workers." Regretfully, Dr. Mastrapa never deciphers what all this means, nor how widely it is implemented.

We are then introduced to the Military Industries Union, described as a powerful aggregate of 12 enterprises throughout Cuba. We are told that MIU is involved with the production of military items and that it is also into biotechnology, sugar mills and the manufacturing of pharmaceutical products. In a future study it may be important to know the relative importance of the 12 enterprises to the total economy, as well as who are they. We do learn from Dr. Mastrapa, however, that the marginal success of the MIU gave FAR officers the necessary experience to now oversee the sugar and tourism sectors of the economy.

In reference to sugar, we are provided statistics that reflect a gradual improvement in production from 1997 to the estimates for the 2000 season. In reference to tourism, we are told that the FAR oversees the tourist sector through Gaviota, S.A. Yet we are also told that Gaviota controls 7% of the existing rooms of the country. This relation between the FAR and tourism requires more clarification.

Dr. Mastrapa then provides his conclusions and we learn that the special period brought the FAR into the new mission of assuming the active management of important economic sectors. This is not debatable. And that by adopting Western style management and organizational techniques, the FAR replaced economic socialist theory with a capitalist one. We understand this to be limited to the areas that come under FAR management, and we would need to know more about the theory and practices of *perfeccionamiento empresarial*. Moreover, for all the techniques applied, the FAR functions within a monopolistic context, where King Castro bestows all production and export rights. This defines the model as a "mercantilist" one, rather than a capitalist one.

That the modest successes of these economic sectors does not resolve the major problem that the Cuban economy faces, because the inefficiencies of centrally planned economies, remains Cuba's major economic hurdle to modernization and the FAR's management of just two sectors does not sustain the failures of an economy based on this model.

These conclusions bring us to think about a very complex set of issues, and requires significant analysis by all of us. As a first step I would contrast this conclusion to what I understand to be the thesis of Mr. Amuchastegui's paper from last year's conference. In that paper he stated that the FAR were in the past, and continue to be, the single most important institution in providing leadership in the process of policy-making and in nominating candidates for key positions at the highest level of the state. A brief review of those led by the FAR can very well illustrate this point:

- Ministry of the Sugar Industry
- Instituto Nacional de la Reserva Estatal
- Ministry of Fisheries and Merchant Marine
- Ministry of Transport
- Ministry of Communications
- Ministry of Tourism
- Ministry of Higher Education
- Attorney General
- Cuban Civil Aviation Corporation, CACSA
- Habanos, S.A.
- Gaviota, S.A.
- Metropolitan Bank

- GeoCuba Entrepreneurial Group
- TECNOTEC
- Industrial Military Union
- Plan Turquino-Manati (covering 20% of the Cuban Territory)
- Plan de Perfeccionamiento Empresarial
- Ideological Department of the Central Committee

Dr. Amuchastegui concludes that, by every possible standard, this is well beyond the "lion's" share. If the FAR is in charge of the economy then the real conclusion may very well be that there remains an inherent contradiction between actual "Stalinist" policies and professed entrepreneurial practices within the FAR itself. The Cuban economy remains closed.

That key officers involved in the FAR's enterprises are loyal to Raul Castro and their entrepreneurial success are linked to the survivability of the regime. That they have built a power-base that will be important during the post-Castro transition period.

Here Amuchastegui also agrees with Mastrapa when he states that: "This (FAR) is a political elite, with or without uniform, highly unified, fighting for its survival, recovery and continuity; they are not a segment of society and state, known as 'the military,' isolated in their drills and barracks. They are building the new systems and spaces to which they can reinsert once they retire and that will meet, as well, the expectations of the generations that are still loyal to the existing power structure."

This conclusion is of outmost importance. The race is on for the future of Cuba, and it is between those who look to the consolidation of the regime along the lines of the Chinese Model — The Succession Model — and those who would want to achieve full transition to political democracy and market economy — The Transition Model. It appears that the FAR is leading the Succession Model.

In this connection, a situation analysis would be most interesting to determine who are the Cuban stockholders of the mixed enterprises? (There are some 450 in 34 sectors according to the most recent count.) And, how much of Cuba's territory and productive assets is currently under, or could still be transferred to the military and other accomplices of the regime, e.g., Ramiro Valdés Menéndez taking over electronics.

Indeed, paraphrasing Dr. Mastrapa, it appears that the FAR has shown to have a significant capacity to adapt and evolve as an institution able to lead in the process of survival and succession of the Cuban Revolution. The FAR has assumed the responsibility of guiding the Cuban economy in its most difficult of times. By providing military officers with a financial stake in the economic successes of the enterprises within the Military Industrial Union, and other business enterprises of the FAR, the regime has assured their loyalty and directly linked the survival of the revolution to them.

Notwithstanding the growing importance of the FAR, we should keep in mind that there are 11 million individuals in the island submitted to conditions of material and spiritual deprivation. There are an-

other 2 million in exile that out-produce the Cuban economy. When the rubber hits the road at some point in the future, all of the formulations of *perfeccionamiento empresarial* and similar reforms conducted by the FAR will hopefully be peacefully integrated into a market economy, or, in my modest estimation, they will be washed away by the power of historical forces and the will of a Cuban people that craves for freedom.

Let's be clear on this point. The FAR should be accountable for representing and guiding the system that sustains totalitarian practices and the exploitation of the Cuban worker by both foreign entities and the State. They control two and one-half of the three legs that sustain the regime: the FAR, the MININT, and now a significant portion of the Civil Sector. Who else, I ask, is responsible for the lack of freedom and impoverishment of the Cuban people?

A SURVEY OF SIGNIFICANT LEGAL CHANGES DURING CUBA'S SPECIAL PERIOD: SETTING PARAMETERS FOR CHANGE

Stephen J. Kimmerling

When Cuba lost the former Soviet Union's economic support, the island entered what is commonly called the Special Period. Stretching now for over a decade, the Special Period has been marked by material deprivation, ongoing legal and illegal emigration, societal malaise, and government efforts to prop up revolutionary fervor.

But the Special Period has also featured domestic legal changes[1] aimed at implementing economic recovery and long-term development strategies based on diversified foreign and domestic investment in capitalistic ventures. While the efficacy of these legal developments and the goals and planning behind them remain hotly debated, Cuba has indeed formed significant legal structures that are fomenting economic (and perhaps, ultimately, political) change within closely guarded parameters. This paper will summarize some of the more significant of these legal developments, emphasize how they interrelate to set limits

for change, and briefly explore those limits' implications and consequences.

The most important Cuban laws passed during the Special Period are those setting the structures and boundaries for economic development. Those meriting special attention are:

- The Constitution of 1992[2]

- The Law of Foreign Investment[3]

- Decree-Law No. 165: Duty-Free Zones and Industrial Parks[4]

- Decree-Law No. 173: Banks and Non-Banking Financial Institutions[5]

This is hardly an exhaustive list, and it by no means intends to give short shrift to laws affecting civil and political rights. Rather, its length acknowledges this paper's limits in discussing what even multiple volumes could not completely cover. Secondly, it re-

---

1. This paper will not explore Cuba's entry into bilateral or multilateral agreements during the Special Period. Though such agreements are certainly important, this paper looks at how domestic laws are laying the groundwork — and setting the limits — for change.

2. Constitución de la República de Cuba [hereinafter Constitution of 1992]. The full text is available on the Internet at http://www2.cuba.cu/gobierno/cuba.htm, accessible through Cuba's official website, http://www.cubaweb.cu. The Constitution was originally published in the Gaceta Oficial de la República de Cuba, no. 7, Aug. 1, 1992, and was printed in book format by Editora Política (1992). The 1992 Constitution is a revised version of the Constitution of 1976 and contains reforms approved by the Asamblea Nacional del Poder Popular in July 1992.

3. Ley No. 77 Sobre las Inversiones Extranjeras [Law No. 77: Foreign Investments] (1995) [hereinafter Foreign Investment Act], translated at http://www.geo.unipr.it/~davide/cuba/economy/LAW95/law1.html.

4. Decreto-Ley Número 165 de las Zonas Francas y Parques Industriales [Decree-Law 165: Duty-Free Zones and Industrial Parks] (1996) [hereinafter Duty-Free Zones and Industrial Parks Law], translated at http://www.giraldilla.com/lawsDL165.htm).

5. Decreto-Ley Numero 173 Sobre los Bancos e Instituciones Financieras no Bancarias [Decree-Law 173: Banks and Non-Banking Financial Institutions] (1997) [hereinafter Banks and Non-Banking Financial Institutions Law].

flects an admittedly subjective (and perhaps jaundiced) view that, to a large extent, economics, finance, and money flows are and will continue to be key foundational factors in Cuba's development. According to this perspective, the strong arm of corporate investment, rather than human rights campaigns, will do far more to bring structural change. Thirdly, and in any case, most laws enacted during the Special Period that touch on civil, human, and political rights have done little to advance the cause of democracy and individual liberty. In addition, such laws' reach, viability, practical application, and developmental effects are, at present, unclear.

THE CONSTITUTION OF 1992

The Constitution of 1992 (a reformed version of the 1976 document) sets the framework for economic change within government parameters. It sets the stage for a tension — a push and pull, as it were — that has existed over the last decade between the need for economic opening and private capital on the one hand and, on the other, the desire to maintain centralized, socialist control; Cuban national sovereignty; and the sanctity of the environment and public health. Thus, while the Constitution envisions joint ventures and establishes a rationale for later-enacted laws governing limited private enterprise and wholly foreign-owned property, it lays strict ground rules and establishes the tough tone and approach Cuba has taken toward economic reforms. The result is like a scale that balances, however unevenly at times, legal and economic reforms and absolute government control.

Though later laws would change the balance somewhat, the Constitution keeps the scales in favor of the government. For example, in the Constitution, the government forcefully asserts its sovereignty and socialist orientation. We find this in several sections of the Constitution, including the passionate preamble,[6] the statement that Cuba is a socialist workers' state, and provisions such as the following:

> Artículo 5o.- El Partido Comunista de Cuba, martiano y marxista-leninista, vanguardia organizada de la nación cubana, es la fuerza dirigente superior de la sociedad y del Estado, que organiza y orienta los esfuerzos comunes hacia los altos fines de la construcción del socialismo y el avance hacia la sociedad comunista.[7]

The Constitution also reserves territorial sovereignty, including over the environment and natural resources ("Artículo 11o.- El Estado ejerce su soberanía (a) sobre todo el territorio nacional, . . . [y] (b) sobre el medio ambiente y los recursos naturales del país …"),[8] while reasserting its "anti-imperialist" stance[9] and affirming state control over most real and commercial property.[10]

Although the Constitution expresses the critical need for economic development, the process is clearly meant to be closely moderated and government-controlled. Article 16, for example, assigns to the state the role of "organizing, directing, and controlling national economic activity in conformity with a plan that guarantees the country's programmed development."[11] Because such activity could conceivably include foreign capital, it is of course reined in through centralized controlled of economic initiatives that must meet certain criteria: "fortalecer el sistema socialista, satisfacer cada vez mejor las necesidades materiales y culturales de la sociedad y los ciudadanos,

---

6. Constitution of 1992, *supra* note 2, at pmbl. ("Nosotros, ciudadanos cubanos, herederos y continuadores del trabajo creador y de las tradiciones de combatividad, firmeza, heroismo y sacrificio forjadas por nuestros antecesores; por los aborígenes que prefirieron muchas veces el exterminio a la sumisión; por los esclavos que se rebelaron contra sus amos; … [d]eclaramos nuestra voluntad de que la ley de leyes de la República este presidida por este profundo anhelo, al fin logrado, de José Martí: 'Yo quiero que la ley primera de nuestra República sea el culto de los cubanos a la dignidad plena del hombre.'").

7. *Id.* at art. 5.

8. *Id.* at art.11 (a)-(b).

9. *Id.* at art. 12 ("La República de Cuba hace suyos los principios antiimperialistas e internacionalistas …").

10. *Id.* at art. 15.

11. *Id.* at art. 16 ("Artículo 16o.- El Estado organiza, dirige y controla la actividad económica nacional conforme a un plan que garantice el desarrollo programado del país …") (translation in main text by author).

promover el desenvolvimiento de la persona humana y de su dignidad, el avance y la seguridad del país."[12]

Similarly, while the Constitution recognizes the validity of joint ventures and other corporate entities,[13] this is counterbalanced by (among other things) government control over external commerce, including the authority to create commercial entities, regulate imports and exports, and determine who has legal authority to handle relevant operations and enter contracts.[14] Finally, Article 27 places strictures on economic initiatives by recognizing the need for development that is socially beneficial (or at least not harmful) and environmentally sound.[15]

None of these commercial provisions constitutes a government concession. Those would come later. Rather, the Constitution establishes a vision of controlled growth and leaves for more specific laws the task of rolling out economic reforms. The latter would open the door to foreign capital and the influence of foreign economic power.

THE FOREIGN INVESTMENT ACT OF 1995[16]

In 1995, Cuba opened itself more broadly to foreign capital with passage of the Foreign Investment Act. This much-heralded law provides for:

- Direct foreign investment in the Cuban economy, though barring investments in education, health care, and noncommercial military operations.[17]

- Property protection guarantees through a bar on expropriations, while ensuring indemnification for expropriations valid for reasons of "the public good or in the interest of society."[18]

- Establishment of joint ventures ("registered-share corporations"[19] having a "legal status distinct from that of any one of the parties"[20] and whose shareholders are both Cuban and foreign); international economic-association contracts (agreements between two or more parties, typically Cuban and foreign, without the creation of a separate legal entity);[21] and totally foreign capital companies (foreign-owned and capitalized companies whereby "the foreign investor manages the company, [and] enjoys all the rights pertinent to it.").[22]

- Investments in and ownership of real estate (subject to restrictions).[23]

- Procedures for Cuban government authorization of proposed investments.[24]

---

12. *Id.*

13. *Id.* at art. 23 ("El Estado reconoce la propiedad de las empresas mixtas, sociedades y asociaciones económicas que se constituyen conforme a la ley.").

14. *Id.* at art. 18 ("El Estado dirige y controla el comercio exterior. La ley establece las instituciones y autoridades estatales facultadas para: —crear empresas de comercio exterior; —normar y regular las operaciones de exportación e importación; y —determinar las personas naturales o jurídicas con capacidad legal para realizar dichas operaciones de exportación e importación y concertar convenios comerciales.").

15. *Id.* at art. 27 ("El Estado protege el medio ambiente y los recursos naturales del país. Reconoce su estrecha vinculación con el desarrollo económico y social sostenible para hacer más racional la vida humana y asegurar la supervivencia, el bienestar y la seguridad de las generaciones actuales y futuras.").

16. Foreign Investment Act, *supra* note 3.

17. *Id.* at ch. IV, art. 10.

18. *Id.* at ch. III, art. 3.

19. *Id.* at ch. V, art. 13.

20. *Id.*

21. *Id.* at ch. V, art. 14.

22. *Id.* at ch. V, art. 15.

23. *Id.* at ch. VI, art. 16.

24. *Id.* at ch. VIII, art. 20-25.

- Requirement that all three types of approved investment entities establish "accounts in freely convertible currency"[25] through the Cuban National Banking System.

- Strict labor requirements obligating joint ventures, international economic-association contract parties, and totally foreign capital companies to hire their Cuban employees through a Cuban "employing entity" specified by the Cuban government.[26] The investing company pays wages to the employing entity in "convertible foreign currency"[27] (typically U.S. dollars), while the employees receive their wages from that entity in Cuban pesos.[28] (The rub here is that employees receive the official one-to-one exchange rate. This significantly lowers their purchasing power and their ability to accumulate wealth.).

- Imposition of a 30% corporate income tax[29] (subject to increase for companies exploiting "renewable or nonrenewable natural resources")[30] that can be reduced by a labor utilization discount[31]; a 14% social security tax;[32] "customs duties and other payments";[33] a "land transportation tax";[34] and a "document tax."[35]

- Authorization of duty-free zones and industrial parks.[36] The former are "areas in which ... a special system can be established covering customs duties, exchange rates, taxation, labor, migration, public order, capital investment and foreign trade, and in which foreign investors can participate for the purposes of financial operations[37] and specified commercial activities."[38] Industrial parks are "areas in which ... a special system can be established covering customs duties, taxation, labor, capital investment and foreign trade, for the development of productive activities with the participation of foreign capital."[39]

- Submission of relevant investment proposals to determine an "investment's suitability from the environmental point of view and [to] determine whether an environmental impact evaluation is required."[40] The Ministry of Science, Technology and the Environment may institute measures to control "damage, dangers or risks for the environment"[41] resulting from investments. Finally, those "responsible for . . . damage or harm . . . [must] . . . reestablish the previous environmen-

---

25. *Id.* at ch. IX, art. 26.

26. *Id.* at ch. XI, art. 33. It is important to note that article 31 provides that "workers in activities corresponding to foreign investments shall be, as a rule, Cubans or foreigners permanently residing in Cuba."); *see also Id.* at ch. XI, art. 34 (1) ("The employing entity ... individually contracts and directly hires Cuban workers and permanent residents. This employing entity pays those workers their wages.").

27. *Id.* at ch. XI, art. 33 (4).

28. Foreign Investment Act, *supra* note 3, at ch. XI, art. 33 (4).

29. *Id.* at ch. XII, art. 39(a).

30. *Id.* at ch. XII, art. 39(b).

31. *Id.* at ch. XII, art. 39(c)(1).

32. *Id.* at ch. XII, art. 39(c)(2).

33. *Id.* at ch. XII, art. 38(c).

34. *Id.* at ch. XII, art. 38(d).

35. *Id.* at ch. XII, art. 38(e).

36. *Id.* at ch. XV, art. 50.

37. *Id.* at ch. XV, art. 51(1).

38. *Id.*

39. *Id.* at ch. XV, art. 51(2).

40. *Id.* at ch. XVI, art. 55.

41. *Id.* at ch. XVI, art. 56(1).

tal situation, repair the material damage and indemnify the injured parties."[42]

The Foreign Investment Act brings to fruition the Constitution of 1992's validation of certain commercial enterprises and its presaging greater foreign commercial ties. Article 23 of the Constitution, for example, clearly states that the government "recognizes joint ventures, companies and economic associations."[43] This was later confirmed by Ricardo Alarcón who noted in the Foreign Investment Act's introductory text that "the Constitution ... [of 1992] ... recognizes ... joint ventures, companies and economic associations ... [and] provides for the partial or total transference of ownership of economic objectives."[44]

In addition, the 1995 law concretizes the Constitution's arguably subtextual references to coming foreign investment. Such references can be inferred in articles that, for example, reassert government oversight over foreign trade[45] and that recognize joint ventures.[46] Of course, the Constitution also reminds us that such trade is subject to the preemptive assertion that the "state organizes, directs, and controls the nation's economic activity."[47]

While the Foreign Investment Act is the realization of constitutionally legitimated corporate activity, it is also another example of the moderated, modulated approach Cuba takes toward development. Even as the act opens the doors to capitalist ventures in Cuba, its provisions and accompanying documentation restate the government's intention of balancing capitalistic development measures against centralized control. That intent is expressed in the Presentation of the Draft of a Law on Foreign Investment, a document accompanying the law when the latter was submitted to the National Assembly of the People's Power:

> This process [i.e., opening the economy to foreign investment] has been carried forward in an orderly way, with negotiations examined one by one, based on the criterion of what is beneficial for the country, without permitting the interests of sectors, territories or institutions to take precedence over those of the nation. In every phase of the process, the economic and social development of the country is present and holds first place.
>
> We speak with complete clarity to the entrepreneurs of other countries with whom we associate. We are a socialist country that has been and is respectful of the agreements to which we have committed and will commit ourselves.
>
> The aim of this Law is to promote and provide incentives for foreign investment within our territory. ... This Law confirms the seriousness with which Cuba is pursuing its policy of opening up to foreign investment within the context of its socialist principles...[48]

In his statement of the law's approval by the National Assembly, Ricardo Alarcón confirms the intent to maintain the balance between foreign commercial engagement and sovereign control:

> WHEREAS: In today's world, without the existence of the socialist bloc, with a globalizing world economy and strong hegemonistic tendencies in the economic, political and military fields, Cuba, in order to preserve its accomplishments despite the fierce blockade to which it is subjected[,] ... can benefit from foreign investment on the basis of the strictest respect for

---

42. *Id.* at ch. XVI, art. 56(2).

43. Constitution of 1992, *supra* note 2, at ch. I, art. 23 ("El Estado reconoce la propiedad de las empresas mixtas, sociedades y asociaciones económicas ...") (translation in main text by author).

44. Foreign Investment Act, *supra* note 3, at introductory text (*The Aim of the Law Is to Promote and Provide Incentives for Foreign Investment Within our National Territory.*).

45. Constitution of 1992, *supra* note 2, at ch. I, art. 18 ("El Estado dirige y controla el comercio exterior.").

46. *Id.* at ch. I, art. 23 ("El Estado reconoce la propiedad de las empresas mixtas, sociedades y asociaciones económicas ...").

47. *Id.* at ch. I, art. 16 ("El Estado organiza, dirige y controla la actividad económica nacional ...").

48. *Presentation of the Draft of a Law on Foreign Investment*, 5th Ordinary Period of Sessions, National Assembly of the People's Power (Sept. 4, 1995), *translated* at http://www.geo.unipr.it/~davide/cuba/economy/ LAW95/ intro1.html.

national independence and sovereignty, given that such investment can ... reinforce the efforts the country must undertake for its economic and social development.[49]

The law's own text then clearly confirms this goal: "This Act has the purpose of promoting and encouraging foreign investment in the territory of the Republic of Cuba ... on the basis of respect for the country's sovereignty and independence and the protection and rational use of natural resources ..."[50] The law attempts to ensure that sovereignty through provisions (discussed *supra*) such as those restricting the hiring of Cuban employees[51] and others requiring environmental impact studies before granting approval of investment proposals.[52]

DECREE-LAW NO. 165: DUTY-FREE ZONES AND INDUSTRIAL PARKS[53]

The 1996 Duty-Free Zones and Industrial Parks Law sets guidelines according to which foreign investors can pursue their Cuba-based economic ventures under advantageous circumstances. This law is the "special legislation"[54] referred to in Article 53 of the Foreign Investment Act of 1995 and is the product of the 1995 Act's authorization of "the establishment of duty-free zones and industrial parks, in delimited areas of national territory."[55]

The law's introductory text lays out the reasoning behind this legislation:

The creation and development of Free Zones and Industrial Parks in the national territory offer new opportunities for foreign investment, as the investors established therein enjoy a special regime as to customs, banking, taxation, labor, migration, public order, capital investment and foreign trade, and this will mean the generation of new jobs, a source of hard currency and technological, economic and social progress for the country.

... Cuba offers great attractions for the development of Free Zones and Industrial Parks, through foreign investment, because of its facilities for international maritime and air communications due to its geographic position, its sociopolitical stability and the availability of skilled labor, among other favorable factors.[56]

By establishing duty-free zones and industrial parks, the law is seen to "contribute ... to economic and social development ... [and] stimulate ... international trade[,] and, besides attracting foreign capital, ... [it will] ... (a) generat[e] new jobs and rais[e] ... workers' skills; ... (b) incorporat[e] a greater domestic industrial value added, making use of the country's resources; and (c) develop ... new national industries through the assimilation of advanced technologies and the export of national products."[57] The law attempts to accomplish this through "regulations of a special customs, banking, tax, labor, migratory and public order regime, which imply facilities and incentives for foreign investment."[58]

---

49. Foreign Investment Act, *supra* note 3, at introductory text (*The Aim of the Law Is to Promote and Provide Incentives for Foreign Investment Within our National Territory.*).

50. *Id.* at ch. I, art. 1 (1).

51. *Id.* at ch. XI, art. 30-37.

52. *Id.* at ch. XVI, art. 54-56.

53. Duty-Free Zones and Industrial Parks Law, *supra* note 4.

54. Foreign Investment Act, *supra* note 3, at ch. XV, art. 53.

55. *Id.* at ch. XV, art. 50.

56. Duty-Free Zones and Industrial Parks Law, *supra* note 4, at introductory text.

57. *Id.* at ch. I, art. 1.3 (a)-(c).

58. *Id.* at ch. I, art. 1.4.

The Duty-Free and Industrial Parks law defines a Free Zone as "a space within the national territory, duly delimited, without any residing population, with free import and export of goods, not linked to the customs demarcation, where industrial, commercial, technological and service-rendering activities are carried out with the application of a special regime."[59] That regime consists of the "rules related to customs, banking, taxation, labor, migratory and public order systems, less onerous and rigid than common or ordinary ones, applicable to grantees and operators of Free Zones as an incentive for investment."[60] An Industrial Park, however, is defined as a "space within the national territory with similar characteristics to those of the Free Zone, but where industrial activities and those service-rendering activities that serve to support them are predominantly carried out."[61]

The law provides that the Cuban government must grant a concession in order for a person or entity "to develop and exploit a Free Zone."[62] Authorized actors within a Free Zone are either grantees or operators. A grantee is "[t]he natural or legal person, with a foreign domicile and foreign capital, or the national legal person which, in the exercise of the corresponding concession and with its own resources, promotes and develops the necessary, sufficient infrastructure for the establishment and functioning of the Free Zone and subsequently assumes the government and management of it."[63] An operator is "[t]he natural or legal person, with a foreign domicile and foreign capital, or the national legal person which the Ministry for Foreign Investment and Economic Cooperation, at the grantee's proposal, authorizes to establish itself in the Free Zone to conduct one or various activities comprised within the legal framework of this occupation."[64]

The Duty-Free Zones and Industrial Parks Law sets logistical and legal parameters for these types of foreign commercial activity within Cuba by providing for:

- Authorization of the Executive Committee of the Council of Ministers to govern the establishment of Free Zones,[65] while authorizing the Ministry for Foreign Investment and Economic Cooperation to regulate and control Free Zone activities,[66] to propose concession grants to the Executive Committee,[67] and to regulate and monitor Free Zones to ensure compliance with conditions imposed on grantees and operators.[68]

- Creation of a Free Zone Commission which advises the Ministry for Foreign Investment and Economic Cooperation.[69] The commission is comprised of the Minister for Foreign Investment and Economic Cooperation and a representative from the Ministries of Economy and Planning; Finance and Prices; Foreign Trade; Labor and Social Security; the Revolutionary Armed Forces; the Interior; Science, Technology, and the Environment; and Transportation, as well as a representative from the National Bank and the General Customs House.[70]

59. *Id.* at ch. II, art. 2.2.

60. *Id.*

61. *Id.*

62. *Id.*

63. *Id.*

64. *Id.*

65. *Id.* at ch. III, art. 3.

66. *Id.* at ch. III, art. 4.1.

67. *Id.* at ch. III, art. 4.2(a).

68. *Id.* at ch. III, art. 5.1.

69. *Id.* at ch. IV, art. 6.1.

70. *Id.* at ch. IV, art. 6.2.

- The process by which investors apply for Free Zone grantee status and what their obligations would be as grantees.[71] The law also covers similar information for would-be operators.[72]

- The special regime under which grantees and operators may develop their investments within Free Zones.[73] Consisting of regulations designed to be "more appealing and less rigid and onerous than common, ordinary ones,"[74] the regime includes: (a) exemptions from "tariffs and other customs duties for introducing in the Free Zones products intended for carrying out . . . authorized activities";[75] (b) exemptions from profit and labor use taxes;[76] (c) tax-free transference abroad, "in freely convertible currency,"[77] of Free Zone grantees' and operators' "net profits or dividends ... [that are] obtain[ed] from their activities";[78] (d) a requirement that Free Zone grantees' and operators' workers "be, as a general rule, Cubans or foreigners who are permanent residents in Cuba."[79] The Ministry of Labor and Social Security sets minimum salaries for each occupation.[80] Grantees "with Cuban or joint capital directly hire ... Cuban workers ... and also act ... as the employing entit[ies] in relation

to the workers required by the operators."[81] However, grantees and operators operating with solely foreign capital must hire Cuban workers and permanent resident foreigners "through a contract ... with an employing entity proposed by the Ministry for Foreign Investment and Economic Cooperation and approved by the Ministry of Labor and Social Security."[82] In this latter instance, the grantee or operator pays employee salaries to the government-owned employing entity in "convertible foreign currency,"[83] while the employees are paid by that entity in Cuban pesos.[84]

DECREE-LAW NO. 173: BANKS AND NON-BANKING FINANCIAL INSTITUTIONS[85]

After passing the 1997 law creating the Central Bank of Cuba,[86] Cuba passed Decree-Law No. 173, which establishes the Registro General de Bancos e Instituciones Financieras No Bancarias (General Registry of Banks and Non-Banking Financial Institutions), which falls under the Central Bank.[87] All financial institutions in Cuba, including foreign institutions with offices in Cuba, must be part of this registry.[88] Decree-Law No. 173 also provides the following:

---

71. *Id.* at ch. V, art. 7-16.

72. *Id.* at ch. VI, art. 17-27.

73. *Id.* at ch. VIII, §§ 1-6.

74. *Id.* at ch. VIII, § 1, art. 31.1.

75. *Id.* at ch. VIII, § 2, art. 32.1.

76. Duty-Free Zones and Industrial Parks Law, *supra* note 4, at ch. VIII, § 3, art. 35.1-35.2 (Note specifications in how exemptions are granted depending on the grantor's or operator's activities.).

77. *Id.* at ch. VIII, § 4, art. 38.1.

78. *Id.*

79. *Id.* at ch. VIII, § 5, art. 43.1.

80. *Id.* at ch. VIII, § 5, art. 44.

81. *Id.* at ch. VIII, § 5, art. 45.1.

82. *Id.* at ch. VIII, § 5, art. 45.4.

83. Foreign Investment Act, *supra* note 2, at ch. XI, art. 33 (4).

84. *Id.*

85. Banks and Non-Banking Financial Institutions Law, *supra* note 5.

86. Decreto-Ley Número 172 Sobre el Banco Central de Cuba [Decree-Law 172: The Central Bank of Cuba] (1997).

87. Banks and Non-Banking Financial Institutions Law, supra note 5, at ch. II, § 1, art. 11.

88. *Id.* at ch. II, § 1, art. 2.

The Central Bank is the governing authority over all financial institutions (in Cuba), their branches, and Cuba-based representative offices of foreign financial entities.[89] The Central Bank retains complete authority to supervise all financial institutions and foreign financial institutions' Cuban offices.[90] The Central Bank can impose fines for noncompliance with its orders and stipulations.[91]

Foreign financial organizations seeking to set up office in Cuba and financial institutions in general must obtain a license from the Central Bank before establishing operations.[92] An applicant must follow the law's procedures for obtaining the license.[93] Those seeking to establish state-related financial institutions must, after securing their license, receive final approval from the Executive Committee of the Council of Ministers.[94] Non-governmental Cuban banks, however, need only secure a license and ensure that their operations are fundamentally linked to international financial credit transactions.[95]

There are several types of licenses, each tailored to the scope of activities in which a given financial institution will engage.[96]

Those who would occupy executive positions in financial institutions must possess a solid and well-recognized moral reputation, have legal capacity to run the day-to-day business, and carry out (or have experience carrying out) important activities in the areas of economics, banking, or finance.[97]

Financial institutions must obtain Central Bank authorization for capital investments in national or foreign entities.[98] The Central Bank governs all aspects of off-shore banking as well as the operation of financial institutions in duty-free zones and industrial parks.[99] The bank also approves financial institutions' accounting and auditing systems to ensure legal compliance.[100]

Any person or entity acting as a financial intermediary must have at least a baseline amount of capital as set and required by the Central Bank.[101] Every financial institution must contribute a percentage of its net profits at least once a year so as to create and build a legal reserve fund to cover risks and possible future losses until such time as the fund holds an amount at least equal to the institution's capital.[102] No financial institution may declare or pay a dividend or pay out any profits if it has not made sufficient provision for covering possible capital losses.[103] The Central Bank can use reserve funds to maintain a financial institution's solvency.[104]

All banks may open Central Bank accounts and maintain a minimum of cash in them.[105] Financial institutions may, within the bounds of their licenses

---

89. *Id.* at ch. II, § 1, art. 3.
90. *Id.*
91. *Id.* at ch. II, § 1, art. 4.
92. *Id.* at ch. II, § 2, art. 6.
93. *Id.* at ch. II, § 1, art. 7-8.
94. *Id.* at ch. II, § 1, art. 9.
95. *Id.* at ch. II, § 1, art. 10.
96. *Id.* at ch. II, § 3, art. 13.
97. *Id.* at ch. II, § 4, art. 20.
98. *Id.* at ch. II, § 4, art. 21.
99. *Id.* at ch. II, § 4, art. 22.
100. *Id.* at ch. II, § 4, art. 23.
101. *Id.* at ch. III, § 1, art. 24.
102. *Id.* at ch. III, § 1, art. 26.
103. *Id.* at ch. III, § 1, art. 27.
104. *Id.* at ch. III, § 1, art. 29.
105. *Id.* at ch. III, § 2, art. 33.

and the law, buy, sell, look after, and administer financial and other assets.[106] A financial institution with license to operate in off-shore banking, duty-free zones, and industrial parks must form a separate, independent unit dedicated exclusively to those operations.[107]

The Central Bank oversees the functioning of the country's payment system, dictates the system's rules and norms, and establishes the necessary supervision to ensure efficient clearing of check payments and payments of other value as between banks.[108] The Central Bank is also empowered to set down the regulations it deems necessary for the smooth functioning of financial institutions and representative offices of foreign entities.[109] Loans issued by a financial institution to one debtor may not exceed the aggregate risks relative to financial institutions' capital and reserves.[110]

Banks are subject to a legal reserve (i.e., hold), equal to an amount established by the Central Bank, to be applied to deposits and debts.[111]

The Central Bank has the authority to dictate the norms, procedures, and regulations it deems necessary for carrying out its supervisory role and its auditing and inspection of financial institutions, offices of representation, and the Central Bank itself.[112] The superintendent of the Central Bank is responsible for supervising, inspecting, regulating, overseeing, and controlling financial institutions and representative offices of foreign entities.[113] The superintendent is authorized to examine these organizations' books and request any additional information deemed necessary to fulfilling his supervisory functions.[114] The Central Bank determines the amount and form in which financial institutions contribute to cover the cost of this supervision.[115] Finally, the Central Bank may, in order to safeguard financial institutions' stability and integrity, arrange a reorganization, assume administration, declare an intervention, and following a judicial decision, take possession of the property or proceed with a forced liquidation.[116]

Financial institutions whose circumstances impede their normal operation can be subjected to voluntary liquidation, intervention, or forced liquidation.[117] Voluntary liquidation applies to institutions that have the resources to settle their obligations with creditors so that they can proceed with liquidation or dissolution, subject to the Central Bank's prior authorization.[118] Intervention, permissible under specific circumstances, involves the Central Bank stepping in to take possession of the property and assuming the institution's administration.[119] The Central Bank then decides whether to conduct a reorganization, seek a forcible liquidation and cancel the institution's license, or withdraw from the intervention.[120] In a forced liquidation, the Central Bank obtains court permission to proceed with the institution's dissolu-

---

106. *Id.* at ch. III, § 2, art. 38.

107. *Id.* at ch. III, § 2, art. 40.

108. *Id.* at ch. IV, art. 45.

109. *Id.* at ch. V, § 1, art. 46.

110. *Id.* at ch. V, § 1, art. 47.

111. *Id.* at ch. V, § 2, art. 49.

112. *Id.* at ch. VI, art. 54.

113. *Id.*

114. *Id.* at ch. VI, art. 56.

115. *Id.* at ch. VI, art. 57.

116. *Id.* at ch. VI, art. 58.

117. *Id.* at ch. VII, art. 60.

118. *Id.* at ch. VII, § 1, art. 61.

119. *Id.* at ch. VII, § 2, art. 68.

120. *Id.* at ch. VII, § 2, art. 71.

tion and then advises the institution's legal representative, shareholders, depositors, and other creditors.[121]

PARAMETERS FOR CHANGE

The Constitution, the Foreign Investment Act, and the laws establishing free-trade zones and the Central Bank registry system are but a few of the important legal developments during the Special Period that have facilitated foreign investment and economic development. Others include laws governing taxation, real estate, and intellectual property. Yet the four covered in this paper have been highlighted because they are the structural building blocks that form a broad and deep foundation upon which tax, real estate, and other laws and regulations are built. In addition, they form a natural progression both chronologically and in terms of increasing specificity. Thus, while the Constitution quite rightly sets out broad provisions, the other three laws proceed from and are built upon that document. They provide the details and rubrics that aim to execute and make real the government's development vision and goals.

These four laws, however, also set parameters for — and limits on — such development in the near and far term. They and other laws, including the Law of the Environment and the Law of Mines, form a matrix of legal requirements, policy, and centralized control that moderate and modulate the pace, scope, quantity, and quality of foreign investment. The goal seems to be to allow foreign capital inflows without compromising certain national interests — in particular, government supremacy, the environment (the protection of which ensures the viability of tourism, among other things), and public health.

These goals and the built-in restrictions designed to achieve them raise serious and as-yet unanswered questions. For example, what effect will these laws have on foreign companies' willingness to invest seriously in Cuba? Furthermore, what concessions might Cuba be forced to make to attract and retain qualified investors? After all, making investment proposals' approval contingent on assurances of minimal environmental harm may dismay important sources of capital. As some companies are turned away, others will opt not to apply at all. In addition, compa-

nies face the disincentive of being barred from paying employees directly in U.S. dollars (or other freely convertible currency) and instead of having to pay workers' dollar salaries to the Cuban government. This not only stands to demoralize employees and make them resentful but also removes an important incentive for ensuring productivity and quality. Companies also confront the hurdle of financial oversight by the Central Bank. Not only must investors contribute to a risk fund, but they are also subject to forcible intervention and liquidation.

These and many other concerns raise the risk that Cuba is discouraging rather than fostering healthy investment and capital flows. Such circumstances also increase the likelihood that the most determined investors will be able to buy flexibility or nonenforcement through bribes or other perks extended to military or civilian gatekeepers of foreign investment. In addition, it is unclear whether and to what extent Cuba is prepared to resist pressure (from corporations and other sources) to make concessions in exchange for corporate willingness to invest. Cuba is a hungry and needy country; the prospect of money, jobs, and economic growth are hard to forgo on an empty stomach.

Finally, since the military is the primary shareholder in Cuban corporations investing in Cuban tourism, and since tourism is an economic staple, there is concern that Cuba's future rests in a capitalist military dictatorship. Under this scenario, the military would be the principle shareholder in and key beneficiary of key economic growth sectors. A Pinochet-style government is therefore not beyond the pale. Others speculate that even if a civilian government assumes control, the military will maintain the greatest hold on Cuba's purse strings.

All of these questions, along with reports of Cuba's recent retreat from economic reforms, raise significant concerns about the country's willingness to travel the necessary road to recovery, growth, and prosperity. The four structural legal changes discussed above were a hopeful first sign of evolution. It remains to be seen what positive, specific, and effective steps will come next.

---

121. Id. at ch. VII, § 3, art. 78-79.

THE CONTRIBUTION OF BITs
TO CUBA'S FOREIGN INVESTMENT PROGRAM

Jorge F. Pérez-López and Matías F. Travieso-Díaz

Bilateral investment treaties (BITs), intended to promote and protect foreign investment, are relatively new but increasingly common instruments in international economic relations.[1] According to the specialized agency of the United Nations that tracks international investment, 1,332 BITs had been concluded by the end of 1996.[2] While BITs were originally conceived as accords between developed and developing countries, motivated by interest on the part of the former to protect their investments in the latter, this is no longer the case. A growing number of BITs concluded in the 1980s and 1990s have been entered between developing countries; other BITs have involved developing nations and countries with economies in transition.[3]

Cuba has recently joined the worldwide trend towards negotiating BITs. Its government, which is actively courting foreign capital, often refers to the BITs that Cuba has concluded — over 40 through the end of 1999 — as evidence of a positive climate in Cuba for foreign investment. The purposes of this paper are to assess whether Cuba's BITs have improved the framework for investment in the island,

and to estimate the potential impact of these BITs on the economic measures that the Cuban government may take following the country's transition to a free-market society.

The paper begins with a brief description of the historical development of BITs and the rationale for their existence. The next section discusses Cuba's general framework for foreign investment, which provides the legal and economic backdrop for the BITs. The third section examines key provisions of several of the BITs that Cuba has signed. The paper then examines some issues relating to the role of BITs during Cuba's market transition, and closes with some conclusions on the contributions that BITs have made and are likely to make to foster foreign investment in the country.

THE HISTORICAL DEVELOPMENT OF BITs

The concept of negotiating treaties aimed specifically at the promotion and protection of foreign investment originated in Germany.[4] The first BIT was signed between the Federal Republic of Germany and Pakistan on November 25, 1959. Subsequently, Germany signed similar agreements with the Domin-

---

1. Jeswald W. Salacuse, "BIT by BIT: The Growth of Bilateral Investments Treaties and Their Impact on Foreign Investment in Developing Countries," *The International Lawyer* 24:3 (Fall 1990), p. 655.

2. United Nations Conference on Trade and Development, *Bilateral Investment Treaties in the Mid-1990s* (Geneva: UNCTAD, 1998), [hereinafter UNCTAD], p. 10. The United Nations Centre on Transnational Corporations became part of the UNCTAD in 1993.

3. *Id.*

4. United Nations Centre on Transnational Corporations (UNCTC), *Bilateral Investment Treaties* (London: Graham & Trotman, 1988) [hereinafter UNCTC], p. 8. According to this treatise, Germany was said to be particularly sensitive to investment protection as its investors had lost their foreign assets in many countries following the two world wars.

ican Republic and with several other countries,[5] as did France, Switzerland, the Netherlands, Italy, Belgium, Sweden, Denmark, and Norway.[6] By the end of 1996, 162 countries and territories from all regions of the world had signed at least one BIT.[7]

The trend to seeking protection for foreign investments long precedes the emergence of the BIT. Under customary international law, aliens engaged in business ventures (e.g., foreign traders or investors) have often been accorded fewer rights by States than those given to domestic citizens.[8] In order to protect the foreign trade activities of their nationals, by the late eighteenth century, capital-exporting countries (e.g., the United States and the Western European countries) concluded Friendship, Commerce and Navigation (FCN) treaties, Treaties of Establishment, or Treaties of Amity and Commerce, that included property protection provisions, such as restrictions on a host country's right of expropriation.[9] These agreements, however, had very broad scope and were more concerned with facilitating trade than regulating investment, so they covered numerous topics, among them right to enter, access to local courts, enforceability of arbitral awards, the right to engage technical experts, questions concerning the right to purchase or lease land, patents, trademarks, tax issues, exchange rates, customs treatment of commercial travelers, and consultations regarding restrictive business practices.[10]

Over time, it became desirable to develop specialized instruments to address the investment-related concerns that were only partially covered by the FCNs and like agreements. Moreover, the emergence of newly independent states in the 1950s created new opportunities for investment. FCNs and like agreements, which implicitly assumed cultural, political and legal affinity between partner countries, were deemed unsuitable to frame the economic relations between developed countries and these newly independent states.

The use of BITs developed slowly at first. Over the period 1959-69, 75 BITs were concluded worldwide, while 92 were concluded in the 1970s.[11] In the 1980s, however, the debt crisis forced countries that had relied on foreign loans for development financing to turn to foreign direct investment (FDI) as an important source of capital. As a result, developing countries began then to encourage foreign investors to locate within their borders and signed BITs as a way to signify their willingness to accept foreign participation in their economies. The decade saw 219 BITs signed, including a significant number between developing countries as well as the first BITs signed

---

5. By the end of 1996, Germany had concluded 113 BITs. See UNCTAD, *supra* n.4, p. 12.

6. A useful list of BITs concluded during 1959-92, in chronological order as well as by signatory countries, is included as an appendix to Margrete Stevens and Ruvan de Alwis, "References on Bilateral Investment Treaties," *ICSID Review* 7:1 (Spring 1992), pp. 229-283.

7. UNCTAD, *supra* n. 4, p. 10.

8. Rudolf Dolzer and Margrete Stevens, *Bilateral Investment Treaties* (The Hague: Martinus Nijhoff Publishers, 1995) [hereinafter DOLZER AND STEVENS], p. 10.

9. UNCTAD, *supra* n. 4, p. 8.

10. DOLZER AND STEVENS, *supra* n. 10, p. 10; UNCTC, *supra* n. 6, p. 4.

11. UNCTAD, *supra* n. 4, p. 9. Most of the early BITs were concluded between Western European countries and African nations. Asian and Latin American countries were less engaged at first in the negotiation of BITs. In the case of Latin America, a significant stumbling block to the negotiation of BITs was the adherence of many countries in this region to a traditional doctrine opposing any international rules on foreign investment, generally known as the Calvo Doctrine. Argentine jurist Carlos Calvo asserted in 1896 that foreign investment should be governed by domestic law and should not be subject to international law rules. See DOLZER AND STEVENS, *supra* n. 10, p. 8.

by China[12] and by the United States.[13] An additional 946 BITs were signed between 1990 and 1996. At the end of 1996, developed countries had signed 924 BITs (62 percent of the total number of BITs), while developing countries and economies in transition had signed 508 (38 percent).[14]

The boom in BITs in the 1990s is attributable to a number of factors, among them:

- The opening to foreign investment brought about by changes toward a market economy in the former socialist countries of Eastern and Central Europe and in the newly independent states of the former Soviet Union;

- The recognition among developing countries of the positive role in economic development that can be played by FDI and the intense competition among countries to attract FDI;

- Shrinkages in foreign aid generally, and difficulties on the part of many developing countries in

obtaining additional foreign financing via debt; and

- The consensus among developed and developing countries, as well as transition economies, that it is in a country's national interest to provide increased legal protection to FDI.[15]

CUBA'S LEGAL FRAMEWORK FOR FOREIGN INVESTMENT

The Cuban revolutionary government nationalized foreign holdings and proscribed all forms of foreign investment in the early 1960s. It was not until 1982 that it issued legislation to permit foreign investment in the island, in the form of joint ventures between foreign entities and Cuban enterprises.[16] Although passage of legislation authorizing foreign investment had symbolic value, its practical effect was limited, as it was largely unsuccessful in generating foreign investment flows.[17] Further changes to the legal framework for foreign investment were instituted in the 1990s with the adoption of a new foreign investment

12. China signed its first BIT (with Sweden) in 1982, shortly after its opening policy in 1979. Within 5 years, China had signed 17 BITs. See Li Shishi, "Bilateral Investment Promotion and Protection Agreements: Practice of the People's Republic of China," in Paul De Waart, Paul Peters, and Erik Denters, editors, *International Law and Development* (Dostrecht: Martinus Nijhoff Publishers, 1998), p. 164.

13. The United States concluded its first two BITs (with Egypt and Panama) in 1982. For the evolution of U.S. policy regarding protection of foreign investment and the development of the U.S. BIT Program, see, e.g., Kenneth J. Vandevelde, "The BIT Program: A Fifteen-Year Appraisal," *American Society of International Law Proceedings* (1992), pp. 532-540. Through March 1999, the United States had signed 44 BITs. See "U.S. Bilateral Investment Treaty Program," at http://www.ustr.gov/agreements/bit (site last visited April 9, 2000).

14. UNCTC, *supra* n. 6, p. 10.

15. UNCTAD, *supra* n. 4, p. 15.

16. "Decreto-Ley No. 50—Sobre asociaciones económicas entre entidades cubanas y extranjeras," *Gaceta Oficial* (February 15, 1982) ("Law 50"), pp. 11-15. For commentaries and analysis of the law see, e.g., Chamber of Commerce of the Republic of Cuba, *Possibility of Joint Ventures in Cuba* (La Habana, 1982); Jean Zorn and Harold Mayerson, "Cuba's Joint Venture Law: New Rules for Foreign Investment," *Columbia Journal of Transnational Law* 21:2 (1982), pp. 272-303; Patrick L. Schmidt, "Foreign Investment in Cuba: A Preliminary Analysis," *Law and Policy in International Business* 15:2 (1983), pp.698-710; Lynn Macgilvray-Saltzman, "Cuba's Joint Venture Associations," *Florida International Law Journal* 1:1 (1984), pp. 45-60; Sula Fiszman, "Foreign Investment Law: Encouragement vs. Restriction—Mexico, Cuba and the Caribbean Basin Initiative," *Hastings International and Comparative Law Review* 8:2 (1985), pp. 147-183; and Jorge F. Pérez-López, *The 1982 Cuban Joint Venture Law: Context, Assessment and Prospects* (Coral Gables: Graduate School of International Studies, University of Miami, 1985). For the changes to the 1982 law in the area of property rights see, e.g., Jorge F. Pérez-López, "Islands of Capitalism in an Ocean of Socialism: Joint Ventures in Cuba's Development Strategy," pp.190-219, in Pérez-López, editor, *Cuba at a Crossroads* (Gainesville: University Press of Florida, 1994).

17. Cuba's first joint venture with a foreign investor was completed in 1990, eight years after Law 50 went into effect. *See, e.g.,* Business International Corporation, "Developing Business Strategies for Cuba" 23 (1992).

law, Law No. 77 on Foreign Investment, in September 1995.[18] This legislation, combined with an aggressive government campaign to attract foreign investors, has resulted in significant foreign investment locating in Cuba in the second half of the 1990s.

Cuba's regulatory framework for foreign investment consists of (1) the above-mentioned Law No. 77; (2) decrees and regulations implementing that law; and (3) some complementary legislation, such as the tax code, a new mining law, and reforms to the banking system. As will be seen below, the BITs serve to complement this limited legal framework.

Foreign Investment Law

Law No. 77 codified the rules under which enterprises that included foreign participation had been operating and introduced some innovations to the legal framework for foreign investment, among them:[19]

Wholly-owned foreign investments: Unlike the previous legislation, which limited foreign investors to 49 percent ownership in joint ventures with domestic (state) investors, Law No. 77 allows for the possibility of investments that are 100 percent-owned by foreigners.

Simplified approval process: Law No. 77 streamlines the administrative approval process for foreign investments. For example, for relatively small and non-sensitive investments, case-by-case approval by the Executive Committee of the Council of Ministers is no longer required, with the approval decision relegated to a Government Commission appointed by the Executive Council.[20] Similarly, pursuant to Law

No. 77, a decision on whether to approve a foreign investment must be handed down within 60 days from the date on which the request was presented; no time frame for handing down such decision was specified in the previous legislation.

Opening up economic sectors to foreign investment: All sectors of the economy are open to foreign investment, subject to approval procedures, with the exception of health and education services and national defense (other than commercial enterprises of the armed forces).

Investments in real estate: Law No. 77 for the first time permits foreign investments in the real estate sector. However, such foreign investments are limited to: (1) housing or tourism facilities for the use of persons who are not permanent residents of Cuba; (2) purchase of real estate for corporate activities; and (3) real estate development for the tourism industry.

Incentives for investments in export processing zones: Law No. 77 foresees the designation, by the Executive Committee of the Council of Ministers, of areas in the national territory where duty-free zones or industrial parks might operate. The law further provides that certain incentives may be offered to investors who locate in these areas.

Ability to export and import: Joint ventures or wholly foreign-owned enterprises are given the right, in accordance with domestic legislation "to export their products directly and to import, also directly, whatever is needed to meet their needs."

---

18. "Ley No. 77—Ley de las inversiones extranjeras," *Gaceta Oficial* (6 September 1995)("Law No. 77"), pp. 5-12. For legal analyses and commentaries to Law No. 77 see, e.g., Matías F. Travieso-Díaz and Alejandro Ferraté, Recommended Features of a Foreign Investment Code for Cuba's Free-Market Transition, 21 N.C. J. INT'L L. & COM. REG. 511 (1996); René Burguet Rodríguez, *Ley de la Inversión Extranjera en Cuba* (Madrid: Consultoría Jurídica Internacional, 1995); Juan Vega Vega, *Cuba: Inversiones Extranjeras a Partir de 1995* (Madrid: Ediciones Endymion, 1996); Ghassan Ossman, "Recent Developments Relating to the Role of the Public Administration in Regulating Investment in Cuba," *The Journal of International Banking Law* 11:10 (October 1996), pp. 415-423; and Dídac Fábregas I Guillén, *La ley de la inversión extranjera y la situación económica actual de Cuba* (Barcelona: Viena, S.L., 1998).

19. Law No. 77, art. 12-15.

20. Article 21 of Law No. 77 reserves for the Executive Committee of the Council of Ministers decisions on the following investments: (1) those whose total value (including the national contribution) exceeds $10 million; (2) wholly foreign-owned enterprises; (3) investments in public services such as transportation, communications, water supplies, electricity, or the operation of a public work; (4) those that involve the exploitation of a natural resource; (5) those that entail the transfer of state property or of a right which is the property of the state; and (6) those that involve commercial enterprises of the armed forces.

In the crucial area of protection against expropriation, Law No. 77 states:

> Foreign investments within the national territory shall enjoy full protection and security and shall not be expropriated, except for reasons of public utility or social interest declared by the Government in accordance with the Constitution of the Republic, legislation in force, and international agreements for the reciprocal promotion and protection of investments subscribed by Cuba, after compensation for their commercial value as determined by mutual agreement and in freely convertible currency.

> If agreement is not reached, the value of the investment shall be determined by an international organization with international reputation in the valuation of businesses, authorized by the Ministry of Finance and Prices and engaged for that purpose by mutual agreement among the parties, or by agreement between the foreign investor and the Ministry for Foreign Investment and Economic Cooperation if the affected party were a wholly foreign-owned corporation.[21]

Article 25 of the Cuban Constitution of 1992 also addresses the issue of expropriation/compensation, stating:

> The expropriation of property for reasons of public utility or social interest and with due compensation is authorized.

> The law establishes the procedure for the expropriation and the bases on which the need for and the utility of this action is to be determined, as well as the form of the compensation considering the interests and economic and social needs of the owner.[22]

Finally, domestic legislation governing forced expropriations, the Civil, Administrative and Legal Procedures Act ("CALPA"), sets up a mechanism for carrying out such actions, including the designation of the government agencies authorized to make the determination that public benefit or social interest is involved, valuation of the assets, and procedures to appeal the valuation.[23]

Implementing Decrees and Regulations

Instrumentalities of the Cuban government have issued several decrees and regulations fleshing out as-

---

21. Law No. 77, art. 3. Interestingly, this Article makes explicit reference to the BITs subscribed by Cuba as one of the legal instruments that provide "full protection and security" to foreign investment located in the island.

22. Constitución de la República de Cuba (1992), *published in* Gaceta Oficial (Aug. 1, 1992) [hereinafter CONSTITUCION DE 1992], art. 25. This provision, which appeared in the Constitution of 1976, was not changed when the Constitution was amended and reissued in 1992.

23. On this legislation and procedures see Burguet Rodríguez, *Ley de la inversión extranjera en Cuba*, pp. 21-22 and Vega y Vega, *Cuba: Inversiones extranjeras a partir de 1995*, pp. 47-49. There is a potentially important discrepancy between the CALPA, which foresees valuation of assets by domestic experts and domestic currency, and the provision authorizing the use of international appraisers and valuation in convertible currency in Law No. 77. Also, under the CALPA, appeal procedures are applicable only to domestic courts, whereas Art. 57 of Law No. 77 states:

> Conflicts that may arise in relations between partners in a joint venture, or between foreign investors and national investors, or between the partners in a wholly foreign-owned investment taking the form of a stock corporation shall be resolved in accordance with the constitutive documents.

> The same rule shall apply when the conflict arises between one or more partners and the joint venture or the wholly foreign-owned corporation with which the foreign partner or partners are associated.

A companion article (Art. 58 of Law No. 77) makes it abundantly clear that domestic courts have jurisdiction in disputes regarding the execution of commercial contracts between foreign investors and state enterprises:

> Disputes over the execution of contracts of joint ventures, foreign investors and domestic investors who are parties to international economic associations and wholly foreign-owned corporations with domestic enterprises and other domestic entities fall under the jurisdiction of the Economic Courts of the People's Courts, as may be established by the Supreme People's Court.

There is no express right under the above article for foreign investors to refer a dispute regarding execution of a contract by a Cuban enterprise to an international dispute resolution tribunal, but the above-quoted Article 57 permits such referrals if provided in the agreements between the joint venturers.

pects of Law No. 77. Briefly summarized, these include:

Labor contracting and labor relations: Resolution No. 3/96 of the Ministry of Labor and Social Security, issued on 27 March 1996,[24] establishes rules for workers of foreign-invested companies operating in Cuba. The resolution elaborates on Article 33 of Law No. 77, which sets out that workers of foreign-invested companies are hired by an "entity" designated by the Ministry for Foreign Investment and Economic Cooperation and authorized by the Ministry of Labor and Social Security; this entity, in turn, contracts with foreign-invested enterprises for the use of labor. Further, the entity pays Cuban workers their salaries and benefits in domestic currency (pesos), while the foreign-invested enterprise pays the entity in convertible currency. Resolution No. 3/96 also sets out criteria for dismissing workers from foreign-invested enterprises, including for conduct "that affects the prestige that every worker of the enterprise should possess" (Article 15.d) and considered to violate worker "suitability" (*idoneidad*) standards spelled out in an Annex to the resolution.

Export processing zones: Article 53 of Law No. 77 contemplates the issuance of laws and regulations governing the creation and operation of export processing zones. In June 1996, the Council of State approved a decree-law setting out the rules for the creation and operation of export processing zones (*zonas francas y parques industriales*).[25] On 24 October 1996, the Ministry for Foreign Investment and Economic Cooperation, issued regulations regarding the establishment of zones and of foreign-invested enterprises within the zones and the creation of a registry of export processing zones and enterprises within the zones.[26]

Application process for foreign investment: Pursuant to Chapter VIII of Law No. 77, Resolution No. 116/95 of the Ministry for Foreign Investment and Economic Cooperation, issued on 1 November 1995, sets out the application process for foreign investment, including documentary requirements and negotiations between foreign investors and the Ministry.[27] It is the responsibility of the Ministry for Foreign Investment and Economic Cooperation to submit the completed investment proposals to the Executive Committee of the Council of Ministers or the Government Commission for approval.

Foreign investment registry: Resolution No. 26 of the Chamber of Commerce of the Republic of Cuba, issued on 5 December 1995, creates a registry of foreign-invested enterprises.[28] Registration is a prerequisite for operating in the country. The resolution also sets the schedule of fees — in convertible currency — for registering joint ventures or wholly foreign-owned corporations and for issuing official certificates of establishment.

Regulation of foreign investment: Resolution No. 127/95 of the Ministry for Foreign Investment and Economic Cooperation, issued on 15 December 1995, proclaims regulatory activities of the Ministry

24. "Resolución No. 3/96, Ministerio de Trabajo y Seguridad Social—Reglamento sobre el regimen laboral en la inversión extranjera," *Gaceta Oficial* (24 May 1996), pp. 266-272.

25. "Decreto-ley No. 165—Ley sobre zonas francas y parques industriales" (3 June 1996), http://www2.cuba.cu/negocios/DL165E/htm.

26. "Procesamiento para la presentación de la solicitud de otorgamiento de una concesión administrativa respecto a una zona franca y su tramitación," Ministerio para la Inversión Extranjera y la Colaboración Económica (24 October 1996), http://www2.cuba.cu/negocios/ INST1E/htm; "Instrucción Z.F. No. 2/96—Procedimiento para la autorización del establecimiento de operadores en las instalaciones de las zonas francas," Ministerio para la Inversión Extranjera y la Colaboración Económica (24 October 1996), http://www2.cuba.cu/ negocios/INST2E/htm; and "Resolución No. 66/96," Ministerio para la Inversión Extranjera y la Colaboración Económica (24 October 1996), http://www2.cuba.cu/negocios/RESOL66E/htm.

27. "Resolución No. 116/95," Ministerio para la Inversión Extranjera y la Colaboración Económica, *Gaceta Oficial* (11 December 1995), pp. 488-490.

28. "Resolución No. 26—Reglamento del Registro de inversiones extranjeras," Cámara de Comercio de la República de Cuba, *Gaceta Oficial* (15 December 1995), pp. 504-506.

over foreign-invested enterprises.[29] They include, among others, the requirement of a detailed annual report by each foreign-invested enterprise; rules regarding the establishment of an economic stimulus fund for workers within each enterprise; and procedures for amending the documents establishing individual foreign-invested enterprises and for purchasing motor vehicles by these enterprises.

Statistical reporting: Resolution No. 159 of the Ministry of the Economy and Planning, issued on 22 December 1995, sets out statistical information required from foreign-invested enterprises.[30] The following information is to be provided to the National Statistical Office either directly by the foreign-invested enterprise or by an agency of the Cuban government that has already received the information: (1) information contained in financial statements submitted to the Ministry of Finance and Prices; (2) information on the work force, submitted by the hiring entity to the Ministry of Labor and Social Welfare; (3) information on exports and imports, submitted to the Ministry of Foreign Commerce; and (4) other information, especially volume of production of goods and services.

Other Laws

While the overall climate for foreign investment is affected by all economic legislation, certain laws adopted by the Cuban Government are particularly relevant for the foreign investment decision. These include: (1) A tax code, adopted in August 1994, that levies taxes on the income of enterprises, including joint ventures with foreign investors.[31] (2) A new mining law, passed in December 1994, that sets the parameters for granting of concessions for the exploitation of Cuban mineral resources, except oil resources.[32] (3) Reforms to the banking system, instituted in May 1997, that separated the central bank from the commercial banking system and sets out the legal framework for registration and operation of commercial banks and financial institutions under the supervision of the Cuban Central Bank.[33]

The combined effect of these new laws is the establishment of an improved, but by no means sufficient, legal framework for foreign investment in the island.[34]

CUBA'S BITs

Chronology

Cuba's first BIT, with Italy, was concluded on 7 May 1993. Cuba signed a second BIT later in 1993 (with Russia); two others in 1994 (Spain and Colombia); eight in 1995 (United Kingdom, China, Ukraine, Bolivia, Vietnam, Lebanon, Argentina and South Africa), seven in 1996 (Chile, Romania, Barbados, Germany, Switzerland, Greece and Venezuela); twelve in 1997 (Slovakia, Hungary, France, Laos, Ecuador, Cape Verde, Jamaica, Brazil, Namibia, Indonesia, Malaysia and Turkey), four in 1998 (Belize, Belgium-Luxembourg, Portugal and Bulgaria), and seven in 1999 (Suriname, Panama, Trinidad and Tobago, Hungary, The Netherlands, Ghana and the Dominican Republic). Thus, between 1993 and the

---

29. "Resolución No. 127/95—Normas relativas a la actividad de supervisión y control de las Inversiones Extranjeras," Ministerio para la Inversión Extranjera y la Colaboración Económica, *Gaceta Oficial* (2 January 1996), pp. 7-15.

30. "Resolución No. 159," Ministerio de Economía y Planificación, *Gaceta Oficial* (15 January 1996), pp. 20-21.

31. "Ley No. 74—Del sistema tributario," *Gaceta Oficial* (5 August 1994). (Some other taxes that may be applicable to foreign investments and their employees include taxes on the value of assets owned; earned income; sales; consumption of public services; real estate holdings; vehicles; and transfer of property. The tax code also sets employer contributions to social security, user fees (e.g., roads tolls), and charges on advertising of products or services.).

32. "Ley No. 76—Ley de minas," *Gaceta Oficial* (23 January 1995), pp. 33-44. (This law is particularly important to foreign entities considering investments in the mining and processing of nickel, copper, gold and other minerals.)

33. Decree-Law No. 172, creating the Cuban Central Bank, and Decree-Law No. 173, setting out the regulations for commercial banks. *See* "Central Bank of Cuba established," *Granma International Electronic Edition*, no. 25 (1997).

34. For an analysis of the requirements of an adequate legal regime for foreign investment in Cuba, *see* Matías F. Travieso-Díaz and Alejandro Ferraté, *Recommended Features of a Foreign Investment Code for Cuba's Free-Market Transition*, 21 N.C. J. INT'L L. & COM. REG. 511 (1996).

end of 1999, Cuba signed 45 BITs, as seen in Table 1.[35]

The Cuban government does not publish the BITs it has concluded. Thus, for this study, we have relied on the BITs as published by Cuba's partner countries. Obtaining the agreements from the partner country has been made difficult by the fact that few of the Cuba BITs appear to have entered into force.[36] It is usually in the context of fulfilling the legal formalities for the entry into force of the BITs — normally the process of ratification by the legislature — that the text of the instrument is published in official legal journals. We have been able to obtain texts of six Cuban BITs (in chronological order of signature): the BITs with Italy,[37] Spain,[38] Colombia,[39] the United Kingdom,[40] Chile,[41] and Portugal.[42] The analysis that follows is based on these six BITs.

Contents of the BITs

The Cuban BITs that we examined are very similar in structure and substantive provisions. Following is a description of the main elements of the six agreements, highlighting where appropriate any differences across them and with model agreements used worldwide by countries entering into BITs.[43]

Preamble: The Preamble of each of the six BITs sets out the rationale for the instrument. Although the language varies across agreements, the rationale generally includes:

• strengthening state-to-state economic cooperation;

---

35. The treaties break down in terms of geographic location of Cuba's signing partner as follows: Europe 15, Latin America and Caribbean 14, Asia 6 and Africa 4. The predominance of BITs with European countries is not surprising, given that Europe is the home of many of Cuba's largest foreign investors.

36. As of July 15, 1996, only three Cuban BITs — with Italy, Spain and the United Kingdom — had entered into force. See "Recent Actions Regarding Treaties to Which the United States is Not a Party: Status of Investment Treaties," 35 *International Legal Materials* (1996), p. 1133. This same information regarding BITs that have entered into force is given in the database of the Centre for Settlement of Investment Disputes, www.worldbank.org/icsid/treaties/cuba.htm. Typically, for a BIT to become effective, it must be ratified by the parliament or other legislative bodies of both countries. Apparently, action by the legislatures of most countries with which Cuba has negotiated BITs has been slow.

37. "Legge 12 maggio 1995, n. 214, Ratifica ed esecuzione dell'accordo fra il Governo della Repubblica italiana ed il Governo della Repubblica di Cuba sulla promozione e protezione degli investimenti, con protocollo e scambio di lettere, fatto a Roma il 7 maggio 1993," *Gazzetta Ufficiale della Repubblica Italiana*, no. 126 (1 June 1995), pp. 109-126 [hereinafter Italy BIT.]

38. "Acuerdo entre el Reino de España y la República de Cuba Sobre la Promoción y Protección Recíproca de Inversiones," *Boletín Oficial del Estado*, no. 276 (18 November 1995), pp. 33522-33524 [hereinafter Spain BIT.]

39. "Ley 245 de 1995, por medio de la cual se aprueba el 'Convenio entre el Gobierno de la República de Colombia y el Gobierno de la República de Cuba sobre Promoción y Protección de Inversiones,' suscrito en Santafé de Bogotá el 16 de julio de 1994," *Diario Oficial* (29 December 1995), pp. 14-18 [hereinafter Colombia BIT.]

40. Agreement between the Government of the United Kingdom of Great Britain and Northern Ireland and the Government of the Republic of Cuba for the Promotion and Protection of Investments, Treaty Series No. 50 (1995). London: HMSO, 1995 [hereinafter UK BIT.]

41. "Acuerdo Privado entre el Gobierno de la República de Chile y la República de Cuba sobre la Promoción y la Protección Recíproca de las Inversiones," Ministerio de Relaciones Exteriores de Chile, Dirección General de Relaciones Económicas Internacionales, at http://www.direcon.cl/acuerdos/acuerdos_inversion/textos/cuba/htm.[hereinafter Chile BIT.]

42. "Decreto no. 45/98, Aprova o Acordo entre a República Portuguesa e a República de Cuba sobre a Promoção e a Protecção Recíprocas de Investimentos, assinado em Havana em 8 de Julho de 1998," *Diario da República*, No. 280/98 (4 December 1998), pp. 6662-6669 [hereinafter Portugal BIT.]

43. There is a great deal of commonality in BITs. Countries contemplating their negotiation typically have already negotiated similar agreements with other countries or have available model agreements. Significant in the convergence of the substantive provisions of BITs has been the work of the Organization for Economic Cooperation and Development (OECD), whose 1967 Draft Convention on the Protection of Foreign Property served as a basis for the model treaties of many developed countries, and the Asian-African Legal Consultative Committee, which developed model agreements used by many developing countries. Also noteworthy in this regard is the work of the United Nations Centre on Transnational Corporations, which has collected, analyzed and disseminated the large body of BITs, making such information widely available to potential BIT signatories. *See generally,* DOLZER AND STEVENS, *supra* n. 10.

Table 1. Chronology of Cuban Investment Promotion and Protection Agreements ("BITs")

Year	Month	Country	Year	Month	Country
1993	May	Italy	1997	April	Laos
	July	Russia		May	Ecuador
				May	Cape Verde
1994	May	Spain		June	Jamaica
	July	Colombia		June	Brazil
				June	Namibia
1995	January	United Kingdom		September	Indonesia
	April	China		September	Malaysia
	May	Ukraine		December	Turkey
	May	Bolivia			
	October	Vietnam	1998	April	Belize
	October	Lebanon		May	Belgium-Luxembourg
	November	Argentina		July	Portugal
	December	South Africa		December	Bulgaria
1996	January	Chile	1999	January	Suriname
	January	Romania		January	Panama
	February	Barbados		March	Mongolia
	May	Germany		May	Trinidad and Tobago
	June	Switzerland		August	Guatemala
	June	Greece		September	Algeria
	December	Venezuela		October	Hungary
				October	Guyana
1997	March	Slovakia		November	The Netherlands
	April	France		November	Ghana

Source: U.S.-Cuba Trade and Economic Council, *Realities of Market Cuba*, available online at http://www.cubatrade.org/market.html (last visited April 6, 2000); Omar Everleny Pérez Villanueva, "La Inversión Extranjera Directa en Cuba: Peculiaridades," in *Balance de la Economía Cubana a Finales de los 1990's* (La Habana: Centro de Estudios de la Economía Cubana, Universidad de La Habana, March 1999); Marta Veloz, "Inversión Extranjera, Un Complemento al Desarrollo del País" (OPCIONES, November 14, 1999, available online at http://www.opciones.cubaweb.cu/en98/index.html.)

- creating the conditions that would encourage foreign investment in both countries; and

- recognizing that the promotion and protection of investment through an international accord (i.e., through the BIT itself) can contribute to attracting investment and to the prosperity of both nations.[44]

Scope: The scope of Cuban BITs — framed through the definition of investments, returns, investors, territory, and time period of application — follow closely the general model of other BITs.

Investments: The Cuban BITs define "investments" as every kind of asset or right accrued in accord with domestic legislation of the country where the invest-

ment took place.[45] For further clarification, the BITs include a non-exhaustive illustrative list of "investments," among them:

- movable and immovable property as well property rights such as mortgages, liens, rights-of-way and usufructs;

- shares in stock and any other form of participation or economic interest in a company;

- claims to money or to any other right that has an economic value;

- intellectual property rights, including copyrights, patents, trademarks, labels, commercial appella-

---

44. This rationale is not included in the Chile BIT.

45. The further clarification that the investment be in accord with domestic legislation of the host country is not present in the UK and Colombia BITs.

tions, industrial designs, know-how and good-will; and

• concessions granted by domestic law or pursuant to contracts, including concessions to explore, cultivate, extract, or exploit natural resources.

The UK[46] and Portugal[47] BITs specify that a change in the form of assets does not affect their character as investments. The Colombia BIT[48] states that "notwithstanding [the definitions in the BIT] ... the Government of Colombia will not consider loans as investments for the purposes of this Agreement," while the Spain BIT[49] expressly includes as investments "those loans granted for this purpose, whether or not capitalized." Despite these differences in scope, it is clear that all BITs are intended to cover most if not all of the vehicles normally utilized in foreign investments.

Investment Returns: Most of the Cuban BITs define[50] returns on investment (called either "réditos," "ganancias" or "rentas de inversión" in the Spanish language) as the amounts yielded by an investment, as defined by the BIT. The BITs provide a non-exhaustive list of such returns: profits, interest, capital gains, dividends, royalties, fees, and payments for technical assistance.

Investors: For purposes of the Cuban BITs, investors can be either natural persons or juridical entities. The definition of natural person that can benefit from the provisions of the agreement varies across BITs. Under the Colombia and Spain BITs, investors are defined as natural persons who are nationals of one of the two countries; under the Italy BIT, investors are natural persons who are citizens of one of the two countries; under the Chile and UK BITs, investors are nationals of Chile or the United Kingdom

and persons who are Cuban citizens; and under the Portugal BIT, investors can be either nationals or citizens of each of the two countries. It is not clear why these differences in definition of natural persons arise, but it would appear that Cuba has a preference for granting the benefits of the agreement to its citizens as opposed to its nationals.

Juridical persons or entities defined as investors include companies, business associations and other organizations established or organized under the laws of one of the two countries and headquartered within the territory of that same country. The Chile BIT adds the further requirement that the juridical person or entity also have "its effective economic activities" within the territory of the country. The Italy and UK BITs clarify that the definition of investor for juridical purposes is not restricted to entities that enjoy limited liability.

Territory: In the Cuban BITs, territory is defined as land and maritime areas under the jurisdiction of each of the states, plus the maritime and submarine areas over which each has sovereignty pursuant to domestic and international law. The Colombia and Chile BITs extend the definition of territory also to include air space. The Spain BIT specifies that territory also includes "the exclusive economic zone and the continental platform which extends beyond the territorial maritime limits of each of the Contracting Parties over which they have or may have, according with international law, jurisdiction and sovereign rights with respect to the exploitation, exploration and preservation of natural resources." Unique among the six BITs under review, a provision in the UK BIT would allow the United Kingdom to extend the territory of application of the agreement as may be agreed by the parties.[51]

---

46. UK BIT, Article 1.

47. Portugal BIT, Article 1.

48. Colombia BIT, Article 1.

49. Spain BIT, Article 1.

50. The Chile BIT does not define the term returns.

51. Article 12 of the UK BIT states: "At the time of entry into force of this Agreement, or at any time thereafter, the provisions of this Agreement may be extended to such territories for whose international relations the Government of the United Kingdom are responsible as may be agreed between the Contracting Parties in an Exchange of Notes."

Timing of Application: The Cuban BITs stipulate that they will become effective 30 days after the parties notify each other that they have met their respective constitutional formalities for entry into force; the exception is the Italy BIT, where entry into force commences at the time of notification of completion of formalities for entry into force. The BITs are to be in force initially for 10 years (Italy, Spain, United Kingdom, Colombia and Portugal) or 15 years (Chile); they will be automatically renewed for successive periods of 2 years (Spain), 5 years (Italy), 10 years (Portugal) or indefinite duration (United Kingdom, Chile and Colombia) unless one of the parties gives notice of its intention to terminate it. Investments made prior to the termination of the agreement will be subject to its terms for the same period of time as the agreement's initial duration (i.e., 10 years for Spain, Colombia and Portugal and 15 years for Chile), with the exception of Italy, in which the period is 5 years, and the United Kingdom, in which it is 20 years. The Chile, Colombia and Italy BITs specify that their provisions will remain in place whether or not there are consular and diplomatic relations between the contracting parties.

The BITs apply to investments made after the entry into force of the agreements as well as those made before, as long as investments predating the BIT were lawful. The Chile[52] and Portugal[53] BITs specify that disagreements or disputes ongoing prior to the entry into force of the agreement would not be subject to the BIT's dispute settlement provisions. Thus, while the BITs are intended to provide after-the-fact protection to foreign investments already in place, they are not to be used as tools to aid foreign investors in the resolution of their ongoing disputes with the host country.

Admission and Treatment: Each of the parties to the Cuban BITs commits to promote, within its territory, investments by investors of the other party, and to admit such investments consistent with domestic law.[54] Each of the parties also commits to protect investments of investors from the other party.[55] Moreover, each party also commits not to "raise obstacles, through unjustified or discriminatory measures, the management, maintenance, growth, use, expansion, sale or, as appropriate, liquidation of such investments."[56] The Spain BIT specifies that each of the parties will grant all necessary permits required by the investments, and will "permit," consistent with domestic law, the execution of labor contracts, licensing arrangements, and technical assistance, commercial, financial and management contracts (Article 3.2), as well as arrangements related to the activities of consultants and experts hired by the other party (Article 3.3).

National Treatment and Most-Favored-Nation Treatment: The willingness of capital-exporting countries to enter into BITs often turns on obtaining national and most-favored-nation treatment for their investors.[57] Capital-exporting countries generally demand both standards in BITs, so that their investors can avail themselves of whichever is more favorable.[58]

- **National treatment** requires that foreigners (i.e., foreign investors) be treated the same as nationals. Often, national treatment is qualified in BITs to apply to instances where foreign and domestic investors are in "identical" or "similar" situations. Another limitation in some BITs is the so-called "developmental clause," whereby national treatment is granted to foreign investors

---

52. Chile BIT, Article 2.

53. Portugal BIT, Article 11.

54. The Chile BIT (Article 3) is silent on the commitment to admission of investments.

55. Article 7.5 of the Colombia BIT states: "Nothing in this agreement shall obligate either of the Contracting Parties to protect investments of persons involved in criminal activities."

56. The quote is from the Spain BIT, Article 3.1. Very similar language is included in the other BITs.

57. UNCTC, Bilateral Investment Treaties, pp. 46-47.

58. *Id.*, p. 49.

subject to the developmental polices of the host country.

- **Most-favored-nation treatment** means that investors from the capital-exporting country concluding the BIT will be granted no less favorable treatment than that given to investors from any other nation. Among the exceptions to most-favored-nation treatment in some BITs is denial of preferential treatment that arises from the host State's membership in a customs union or a regional organization.

The Cuban BITs seek to give effect to these internationally-accepted principles. In the BITs, each party commits to grant to investors of the other party the same treatment (i.e., no less favorable treatment) to that accorded to domestic investors (national treatment) or to investors of a third country (most-favored-nation) treatment engaged in similar activities. With the exception of the Chile BIT, the Cuban BITs also explicitly grant national treatment and most-favored-nation treatment to the returns of investments by investors of the two parties.

Compensation for losses that arise from circumstances beyond the control of the investors is also subject to national treatment and most-favored-nation treatment pursuant to the Cuban BITs. For example, the Portugal BIT (Article 5) provides:

> Investors of one of the Contracting Parties whose investments in the territory of the other Contracting Party suffer losses as a result of wars or other armed conflicts, a state of national emergency and other equivalent events pursuant to international law, shall not receive from such Contracting Party treatment less favorable than that which the latter Contracting Party grants to domestic investors or investors from a third party with respect to restitution, indemnification or other pertinent issues. Compensation pursuant to such losses should be transferred freely and without delay, in convertible currency, in accord with

legislation of the Contracting Party where the investments were made.

The UK and Colombia BITs extend national and most-favored-nation treatment to compensation from losses to investors from one of the parties that might arise from actions by the other party, such as requisitioning or destruction of their property not required by the needs of the situation. Compensation[59] shall be freely transferable and in convertible currency.

The Cuban BITs, with the exception of the Chile BIT, include a provision whereby if either of the contracting parties modifies its domestic legislation, or if its international obligations change so that it offers more favorable treatment to foreign investors than that accorded at the time the BIT was signed, the more favorable rules will apply. For instance, the UK BIT (Article 11) states:

> If the provisions of law of either Contracting Party or obligations under international law existing at present or established hereafter between the Contracting Parties contain rules, whether general or specific, entitling investments by nationals or companies of the other Contracting Party to a treatment more favourable than is provided for by the present Agreement, such rules shall to the extent that they are more favourable prevail over the present Agreement.

Exceptions to National and Most-Favored-Nation Treatment: Some exceptions to national and most-favored-nation treatment of investors are carved out in the Cuban BITs. These exceptions are granted for the benefit of domestic investors or those from third countries in case of: (1) an existing or future customs union, common market, free trade area, or similar arrangement in which one of the parties either participates or might participate; and (2) agreements, international conventions, or domestic legislation dealing wholly or primarily with taxation.[60] The Cuban BITs, however, do not grant exemptions from na-

---

59. The UK BIT foresees compensation either in the form of restitution or adequate compensation. The Colombia BIT explicitly provides for restitution in the case of property requisitioned by the authorities of a party, and adequate compensation in the case of destruction of property.

60. The Spain BIT clarifies that the taxation instruments in question include double taxation agreements.

tional treatment related to the so-called "developmental clause" sometimes found in BITs, under which special and preferential treatment is allowed for domestic investors in certain areas in order to stimulate the host country's internal development. This may be the case because Cuba does not currently allow "investment" activities by its nationals.[61]

Transfers: The Cuban BITs commit each of the parties to allow the investors of the other party to transfer freely, in convertible currency and without delay,[62] their investments and any returns thereon. Unless otherwise agreed by the investor, transfers are to be made at the exchange rate prevailing at the time of the transfer.

Some of the Cuban BITs specify the same commitments with regard to other forms of transfers, for example funds from the partial or full liquidation of investments (Chile, Spain, Colombia, Italy and Portugal BITs), funds necessary to service debts associated with the investment (Chile, Spain, Italy and Portugal BITs), compensation for losses or awards associated with the resolution of disputes (Chile, Italy and Portugal BITs), and funds for the payment of salaries and other forms of compensation to employees of the investment who have been granted work permits (Spain BIT). The Colombia BIT (Article 6.3) allows either of the contracting parties to restrict transfers in case of "serious balance of payments difficulties"; these restrictions would be in place "for a limited period of time, and would be administered in an equitable manner, in good faith, and on a non-discriminatory basis." A protocol annexed to the Chile BIT states that funds can only be transferred starting one year after they have been invested, unless domestic legislation provides for more favorable treatment.

Finally, all Cuban BITs contain a subrogation clause, whereby a party may assume the rights of an investor if the party, or an agency of the party, has made one or more payments to an investor to compensate for a non-commercial risk.

Expropriation: The Cuban BITs provide that expropriation of investments of the parties will be made exclusively for reasons of public utility in accord with domestic law, on a non-discriminatory basis, and pursuant to compensation that is:

- immediate, adequate and effective (Chile and UK BITs; prompt, adequate and effective in the Colombia BIT);
- without unjustifiable delay and adequate (Spain BIT);
- immediate (Portugal BIT); or
- adequate (Italy BIT).

---

61. Under Cuban law, the country's citizens are only allowed very limited economic/commercial activities, and none that would qualify them as "domestic investors" as the term is usually understood. The most significant activities for private gain permitted in Cuba are those related to food production and distribution, as agriculture was the only sector of the economy not taken over by the state in the early 1960s. Before they are able to sell their output directly to the public, private farmers must sell a predetermined amount to the state for distribution through the *acopio* system. In September 1993, the Cuban Council of State passed legislation that ratified the concept of self-employment and provided the basis for its expansion ("Decreto-Ley No. 141—Sobre el ejercicio del trabajo por cuenta propia," *Gaceta Oficial* (8 September 1993), p. 11); subsequently, the Ministries of Labor and Social Security and of Finance issued regulations identifying occupations (in the services sector) in which self-employment would be permitted and setting out rules governing such self-employment, including permits, fees, taxes, and prohibitions, such as hiring helpers or employees and professionals engaging in self-employment in their professional field. ("Resolución Conjunta No. 1 CETSS-CEF," *Gaceta Oficial* (8 September 1993), pp. 11-14.) On these forms of private enterprises in Cuba see Jorge Pérez-López, *Cuba's Second Economy* (New Brunswick: Transaction Publishers, 1995). However, state-owned enterprises do engage in a wide range of economic/commercial activities, often in partnership or "joint venture" with foreign investors.

62. The Portugal BIT defines "without delay" as occurring within 30 days of the request for transfer; the Chile BIT as 60 days; and the Spain BIT as 3 months.

The above conditions apply to nationalizations, expropriations, or measures with the equivalent characteristics or effects.[63]

The value of compensation is to be established on the basis of the "genuine" value of the investment at the time immediately preceding the taking or announcement of the action, and should include interest until the date of payment calculated using a normal commercial rate. Two of the agreements (Chile and Italy BITs) provide that if there is no agreement between the parties on the commercial interest rate, the LIBOR (London Inter Bank Offer Rate) rate is to be used.

The Cuban BITs provide that the investor subject to the expropriation shall have recourse to judicial authorities in the host country to challenge the legality of the expropriation action or the value of compensation. The exception is the Spain BIT, which indicates that disagreements regarding the amount of compensation should be resolved via the dispute settlement procedures in the Agreement.

Dispute Settlement: The Cuban BITs contain mechanisms to deal with disputes that may arise between states and between an investor or investors and the state.

State-to-State Disputes: Cuban BITs provide that disputes between the parties regarding the interpretation and implementation of the agreement should be resolved, to the extent possible, through diplomatic means (Italy, UK, Colombia and Portugal BITs) or "friendly consultations" (Spain and Chile BITs). If after 6 months[64] this approach has not been successful, either of the parties may request the formation of an ad hoc arbitral panel following the rules set out in the agreement.

The composition of the arbitral panel will be as follows:

- the panel will be composed of three members

- each of the parties will designate one member of the panel

- the two members will select a national of a third country[65] who will be proposed to the parties as the head of the arbitral panel and will assume such role if accepted by the parties

- the designation by the parties of the first two arbitrators will be made within 2 months[66] of the request for the formation of the panel

- the designation of the head of the panel will be made within 3 months of the designation of the other panel members.[67]

- if the parties are unable to agree on the composition of the panel within the specified time limits, either party can request that the President of the International Court of Justice to make the necessary appointments;

- in the eventuality that the President of the International Court of Justice is of the nationality of one of the contracting parties or is unable to fulfill the responsibility of making the appointments, the task shifts to the Vice President of the Court, to the senior member of the Court who is not a national of one of the parties, and so on.

---

63. All these formulations echo to a degree the "Hull Formula," in reference to former U.S. Secretary of State Cordell Hull who, in a diplomatic note of August 22, 1938 to the Mexican Ambassador regarding the Mexican expropriations of U.S. agrarian and oil properties, declared that "under every rule of law and equity, no government is entitled to expropriate private property, for whatever purpose, without provision for prompt, adequate and effective payment therefor." Henry J. Steiner, Detlev E. Vagts, and Harold Hongju Koh, *Transnational Legal Problems: Materials and Text,* Fourth Edition (Westbury, New York: The Foundation Press, 1994), p. 458.

64. Three months in the Italy BIT; there is no time limit in the UK BIT.

65. In the Chile and Portugal BITs, the president of the arbitral panel must be national of a country that has diplomatic relations with both parties.

66. Three months in the Italy BIT.

67. In the Chile BIT, the time limits are 30 days to select the candidate for head of the panel and 30 days for the countries to approve such selection.

The decision of the arbitral panel will be made by majority vote and will be binding on both parties. The panel will determine its own procedure.[68] Each of the parties will be responsible for the costs of its own member of the panel and its representation before it, and will share equally the costs of the Chairman and other costs.[69]

Investor-State Disputes: Most BITs negotiated since the 1970s provide for arbitration to settle disputes between an aggrieved foreign investor and the host State. Typically, BITs initially call for "amicable" discussions for a specified period of time (generally 6 months) to seek to settle the dispute. If the dispute remains unresolved, it can be referred at the request of either Party for binding arbitration using international dispute settlement mechanisms, such as those established under the Convention on the Settlement of Investment Disputes between States and Nationals of Other States,[70] the United Nations Commission on International Trade Law (UNCITRAL),[71] or the International Chamber of Commerce (ICC).[72]

The Cuban BITs follow this international practice. Differences between an investor from a party to a Cuban BIT and the other state should be resolved, in the first instance, through friendly consultations. If such consultations fail in resolving the differences, within 6 months from the request for consultations (3 months in the UK and Chile BITs), the investor may request[73] that the dispute be submitted to a dispute resolution body.

The six Cuban BITs we reviewed differ significantly with regard to the dispute settlement body:

- **Italy:** (a) the competent tribunal of the country where the dispute has taken place; or (b) an ad hoc arbitral panel, constituted in accord with the provisions in the agreement for state-to-state disputes.

- **Spain:** (a) the competent tribunal of the country where the controversy has taken place; (b) an ad hoc arbitral panel, constituted in accord with the UNCITRAL Arbitration Rules; or (c) the International Court of Arbitration of the International Chamber of Commerce.

---

68. The Colombia BIT indicates that the contracting parties might establish the rules of procedure for the panel.

69. The UK and Portugal BITs foresee the possibility that the panel might decide to divide the latter costs other than equally.

70. The Convention on the Settlement of Investment Disputes between States and Nationals of Other States (the Convention) came into force on October 14, 1966; 146 States (Cuba excluded) had signed the Convention as of October 1998. The International Centre for Settlement of Investment Disputes (ICSID), which operates as part of the World Bank Group, was created in 1966 pursuant to the Convention. ICSID provides facilities for the conciliation and arbitration of disputes between member countries and investors who qualify as nationals of other member countries. Recourse to ICSID conciliation and arbitration is voluntary; however, once the parties have consented to ICSID arbitration, neither can unilaterally withdraw its consent. Moreover, all Convention signatories, whether or not parties to the dispute, are required by the Convention to recognize and enforce ICSID arbitral awards. See http://www.worldbank.org/icsid/about/main.htm.

71. The Convention on the Recognition and Enforcement of Arbitral Awards (New York, 1958) came into force on June 7, 1959. Cuba ratified this Convention on December 30, 1974, and it entered into force in Cuba on March 30, 1975. See http:/www.uncitral.org. In 1976, UNCITRAL issued Arbitration Rules which provide a comprehensive set of procedural rules upon which parties may agree for the conduct of arbitral proceedings arising out of their commercial relationships. The text of the 1976 UNCITRAL Arbitral Rules are available at http://www.uncitral.org/english/texts/arbconc/arbitrul.htm.

72. The International Chamber of Commerce, founded in 1919 and headquartered in Paris, is the foremost world business organization, holding consultative status at the highest level with the United Nations and its specialized agencies. In 1923, the ICC founded the International Court of Arbitration to conduct international commercial arbitration, settling disputes in a final and binding manner. The Court operates pursuant to Rules of Arbitration first issued in the 1970s and revised periodically thereafter. See http://www.iccwbo.org.

73. The Italy, Spain, Chile and Colombia BITs are clear in stating that the decision of what dispute settlement venue to use is the choice of the investor. The UK BIT seems to grant this right to the investor to seek international arbitration, but suggests that the decision on the venue to use is to be made by both parties. The Portugal BIT indicates that either of the parties could make the decision to seek arbitration and decide on the venue.

- **United Kingdom:** (a) the International Court of Arbitration of the International Chamber of Commerce; or (b) an international arbitrator or an ad hoc arbitral panel constituted in accord with the UNCITRAL Arbitration Rules.

- **Colombia:** (a) the competent tribunal of the country where the dispute has taken place; or (b) an ad hoc arbitral panel, constituted in accord with the provisions in the agreement for state-to-state disputes and operating in accord in accord with the UNCITRAL 1976 Arbitration Rules.

- **Chile:** (a) the competent tribunal of the country where the dispute has taken place; (b) an ad hoc arbitral panel, constituted in accord with the UNCITRAL Arbitration Rules; or (c) an ad hoc arbitral panel, constituted in accord with the provisions in the agreement for state-to-state disputes.

- **Portugal:** (a) the competent tribunal of the country where the dispute has taken place; (b) the International Court of Arbitration of the International Chamber of Commerce; or (c) an ad hoc arbitral panel, constituted through special agreement among the parties or in accord with the UNCITRAL Arbitration Rules. Article 4 of a Protocol annexed to the Portugal BIT provides that, should the parties be signatories to the Convention on the Settlement of Investment Disputes between States and Nationals of Other States, investor-state disputes may be referred to the International Centre for the Settlement of Investment Disputes. As noted earlier, Cuba is not currently a signatory to such Convention and therefore this arbitration venue is not currently available.

The Spain BIT adds that the arbitration will be based on: (a) provisions of the BIT and other agreements between the parties; (b) generally accepted rules and principles of international law; and (c) domestic law of the party where the investment was made, including rules regarding legal disputes.

The BITs are silent on time frames for the commencement of the arbitration process. The UK BIT provides that, if after three months from the date of the request, the arbitration venue has not been agreed by the parties (recall that in the UK BIT, the two parties have to agree on the arbitration venue), the arbitration venue itself can become the subject of arbitration, in accord with UNCITRAL Arbitration Rules.

The Spain and Chile BITs proclaim that arbitral awards will be final and binding; they will be executed in accord with the law of the country where the investment was made. The Portugal BIT proclaims that arbitral awards will be binding for all parties and will only be subject to appeal only to the extent that such process is available within the arbitration venue.

The Chile and Portugal BITs specify that once the arbitral process has begun, the parties shall refrain from dealing with the disputed issue through diplomatic means. Once an arbitral award has been made, the parties might engage in a diplomatic dialogue to promote the enforcement of such award.

SIGNIFICANCE OF CUBAN BITs
This section of the paper discusses the current significance of Cuban BITs in two respects: (1) the contribution they make to Cuba's overall legal framework for foreign investment; and (2) their impact on attracting foreign investment into the island.

Contribution of BITs to
Cuba's Legal Framework for Foreign Investment
BITs protect investors from a signatory country by providing a framework in the host country for national treatment of the investors and setting up dispute settlement procedures, methods for compensation for expropriation, and guarantees of the convertibility and repatriation of profits.[74]

- In the area of expropriation/compensation—particularly relevant in the Cuban case given the nationalizations of foreign investment that occurred in the early 1960s[75]—the Cuban BITs add the notion of *non-discrimination* to the al-

---

74. Matías Travieso-Díaz, *The Laws and Legal System of a Free-Market Cuba* (Westport: Connecticut: Quorum Books, 1996), p. 114.

ready existing standard for expropriation in the Cuban legislation (i.e., that the expropriation be for a public purpose or public interest; in accord with due process of law; and subject to compensation). This means that that the investments of the nationals of a signatory country should not be singled out for expropriation in any particular respect vis-à-vis those of the citizens of other countries.[76]

- As discussed above, the BITs with Chile and the United Kingdom also call for compensation to be "immediate, adequate and effective" and in the BIT with Colombia, "prompt, adequate and effective,"[77] while the others use a somewhat different formulation, calling for compensation to be "adequate" (Italy), "immediate" (Portugal), and "without unjustified delay and adequate" (Spain). Thus, in this area at least some of the BITs create a more favorable compensation standard for the foreign investor than the vague "proper" standard set forth in the Cuban legislation.

- With regard to dispute settlement, Cuba's investment framework legislation is permissive, stating that it is up to the parties in constitutive documents of a joint venture to determine the methodology for such process. Presumably, in the constitutive documents, the parties could designate an international body to settle potential disputes.[78] Should the parties not designate an alternative mechanism, disputes will be resolved by the Arbitral Court of the Cuban Chamber of Commerce, which is the normal procedure for resolving economic disputes in the nation pursuant to the CALPA.[79]

For disputes between investors and the host state, BITs give the investor the choice of whether to submit to domestic or international arbitration; in 5 of the BITs reviewed (Spain, United Kingdom, Colombia, Chile and Portugal), investors may submit a dispute with the host country to an ad hoc panel operating in accord with UNCITRAL rules, while in two of the BITs (Spain and the United Kingdom) the dispute may also be submitted to the Court of Arbitration of the International Chamber of Commerce. Given that an instrumentality of the Cuban State is always one of the joint venturers, the BITs might allow a dispute between business partners to become subject to international arbitration.[80] In this respect, the BITs may provide substantial additional protection to some foreign investors in Cuba by giving them access to international dispute-resolution

---

75. On the expropriation of foreign property by the Cuban government in the early 1960s see, e.g., Paul Sigmund, *Multinationals in Latin America: The Politics of Nationalization* (Madison: University of Wisconsin Press, 1980).

76. This is particularly important in the Cuban context because, in the early years of the Revolution, Cuba singled out for expropriation the assets of U.S. nationals, causing the United States to denounce the expropriations as unlawful. *See, e.g., United States Protests New Cuban Law Directed at American Property*, 43 Dep't State Bull. 171 (1960). For a detailed description of the process by which Cuba expropriated the assets of U.S. nationals, *see* Michael W. Gordon, THE CUBAN NATIONALIZATIONS: THE DEMISE OF PROPERTY RIGHTS IN CUBA 69-108 (1975).

77. As discussed above, this is the so-called "Hull Formula."

78. According to Vega y Vega, *Cuba: Inversiones extranjeras a partir de 1995*, p. 194, some of the joint ventures established pursuant to Law No. 50 of 1982 designated Arbitral Courts outside of Cuba, including UNCITRAL rules.

79. Vega y Vega, *Cuba: Inversiones extranjeras a partir de 1995*, p. 194.

80. There is a considerable question, however, whether a Cuban entity entering into a joint venture with a foreign investor will be deemed to be an extension of the Cuban state such that a dispute between the foreign investor and its Cuban partner becomes a dispute between a foreign investor and the State such as to trigger the dispute resolution provisions of the BIT. In the United States, there is a presumption of separate juridical status by a state instrumentality from the State itself; this presumption can be overcome under two circumstances: when the corporate entity is so extensively controlled by the State that a relationship of principal and agent is created, and when to recognize the separation would work fraud or injustice or defeat overriding public policies. First National City Bank v. Banco Para el Comercio Exterior de Cuba, 462 U.S. 611, 629-30 (1983); Alejandre v. Telefonica Larga Distancia de Puerto Rico, 183 F. 3d 1277, 1284-95 (11ᵗʰ Cir. 1999). The party claiming that the instrumentality is not entitled to separate recognition bears the burden of proving so. See Alejandre, *supra*, 905 F.2d 438, 447 (D.C. Cir., 1990).

Table 2. Committed/Delivered Foreign Investment in Cuba, as of March 30, 1999

Country and year (if any) of Signing of BIT with Cuba	Value of Committed/ Delivered Investment ($U.S. million)
Canada (None)	$600.0
Mexico (None)	$450.0
Italy (1993)	$387.0
Spain (1994)	$100.3
France (1997)	$50.0
United Kingdom (1995)	$50.0
Netherlands (1999)	$40.0
Chile (1996)	$30.0
Brazil (1997)	$20.0
Portugal (1998)	$10.0
Israel (None)	$7.0
South Africa (1995)	$5.0
China (1995)	$5.0
Venezuela (1996)	$3.0
Russia (1993)	$2.0
Germany (1996)	$2.0
Dominican Republic (1999)	$1.0
Jamaica (1997)	$1.0
Honduras (None)	$1.0
Sweden (None)	$1.0
Japan (None)	$0.5
Greece (1996)	$0.5
Panama (1999)	$0.5
Uruguay (None)	$0.3
Austria (None)	$0.1
TOTAL	$1767.2

Source: U.S.-Cuba Trade and Economic Council, "Foreign Investment and Cuba," http://www.cubatrade.org/foreign.html.

mechanisms that may provide fairer and more effective procedures than resort to Cuban courts.

Foreign Investment Performance and BITs

Quantitative information on the status of foreign investment in Cuba is scarce and inconsistent. In October 1991, Julio García Oliveras, chairman of the Cuban Chamber of Commerce, mentioned that negotiations were ongoing with investors accounting for potential investments of $1.2 billion.[81] Vice President Carlos Lage stated in November 1994 that by the end of 1994, joint ventures would have provided Cuba with $1.5 billion in investment.[82] By the end of 1995, according to unnamed official sources, investment had reached more than $2.1 billion.[83] Another Cuban official has reported that foreign investment at the end of 1997 amounted to $2.2 billion.[84]

Official balance of payments statistics issued by the Cuban National Bank and Cuban Central Bank suggest that foreign investment over the period 1993-98 amounted to over $1.3 billion.[85]

Meanwhile, an organization with contacts in Cuba has reported that "committed/realized" foreign investment from 1990 through March 20, 1999 was $1.767 billion.[86] This last source also contains information on the magnitude of foreign investment in the island by country of origin; these data are reported in Table 2. According to this source, Cuba's six largest sources of foreign investment were Canada, Mexico, Italy, Spain, France and the United Kingdom.

Another way to examine the country of origin of foreign investment is through the number of joint ven-

81. Cited in Business International Corporation, *Developing Business Strategies for Cuba* (New York: Business International Corporation, 1992), p. 24.

82. "Carlos Lage Addresses Conference 21 November," Havana Tele Rebelde Network (23 November 1994), as reproduced in *FBIS-LAT-94-229-S* (29 November 1994).

83. "Support for Economic Changes," Havana Radio Havana Cuba (12 July 1995), as reproduced in FBIS-LAT-*95-137* (18 July 1995).

84. Information released by Osvaldo Martínez, Director of the Center for the Study of the World Economy, as reported from La Habana by EFE (17 May 1998).

85. Banco Nacional de Cuba, *Economic Report 1994* (La Habana, August 1995) and *Informe económico 1995* (La Habana, May 1996); Banco Central de Cuba, *Informe económico 1997* (La Habana, May 1998) and *Informe económico 1998* (April 1999). These figures are reported in pesos and converted to U.S. dollars at the official exchange rate for commercial transactions of 1 peso = 1 U.S. dollar, even though the exchange rate of the peso in exchange houses operated by the Cuban government is about 20 pesos for one U.S. dollar.

86. U.S.-Cuba Trade and Economic Council, Inc., "Foreign Investment and Cuba," at http://www.cubatrade.org/foreign/htm, last visited Apr. 10, 2000.

Table 3.   New Joint Ventures for Top Countries Investing in Cuba, 1990-97

Country	1990	1991	1992	1993	1994	1995	1996	1997	Total
All Countries	1	12	25	40	64	51	54	69	317
Spain	1	2	5	7	10[a]	14	10	13	62
Canada		1	8	6	20	7	9	8	59
Italy			1	58[a]	4	6	5	13	34
France			3	6		3	2	2[a]	16
U.K.				1	2	2*	5	5	15
Mexico		3	1	1	4	2	1	1	13

Source: Based on information presented in Omar Everleny Pérez Villanueva, "La inversión extranjera directa en Cuba: Peculiaridades," mimeographed (1998), p. 16.

a.   Denotes the year that the country's BIT was signed with Cuba.

tures consummated. As of the end of 1997, a total of 317 joint ventures with foreign investors had been created. The distribution of joint ventures by country of origin for the six main sources of foreign investment is shown in Table 3.[87] The six countries indicated in the table accounted for 199 joint ventures, or 62.8 percent of the total number of joint ventures established through 1997. According to another source, the total number of joint ventures by 1998 had risen to 345, of which 70 were with investors from Spain, 66 from Canada, 52 from Italy, 15 from the United Kingdom and 14 from France.[88]

Table 4 combines information on the existence of BITs with magnitudes of foreign investment. The first row of the table lists countries with which Cuba has concluded a BIT, while the second row does the same for countries with which Cuba has not concluded a BIT. The columns list countries according to the magnitude of foreign investment their nationals have made in Cuba through March 10, 1999, based on the information in Table 2; the amount of investment in million U.S. dollars is given in parenthesis for each country that has non-zero investment. It should be noted that the range of the amount of investment is very wide, with investment as small as

$100,000 (from Austrian nationals) reported in the table.

While Cuba has concluded BITs with countries responsible for significant flows of foreign investment in the island, a much larger set of countries appear not to have made any investments. Thus, out of the 45 countries with which Cuba has negotiated BITs to date, 24 (58 percent) appear not to have made any investment in Cuba to date.[89]

On the other hand, four of the six countries listed in Table 2 as accounting for the greatest amount of foreign investment in Cuba ($50 million or more) had signed BITs with Cuba. Table 3 shows that for three of those countries, the number of joint ventures increased significantly after execution of the BITs. For Spain, there were 25 joint ventures up to 1994, when the BIT was signed, and 37 in the following three years. For Italy, there were six joint ventures up to 1993, when the BIT was signed, and ten in the following four years; and for the U.K., there were five joint ventures up to 1995, when the BIT was signed, and ten more in the following two years. (The fourth country, France, signed its BIT in 1997, so no statis-

87.   Based on information presented in Omar Everleny Pérez Villanueva, "La inversión extranjera directa en Cuba: Peculiaridades," mimeographed (1998), p. 16.

88.   Philip Peters, *A Different Kind of Workplace: Foreign Investment in Cuba* (Arlington, Virginia: Alexis de Tocqueville Institution, March 1999), p. 9.

89.   Many of the countries with which Cuba has negotiated BITs (e.g., Belize, Cape Verde, Laos, Namibia, Suriname) are less advanced developing countries that are unlikely to have capital to invest in Cuba. Thus, it would seem that Cuban BIT-making is at least in part politically motivated, using these instruments to signal friendship between nations and confluence of political agendas. This is not a phenomenon unique to Cuba. The United States, for example, has also entered into certain BITs, at least in part, to further the country's political objectives. *See* Vandevelde, "The BIT Program," p. 539.

Table 4.   BITs and Magnitude of Foreign Investment

Is There a BIT?	Magnitude of Foreign Investment (in million US dollars)			
	None	Low (less than 5 million)	Medium (5 to 49 million)	High (50 million or more)
Yes	Algeria Argentina Barbados Belgium/Luxemb. Belize Bolivia Bulgaria Cape Verde Colombia Ecuador Hungary Ghana Guatemala Guyana Indonesia Laos Lebanon Malaysia Mongolia Namibia Romania Slovakia Suriname Switzerland Trinidad and Tobago Turkey Ukraine Vietnam	Venezuela (3) Russia (2) Germany (2) Jamaica (1) Dominican Rep. (1) Greece (0.5) Panama (0.5)	Netherlands (40) Chile (30) Brazil (20) Portugal (10) China (5) South Africa (5)	Italy (387) Spain (100) United Kingdom (50) France (50)
No	Rest of the World	Honduras (1) Sweden (1) Japan (0.5) Uruguay (0.3) Austria (0.1)	Israel (7)	Canada (600) Mexico (450)

Note: Figures in parenthesis represents value of investment in million U.S. dollars from Table 2.

tics on post-BIT investment performance can be provided based on the data available to the authors.)

Thus, an argument could be made that the signing of a BIT between a country and Cuba serves to encourage investment by the nationals of that country in Cuba. However, there is no empirical evidence showing that the existence of BITs significantly affects investor decision-making and increases foreign investment, whether in Cuba or elsewhere.[90] As an analyst put it,

> ... the existence of a bilateral investment treaty is only one of several factors that enter into the investor's de-

cision making process and, thus affect the flow of direct investment. It is certainly not the most decisive one. Its importance varies from case to case. For some countries it is insignificant, yet for others it may be the decisive element in attracting foreign investment to a country where it not otherwise go. This is particularly the case when national investment guarantees require the existence of a bilateral investment treaty.[91]

The converse is perhaps just as interesting. Returning to Table 4, Cuba has not concluded BITs with Canada and Mexico, the two countries that are reported to be the largest sources of foreign investment in the island, at $600 million and $450 million, respective-

---

90. Salacuse, "BIT by BIT," p. 673.

91. UNCTC, Bilateral Investment Treaties, p. 14.

ly.[92] In all, Cuba has not concluded BITs with 8 out of the 25 countries that had investments in the island. These eight countries accounted for approximately $1.06 billion in investment, or about 59% of the approximately $1.8 billion foreign investment in the island through March 30, 1999. Thus, the absence of a BIT has not been shown to be a restraining factor for several of Cuba's most significant sources of foreign investment.[93]

All things considered, it can be concluded that for the citizens of a capital-exporting nation, the existence of a BIT between their country and Cuba should be a positive factor, albeit not a decisive one, in the decision whether to invest in Cuba. This is so because the BIT provides some protection to the investor beyond that which he can obtain through direct negotiations with its prospective Cuban partner. In addition, the signing of a BIT is a clear message that Cuba, at least for the time being, intends to respect and give adequate legal protection to foreign investment in the island. Finally, the signing of a BIT signals to the citizens of a country that their government stands ready to act to protect their interests in the event of an investment dispute in Cuba.

An interesting additional question is whether the advantages now afforded by the BITs that Cuba has signed with many nations will remain available to those nations' citizens when Cuba makes a transition to a free-market society. This question will be examined in the next section.

THE STATUS OF BITs IN A POST-TRANSITION CUBA

This section addresses some BIT issues that are likely to arise when Cuba starts its transition to a free-market society. The discussion that follows assumes that Cuba is moving towards a market economy and is seeking to resume trade and other economic relations with the United States. A post-transition environment may present Cuban leaders with the opportunity to reexamine the economic relationships that have been established with other countries and decide whether Cuba wishes to continue to encourage investment by citizens of those countries. This section discusses the impact that the BITs that Cuba has signed could have on these issues and other aspects of the country's foreign investment policies.

Should Cuba Continue Entering Into BITs?

Cuba has now signed BITs with its current and anticipated future trading partners, with four major exceptions: Canada and Mexico, which are source of major investments in the island; Japan, whose level of investment in Cuba thus far has been low; and the United States, whose nationals are prohibited by law from investing in Cuba.[94] If Cuba has not concluded BITs with these countries prior to its economic transition, a question arises whether Cuba's interests

---

92. According to the ICSID database, Canada has been a fairly active participant in BITs, with 17 such agreements concluded through the end of 1996. The same source only records two BITs for Mexico through the end of 1996. The database is given at http://www.worldbank.org/icsid/treaties/main.htm.

93. Because BITs are reciprocal agreements, some of Cuba's BITs might be seen as seeking to protect future Cuban investments abroad. A Cuban analyst refers to over 100 enterprises in foreign countries operating with Cuban capital, although most of these appear to be sales/marketing offices for Cuban state-owned enterprises. Pérez Villanueva, "La inversión extranjera directa en Cuba: Peculiaridades," p. 27. Some enterprises which do appear to represent Cuban investments in the manufacturing and services sectors include: (1) In Mexico, BIOTER, a Cuban-Mexican joint venture producing soybean derivatives, and Agroingeniería, S.A. de CV, a company producing agricultural implements located in the Mexican state of Michoacán; (2) In Vietnam, a construction company that began operations in 1995 and several joint ventures operating cattle farms; (3) In Uganda, Labiofam Pharmaceutical Uganda, Ltd., a joint venture that produces medical products, serums and children's food supplements. *Id.*, pp. 27-30. However, Cuba's status as a capital-importing nation and its current economic crisis make it unlikely that Cuba will be the source of many significant investments in other countries for the foreseeable future.

94. As is well known, the United States has in place a comprehensive embargo against trade and other economic transactions involving Cuba. The embargo is founded on several statutes, and is implemented by detailed regulations, the Cuban Assets Control Regulations (CACR), issued and administered by the U.S. Department of the Treasury. For a detailed discussion of the U.S. trade embargo and its legal foundations see Matías Travieso-Díaz, *The Laws and Legal System of a Free-Market Cuba* (Westport: Connecticut: Quorum Books, 1996), Ch. 2.

would be best served by seeking to negotiate BITs with those countries in an economic transition environment.[95]

While BITs provide benefits to both capital-exporting countries (by providing additional protection to the investments made abroad by their nationals) and capital-importing nations (by tending to stimulate foreign investment), BITs also impose restrictions on a capital-importing country's ability to impose economic measures that may be considered desirable at a particular point in time. For example, while a transition government in Cuba may wish to protect nascent local industries from competition from foreign sources, the BITs that the United States and other capital-exporting countries seek to negotiate prohibit the imposition of protectionist policies by the country with which the treaty is negotiated.[96] The merits of local content rules, export quotas and other protectionist measures can be debated; on the other hand, were Cuba to sign a BIT with the United States that included the standard U.S. terms[97] the imposition of such measures would become unavailable to the Cuban government.[98]

On the whole, it appears that the potential stimulation of foreign investment provided by the BITs outweighs the domestic economic policy limitations introduced by the treaties. Therefore, it is our conclusion that a transition period Cuba should seek to enter into BITs with those countries whose nationals are a potential source of significant foreign investment and with which Cuba has no such treaties at the start of the transition, particularly the United States.

Should Cuba Move to Terminate Any of Its Existing BITs?

Under well settled international law principles, the BITs executed by Cuba with a number of foreign nations are binding agreements between the contract-

---

95. Two implicit assumptions in this discussion are (1) that Cuba is unlikely to become a major capital-exporting country in the foreseeable future, so it will not need to enter into BITs to protect the interests of its investors abroad, and (2) that whether Cuba should enter into additional BITs with developing countries is an interesting political question whose answer should have no material impact on bringing additional investment into Cuba.

96. U.S. BITs provide investors of one party to the treaty who invest in the other party's territory with six basic guarantees:

First, BITs ensure that a party's companies will be treated as favorably as their competitors. They receive the better of national or most favored nation (MFN) treatment when they seek to initiate investment and throughout the life of that investment, subject to certain limited and specifically described exceptions.

Second, BITs establish clear limits on the expropriation of investments and ensure that investors covered by the treaty will be fairly compensated. Expropriation can occur only in accordance with international law standards, that is, for a public purpose, in a nondiscriminatory manner, under due process of law, and accompanied by payment of prompt, adequate, and effective compensation.

Third, BITs guarantee that a party's investors have the right to transfer funds into and out of the country without delay using a market rate of exchange. This covers all transfers related to an investment, including interest, proceeds from liquidation, repatriated profits and infusions of additional financial resources after the initial investment has been made.

Fourth, BITs limit the ability of host governments to require a party's investors to adopt inefficient and trade distorting practices. In particular, performance requirements, such as local content or export quotas, are prohibited.

Fifth, BITs give a party's investors the right to submit an investment dispute with the treaty partner's government to international arbitration. There is no requirement to use that country's domestic courts.

Sixth, BITs give a party's investors the right to engage the top managerial personnel of their choice, regardless of nationality.

U. S. Department of State, "Fact Sheet on the U.S. Bilateral Investment Treaty (BIT) Program," available at http://www.usis-israel.org.il/publish/press/trade/archive/1997/april/et20417.htm

97. For an example of a standard U.S. BIT, see "Treaty Between the Government of the United States of America and The Government of the Republic of Azerbaijan Concerning the Encouragement and Reciprocal Protection of Investment," available online at http://www.state.gov/www/issues/economic/6proto.html

98. Imposing such limitations on the government's ability to act is not necessarily a bad result from the economic standpoint. For example, avoiding protectionist measures may be a good economic policy, and the existence of prohibitions in the BITs against such measures may serve to fend off attempts by local interests to achieve privileged positions.

ing states and remain in effect until their expiration or termination.[99] In addition, international treaties like the BITs have the same binding effect on countries as their domestic legislation.[100] Therefore, the BITs negotiated by Cuba since 1993 should remain in effect unless terminated by one of the parties, and their provisions should be controlling on the domestic policies of the current Cuban government and any successors thereto.

Unilateral termination by a party to one of Cuba's BITs requires in most cases a one year notice.[101] Even after termination, investments in place at the time of termination remain protected by the BIT for a period that varies with the treaty, ranging for example from five years for the Italy BIT to twenty for the UK BIT. Therefore, were the Cuban government to terminate any of the BITs, the investments by the nationals of the countries whose BITs were terminated would still enjoy the protection of the BITs for some period of time.

Potential Effect of Existing BITs on Resolution of Expropriation Claims

The Cuban government may consider seizing properties subject of investment by the nationals of a country with which Cuba has a BIT as part of the process of resolving outstanding expropriation claims involving those properties. As noted earlier, Cuba

seized the properties of U.S. and other foreign nationals on the island starting in 1959, and in the vast majority of cases has failed to either return them to their former owners or pay compensation for the expropriations, although it later entered into global settlement agreements with the governments of several countries.[102] The expropriation claims of several thousand U.S. nationals and potentially hundreds of thousands of Cuban nationals remain pending and represent a serious and potentially explosive issue that must be addressed early by the Cuban government at the time of the country's transition to a free-market economy.

One of the charges frequently made by the former owners of confiscated Cuban properties is that investments made in Cuba by third country nationals are illegal to the extent that they involved property taken without compensation from their former owners. This sentiment has been reflected in the "Cuban Liberty and Democratic Solidarity (LIBERTAD) Act of 1996,"[103] also known as the "Helms-Burton Law," which declares that any commercial activity using or otherwise benefiting from property confiscated from a U.S. national constitutes "trafficking"[104] that would subject those who engage in it to potential civil liability in U.S. courts and exclusion from the territory of

99. See, e.g., Vienna Convention on the Law of Treaties Between States and International Organizations or Between International Organizations ("Vienna Convention"), available online at http://www.un.org/law/ilc/texts/trbtstat.htm. Art. 26 of the Vienna Convention reflects the time-honored principle of *pacta sunt servanda,* stating: "Every treaty in force is binding upon the parties to it and must be performed by them in good faith."

100. Art. 27.1 of the Vienna Convention indicates: "A State party to a treaty may not invoke the provisions of its internal law as justification for its failure to perform the treaty."

101. The Spain BIT requires only six months notice.

102. For a detailed discussion of the Cuban expropriation issue see Matías Travieso-Díaz, *The Laws and Legal System of a Free-Market Cuba* (Westport: Connecticut: Quorum Books, 1996), p. 71-104.

103. Pub. L. No. 104-114, 110 Stat. 785, *codified in scattered sections of* 22 U.S.C.

104. Section 4(13) of the Helms-Burton Law states that a person "traffics" in confiscated property if "that person knowingly and intentionally —

(i) sells, transfers, distributes, dispenses, brokers, manages, or otherwise disposes of confiscated property, or purchases, leases, receives, possesses, obtains control of, manages, uses, or otherwise acquires or holds an interest in confiscated property,

(ii) engages in a commercial activity using or otherwise benefiting from confiscated property, or

(iii) causes, directs, participates in, or profits from, trafficking (as described in clause (i) or (ii) by another person, or otherwise engages in trafficking (as described in clause (i) or (ii)) through another person, without the authorization of any United States national who holds a claim to the property.

the United States.[105] Cuba may decide that resolution of the expropriation claims requires that some of the properties now subject to joint ventures between Cuban entities and foreign investors should be sold or returned to their former owners.[106]

If that decision were to be made, the expropriation protection provisions in the BITs could come to be tested. One probable test would come in the event that expropiatory actions by the Cuban government in Cuba were seen as directed exclusively or disproportionately against the nationals of one particular country. Discriminatory actions by a State against the nationals of a foreign country are a violation of international law.[107] In addition, as noted above, all Cuban BITs include a prohibition against discriminatory takings of the property of the nationals of the signatory countries. Therefore, any actions by a successor Cuban government directed exclusively against the property interests of the nationals of a country that has signed a BIT with Cuba would be in direct violation of the BIT and should trigger the state-to-state dispute resolution mechanisms described in the previous section.

Another test of the BITs could come even if the actions by the Cuban government against foreign-owned assets were not discriminatory and were leveled equally at all foreign investments similarly situated (e.g., all investments in real property). In such instance, other provisions in the BITs might come

into play. To the extent that Cuba implements actions to expropriate foreign holdings, it must do so in accordance with its domestic law and the provisions of the various treaties in force.[108] In particular, the BIT provisions regarding the amount and form of payment become applicable and ordain that payment for the value of the expropriated assets be made in accordance with the Hull formula or a similar formulation.[109] Failure to abide by these requirements may trigger the dispute resolution provisions of the BITs and eventually lead to international arbitration.[110]

Still another test of the BITs could come if individual investors complained that the actions taken to provide them with compensation for the taking of their assets were deficient (e.g., improper valuation, inadequate or dilatory payments, etc.) Such complaints might trigger not only the mechanisms in the BITs to resolve differences between individual investors and the Cuban State, but also cause a country-to-country dispute under the BITs.

The existence of the BIT provides some assurance to an investor from the country that signed the BIT with Cuba that the current Cuban government or its successor will not take measures that adversely affect the investment without providing adequate compensation. Conversely, the BITs provide a boundary condition that must be observed in setting in place mechanisms to resolve expropriation claims in a transition-period Cuba.

---

105. *See* Helms-Burton Law, Titles III and IV

106. *See* Matías Travieso-Díaz, *The Laws and Legal System of a Free-Market Cuba* (Westport: Connecticut: Quorum Books, 1996), p. 71-104, for a discussion of potential methods for the resolution of outstanding expropriation claims by U.S. and Cuban nationals.

107. See, e.g., Banco Nacional de Cuba v. Sabbatino, 193 F.Supp. 375, 385 (S.D.N.Y. 1961), *aff'd*, 307 F.2d 845 (2d Cir. 1962), *rev'd on other grounds*, 376 U.S. 398 (1964).

108. As noted earlier, both Art. 25 of the current Cuban Constitution and Law No. 77 recognize the right of the State to expropriate foreign investments, but only "for reasons of public utility or social interest" and subject to the payment of compensation for "the commercial value" of the property being expropriated.

109. As indicated earlier, the various BITs include different descriptions of the compensation formula, but they all have in common the requirements that the payment must be prompt and adequate and based on the fair market value of the investment at the time of the taking.

110. This does not necessarily mean that the investor would prevail in the dispute or that Cuba would be required to pay damages for the taking of the investor's property. The question whether foreign investors in Cuba have acquired good title to their assets is one that will need to be decided in the Cuban courts; the answer to that question would in part dictate the ultimate outcome of any investor-initiated arbitration.

CONCLUSIONS

Cuba has been somewhat successful in attracting foreign investment in the 1990s. As part of the measures implemented to foster such investment, Cuba has negotiated over 40 bilateral investment promotion and protection agreements, following the formats used internationally for such agreements.

The main contributions BITs have made to the framework for foreign investment in Cuba are: (1) to set out more clearly the standard for compensation in potential expropriations of foreign investment; and (2) to give foreign investors the right to take disputes to international tribunals outside of the jurisdiction of the Cuban arbitration system in those instances in which the constitutive documents of a joint venture may not already provide this venue. These improvements to the legal framework are not likely by themselves to have much influence on Cuba's ability to attract foreign investment in the near future, although their existence probably has an intangible positive impact on the investment climate.

CUBAN LABOR LAW: ISSUES AND CHALLENGES

Aldo M. Leiva

Labor laws supposedly designed to safeguard the interests of Cuban workers has been one of the bulwarks of the political mythology of the Castro Revolution since the early 1960s. Such a mythification has served several purposes: (1) denigrate or deny any accomplishments of the Cuban Republics that predated the 1959 Revolution; (2) re-write Cuban history to convert what was essentially a middle-class revolution to one that was spearheaded by the traditional Marxist protagonists of peasants and workers; and (3) present a "progressive" labor policy that recognizes and guarantees basic labor rights albeit within the strict confines of a totalitarian system that selectively denies such rights at its discretion. The result is a body of propaganda that trumpets Cuba as the stereotypical "worker's paradise." Like so many other aspects of Cuban reality, when dogma and official statistics surrounding labor rights are peeled away, a very different reality is evident, where Cuban workers emerge as one of the most exploited and manipulated labor forces in the world. In any transition from totalitarianism to democracy, the role of workers and the rights to be afforded to the working class will be key issues facing legislators and policy-makers in the creation of a new Cuban society.

Presented in this essay is a brief survey of Cuban labor law during the Republican era (1902-1952), followed by an analysis of labor law as legislated and as practiced under the Castro regime, and concluding with a discussion of issues facing drafters of new Cuban labor laws in a post-Castro Cuba. This analysis is not intended to serve as a blueprint for future policy makers, but rather as a point of initiation for a national debate that will allow Cubans to determine the morals, laws, culture and society that will comprise a new Cuban Republic. Ultimately, the Cuban people possess the sovereign right to determine such issues and the scope and quality of presentations and studies that have been completed through the Association for the Study of the Cuban Economy will serve as a potential resource during the transition process.

CUBAN LABOR LAW DURING THE REPUBLICAN ERA (1902-1952)

Constitutional Guarantees of Labor Rights

Since the establishment of the Cuban Republic in 1902, Cuban Constitutions and legislation have mirrored Cuban sociopolitical events, which at times have been turbulent. The constitutions of 1901, 1934, and 1935 all recognized and guaranteed basic civil rights that bear directly on labor rights, such as freedom of assembly and freedom of association.[1] However, the 1940 Constitution provides the most extensive treatment of labor rights within a Constitutional setting, continuing traditional provisions of civil, political, and procedural guarantees, but including extensive legislative provisions governing family, culture, property and work.[2] Such issues had not been addressed by earlier Constitutions.

---

1. "The Socialist Constitution of Cuba," Columbia Journal of Transnational Law 17:45, p. 470, 1978.

2. Id., at 470.

The 1940 Constitution recognized basic labor and economic guarantees, such as the right to work, a forty hour maximum work week, one month of annual vacations, minimum wages, equal pay for equal work, social security, the rights to form and join unions, and right to strike, and provided working women the right to paid maternity leave. These expansive rights were widely praised at the time by the Cuban Socialist Party, which had sent delegates to the constitutional assembly.[3]

Administrative Organization

The Secretariat of Labor was created in 1933 and its functions were identified as "the enforcement of social laws, services of social assistance, inspection of labor conditions and lodging, supervision of labor courts, supervision and control of ... social insurance ... and the supervision over compliance with international labor agreements."[4] Resolutions of the Secretary of Labor were enforced through "interventors," who were appointed by the Executive Branch to private enterprises by the Secretariat of Labor. Interventors would ensure compliance with labor resolutions and those enterprises that did not comply were temporarily managed by interventors until labor practices were brought into compliance.[5]

The Secretariat of Labor was also advised by the Superior Labor Council, consisting of representatives from government, management and labor. Appeals in labor matters were heard by the Court of Constitutional and Social Guarantees.[6]

Labor problems were addressed by tripartite (government-employer-employee), bipartite (employer-employee), and governmental councils. For example, the Intelligence Commission of Port Workers had jurisdiction over labor matters within the maritime sector, and was composed of employers, employees and was presided over by a member of the judiciary.[7]

Protection of Worker Rights

During the Republican era, labor was nationalized, meaning that Cubans were guaranteed at least 50% of the employment and salary of all businesses and 100% of the employment and salary of future enterprises. Three exemptions were established: (1) foreign technical/professional personnel (unless Cuban technicians/professionals were available); (2) veterans; and (3) owner representatives having administrative or supervisory functions.[8] If employees had to be terminated from employment, foreign workers had to be fired before Cuban nationals and new positions had to be filled by Cuban citizens. By the 1950s, however, the Ministry of Labor modified and relaxed this strict policy to allow additional foreigners with specialized technical knowledge and experience to retain key positions, especially in areas where Cuban professional/technical schools could not keep up with labor demands.

Cuban workers were protected from arbitrary discharge and the law set forth detailed procedures and causes through which employees could be discharged. Examples of justified causes were unauthorized absence, incompetence/negligence, fraud/theft, divulging trade secrets, and decline in work performance.[9] Causes for which an employer could not discharge an employee were maternity, transfer of the enterprise, military duty, and, in some sectors, mechanization.[10] Certain classes of employees, such as domestic servants and some non-sugar agricultural workers, were exempted from these requirements. In practice, the process of discharging employees was slow and complicated, and consisted of filing of pa-

3. Id., at 471.

4. Vidana, Evangelina, "Labor Legislation during the Republic of Cuba: 1902-1958," Thesis, University of Miami, Florida, 1970.

5. Id.

6. Id.

7. Id.

8. Id.

9. Id.

10. Id.

pers by the employer, followed by an administrative stage and judicial stage. The ultimate decision was subject to appeal.[11]

Cuban workers had the right to enter into labor contracts individually or collectively. Collective bargaining was well-protected and was recognized as a compulsory right by the 1940 Constitution. Collective agreements were registered with the Ministry of Labor, whereby they became enforceable.[12]

In 1933, the right of workers to organize into labor unions was established under Cuban law, abandoning the colonial-era Law of Association of 1888, and new regulations on labor unions were established. Only government employees were exempted from these provisions. The 1940 Constitution also guaranteed the right to unionize and labor unions could not be dissolved.[13] Under the law, all labor leaders had to be Cuban citizens, delegates from the Secretariat of Labor could attend union meetings, union leaders had to elected by ballot instead of by acclamation, and payment of union dues was compulsory.[14] Unions were forbidden from participating in political activities.

The right of workers to strike was recognized under Cuban law, provided prior notice was given to the Secretariat of Labor. Labor disputes that could potentially lead to a strike had to be brought before Commissions for Social Cooperation,[15] before exercising the right to strike. If the Commission ruled against the union, the strike was unauthorized and therefore illegal. The union had a right of appeal to the Supreme Court. General strikes and lockouts

were illegal, especially in such key sectors as electricity, water, telephone, and medical services.[16]

Under the 1940 Constitution, the State's key responsibility to workers was to provide and ensure favorable living and working conditions. As to living conditions, the State was to sponsor and develop housing for labor and was required to ensure the economic conditions necessary for a dignified standard of living, employment for the unemployed, nationalization of labor, non-discriminatory practices regarding sex, race, or class, non-monopolization, and equality in the application of social laws. Voluntary (uncompensated) work was expressly forbidden by law.

In the area of benefits, the State was to contribute one third of the pension and retirement funds. It was also responsible for mediating conflicts between management and labor. The government recognized a maximum 8 hour workday, a maximum 44 hour workweek, one month paid vacation, 4 paid holidays, minimum salary, equal pay for equal work, collective bargaining, unionization, right to strike, and social security. Labor rights, including the right to work, were declared inalienable, and were to be safeguarded by the Constitutionally-created Tribunal of Constitutional and Social Guarantees.[17]

Social security guaranteed by the 1940 Constitution addressed risks of unemployment, labor accidents, illnesses, occupational diseases, labor maternity, old age, disability, retirement, and death.[18] The protection against illnesses covered medical assistance free of charge. Social insurance for labor accidents and occupational diseases were paid for by the employer,

---

11. Id.

12. Id.

13. Id.

14. Id.

15. Prior to creation of the Commissions for Social Cooperation, Cuban legislation attempted to created two types of systems, both independent of the Ministry of Labor, one which provided for an employer-employee direct approach, and the other provided for a National Arbitration Commission. Both were subsequently declared unconstitutional and annulled in 1943. Vidana, Evangelina, "Labor Legislation during the Republic of Cuba: 1902-1958," Thesis, University of Miami, Florida, 1970.

16. Id.

17. Id.

18. Id.

while social insurance related to unemployment, old age and disability were paid equitably among the government, employer, and employee. Social insurance institutions were to be administered by organizations comprised of representatives elected by employers, employees, and by a government representative.[19]

Critiques of the Cuban Labor Code in Practice

Despite the extensive laws and rights protecting workers' interests, actual practice and experience differed from the ideal concepts enshrined in Cuban law. The Cuban labor movement passed through several phases during the Republican era. Only occupational accident compensation and social security measures for railway men and mineworkers were in place before 1933. The Machado Regime of the 1920s had been openly hostile to labor interests, resulting in murders of several labor leaders, strike-breaking by force, and outright bans on labor organizations.[20]

However, as labor organizations grew in political power, successive governments sought labor support by passing the above-described comprehensive labor laws. Labor influence continued growing into the 1950s.[21] By 1958, a million workers, approximately half of the Cuban labor force, belonged to a labor union.[22] In 1938, the unions had been grouped together into a national confederation, the CTC (Cuban Confederation of Workers), composed of 32 industrial federations.[23] Government decrees usually settled labor disputes, and collective bargaining in

practice was infrequent, since all disputes had to be presented before the Ministry of Labor if a majority of the workers in the business chose the option. The Ministry of Labor was composed of political appointees and, especially in the 1940s, was filled with appointees friendly to labor unions.[24] One employer appeared before the labor courts sixty times without a favorable decision. Employers often complained of the difficulty in discharging employees.[25] For example, one company filed 200 applications to discharge employees for justifiable causes and failed each time.[26] Many foreign investors were aware of the protective labor laws and refused to invest in the Cuban economy, based on the experience of Cuban businesses.[27] The rigidity of labor legislation was also severely criticized in the World Bank's 1951 report on Cuba.[28]

In addition, despite the labor guarantees, by the 1950s, a large portion of the Cuban population was either unemployed or partially employed, and were not unionized. During the five months of the sugar harvest, the unemployment rate was 8%, while during the rest of the year ("tiempo muerto") rose to as high as 32%.[29] For such workers, family ties and acquaintances were part of an informal social/economic network, which provided support where labor unions and the government could not or would not.[30]

Originally, administrative enactment of worker rights was to be accomplished through a number of Constitutionally-created instruments for social reform and economic development, such as a national

---

19. Id.

20. Thomas, Hugh, *Cuba or The Pursuit of Freedom*, p. 1173, Da Capo Press, New York,1998.

21. Id. at 1174.

22. Id. at 1178.

23. Id. at 1178-79.

24. Id. at 1174.

25. Id. at 1174.

26. Id. at 1176.

27. Id. at 1177.

28. Id. at 1177.

29. Id. at 1175.

30. Id. at 1175.

bank, and a program to achieve full employment. These far-reaching goals were not attained, however, in part due to delays in passing legislation enacting such rights and inability to enact legislation on the more ambitious goals, such as full employment, during the 12-year period when the 1940 Constitution was in effect.[31]

CUBAN LABOR LAW UNDER THE CASTRO REGIME (1959-PRESENT)

The Socialist Constitution

When the Castro regime seized power in 1959, Fidel Castro suspended the 1940 Constitution and enacted the Fundamental Law of 1959, which nonetheless included many of the socioeconomic rights of the 1940 Constitution. Similarly, the socialist Constitution of 1976 includes several of the social and economic rights of the 1940 Constitution, although on the premise that such rights are reality and not just ideals to be pursued.[32] Although the most recent Cuban Constitution (1992) lists such rights, it suffers from the Castro regime's disregard for the rule of law, an official practice that has been in place since the regime's seizure of power in 1959. Like other totalitarian governments, Cuba's laws are purposefully vague on key issues, to allow ample state control and discretion. Many laws that are on the books are simply disregarded or are subject to exceptions grounded on the overriding principle of absolute control over Cuban society by the regime.

The Cuban socialist constitution is a radical departure from pre-existing legal norms in Cuba. First, unlike the 1940 Constitution, which was the last legitimate political expression of the Cuban people, both the 1976 and 1992 constitutions were drafted and approved by the Castro regime with virtually no public participation or consent. Second, all constitutional guarantees are subordinated to the dictates and dis-

cretion of the State. Third, as the means of production are state-owned, all workers are employees of the state, the same entity supposedly responsible for guaranteeing worker rights. The result of these factors is that current Cuban labor law primarily imposes requirements on the Cuban state's workers/employees and any of the rights and privileges that are afforded to Cuban workers are subject to suspension and broad interpretation by Cuban courts.

This problem is further compounded by the fact that there is no independent judiciary, as the Cuban courts are subordinate to the National Assembly and the Council of State, of which Castro is president.[33] Article 123 of the Constitution provides that a key purpose of the judiciary is to educate citizens on socialism, a goal inconsistent with the judicial concept of neutrality. Therefore, any Cuban worker seeking legal redress against his employer — the Cuban State — faces a judge committed to ideological conformity with the State.

All these principles are consistent with the Stalinist model that has been in place in Cuba since the 1960s. As the Castro regime consolidated its power by adopting this model, a new concept of labor relations arose, which consists of the following features:

- Work is a right, duty and source of pride for each citizen;

- Non-paid voluntary work is an essential element;

- Brigades and other forms of militarized labor are utilized;

- Self-employment is discouraged through official policy;

- Workers are subjected to intensive social mobilization through propaganda and coercion; and

---

31. Former President Fulgencio Batista's coup in 1952 suspended the 1940 Constitution, replacing it with the Constitutional Law of 1952, which recognized many of the socioeconomic rights that had been guaranteed under its predecessor. Although the 1940 Constitution was briefly reinstated by the Batista regime after election of Fulgencio Batista to the presidency in 1955, constitutional guarantees were suspended thereafter and remained suspended through 1958.

32. "The Socialist Constitution of Cuba," Columbia Journal of Transnational Law 17:45, p. 470, 1978.

33. Hernández, Esperanza and Truyol, Berta, "Out in Left Field: Cuba's Post-Cold War Strikeout," 18 Fordham Int'l L.J. 15, 1994.

- Strikes are prohibited and voluntary collective bargaining does not exist.[34]

These key points of the Stalinist model are incorporated into the Constitution and into Cuba's Labor Code. Article 45 of the Constitution provides that work in socialist society is a right as well as a duty. It further officially declares the elimination of unemployment. Most importantly, Cuban workers must participate in uncompensated "voluntary" work, usually in the form of field labor. On its face, this voluntary work requirement is a legal fiction, as it is a constitutionally-created obligation on every Cuban citizen.

Article 53 provides for freedom of speech and of the press so long as they conform with the goals of socialist society. Article 54 also seemingly guarantees the right of assembly, protest, and association to all workers. Article 46 guarantees a right to leisure time, an 8 hour work day and annual paid vacations. Articles 47 and 48 provide for social security to disabled workers, sick workers and the elderly. Article 49 provides for compensation for job related injuries, and guarantees worker safety.

Despite these guarantees, Article 62 provides that none of the liberties guaranteed under the Constitution "can be exercised against the Constitution and Cuban laws, nor against the socialist state." Article 62 therefore acts as a catch-all provision where any Cuban seeking to assert a legal right is subject to unlimited state discretion in determining whether such an act is "against the socialist state." This applies to any workers who attempt to organize independent labor unions or seek to assert other essential labor rights, such as the right to safe working conditions.

Labor Code

In 1984, the National Assembly of People's Power proposed and adopted a Labor Code governing all labor matters.[35] A review of the Cuban Labor Code's provisions demonstrate that 21% of its articles are focused on establishing requirements and duties of Cuban workers, including disciplinary actions and "voluntary" work requirements. The Labor Code creates a reward/disciplinary system to motivate workers to perform their duties.[36] Rewards consist of moral and material awards, such as public recognition and access to scarce goods and services.[37] Pursuant to the Code, Cuban workers are obligated to (1) be regular and punctual in attendance; (2) make fullest use of the work day; (3) fulfill requirements of their occupation; (4) abide by occupational health and safety regulations; (5) care for socialist property; and (6) perform other duties required by law.[38]

The Cuban Labor Code creates several administrative structures primarily oriented toward governing and managing workers. Evaluation Committees set forth work requirements for Cuban workers, technical norms, and means by which workers are evaluated. Labor councils address labor disputes and Wage Committees set worker wages for specific sectors. The Law for Labor Justice (1992) adds additional disciplinary measures to enforce compliance with labor requirements.[39]

An added component to the above work/disciplinary requirements is the aspect of ideological control. All Cuban workers have an official work record that tracks and evaluates the "ideological integration" of each worker.[40] Therefore, any workers who fail to demonstrate adequate levels of commitment to the Castro Revolution, or who fail to participate in such

---

34. Córdova, Efrén, "Legal Changes in the Area of Labor Relations," *Cuba in Transition—Volume 3*, Association for the Study of the Cuban Economy, Washington, 1993.

35. Pérez-López, Jorge F., "Cuba's Thrust to Attract Foreign Investment: A Special Labor Regime for Joint Ventures in International Tourism," University of Miami Inter-American Law Review, 24:2, page 261, 1992.

36. Id. at 268-69.

37. Id.

38. Id.

39. Córdova, Efrén, Op. Cit.

40. Hernandez, Esperanza and Truyol, Berta, "Out in Left Field: Cuba's Post-Cold War Strikeout," 18 Fordham Int'l L.J. 15, 1994.

events as state-sponsored rallies, can face disciplinary actions, demotions, or other professional setbacks.

A compounding issue is the fact that suitability for employment is vaguely defined in the Labor Code as that "set of qualities that a worker must possess [to] make him or her apt, given work requirements, for a specific observation or post."[41] Unfortunately, the specific qualities that make a worker suitable or apt are not defined anywhere in the Code. The result is that such ambiguous legislation lends itself for use as a repressive instrument, wherein a worker who is not deemed to be ideologically committed to socialism may find himself or herself terminated under this broad and vague language. Again, the law is another tool of control rather than a source of protection for the Cuban worker.

Worker Rights

Under the current legal structure of Cuba, the State occupies the dual role of employer and guarantor of worker rights. More importantly, the State decides where and when people work, whether they receive promotions, and whether they may even purchase appliances at workplace credit unions.[42] While the State occupies the unique role of sole employer in Cuba, it also has broad discretion in determining the extent and operation of constitutionally guaranteed worker rights.

Many of the Constitutional guarantees provided in earlier constitutions are disregarded by the current legal system. Despite constitutional guarantees, rights to freedom of assembly and association are essentially non-existent. Workers can be forced to work 10, 12 or 14 hours a day, in violation of pre-1959 limits to eight hour workdays[43] and in violation of international norms.[44]

The Secretary General of the Cuban Confederation of Workers has lauded workers who labored 18 hours a day as exemplary models of the ideal Cuban worker.[45] Sugar harvests frequently require 14 to 16 hour workdays.[46]

One of the greatest omissions in current Cuban labor law is the complete absence of the right to strike. This right has been proscribed by the Castro regime, perhaps in recognition of the political success of strikes in the struggle against the Batista dictatorship. Similarly, as to collective bargaining, labor agreements with state-run enterprises are not subject to negotiation.

Official labor unions are controlled by the State and therefore do not oppose these violations of internationally-recognized labor rights. Cuban labor unions are integrated into the government's network of mass organizations, such as youth groups, women's groups, and professional organizations. Adopting the totalitarian model utilized in other socialist dictatorships, each sector of Cuban society is pooled into large mass organizations which orient that sector and collect information for the state regarding its constituency. The absolute control of the Cuban Communist Party is enshrined in the bylaws of the Cuban Workers' Central (CTC) which provides that the labor movement recognizes the commanding role of the Party. The result is that unions are reshaped into sources of labor discipline, socialist emulation, voluntary work and social mobilization.

As a consequence, the Castro regime also suppresses all efforts to create independent labor unions. During the "Special Period" after the collapse of Soviet Communism, several independent labor organizations evolved among them the Consejo Unitario de Trabajadores Cubanos, Confederación de Trabajadores Democráticos de Cuba, Confederación de Trabaja-

---

41. Pérez-López, Jorge F. Op. Cit. at 264.

42. Hernandez, Esperanza and Truyol, Berta, "Out in Left Field: Cuba's Post-Cold War Strikeout," 18 Fordham Int'l L.J. 15, 1994.

43. The current Cuban Constitution also includes a right to an eight hour workday.

44. Córdova, Efrén. Op. Cit.

45. Id.

46. Id.

dores Libres de Cuba, and others.[47] Leaders of these organizations have been persecuted, arrested, incarcerated or subjected to mob violence. Despite repression, similar groups are showing recent signs of growth throughout the island. However, they still remain small, isolated, weakly organized and easily infiltrated by Cuban state security.

Independent labor organizations within the island have successfully criticized the Castro regime for the following deficiencies: prohibition of strikes and other forms of peaceful labor protest, poor safety conditions, indiscriminate firing and discrimination for political and ideological reasons, being forced to engage in non-labor related activities of primarily ideological content, political activities during the workday, no independent labor, and violation of privacy rights due to investigations and searches of residences of workers.[48]

In the growing tourist sector, manipulation of workers by the regime is perhaps most evident. Foreign-managed enterprises cannot directly contract with Cuban workers. Rather, they must hire official state worker service agencies, who then contract Cuban workers. Foreign enterprises, in any sector, must pay worker salaries in dollars to the Cuban state, which then pays Cuban workers in almost worthless Cuban pesos. The result is that Cuban workers are paid at a fraction of the value of the labor they provide to foreign entities. For this reason, the average monthly income of the Cuban worker is approximately ten dollars.

In summary, the legal concepts expressed in the current Cuban Constitution are not applied. Through exceptions and broad discretion, the regime exempts itself from having to comply with its own laws, often sacrificing what few rights it supposedly guarantees to workers. The Cuban Labor Code is primarily designed as a means to control and manage Cuban workers and basic rights, such as unionization and striking, are omitted from Cuban law. Any future government must reincorporate such basic laws into new legislation, so that Cuban workers may enjoy the same protections and rights enjoyed by workers in Western democracies.

PROPOSALS FOR LABOR LAW IN A POST-CASTRO CUBA

New Cuban labor legislation should meet several essential criteria during the transition from totalitarianism to democracy: (1) transparency; (2) flexibility; and (3) balance of interests. During the transition period, labor laws must be clearly defined for the benefit of both employers and employees. Such transparency will fully advise employees of their rights while ensuring employers and potential investors of labor requirements. Labor laws should also be flexible, to reflect changing conditions of the Cuban economy. Lastly, drafting of labor laws should provide ample opportunity for participation by all sectors of Cuban society.

Several legal sources exist for the creation of new labor legislation. A primary source is the fifty-year legislative legacy of the Republican era. While many provisions in earlier legislation, as seen in Cuban Constitutions and Cuban Labor Codes, now seem antiquated and not in conformity with current international standards,[49] Cuba nonetheless had a highly developed system of substantive and procedural laws that can provide a starting point for discussion. The object here will be not to blindly follow and adopt legal precedents that have not been in effect for almost fifty years, but rather serve as a framework within which to adopt new legal principles.

Another source for legal guidance is the International Labor Organization (ILO), created to promote worldwide labor standards.[50] Founded in 1919 as a component of the League of Nations, the ILO is now

---

47. 7 Brito, Joel, "El Sindicalismo en la Cuba de Hoy," CEON, Colección Actualidad, Vol. 1, Num. 1, August 1999.

48. Id.

49. Such as the stringent standards for dismissing employees, criticized even during the Republican era.

50. Erickson, Christopher L., and Mitchell, Daniel J.B. "Labor Standards in International Trade Agreements, the Current Debate," Labor Law Journal, p. 764, 1996.

affiliated with the United Nations. The ILO can provide technical assistance in developing labor legislation. The ILO consults with developing countries in creating new legislation that permits such nations to compete in the global economy while ensuring adequate protection of worker's rights. The ILO advocates for such basic labor standards as: right of association, right to unionize and collective bargaining, free choice of employment, prohibitions on child labor, non-discrimination in employment, adequate wages, limits on working hours, health care, social security and occupational safety and health protection. The ILO may provide technical assistance to the new Cuban government and may also investigate complaints of violations of labor standards and assist a Cuban Ministry of Labor in ensuring adequate protection of Cuban worker rights.

In addition, as Cuba transitions into a participant of the international free market economy, it will no doubt enter into new agreements with trading partners. Such trade agreements often include provisions relating to worker rights and labor rights, with varying degrees of specificity and enforceability.[51] Although the issue of inclusion of labor standards into trading agreements is contested, trading partners may seek minimum labor standards applicable to each signatory. Foreign labor unions may play a key role in insisting upon such standards.

Multilateral Human Rights Conventions also provide a source for discussion of labor rights. The United Nations Universal Declaration of Human Rights and its Bill of Rights recognize such basic rights as rights of association and trade union organizing and bargaining, favorable wages and working conditions, and prohibitions against forced labor, child labor and discrimination.[52]

Lastly, voluntary labor codes adopted by multinational enterprises may provide another source of norms for labor practice in Cuba. Such codes have been promoted by non-governmental organizations, industry associations, and individual companies with the purpose of standardizing labor practices and rights in the international economy. Of course, the key deficiency with such codes is that they are not enforceable and are subject to changes in corporate policy.

A review of the above sources suggests the following unconditional basic labor rights should be guaranteed to Cuban workers during the transition period to democracy and free market participation:

- Right of Association;

- Right to independent unions;

- Right to strike;

- Collective bargaining;

- Prohibition against forced labor;

- Prohibition against discrimination;

- Minimum health and safety requirements; and

- Limits on work hours and work weeks.

Other rights, such as wage levels, access to medical services, social security, worker's compensation for on the job injuries, should be guaranteed to Cuban workers, though the ability of the state to provide such benefits will be conditioned on the status of the economy and on Cuba's level of development. Creation and maintenance of pension plans and tax structures to supplement and support a social safety net will be an essential component of drafting new Cuban labor legislation.[53]

The form in which these rights will be incorporated into Cuban legislation is dependent on the prevailing concept of the relationship between the State and the individual. Unlike the United States, Cuban legal and social norms have accepted (and insisted upon) a large role for the state. Prior to the Castro Revolu-

---

51. Compa, Lance, "Labor Rights and Labor Standards in International Trade," Law and Policy in International Business, vol. 25, p. 179, 1993.

52. Id.

53. Travieso-Díaz, Matías F., *The Laws and Legal System of a Free-Market Cuba: A Prospectus for Business*, p. 171.

tion, the Cuban state certainly played a central role in society and expected the state to provide a social safety net, as seen in the expansive rights accorded to workers in the 1940 Constitution and earlier legislation. After more than forty years of a centralized State system, Cubans on the island will no doubt expect continuity in minimum social benefits, among which are social security, free access to health care, and free education. This has been the experience of those Central and Eastern European countries, which chose, or were forced to preserve, well-developed but costly social safety nets.[54] Of course, such benefits are never "free," and any new Cuban government will need to develop the proper tax structure and policies to permit the existence of even the most basic of these benefits.

Such a pressing societal need will have to be balanced against competing needs of attracting investment and growing the economy. Labor laws and regulations impose costs on employers.[55] During a transition, the new Cuban government will have to consider the trade-offs between providing worker benefits and social safety nets to promote social stability, while cutting operational costs to employers.[56] In the area of foreign investment, an extensive (and expensive) social safety net may also discourage foreign investment, as in East Germany after its reunification with West Germany.[57]

During the transition away from a centralized economic and political system, Cuba will require a massive capital investment, in such basic areas as its infrastructure and communications, as well as a perhaps greater investment in the Cuban people, to provide them with the proper education, training, and job skills necessary for a competitive economy. Such training may be provided by state programs or by state-employer joint programs, perhaps in exchange for tax credits.

The role of foreign labor in rebuilding Cuba must also be debated. The new Cuban government may be pressured to place restrictions on the ability of enterprises to hire foreign workers, through such measures as work permits and quotas.[58] Such restrictions are also consistent with Cuba's tradition of nationalized labor. Many countries have also adopted such measures,[59] such as Costa Rica where no more than 10% of employees of an enterprise may be foreigners. However, during the transition period, any such restrictions should be liberalized to permit new investors to freely choose qualified employees, especially in areas where employees with technical skills will be in short supply.[60]

Other issues during the transition era will center on the status of employees of former state-owned enterprises. Legislation and guidelines will need to be developed to determine which employees will be transferred to newly-privatized enterprises, and how employees who lose their jobs will be compensated.[61]

These issues and challenges will be faced by a Cuban society burdened by decades of totalitarian control, where civic debate and public participation have been non-existent. Many cultural features of totalitarian control, such as intolerance and inability to compromise, may have a negative impact on consensus-building. Nonetheless, these barriers will have to be faced by the Cuban people as they reshape Cuba with new laws, new goals, and new life. At the center

---

54. Travieso-Díaz, Matías F., "Recommended Features of a Foreign Investment Code for Cuba's Free Market Transition," 21 N.C. J. Int'l L. & Com. Reg. 511, 1996.

55. Id.

56. Id.

57. Travieso-Díaz, Matías F., *The Laws and Legal System of a Free-Market Cuba: A Prospectus for Business*, p. 172.

58. Travieso-Díaz, Matías F., "Recommended Features of a Foreign Investment Code for Cuba's Free Market Transition," 21 N.C. J. Int'l L. & Com. Reg. 511, 1996.

59. Id.

60. Id.

61. Travieso-Díaz, Matías F., *The Laws and Legal System of a Free-Market Cuba: A Prospectus for Business*, p. 171.

of the physical and spiritual reconstruction of Cuba will be Cuban workers, whose rights and privileges will be debated by policy makers and legislators. Cuban workers' interests must be seriously considered in the formulation of new laws but must be balanced against competing national interests of economic growth and stability. The debate, though long and difficult, should be anticipated with research on the above issues so that Cuba may strive to attain José Martí's goal of existing "with all, for the good of all."[62]

---

62. José Martí (1853-1895), Cuban statesman, journalist, poet and lawyer, is considered by many Cubans to be an intellectual and spiritual guiding force for Cuban nationalism and Cuban identity.

COMMENTS ON

"ACTUARIAL MODEL OF THE IMPACT OF LINKING ECONOMIC VARIABLES TO A LIFE SURVIVAL FUNCTION" BY DONATE-ARMADA[1]

Diego R. Roqué

In order to fully appreciate the significance of the vast contribution this work is making towards providing a clear understanding of the difficult situation traversed by the Cuban nation today, a brief background discussion leading to the introduction of Donate-Armada's theme, development and conclusions is a clear necessity. The commentary will be direct and to the point, hopefully not deviating much from the central point but certainly adding color to the discussions and debate.

COMMENTARY

Almost everybody is familiar with Newton's Laws of Mechanics. One in particular, the Law of Inertia, is very insightful. This law tells us about the natural tendency to resist change as it describes the most natural states of motion. An object at rest will remain at rest or an object moving at a constant velocity will remain moving at that constant velocity unless a force is applied to change the object's state of motion.

Imagine then taking the trouble to forecast that an object at rest will remain at rest or that an object moving with a constant speed and direction will remain moving with the same velocity. From the point of view of the art and science of forecasting there

would be nothing particularly meritorious or intelligent about these predictions. The real challenge in forecasting, requiring insight and analytical skills, would be to as accurately as possible predict the exceptional event, namely when forces will come into play that will change the states in the entity of interest.

Inertia is also applicable in social situations albeit not with the exactitude of physics. This is one of the reasons why most contemporary social scientists that venture forecasts predict no change in Cuba's future. The consensus seems to be that the current hardline Cuban leadership will be allowed to expire naturally. Only then, at their expiration, do the expectations of forces changing the Cuban social scene appear to come alive. Most of these predictions, however, are blind in the sense that no one has been able to determine with any degree of accuracy when the natural expiration of the current Cuban leadership will occur; so in a sense they are predicting that an object at rest will simply remain at rest. Clearly the death of Fidel Castro is viewed by many as the exceptional event that will unleash the forces of change in the island. It is here where Donate-Armada, armed with his vital actuarial statistics, is making one of many

---

1. Editors' Note: This is a corrected version of Mr. Roqué's paper. Regrettably, the version included in *Cuba in Transition—Volume 9*, contained serious errors. Apologies are hereby extended to Mr. Roqué.

important contributions. There is more than just inertia, however, inducing social scientists to predict no major changes in the Cuban social scene.

From the very beginning of Castro's revolution, intelligent and courageous Cubans, men women and children, ultimately had to opt for the "Strategic Retreat" (see Sun-tzu's *The Art of War*) much in the manner of General MacArthur in the Phillippines or for that matter the Chinese Nationalists fleeing the mainland. Proximity and American policy permitted them to do this possibly avoiding for our own hemisphere another carnage a la Stalin, Hitler or Pol Pot. The momentum that carried Castro to power helped explain why this was the intelligent choice for Cubans. But this explanation seems to have run out of gas when 40 years after the takeover, young Cubans, in defiance of sharks, still jump into rafts headed for the United States. But even worse than this is to hear the explanations given by the recent arrivals as to why they left Cuba.

Asking some of them why they left is quite an eye opener. The responses range from "my husband had to pay thirty pesos for a beer" to " there were no toys for my children" to "I had no access to dollars" and so on. At first glance, they appear to be economic refugees. But this is just an impression. These are the children of the revolution who are fleeing and one must come to the horrible conclusion that there is absolutely no consciousness in Cuba as to what it is that is so terribly oppressing them. In reality, it is impossible not to be a political refugee fleeing Cuba; they just do not know it. Explanations for this abound. They are the subject for another treatise. Suffice to say that ignorance of communism and of the problems communist totalitarianism unleashes in a society is probably the primary reason why the people can not shake off their yoke and why there really seems to be little possibility for change inside Cuba. Social scientists see very little possibility of an open rebellion, much less a successful one, in Cuba. The hard reality seems to be that the possibility of other exceptional events competing with the death of Castro for impact appear remote at best.

Very little has been discussed publicly about the heavy costs incurred by Cuban society throughout its revolutionary period. Communist ideologues maintain the premise that their system sacrifices traditional Western human rights in order to give priority to their Socialist human rights. They point out their constitution guarantees rights such as education, health care and employment among others. For forty years Cubans have heard nothing but how good they have it in these areas. The international media and academia have echoed these claims. Socialist rights are not known in the West as rights but rather as basic or elementary human needs that must be satisfied as best as is possible. What seems to escape the attention of most is the fact that Western societies can give emphasis to the satisfaction of these basic human needs in a far more constructive manner than communism does. In fact, the communist legacy is in reality a mythological one.

Western human rights seek to protect the citizenry by rendering the government passive in the face of an active private sector. When basic human needs are declared Socialist human rights guaranteed by the constitution, this de facto creates a very active government that must render the citizenry passive in order to procure these rights. The private sector must be destroyed and along with it goes such rights as those guaranteed by the Bill of Rights in the United States. This is the basic flaw inherent in the structure of communist societies. The government must exercise sovereignty over the citizenry. In free societies, the citizenry exercise sovereignty over their government.

The sacrifice might still be worth it to some if in fact the goals of guaranteeing Socialist human rights were to be attainable and everlasting. But even this is questionable. Here one must make a distinction between the transient and the enduring and between a propagandistic effort and permanent effective institutionalization. It stands to reason that it takes a solid, robust and growing economy for any nation to really be able to meet over the long haul its commitments in terms of the social services provided to the citizenry. This brings us to the second inherent failure of communism, the economy. It is no wonder health care and education are rapidly decaying in Cuba today. Unemployment and subemployment are rampant.

Housing is either non existent or completely run down, and all of these just scratch the surface. The social and economic costs paid by Cuban society are astronomical. There are only a few romantics left who refuse to recognize this and there are those who think Socialist priorities are worth rescuing and still pay lip service to the Cuban revolution.

Ever since the inception of ASCE, a lot of effort has been devoted towards measuring some of these social and economic costs in the hopes of encouraging and expediting a transition towards a more rational regime in Cuba. Social costs are easy to point out but very difficult to measure. They take a severe toll in terms of human suffering as every aspect of an individual's life is controlled by the state. This is really the realm of psychologists and sociologists. Economic costs, on the other hand, are easier to quantify and analyze. Cuban society (its people) must be made aware of these costs and aware of the inherent flaws of communism as a first step in the road towards their recapturing their sovereignty over their government along with their freedom and rights.

It took an MIT physicist currently practicing as an actuarial scientist to have come up with a very rational methodology to measure the actual costs Cuban society is going to incur in waiting for the natural expiration of the current leadership. The longer it waits, the higher the costs. The analysis assumes, of course, that a transition towards a more viable economic system will commence upon the death of Fidel Castro. It also assumes that Castro will maintain his current hardline stand for as long as he lives as in "Socialism or Death." Herein lies the most valuable contribution Ricardo Donate-Armada makes in his paper. It is a sound and rigorous analysis of a reality many inside and outside Cuba do not want to face up to.

To quote Donate-Armada: "Making a particular economic variable dependent on the survival status of the current Cuban leadership, and making the leadership's survival status a random variable dependent on time elapsed is what defines an actuarial model for that economic variable." Two types of economic variables are discussed. They are those based on annuity payments and those that reflect the relative val-

ues of macroeconomic amounts. Along with mortality tables, one calculated specifically for Cuba, the results of the economic analyses are completely tabulated as well. The most impressive of these by far is in the realm of macroeconomic variables. It is the expected Ultimate Scaled GNP Loss (in units of a projected base GNP) as a result of waiting for the current leadership to expire naturally. The resulting scaled loss depends mostly on the ratio of the GNP growth factor while the leadership survives and the GNP growth factor after the leadership dies. It assumes the current leadership is 73 years old in order to do the calculations.

In a similar vein, the report also gives the expected Scaled GNP Loss as a function of elapsed years assuming the current leadership is 73 years old. It places in evidence that the GNP loss grows to its ultimate value relatively fast for the several scenarios considered. Of course, the calculations cited, both Ultimate and dependent on elapsed time, definitely establish the GNP loss dependence on the assumed leadership mortality. Donate-Armada's paper gives a very refined analysis of this economic reality with good explanations and luxury of detail.

THE MODEL

The actuarial models used depend in turn on the existence of a survival model. The latter is reflected in the use of a fundamental underlying random variable measuring the time until death in the lifetime of an arbitrary Cuban citizen. This random variable is nonnegative, continuous and in units of years. Here it is labeled T. One can construct probability statements with it. Examples are:

$P[T \leq x]$: The probability the citizen dies on or before attaining age x years.

$P[T > x]$: The probability the citizen's life will exceed x years of age.

By using this random variable, one can characterize such things as the life expectancy at birth for an arbitrary citizen. This concept is denoted the expected value of T and labeled $E[T]$. In formal mathematical terms it is given by: $\int_0^\infty P[T>t]dt$

Two probabilities in particular play a fundamental role in the development of the theory. They are: First the probability the life will exceed t more years of age after having attained the age of x years given that age x has been attained. This probability may be labeled t_P_x. Then there is its complement labeled t_Q_x which is the probability the life will cease on or before t more years after having attained the age of x years given that age x has been attained. Please note that this two probabilities add up to one. The key probabilities, however, are t_P_x and $1\_Q\_(x + t)$ which are described formally as :

$$t\_P\_x = P [T > x + t \mid T > x] \text{ and}$$
$$1\_Q\_(x + t) = P [T \leq x + t + 1 \mid T > x + t] \quad (1)$$

These two probability statements are used to relate the two events in question. The two conditional events themselves deserve notice. They are:

$$\text{Event 1} : \{ T > x + t \mid T > x \} \text{ and}$$
$$\text{Event 2} : \{ T \leq x + t + 1 \mid T > x + t \} \quad (2)$$

By virtue of the conditioning (reduction in the respective sample spaces) the two events are statistically independent and hence their joint probability is given by the product of the two probabilities. This product is denoted $(t\_P\_x)(1\_Q\_(x + t))$ and it represents the probability that the life will exceed t more years after having attained the age of x years and that the life will cease on or before one more year after having attained the age of x + t years. That the two events are statistically independent can be shown in more general terms. Consider the following proposition:

Proposition: Events 1 and 2 are statistically independent.

Proof: Let event 1 be $\{ A \mid B \}$ (read A given B)

and let event 2 be $\{ C \mid A \}$ (read C given A),

where A is a subset of B and hence it is the case that given A ====> given B

and for any set X it is also the case that given X ====> given X.

One may then use the general probability rule:

$$P [A \mid B] P [B] = P [A \text{ and } B].$$

Consider the following product:

$$P [C \mid A] P [A \mid B] \quad (3)$$

$$= P [C \mid A \mid A] P [A \mid B] \text{ since given A ====> given A} \quad (4)$$

$$= P [C \mid A \mid A \mid B] P [A \mid B] \text{ since given A ====> given B} \quad (5)$$

$$= P [(C \mid A) \mid (A \mid B)] P [(A \mid B)] \text{ by organizing or simply} \quad (6)$$

given A ====> given A given B

$$= P [(C \mid A) \text{ and } (A \mid B)] \text{ by the general rule.}$$
QED $\quad (7)$

It is then possible to define the discrete curtate survival random variable T_x with

$\{(t\_P\_x)(1\_Q\_(x + t))\}$ as its probability mass function for some age x > 0 and t = 0,1,2,..... .

This random variable represents, in a discrete scale, the residual lifetime of a life already shortened by x years. One can then calculate the residual life expectancy of someone who has attained the age of x years by taking the expected value $E [T\_x]$. As pointed by Donate-Armada, one can also define economic variables dependent on the survival after age x, $f (T\_x)$, and obtain their expected value $E [f (T\_x)]$. He also shows us how one can project at age x the value of an economic variable n years into the future and even obtain a projected expected value useful for comparison purposes and in assessing how rapidly the economic variable reaches its ultimate value.

CONCLUSIONS

The quantification of the economic costs incurred by Cuban society while it waits for the natural expiration of its current leadership is based on very realistic scenarios reflecting the possibility of economic recovery once a real transition to a more viable system commences in Cuba (see for example the work by Alonso and Lago in previous editions of *Cuba in Transition*). This work constitutes clear evidence that the woes afflicting the Cuban nation today have very little or nothing to do with American foreign policy and a lot to do with Cuba's own internal structure and management.

If Fidel Castro had been the CEO of an American firm, he would have already been forced to resign in the decade of the sixties. Unfortunately, he is also the Chairman of the Board and he owns all the stocks. It is rare to see a nation for so long led by such an incompetent, misguided and arrogant figure. The cult to his personality and the man's own delusions of grandeur as reflected in his still firmly held belief of his own inevitable triumph over Capitalism continues to blind him and prevents him from doing what is right and best for the Cuban nation and its people.

According to the mortality tables compiled by Donate-Armada for Cuban society, the residual life expectancy of an arbitrary Cuban citizen who has attained the age of 73 years is approximately 10 years. The implications of this statistic are enormous. It represents bad news for the Cuban nation. It could be a while longer before responsible Cuban citizens are able to put their house in order. This statistic may

or may not be valid for the person of Fidel Castro. He is not an arbitrary citizen. Yet it is an indicator that can not be ignored by planners both inside and outside Cuba. It appears that the Cuban nation will continue to pile up immense costs while Fidel continues to wage his one man war against the Yankees. If it were not such an irresponsible act to give this man (Fidel) any kind of resources he could manipulate, one would almost be tempted to suggest that the best American policy under the circumstances would be to bow to the tyrant and capitulate even if Jefferson turns in his grave. But steady as she goes continues to be the best American response to his madness. The payoff and return for this patience will some day be enormous because the changes will be swifter and Cuban culture and values will be restored on a much healthier foundation. The one fact that is certain is that the natural expiration of the current Cuban leadership will occur in the very near future. If one considers all the costs incurred and all the suffering and sacrifice, it is well worth the wait for such an event to take place. It will be most welcomed by everyone.

Appendix A
Authors and Discussants

Charles M. Adams is Professor in the Department of Food and Resource Economics at the University of Florida and Extension Economist/Marine Economics Specialist with the Florida Sea Grant Program. Since 1995, Dr. Adams has been conducting research on fisheries with the University of Havana and the Cuban Ministry of Fisheries as part of the International Agricultural Trade and Development Center's collaborative research project.

Benigno Aguirre is Professor of Sociology at Texas A&M University.

José Alvarez is Professor, Food and Research Economics Department, Institute of Food and Agricultural Sciences, University of Florida, where he works as the Area Economist at the Everglades Research and Education Center, Belle Glade, Florida. He has traveled to Cuba in the past few years as one of the principal investigators in two grants from the John D. and Catherine T. MacArthur Foundation to study Cuban agriculture and the potential economic impact on the agricultural economies of Florida and Cuba after the lifting of the U.S. economic embargo. He earned a B.A. in Economics (1971) and M.S. (1974) and Ph.D. (1977) in Food and Resource Economics all from the University of Florida.

Nelson Amaro is Dean of the Faculty of Social Sciences and Director of the Masters Program on Development at the Universidad del Valle de Guatemala. For more than 30 years, he has been a consultant to international agencies on community development, social participation and education issues.

Domingo Amuchastegui is a former Political Officer of the General Staff and Intelligence Officer in Cuba's DGI. He is also a former Professor at the Higher Institute of International Relations and Guest Professor at the National Defense College. He is currently a Ph.D. Candidate in International Relations, School of International Studies, University of Miami and an independent researcher on Cuban affairs, established in Miami.

Juan A. B. Belt has been a Senior Economist at the Inter-American Development Bank since 1998. He works on infrastructure and financial sector programs in the Andean countries and the Caribbean. Before joining the IDB, he was the Chief Economist of the Global Bureau of USAID, and also served in USAID missions in Guatemala, El Salvador, Costa Rica and Panama. Prior to his work at USAID, he worked for the World Bank and for the World Bank/FAO Program, mostly in Latin America, Europe and Africa. He studied economics at Georgetown, American and Cornell universities.

Ernesto Betancourt is a consultant on government reform. Has an MPIA from the University of Pittsburgh and studied Advertising and Marketing at American University. He was the first Director and organizer of Radio Marti and represented Castro in Washington in 1957-58. Has written extensively on the Cuban Revolution.

Hans-Jürgen Burchardt is a Professor and Researcher at the University of Hannover, Germany. The holder of a Doctorate in Economic Sciences and Sociology, Dr. Burchardt specializes on the study of transition economies, regional integration and agrarian issues, among others. His best known publications in Germany are the monographs *Cuba — El largo adiós de un mito* (Stuttgart, 1996) and *Cuba — En el otoño del patriarca* (Stuttgart, 1999) and his edited collection *La última reforma agraria del siglo* (Caracas, 2000).

Evaldo A. Cabarrouy is professor of economics and finance at the University of Puerto Rico, Río Piedras Campus, where he has been on the faculty since 1985. He previously served as faculty and director of the MBA Program at the Universidad del Turabo. From 1990 to 1991 he was Program Economic Advisor for the USAID in El Salvador and in 1992 adviser to the governor of the Commonwealth of Puerto Rico on economic development. Dr. Cabarrouy has been a Latin American Teaching Fellow, a Fulbright Scholar in Colombia and has participated in the USIA Overseas Speakers Program.

Rolando H. Castañeda is currently Principal Project Specialist for the Inter-American Development Bank (IDB), based in Santiago, Chile, an organization in which he has held different positions since 1974. Before joining the IDB, he worked as an economist at the Organization of American States; the Rockefeller Foundation at the University of Cali, Colombia; the University of Puerto Rico at Río Piedras; and the Puerto Rico Planning Board. He holds an M.A. and is a Ph.D. candidate at Yale University, concentrating in monetary policy and econometrics.

Eudel Eduardo Cepero, geographer and environmentalist, is currently at the South Florida Environmental Center, Florida International University. In 1996 he founded the Agencia Ambiental Entorno Cubano (AAMEC) in Camagüey, an NGO devoted to protecting the Cuban environment. He has continued AAMEC's work in Miami, where he resides since 1999.

Nicolas Crespo is a hotel industry and tourism specialist, President of Phoenix Hospitality and Consulting Corporation and Latin America Hospitality and Consulting, a consulting firm based in Key Biscayne, Florida. He also presides the Cuban Society of Tourism Professionals, a research organization specialized on Cuban tourism and a depository of vast information on the Island's tourism industry. Mr. Crespo is a graduate of the School of Commercial Sciences of Havana University.

Alfred G. Cuzán is Professor of Political Science at The University of West Florida, where he teaches and writes in the areas of American Politics, Latin American Politics, and Political Economy. He is a Henry Salvatori Fellow of the Heritage Foundation and a Reuben Askew Fellow of the Florida Institute of Government. His published bibliography includes over forty items appearing in such journals as *Behavioral Science*, *Latin American Research Review*, *Political Science Quarterly*, *Presidential Studies Quarterly*, and *Public Choice*. He holds a B.A. in Government and Economics from the University of Miami and and M.A. and Ph.D. in Political Science from Indiana University.

Larry Daley (García-Iñiguez Enamorado) is professor in the Department of Horticulture, Oregon State University, Corvallis, Oregon. His interests are the biophysics and biochemistry of plant germplasm. Professor Daley comes from an old and rural Cuban family, rooted in the forested hills and mountains of Guamá, Sierra Maestra, Oriente province.

Sergio Díaz-Briquets is Vice President of Casals & Associates, Inc. (C&A), a Washington area-based consulting firm. For the last six years, C&A has conducted, under contract to the U.S. Agency for International Development, the America's Accountability and Anti-Corruption (AAA) project. Other C&A projects address similar concerns in specific countries and on a global basis.

María Dolores Espino is Associate Professor of Business Administration at St. Thomas University in Miami, Florida. She received a Ph. D. in Economics from Florida State University, where her dissertation dealt with the economic impact of tourism on Florida's economy. She has written a number of articles on the Cuban tourism industry and other economic issues.

Oscar Espinosa Chepe is an independent economist residing in La Habana.

José Antonio Font is an activist, entrepreneur and strategic advisor in finance and development. He has assisted in the establishment of several institutions promoting private enterprise and political democracy. Mr. Font received his B.A. in International Business and Economics from the School of International Service, The American University (1969) and did graduate work in Development Banking and International Finance also at The American University (1973-1975).

Ted Henken is a Ph.D. candidate at the Stone Center for Latin American Studies of Tulane University. Trained as a sociologist, his research interests include Cuban and Mexican immigration to the United States and Cuba's "second economy." He has been to Cuba to carry out research on these issues on four different occasions. He has also worked with Cuban balseros and Mexican migrant workers in southern Alabama.

Ernesto Hernández-Catá is Associate Director of the African Department, International Monetary Fund (IMF). Previously, he served as Deputy Director of the IMF's Western Hemisphere Department and of the European II Department (in charge of relations with Russia and other states of the former Soviet Union) and held other positions at the IMF and at the Board of Governors of the Federal Reserve System. He received a License from the Graduate Institute of International Studies in Geneva (1967) and M.A. (1970) and Ph.D. (1974) in economics from Yale University.

Stephen J. Kimmerling is an attorney who researches and writes about legal issues surrounding U.S.-Cuban relations. He served the New York University School of Law as Cuba Conferences Director, organizing symposia at the Law School on vanguard legal issues in U.S.-Cuban affairs. Mr. Kimmerling holds a J.D. from the New York University School of Law and is a member of the New York and Florida Bars, the Association for the Study of the Cuban Economy, the American Society of International Law, and the Cuban-American Bar Association.

William E. Kost is a senior economist in the Asia/Western Hemisphere Branch, Market and Trade Economics Division, Economic Research Service, U.S. Department of Agriculture. He is currently focusing a portion of his time on Cuban agriculture.

Aldo M. Leiva is an attorney, writer, and public speaker in Miami, Florida. Mr. Leiva has researched and published articles and papers addressing Cuban policy issues. He is a member of the Association for the Study of the Cuban Economy, Cuban American Bar Association, and the Florida Bar.

Armando Linde is Deputy Secretary of the International Monetary Fund. Previously, he has served in a number of senior positions at the IMF, including that of Senior Advisor in the Western Hemisphere Department, Senior Resident Representative in India, and Chief of the River Plate Division in the Western Hemisphere Department. He did his graduate work in Economics at the University of Maryland.

Manuel Madrid-Aris is an Adjunct Professor at Florida International University's Department of Economics and an international consultant on economic and public policy issues in developing countries. His areas of specialization include economic development, economics of regulation and antitrust and environmental economics. He has provided economic, environmental and public policy consulting services on a variety of subjects to private enterprises, governments, and international organizations. He holds a Civil Engineering degree from UTFSM-Chile and a Master of Arts degree in Economics and a Ph.D. in Political Economy and Public Policy from the University of Southern California.

Armando F. Mastrapa, III is the publisher of the *Cuban Armed Forces Review* Internet Web Site and a graduate of Government and Politics from St. John's University in New York City.

Emily Morris is a Senior Editor/Economist with the Country Analysis and Forecasting Division, Latin American Region, The Economist Intelligence Unit, London.

Manuel David Orrio is an independent economist residing in La Habana.

Roberto Orro Fernández is a Lecturer-Researcher at the Escuela de Economía, Universidad de Guanajuato, Mexico, a position he has held since 1995. He held a similar position at the Escuela de Economía, Universidad de la Habana, from 1989 to 1993. He received an M.A. in Economics from El Colegio de México in 1995 and a degree in economic planning from the Universidad de la Habana in 1986.

Silvia Pedraza is an Associate Professor of Sociology at the University of Michigan, Ann Arbor. She is the author of numerous articles in professional journals and two books, *Origins and Destinies: Immigration, Race, and Ethnicity in America* (Wadsworth, 1996), co-edited with Ruben G. Rumbaut, and *Political and Economic Migrants in America: Cubans and Mexicans* (University of Texas Press, 1985). Her research interests are in the areas of the sociology of immigration, race, and ethnicity in America, as well as the sociology of Cuba's revolution and exodus. She holds a Ph.D. in Sociology from the University of Chicago.

Lorenzo L. Pérez is Senior Resident Representative of the International Monetary Fund (IMF) in Brazil. Previously, he served in the IMF's Fiscal Affairs, Western Hemisphere, Exchange and Trade Relations and European Departments and held positions at the U.S. Department of the Treasury and the U.S. Agency for International Development. He received a Ph.D. in economics from the University of Pennsylvania.

Jorge F. Pérez-López is an international economist with the Bureau of International Labor Affairs, U.S. Department of Labor. He is the author of *Cuba's Second Economy: From Behind the Scenes to Center Stage* (Transaction Publishers, 1995), co-editor of *Pespectives on Cuban Economic Reforms* (Arizona State University Press, 1998) and co-author of *Conquering Nature: The Environmental Legacy of Socialism in Cuba* (University of Pittsburgh Press, 2000). He received a Ph.D. in Economics from the State University of New York at Albany.

Joseph M. Perry is Professor of Economics and Chairperson of the Department of Economics and Geography at the University of North Florida, where he has been a faculty member since 1971. He was previously a member of the economics faculty of the University of Florida. Dr. Perry received his Ph. D in Economics from Northwestern University in 1966, after completing undergraduate studies at Emory University and Georgia State University. His recent research has focussed on regional economic development, with specific reference to Central American and Caribbean nations, and their trade relationships with the United States.

Federico Poey is a Cuban born agronomist with intimate knowledge of Cuba's agricultural and natural resources while living in Cuba until 1963 and more recently through the preparation of research papers on agricultural and economic issues for the US-Cuba Business Council. He is currently President of Agricultural Development Consultants, Inc.—AGRIDEC—in Miami, Florida.

Carmen M. Rinehart is a Professor at the University of Maryland School of Public Affairs and the Department of Economics. She is also a Research Associate at the National Bureau of Economic Research and on the editorial board of the *Journal of International Economics*, the *Review of International Economics* and the *World Bank Economic Review*. She received her Ph.D. from Columbia University.

Mario A. Rivera, Ph.D., is Associate Professor of Public Administration, School of Public Administration, Anderson School of Management, University of New Mexico. Current research interests center on network economics, including the political economy of the Internet.

Jorge Luis Romeu is a Senior Engineer with IIT Research Institute's (IITRI) Assurance Technology Center in Rome, NY. He was a member of the mathematics faculty at SUNY-Cortland, from which he retired Emeritus after fourteen years and is an Adjunct Professor in the Engineering Program at Syracuse University. He is the lead author of the book *A Practical Guide to Statistical Analysis of Materials Property Data*. Romeu holds a Ph.D. in Operations Research, is a Chartered Statistician Fellow of the Royal Statistical Society, a member of the American Statistical Association (ASA) and the International Association for Statistical Education (IASE).

Marta Beatriz Roque is Director of the Instituto Cubano de Economistas Independientes and a member of the Grupo de Trabajo de la Disidencia Interna para el Análisis de la Situación Socio-Económica. She is one of the authors of *La Patria es de Todos*, for which she was jailed by the Cuban Government. She resides in La Habana.

James E. Ross is Courtesy Professor and Program Adviser, International Agricultural Trade and Development Center, Institute of Food and Agricultural Sciences, University of Florida. He has served in his present position since retiring from the Foreign Agricultural Service in 1992. He served as Agricultural Counselor in Venezuela, Egypt, Italy and Korea. With the University of Florida, he served as Chief of Party in Costa Rica and Ghana.

Joaquín Roy is Professor of International Studies and Senior Research Associate of the North-South Center of the University of Miami. He was previously on the faculty of the School of International Studies of Johns Hopkins University and Emory University. His research and teaching areas are the history of political ideas, Latin American thought, intellectual history and literature, contemporary ideologies, regional integration, transitions to democracy, and human rights policies. Among his recent books are *La siempre fiel* (University of Madrid, 1998) and *Cuba, the U.S. and the Helms-Burton Doctrine* (University of Florida Press, 2000).

Joseph L. Scarpaci is a Professor of Urban Affairs and Planning in Virginia Tech's College of Architecture and Urban Studies. New editions of his co-authored book, *Havana: Two Faces of the Antillean Metropolis* are fortchoming by the University of North Carolina Press and the Casa de las Américas. His forthcoming book, *Plazas and Skyscrapers: The Transformation of the Latin American Historic District* will be published by the University of Arizona Press in late 2001.

Stephen L. Shapiro is Professor of Economics at the University of North Florida, where he has been a faculty member since 1972. Dr. Shapiro received his Ph. D. Degree in Economics from the University of South Carolina in 1972, after prior graduate study at the University of Utah. He has published extensively on the impact of state lotteries on education and taxes. His most recent research has been focussed on regional economic development.

Jeffrey W. Steagall is Associate Professor of Economics and Director of the International Studies in Business Program at the University of North Florida. Dr. Steagall received his Ph. D. in Economics from the University of Wisconsin at Madison in 1990. His

undergraduate studies were completed at St. Norbert College. Dr. Steagall is an international trade and finance specialist, with a particular interest in the trade relationships of developing countries.

Charles Suddaby is a consultant specializing in the hospitality and tourism sectors. He has been working on projects in Cuba since 1994, and is currently evaluating the potential for a 3,000-room resort to be developed in the Jardines del Rey region.

Matías F. Travieso-Díaz is a partner in Shaw Pittman, a 250-lawyer law firm with offices in Washington, D.C., New York City and Northern Virginia. He is the author of *The Laws and Legal System of a Free-Market Cuba* (Quorum Books, 1996) and numerous law review articles, papers and newspaper columns on matters related to Cuba's transition to a free-market, democratic society. He hold B.S. and M.S. degrees in Electrical Engineering from the University of Miami and a Ph.D. in Electrical Engineering from Ohio State University. He earned a J.D. degree from Colombia Law School.

Charles Trumbull is currently a third year student at Dartmouth College majoring in philosophy.

Alberto Vega is a senior environmental planner with more than twenty years of professional, worldwide experience in environmental impact assessments, watershed management, water and soil resources, wetlands and institutional development and environmental policy. He is currently Associate Environmental Planner at Dames & Moore, a URS corporation firm in Miami, Florida.

Sidney Weintraub holds the William E. Simon Chair in Political Economy at the Center for Strategic and International Studies, Washington, D.C. He is also Dean Rusk Professor Emeritus at the Lyndon B. Johnson School of Public Affairs, University of Texas at Austin. A member of the U.S. Foreign Service from 1949 to 1975, Dr. Weintraub held the post of Deputy Assistant Secretary of State for International Finance and Development from 1969 to 1974 and Assistant Administrator of the U.S. Agency for International Development in 1975. His most recent books include *Financial Decision-Making in Mexico: To Bet A Nation* (Macmillan and University of Pittsburgh Press, 2000) and *Development and Democracy in the Southern Cone: Imperatives for Policy in South America* (Center for Strategic and International Studies, 2000).

Louis A. Woods is Professor of Geography and Economics at the University of North Florida, where he has been a faculty member since 1972. Dr. Woods received his Ph. D. in Geography from the University of North Carolina at Chapel Hill in 1972, after completing undergraduate studies in Geography at Jacksonville University. He completed postgraduate work in Economics at East Carolina University. His recent research has focussed on the determinants of regional economic development, and the constraints imposed by environmental concerns.

Appendix B
Acknowledgements

We want to take the opportunity to acknowledge the continued financial support provided to ASCE's activities by the following sponsoring members:

Alonso, José F.

Amaro, Nelson R.

Batista-Falla, Victor

Betancourt, Roger R.

Bravo, Jorge, Ing.

Calzón, Frank

Cox, Tomas E.

Crespo, Nicolas

Crews, Eduardo T.

de la Hoz, José M.

Espinosa, Juan Carlos

Esteve-Abril, Humberto G.

Fernández, Carlos J.

García-Aguilera Hamshaw, Carolina

Gayoso, Antonio

Gómez, Andy S.

Gómez Martín, Leopoldo

Gutiérrez, Ariel E.

Gutiérrez, Alfredo D.

Hernández-Catá, Ernesto

Linde, Armando

López, Roberto I.

Luis, Luis R.

Luzarraga, Alberto

Maidíque, Modesto A.

Mayer, Alfonso

Miranda, Jose E.

Morán, Ricardo J.

Padial, Carlos M.

Pérez, Lorenzo

Pérez-López, Jorge

Perry, Joseph M.

Piñón Cervera, Jorge

Prado, Juan A.

Pujol, Joaquín P.

Pujol, Michelle

Quijano, Carlos N.

Reich, Otto J.

Roca, Rubén A.

Rodríguez, José Luís

Sánchez, Juan T.

Sánchez, Federico F.

Sánchez, Nicolás

Sanguinetty, Jorge

Vallejo, Jorge I.

ASCE would like to thank the principal sponsor of the Tenth Annual Meeting, the University of Miami Institute for Cuban and Cuban American Studies (ICCAS).

ASCE also acknowledges the support of the World Council of Credit Unions and of Shaw Pittman in facilitating our board meetings over the last four years.

503

Heterick Memorial Library
Ohio Northern University

DUE	RETURNED	DUE	RETURNED
FEB 17 JUL 14 2008		13.	
2.		14.	
3.		15.	
4.		16.	
5.		17.	
6.		18.	
7.		19.	
8.		20.	
9.		21.	
10.		22.	
11.		23.	
12.		24.